FOURTH
New
EDITION

Provence and the Côte d'Azur

by Nancy Coons

The complete guide, thoroughly up-to-date

Packed with details that will make your trip

The must-see sights, off and on the beaten path

What to see, what to skip

Mix-and-match vacation itineraries

City strolls, countryside adventures

Smart lodging and dining options

Essential local do's and taboos

Transportation tips, distances and directions

Key contacts, savvy travel tips

When to go, what to pack

Clear, accurate, easy-to-use maps

Books to read, videos to watch, background essay

Fodor's Travel Publications, Inc.
New York • Toronto • London • Sydney • Auckland
www.fodors.com

Fodor's Provence and the Côte d'Azur

EDITOR: Natasha Lesser

Editorial Contributors: David Brown, Nancy Coons, Nigel Fisher, Helayne Schiff, M. T. Schwartzman (Gold Guide editor)

Editorial Production: Tom Holton

Maps: David Lindroth, Inc.; Mapping Specialists Ltd., *cartographers;* Robert Blake, *map editor*

Design: Fabrizio La Rocca, *creative director;* Guido Caroti, *associate art director;* Jolie Novak, *photo editor*

Production/Manufacturing: Robert B. Shields

Cover Photograph: Sonja Bullaty © 1991

Design: Between the Covers

Copyright

Special Sales

CONTENTS

Maps

ON THE ROAD WITH FODOR'S

WHEN I PLAN A VACATION, the first thing I do is cast around among my friends and colleagues to find someone who's just been where I'm going. That's because there's no substitute for a recommendation from a good friend who knows your tastes, your budget, and your circumstances, someone who's just been there. Unfortunately, such friends are few and far between. So it's nice to know that there's *Fodor's Provence and the Côte d'Azur*.

In the first place, this book won't stay home when you hit the road. It will accompany you every step of the way, steering you away from wrong turns and wrong choices and never expecting a thing in return. It includes a wonderful, full-color map from Rand McNally, the world's largest commercial mapmaker. Most important of all, it's written and assiduously updated by the kind of people you *would* hit up for travel tips if you knew them. They're as choosy as your pickiest friend, except they've probably seen a lot more of Provence and the Côte d'Azur. In these pages, they don't send you chasing down every town and sight in Provence and the Côte d'Azur, but have instead selected the best ones, the ones that are worthy of your time and money. To make it easy for you to put it all together in the time you have, they've created short, medium, and long itineraries and, in cities, neighborhood walks that you can mix and match in a snap. Just tear out the map at the perforation, and join us on the road in Provence and the Côte d'Azur.

About the Writer

Our success in achieving our goals—and in helping to make your trip the best of all possible vacations—is a credit to the hard work of our extraordinary writer and editor.

Nancy Coons devoted a year to the research and writing of this new version of *Provence and the Côte d'Azur,* living in *gîtes* (vacation rentals) and sleeper trains, tasting obscure regional specialties, testing hotel mattresses and sizing up pools, comparing palm trees and plane trees, beaches, views and sunsets. Then she wrote the book in her 300-year-old farmhouse in Lorraine, describing the golden light of Arles from under iron-gray skies. She has worked on many other Fodor's projects, including the guide to Switzerland as well as chapters on Luxembourg, Belgium, Alsace, and her own Lorraine. Her writing on European culture and food has appeared in the *Wall Street Journal, Opera News,* and *National Geographic Traveler.* When she isn't researching for Fodor's, she sings alto in an 8-voice a capella vocal ensemble, performing in embassies, châteaux, Baroque churches, and Romanesque chapels, and—in full costume—in her village's medieval fair. Her husband Mark Olson, and their daughters, Elodie (10) and Alice (5), accompany her on her travels when French school holidays permit, which is often.

Editor **Natasha Lesser** escaped to live in Paris—not even in the bloom of her youth—and discovered the joys of France (and its quirks). Although she explored every boulevard and back rue in Paris, many a mile of coast in Normandy, and the heights of the French Alps, it wasn't until later that she made it to the south of France—and came to understand its warm appeal. Her favorite time to go? In October when the crowds have gone but the sun still shines strong.

Connections

We're pleased that the American Society of Travel Agents continues to endorse Fodor's as its guidebook of choice. ASTA is the world's largest and most influential travel trade association, operating in more than 170 countries, with 27,000 members pledged to adhere to a strict code of ethics reflecting the Society's motto, "Integrity in Travel." ASTA shares Fodor's devotion to providing smart, honest travel information and advice to travelers, and we've long recommended that our readers—even those who have guidebooks and traveling friends—consult ASTA member agents for the experience and professionalism they bring to your vacation planning.

On Fodor's Web site (www.fodors.com), check out the new Resource Center, an on-line companion to the Gold Guide chapter of this book, complete with useful hot links to related sites. In our forums, you can also get lively advice from other travelers and more great tips from Fodor's experts worldwide.

How to Use This Book

Organization

Up front is the **Gold Guide,** an easy-to-use section arranged alphabetically by topic. Under each listing you'll find tips and information that will help you accomplish what you need to in France. You'll also find addresses and telephone numbers of organizations and companies that offer destination-related services and detailed information and publications.

The first chapter in the guide, **Destination: Provence and the Côte d'Azur,** helps get you in the mood for your trip. New and Noteworthy cues you in on trends and happenings, What's Where gets you oriented, Pleasures and Pastimes describes the activities and sights that make France unique, Great Itineraries lays out a selection of complete trips, Fodor's Choice showcases our top picks, and Festivals and Seasonal Events alerts you to special events to seek out.

Chapters in *Provence and the Côte d'Azur* are arranged regionally, beginning with the northwestern section of Provence, then moving north into the Vaucluse, east toward Aix and Marseille, and finally along the coast from west to east. Each chapter is divided by geographical area; within each area, towns are covered in logical geographical order, and attractive stretches of road and minor points of interest between them are indicated by the designation *En Route.* And within town sections, all restaurants and lodgings are grouped. For many major cities and towns, walking tours are recommended and sights are listed alphabetically.

To help you decide what to visit in the time you have, all chapters begin with our recommended itineraries. The A to Z section that ends all chapters covers getting there and getting around. It also provides helpful contacts and resources.

At the end of the book you'll find **Portraits,** a chronology and an evocative essay on

the region by Peter Mayle followed by suggestions for pretrip research, from recommended reading to movies on video that use France as a backdrop.

Icons and Symbols

★   Our special recommendation
✕   Restaurant
🏠   Lodging establishment
✕🏠   Lodging establishment whose restaurant warrants a special trip
🐤   Good for kids (rubber duck)
☞   Sends you to another section of the guide for more information
✉   Address
☎   Telephone number
🕓   Opening and closing times
💰   Admission prices (those we give apply to adults; substantially reduced fees are almost always available for children, students, and senior citizens)

Numbers in white and black circles ③ ❸ that appear on the maps, in the margins, and within the tours correspond to one another.

Dining and Lodging

The restaurants and lodgings we list are the cream of the crop in each price range. Price charts appear in the Pleasures and Pastimes section that follows each chapter introduction.

Hotel Facilities

We always list the facilities that are available—but we don't specify whether you'll be charged extra to use them: When pricing accommodations, always ask what's included. In addition, assume that all rooms have private bathrooms unless otherwise noted (and then be sure to ask for a private bathroom, if you want one). Note that private bathrooms may have either a bathtub *or* a shower (which is not noted), and not necessarily both; if you prefer one or the other, be sure to ask when making the reservation. In addition, when you book a room, be sure to mention if you have a disability or are traveling with children, if you prefer a certain type of bed, or if you have specific dietary needs or other concerns.

Restaurant Reservations and Dress Codes

Reservations are always a good idea; we mention them only when they're essential or are not accepted. Book as far ahead as you can, and reconfirm as soon as you arrive. Unless otherwise noted, the restaurants listed are open daily for lunch and dinner. We mention dress only when men are required to wear a jacket or a jacket and tie. Look for an overview of local dining-out habits in the Gold Guide and in the Pleasures and Pastimes section that follows each chapter introduction.

Credit Cards

The following abbreviations are used: **AE**, American Express; **DC**, Diners Club; **MC**, MasterCard; and **V**, Visa.

Don't Forget to Write

You can use this book in the confidence that all prices and opening times are based on information supplied to us at press time; Fodor's cannot accept responsibility for any errors. Time inevitably brings changes, so always confirm information when it matters—especially if you're making a detour to visit a specific place.

Were the restaurants we recommended as described? Did our hotel picks exceed your expectations? Did you find a museum we recommended a waste of time? Keeping a travel guide fresh and up-to-date is a big job, and we welcome your feedback, positive *and* negative. If you have complaints, we'll look into them and revise our entries when the facts warrant it. If you've discovered a special place that we haven't included, we'll pass the information along to our correspondents and have them check it out. So send us your thoughts via e-mail at editors@fodors.com (specifying the name of the book on the subject line) or on paper in care of the Provence and the Côte d'Azur editor at Fodor's, 201 East 50th Street, New York, New York 10022. In the meantime, have a wonderful trip!

Karen Cure

Karen Cure
Editorial Director

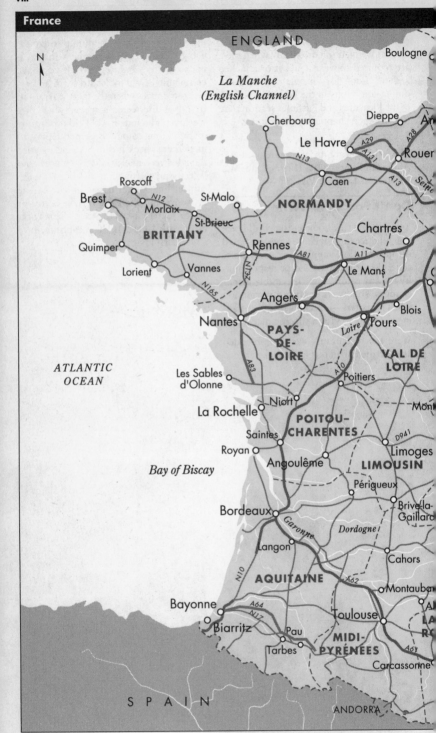

Calais

BELGIUM

NORTH

Lille

Arras

PICARDY

niens

Cambrai

St. Quentin

LUXEMBOURG

Beauvais

CHAMPAGNE-
ARDENNES

Reims

Metz

ILE-DE-
FRANCE

Paris

Châlons-en-
Champagne

ALSACE-
LORRAINE

Nancy

Sens

Strasbourg

GERMANY

Orléans

Troyes

Colmar

Auxerre

Mulhouse

Belfort

Bourges

Dijon

Besançon

Nevers

Beaune

FRANCHE-
COMTÉ

SWITZERLAND

BURGUNDY

çon

Mâcon

Bourg-en-
Bresse

Clermont-
Ferrand

Lyon Rhône

ALPES

ITALY

UVERGNE

Le Puy

Chambéry

Aurillac

RHÔNE
VALLEY

Grenoble

Rodez

Montélimar

Gap

Millau

PROVENCE

Sisteron

Nîmes

Avignon

CÔTE
D'AZUR

GUEDOC
SSILLON

Montpellier

Aix-en-Provence

Nice

MONACO
Monte Carlo

Cannes

Narbonne

Marseille

Perpignan

Toulon

Mediterranean Sea

Corsica

0   50 mi
0   75 km

Corsica

Calvi

Bastia

Corte

Ajaccio

N198

Bonifacio

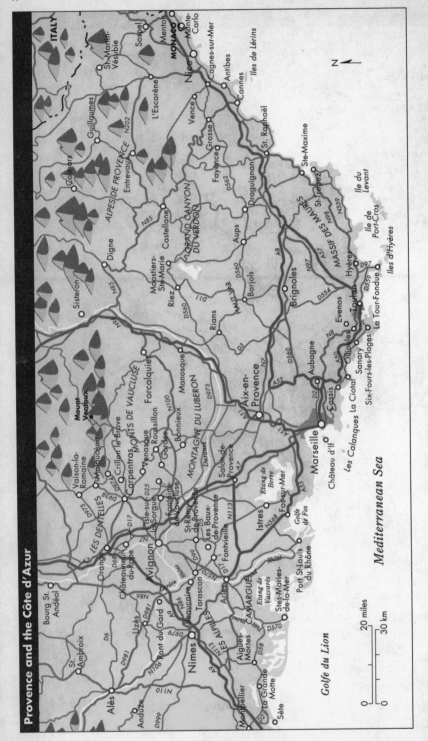

Provence and the Côte d'Azur

SMART TRAVEL TIPS A TO Z

Basic Information on Traveling in Provence and the Côte d'Azur, Savvy Tips to Make Your Trip a Breeze, and Companies and Organizations to Contact

AIR TRAVEL

BOOKING YOUR FLIGHT
CARRIERS

Most airlines fly to Paris and have connecting flights to the south of France on domestic airlines. The one exception is Delta, which has frequent nonstop flights to Nice from New York.

➤ DOMESTIC AIRLINES: **Air France** (☎ 800/237–2747 in the U.S., 08–02–80–28–02 in France), flies from Paris to Avignon, Marseille, Nice, Toulon, and other cities in the south of France. **Air Liberté** (☎ 02–47–88–48–48 or 08–03–80–58–05) flies from Paris to Nice and Toulon. **AOM** (☎ 01–49–79–12–34 or 08–03–00–12–34) flies from Paris to Nice, Marseille, and Toulon.

➤ MAJOR AIRLINES: **Air France** (☎ 800/237–2747 in the U.S., 08–02–80–28–02 in France) flies to Paris Charles de Gaulle and has connecting flights on its domestic airline to Avignon, Marseille, Nice, and Toulon. **American Airlines** (☎ 800/433–7300 in the U.S., 01–69–32–73–07 in France) flies to Paris Charles de Gaulle and Orly and connects with domestic airline flights to Marseille and Nice. **Continental** (☎ 800/231–0856 in the U.S., 01–42–99–09–09 in France) flies to Paris Charles de Gaulle and connects with domestic airline flights to the south. **Delta** (☎ 800/241–4141 in the U.S., 01–47–68–92–92 in France) flies to Paris Charles de Gaulle and is the only airline with nonstop flights from the U.S. to Nice (availability varies according to time of year). **Northwest** (☎ 800/225–2525 in the U.S., 01–42–66–90–00 in France) flies to Paris Charles de Gaulle and connects with domestic airline flights to the south. **TWA** (☎ 800/892–4141 in the U.S., 01–49–19–20–00 in

France) flies to Paris Charles de Gaulle and connects with domestic airline flights to the south. **United** (☎ 800/538–2929 in the U.S., 08–01–72–72–72 in France) flies to Paris Charles de Gaulle and connects with domestic airline flights to the south. **US Airways** (☎ 800/428–4322 in the U.S., 01–49–10–29–00 in France) flies to Paris Charles de Gaulle and connects with domestic airline flights to the south.

➤ FROM THE U.K.: **Air France** (☎ 0181/742–6600 in the U.K., 08–02–80–28–02 in France). **British Airways** (☎ 0990/074–074 in the U.K., 08–02–80–29–02 in France). **British Midland** (☎ 0345/554–554 in the U.K., 01–48–62–55–65 in France). **Easyjet** (☎ 0990/292–929 in the U.K., 04–93–21–48–33 in France) runs scheduled services to Nice from Luton and Liverpool.

CHARTERS

Charters usually have the lowest fares but are the least dependable. Departures are infrequent and seldom on time, flights can be delayed for up to 48 hours or can be canceled for any reason up to 10 days before you're scheduled to leave. Itineraries and prices can change after you've booked your flight.

In the U.S., the Department of Transportation's Aviation Consumer Protection Division has jurisdiction over charters and provides a certain degree of protection. The DOT requires that money paid to charter operators be held in escrow, so if you can't pay with a credit card, **always make your check payable to a charter carrier's escrow account.** The name of the bank should be in the charter contract. If you have any problems with a charter operator, contact the DOT (☞ Airline Complaints, *below*). If you buy a charter package that includes both air and land arrangements, remember that the escrow requirement applies only to the air component.

➤ CHARTER CARRIER: **Tower Air** (☎ 800/34–TOWER) flies to Paris.

CONSOLIDATORS

Consolidators buy tickets for scheduled international flights at reduced rates from the airlines, then sell them at prices that beat the best fare available directly from the airlines, usually without restrictions. Sometimes you can even get your money back if you need to return the ticket. Carefully read the fine print detailing penalties for changes and cancellations, and **confirm your consolidator reservation with the airline.**

➤ CONSOLIDATORS: **Cheap Tickets** (☎ 800/377–1000). **DER Travel Services** (☎ 800/717–4247). **Up & Away Travel** (☎ 212/889–2345). **Discount Travel Network** (☎ 800/576–1600). **Unitravel** (☎ 800/325–2222). **World Travel Network** (☎ 800/409–6753).

COURIERS

When you fly as a courier, you trade your checked-luggage space for a ticket deeply subsidized by a courier service. It's all perfectly legitimate, but there are restrictions: You can usually book your flight only a week or two in advance, your length of stay may be set for a certain number of days, and you probably won't be able to book a companion on the same flight.

➤ COURIER COMPANIES: **Air Courier Association** (✉ 15000 W. 6th Ave., Suite 203, Golden, CO 80401, ☎ 800/282–1202, www.aircourier.org). **International Association of Air Travel Couriers** (✉ 220 South Dixie Highway #3, P.O. Box 1349, Lake Worth, FL, 33460, ☎ 561/582–8320, FAX 561/582–1581. www.courier.org). **Now Voyager Travel** (✉ 74 Varick St., Suite 307, New York, NY 10013 ☎ 212/431–1616, FAX 212/219–1753 or 212/334–5243, www.nowvoyagertravel.com).

CUTTING COSTS

The least-expensive airfares to France are priced for round-trip travel and usually must be purchased in advance. It's smart to **call a number of airlines, and when you are quoted a good price, book it on the spot**—the same fare may not be available the next day. Airlines generally allow you to change your return date for a fee. However, most low-fare tickets are nonrefundable. To get the lowest airfare, **check different routings.** Compare prices of flights to and from different airports if your destination or home city has more than one gateway. Also price off-peak flights.

Travel agents, especially those who specialize in finding the lowest fares (☞ Discounts & Deals, *below*), can be especially helpful when booking a plane ticket. When you're quoted a price, **ask your agent if the price is likely to get any lower.**

CHECK IN & BOARDING

The first passengers to get bumped are those who checked in late and those flying on discounted tickets, so **get to the gate and check in as early as possible,** especially during peak periods. Note, too, that for international flights you are asked to check in at least 2 hours before the flight.

Although the trend on international flights is to drop reconfirmation requirements, many airlines still ask you to reconfirm each leg of your international itinerary. Failure to do so may result in your reservation being canceled.

To enter France, you need to **carry your passport.** You will be asked to show it when you check in. For more information, *see* Passports & Visas, *below.*

DISCOUNT PASSES

You can **save on air travel** within Europe if you plan on traveling to and from Paris aboard Air France. As part of their Euro Flyer program, you then can buy between three and nine flight coupons, valid on these airlines' flights to more than 100 European cities including many French cities. At $120 each (April–September) and

$99 each (October–April 1), these coupons are a good deal, and the fine print still allows you plenty of free-dom.

ENJOYING THE FLIGHT

For more legroom, **request an emergency-aisle seat.** Don't sit in the row in front of the emergency aisle or in front of a bulkhead, where seats may not recline.

If you don't like airline food, **ask for special meals when booking.** These can be vegetarian, low-cholesterol, or kosher, for example.

When flying internationally, try to maintain a normal routine, to help fight jet-lag. At night, **get some sleep.** By day, **eat light meals, drink water (not alcohol), and move around the cabin** to stretch your legs.

Many carriers have prohibited smok-ing on all of their international flights; others allow smoking only on certain routes or certain departures, so **contact your carrier regarding its smoking policy.**

FLYING TIMES

Flying time to Paris is 7½ hours from New York, 9 hours from Chicago, and 11 hours from Los Angeles. Flying time between Paris and Nice is approximately 1 hour.

HOW TO COMPLAIN

If your baggage goes astray or your flight goes awry, complain right away. Most carriers require that you **file a claim immediately.**

➤ AIRLINE COMPLAINTS: U.S. Depart-ment of Transportation **Aviation Consumer Protection Division** (✉ C-75, Room 4107, Washington, DC 20590, ☎ 202/366–2220). **Federal Aviation Administration Consumer Hotline** (☎ 800/322–7873).

AIRPORTS

The major gateways to France are Paris's Orly and Charles de Gaulle airports. Nice, Marseille, and Mont-pellier airports are also served by frequent flights from Paris and Lon-don, and daily connections from Paris arrive at the smaller airports in Avi-gnon and Nîmes.

➤ AIRPORT INFORMATION: **Charles de Gaulle** (☎ 01–48–62–12–12). **Marseille** (☎ 04–42–78–21–00). **Montpellier** (☎ 04–67–20–85–00). **Nice** (☎ 04–93–21–30–30). **Nîmes** (☎ 04–66–70–06–88). **Orly** (☎ 01–49–75–15–15).

BEACHES

If you're planning to devote a lot of time to beaches and haven't tackled the French coast before, get to **know the distinction between private and public.** All along the coast, the water-front is carved up into private frontage, roped off and advertised by coordinated color awnings, parasols, and mattresses. These private beaches usually offer full restaurant and bar service, and rent mattresses, umbrel-las, and lounge chairs by the day and half-day. Dressing rooms and showers are included; some even rent private cabanas. Prices can run from 60 francs a day to 120 or more. Private beaches compete with each other not only via fashionable cuisine and flashy colors, but by offering enter-tainment—children's wading pools, waterskiing, or parasailing.

But interspliced between these com-mercial beaches is plenty of public space, with open access and (usually) the necessary comforts of toilets and cold rinse "showers" for washing off the salt. At these you must provide your own mattress or mat (indispens-able on the rocks) and you can profit from the democratic bar service provided by enterprising vendors who cruise the waterfront with drinks and snacks.

BIKE TRAVEL

The French are great bicycling enthusiasts—witness the Tour de France—and there are tremendous opportunities to practice this Gallic sport in the south. From the Vaucluse, where cyclists pedal through the Luberon, to the Côte d'Azur, where they criss-cross the Esterel over the sea, Provence and the coast provide good biking conditions and multiple options for rental and transport. For 44 francs a day (55 francs for a 10-speed touring bike) **you can rent bikes from many train stations;** you need to show your passport and leave a deposit of 1,000 francs or a Visa or

MasterCard. Mountain bikes (known as VTT or *vélo touts terrains*) can be rented from many shops, as well as from some train stations. Bikes may be taken as accompanied luggage from any station in France; some trains in rural areas don't even charge for this. Tourist offices supply details on the more than 200 local shops that rent bikes, or you can get the SNCF brochure "Guide du Train et du Vélo" from any station.

Contact the Fédération Française de Cyclotourisme for information on bicycling routes in Provence and the Côte d'Azur. The yellow Michelin maps (1:200,000 scale) are fine for roads, but for off-road bicycling you may want to get one of the Institut Géographique National's detailed, large-scale maps. Try their blue series (1:25,000) or orange series (1:50,000). For more bicycling trips, *see* Theme Trips *in* Tour Operators, *below.*

➤ BICYCLING INFORMATION: **Fédération Française de Cyclotourisme** (✉ 8 rue Jean-Marie-Jégo, 75013 Paris, ☎ 01–44–16–88–88). **Institut Géographique National** (✉ IGN, 107 rue La Boétie, 75008 Paris, ☎ 01–42–56–06–68).

BIKES IN FLIGHT

Most airlines will accommodate bikes as luggage, provided they are dismantled and put into a box. Call to see if your airline sells bike boxes (about $5; bike bags are at least $100) although you can often pick them up free at bike shops. International travelers can sometimes substitute a bike for a piece of checked luggage for free; otherwise, it will cost about $100. Domestic and Canadian airlines charge a $25–$50 fee.

BUS TRAVEL

France's excellent train service means that long-distance buses are rare; **regional buses are found mainly where train service is spotty.** The weakest rail links in the south lie in the Luberon region of the Vaucluse, in the Alpilles, and in the backcountry of the Haut Var, Haute Provence, and the pre-Alpes behind Nice. To explore these lovely regions, you must work closely with a bus schedule (available at most train stations) and plan connections carefully. Don't plan on too much multi-stop sightseeing if you're limited to bus connections, as they rarely dovetail with your plans. To visit the popular hill towns just behind the Côte d'Azur—Grasse, St-Paul, Vence, and Biot—you can catch a regional bus or watch for commercial bus excursions advertised in the bigger coastal resorts. Tourist offices provide information on accompanied excursions. Excursions and bus holidays are organized by the SNCF and a plethora of private tour companies. Ask for a brochure at any major travel agent or contact France-Tourisme. Bus tours from the U.K. generally depart from London.

➤ TO THE U.K. AND OTHER EUROPEAN COUNTRIES: **Eurolines** (✉ 28 av. Général-de-Gaulle, Bagnolet, ☎ 01–49–72–51–51 in France, 0171/730–3499 in the U.K.) runs bus trips (via Hovercraft or ferry) from London to Paris.

➤ WITHIN FRANCE: **SNCF** (✉ 88 rue St-Lazare, 75009 Paris, ☎ 08–36–35–35–35 in English).

BUSINESS HOURS

BANKS

Bank hours vary from branch to branch, but are usually open weekdays, generally from 8:30 to 5. Most take a one-hour, or even a 90-minute, lunch break. But **money can also be exchanged at 24-hour exchange offices or withdrawn from ATM machines** in the larger cities and towns (☞ Money, *below*).

MUSEUMS

Museum hours are somewhat lax in the south, with seasonal variations and a tendency to change slightly and often. Usual opening times are from 9:30 or 10 to 5 or 6, but many close for lunch (noon–2). To allow for long terrace lunches and an afternoon lag in business due to beach time, the lunch hour may be even longer in summer, with some later evening hours to compensate. Most museums are closed one day a week (generally Monday or Tuesday) and on national holidays: **check museum hours before you go.**

SHOPS

Large stores in big towns are open from 9 or 9:30 until 7 or 8. Smaller shops often open earlier (8 AM) and close later (8 PM) but take a lengthy lunch break (1–3) in the south of France. Corner groceries frequently stay open until around 10 PM.

CAMERAS & COMPUTERS

EQUIPMENT PRECAUTIONS

Always **keep your film, tape, or computer disks out of the sun.** Carry an extra supply of batteries, and **be prepared to turn on your camera, camcorder, or laptop** to prove to security personnel that the device is real. Always **ask for hand inspection of film,** which becomes clouded after successive exposure to airport X-ray machines, and **keep videotapes and computer disks away from metal detectors.**

➤ PHOTO HELP: **Kodak Information Center** (☎ 800/242–2424). *Kodak Guide to Shooting Great Travel Pictures,* available in bookstores or from Fodor's Travel Publications (☎ 800/533–6478; $16.50 plus $4 shipping).

ONLINE ON THE ROAD

If you use a major Internet provider, getting on line in major cities in the south of France shouldn't be difficult. Call your Internet provider to get local access numbers. Some hotels even have in-room modem lines. You may, however, need an adapter for your computer.

➤ ACCESS NUMBERS IN PARIS: **AOL** (☎ 01–40–64–16–70). **Compuserve** (☎ 08–36–06–13–19).

CAR RENTAL

Though renting a car in France is expensive—about twice as much as in the United States—as is gas (5.80 francs to 6.80 francs per liter), it may pay off if you are traveling with two or more people. In addition, renting a car gives you the freedom to move around at your own pace that the train does not. Rates in Nice begin at about $50 a day and $200 per week

for an economy car with air conditioning, a manual transmission, and unlimited mileage. The price doesn't usually take into account the 20.6% VAT tax or, if you pick it up from the airport, the airport tax.

If you're flying into Paris, it may be more economical to connect via a smaller airline directly to Nice or Marseille, then rent your car in the south. Or consider a rail-drive pass with one of the larger car rental companies, which allow a few days' rail travel—say, from Paris to Nice—and a block of car-rental time. By using the train to cover the long distances, then exploring the region in depth by car, you can make the most of both styles of transit.

➤ MAJOR AGENCIES: **Alamo** (☎ 800/ 522–9696, 0800/272–2000 in the U.K.). **Avis** (☎ 800/331–1084, 800/ 879–2847 in Canada, 008/225–533 in Australia). **Budget** (☎ 800/527– 0700, 0800/181181 in the U.K.). **Dollar** (☎ 800/800–4000; 0990/ 565656 in the U.K., where it is known as Eurodollar). **Hertz** (☎ 800/ 654–3001, 800/263–0600 in Canada, 0345/555888 in the U.K., 03/9222–2523 in Australia, 03/358– 6777 in New Zealand). **National InterRent** (☎ 800/227–3876; 0345/ 222525 in the U.K., where it is known as Europcar InterRent).

➤ LOCAL AGENCIES: Most major companies—Hertz, Avis, Europcar— are represented in the cities with major airports (Nice, Marseille) and important rail stops (Avignon, Marseille, Toulon, Fréjus/St-Raphaël, Cannes, Nice, and Menton). *See* individual chapters for major rental outlets.

CUTTING COSTS

To get the best deal, **shop around** and book before you leave home.

Also **ask your travel agent about a company's customer-service record.** How has the company responded to late plane arrivals and vehicle mishaps? Are there often lines at the rental counter? If you're traveling during a holiday period, does a confirmed reservation guarantee you a car?

SMART TRAVEL TIPS / THE GOLD GUIDE

Be sure to **look into wholesalers,** companies that do not own fleets but rent in bulk from those that do and often offer better rates than traditional car-rental operations. Prices are best during off-peak periods. Rentals booked through wholesalers must be paid for before you leave the United States.

If you are planning on being in France for at least 17 days, **look into leasing a car;** rates include all taxes, insurance, and unlimited mileage.

In addition, **look into car rental and train travel or fly/drive packages,** these may end up saving you some money and time.

➤ LONG-TERM LEASING: **Renault Eurodrive** (☎ 800/221–1052 east; ☎ 800/477–7716 west; and ☎ 800/777–7131 FL and Puerto Rico).

➤ RENTAL WHOLESALERS: **Auto Europe** (☎ 207/842–2000 or 800/223–5555, FAX 800–235–6321). **Europe by Car** (☎ 212/581–3040 or 800/223–1516, FAX 212/246–1458). **DER Travel Services** (✉ 9501 W. Devon Ave., Rosemont, IL 60018, ☎ 800/782–2424, FAX 800/282–7474 for information or 800/860–9944 for brochures). **Kemwel Holiday Autos** (☎ 914/835–5555 or 800/678–0678, FAX 914/835–5126).

INSURANCE

When driving a rented car you are generally responsible for any damage to or loss of the vehicle. Before you rent, **see what coverage you already have** under the terms of your personal auto-insurance policy and credit cards, and ask what coverage you may be able to get when you rent the car. Collision policies that car-rental companies sell for European rentals typically do not cover stolen vehicles.

REQUIREMENTS

In France your own driver's license is acceptable. You don't need an International Driver's Permit, unless you are planning on a long-term stay; you can get one from the American or Canadian automobile association, and, in the United Kingdom, from the Automobile Association or Royal Automobile Club.

➤ AUTO CLUBS: **American Automobile Association** (☎ 800/564–6222). **Australian Automobile Association** (☎ 06/247–7311). **Canadian Automobile Association** (CAA, ☎ 613/247–0117). **New Zealand Automobile Association** (☎ 09/377–4660). **United Kingdom Automobile Association** (☎ 0990/500600), or **Royal Automobile Club** (☎ 0990/722722 for membership inquiries, 0345/121345 for insurance).

SURCHARGES

Before you pick up a car in one city and leave it in another, **ask about drop-off charges or one-way service fees,** which can be substantial. Note, too, that some rental agencies charge extra if you return the car before the time specified in your contract. To avoid a hefty refueling fee, **fill the tank just before you turn in the car,** but be aware that gas stations near the rental outlet may overcharge.

CAR TRAVEL

EMERGENCY SERVICES

If your car breaks down on an expressway, **go to a roadside emergency telephone** and call the breakdown service. If you have a breakdown anywhere else, find the nearest garage or contact the police (dial 17).

GASOLINE

Gas is expensive, especially on expressways and in rural areas. When possible, **buy gas before you get on the expressway** and keep an eye on pump prices as you go. These vary enormously; anything from 5.80 to 6.80 francs per liter. The cheapest gas can be found at *hypermarchés* (very large supermarkets). It is possible to go for many miles in the country without passing a gas station—**don't let your tank get too low in rural areas.**

PARKING

Parking can be difficult in large towns; your best option (especially in a metropolis like Nice or Marseille) is to duck into the parking garage nearest the neighborhood you want to visit. Carry the ticket with you, and pay at the vending-machine-style ticket dispenser before you go back to your car. On the street, meters and ticket machines (pay and display) are common: Make sure you **have a supply of 1-, 2-, 5-, and 10-franc coins. Be sure to check the signs before you park, as rules vary.** In smaller towns, parking may be permitted on one side of the street only—alternating every two weeks—so pay attention to signs.

The coastal area of Provence—especially the Camargue and the Calanques—as well as overlooks along the Côte d'Azur are extremely vulnerable to car break-ins, and the parking lots are often littered with broken windshield glass. It's important that you **never leave valuables visible in the car,** and think twice about leaving them in the trunk. Any theft should be reported formally to the police.

ROADS

France's roads are classified into five types, numbered and prefixed *A, N, D, C,* or *V.* For the fastest roads between two points, **look for roads marked** *A* **for** *autoroutes.* A *péage* (toll) must be paid on most expressways: The rate varies but can be steep.

The *N* (Route Nationale) roads, which are sometimes divided highways, are the route of choice for heavy freight trucks, and are often lined with industry and large chain stores. More scenic, though less trafficked than the RNs are the *D* (Route Départementale) roads, often also wide and fast. Don't be daunted by smaller (*C* and *V*) roads, either; they're often the most scenic.

Though routes are numbered, the French generally guide themselves from city to city and town to town by destination name. When reading a map, keep one eye on the next big city toward your destination as well as the next small town; most snap decisions will have to be based on town names, not road numbers.

Negotiating the back roads requires a careful mix of map and sign reading, often at high speeds around suburban *giratoires* (rotaries). But by the time you head out into the hills and the tiny roads—one of the best parts of Provence and the Côte d'Azur—give yourself over to road signs and pure faith: As is the case throughout France, **directions are indicated by village name only, with route numbers given as a small-print afterthought.** Of course, this means you have to recognize the minor villages en route.

To leave Paris by car, figure out which of the *portes* (gates) corresponds to the direction you are going. Major highways connect to Paris at these points, and directions are indicated by major cities. For instance, heading north, look for Porte d'Orléans (direction Lyon and Bordeaux). It's best to **steer clear of rush hours** (7–9:30 AM and 4:30–7:30 PM).

ROAD MAPS

If you plan to drive through France, **get a yellow Michelin map** for each region you'll be visiting. The maps are available from most bookshops and newsagents.

RULES OF THE ROAD

In France, **you may use your own driver's license,** but you must be able to prove you have third-party insurance. Drive on the right and **yield to drivers coming from streets to the right.** However, this rule does not necessarily apply at roundabouts, where you are obligated to yield to those already within (to your left)–but should watch out for just about everyone. You must **wear your seat belt,** and children under 12 may not travel in the front seat. Speed limits are 130 kph (80 mph) on expressways, 110 kph (70 mph) on divided highways, 90 kph (55 mph) on other roads, 50 kph (30 mph) in towns. French drivers break these limits and police dish out hefty on-the-spot fines with equal abandon.

CHILDREN & TRAVEL

CHILDREN IN FRANCE

Be sure to plan ahead and **involve your youngsters** as you outline your trip. When packing, include things to keep them busy en route. On sightseeing days try to schedule activities of special interest to your children. If you are renting a car don't forget to **arrange for a car seat** when you reserve.

There are plenty of diversions for the young (noted by a duck icon throughout this book), and **almost all museums and movie theaters offer discounted rates** to children.

Playgrounds can be found off many toll roads. Most rest-stop bathrooms have changing tables.

Supermarkets carry several major brands of diapers (*couches à jeter*), universally referred to as Pampers (pawm-paires). Junior sizes are hard to come by, as the French toilet-train early. There's always plenty of baby food, and pharmacies provide the essentials.

DINING

The best restaurants in France do not welcome small children; except for the traditional family Sunday-noon dinner, fine dining is considered an adult pastime. Aim for more modest *auberges* (country inns), and if there's a choice **consider having your meal in the café or bar** rather than in the linen-and-goblet filled dining room. In cities, brasseries offer a casual option and the flexible meal times that children often require. Many mainstream restaurants have highchairs and serve children's portions (*menu enfant*), usually spaghetti or the ubiquitous *steak-frites,* a mountain of fries with a thin steak or fat patty of ground beef, usually extremely rare. If you're queasy about this, ask for it *à point* (well done). If your children go to bed early, opt for your hot meal at noon (there are cheaper prix-fixe menus, too) and consider having a sandwich, quiche, or pizza at a café or brasserie in the early evening; full-service restaurants usually do not serve before 7 PM.

FLYING

If your children are two or older, **ask about children's airfares.** As a general rule, infants under two not occupying a seat fly at greatly reduced fares or even for free.

In general the adult baggage allowance applies to children paying half or more of the adult fare. When booking, **ask about carry-on allowances for those traveling with infants.** In gen-

eral, for babies charged 10% of the adult fare you are allowed one carry-on bag and a collapsible stroller, which may have to be checked; you may be limited to less if the flight is full.

Experts agree that it's a good idea to use safety seats aloft for children weighing less than 40 pounds. Airlines, however, can set their own policies: U.S. carriers allow FAA-approved models but usually require that you buy a ticket, even if your child would otherwise ride free, since the seats must be strapped into regular seats. Airline rules vary, so it's important to **check your airline's policy about using safety seats during takeoff and landing.** (That safety seat may serve in your rental car, too, if you choose.) Safety seats cannot obstruct the movement of other passengers in the row, so get an appropriate seat assignment as early as possible.

When making your reservation, **request children's meals or a free-standing bassinet** if you need them; the latter are available only to those seated at the bulkhead, where there's enough legroom. Remember, however, that bulkhead seats may not have their own overhead bins, and there's no storage space in front of you—a major inconvenience.

GROUP TRAVEL

When planning to take your kids on a tour, look for companies that specialize in family travel.

➤ FAMILY-FRIENDLY TOUR OPERATORS: **Grandtravel** (✉ 6900 Wisconsin Ave., Suite 706, Chevy Chase, MD 20815, ☎ 301/986–0790 or 800/247–7651) for people traveling with grandchildren ages 7–17. **Families Welcome!** (✉ 92 N. Main St., Ashland, OR 97520, ☎ 541/482–6121 or 800/326–0724, FAX 541/482–0660). **A Touch of France** (✉ 660 King George Rd., Fords, NJ 08863, ☎ 800/738–5240).

LODGING

If you're planning to stay in hotels, be sure to book ahead. Many small hotels have only one or two rooms that sleep four (triples are much more common); if there are more of you, you'll have to book two neighboring rooms or a suite. If you want a family-size room or a pair of adjoining rooms, book ahead. Larger hotels will often provide cribs free to guests with young children, which is not usually the case at inns and smaller hotels. Older children are charged at adult rates unless the hotel offers a special family rate. Be sure to **ask about the cutoff age for children's discounts** when booking.

Another option: **consider a gîte, a short-term apartment or house rental,** or a home exchange. *See* Lodging, *below* for information about rental and home exchange organizations.

TRAIN TRAVEL

The SNCF allows children under 4 to travel free (provided they don't occupy a seat) and children 4 to 11 to travel at half fare. The Carte Kiwi (285 francs) allows children under 16 and as many as four accompanying adults to make four journeys at 25%–50% off.

Changing compartments for infants are available on all TGVs, although not on all local trains. For more information, *see* Train Travel, *below.*

CONSUMER PROTECTION

Whenever possible, **pay with a major credit card** so you can cancel payment or get reimbursed if there's a problem, provided that you can provide documentation. This is the best way to pay, whether you're buying travel arrangements before your trip or shopping at your destination.

If you're doing business with a particular company for the first time, **contact your local Better Business Bureau and the attorney general's offices** in your state and the company's home state, as well. Have any complaints been filed?

Finally, if you're buying a package or tour, always **consider travel insurance** that includes default coverage (☞ Insurance, *below*).

➤ LOCAL BBBs: **Council of Better Business Bureaus** (✉ 4200 Wilson Blvd., Suite 800, Arlington, VA 22203, ☎ 703/276–0100, FAX 703/525–8277).

CUSTOMS & DUTIES

When shopping, **keep receipts** for all of your purchases. Upon reentering the country, **be ready to show customs officials what you've bought.** If you feel a duty is incorrect, appeal the assessment. If you object to the way your clearance was handled, get the inspector's badge number. In either case, first ask to see a supervisor, then write to the appropriate authorities, beginning with the port director at your point of entry.

IN FRANCE

There are two levels of duty-free allowance for travelers entering France: one for goods obtained (tax paid) within another European Union (EU) country and the other for goods obtained anywhere outside the EU or for goods purchased in a duty-free shop within the EU.

In the first category, you may import duty-free: 300 cigarettes or 150 cigarillos or 75 cigars or 400 grams of tobacco; 5 liters of table wine and (1) 1½ liters of alcohol over 22% volume (most spirits), (2) 3 liters of alcohol under 22% by volume (fortified or sparkling wine), or (3) 3 more liters of table wine; 90 milliliters of perfume; 375 milliliters of toilet water; and other goods to the value of 2,400 francs (620 francs for those under 15).

In the second category, you may import duty-free: 200 cigarettes or 100 cigarillos or 50 cigars or 250 grams of tobacco (these allowances are doubled if you live outside Europe); 2 liters of wine and (1) 1 liter of alcohol over 22% volume (most spirits), (2) two liters of alcohol under 22% volume (fortified or sparkling wine), or (3) 2 more liters of table wine; 60 milliliters of perfume; 250 milliliters of toilet water; and other goods to the value of 300 francs (150 francs for those under 15).

IN AUSTRALIA

Australia residents who are 18 or older may bring back A$400 worth of souvenirs and gifts (including jewelry), 250 cigarettes or 250 grams of tobacco, and 1,125 ml of alcohol (including wine, beer, and spirits). Residents under 18 may bring back A$200 worth of goods.

➤ INFORMATION: **Australian Customs Service** (Regional Director, ⊠ Box 8, Sydney, NSW 2001, ☎ 02/9213–2000, FAX 02/9213–4000).

IN CANADA

Canadian residents who have been out of Canada for at least 7 days may bring in C$500 worth of goods duty-free. If you've been away less than 7 days but more than 48 hours, the duty-free allowance drops to C$200; if your trip lasts 24–48 hours, the allowance is C$50. You may not pool allowances with family members. Goods claimed under the C$500 exemption may follow you by mail; those claimed under the lesser exemptions must accompany you. Alcohol and tobacco products may be included in the 7-day and 48-hour exemptions but not in the 24-hour exemption. If you meet the age requirements of the province or territory through which you reenter Canada, you may bring in, duty-free, 1.14 liters (40 imperial ounces) of wine or liquor or 24 12-ounce cans or bottles of beer or ale. If you are 16 or older you may bring in, duty-free, 200 cigarettes and 50 cigars.

You may send an unlimited number of gifts worth up to C$60 each duty-free to Canada. Label the package UNSOLICITED GIFT—VALUE UNDER $60. Alcohol and tobacco are excluded.

➤ INFORMATION: **Revenue Canada** (⊠ 2265 St. Laurent Blvd. S, Ottawa, Ontario K1G 4K3, ☎ 613/993–0534, 800/461–9999 in Canada).

IN NEW ZEALAND

Homeward-bound residents with goods to declare must present themselves for inspection. If you're 17 or older, you may bring back $700 worth of souvenirs and gifts. Your duty-free allowance also includes 4.5 liters of wine or beer; one 1,125-ml bottle of spirits; and either 200 cigarettes, 250 grams of tobacco, 50

cigars, or a combo of all three up to 250 grams.

➤ INFORMATION: **New Zealand Customs** (⊠ Custom House, ⊠ 50 Anzac Ave., Box 29, Auckland, New Zealand, ☎ 09/359–6655, ☎ 09/309–2978).

IN THE U.K.

If you are a U.K. resident and your journey was wholly within the European Union (EU), you won't have to pass through customs when you return to the United Kingdom. If you plan to bring back large quantities of alcohol or tobacco, check EU limits beforehand.

➤ INFORMATION: **HM Customs and Excise** (⊠ Dorset House, ⊠ Stamford St., London SE1 9NG, ☎ 0171/202–4227).

IN THE U.S.

U.S. residents may bring home $400 worth of foreign goods duty-free if they've been out of the country for at least 48 hours (and if they haven't used the $400 allowance or any part of it in the past 30 days).

U.S. residents 21 and older may bring back 1 liter of alcohol duty-free. In addition, regardless of your age, you are allowed 200 cigarettes and 100 non-Cuban cigars. Antiques, which the U.S. Customs Service defines as objects more than 100 years old, enter duty-free, as do original works of art done entirely by hand, including paintings, drawings, and sculptures.

You may also send packages home duty-free: up to $200 worth of goods for personal use, with a limit of one parcel per addressee per day (and no alcohol or tobacco products or perfume worth more than $5); label the package PERSONAL USE, and attach a list of its contents and their retail value. Do not label the package UNSOLICITED GIFT, or your duty-free exemption will drop to $100. Mailed items do not affect your duty-free allowance on your return.

➤ INFORMATION: **U.S. Customs Service** (Inquiries, ⊠ Box 7407, Washington, DC 20044, ☎ 202/

927–6724; complaints, Office of Regulations and Rulings, ✉ 1301 Constitution Ave. NW, Washington, DC 20229; registration of equipment, Resource Management, ✉ 1301 Constitution Ave. NW, Washington DC 20229, ☎ 202/927–0540).

DINING

The sooner you relax and go with the French flow, the more you'll enjoy your stay. Expect to spend at least two hours for lunch in a restaurant, savoring three courses and talking over the wine; dinner lasts even longer. If you keep one eye on your watch and the other on the waiter, you'll miss the point and spoil your own fun.

If you're antsy to get to the next museum, or if you plan to spend the evening dining in grand style, consider lunching in a brasserie, where quick, one-plate lunches and full salads are available. Cafés often serve *casse croûtes* (snacks), including sandwiches, which are simply baguettes lightly filled with ham or cheese; or *croques monsieurs,* grilled ham and cheese open-face sandwiches with a minimum of grease. Bakeries and *traiteurs* (delis) often sell savory items like quiches, tiny pizzas, or pastries filled with pâté. On the Côte d'Azur, you can profit from a wealth of street food, from the chick-pea-based crêpes called *socca* to *pissaladière* (onion-olive pizza) and pan bagnat (a tuna-and-egg-stuffed pita-style bun).

You may benefit from a few pointers on French dining etiquette: Diners in France don't negotiate their orders much, so don't expect serene smiles when you ask for sauce on the side. Order your coffee after dessert, not with it. When you're ready for the check, ask for it: No professional waiter would dare put a bill on your table while you're still enjoying the last sip of coffee. And don't ask for a doggy bag; it's just not done.

Also a word on the great mineral-water war: The French usually drink wine or mineral water—not soda or coffee—with their food. You may ask for a carafe of tap water, but not always: In general, diners order mineral water if they don't order wine. It's not that the tap water is unsafe; it's usually fine—just not as tasty as Evian or slightly fizzy Badoit.

One of the wonderful aspects of breakfast in Provence and on the Côte d'Azur is eating outdoors, whether on the restaurant terrace or on your own tiny balcony. Breakfasts are light: consisting of croissants and bread, jam and butter, and wonderful coffee. More hotels are also serving yogurt, fruit juice, cereal, cheese, and even eggs upon request.

There is no need to wear a tie and jacket at most restaurants (unless specified), even fancy ones. For more on what to wear in the south of France, *see* Packing for Provence & the Côte d'Azur, *below*. Restaurants along the coast are generally more expensive than those inland; basic regional fixed-price menus average 90 francs–125 francs, though the high end of this figure represents the usual cost of seafood so often featured on restaurant menus. In high summer reserve at popular restaurants, especially if you want a coveted outdoor table.

MEALTIMES

You'll notice here more than anywhere in France that the lunch hour begins after 1; some places don't even open before that. If you don't mind being a gauche foreigner, eating at noon is one way to get into those sought-after restaurants that do open at 12. If you want to really do as the Romans do, reserve for a lunch at 1 or 1:30.

Breakfast usually is served from 8:30 to 10:30; if you want it earlier, arrange a time the night before. Dinner is usually eaten after 8.

DISABILITIES & ACCESSIBILITY

ACCESS IN FRANCE

Although the French government is doing much to ensure that public facilities provide for visitors with disabilities, it still has a long way to go. A number of monuments, hotels, and museums—especially those constructed within the past decade—

THE GOLD GUIDE / SMART TRAVEL TIPS

are equipped with ramps, elevators, and special toilet facilities. Lists of regional hotels include a symbol to indicate which hotels have rooms that are accessible to people using wheelchairs. The SNCF has special cars on some trains that have been reserved exclusively for people using wheelchairs and can arrange for those passengers to be escorted on and off trains and assisted in making connections (the latter service must, however, be requested in advance).

If you have a hearing aid, bring batteries with you, as battery types are not coded in the same way. When buying replacements, carry the dead battery with you for a perfect match.

➤ LOCAL RESOURCES: **Association des Paralysés de France** (✉ 17 bd. Auguste-Blanqui, 75013 Paris, 01–40–78–69–00) for a list of Paris hotels. **Comité Nationale Français de Liaison pour la Réadaptation des Handicapés** (✉ 236-B rue de Tolbiac, 75013 Paris, ☎ 01–53–80–66–66).

MAKING RESERVATIONS

When discussing accessibility with an operator or reservations agent, be sure to **discuss your needs before booking.** Are there any stairs, inside *or* out? Are there grab bars next to the toilet *and* in the shower/tub? How wide is the doorway to the room? To the bathroom? For the most extensive facilities meeting the latest legal specifications, **opt for newer accommodations,** which are more likely to have been designed with access in mind. Older buildings or ships may have more limited facilities.

TRAVEL AGENCIES & TOUR OPERATORS

As a whole, the travel industry has become more aware of the needs of travelers with disabilities. In the U.S., the Americans with Disabilities Act requires that travel firms serve the needs of all travelers. Note, though, that some agencies and operators specialize in making travel arrangements for individuals and groups with disabilities.

➤ TRAVELERS WITH MOBILITY PROBLEMS: **Access Adventures** (✉ 206 Chestnut Ridge Rd., Rochester, NY 14624, ☎ 716/889–9096), run by a former physical-rehabilitation counselor. **Accessible Journeys** (✉ 35 W. Sellers Ave., Ridley Park, PA 19078, ☎ 610/521–0339 or 800/846–4537, FAX 610/521–6959), for escorted tours exclusively for travelers with mobility impairments. **CareVacations** (✉ 5019 49th Ave., Suite 102, Leduc, Alberta T9E 6T5, ☎ 403/986–6404, 800/648–1116 in Canada) has group tours and is especially helpful with cruise vacations. **Flying Wheels Travel** (✉ 143 W. Bridge St., Box 382, Owatonna, MN 55060, ☎ 507/451–5005 or 800/535–6790, FAX 507/451–1685), a travel agency specializing in customized tours and itineraries worldwide. **Hinsdale Travel Service** (✉ 201 E. Ogden Ave., Suite 100, Hinsdale, IL 60521, ☎ 630/325–1335), a travel agency that benefits from the advice of wheelchair traveler Janice Perkins.

DISCOUNTS & DEALS

Be a smart shopper and **compare all your options** before making any choice. A plane ticket bought with a promotional coupon may not be cheaper than the least expensive fare from a discount ticket agency. For high-price travel purchases, such as packages or tours, keep in mind that what you get is just as important as what you save. Just because something is cheap doesn't mean it's a bargain.

CREDIT-CARD BENEFITS

When you use your credit card to make travel purchases you may get free travel-accident insurance, collision-damage insurance, and medical or legal assistance, depending on the card and the bank that issued it. American Express, MasterCard, and Visa provide one or more of these services, so **get a copy of your credit card's travel-benefits policy.** If you are a member of an auto club, always **ask hotel and car-rental reservations agents about auto-club discounts.** Some clubs offer additional discounts on tours, cruises, and admission to attractions.

DISCOUNT RESERVATIONS

To save money, **look into discount-reservations services** with toll-free numbers, which use their buying power to get a better price on hotels, airline tickets, even car rentals. When booking a room, always **call the hotel's local toll-free number** (if one is available) rather than the central reservations number—you'll often get a better price. Always ask about special packages or corporate rates.

When shopping for the best deal on hotels and car rentals, **look for guaranteed exchange rates,** which protect you against a falling dollar. With your rate locked in, you won't pay more, even if the price goes up in the local currency.

➤ AIRLINE TICKETS: ☎ **800/FLY–4–LESS.**

➤ HOTEL ROOMS: **Hotels Plus** (☎ 800/235–0909). **Hotel Reservations Network** (☎ 800/964–6835). **International Marketing & Travel Concepts** (☎ 800/790–4682). **Steigenberger Reservation Service** (☎ 800/223–5652). **Travel Interlink** (☎ 800/888–5898).

PACKAGE DEALS

Packages and guided tours can save you money, but don't confuse the two. When you buy a package, your travel remains independent, just as though you had planned and booked the trip yourself. Fly/drive packages, which combine airfare and car rental, are often a good deal. In cities, ask the local visitor's bureau about hotel packages. These often include tickets to major museum exhibits and other special events. With a **a rail/drive pass, you may get substantial savings** on train tickets and car rentals. All Eurail- and Europass holders get a discount on Eurostar fares through the Channel Tunnel.

ELECTRICITY

To use your U.S.-purchased electric-powered equipment, **bring a converter and adapter.** The electrical current in France is 220 volts, 50 cycles alternating current (AC). French electrical outlets have two round holes ("female") and a "male" ground; your appliances must either have a slender, two-prong plug that bypasses that ground, or a plug with two round prongs and a hole.

If your appliances are dual-voltage, you'll need only an adapter. Don't use 110-volt outlets, marked FOR SHAVERS ONLY, for high-wattage appliances such as blow-dryers. Most laptops operate equally well on 110 and 220 volts and so require only an adapter.

EMBASSIES

If you need assistance in an emergency you can go to your country's embassy or consulate. Proof of identity and citizenship are generally required to enter. If your passport has been stolen, get a police report then contact your embassy for assistance.

➤ EMBASSY ADDRESSES: **Australia** (✉ 4 rue Jean-Rey, Paris, 15ᵉ, ☎ 01–40–59–33–00, métro Bir Hakeim, ☉ weekdays 9:15–12:15) **Canada** (✉ 35 av. Montaigne, Paris, 8ᵉ, ☎ 01–44–43–29–00, métro Franklin-D.-Roosevelt, ☉ weekdays 8:30–11). **New Zealand** (✉ 7 ter rue Léonardo da Vinci, Paris, 16ᵉ, métro Victor Hugo ☎ 01–45–00–24–11, ☉ weekdays 9–1).

United Kingdom (✉ 35 rue du Faubourg-St-Honoré, Paris, 8ᵉ, ☎ 01–44–51–31–00, métro Madeleine, ☉ weekdays 9:30–12:30 and 2:30–5; ✉ 24 av. du Prado, Marseille, ☎ 04–91–15–72–10 for 24-hour emergency help, ☉ weekdays 9–noon and 2–5).

United States (✉ 2 rue St-Florentin, Paris, 1ᵉʳ, ☎ 01–43–12–22–22 in English or ☎ 01–43–12–23–47 in emergencies, métro Concorde, ☉ weekdays 9–3; ✉ 12 bd. Paul Peytral, Marseille, ☎ 04–91–54–92–00, ☉ weekdays 8:30–12:30 and 1:30–5:30 and until 4:30 on Friday.

EMERGENCIES

France's emergency services are conveniently streamlined and universal, so no matter where you are in the country, you can dial the same phone numbers, listed below. Every town and village has a *médecin de garde* (on-duty doctor) for flus, sprains, tetanus shots, etc. To find out who's on any given evening, call any *généraliste* (general practitioner) and a recording will refer you. If you need an x-ray or emergency treatment, call the ambulance number (☎ 15) and you'll be whisked to the hospital of your choice—or the nearest one. Note that outside of Paris it's very difficult to find English-speaking doctors.

In case of fire, hotels are required to post emergency exit maps inside every room door and multilingual instructions.

➤ EMERGENCIES: **Ambulance** (☎ 15). **Fire Department** (☎ 18). **Police** (☎ 17).

GAY & LESBIAN TRAVEL

In Provence and the Côte d'Azur, the gay and lesbian communities are low-key and reserved in public, although active and easily accessible to visitors. Discos and nightclubs are numerous and popular. To find out where they are, look for the *Guide Gay Grand Sud* for men and the *Guide Lesbien,* available in most gay and lesbian bars and clubs.

➤ GAY- AND LESBIAN-FRIENDLY TRAVEL AGENCIES: **Corniche Travel** (✉ 8721 Sunset Blvd., Suite 200, West Hollywood, CA 90069, ☎ 310/854–6000 or 800/429–8747, FAX 310/659–7441). **Islanders Kennedy Travel** (✉ 183 W. 10th St., New York, NY 10014, ☎ 212/242–3222 or 800/988–1181, FAX 212/929–8530). **Now Voyager** (✉ 4406 18th St., San Francisco, CA 94114, ☎ 415/626–1169 or 800/255–6951, FAX 415/626–8626). **Yellowbrick Road** (✉ 1500 W. Balmoral Ave., Chicago, IL 60640, ☎ 773/561–1800 or 800/642–2488, FAX 773/561–4497). **Skylink Travel and Tour** (✉ 3577 Moorland Ave., Santa Rosa, CA 95407, ☎ 707/585–8355 or 800/225–5759, FAX 707/584–5637), serving lesbian travelers.

➤ GAY- AND LESBIAN-FRIENDLY TRAVEL AGENCY IN FRANCE

Mistral Tours (✉ 4 rue Pissantour, 13150 Boulbon, ☎ FAX 04–90–43–86–90) has pre-planned packages with specific cultural themes—van Gogh in Provence, say, or Roman Provence—and can include hikes and bike tours.

HEALTH

See Emergencies, *above.*

DOCTORS & HOSPITALS

For information on doctors and hospitals throughout Provence and Côte d'Azur, *see* A to Z sections *in* individual chapters.

MEDICAL PLANS

No one plans to get sick while traveling, but it happens, so **consider signing up with a medical-assistance company.** Members get doctor referrals, emergency evacuation or repatriation, 24-hour telephone hot lines for medical consultation, cash for emergencies, and other personal and legal assistance. Coverage varies by plan, so **review the benefits of each carefully.**

➤ MEDICAL-ASSISTANCE COMPANIES: **International SOS Assistance** (✉ 8 Neshaminy Interplex, Suite 207, Trevose, PA 19053, ☎ 215/245–4707 or 800/523–6586, FAX 215/244–9617; ✉ 12 Chemin Riantbosson, 1217 Meyrin 1, Geneva, Switzerland, ☎ 4122/785–6464, FAX 4122/785–6424; ✉ 10 Anson Rd., 14-07/08 International Plaza, Singapore, 079903, ☎ 65/226–3936, FAX 65/226–3937).

HIKING

In Provence and the Côte d'Azur, there are many good places to hike, especially along the extensive network of mapped-out *Grands Randonnées* (GRs or Big Trails) that range from easy to challenging. For details on hiking in France and guides to GRs in specific areas, contact the Club Alpin Français or the Fédération Française de la Randonnée Pédestre, which also publishes good topographical maps. The IGN maps sold in many bookshops are also invaluable (☞ Bicycling, *above*).

Note that some of the best hiking wilderness along the coast—especially around the Calanques between Marseille and Cassis, and the Esterel between Fréjus and Cannes—are closed in July and August because of wildfire danger. Before you plan a summer of seaside hikes, **check with local tourist offices to confirm that trails are open.**

➤ HIKING ORGANIZATIONS: **Club Alpin Français** (✉ 24 av. Laumière,

75019 Paris, ☎ 01–53–72–87–00).
**Comité Départemental de Randonée
Pedestre Bouches-du-Rhône** (✉ 24
av. Prado, 13006 Marseille, ☎
04–91–81–12–08). **Comité Départe-
mental de Randonée Pedestre Alpes-
Maritime** (✉ 83 av. Joseph-Raybaud,
06300 Nice, ☎ 04–93–13–07–60).
**Comité Départemental de Randoné]e
Pedestre Var** (✉ L'Helianthe, rue
Emile Olivier La Rode, Toulon
83000, ☎ 04–94–42–15–01).
**Comité Départemental de Randonée
Pedestre Vaucluse** (Daniel Locci, Les
Fontaines du Levant, ✉ 63 av. César-
Franck, 84000 Avignon, written
requests only). **Fédération Française
de la Randonnée Pédestre** (✉ 14 rue
Riquet, 75019 Paris, ☎ 01–44–89–
93–93, FAX 01–40–35–85–67, email
ffrp.paris@wannado.fr).

HOLIDAYS

With 11 national *jours feriés* (holidays) and 5 weeks of paid vacation,
the French have their share of repose.
In May, there is a holiday nearly
every week, so be prepared for stores,
banks, and museums to shut their
doors for days at a time. Be sure to
**call museums, restaurants, and hotels
in advance to make sure they will be
open.**

Dates in 1999 and 2000: January 1
(New Year's Day); April 5, April 24
(Easter Monday); May 1 (Labor
Day); May 8 (VE Day); May 13, June
1 (Ascension); May 23, June 12
(Pentecost Monday); July 14 (Bastille
Day); August 15 (Assumption);
November 1 (All Saints); November
11 (Armistice); December 25 (Christ-
mas).

It's also useful to bear in mind France's
school vacations, which tend to
unleash hordes of families and *classes
de mer* (school trips to the coast) on
museums, castles, and family hotels.
School vacations are divided by
region and are spread out over
about three weeks in late October–
November, Christmas–New Year's,
again in February, and finally in
April.

INSURANCE

Travel insurance is the best way to
protect yourself against financial loss.

The most useful plan is a comprehensive policy that includes coverage for
trip cancellation and interruption,
default, trip delay, and medical expenses (with a waiver for preexisting
conditions).

Without insurance, you will lose all
or most of your money if you cancel
your trip, regardless of the reason.
Default insurance covers you if your
tour operator, airline, or cruise line
goes out of business. Trip-delay
covers unforeseen expenses that you
may incur due to bad weather or
mechanical delays. It's important to
compare the fine print regarding trip-
delay coverage when comparing
policies.

For overseas travel, one of the most
important components of travel
insurance is its medical coverage.
Supplemental health insurance will
pick up the cost of your medical bills
should you get sick or injured while
traveling. U.S. residents should note
that Medicare generally does not
cover health-care costs outside the
United States, nor do many privately
issued policies. Residents of the
United Kingdom can buy an annual
travel-insurance policy valid for most
vacations taken during the year in
which the coverage is purchased. If
you are pregnant or have a preexisting condition, make sure you're
covered. British citizens should buy
extra medical coverage when traveling overseas, according to the Association of British Insurers. Australian
travelers should buy travel insurance,
including extra medical coverage,
whenever they go abroad, according
to the Insurance Council of Australia.

Always **buy travel insurance directly
from the insurance company**; if you
buy it from a cruise line, airline, or
tour operator that goes out of business you probably will not be covered
for the agency or operator's default, a
major risk. Before you make any
purchase, **review your existing health
and home-owner's policies** to find out
whether they cover expenses incurred
while traveling.

➤ TRAVEL INSURERS: In the U.S.,
Access America (✉ 6600 W. Broad
St., Richmond, VA 23230, ☎ 804/
285–3300 or 800/284–8300). **Travel**

Guard International (⊠ 1145 Clark St., Stevens Point, WI 54481, ☎ 715/345–0505 or 800/826–1300). In Canada, **Mutual of Omaha** (⊠ Travel Division, ⊠ 500 University Ave., Toronto, Ontario M5G 1V8, ☎ 416/598–4083, 800/268–8825 in Canada).

➤ INSURANCE INFORMATION: In the U.K., **Association of British Insurers** (⊠ 51 Gresham St., London EC2V 7HQ, ☎ 0171/600–3333). In Australia, the **Insurance Council of Australia** (☎ 613/9614–1077, FAX 613/9614–7924).

LANGUAGE

Although many French people, especially in major tourist areas, speak some English, it's important to remember that you are going to France and that people speak French. However, generally at least one person in most hotels can explain things to you in English (unless you are in a very rural area). Be patient, and speak English slowly.

The French may appear prickly at first to English-speaking visitors. But it usually helps if you **make an effort to speak a little French.** So even if your own French is terrible, try to master a few words. A simple, friendly "bonjour" (hello) will do, as will asking if the person you are greeting speaks English ("Parlez-vous anglais?").

LANGUAGES FOR TRAVELERS

A phrase book and language tape set can help get you started.

➤ PHRASE BOOKS AND LANGUAGE-TAPE SETS: *Fodor's French for Travelers* ($7; 800/533–6478 to order).

LODGING

Provence and the Côte d'Azur may be the most accommodating region in France, with every kind of hotel, country inn, converted *mas* (Provençal farmhouse), luxury palace, bed-and-breakfast, and vacation rental imaginable. Consider the kind of vacation you want to spend— going native in a country *gîte* (rental house), being pampered in a luxury penthouse over the Mediterranean in Cannes, or getting to know the locals in a cozy B&B. Then check the

Fodor's recommendations in each chapter, or contact the local tourist offices for more specific information.

B&BS

Bed-and-breakfasts, known in France as *chambres d'hôte,* are common in rural Provence, and less so along the Côte d'Azur. Check local tourist offices for details or contact Gîtes de France, the national vacation-lodging organization that lists B&Bs all over the country, from rustic to more luxurious. Often table d'hôte dinners (meals cooked by and eaten with the owners) can be arranged for an extra, fairly nominal fee. Note that in B&Bs, unlike hotels, it is more likely that the owners will only speak French. Staying in one may, however, give you more of an opportunity to meet French people.

➤ B&B GUIDES: **Karen Brown's France: Charming Bed & Breakfasts** and **Rivages Bed & Breakfasts of Character and Charm in France** available in bookstores or from Fodor's Travel Publications (☎ 800/533–6478).

➤ RESERVATION SERVICES: **Gîtes de France** (⊠ 59 rue St-Lazare, 75439 Paris cedex 09, ☎ 01–49–70–75–75, FAX 01–42–81–28–53); request the brochure, "Chambres d'Hôtes: Campagne, Mer et Montagne," which covers Provence, the Alps, and the Côte d'Azur.

CAMPING

French campsites have a good reputation for organization and amenities but are crowded in July and August. Many campsites welcome reservations, and in summer, it makes sense to book in advance.

➤ CAMPSITE GUIDE: **Fédération Française de Camping et de Caravaning** (⊠ 78 rue de Rivoli, 75004 Paris, ☎ 01–42–72–84–08) publishes a guide to France's campsites; they'll send it to you for 100 francs, plus shipping.

HOME EXCHANGES

If you would like to exchange your home for someone else's, **join a home-exchange organization,** which will send you its updated listings of available exchanges for a year and will include your own listing in at least one of them. It's up to you to make specific arrangements. You might also look in the weekly journal *France-USA Contacts* (also known as *FUSAC*), which lists people interested in apartment exchanges.

➤ EXCHANGE CLUBS: **HomeLink International** (✉ Box 650, Key West, FL 33041, ☎ 305/294–7766 or 800/638–3841, 𝔽𝔸𝕏 305/294–1148; $83 per year).

➤ EXCHANGE LISTINGS: **FUSAC** (✉ 3 rue Larochelle, 75014, ☎ 01–45–38–56–57; ✉ Box 115, Cooper Station, NY, NY, 10276, ☎ 212/929–2929).

HOSTELS

No matter what your age, you can **save on lodging costs by staying at hostels** (though some do have age restrictions.) In some 5,000 locations in more than 70 countries around the world, Hostelling International (HI), the umbrella group for a number of national youth hostel associations, offers single-sex, dorm-style beds and, at many hostels, "couples" rooms and family accommodations. Membership in any HI national hostel association, open to travelers of all ages, allows you to stay in HI-affiliated hostels at member rates (one-year membership is about $25 for adults; hostels run about $10–$25 per night). Members also have priority if the hostel is full; they're eligible for discounts around the world, even on rail and bus travel in some countries.

➤ HOSTEL ORGANIZATIONS: **Hostelling International—American Youth Hostels** (✉ 733 15th St. NW, Suite 840, Washington, DC 20005, ☎ 202/783–6161, 𝔽𝔸𝕏 202/783–6171). **Hostelling International—Canada** (✉ 400-205 Catherine St., Ottawa, Ontario K2P 1C3, ☎ 613/237–7884, 𝔽𝔸𝕏 613/237–7868). **Youth Hostel Association of England and Wales** (✉ Trevelyan House, ✉ 8 St. Stephen's Hill, St. Albans, Hertfordshire AL1 2DY, ☎ 01727/855215 or 01727/845047, 𝔽𝔸𝕏 01727/844126); membership in the U.S. $25, in Canada C$26.75, in the U.K. £9.30). **Fédération Unie des Auberges de Jeunesse** (✉ 27 rue Pajol, 75018 Paris, ☎ 01–

44–89–87–27, 𝔽𝔸𝕏 01–44–89–87–10, www.fuaj.org).

HOTELS

Hotels are officially classified from one-star to four-star-deluxe. Prices must, by law, be posted at the hotel entrance and should include taxes and service. Rates are always by room, not per person.

You should always **check what bathroom facilities the price includes,** if any. Because replumbing drains is often prohibitive, if not impossible, old hotels may have added bathrooms—often with *douches* (showers), not *baignoires* (tubs)—to the guest rooms, but not toilets. If you want a private bathroom, state your preference for shower or tub—the latter always costs more. Unless otherwise noted, lodging listings in this book include a private bathroom with a shower *or* tub.

When making your reservation, **ask for a *grand lit* if you want a double bed.** The quality of accommodations, particularly in older properties and even in luxury hotels, can vary greatly from room to room, as hotels are often renovated floor by floor; **if you don't like the room you're given, ask to see another.**

If you're counting on air-conditioning you should **make sure, in advance, that your hotel room is *climatisé*** (air-conditioned). As the French generally haven't fallen in step with American tastes for cold air in a heat-wave, air-conditioning is not a given, even at hotels in inland Provence far from sea breezes. If air-conditioning is not noted in a hotel review, don't assume there will be air-conditioning. And when you throw open the windows, **don't expect screens** *(moustiquaires)*. Nowhere in Europe are they standard equipment, and the only exceptions are found occasionally in the Camargue marshlands, where mosquitos are actually a problem.

Breakfast is not always included in the price, but you are sometimes expected to have it and are occasionally charged for it regardless. Make sure to inform the hotel if you are not going to be breakfasting there. In smaller rural hotels you may be

THE GOLD GUIDE / SMART TRAVEL TIPS

expected to have your evening meal at the hotel, too.

Logis de France hotels are small and inexpensive and can be relied on for comfort, character, and regional cuisine. Look for its distinctive yellow and green sign. The Logis de France paperback guide is widely available in bookshops (100 frs) or from Logis de France.

Relais & Châteaux, Small Luxury Hotels of the World, and Leading Hotels of the World are three prestigious international groups with numerous converted châteaux and manor houses among its members. Not as luxurious, but strong on charm, is the Châteaux et Hôtels Independents group, which, despite the name, has banded together and published its own catalogue.

It's always a good idea to **make hotel reservations as far in advance as possible,** especially in late spring, summer, or fall. If you arrive without a reservation, however, the tourist office may be able to help.

➤ HOTEL DIRECTORIES: **Châteaux et Hôtels Independents** (✉ 12 rue Auber 75009 Paris, ☎ 01–40–07–00–20, FAX 01–40–07–00–30). **Leading Hotels of the World** (✉ 99 Park Ave., NY, NY 10016, ☎ 212/838–7874, FAX 212/758–7367). **Logis de France** (✉ 83 av. d'Italie, 75013 Paris, ☎ 01–45–84–70–00, FAX 01–45–83–59–66). **Relais & Châteaux** (✉ 15 rue Galvani, 75017 Paris, ☎ 01–45–72–96–50, FAX 01–45–72–96–69; ✉ 11 E. 44th St., Suite 707, New York, NY 10017, ☎ 212/856–0115 or 800/860–4930, FAX 212/856–0193). **Small Luxury Hotels of the World** (✉ 1716 Banks St., Houston, TX 77098, ☎ 713/522–9512 or 800/525–4800 in the U.S., FAX 713/524–7412; ✉ James House, Bridge St., Leatherhead, Surrey, KT22 7EP, U.K., ☎ 44/01372–361873, FAX 44/01372–361874).

VACATION RENTALS

If you want a home base that's roomy enough for a family or group and comes with cooking facilities, **consider a furnished rental.** Renting an apartment or a *gîte rural*—a furnished house in the country—for a week or month can save you money if you're traveling with family or with a group. It's possible to even rent quite luxurious properties.

The national rental network, the Fédération Nationale des Gîtes de France, rents rural homes with regional flavor, often restored farmhouses or village row houses in pretty country settings (☞ Close-Up Box, "The Gîte Way," *in* Chapter 1). In fact, the system grew out of a subsidized movement to salvage wonderful old houses falling to ruin. Gîtes-de-France are nearly always maintained by on-site owners, who greet you on your arrival and provide information on groceries, doctors, and nearby attractions.

A nationwide catalogue (105 francs) is available from the Fédération Nationale des Gîtes de France listing gîtes ruraux for rent. Called "Nouveaux Gîtes Ruraux," the catalogue only lists the newest additions to the network because a comprehensive nationwide listing of all gîtes wouldn't fit between two covers. If you know what region you want to stay in, contact the departmental branch directly and order a photo catalogue that lists every property. If you specify which dates you plan to visit, the office will narrow down the choice to rentals available for those days. ☞ Vacation Rentals *in* A to Z sections of each chapter for how to contact regional offices.

Individual tourist offices often publish lists of *locations meublés* (furnished rentals); these are often inspected by the tourist office and rated by comfort standards. Usually they are booked directly through the individual owner, which generally requires some knowledge of French. Rentals that are not classified or rated by the tourist office should be undertaken with trepidation, and can fall well below your minimum standard of comfort.

Vacation rentals in France always book from Saturday to Saturday (with some offering weekend rates off-season). Most do not include bed linens and towels, but make them available for an additional fee. Always check on policies on pets and children, and specify if you need an enclosed garden for toddlers, a washing machine, a fireplace, etc. If you plan to have overnight guests during your stay, let the owner know; there may be additional charges. Insurance restrictions prohibit loading in guests beyond the specified capacity.

➤ CONTACTS: **Fédération Nationale des Gîtes de France** (⌂ 59 rue St-Lazare, 75439 Paris cedex 09, ☎ 01–49–70–75–75, 𝖥𝖠𝖷 01–42–81–28–53). **French Government Tourist Office** (☞ Visitor Information, *below*) is another source for information about vacation rentals.

➤ RENTAL AGENTS: **Chez Vous** (⌂ 1001 Bridgeway, Suite 245, Sausalito, CA 94965, ☎ 415/331–2535, 𝖥𝖠𝖷 415/331–5296). **Drawbridge to Europe** (⌂ 5456 Adams Rd., Talent, OR 97540, ☎ 541/512–8927 or 888/268–1148, 𝖥𝖠𝖷 541/512–0978). **French Experience** (⌂ 370 Lexington Ave., New York, NY 10017, ☎ 212/986–1115, 𝖥𝖠𝖷 212/986–3808). **Hometours International** (⌂ Box 11503, Knoxville, TN 37939, ☎ 423/690–8484 or 800/367–4668). **Interhome** (⌂ 1990 NE 163rd St., North Miami FL, 33162, ☎ 305/940–2299, 𝖥𝖠𝖷 305/940–2911). **Orion** (⌂ 140 E. 56th St., New York, NY 10022, ☎ 800/755–8266, 𝖥𝖠𝖷 212/688–9467). **Property Rentals International** (⌂ 1008 Mansfield Crossing Rd., Richmond, VA 23236, ☎ 804/378–6054 or 800/220–3332, 𝖥𝖠𝖷 804/379–2073). **Rental Directories International** (⌂ 2044 Rittenhouse Sq., Philadelphia, PA 19103, ☎ 215/985–4001, 𝖥𝖠𝖷 215/985–0323). **Rent-a-Home International** (⌂ 7200 34th Ave. NW, Seattle, WA 98117, ☎ 206/789–9377 or 800/488–7368, 𝖥𝖠𝖷 206/789–9379). **Vacation Home Rentals Worldwide** (⌂ 235 Kensington Ave., Norwood, NJ 07648, ☎ 201/767–9393 or 800/633–3284, 𝖥𝖠𝖷 201/767–5510). **Villas and Apartments Abroad** (⌂ 420 Madison Ave., Suite 1003, New York, NY 10017, ☎ 212/759–1025 or 800/433–3020, 𝖥𝖠𝖷 212/755–8316). **Villas International** (⌂ 950 Northgate Dr., Suite 206, San Rafael, CA 94903, ☎ 415/499–9490 or 800/221–2260, 𝖥𝖠𝖷 415/499–9491).

Hideaways International (⌂ 767 Islington St., Portsmouth, NH 03801, ☎ 603/430–4433 or 800/843–4433, 𝖥𝖠𝖷 603/430–4444; membership $99) is a club for travelers who arrange rentals among themselves.

MAIL

POSTAL RATES

Letters and postcards to the United States and Canada cost 4.40 francs (about 75¢) for 20 grams. Letters and postcards to the United Kingdom cost 3 francs (about 33p) for up to 20 grams. Letters and postcards within France cost 3 francs. Stamps can be bought in post offices (La Poste) and cafés sporting a red TABAC sign outside.

RECEIVING MAIL

If you're uncertain where you'll be staying, **have mail sent to the local post office,** addressed as "poste restante," or to American Express, but remember that during peak seasons, American Express may refuse to accept mail.

MONEY

ATMS

ATMs are fairly common in major cities and larger towns and are one of the easiest ways to get francs; don't, however, count on finding ATMs in smaller towns and very rural areas. Banks usually offer excellent, wholesale exchange rates through ATMs.

To get cash at ATMs in France, **your PIN must be four digits long.** You may have more luck with ATMs if you are using a credit card or a debit card that is also a Visa or MasterCard, rather than just your bank card. Note, too, that you may be charged by your bank for using ATMs overseas; inquire at your bank about charges.

Using a debit card (with a Visa or MasterCard symbol on it) makes it easier to find ATMs that you can use.

Before you go, it's a good idea to **get a list of ATM locations that you can use** in France from your bank.

➤ ATM LOCATIONS: **Cirrus** (☏ 800/424–7787). **Plus** (☏ 800/843–7587) for locations in the U.S. and Canada, or visit your local bank.

COSTS

The following prices are to give you an idea of costs. Note that it is less expensive to eat or drink standing at a café or bar counter than it is to sit at a table. Two prices are listed, *au comptoir* (at the counter) and *à salle* (at a table). Coffee in a bar: 6–7 francs (standing), 10–30 francs (seated); beer in a bar: 10 francs (standing), 15–40 francs (seated); Coca-Cola: 6–10 francs a can; ham sandwich: 15–25 francs; one-mile taxi ride: 35 francs; movie: 50 francs (sometimes 15%–35% cheaper on Monday and Wednesday); foreign newspaper: 10–15 francs.

CREDIT & DEBIT CARDS

Many restaurants and stores take both credit and debit cards, though there is often a 100-franc minimum.

➤ REPORTING LOST CARDS: **American Express** (☏ 910/668-5309; call collect). **Diner's Club** (☏ 303/799–1504; call collect). **Mastercard** (☏ 0800/90–1387). **Visa** (☏ 0800/90–1179).

CURRENCY

The units of currency in France are the franc (fr) and the centime. Bills are in denominations of 500, 200, 100, 50, and 20 francs. Coins are 20, 10, 5, 2, and 1 francs and 50, 20, 10, and 5 centimes. At press time (1998), the exchange rate was about 6 francs to the U.S. dollar, 4.09 to the Canadian dollar, 10.07 to the pound sterling, 3.66 to the Australian dollar, 3.12 to the New Zealand dollar, and 8.45 to the Irish punt.

EXCHANGING MONEY

There are a variety of ways to exchange money, though you have greater options in major cities than in rural areas. In general, the **Banque de France has the best rates** of all the banks. In general, however, banks don't always offer great exchange rates.

Another option is to compare rates between booths and banks and **look for exchange booths that clearly state "no commission."** If you are exchanging a large amount of money, you may be able to get a better deal; it's worth asking. Exchange booths in airports, train stations, hotels, and stores generally offer the worst rates, though you may find their hours more convenient.

Although fees charged for ATM transactions may be higher abroad than at home (you may want to check on this before leaving), **ATM exchange rates are often excellent,** because they are based on wholesale rates offered only by major banks. ATMs are also convenient (you get francs right out of the machine), and are found in large cities and towns, and in major airports and train stations (☞ ATMs, *above* for more information).

If you are concerned that you may not be able to use your bank or debit card at the airport or train station when you first arrive, or you want to avoid lines at airport or train station exchange booths, **consider getting a bit of local currency before you leave home.**

➤ EXCHANGE SERVICES: **Chase Currency To Go** (☏ 800/935–9935; 935–9935 in NY, NJ, and CT). **International Currency Express** (☏ 888/842–0880 on the East Coast, 888/278–6628 on the West Coast). **Thomas Cook Currency Services** (☏ 800/287–7362 for telephone orders and retail locations).

TRAVELER'S CHECKS

Do you need traveler's checks? It depends on where you're headed.

If you're going to rural areas and small towns, go with cash; traveler's checks are best used in cities or popular tourist areas.

Although you can usually get cash from ATMs, it makes sense to **bring some money in traveler's checks, just in case.**

If you get traveler's checks in dollars or your country's currency, you can easily exchange these at banks or exchange bureaus, though you must bring along your passport; traveler's checks are almost never accepted by merchants, restaurants, or hotels.

Lost or stolen checks can usually be replaced within 24 hours. To ensure a speedy refund, buy your own traveler's checks—don't let someone else pay for them: Irregularities like this can cause delays. The person who bought the checks should make the call to request a refund.

OUTDOOR ACTIVITIES & SPORTS

Provence and the Côte d'Azur have no shortage of sports facilities. Seaside resorts are well equipped for water sports, such as windsurfing, waterskiing, diving, and jetskiing, and private and public beaches compete to please the crowds. In inland Provence, there are public swimming pools in almost every town.

Bicycling (☞ Bicycling, *above*) and hiking (☞ Hiking, *above*) are popular, especially in the Vaucluse and the hills behind the Côte d'Azur.

Équitation (horseback riding) is possible in many rural areas; a horseback tour of the Camargue is de rigeur. The rivers draining off the Alps offer excellent fishing (check locally for authorization rights), canoeing, and kayaking.

Tennis is phenomenally popular, and courts are everywhere: Try to find a typical *terre battue* (clay court) if you can.

The French are not so keen on jogging, but you'll have no difficulty locating a suitable local park or avenue.

Golf is probably the most popular sport in along the coast, with dozens of slickly maintained, beautifully landscaped courses stretching from St-Tropez to Menton. *See* individual chapters for specific outdoor activities and sports listings.

PACKING

LUGGAGE

How many carry-on bags you can bring with you is up to the airline. Most allow two, but the limit is often reduced to one on certain flights. Gate agents will take excess baggage—including bags they deem oversize—from you as you board and add it to checked luggage. To avoid this situation, make sure that everything you carry aboard will fit under your seat. Also, get to the gate early, and request a seat at the back of the plane; you'll probably board first, while the overhead bins are still empty. Since big, bulky baggage attracts the attention of gate agents and flight attendants on a busy flight, make sure your carry-on is really a carry-on. Finally, a carry-on that's long and narrow is more likely to remain unnoticed than one that's wide and squarish.

On international flights, baggage allowances may be determined not by piece but by weight—generally 88 pounds (40 kilograms) in first class, 66 pounds (30 kilograms) in business class, and 44 pounds (20 kilograms) in economy.

Airline liability for baggage is limited to $1,250 per person on flights within the United States. On international flights it amounts to $9.07 per pound or $20 per kilogram for checked baggage (roughly $640 per 70-pound bag) and $400 per passenger for unchecked baggage. You can buy additional coverage at check-in for about $10 per $1,000 of coverage, but it excludes a rather extensive list of items, shown on your airline ticket.

Before departure, **itemize your bags' contents** and their worth, and label the bags with your name, address, and phone number. (If you use your home address, cover it so that potential thieves can't see it readily.) Inside each bag, **pack a copy of your itinerary.** At check-in, **make sure that each bag is correctly tagged** with the destination airport's three-letter code. If your bags arrive damaged or fail to arrive at all, file a written report with the airline before leaving the airport.

PACKING LIST

In your carry-on luggage **bring an extra pair of eyeglasses or contact lenses** and **enough of any medication** you take to last the entire trip. You may also want your doctor to write a spare prescription using the drug's generic name, since brand names may

THE GOLD GUIDE / SMART TRAVEL TIPS

THE GOLD GUIDE / SMART TRAVEL TIPS

vary from country to country. **Never put prescription drugs or valuables in luggage to be checked.** To avoid customs delays, carry medications in their original packaging.

It's a good idea to **pack a photocopy of your passport in your suitcase,** well removed from the original. And don't forget to copy down and carry addresses of offices that handle refunds of lost traveler's checks.

Although you'll usually have no trouble finding a baggage cart at the airport, luggage restrictions on international flights are tight and baggage carts at railroad stations are not always available, so **pack light.** Even hotel staffs are becoming less and less tolerant of heavy suitcases and heaps of luggage worthy of a Titanic crossing.

Over the years, casual dress has become more acceptable, although the resorts along the Côte d'Azur still feature smart-dressers and fashion-plates.

Jeans are very common, though they, too, are worn very stylishly, with a nice button-down shirt, polo, or t-shirt without writing. Shorts, though longish per current trends, are now a popular item for the younger crowd in most cities. More and more people are wearing sneakers, although you may still stand out as a tourist with them on, especially if you wear them when you go out at night.

There is no need to wear a tie and jacket at most restaurants (unless specified), even fancy ones, though you should still try to look nice. Most casinos and upscale nightclubs along the Côte d'Azur, however, require jackets and ties.

For beach resorts, take a decent cover-up; wearing your bathing suit on the street is frowned upon.

Most of France is hot in the summer, cool in the winter. Since it rains all year round, **bring a raincoat and umbrella.** You'll need a sweater or warm jacket for the Mediterranean in winter.

If you are staying in budget hotels, **take along soap; many hotels either** do not provide it or give you a very limited number. You might also want to bring a washcloth.

PASSPORTS & VISAS

When traveling in France, **carry your passport even if you don't need it** (it's always the best form of I.D.); just be sure to keep it in a very safe place. Also, make **two photocopies of the data page** (one for someone at home and another for you, carried separately from your passport).

If you lose your passport, promptly call the nearest embassy or consulate and the local police; having the data-page information can speed replacement.

ENTERING FRANCE

All Australian, Canadian, New Zealand, U.K, and U.S. citizens, even infants, need only a valid passport to enter France for stays of up to 90 days.

PASSPORT OFFICES

➤ CONTACTS: **Australian Passport Office** (☎ 131–232). **Canadian Passport Office** (☎ 819/994–3500 or 800/567–6868).**New Zealand Passport Office** (☎ 04/494–0700 for information on how to apply, 0800/ 727–776 for information on applications already submitted). **United Kingdom Passport Office, London** (☎ 0990/21010), for fees and documentation requirements and to request an emergency passport. **United States National Passport Information Center** (☎ 900/225–5674; calls are charged at 35¢ per minute for automated service, $1.05 per minute for operator service).

SAFETY

Car break-ins have become part of daily life in the south, especially in the isolated parking lots where hikers set off to explore for the day. Be especially careful around the marshes of the Camargue, the departure point for the Iles d'Hyères ferries, the rocky Esterel between Fréjus and Cannes, and the coastal path around St-Tropez: **Take valuables with you and, if possible, leave your luggage at your hotel.**

Also beware of petty theft—purse snatching and pickpocketing. Use common sense: Avoid pulling out a lot of money in public; and wear a handbag with long straps that you can sling across your body, bandolier-style, with a zippered compartment for your money and passport. It's also a good idea to wear a money belt. Men should keep their wallets up front, as safely tucked away as possible.

SENIOR-CITIZEN TRAVEL

Older travelers to France can take advantage of many discounts, such as reduced admissions of 20%–50% to museums and movie theaters. Seniors 60 and older should **buy a Carte Vermeil,** which entitles the bearer to discounts on rail travel outside Paris (☞ Train Travel, *below*).

To qualify for age-related discounts, **mention your senior-citizen status up front** when booking hotel reservations (not when checking out) and before you're seated in restaurants (not when paying the bill). Note that discounts may be limited to certain menus, days, or hours. When renting a car, **ask about promotional car-rental discounts,** which can be cheaper than senior-citizen rates.

➤ ADVENTURES: **Overseas Adventure Travel** (✉ Grand Circle Corporation, ✉ 625 Mt. Auburn St., Cambridge, MA 02138, ☎ 617/876–0533 or 800/221–0814, FAX 617/876–0455).

➤ EDUCATIONAL PROGRAMS: **Elderhostel** (✉ 75 Federal St., 3rd floor, Boston, MA 02110, ☎ 617/426–8056). **Interhostel** (✉ University of New Hampshire, ✉ 6 Garrison Ave., Durham, NH 03824, ☎ 603/862–1147 or 800/733–9753, FAX 603/862–1113).

SHOPPING

People don't usually bargain in shops where **prices are clearly marked.** But at outdoor and flea markets and in antiques stores, bargaining is a way of life. If you're thinking of buying several items, you've nothing to lose by cheerfully suggesting to the propri-

etor, *"Vous me faites un prix?"* ("How about a discount?").

A number of shops offer VAT taxes to foriegn shoppers (☞ Taxes, *below*).

CLOTHING SIZES

To figure out the French equivalent of U.S. clothing and shoe sizes, **do the following, simple calculations.**

To change U.S. men's suit sizes to French suit sizes, add 10 to the U.S. suit size. For example, a U.S. size 42 is a French size 52.

French men's collar sizes vary in their relation to U.S. collar sizes. But you can get the approximate size by multiplying the U.S. collar size by 2 and adding 8. For example, a U.S. size 15 is a French size 38. A U.S. size 15½ is a French size 39 or 40.

French men's shoe sizes vary in their relation to U.S. shoe sizes. A U.S. men's size 7½ is a French size 40; an 8½ is a 41; a 9½ is a 42.

To change U.S. dress/coat/blouse sizes to French sizes, add 30 to the U.S. size. For example, a U.S. women's size 8 is a French size 38 and a U.S. size 10 is a French size 40.

To change U.S. women's shoe sizes to French shoe sizes, add approximately 31 to the U.S. shoe size. For example, a U.S. size 7 is a French size 38.

STUDENT TRAVEL

There are bargains for students holding a valid college or international student I.D. almost everywhere in the south of France, on train and plane fares, and for movie and museum tickets. So, **carry your valid university or international I.D. card with you at all times so you can get discounts.**

TRAVEL AGENCIES

To save money, **look into deals available through student-oriented travel agencies.** To qualify you'll need a bona fide student I.D. card. Members of international student groups are also eligible.

➤ STUDENT I.D.s & SERVICES: **Council on International Educational Exchange** (☞ *above*), for mail orders only, in the United States. **Travel Cuts** (✉ 187 College St., Toronto, Ontario M5T 1P7, ☎ 416/979–2406 or 800/667–2887) in Canada.

➤ STUDENT TOURS: **Contiki Holidays** (✉ 300 Plaza Alicante, Suite 900, Garden Grove, CA 92840, ☎ 714/740–0808 or 800/266–8454, FAX 714/740–2034). **AESU Travel** (✉ 2 Hamill Rd., Suite 248, Baltimore, MD 21210-1807, ☎ 410/323–4416 or 800/638–7640, FAX 410/323–4498).

TAXES

All taxes must be included in posted prices in France. The initials TTC (*toutes taxes comprises*—taxes included) sometimes appear on price lists but, strictly speaking, are superfluous. By law, **restaurant and hotel prices must include 20.6% taxes and a service charge.** If they show up as extra charges on your bill, complain.

VALUE-ADDED TAX (V.A.T.)

A number of shops offer VAT refunds to foreign shoppers. You are entitled to an Export Discount of 20.6%, depending on the item purchased, but it is often applicable only if your purchases in the same store reach a minimum of 2,800 francs (for U.K. and EU residents) or 1,200 francs (other residents, including U.S. and Canadian residents). Remember to **ask for the refund, as some stores—especially larger ones—offer the service only upon request.**

TELEPHONES

COUNTRY CODES

The country code for France is 33 and for Monaco, 337. All phone numbers in France have a two-digit prefix determined by zone: Paris and the Ile de France, 01; the northwest, 02; the northeast, 03; the southeast, 04; and the southwest, 05. Numbers beginning with 08 are either toll-free or toll calls (with an additional charge on top of making the call).

CALLING FRANCE

When dialing a French number from abroad, drop the inital 0 from the two-digit prefix. To call France from the United States, for instance, dial

011 (for all international calls), then dial 33 (the country code), and the number in France, minus the inital 0. To call France from the United Kingdom, dial 00–33, then dial the number in France minus any initial 0.

CALLING HOME

To call out of France, dial 00 and wait for the tone, then dial the country code (1 for the United States and Canada, 44 for the United Kingdom) and the area code (minus any intial 0) and number. Expect to be overcharged if you call from your hotel.

AT&T, MCI, and Sprint international access codes make calling the United States relatively convenient, but you may find the local access number blocked in many hotel rooms. First ask the hotel operator to connect you. If the hotel operator balks, ask for an international operator, or dial the international operator yourself. One way to improve your odds of getting connected to your long-distance carrier is to travel with more than one company's calling card (a hotel may block Sprint, for example, but not MCI). If all else fails, call from a pay phone in the hotel lobby.

➤ ACCESS CODES: **AT&T Direct** (☎ 08–00–99–00–11; 800/874–4000 for information). **MCI Call USA** (☎ 08–00–99–00–19; 800/444–4444 for information). **Sprint Express** (☎ 08–00–99–00–87; 800/793–1153 for information).

LONG-DISTANCE CALLS

To call any region in France from another region, dial the full 10-digit number (including the two-digit prefix).

LOCAL CALLS

To make calls in the same city or town, or in the same region, dial the full 10-digit number.

OPERATORS & INFORMATION

To find a number **in France, dial 12 for information.** For international inquiries, dial 00–33–12 plus 11 for the U.S., 44 for the U.K.

Another source of information is the Minitel, an online network similar to the Internet. You can find one—they look like a small computer terminal—in most post offices. Available (free for the first three minutes) is an online phone book covering the entire country. To find simple telephone information in France, hit the *appel* (call) key, then the number 3611. When prompted, type the name you are looking for and hit *envoi* (return). This information number is also useful for tracking down services: choose *activité* (activity), tap in *piscine* (swimming pool), then Chartres, for example, and it will give you a list of all the pools in Chartres. Go to other lines or pages by hitting the *suite* (next) key. Newer models will connect automatically when you hit the book-icon key. To disconnect, hit *fin* (end).

PUBLIC PHONES

Telephone booths **can almost always be found at post offices, and often in cafés.** A local call costs 74 centimes for every three minutes; half-price rates apply weekdays between 9:30 PM and 8 AM, from 1:30 PM Saturday, and all day Sunday.

Most **French pay phones are operated by *télécartes* (phone cards),** which you can buy from post offices, métro stations, and some tabacs (tobacco shops) for a cost of 40.6 francs for 50 units and 97.5 francs for 120. Coin operated pay phones are scarce, existing only in cafés (who can set their own rates) and post offices. Phone cards are accepted everywhere else, even the métro. The easiest but most expensive way to phone is to use your own Visa card, which is accepted in all phone booths and works like a télécarte.

TIPPING

The French have a clear idea of when they should be tipped. Bills in bars and restaurants include service, but **it is customary to round out your bill with some small change** unless you're dissatisfied. The amount of this varies: anywhere from 50 centimes if you've merely bought a beer, to 10 francs after a meal. Tip taxi drivers and hairdressers about 10%. Give ushers in theaters and movie theaters 1 or 2 francs. In some theaters and hotels, coat check attendants may expect nothing (if there is a sign saying POURBOIRE INTERDIT—tips forbidden); otherwise give them 2–5 francs. Washroom attendants usually get 2 francs, though the sum is often posted.

If you stay in a hotel for more than two or three days, it is customary to leave something for the chamber-maid—about 10 francs per day. In expensive hotels you may well call on the services of a baggage porter (bell boy) and hotel porter and possibly the telephone receptionist. All expect a tip: Plan on about 10 francs per item for the baggage boy, but the other tips will depend on how much you've used their services—common sense must guide you here. In hotels that provide room service, give 5 francs to the waiter (this does not apply to breakfast served in your room). If the chambermaid does some pressing or laundering for you, give her 5 francs on top of the charge made.

Gas-station attendants get nothing for gas or oil, and 5 or 10 francs for checking tires. Train and airport porters get a fixed 6–10 francs per bag, but you're better off getting your own baggage cart if you can (a 10-franc coin—refundable—is necessary in train stations only). Museum guides should get 5–10 francs after a guided tour, and it is standard practice to tip tour guides (and bus drivers) 10 francs or more after an excursion, depending on its length.

TOUR OPERATORS

Buying a prepackaged tour or independent vacation can make your trip to Provence and the Riviera less expensive and more hassle-free. Because everything is prearranged, you'll spend less time planning.

Operators that handle several hundred thousand travelers per year can use their purchasing power to give you a good price. Their high volume may also indicate financial stability. But some small companies provide more personalized service; because they tend to specialize, they may also

THE GOLD GUIDE / SMART TRAVEL TIPS

be more knowledgeable about a given area.

BOOKING WITH AN AGENT

Travel agents are excellent resources. In fact, large operators accept bookings made only through travel agents. But it's a good idea to **collect brochures from several agencies,** because some agents' suggestions may be influenced by relationships with tour and package firms that reward them for volume sales. If you have a special interest, **find an agent with expertise in that area**; ASTA (☞ Travel Agencies, *below*) has a database of specialists worldwide.

Make sure your travel agent knows the accommodations and other services. Ask about the hotel's location, room size, beds, and whether it has a pool, room service, or programs for children, if you care about these. Has your agent been there in person or sent others you can contact?

Do some homework on your own, too: Local tourism boards can provide information about lesser-known and small-niche operators, some of which may sell only direct.

BUYER BEWARE

Each year consumers are stranded or lose their money when tour operators—even very large ones with excellent reputations—go out of business. So **check out the operator.** Find out how long the company has been in business, and ask several travel agents about its reputation. If the package or tour you are considering is priced lower than in your wildest dreams, **be skeptical.** Try to **book with a company that has a consumer-protection program.** If the operator has such a program, you'll find information about it in the company's brochure. If the operator you are considering does not offer some kind of consumer protection, then ask for references from satisfied customers.

In the U.S., members of the National Tour Association and United States Tour Operators Association are required to set aside funds to cover your payments and travel arrangements in case the company defaults.

It's also a good idea to choose a company that participates in the American Society of Travel Agent's Tour Operator Program (TOP). This gives you a forum if there are any disputes between you and your tour operator; ASTA will act as mediator.

➤ TOUR-OPERATOR RECOMMENDATIONS: **American Society of Travel Agents** (☞ Travel Agencies, *below*). **National Tour Association** (✉ NTA, ✉ 546 E. Main St., Lexington, KY 40508, ☎ 606/226–4444 or 800/755–8687). **United States Tour Operators Association** (✉ USTOA, ✉ 342 Madison Ave., Suite 1522, New York, NY 10173, ☎ 212/599–6599 or 800/468–7862, FAX 212/599–6744).

COSTS

The more your package or tour includes, the better you can predict the ultimate cost of your vacation. Make sure you know exactly what is covered, and **beware of hidden costs.** Are taxes, tips, and service charges included? Transfers and baggage handling? Entertainment and excursions? These can add up.

Prices for packages and tours are usually quoted per person, based on two sharing a room. If traveling solo, you may be required to pay the full double-occupancy rate. Some operators eliminate this surcharge if you agree to be matched with a roommate of the same sex, even if one is not found by departure time.

GROUP TOURS

Among companies that sell tours to Provence and the Riviera, the following are nationally known, have a proven reputation, and offer plenty of options. The classifications used below represent different price categories, and you'll probably encounter these terms when talking to a travel agent or tour operator. The key difference is usually in accommodations, which run from budget to better, and better-yet to best.

➤ SUPER-DELUXE: **Abercrombie & Kent** (✉ 1520 Kensington Rd., Oak Brook, IL 60521-2141, ☎ 630/954–2944 or 800/323–7308, FAX 630/954–3324). **Travcoa** (✉ Box 2630,

2350 S.E. Bristol St., Newport Beach, CA 92660, ☎ 714/476–2800 or 800/992–2003, ℻ 714/476–2538).

➤ DELUXE: **Maupintour** (✉ 1515 St. Andrews Dr., Lawrence, KS 66047, ☎ 785/843–1211 or 800/255–4266, ℻ 785/843–8351). **Tauck Tours** (✉ Box 5027, 276 Post Rd. W, Westport, CT 06881-5027, ☎ 203/226–6911 or 800/468–2825, ℻ 203/221–6866).

➤ FIRST-CLASS: **Brendan Tours** (✉ 15137 Califa St., Van Nuys, CA 91411, ☎ 818/785–9696 or 800/421–8446, ℻ 818/902–9876). **Caravan Tours** (✉ 401 N. Michigan Ave., Chicago, IL 60611, ☎ 312/321–9800 or 800/227–2826, ℻ 312/321–9845). **Collette Tours** (✉ 162 Middle St., Pawtucket, RI 02860, ☎ 401/728–3805 or 800/340–5158, ℻ 401/728–4745). **DER Tours** (✉ 9501 W. Devon St., Rosemont, IL 60018, ☎ 800/937–1235, ℻ 847/692–4141 or 800/282–7474, 800/860–9944 for brochures). **Insight International Tours** (✉ 745 Atlantic Ave., #720, Boston, MA 02111, ☎ 617/482–2000 or 800/582–8380, ℻ 617/482–2884 or 800/622–5015). **Trafalgar Tours** (✉ 11 E. 26th St., New York, NY 10010, ☎ 212/689–8977 or 800/854–0103, ℻ 800/457–6644).

➤ BUDGET: **Trafalgar** (☞ *above*).

PACKAGES

Like group tours, independent vacation packages are available from major tour operators and airlines. The companies listed below offer vacation packages in a broad price range.

➤ AIR/HOTEL: **DER Tours** (☞ First-Class, *above*). **4th Dimension Tours** (✉ 7101 S.W. 99th Ave., #105, Miami, FL 33173, ☎ 305/279–0014 or 800/644–0438, ℻ 305/273–9777).

➤ FROM THE U.K.: **British Airways Holidays** (✉ Astral Towers, Betts Way, London Rd., Crawley, West Sussex RH10 2XA, ☎ 01293/722–727, ℻ 01293/722–624). **Cresta Holidays** (✉ Tabley Ct., Victoria St., Altrincham, Cheshire WA14 1EZ, ☎ 0161/927–7000) for hotel and apartment holidays. **Invitation to France**

(✉ 4 Alice Ct., 116 Putney Bridge Rd., London SW15 2NQ, ☎ 0181/871–3300) for chateaux and country-house hotels. **Thomas Cook** (✉ 45 Berkeley St., London W1A 1EB, ☎ 0171/499–4000) offers fly-drive holidays that may include Disneyland Paris.

THEME TRIPS

➤ ART AND ARCHITECTURE: **Endless Beginnings Tours** (✉ 12650 Sabre Springs Pkwy., Ste. 207-105, San Diego, CA 92128–4114, ☎ 619/566–4166 or 800/822–7855, ℻ 619/679–5376).

➤ BARGE CRUISES: **Abercrombie & Kent** (☞ Group Tours, *above*). **Alden Yacht Charters** (✉ 1909 Alden Landing, Portsmouth, RI 02871, ☎ 401/683–4200 or 800/253–3654, ℻ 401/683–3668). **European Waterways** (✉ 140 E. 56th St., Suite 4C, New York, NY 10022, ☎ 212/688–9489 or 800/217–4447, ℻ 212/688–3778 or 800/296–4554). **KD River Cruises of Europe** (✉ 2500 Westchester Ave., Purchase, NY 10577, ☎ 914/696–3600 or 800/346–6525, ℻ 914/696–0833). **Le Boat** (✉ 10 S. Franklin Turnpike, #204B, Ramsey, NJ 07446, ☎ 201/236–2333 or 800/922–0291). **Maupintour** (☞ Group Tours, *above*).

➤ BICYCLING: **Backroads** (✉ 801 Cedar St., Berkeley, CA 94710-1800, ☎ 510/527–1555 or 800/462–2848, ℻ 510-527–1444). **Bridges Tours** (✉ 2855 Capital Dr., Eugene, OR 97403, ☎ 541/484–1196 or 800/461–6760, ℻ 541/687–9085). **Butterfield & Robinson** (✉ 70 Bond St., Toronto, Ontario, Canada M5B 1X3, ☎ 416/864–1354 or 800/678–1147, ℻ 416/864–0541). **Chateaux Bike Tours** (✉ Box 5706, Denver, CO 80217, ☎ 303/393–6910 or 800/678–2453, ℻ 303/393–6801). **Euro-Bike Tours** (✉ Box 990, De Kalb, IL 60115, ☎ 815/758–8851 or 800/321–6060). **Europeds** (✉ 761 Lighthouse Ave., Monterey, CA 93940, ☎ 800/321–9552, ℻ 408/655–4501). **Himalayan Travel** (✉ 110 Prospect St., Stamford, CT 06901, ☎ 203/359–3711 or 800/225–2380, ℻ 203/359–3669). **Naturequest** (✉ 934 Acapulco St., Laguna Beach, CA

THE GOLD GUIDE / SMART TRAVEL TIPS

92651, ☎ 714/499–9561 or 800/
369–3033, FAX 714/499–0812).
Progressive Travels (✉ 224 W. Galer
Ave., Suite C, Seattle, WA 98119, ☎
206/285–1987 or 800/245–2229, FAX
206/285–1988). **Rocky Mountain
Worldwide Cycle Tours** (✉ 333
Baker St., Nelson, BC0, Canada V1L
4H6, ☎ 250/354–1241 or 800/661–
2453, FAX 250/354–2058). **Safaricen-
tre** (✉ 3201 N. Sepulveda Blvd.,
Manhattan Beach, CA 90266, ☎
310/546–4411 or 800/223–6046, FAX
310/546–3188). **Uniquely Europe** (✉
1940 116th Ave. NE, Bellevue, WA
98004, ☎ 425/455–4445 or 800/
927–3876, FAX 425/455–2111).
Vermont Bicycle Touring (✉ Box
711, Bristol, VT, 05443-0711, ☎
802/453–4811 or 800/245–3868, FAX
802/453–4806).

➤ CUSTOMIZED PACKAGES: **Abercrombie & Kent** (☞ Group Tours, *above*).
Alekx Travel (✉ 519A S. Andrews
Ave., Fort Lauderdale, FL 33301, ☎
954/462–6767, FAX 954/462–8691).
Five Star Touring (✉ 60 E. 42nd St.,
#612, New York, NY 10165, ☎ 212/
818–9140 or 800/792–7827, FAX
212/818–9142). **The French Experience** (✉ 370 Lexington Ave., Suite
812, New York, NY 10017, ☎ 212/
986–1115).

➤ FOOD AND WINE: **Cuisine International** (✉ Box 25228, Dallas, TX
75225, ☎ 214/373–1161, FAX 214/
373–1162). **European Culinary
Adventures** (✉ 5 Ledgewood Way,
Suite 6, Peabody, MA 01960, ☎ 508/
535–5738 or 800/852–2625).

➤ GOLF: **Golf International** (✉ 275
Madison Ave., New York, NY 10016,
☎ 212/986–9176 or 800/833–1389,
FAX 212/986–3720). **ITC Golf Tours**
(✉ 4134 Atlantic Ave., #205, Long
Beach, CA 90807, ☎ 310/595–6905
or 800/257–4981).

➤ HOMES AND GARDENS: **Cooper-
smith's England** (✉ Box 900, Inver-
ness, CA 94937, ☎ 415/669–1914,
FAX 415/669–1942). **Expo Garden
Tours** (✉ 70 Great Oak, Redding,
CT 06896, ☎ 203/938–0410 or 800/
448–2685, FAX 203/938–0427).

➤ HORSEBACK RIDING: **Cross Country
International Equestrian Vacations**
(✉ Box 1170, Millbrook, NY 12545,

☎ 800/828–8768, FAX 914/677–
6077). **Equitour FITS Equestrian** (✉
Box 807, Dubois, WY 82513, ☎
307/455–3363 or 800/545–0019, FAX
307/455–2354).

➤ LEARNING: **Fresh Pond Travel
Vacations** (✉ 186 Alewife Brook
Parkway, Cambridge, MA 02138, ☎
617/661–9200 or 800/645–0001, FAX
617/661–3354). **IST Cultural Tours**
(✉ 225 W. 34th St., New York, NY
10122-0913, ☎ 212/563–1202 or
800/833–2111, FAX 212/594–6953).
**Smithsonian Study Tours and Semi-
nars** (✉ 1100 Jefferson Dr. SW,
Room 3045, MRC 702, Washington,
DC 20560, ☎ 202/357–4700, FAX
202/633–9250).

➤ SPAS: **Great Spas of the World** (✉
55 John St., New York, NY 10038,
☎ 212/267–5500 or 800/772–8463,
FAX 212/571–0510). **Spa-Finders** (✉
91 5th Ave., #301, New York, NY
10003-3039, ☎ 212/924–6800 or
800/255–7727). **Spa Trek Travel** (✉
475 Park Ave. S, New York, NY
10016, ☎ 212/779–3480 or 800/
272–3480, FAX 212/779–3471).

➤ TOUR RESOURCES: **Maison de la
France** (☞ Visitor Information,
below) publishes many brochures on
theme trips in France including "In
the Footsteps of the Painters of Light
in Provence" and "France for the
Jewish Traveler." **Travel Contacts** (✉
Box 173, Camberley, GU15 1YE,
England, ☎ 01276/67–7217, FAX
01276/6–3477) represents over 150
tour operators in Europe.

➤ WALKING: **Abercrombie & Kent**
(☞ Group Tours, *above*). **Backroads**
(☞ Bicycling, *above*). **Butterfield &
Robinson** (☞ Bicycling, *above*).
Country Walkers (✉ Box 180, Water-
bury, VT 05676-0180, ☎ 802/244–
1387 or 800/464–9255, FAX 802/
244–5661). **Euro-Bike Tours** (☞
Bicycling, *above*). **Europeds** (☞
Bicycling, *above*). **Fenwick & Lang**
(✉ 1940 116th Ave. NE, Bellevue,
WA 98004, ☎ 425/455–4445 or
800/927–3876, FAX 425/455–2111).
Himalayan Travel (✉ 110 Prospect
St., Stamford, CT 06901, ☎ 203/
359–3711 or 800/225–2380, FAX
203/359–3669). **Mountain Travel-
Sobek** (✉ 6420 Fairmount Ave., El

Cerrito, CA 94530, ☎ 510/527–8100 or 800/227–2384, FAX 510/525–7710). **Naturequest** (☞ Bicycling, *above*). **Overseas Adventure Travel** (✉ 625 Mt. Auburn St., Cambridge, MA 02138, ☎ 800/955–1925, FAX 617/876–0455). **Progressive Travels** (☞ Bicycling, *above*). **Uniquely Europe** (☞ Bicycling, *above*). **Wilderness Travel** (✉ 1102 Ninth St., Berkeley, CA 94710, ☎ 510/558–2488 or 800/368–2794).

➤ YACHT CHARTERS: **Club Voyages** (✉ 43 Hooper Ave., Atlantic Highlands, NJ 07716, ☎ 888/842–2122 or 732/291–8228, FAX 732/291–4277). **Huntley Yacht Vacations** (✉ 210 Preston Rd., Wernersville, PA 19565, ☎ 610/678–2628 or 800/322–9224, FAX 610/670–1767). **Lynn Jachney Charters** (✉ Box 302, Marblehead, MA 01945, ☎ 617/639–0787 or 800/223–2050, FAX 617/639–0216). **The Moorings** (✉ 19345 U.S. Hwy. 19 N, 4th floor, Clearwater, FL 34624-3193, ☎ 813/530–5424 or 800/535–7289, FAX 813/530–9474). **Ocean Voyages** (✉ 1709 Bridgeway, Sausalito, CA 94965, ☎ 415/332–4681 or 800/299–4444, FAX 415/332–7460).

TRAIN TRAVEL

The SNCF is recognized as Europe's best national rail service: It's fast, punctual, comfortable, and comprehensive. You can get to Provence and the coast from all points west, north, and east, though lines out of Paris are by far the most direct. There are various options: local trains, overnight trains with sleeping accommodations, and the high-speed TGV, the *Trains à Grande Vitesse* (High-Speed Trains).

For overnight accomodations, you have the choice between high-priced *wagons-lits* (sleeping cars) and affordable *couchettes* (bunks, six to a compartment in second class, four to a compartment in first, with sheets and pillow provided, priced at around 90 francs).

The TGVs average 255 kph/160 mph on the Lyon/southeast line, but after Valence, they slow to local-train speeds. It's still the fastest way south: You can get from Paris to Avignon in 3½ hours, and from Paris to Nice in 6½ hours. As with other main-line trains, a small supplement may be assessed during peak hours. The laying of high-speed rails from Valence to Avignon and on to Nice will cut travel time considerably; the project is supposed to be completed by 2001.

Certain models of the TGV, called a "train duplex," offer luxurious, state-of-the-art comfort, with double-decker seating and panoramic views. When one of these passes along the coast—especially from Nice to Menton—it makes for a dramatic sightseeing excursion, though it pokes along at a local-train snail's pace. Ask about duplex trains when you're connecting from one coastal city to another (Marseille–Toulon–Fréjus–Cannes–Nice–Menton).

You must **always make a seat reservation for the TGV**—easily obtained at the ticket window or from an automatic machine. Seat reservations are reassuring but seldom necessary on other main-line French trains, except at certain busy holiday times.

Once you're in the south, though, choose your homebase carefully. Places in hill country and the mountains—the Luberon, the Alpilles, and the backcountry hills behind Nice—are not accessible by train, and you'll have to get around by bus or rental car.

If you know what station you'll depart from, you can get a free train schedule there (while supplies last), or you can access the new multilingual computerized schedule information network at any Paris station and at larger stations (Marseille and Nice). You can also make reservations and buy your ticket while at the computer.

If you are traveling from Paris or any other terminus, **get to the station half an hour before departure** to ensure that you'll have a good seat.

Before boarding, you must **punch your ticket (but not Eurailpass) in one of the orange machines** at the entrance to the platforms, or else the ticket collector will fine you 100 francs on the spot.

► INFORMATION: SNCF (☎ 08–36–35–35–35); note that a per minute charge is assessed.

► WEB SITES: Eurail/Eurostar (www.eurail.com/). SNCF (www.sncf.fr/indexe.htm).

DISCOUNT PASSES

If you plan to travel outside of Paris by train, **consider purchasing a France Rail Pass,** which allows three days of unlimited train travel in a one-month period. Prices begin at $130 for two adults traveling together in second class and $165 second class for a solo traveler. First-class rates are $156 for two adults and $195 for a solo traveler. Additional days may be added for $30 a day in either class. Other options include the France Rail 'n Drive Pass (combining rail and rental car), France Rail 'n Fly Pass (rail travel and one air travel journey within France), and the France Fly Rail 'n Drive Pass (a rail, air, and rental car program all in one).

France is one of 17 countries in which you can **use EurailPasses,** which provide unlimited first-class rail travel, in all of the participating countries, for the duration of the pass. If you plan to rack up the miles, get a standard pass. These are available for 15 days ($522), 21 days ($678), one month ($838), two months ($1,148), and three months ($1,468). If your plans call for only limited train travel, **look into a Europass,** which costs less money than a EurailPass. Unlike EurailPasses, however, you get a limited number of travel days, in a limited number of countries, during a specified time period. For example, a two-month Europass ($316) allows between 5 and 15 days of rail travel, but costs $200 less than the least expensive EurailPass. Keep in mind, however, that the Europass is good only in France, Germany, Italy, Spain, and Switzerland, and the number of countries you can visit is further limited by the type of pass you buy.

In addition to standard EurailPasses, **ask about special rail-pass plans.** Among these are the Eurail Youthpass (for those under age 26), the Eurail Saverpass (which gives a discount for two or more people traveling together), a Eurail Flexipass (which allows a certain number of travel days within a set period), the Euraildrive Pass and the Europass Drive (train and rental car).

Whichever of the above you choose, remember that you must **purchase your pass at home before leaving for Europe.**

Don't assume that your rail pass guarantee you a seat on the train you wish to ride. You need to **book seats ahead even if you are using a rail pass;** seat reservations are required on high-speed trains, and are a good idea on trains that may be crowded—particularly in summer on popular routes. You will also need a reservation for sleeping accommodations.

TICKET AGENTS

Eurail- and Europasses are available through travel agents and a few authorized organizations. **CIT Tours Corp.** (⊠ 15 West 44th St., 10th Floor, New York, NY 10036, ☎ 800/248–7245 for rail or 800/248–8687for tours and hotels). **DER Travel Services** (⊠ 9501 W. Devon Ave., Rosemont, IL 60018, ☎ 800/782–2424). **Rail Europe**(⊠ 226–230 Westchester Ave., White Plains, NY 10604, ☎ 800/438–7245, FAX 800/432–1329; ⊠ 2087 Dundas E., Suite 105, Mississauga, Ontario L4X 1M2, ☎ 905/602–4195),

FRENCH RAIL PASSES

SNCF offers a number of discount rail passes available only for purchase in France. When traveling together, **two people (who don't have to be a couple) can save money with the Prix Découverte à Deux.** You'll get a 25% discount during "périodes bleus" (blue periods; weekdays and not on or near any holidays). Note that you have to be with the person you said you would be traveling with.

You can **get a reduced fare if you are a senior citizen (over 60)** with the Carte Vermeil. There are two options: The first, the Carte Vermeil Quatre Temps, costs 143F and gives you a reduction on 4 trips: 50% off in the blue periods and 20% off during the more crowded "périodes blanches" (white periods; weekends or on or around holidays). The second, the Carte Vermeil Plein Temps, is 279F and allows you, for one year, an unlimited number of 30% reductions on trips within France and a 30% discount on trips outside of France.

With the Carte Kiwi, **children under 16 can get 25%–50% off** four trips for 285 francs, or for a full year of travel for 444 francs. There's a wonderful bonus, too: Up to four accompanying passengers, whether blood relatives or not, get the discount, too.

If you purchase an individual ticket from SNCF in France and you're under 26, you will automatically get a 25% reduction (a valid ID, such as an ISIC card or your passport, is necessary). If you're going to be using the train quite a bit during your stay in France and **if you're under 26, consider buying the Carte 12–25** (270F), which offers unlimited 50% reductions for one year (provided that there's space available at that price, otherwise you'll just get the standard 25% discount).

If you don't benefit from any of these reductions and **if you plan on traveling at least 1,000 km (620 mi) roundtrip (including several stops), look into purchasing a Billet Séjour.** This ticket gives you a 25% reduction if you stay over a Sunday and if you travel only during blue periods. It may be a major organizational feat, but you can save a lot of cash this way.

FROM THE U.K.

Short of flying, the "Chunnel" is the fastest way to cross the English Channel: 3 hours from London's central Waterloo Station to Paris's central Gare du Nord. Round-trip tickets range from 3,400 francs for first class to 690 francs for second class. From Paris, there's direct service on the TGV that whisks you at high speeds as far south as Valence, then putters along at local speeds through Avignon, Marseille, Fréjus, and Nice. For other stops along this coastal route, you may have to change to a local train.

British Rail also has four daily departures from London's Victoria Station, all linking with the Dover-Calais/Boulogne ferry services through to Paris. There is also overnight service on the Newhaven-Dieppe ferry and those out of Hull as well. Journey time is about eight hours. Credit-card bookings are accepted by phone or in person at a British Rail Travel Centre.

➤ CAR TRANSPORT: **Le Shuttle** (☎ 0990/353535 in the U.K.).

➤ PASSENGER SERVICE: In France, **Eurostar** (☎ 08–36–35–35–39). In the U.K., **Eurostar** (☎ 0345/881881), **InterCity Europe** (✉ Victoria Station, London, ☎ 0171/834–2345, 0171/828–0892 for credit-card bookings). In the U.S., **BritRail Travel** (☎ 800/677–8585), **Rail Europe** (☎ 800/942–4866).

➤ SCHEDULE INFORMATION: **British Rail** (☎ 0171/834–2345).

➤ TRAIN-FERRY LINK: **British Rail International** (☎ 0171/834–2345) and **Sealink** (☎ 01–44–94–40–40) provide train-ferry travel between the U.K. and France.

TRANSPORTATION

It's possible to have a satisfying initiation to this broad region by train alone: There are sweeping, comprehensive connections all the way from Montpellier to Avignon to Marseille and on to the full length of the Italian coast. There are good regional bus networks, too, that connect out of train stations, but they're not very efficient for village-hopping and multi-stop sightseeing, as their schedules rarely intersect with yours. And sooner or later you may feel restless and want to burrow inland a bit, and here the trains are much more limited. A rental car is an obvious solution, but if you've flown into Paris, it's a long drive south (7 hours). For an extended vacation in the region, a rail-drive pass allows you to cover a few direct rail trajectories between bases, then take a rental car onto the back roads and byways. Or you could fly to the south of France and rent a car from the airport. If you really want to sit back and let someone else do the work, consider a holiday bus excursion, where the tour company books all lodging and meals and guides you from sight to sight.

TRAVEL AGENCIES

A good travel agent puts your needs first. Look for an agency that has been in business at least five years, emphasizes customer service, and has someone on staff who specializes in your destination. In addition, **make sure the agency belongs to a professional trade organization,** such as ASTA in the United States. If your travel agency is also acting as your tour operator, *see* Buyer Beware in Tour Operators, *above*).

➤ LOCAL AGENT REFERRALS: American Society of Travel Agents (ASTA, ☎ 800/965–2782 24-hr hot line, FAX 703/684–8319). **Association of Canadian Travel Agents** (✉ Suite 201, 1729 Bank St., Ottawa, Ontario K1V 7Z5, ☎ 613/521–0474, FAX 613/521–0805). **Association of British Travel Agents** (✉ 55–57 Newman St., London W1P 4AH, ☎ 0171/637–2444, FAX 0171/637–0713). **Australian Federation of Travel Agents** (☎ 02/9264–3299). **Travel Agents' Association of New Zealand** (☎ 04/499–0104).

➤ FRANCE-FOCUSED AGENCY: **New Frontiers** (✉ 12 E. 33 St., 11th floor, NY, NY 10016, ☎ 800/366–6387 or 212/779-0600, FAX 212/779–1007) books domestic air flights, trains, car rentals, and hotels in France.

TRAVEL GEAR

Travel catalogs specialize in useful items, such as compact alarm clocks and travel irons, that can **save space when packing.** They also offer dual-voltage appliances, currency converters, and foreign-language phrase books.

➤ CATALOGS: **Magellan's** (☎ 800/962–4943, FAX 805/568–5406). **Orvis Travel** (☎ 800/541–3541, FAX 540/343–7053). **TravelSmith** (☎ 800/950–1600, FAX 800/950–1656).

VISITOR INFORMATION

TOURIST INFORMATION

➤ FRENCH GOVERNMENT TOURIST OFFICE: **France On-Call** (☎ 202/659–

7779; Mon.–Fri. 9–9. **Chicago** (✉ 676 N. Michigan Ave., Chicago, IL 60611, ☎ 312/751–7800). **Los Angeles** (✉ 9454 Wilshire Blvd., Suite 715, Beverly Hills, CA 90212, ☎ 310/271–6665, FAX 310/276–2835). **New York City** (✉ 444 Madison Ave., 16th floor, New York, NY 10022, ☎ 212/838–7800). **Canada** (✉ 1981 Ave. McGill College, Suite 490, Montréal, Québec H3A 2W9, ☎ 514/288–4264, FAX 514/845–4868. **U.K.** ✉ 178 Piccadilly, London W1V OAL, ☎ 171/629–2869, FAX 0171/493–6594.

➤ REGIONAL TOURIST OFFICE: The mother lode of general information on the region covered in this book is the **Comité Régional du Tourisme de Provence-Alpes-Côtes d'Azur** (PACA, Regional Committee on Tourisme in Provence, the Alps, and the Côte d'Azur, ✉ 14 rue Ste-Barbe, Espace Colbert, 13001 Marseille, ☎ 04–91–39–38–00, FAX 04–91–56–66–61).

➤ LOCAL TOURIST OFFICES: *See* the A to Z sections *in* individual chapters for local tourist office telephone numbers and addresses.

WORLD WIDE WEB

Do **check out the World Wide Web** when you're planning. You'll find everything from up-to-date weather forecasts to virtual tours of famous cities. The Fodor's Web site, www.fodors.com, is a great place to start your on-line travels. For more information specifically on France, visit the following.

➤ RECOMMENDED WEB SITES: **Eurail/Eurostar** (www.eurail.com/). **French Youth Hostel Federation** (ww.fuaj.org). **Maison de la France/ French Government Tourist Office** (www.francetourism.com and www.maison-de-la-france.com:8000/). **Monaco Tourist Office** (www.monaco.mc/usa/). **Provence Tourist Office** (www.visitprovence.com). **Riviera Tourist Office** (www.crt-riviera.fr/). SNCF (www.sncf.fr/indexe.htm).

WHEN TO GO

July and August in Provence and the Côte d'Azur can be stifling, not only because of the intense heat but the crowds of tourists and vacationers. June and September are the best months to be in the region, as both are free of the midsummer crowds and the weather is summer-balmy. June offers the advantage of long daylight hours, while cheaper prices and many warm days, often lasting well into October, make September attractive. Try to avoid the second half of July and all of August, when almost all of France goes on vacation. Huge crowds jam the roads and beaches, and prices are jacked up in resorts. Don't travel on or around July 14 and August 1, 15, and 31, when every French family is either going on vacation or driving home. Watch out for May, riddled with church holidays—one a week—and

the museum closings they entail. Anytime between March and November will offer you a good chance to soak up the sun on the Côte d'Azur. After All Saints (November 1) the whole region begins to shutter down for winter, and won't open its main resort hotels until Easter. Still, off-season has its charms—the pétanque games are truly just the town folks' game, the most touristy hill towns are virtually abandoned, and when it's nice out—more often than not—you can bask in direct sun in the cafés.

➤ FORECASTS: **Weather Channel Connection** (☎ 900/932–8437), 95¢ per minute from a Touch-Tone phone.

CLIMATE

What follows are average daily temperatures for Provence and the Côte d'Azur.

Jan.	54F	12C	May	70F	21C	Sept.	77F	25C
Feb.	54F	12C	June	80F	27C	Oct.	72F	22C
Mar.	58F	14C	July	83F	28C	Nov.	62F	17C
Apr.	65F	19C	Aug.	83F	28C	Dec.	57F	14C

THE GOLD GUIDE / SMART TRAVEL TIPS

1 Destination: Provence and the Côte d'Azur

STONE, SUN, AND SEA: PROVENCE PRIMORDIAL

THE ROASTED RED ROOFS skew downhill at Cubist angles, sunbleached and mottled with age. Stone and stucco walls emerge from the bedrock all of a hue—amber, saffron, honey. The sky is a prism, scoured to clarity by the juggernaut winds of the mistral; it radiates an azure of palpable intensity and bottomless depth. A rhythm of Romanesque tiles overlap in sensual snaking rows; they were, after all, mixed from the wet clay and molded over the thighs of women, and like their models are as alike and as varied as the reeds in a Pan pipe. Their broad horizontal flow forms a foil for the dark, thrusting verticals of the funeral cypress and the ephemeral, feminine puff of the silvery olive. In the fields behind, white-hot at midday, chill and spare at night, you crunch through an abundance of wild thyme, rosemary, and lavender dried in the arid breeze, their acrid-sweet scent cutting through the crystal air like smelling salts. Sheep bells tinkle behind dry rock walls and churchbells sound across valleys as easily as over the village wall; in the distance is the pulsing roar of the sea. Nowhere in France, and rarely in the Western world, can you touch antiquity with this intimacy—its exoticism, its purity, eternal and alive. Provence and the Côte d'Azur: Together they are, as the French say, primordial.

Basking luxuriously along the sunny southern flank of France, bordered to the east by Italy, sheltered to the northeast by the Alps, and leaning west and southwest toward its Spanish-influenced neighbors in Languedoc and the Basque country, Provence and its famous coast are to the Mediterranean as Eve was to Adam's rib, begotten, as it were, by the Fertile Crescent. The Greeks and Phocaeans first brought classical culture to the Celt-like Ligurian natives of the coast in 600 BC when they founded Massilia (Marseille), which thrived as a cosmopolitan colony—the Athens of a nascent Europe—until their alliance with the upstart Romans in Aix turned sour.

Julius Caesar himself claimed Marseille in 49 BC, and thus it came to be Provincia Romana, the first Roman stronghold in Gaul. The best of Latin culture flourished here until the fall of the Empire, some of it outliving Rome. Under Roman rule, the *indigenes* (natives) were transformed (as one period writer had it) from "mustachioed, abundantly hairy, exuburant, audacious, thoughtless, boastful, passionate warriors" into disciplined hard workers—at least temporarily. In its wake, Rome left its physical mark as well: The theater and triumphal arch in Orange; the amphitheaters in Nîmes and Arles; the magnificent aqueduct bridge called the Pont du Gard; the mausoleum, arch, and village ruins in St-Rémy; the villas and baths in Vaison-le-Romaine—these monuments, still standing today, are considered among the best of their kind in existence, easily rivaling the Colosseum in Rome. The Maison Carrée in Nîmes, built by Agrippa in 16 BC, remains as pure an homage to their Greek forebears as the Romans ever produced. Vivid details in Roman artifacts bring the stories to life: The creamy marble bust of Octavian found in Arles shows a peach-fuzz beard on his all-too-young face—a Roman sign of mourning for the assassination of Julius Caesar.

Yet the noble remains of Rome have taken on a patina and given way to the more modest culture of modern Provence, where the village shops shutter down for the *sieste,* matrons pinch melons with the concentration of wine tasters in Bordeaux, and the menfolk hunch earnestly over a milky glass of pastis and size up the angle of a rolling *pétanque* ball with the skepticism and discretion of a federal judge. In this modern province, Provence, the olives blacken at their own pace to onyx, then ebony, and the melons plump with juice drawn deep under the rocky Alpilles; the world moves slowly in the heat.

Until the cell phone rings. Then the "New South" shows its well-tanned profile as one of the most coveted regions for tourism in France—even, no, especially, by the

French. Today Provence and its Côte d'Azur implies a lazy, laissez-faire lifestyle, a barefoot idyll, three-hour lunches, sultry terrace nights, and a splash in the Mediterranean . . . but *branché,* plugged in, connected by phones and freeways and airports and the TGV to Paris and the world. Many a pale, embittered northerner has found new lust for life in its chic contemporary pulse, converting old *mas* (farmhouses) into summer homes, and opening restaurants and hotels that out-Provence Provence.

These vacation retreats brim over with Provençal architecture (roughly construed in shades of ochre and pink), Provençal decor (sophisticated country prints, cheery-colored pottery, and curves of bronzed iron), and Provençal cuisine (olive oil, garlic, grilled vegetables, and fish). And it doesn't just stop at the borders: The Provence formula is a world-wide fashion now, a panacea of sunshine that brightens the darkest streets of both hemispheres. If the '80s were about Italy, from the dawning of fettuccine Alfredo to Memphis high-tech design to the wholesale invasion of Tuscan villas, the '90s were the Provençal Renaissance—and the fashion shows no sign of abating.

It's a post-industrial phenomenon, this worship of the southern *soleil,* launched by northern aristocrats fleeing the fog and coal smog on which they blamed their pallor, their lassitude, and their very real tuberculosis. The light was a blessing, the Mediterranean breezes a relief, and railroads and steamers cut swaths to the coast, first carrying the sickly, then the privileged and adventurous, then the creative, and ultimately the glamorous to its primal combination of light, rock, and sea.

Everyone from Russian princes to American robber barons to writers and thinkers flocked to the southern coast, constructing a fantasy world of gleaming-white villas, of turquoise swimming pools, and balustrades framing Technicolor sunsets. The Lost Generation found a new home here under the palms—Hemingway, Zelda and Scott Fitzgerald, nurturing a brood of bitter wits like Dorothy Parker, John Dos Passos, and Gertrude Stein and Alice B. Toklas.

And the whole of 20th-century art seemed to bloom under its sun—Picasso, Matisse, Cézanne, van Gogh, Chagall, Monet,

Léger, and Miró. The crystalline light and elemental forms inspired them, and the *volupté* of the Mediterranean saturates their work—sensual fruit, lush flowers, fundamental forms, light and color analyzed, interpreted, transformed, revealed. They, like the literati before them, found in this primeval setting the peace and stimulation to create.

Then came the movie stars, trading the palm trees of Hollywood for the palm trees of the Riviera. Grace Kelly married a prince and led her own tiny principality on a cliff over the sparkling blue waters of Monaco; a tousled and tanned Robert Mitchum was arrested for smoking marijuana and swimming with a topless starlet in Cannes. A teenaged Brigitte Bardot moved heaven and earth when she swayed, flat-footed and full-lipped, through *And God Created Woman* in St-Tropez.

And the world followed, blessed with long vacations, easy air travel, and post-war prosperity. On the slim, rocky beaches of the coast were nurtured the first Perfect Tans, cultivated with tantalizing exhibitionism on every flauntable inch of skin. And still today, oblivious to the ozone hole, rank on rank of nearly bare bodies press flank to flank on the Mediterranean shore.

Yet caveat emptor—the glamour of the Côte d'Azur has, for the most part, been crowded down to the shoreline and swept out to sea: Honky-tonk tourist traps, candy-pink duplexes, and projectlike highrises dominate much of the region, while the wealthy hoard their seaside serenity in private, isolated villas. At greasy brasseries along the waterfront, sunburned visitors and leathery locals fight for the waiter's attention just to gulp down a " 'ot dog" and a lukewarm Coke, or to strain through the canned crab in a mass-produced bourride. Only off-season—early spring, late fall, even fine mid-winter days—can you experience the healing balm of the gentle sun, the mesmerizing rhythm of the waves, the squeaky-clean breeze that flows steady and sure from the infinite blue horizon.

To find the grace and antiquity of the region, and the sun if not the seaside, you'll want to retreat to the noble city old-towns—Nice, Marseille, Aix, and Avignon—and the slow-paced villages, both nestled along the waterfront and rising like ziggurats on stony hilltops behind the coast. Here you'll discover the palpable light, the honeyed hues, the rough-hewn geometry that inspired van Gogh and Cézanne, Picasso and Matisse.

Anywhere in this ancient region you may share their epiphany, whether standing humbled inside the 5th-century baptistery in St-Saveur in Aix; breakfasting on a wrought-iron balcony overlooking turquoise Mediterranean tides; contemplating the orbs and linear perspective of a melon field outside Cavaillon; or sipping the sea-perfumed elixir of a great bouillabaisse (surely the Phocaeans sipped something similar 2,600 years ago) along the docks of Marseille. Evocative, earthy, eternal, primordial: Like a woven rope of garlic, Provence and its coast are the essence of Latin France.

decade. In the 1980s the dark-green pine forests on Cézanne's beloved Montagne Ste-Victoire were razed, leaving the famous profile bald and bleak. Then Marcel Pagnol's beloved countryside, where he set *Manon des Sources* (*Manon of the Springs*), was stripped by wildfire. Now it's the **Calanques** (rocky coves) just east of Marseille—those closest to the city, not to neighboring Cassis—that have suffered repeated arson attacks. The resinous brush and aromatic herbs that crackle underfoot go up in a flash, fed by the ripping winds of the mistral. Forbidding summer hikers to go into the coastal hills hasn't helped; the fires are set deliberately by arsons with a grudge against the world, who wait for the weather report and strike when the mistral offers the full bellows of its force.

NEW AND NOTEWORTHY

This may be your last chance to visit Provence before new waves of visitors roar into the region on the soon-to-be-open **TGV Mediterranée,** the *train à grande vitesse* (high-speed train) that will whisk Parisians to Marseille in 3 hours. Expected to open for service in June 2001, the massive construction site cuts a swath from Valence to Avignon, then forks toward Nîmes to the southwest and toward Marseille to the southeast. The construction is especially visible between Avignon and Salon-de-Provence, sometimes complicating travel on the autoroute. Two new TGV stations are being built in Provence: One below Avignon (best time from Paris projected at 2 hours 40 minutes), one below Aix-en-Provence (best time 2 hours 50 minutes); and the venerable old Gare St-Charles in downtown Marseille is being remodeled to accommodate its slick new visitor. Meanwhile, if you take the TGV *before* the opening, you'll be whisked at hare-like speeds to Valence—then you'll make like a tortoise to Avignon, Marseille, and Nice. Enjoy the scenery: Next time you ride this route it may streak past in a 300-km-an-hour blur.

Forest fires continued to ravage the arid hills above Marseille throughout the summer of 1998, attacking a region that has already stood heavy fire losses over the past

WHAT'S WHERE

The Alpilles, Arles, and the Camargue

On the marshy, windswept flatlands around the Rhône River delta and the raw-rock hills of Les Alpilles, which divert the river west, this region was a major Roman crossroads, profiting from the river, the coast, and a route through the Alps. Nowhere in France will you find such a concentration of antiquities, so superbly preserved: whole arenas, a complete Greco-Roman village, and the impressive aqueduct called the Pont du Gard. It's a region of haunting natural beauty, too, with the Camargue's hypnotic plane of marsh grass stretching to the sea, interrupted only by the occasional explosion of flying flamingos. The scenery is only surpassed by the cities, each cut from its own stamp: Feisty, tatty, Latin Nîmes; graceful Arles, still resonant with the memory of van Gogh; chic, cosmopolitan St-Rémy, a haven for fashionable urbanites; and Montpellier, a hip university town carrying on a humanist tradition dating from the Renaissance.

The Vaucluse

Anchored by the magnificent papal stronghold of Avignon, with its gargantuan medieval palace and crenelled city walls, the Vaucluse spreads luxuriantly north into the prestigious Rhône vineyards of Châteauneuf-du-Pape and east into wild mountain country covered with orchards of olive, apricot, and almond. There are fields of Roman ruins in Vaison-la-Romaine and a fully functional Roman theater in Orange, draped at the foot of Mont Ventoux. But thanks in part to the tantalizing descriptions of British author Peter Mayle, the world beats a path to the Luberon, a long, low mountain covered in dark forests, patchworked with vineyards and olive groves, and punctuated by medieval hilltop villages in shades of ochre and honey gold: Bonnieux, Ménerbes, Roussillon, and Gordes. Like Mayle, others, too, are seeking the sun-blessed lifestyle of fresh-picked melons, cool stone farmhouses, and bare feet.

Aix, Marseille, and the Central Coast

Cézanne lived and died in the city of Aix and painted the rugged, dry countryside around it in rough-hewn daubs of russet and green. Marcel Pagnol, filmmaker and author of *Jean de Florette* and *Manon des Sources* (*Manon of the Springs*) spent a lifetime capturing the scent of thyme and the roar of the fish market in his native territory around Marseille. This is inspirational country, both for the austere beauty of its scenery and the rhythm of its cities: sleek, smart Aix, burgeoning with international students and the arts, both painterly and musical; and the metropolis of Marseille—bold, ancient, larger than life, and dazzling white in the Mediterranean sun.

And then there's the coast, basically ignored by the hordes that jostle along the Côte d'Azur. Along it are pockets of natural beauty that could pass for an Aegean island; the rocky calanques between Marseille and the picture-perfect port of Cassis make for some of the prettiest coastline in France. Along this quiet underbelly are small bays, local beaches, and spectacular views from the coastal highway. There's Bandol, as well known for its beaches as its crystalline pink wine, and the brawny shipyard city of Toulon, full of urban grit. And at the end of the world, the Presqu'île de Giens—the region's southernmost point—ferries leave hourly for the car-free paradise on the Iles d'Hyères.

The Western Côte d'Azur

This is where the legend begins: The palm trees swaying, the crystalline sun, the ocean improbably blue, all framed against a backdrop of the looming green Massif des Maures and the red-rock Massif de l'Esterel. There's the fishing-village cachet of St-Tropez, its port-front cafés thick with young gentry affecting indifference but peeping furtively over their sunglasses in hopes of glimpsing a movie star. There are vast family-beach conglomerates like Ste-Maxime and Fréjus, and *sportif* resorts like St-Raphaël and Mandelieu. And there's Cannes, of course, the ultimate Grand Tour Mediterranean resort town, which maintains its grace and glamour even after the film stars go home.

Yet an important part of the experience of visiting this stellar coastline is to retreat from it, even briefly, and visit the hills behind. Here you'll still find old Provence, palpable in the crumbling medieval stone, the broad and heavy-leafed plane trees, and the chink of the metal balls in a sandlot game of *pétanque* (lawn bowling). All this is just minutes from the coast, in the famous hill towns and *villages perchés* (perched villages), built high on hilltops to fend off attacks from the Moors. There's Mougins, Picasso's final retreat; Fayence, named for its tradition of pottery making; and the sunny perfume-making center of Grasse, where you can nonetheless lose yourself in the narrowest, darkest old-town streets this side of Marseille.

Venture even farther past this most accessible plateau, and you'll enter the wild and wonderful backcountry of Haute Provence, winding on mountain roads from hill town to hill town until you reach one of France's greatest natural wonders: the Gorges du Verdon, a Grand Canyon–like chasm roaring with milky green water and edged by some of Europe's most hair-raising roads.

Nice and the Eastern Côte d'Azur

With its extraordinary climate, cosseted by Mediterranean breezes and sheltered from the mistral by a spectacular backdrop of green cliffs and silver Alps, it's easy to see why this eastern branch of the Côte d'Azur won the heart of the world. But that's its downside, too: The concentration of sun seekers and their concrete villas have scarred the landscape and rendered transit, dining, and sunbathing almost impossible in the August peak. But filter out the excess of tourists, and you have the magnificent natural site and superb light that seduced Matisse, Picasso, Renoir, and Cocteau. They offered their thanks with an outpouring of masterpieces and decorated chapels that alone justify a visit to the region.

Some of the most appealing and varied ports in the south of France are on the eastern Côte d'Azur: The noble old bastion of Antibes and its luxurious peninsula, the Cap d'Antibes; the pretty fishing port of Villefranche-sur-Mer; the yacht port of St-Jean on the tropical peninsula of Cap Ferrat; and the lemon-scented seaside resort town of Menton. The two main urban centers of this region couldn't be more different: There's Nice, full of textures, scents, and history, rich with museums, and colored with its own cuisine and patois. And there's slick, state-of-the-art Monaco, bristling with high-rises and luxury villas—a playground for the wealthy.

From the coast you can drive up into the hills in minutes and visit picturesque hill towns that cater to the crowds: St-Paul-de-Vence, Vence, and Tourrettes-sur-Loup. Or you can take a day or two and leave it all behind, plunging into the deep *arrière-pays* (backcountry) between the coast and the Alps, a world of deep forest gorges, isolated mountain towns, and moving Renaissance painted chapels.

PLEASURES AND PASTIMES

Antiquities

Though France is full of ancient treasures, an extraordinary concentration of them are here along the Mediterranean coast, where dragon's head galleys sailed in from Phoécea, Greece, Rome, and Africa. The south of France flourished in the glory days of Athens and Alexandria, and by the time Julius Caesar conquered the coast it had been long since well tamed. If you visit the ruins of Glanum in St-Rémy, the old Greco-Roman crossroads on a major Alpine route, you'll see the vestiges of baths and of central heating. In Arles and Nîmes, theaters attest to a thriving high culture and arenas to one popular and often cruel. Vaison-la-Romaine has remains of vast libraries, cooking vats, and flush toi-

lets. And the granddaddy of all Roman treasures is the Pont du Gard, the magnificent multitier aqueduct straddling the Gardon River west of Avignon.

Art

Artists have been drawn to the south of France for generations, awed by its luminous colors and crystal-clear light. Monet, Renoir, Gauguin, and van Gogh led the way, followed over the years by Léger, Matisse, Picasso, Chagall, and Cocteau. Cézanne had the good fortune to be born in Aix, and he returned to it, and to his beloved country home nearby, throughout his life.

The artists left behind them a superb legacy of works, utterly individual but all consistently bathed in Mediterranean color and light. That's why a visit to this region can be as culturally rich as a month in Paris and just as intimately allied to the setting that inspired the work. Art museums abound: Aix, Menton, and Nice all have modest Beaux-Arts museums, each with a handful of pieces that rise above the ordinary. And there's the superlative Fondation Maeght in St-Paul-de-Vence, which is devoted to contemporary works. But the real draw is the one-man museum: Cézanne's studio in Aix, Renoir's garden home in Cagnes, Biot's Léger museum, and virtual shrines to Matisse and Chagall in Nice. In Antibes's château is a vast collection of Picasso's work and Menton hosts a bastion full of nothing but the fantasies of Cocteau. And Picasso, Matisse, and Cocteau all decorated chapels with broad frescos, following a tradition that was born on Côte d'Azur soil.

There's earlier art, too, in this region where culture dates back thousands of years. Roman sculptures and mosaics are found throughout Provence, alive with images of the fauna and flora of France. And all along the Côte d'Azur and the backcountry behind Nice, you'll find marvelous "primitive" sacred art, a grave misnomer for paintings in a passionate and graceful style executed in 15th-century churches throughout the region. The leader of this school of painting was the Niçois artist Louis Bréa, and his disciples—often as tender and direct in style as their master—abound.

If you love art, don't miss out on the Carte Musée Côte d'Azur, a museum pass that grants you unlimited access to some

58 museums from Cannes to the Italian border. For 70 francs you have three days to move freely from, say, the Picasso museum in Antibes to the Renoir studio in Cagnes to the Fondation Maeght in St-Paul-de-Vence. For 140 francs you get a pass that's good for seven days. It doesn't work across the border in Monaco, though. Ask for it at any participating museum or in certain *bureaux de changes* (for information call ☎ 04–93–52–33–25).

You'll notice a peculiar phenomenon if you study published museum hours in this most Latin of French regions: In summer the lunch hour expands to accommodate that extra bottle of rosé, with many museums (and shops, too) closing until 3 or even 4, then staying open until 7 or later. Take any published timetable (including those in this guide) with a grain of salt, as even the ticket takers and curators shrug and qualify with " . . . *un peu près*" ("more or less").

Beaches and Swimming Pools

The beaches of the French Riviera have long been reviled for their famous *galets,* round white stones the size of your fist heaped along the shoreline, just where the sand should be. Sit on them for long, and you'll have to shift; lie on them with a book, and you'll feel like a fakir on a rounded bed of nails. Mattresses are de rigueur, and not just for Côte d'Azur cachet. Some resorts ship in truckfuls of sand or shovel in loads from deep water. But there are *some* natural sand beaches on the southern French coast—especially between St-Tropez and Cannes. Provence's coastline—between the Camargue and St-Tropez—alternates sandy pockets with rocky inlets called *criques* and *calanques* where you perch on black rocks and ease yourself into the turquoise water.

But inland Provence gets hot—hotter by far than the breeze-cooled coast. And here you'll find that no matter how you may come to resent the influx of over-landscaped *mas* (farmhouses) and the flocks of tourists, when you're hot, there's nothing like a swimming pool. Thus an entire culture of hotels-with-pools dominates the new Provence, the best of them carefully harmonized with gardens of cypress and lavender. On the Côte d'Azur, given the larger-than-life sense of privilege and indulgence, hotel pools are surprisingly small—even in the luxury hotels of Cannes.

They're just big enough for a cool freshwater dip after a day in the salty waves of the sea.

Châteaux and Villas

The length of the coastline, the hills behind, and the banks of the Rhône River bristle with blunt, thick-stoned fortresses that kept aggressors out, from Saracens (meaning, very loosely, any Islamic peoples—Moors, Arabs, Turks) to feudal contenders. These bastions were so effectively placed and the coastline such a crucial strategic site that these early structures were often reinforced and expanded through the ages, especially in the formidable sloped star shape unique to the 17th-century military engineer Vauban. Tarascon and Beaucaire have daunting castles that face off across the Rhône, and Oppède, Ménerbes, and Lacoste offer the staunch ruins of Vaucluse fiefdoms. Crenelated towers loom high in the mountains above Breil-sur-Roya and on the hilltop in Trigance, deep in Haute Provence. But the Mediterranean coast and the hills just behind bristle belligerently with castles keeping watch over the sea, from St-Tropez's citadelle to Cannes's Le Suquet to Eze's aerie fortress to Menton's waterfront bastion—not to mention the dozens of inland perched villages, each crowned with the remains of its feudal ramparts.

Most of the more delicate, residential châteaux seem to have been converted into hotels to accommodate the huge influx of visitors to the region. On the Côte d'Azur, the extravagances of the Belle Époque left a legacy of fabulous villas of every shape, size, and cultural reference, from Moroccan to Spanish to Greek to Japanese. Many have survived as tourist attractions, while others have metamorphosed into luxury lodgings, and a few still serve as exclusive retreats of the privileged few.

Churches, Abbeys, and Painted Chapels

This isn't Gothic cathedral country, but a treasure trove of smaller church gems offer a moving, more intimate alternative. Provence is peppered with tiny Romanesque churches, as pure and austere in form as a cathedral is flamboyant. The tiniest of these, with rounded apse, single naves, and a minimum of windows, speak of aeons before the turn of the first millennium, though they generally date from the 11th or 12th centuries. Their counterparts, similar in spirit if not in scale: The massive Romanesque abbeys that loom in grim Cistercian austerity over quiet fields in Provence, perfect in their symmetry, their pure geometry, and the ageless antiquity of their form.

All the aesthetic force of chapels in mountain villages are focused on their frescoes, and they lack the extravagance of Gothic arches and cross vaults. These famous painted chapels of the coastal mountains have every inch of their inner surface decorated with images of saints, angels, demons, and the life of Christ. These simple painted chapels often stand side by side with sophisticated, sensual Baroque churches, embellished and garnished and gilded within an inch of their lives. The most extravagant of these churches are in Nice, concentrated in nooks and crannies of the old town. But even some of the most isolated backcountry villages have Baroque churches to rival the finest in town.

You needn't go into them all. This isn't Florence, where if you miss a church you miss a Masaccio. Most of the area's churches don't contain masterworks, and many are architectural hybrids. But in the few you may choose to enter, the sense of cultural nuance, of history, and of the rhythm of form and light will reveal to you part of the essence of the south.

Dining

The sound of a bottle of rosé swirling in a bucket of ice, the sizzle of a fennel-grilled fish when you drizzle a green trail of olive oil over the flesh, the dappling green shade splashed with fuchsia patches of bougainvillea and scarlet trails of geraniums—these are the sensual delights of a long garden lunch in the south of France. At night the colors intensify to chiaroscuro tones, with bright strings of yellow bulbs strung between the pollards and lamplight glowing through broad green leaves. You see it in the faces of the diners around you, who left behind dark city canyons and bland suburbs, who slip into sherbet-color linens and slouch gracefully, gratefully, in a wrought-iron garden chair: lassitude, contentment, and *volupté* (sensuality).

And you won't waddle away from the table at the end of the meal. The cuisine of Provence and the Côte d'Azur has al-ways been light—shunning the beef, pork, and butter of the north for fresh fish, plump vegetables, and the most delicate of olive oils. Produce may be picked year-round in the back *potager* (vegetable patch), and the mesclun salads—sprouts of peppery baby greens—may be tossed and rolled in its vast salad bowl with the earnest attention usually reserved for church ritual so as not to bruise the fresh-cut leaves. None of the north's oozing Livarots and ammoniac jolts of ripe Muenster here: Just cool mozzarella interspersed with basil leaves before the meal, a concise nugget of goat cheese standing, virginally pure, in an emerald pool of oil.

You'll eat late in the south, rarely before 1 for lunch, usually after 9 at night. In summer, shops and museums may shut down until 3 or 4, as much to accommodate lazy lunchers as for the crowds taking sun on the beach. But a late lunch works nicely with a late breakfast—and that's another southern luxury. As morning here is the coolest part of the day and the light is at its sweetest, hotels of every class take pains to make breakfast memorable and whenever possible served outdoors. There may be tables in the garden with sunny-print cloths and a nosegay of flowers, or even a tray on your private balcony table. Accompanied by birdsong and cool morning sun, it's one of the three loveliest meals of the day.

Flora

Although the hot-house crescent of the Côte d'Azur blooms extravagantly with palm trees, lemon trees, bananas, and jungle flowers, the rest of Provence has a flora all its own—austere, hardy, and aromatic. The intense heat of the summer sun alternates with the razor-sharp winds of the mistral—a freight train of air blasting hard down the Rhône Valley. The vegetation battens down and lies low, turning thick, tiny, waxy leaves toward the assault of heat and wind—as if to say, the less surface exposed, the better. Boxwood and holly and dwarf scrub oak cover the hillsides. Rosemary and lavender send out leaves that are matchstick thin and wrap themselves in woody bark dense with aromatic resin. Bushy mimosas send out feathery, fernlike leaves and thick showers of the finest of yellow flowers. Eucalyptus flutters long ribbon strips of aromatic leaves, and olive trees hang clusters of silver ovals, their twisted trunks staked deep into the earth with broad, strong roots. The cork oak develops a thick bark so resistant and watertight, it's harvested in sheets. And the pines define the landscape, the tall black-green silhouettes of the pin d'alep (a species of mediterranean pine) tortured into random forms, the mushroom-shape parasol pine spreading a thick, black dome over the earth.

Yet the plane tree is a paradox. Although its brothers tuck in like sumo wrestlers against heat and wind, these *grandes dames* spread glorious branches wide over city squares, their leaves broad and heavy as palms, creating their own deep shade in summer, then shedding all to let in the gentle winter sun.

But the cypress is the symbol of Provence, its tall evergreen spears flanking mansion and mas and symbolizing hospitality. Tradition has it that one cypress symbolizes the proffering of a glass of water to passersby; two means water and a meal; and three means a night's sleep in the barn.

Pastis and Pétanque

The café is a way of life in Provence, a shady outdoor living room where friends gather like family and share the ritual of the long, cool drink of pastis, the discussion of the weather (hot), and an amble over to the *pétanque* (lawn bowling) court. They stand, somber and intense, hands on hips or folded behind backs, and watch the intricate play of heavy metal balls rolling and clicking. A knot of onlookers gathers, disperses, is reinforced with those with a fresh interest. In this region of the animated debate, the waving gesture, the forefinger punching to chest, it is a surprisingly quiet pastime and deeply ingrained into the rhythm of daily life.

Perched Villages

In the Middle Ages, pirates and brigands, Saracens and acquisitive lords drove village life to put its wagons, as it were, in a circle—and well above the fray. Thus the whole of Provence and its coast sprouted dense stone *villages perchés* (perched villages) from the hilltops, Babel-like towers of canted cubes and blunt cylinders in shades of dove-gray and honey-gold. Built with the stone beneath them, they seem to grow out of the rock, organic and somehow alive. Houses mount several levels, with rooms sometimes covering seven or eight floors; thus freed from obstructing neighbors, their windows take in light and wide-open views. The tiniest of streets weave between these rakish building blocks, and the houses seem tied together by arching overpasses and rhythmic arcades. Wells spring up in miniature *placettes* (little squares), the trickling sound echoing loud in the stone enclosure. The whole of the ensemble is often wrapped in a wall and crowned with the two strongest assurances of protection, sacred and secular: A steeple and a watchtower.

Nowadays many of the hill towns are nearly ghost towns, though more and more are tapping into the tourist boom. Those closest to the coast and to urban centers—in the Luberon and in Nice's backcountry, in particular—have become souvenir malls choked with galleries of dubious quality. As the tourist packs rove on in search of authenticity, the other hill towns develop their commerce and find new life. Only Peillon, above Nice, has resisted development, its citizens voting to ban commerce from its steep-raked streets. There, and deep north in Haute Provence, you can still wander aimlessly through the maze of tunnel-like *ruelles* (alleys) and feel the isolation—often idyllic, sometimes harsh—of these eagle's-nest enclaves, high above the world.

Shopping

Some of the eagle's-nest hilltop villages have their predatory claws unfurled these days, with every house a storefront overflowing with doodads and geegaws in Provençal themes. You'll find olive-wood herb grinders, mass-produced sachets of lavender, and bubble-gum-scented olive-oil soaps. Fabric in bright Indian prints—the country cottons that have come to mean Provence—has been fashioned into any and every salable form, from tea cozies and aprons to toilet-paper holders covered with olive sprigs. There are pottery mugs with good-luck *cigales* (cicadas) and coasters of the famous sunflowers. And galleries flaunt Day-Glo bright paintings—hallucinatory takeoffs on van Gogh and Cézanne.

These items are the bastard children of legitimate crafts and products that are marvelously and intrinsically Provençal. Far from the beaten tourist paths, in the fashionable towns and discreet backstreets of

THE GÎTE WAY

YOU COME HOME from a hard day's sightseeing, slip off your shoes, pull a pitcher of cold water from the fridge, pour a pastis and carry it out to the terrace. There's a basket heavy with goodies from the village market—a fresh rabbit, three different tubs of olives, a cup of fresh-scooped tapenade, apricots and melons warm from the sun. After your drink, you'll sort it all out and fix supper, French pop music sambaing gently on the radio. You'll eat as long and as late as you like, and carry the children to their twin beds in the back room before you take a stroll through the almond grove or crunch through the wild thyme to look at the city lights strung far below. Even doing the dishes in the sink seems okay in this far-away, summer-cottage mode, far from the mini-bars, lobby-lounges, and snotty waiters of the beaten tourist track.

This is the gîte way, the alternative to hotels and restaurants and even to the anonymous seaside vacation flats farmed out by agencies abroad. The national network known as Gîtes de France has organized and catalogued a vast assortment of rural houses, many of them restored farmhouses and old village bastides, most of them rich in regional character and set in the picturesque countryside. The participating houses are inspected and categorized by comfort level (for example, three stars includes a washing machine), with standardized lists of minimum furnishings (from corkscrews to salad spinners to vegetable peelers).

But the key to the charm is the personal touch: Gîtes de France owners greet their guests on arrival, and may pop by (discreetly, rarely) during the week with lettuce from their garden, a bottle from their vineyard, holiday candy for the kids. There's a cupboard full of maps and brochures on local museums, and often the name of a nearby restaurant if you're too sunburned to cook. And they'll come to collect the key a week later and wish you a bon voyage.

There are drawbacks, of course: You'll have to bring towels and linens, and make up the beds yourself (you can often rent linens from the host if you prefer), and you are requested to leave the house in the same condition in which you found it—which usually means impeccable, and requires some mopping and scrubbing.

But the privacy and independence counterbalance any drudgery, and you'll meet people far different from the tourists and supercilious concierges of standardized hotels: farmers, teachers, wine-makers, artists, anyone with the time to care for a cottage, a neighboring farmhouse, a converted stone barn.

Contact the headquarters of the département you plan to visit and request a catalogue of properties, then make a reservation by phone or fax. You must give them a 25% down payment with your reservation, then the rest when you return the contract, one month before your visit. The addresses of Gîte-de-France branches are listed in the Vacation Rentals of A to Z sections in every regional chapter; for more information on the gîte way, *see* Lodging *in* the Gold Guide.

cities, you'll find some of the loveliest products in France. Some of the options: *boutis,* intricately quilted cotton throws; richly textured Provençal fabrics in 18th-century reproduction prints, put to legitimate use as skirts, curtains, and luxurious tablecloths; fine faience from Moustiers, its swirling grotesques dating from the 16th century; bubbled blown glass from Biot; pottery tableware and garden pots from Aubagne, Biot, and Vallauris; marvelously mild and natural *savon de Marseille* (Marseille soap); artisanal olive oil from Nice and the Alpilles; and if you acquire the taste, the sometimes exquisitely rendered *santons,* tiny terra-cotta figurines first made for Provençal Christmas crèches.

Wine

Although Provence has a few fine wines—notably the lower Rhône greats like Châteauneuf-du-Pape and Beaumes-de-Venise and a few excellent whites from Cassis, Bandol, and Palette—the majority of wine drunk here is unpretentious, sunny stuff, with the most by far being rosé. As much as it is identified with olives and cypress trees, the quintessential Provençal landscape is defined by the retreating perspective of row on rocky row of gnarled vines, their green shoots growing heavy through the summer and by fall sagging under the weight of ripe grapes. In winter there's the tantalizing smell of burning clippings as the farmers work their way slowly up one row, down another, trimming off last year's growth.

There are several sub-regions of southern wines. In the eastern Languedoc, above the Camargue, is the region known as Costières-de-Nîmes, and a straightforward table wine from the Côtes-de-Luberon appears on every Vaucluse table, alongside the equally unpretentious Côtes-du-Ventoux. But generally from the Rhône eastward the wines fall under the undemanding umbrella title of Côtes de Provence, meaning simply the hills of Provence.

Remember that in these parts the word *vin* (wine) twangs through the nose like a broken banjo string and sounds more like *vaing. Santé* (to your health)!

FODOR'S CHOICE

Following is a highly subjective compendium of *coups de coeur* (heartthrobs) and favorites, from the humble to the magnificent.

Antiquities

★ **Amphitheater, Arles.** Though a hair less flawlessly preserved than its triple-tiered rival at Nîmes, this Colosseum-style Roman stadium stands at the heart of Arles's quiet old town, and is all the easier to appreciate without Nîmes's roaring traffic.

★ **Les Antiques, St-Rémy.** Just across the highway from the ruined Greco-Roman village of Glanum, these two superbly detailed Roman monuments date from 30 BC, when they marked an important trans-Alpine crossroads.

★ **Pont du Gard.** The granddaddy of Roman treasures in France and surely one of the wonders of the (classical) world, this imposing multitiered aqueduct-bridge deserves the awestruck crowds it attracts.

★ **Quartier de la Villasse, Vaison-la-Romaine.** At these skeletal remains of a Roman village, it's the toilets in the *thermes* (baths) that stick in the memory: They are so perfectly preserved and efficiently constructed, with fresh water used to sweep waste down raked troughs.

★ **Village des Bories, Gordes.** Mysterious origins that trace back to the Celto-Ligurians, primeval forms, and hiding places scattered through the olive groves make these ancient huts the most evocative structures south of Stonehenge.

Beaches

★ **Calanque En Vau, Cassis.** You can only reach this castaway's cove by boat or by hiking the cliff top and clambering down the steep rocks, but it's worth it: Nowhere else on the coast can you find such a tiny slice of paradise, surrounded by massive cliffs and sheltered from the winds of the open sea.

★ **Plage de Pampelonne, St-Tropez.** This pristine stretch of soft sand looks out to the open sea and northeast along the whole of the Côte d'Azur.

Churches

★ **Abbaye de Montmajour, north of Arles.** All the more evocative because it stands empty and ruined on a hilltop at the foot of Les Alpilles, this Romanesque abbey retains its pure vaulting forms.

★ **Abbaye de Sénanque, near Gordes.** With its rhythm of perfectly preserved Romanesque cubes, vaults, and domes, this abbey functions today in pure isolation, surrounded by fields of lavender.

★ **Cathédrale St-Sauveur, Aix-en-Provence.** It's worth planning your visit to Aix around the rare weekly opening of the Nicolas de Froment triptych in this cathedral, itself a marvelous hodgepodge of Merovingian, Romanesque, Gothic, and Baroque styles.

★ **Chapelle de la Miséricorde, Nice.** Of the dozens of florid Baroque chapels scattered throughout Nice's old town, this one is the most magnificent; it's a superbly balanced *pièce-montée* (wedding cake) of half-domes and cupolas, decorated frescoes, faux marble, gilt, and crystal chandeliers.

★ **Église St-Trophime, Arles.** You won't find a more perfectly preserved Romanesque facade in the south of France—its arcing lines and superb figurative detail are enough to rivet you to the place de la République on which it stands.

★ **Groupe Épiscopal, Fréjus.** A superb 5th-century baptistery surrounded by Corinthian columns, a delicate Gothic cloister, and an austere cathedral make up this ensemble at the top of Fréjus's old town.

★ **Notre-Dame-des-Fontaines, Vallée de la Roya.** Isolated in a wooded valley and surrounded by the roar of mountain streams, this tiny chapel was decorated in the 15th century with moving, sometimes naively powerful, images of the life and death of Christ.

Dining

★ **L'Affenage, Arles.** A roaring fireplace grill and a parade of crockery bowls full of Provençal hors d'oeuvres (eggplant, tapenade, and chick-peas with cumin) make this a popular lunch spot. $

★ **Le Boucanier, La Napoule.** Despite the '60s decor, tables by the window look over the port and the château, and you won't find fresh fish less pretentiously served anywhere else on the coast. $$

★ **Bouchon d'Objectif, Cannes.** This bistro mounts photography exhibits and serves simple Provençal fare: fish with aïoli, rabbit terrine, and fresh goat cheese salads. $

★ **Chez Jacotte, Nîmes.** A bright-fauve color scheme, candlelight, cuisine imaginatively spiced, and the warm welcome make this the perfect little hole-in-the-wall, in Nîmes's old town. $

★ **La Cuisine de Reine, Avignon.** A tongue-in-chic commedia dell'arte decor and arcade windows overlooking the green court augment the fresh, eclectic cooking. $$

★ **Le Fournil, Bonnieux.** The hip owners have decorated this little niche, carved deep in a stone cliff, with contemporary art and mismatched linens; the food is fresh, light, and classic. $$–$$$

★ **Galerie des Arcades, Biot.** This restaurant is old-style Provence, adopted by an artsy clientele but maintained in checkered-cloth authenticity. $

★ **Grand Café de Turin, Nice.** This tiny bistro is a Côte d'Azur institution for platters of oysters, clams, and sea urchins. $$

★ **Jacques Maximin, Vence.** Maximin, the thunder-browed bad-boy genius, has fled his triumphs on the coast and opened a country inn where his cooking maintains a standard of cutting-edge chic and inspired imagination. $$$

★ **Le Jardin de Sens, Montpellier.** With numerous awards already under their belts, the unstoppable Pourcel brothers have now been voted Meilleurs Chefs de l'Année by the most discriminating critics of all: their peers. $$$$

★ **Lou Pistou, Nice.** Sample the classics of old-Nice cuisine—*soupe au pistou* (minestrone with pesto), *pissaladière* (a pizzalike dish topped with caramelized onions and anchovy spread), and *petits farcis* (red peppers, zucchini, and eggplant stuffed with spicy sausage)—in this friendly shoebox-size mom-and-pop joint. $–$$

★ **Le Louis XV, Monte Carlo.** Crystal, gilt, and period pomp frame the extraordinary cuisine of Alain Ducasse, certainly one of France's finest chefs—but holding forth in Monaco. $$$$

★ **La Mérenda, Nice.** Making a full retreat from haute cuisine, the great Dominique Le Stanc, formerly of the Negresco Hotel, opened this back-to-bistro hideaway; you have to stop by in person to reserve since there's no phone. $$

★ **Montagard, Cannes.** This place is a rarity in France: it serves imaginative, stylishly prepared vegetarian cuisine in a cool, chic setting. $

Drives

★ **Corniche de l'Estérel (N98), from St-Raphaël to La Napoule.** As you drive along this dramatic cliff-top coastline highway, with the red rock of the Esterel sloping spectacularly down to the azure water, you'll get a glimpse of the coast as it was before the building boom.

★ **Route de la Corniche Sublime, Gorges du Verdon.** Don't drive along here if you suffer from vertigo, because the views from the passenger side drop off a cool mile down to the seething green water below. That's why it's one of the most spectacular drives in Europe.

★ **Routes des Crêtes, Cassis to La Ciotat.** This extraordinary drive takes you to the top of the Cap Canaille, a massive cliff that soars above the rocky coast.

Gardens

★ **Jardin Thuret, Cap d'Antibes.** This is the garden where the botanist Gustave Thuret first introduced the exotic, subtropical greenery that now defines the Côte d'Azur; its position on a peninsula surrounded by the sea is magnificent.

★ **Villa Ephrussi-Rothschild, St-Jean-Cap-Ferrat.** No less than seven gardens designed by theme—rustic Provençal, serene Japanese, the severe symmetry of the French—crown this hilltop estate that takes in sea views from both sides.

Lodging

★ **Aiglon, Menton.** A converted mansion with a luxurious garden, a pool, and a pretty restaurant, this inn stands a block from the ocean. $$-$$$

★ **Arlatan, Arles.** Dainty but aristocratic, this prettily decorated 15th-century mansion sits in the heart of the old town. $$$

★ **Auberge de la Madone, Peillon.** High on a hill at the edge of this boutique-free perched village, this inn is the ultimate Provençal getaway—and it's just miles from the Côte d'Azur. $$-$$$

★ **La Bastides de Moustiers, Moustiers.** Alain Ducasse plays country gentleman here, supervising a protégé chef and tending his herb garden on the grounds of this lovely old stone country house. $$$$

★ **Brise Marine, St-Jean-Cap-Ferrat.** With a balustraded terrace opening toward the sea and homey guest rooms, this "seabreeze" inn provides a rare chance for you to live like the other half who people Cap Ferrat. $$$

★ **Château des Ollières, Nice.** Live like the Russian nobles who flocked to 19th-century Nice in this flamboyantly luxurious hilltop villa. $$$$

★ **Le Clos de Buis, Bonnieux.** This bed-and-breakfast has a pool with a valley view, impeccable regional-style rooms, and the ambience of a home with guests instead of paying customers. $$

★ **La Glycine, Porquerolles, Iles d'Hyères.** This hotel is an unpretentious oasis in the center of the island's village. $$-$$$

★ **Jardin d'Emile, Cassis.** Parasol pines, chalk cliffs, and sea views add charm to this cozy-chic romantic retreat. $$

★ **Lou Cagnard, St-Tropez.** Young, new owners have fixed up this bargain retreat with fresh tiles and a lovely garden. $-$$

★ **Mas de Cacharel, Stes-Maries-sur-Mer.** Serene and isolated along the border of the Camargue's natural reserve, this simple retreat has wild egrets that flutter up when you drive in and white horses that gaze on you by the pool. $$

★ **La Mirande, Avignon.** Arguably the loveliest hotel in Provence, this grand but intimate hotel nestles at the foot of the Popes' Palace and is exquisitely decorated in rich fabrics. $$$$

★ **Muette, Arles.** The results of the hard work and devotion of a couple who love old architecture, this modest old-town inn has exposed stone, beams, and fresh sunflowers in every room. $

★ **La Perouse, Nice.** More Côte d'Azur than old Nice, this cliff-top hideaway has a pool surrounded by lemon trees and sweeping views of the Baie des Anges. $$$$

☆ **Le Petit Nice, Marseille.** Play Nick and Nora Charles in this extravagantly beautiful cliff-top villa with balustraded terrace over the sea. *$$$$*

☆ **Quatre Dauphins, Aix.** In the noble old quarter below the cours Mirabeau, this pretty little hotel is brightened by Provençal fabrics, painted furniture, and a personal welcome. *$–$$*

☆ **Windsor, Nice.** Rooms are decorated by artists, and there's a meditation space upstairs, but it's the tropical garden that makes this downtown hotel a tiny paradise. *$$*

Markets

☆ **Antiques Market, Isle-sur-la-Sorgue.** Lacy linens, crockery, oak washstands, and almost-old-master paintings crowd the banks of the Sorgue canals during the Sunday antiques market.

☆ **City Market, Aix.** Every Provençal delicacy imaginable can be tucked into your basket at this chic city market, augmented by antiques on Tuesday, Thursday, and Saturday.

☆ **Cours Saleya Market, Nice.** Flanked by cafés and overflowing with vivid flowers, this long stretch of stands vaunts olives, fresh crabs, *socca* (a pancake of chick-pea flour), and mesclun salad mix.

☆ **Fish and North African Markets, Marseille.** Both the theatrical fish market on the quai des Belges and the activity-filled North African market on place des Capucins make this big city feel like an international village.

☆ **Local Market, Aubagne.** Authentic, atmospheric, and full of farm stands brimming with local produce, this is the real thing: A Provençal market, with pots, pillows, mesclun, and all.

☆ **Marché Couvert, Menton.** In a Belle-Époque shelter just in from the seaside, fruit, cheese, bread, fish, and game are arranged like jewels in an upscale boutique, but the spirit is pure Provençal.

Museums

☆ **Centre de la Vieille Charité, Marseille.** Its extraordinary neoclassic architecture and fine ethnic and archaeology museums make this converted hospice a must-see.

☆ **Fondation Maeght, St-Paul-de-Vence.** For its serene setting in a hilltop woods and its light-flooded displays of modern works, this gallery-museum is the best mixed-artist exhibition space in the south of France.

☆ **Musée de l'Arles Antique, Arles.** This state-of-the-art shrine to antiquity has magnificent mosaics viewed from platforms and rows of early Christian sarcophagi.

☆ **Musée Matisse, Nice.** In a superb Italianate villa above Nice, Matisse's family has amassed a wide-ranging collection of the artist's works.

☆ **Musée National Message Biblique Marc Chagall, Nice.** This passionate and personal collection of late works shows the artist at his life-affirming best.

☆ **Musée Océanographique, Monaco.** With its atmosphere of Victorian adventure and its aquarium tanks full of exotic sea life, this museum is one of a kind.

☆ **Musée Picasso, Antibes.** This noble old seaside château seems to struggle to contain the energy and inspiration Picasso brings to its walls.

☆ **Museon Arlaten, Arles.** This museum houses the quirky, personal collection of Provençaliana from Frédéric Mistral himself, the 19th-century poet and father of the Provençal revival.

Natural Wonders

☆ **Fontaine de Vaucluse.** Welling out of the center of the earth and sheltered by vertiginous cliffs, this phenomenal spring gushes down to a pretty riverside town.

☆ **Gorges du Verdon, Haute Provence.** France's Grand Canyon mixes dizzying cliff-top views with roaring green water and the scent of wild boxwood.

☆ **Roussillon.** The village seems to grow out of the stone around it, from which the earthy reds and golds of the local ochre are extracted.

Old Towns

☆ **Commune Libre du Safranier, Antibes.** Narrow alley-streets, shutters, laundry, and a riot of flowering vines make this neighborhood off Antibes's old town picture-book pretty.

☆ **Le Panier, Marseille.** This dense maze of improbably tall row houses perched impossibly close looms dark, exotic, and terribly Mediterranean above the old port.

★ **Vieux Nice, Nice.** Far from gentrified, this aromatic neighborhood seethes with unself-conscious life, the energy and texture that sets Nice apart; food stands selling Niçoise specialties and the jewel-box Baroque chapels on every corner add to its charm.

Perched villages

★ **Oppède-le-Vieux.** Isolated above the Luberon, this village stands alone in the mist, lovingly cared for by its residents but utterly uncommercial.

★ **Peillon.** This perfect example of the eagle's-nest villages above the coast has been voted boutique-free forever by its citizens, and remains marvelously ancient, even primeval, in atmosphere.

★ **Saorge.** Watercolor tones and precarious cants over the forest gorge give the old houses of this mountain village surreal beauty.

Ports of Call

★ **Anse Croisette/Les Goudes, Marseille.** The end of the world, they call it, and it feels like it, on a rocky thrust between the city and the calanques of Cassis.

★ **Cassis.** Under the imposing monolith of the Cap Canaille and the picturesque ruins of a medieval château, this pretty pleasure port mixes sophisticated yachts and brightly painted fishing boats.

★ **St-Jean-Cap-Ferrat.** Yachts sail into dock and passengers jump out for lunch at one of the port-side cafés that make this gateway to the cape all the more appealing.

★ **Villefranche.** With a portly citadelle and a medieval old town that spills down to the waterfront cafés, this town is the most picturesque Mediterranean port on the Côte d'Azur.

Walks and Hikes

★ **Promenade Le Corbusier, Roquebrune-Cap Martin.** Wander over rocks and through lush greenery on this contemplative capeside trail that leads to what was once Le Corbusier's waterfront retreat.

★ **Sentier Martel, Gorges du Verdon.** This harrowing canyon trail, clinging to walls above the torrent of the Verdon river, over vertical iron ladders, and through tunnels ankle deep in water, has been called the best of France's Grande Randonées (Great Trails); if you dare take your eyes off your feet, the setting is spectacular.

GREAT ITINERARIES

In a week to 10 days, you can get a good feel for what makes the south of France famous—and wonderful. Here are some suggestions for how to structure a visit. Or create your own route using the suggested itineraries in each chapter.

First-time Tour

To hit on the highlights of the south and mix the best of the arid hills of Provence with the tropical glamour of the Côte d'Azur, settle in to a town for two or three nights at a time and make local excursions from there, taking advantage of the autoroute network that can whisk you from one vastly different experience to the next.

➤ DURATION: 8 days.

➤ THE MAIN ROUTE: **Four nights: Avignon** or **Arles.** Base yourself in these atmospheric Provençal towns, then make day trips to **Les Baux** and **St-Rémy** in the arid Alpilles, to the hilltop villages of **Gordes** or **Bonnieux** in the Luberon, or to **Vaison-la-Romaine** to see the Roman ruins. Also, don't miss the majestic Roman aqueduct, the **Pont du Gard.**

Four nights: Antibes or **St-Jean-Cap-Ferrat.** Here you can experience the history and beauty of the Côte d'Azur and walk along one of the luxurious jungle peninsulas of Cap d'Antibes or Cap Ferrat. You can visit perfume factories in **Grasse,** the hilltop medieval towns of **St-Paul-de-Vence** or **Vence,** and spend a day in urban, exotic Nice.

➤ GETTING AROUND: You'll need a car for this tour, as trains don't penetrate the hill country, and only the most intrepid bikers can tackle the hills. You can try to synchronize train travel with regional bus connections, but must be of a military mindset and live with tight and often inconvenient schedules.

➤ INFORMATION: *See* Chapters 2, 3, 5, and 6.

Great Provençal Towns: Aix, Arles, and Avignon

If you want to focus only on the best of Provence—its history, its architecture, its markets, and its cafés, devote your time to the "three As" and the area between them that anchors the heart of Provence.

➤ DURATION: 6 days.

➤ THE MAIN ROUTE: **Two nights: Avignon.** Visit the Pope's Palace and Les Halles, the covered market. Take a half-day excursion to the **Pont du Gard.** On your way south visit the hauntingly beautiful **Abbaye de Montmajour.**

Two nights: Arles. Visit the Roman monuments—the arena and the theater—and peruse the Musée d'Arles Antique. Sample quirky Provençal history in the Museon Arlaten and study the superb Romanesque proportions of St-Trophime and its cloisters.

Two nights: Aix. View the handful of Cézannes in the Musée Granet, then visit the artist's studio. Wander the twisting streets of the old town and visit the cathedral with its Froment triptych and its 5th-century baptistery. But mainly, pull up a café chair on the grand and graceful cours Mirabeau and watch the world go by.

➤ GETTING AROUND: You can visit everything on this itinerary by train except the Pont du Gard and the Abbaye de Montmajour, for which a rental car or an excursion bus is necessary.

➤ INFORMATION: *See* Chapters 2, 3, and 4.

Peter Mayle Country

You can cover much of the ground the British author brought to life in *A Year in Provence* and subsequent books and in the process see some of the best of the Vaucluse.

➤ DURATION: 6 days.

➤ THE MAIN ROUTE: **Two nights: Isle-sur-la-Sorgue.** Aim for a Sunday to peruse the famous antiques market along the waterwheels and canals of the Sorgue River, enjoy the unpretentious backstreets of the old town, and make a half-day pilgrimage to **Fontaine de Vaucluse,** both for its lovely setting and for its natural wonder, the torrent that wells up from deep under spectacular cliffs.

Two nights: Bonnieux. Use Bonnieux as a base to explore other Luberon hill towns: **Oppède** and **Ménerbes,** ochre-red **Roussil-**lon, and **Gordes,** with its mysterious stone huts called *bories.*

Two nights: Avignon. In addition to enjoying this ancient city's palace and museums, make a pilgrimage to the Les Halles market Mayle describes in *A Year in Provence* and drive up to **Orange** to see the Roman theater, home of the famous annual opera festival.

➤ GETTING AROUND: A car is crucial to visiting the Luberon, as the rail line stops at Isle-sur-la-Sorgue. Biking is hard work in these hills, but the countryside and pretty hill towns make it rewarding if you're in good shape.

➤ INFORMATION: *See* Chapter 3.

20th-Century Art Tour

If you want to make a pilgrimage to the land of the famous light that inspired many of this century's greatest artists, it's easy to follow a line of the villages they loved—and where they left palpable traces.

➤ DURATION: Assuming you're in it only for the art, give yourself six days. Add time for beaches, backcountry drives, wine tasting, or clifftop walks, and you could easily spend two weeks.

➤ THE MAIN ROUTE: **One night: Arles.** His neighbors in Arles had van Gogh evicted and declared dangerous; thus this city he loved neither purchased nor inherited his work. Yet the town bears the traces of his days here, a time of intense engagement and productivity.

One night: Aix. Visit Cézanne's studio, the shop where his father sold hats, and the Musée Granet, where a few of his paintings remain. Drive into the countryside to view his beloved Jas de Bouffan (only from afar, as it's private) and take in views of Ste-Victoire, the mountain that Cézanne immortalized in myriad paintings.

Two nights: Antibes. Visit the château where Picasso experimented on a grand scale and the resulting museum of his works. Drive up to **Biot,** where Fernand Léger left a legacy of bold mosaics, ceramics, and stained glass. In **Cagnes,** visit Renoir's last home and its inspiring garden. Drive up to **St-Paul-de-Vence** to visit the Fondation Maeght, surrounded by Miró sculptures and filled with contemporary art.

Two nights: Nice. Hike or take the bus up to the Cimiez neighborhood, where two marvelous museums enshrine the works of Matisse and Chagall. Make a trip to **Menton** to see Cocteau's bastion and stop at **Villefranche** to view his decorated chapel St-Pierre. If you have time, hike out the Cap Martin to see Le Corbusier's pure, unassuming *cabanon,* a waterfront retreat he designed for himself.

➤ GETTING AROUND: Though most of the towns can be accessed by train, you'll need a car to get to Biot, the heights of Cagnes, and St-Paul-de-Vence. You may be able to book bus excursions to these places out of Nice, but not every sight is serviced every day.

➤ INFORMATION: *See* Chapters 2, 4, 5, and 6.

Cruising the Côte d'Azur

Make like a movie star and follow the coastline from St-Tropez to Cannes to Antibes to Monte Carlo—hitting the best beaches, circling the tropical capes, perusing the markets, and making the requisite hill-town run into St-Paul, Vence, or Grasse. You can base yourself in one or two resorts and make excursions by train or car, or hotel hop from stop to stop. Be sure to wear your sunglasses!

➤ DURATION: 10 days.

➤ THE MAIN ROUTE: **Two nights: St-Tropez.** Make the port-side scene in the cafés, see the Impressionists at the Annonciade, and climb up to the Citadelle. The next day, drive up to **Gassin** and **Ramatuelle** for views and old-town wandering.

Two nights: Cannes. Walk up into Le Suquet, the old town, take a boat to Ile **Ste-Marguerite,** and bask on La Croisette, the waterfront promenade. The next day, consider an excursion up to **Grasse** to visit a perfume factory and explore the Italian-style old town; or shop for ceramics in **Vallauris** and glass art in **Biot.**

Two nights: Antibes. Visit the Picasso museum, stroll the waterfront ramparts, and wander the old town with its Provençal market. Then hike or drive out onto the **Cap d'Antibes** for a day of tropical hedonism. If it's rainy or you're sunburned, opt for an excursion up to the pretty perched village of **St-Paul** or the walled old town of **Vence.**

Two nights: Nice. This is the big-city leg of your trip, so immerse yourself in culture: the Matisse and Chagall museums, or the cutting-edge Modern Art Museum. Then stroll through the labyrinthine old town, and allow time to sit on the pebbly beach on the stunning Baie des Anges.

Two nights: Villefranche-sur-Mer or St-Jean-Cap-Ferrat. Either of these pretty ports take you back to the days before the Riviera became the land of pink concrete, and both offer easy access to the tropical glories of Cap Ferrat. Take in the Villa Kerylos in neighboring **Beaulieu,** or tour the art-charged rooms and expansive gardens of the Villa Ephrussi-Rothschild in **St-Jean-Cap-Ferrat.**

One night: Monte Carlo. Consider ending your vacation with a bang, and splurge on a night at one of the grand hotels in this wealthy urban enclave glittering over the sea. Drop by your neighbors' at the Prince's Palace, and visit the pirhanas at the Museum of Oceanography.

➤ GETTING AROUND: Most of the coastal towns in this itinerary can be visited along the magnificent Provence-Côte d'Azur train lines, with the exception of St-Tropez; its nearest rail stop is at Fréjus/St-Raphaël. Any ventures inland, however—to Ramatuelle, St-Paul or Vence, Grasse, Biot, or Vallauris—must be accomplished by car or by excursion buses, which depart from major towns.

➤ INFORMATION: *See* Chapters 5 and 6.

FESTIVALS AND SEASONAL EVENTS

Much of the year, Provence and the Côte d'Azur has extraordinary weather, dependable sunshine, and balmy summer nights. And while it may not be the land of the midnight sun, France profits from late sunsets June through mid-August (remember, Marseille is on the same northern latitude as Halifax). All this makes Provence and the Côte d'Azur festival country, from moonlit operas in the Roman theater in Orange to sunbaked bullfights in Arles. For general information on festivals and events in this region, write to the **Comité Régional de Tourisme PACA** (Provence-Alpes-Côte d'Azur; ⊠ 14 rue Ste-Barbe, 13001 Marseille, ☎ 04–91–39–38–00). The precise dates of the following festivals vary from year to year, so check with local tourist offices for details.

WINTER

➤ DEC.: Throughout Provence, village churches display charming, sometimes exquisitely executed **crèches,** featuring the tiny terra-cotta figurines called *santons,* which are native to Marseille and Aubagne.

➤ JAN.: On the fourth Sunday of the month, the backcountry hill town of Aups celebrates its specialty with the **Foire aux Truffes** (Truffle Festival).

➤ FEB.: For two weeks before (or even during) Lent, Nice explodes with **Carnival** revelry, celebrating with enormous masks called *grosses-têtes* (fat heads) and gorgeous *batailles des fleurs* (flower battles), actually parades complete with floats, beauty queens, and flying bouquets. Just up the coast, Menton celebrates its **Fêtes des Citrons,** a festival of locally-grown lemons complete with parades and enormous sculptures made of the fruit.

SPRING

➤ APR.: The **Monte Carlo Open,** the prestigious tennis tournament, takes place in the posh Monte Carlo Country Club as the **Printemps des Arts,** Monaco's spring arts festival, unfolds in the opera house.

➤ MAY: With the processions and fireworks of **La Bravade,** St-Tropez reaffirms its Provençal roots before the glitterati arrive, re-enacting the arrival of Saint Tropez's body in a boat guarded by a cock and a dog. Nîmes celebrates Pentecost with a Spanish-accented *féria,* a city-wide festival of parades, bull-races, and *corridas*(bullfights) in the Roman arena. St-Rémy observes Pentecost with another beast—the sheep—through its **Fête de la Transhumance,** the

great migration of the wooly herds from the valley to the highlands; some 4,000 sheep trot through the town center, guided by costumed shepherds. The antithesis, up the coast: the **Cannes Film Festival,** with its glittering crowds of A-list celebrities and wannabes.

SUMMER

➤ JUNE: Arles dusts off traditional costumes for their **féria,** with bullfights and races in their own Roman arena, and parades through the old-town streets.

➤ JULY: Now is the time when the summer arts festival season hits the ground running. Avignon transforms itself into one big theater for the **Festival Annuel d'Art Dramatique** (Annual Dramatic Arts Festival), with some 300 cutting-edge theater productions, including "off" and "off-off" performances. Aix's world-class **Festival International d'Art Lyrique** (International Opera Festival) imports top artists for performances in the courtyard of the Archbishop's Palace. The superb Roman theater in Orange glows with some of the world's best opera productions during **Les Chorégies d'Orange.** Nice and Antibes both feature stellar **jazz festivals** under the stars. And though Arles hosts photography exhibitions throughout the summer, their annual **Rencontres Internationales de la Photographie** (International Meeting of Photography) comes to a five-day climax this month with a summit of celebrity photographers. Be sure to book lodging and tickets well in advance for all of these famous July events.

AUTUMN

➤ OCT.: Early in the month each year the **Fêtes d'Aigues Mortes** sees this Camargue fortress-town go wild with bull-races, parades, and dancing on place St-Louis. In nearby Stes-Maries-de-la-Mer, pilgrims carry wooden statues of Saint Mary Magdelene and Saint Martha from the church to the beach, where they long ago floated ashore. The first weekend in October, St-Tropez stages the competitive **Nioulargue,** a sailing regatta that draws the crème-de-la-crème.

2 The Alpilles, Arles, and the Camargue

The Pont du Gard, Nîmes, the Rhône Delta, and the Languedoc Frontier

From the spare, rugged flatlands in the Languedoc west of the Rhône, through the lunar landscape of the Camargue marshlands and into the painterly highlands known as the Alpilles, this is the region where the Romans left their surest mark. Astonishingly well-preserved arenas in Nîmes and Arles, the traces of the entire village of Glanum outside St-Rémy, and the miraculous aqueduct called the Pont du Gard attest to the vibrancy of the Latin civilization that only found equal in Rome.

SCOURED BY THE MISTRAL and leveled to prairie flat-lands by eons of earth deposits carried south by the Rhône, this is Provence in its rawest form. Only the rude rock outcrops called the Alpilles interrupt the horizon, dusted with silvery olives and bristling with somber cypress spears. To the west, where the Provençal dialect gives way to Languedoc, the ancient language of the southwest, vineyards swathe the countryside in rows of green and black. Along the southern coast, the Camargue's monotonous landscape of reeds and cane secrets exotic wildlife—rich-plumed egrets, rare black storks, clownish flamingos—as well as domestic oddities: dappled white horses and lyre-horned bulls, descended from ancient, indigenous species.

The scenery is only surpassed by the cities: feisty, tatty Nîmes, its raffish urban lifestyle surging obliviously through a ramshackle, gritty-chic old town; graceful, artsy Arles, in harmonious van Gogh hues; chic St-Rémy, a gracious retreat for cosmopolitan regulars, the Hamptons of Provence.

Each of these cities would be fascinating to explore without their trump card: classical antiquities, superbly preserved, unsurpassed in northern Europe. The Colosseum-like arenas in Nîmes and Arles are virtually intact, solid enough to serve their original purpose as stadiums; they date from the time of Christ. The mausoleum and arc de triomphe outside St-Rémy are still so richly detailed, they look like reproductions, but they're signed by the children of Caesar Augustus. And across the street, the vivid high-relief ruins of Glanum trace back to the Hellenism of the 3rd century BC.

Add to these attractions Romanesque châteaux and abbeys, seaside fortresses that launched crusades, and sun-sharpened landscapes seen through the tortured eyes of van Gogh and Gauguin, and you have a region worth exploring in depth.

Pleasures and Pastimes

Architecture and Antiquities

Churches, châteaux, and abbeys sprinkle the countryside of western Provence, a surprising concentration of them pure Romanesque—that is, built in the solid progression of arches and barrel vaults that marked Roman engineering and was mimicked in the hinterlands by architects through the 12th and 13th centuries. Signs point to ÉGLISE ROMANE XII-IÈME—meaning Romanesque. *Romain* refers to Roman remains—just as prolific in the region.

Although you'll find Roman traces throughout Provence (and indeed France), the most beautifully preserved are concentrated here around the Rhône. With two arenas (at Arles and Nîmes), the ancient Hellenistic settlement outside St-Rémy, the miraculously preserved temple in Nîmes (Maison Carrée), and traces of Roman life scattered over the region, this is the place to concentrate if your taste runs to the classical. (You'll also want to run up to Orange and Vaison-la-Romaine; ☞ Chapter 3.)

Bird-Watching

The Camargue marshlands produce a nutty rice much prized by French gastronomes, as well as by birds who migrate through and feast on its chewy grains. A day's walk through the nearly car-free zone around the Etang de Vaccarès may reveal bitterns, egrets, a handful of tern species, hoopoes, and—a thrill even if you're not a birder—great flocks of gawky flamingos.

Dining

If eating is the national pastime in France, it is a vocation in Provence. And the pleasure of relaxing in a shady square over a pitcher of local rosé, a bowl of olives, and a regional plat du jour is only enhanced in western Provence by quirky local specialties. Consider nibbling tiny tellines, salty clams the size of your thumbnail, fresh from the Camargue coast. Or try a crockery bowl of steaming bull stew (*gardianne*), a sinewy daube of lean-and-mean beef from the harsh Camargue prairies, ladled over a scoop of chewy red Camargue rice. The mouth-watering oddity called *brandade* (salt cod pestled with olive oil and milk into a creamy spread) has a peculiar history: Cod isn't even native to Nîmes but was traded, in its leathery salt-dried form, by medieval Breton fishermen in exchange for south-coast salt. The Nîmois mixed in local olive oil and created a local staple.

CATEGORY	COST*
$$$$	Over 400 frs
$$$	250–400 frs
$$	125–250 frs
$	Under 125 frs

per person for a three-course meal, including tax (20.6%) and tip but not wine

Horseback Riding

The wild glamour of the ancient race of Camargue horses becomes downright pedestrian when the now-domesticated beauties are saddled en masse and led through the marsh trails. Rent-a-horse stands proliferate along the marshland highways, and trails are thick with gringos plodding along in subservient lines. But that way you can experience the austerity of the landscape without getting your feet wet.

Lodging

Although Arles, Les Baux, and St-Rémy have stylish, competitive hotels with all the requisite comforts and Provençal touches from wrought iron to *folklorique* cottons, Nîmes doesn't attract—or much merit—the overnight crowds; thus its hotels, with rare exception, have little in the way of charm. But throughout the region and well outside the towns you'll find lovely converted *mas* (farmhouses), blending into the landscape as if they'd been there a thousand years— but offering modern pleasures: gardens, swimming pools, and sophisticated cooking.

If you plan on spending a week or more in the region, a *gîte* (vacation rental) opens up new ways to appreciate the region: market browsing and the sampling of local specialties *comme chez soi* (home style). The local branches of Gîtes-de-France, the national network for vacation rentals, are divided by *départements* (administrative regions): The Hérault offices serve Montpellier and the Camargue region; the Gard offices handle Nîmes and environs, and the Bouches-du-Rhône branch covers the area including Arles, St-Rémy, and the Alpilles. For addresses, *see* Vacation Rentals *in* The Alpilles, Arles, and the Camargue A to Z, below.

CATEGORY	COST*
$$$$	Over 800 frs
$$$	550–800 frs
$$	300–550 frs
$	Under 300 frs

All prices are for a standard double room for two, including tax (20.6%) and service charge.

Wine

Though all of Provence is known for its rosés, some wines produced west of the Rhône merit special mention. Lirac and Tavel, world famous and highly commercial rosés, come from the Rhône Valley just up from road from the Pont du Gard. An obscure sand wine, or *vin de Sables*, from the coast of the Camargue gets drunk in quantities it doesn't really deserve, thanks to the crowds of thirsty tourists who pack into nearby purpose-built resorts.

Exploring the Alpilles, Arles, and the Camargue

This is the kind of country that inspires a Latin latitude (if not lassitude), so with all the ruins and châteaux to visit, allow yourself time to wander through food markets and to sit on a shady terrace watching the painterly changes in light.

Great Itineraries

Although Montpellier and Nîmes belong in spirit to the Languedoc, their proximity to the Camargue and Arles makes them a logical travel package. With their rugged hills and rich olive groves, the Alpilles are a world apart, but easily accessible from Arles and environs. You can move from site to site, or choose a central base—say, Arles—and explore them all without driving more than an hour to any one attraction. A couple of days passing through the region would allow you to see world-class antiquities; five days would allow time to wander the Camargue; a week would let you see the principal sites, enjoy a nature tour, and take a break by the sea. And don't forget that the ravishing old city of Avignon is just an hour's easy run up from Arles (☞ Chapter 3).

Numbers in the text correspond to numbers in the margin and on the Alpilles, the Camargue, and the Languedoc Frontier, Nîmes, Montpellier, and Arles maps.

IF YOU HAVE 3 DAYS

Consider basing yourself in ⚏ **Arles** ㉒–㉝ to see the Roman treasures (including the Musée d'Arles Antique), visit the Romanesque Église St-Trophime and its cloister, and wander the old-town streets and squares, as Vincent van Gogh did. Then on day two head up to **Nîmes** ②–⑪ for a look at the Maison Carrée and the arena. From Nîmes you can drive to the ancient fortress-port of **Aigues-Mortes** ⑳ and through the austere Camargue. Or if you prefer culture to nature, head north from Nîmes to the magnificent Roman aqueduct called the Pont du Gard. Spend the third day in the hills, visiting the spectacular hilltop château-village of **Les Baux-de-Provence** ㊲ and serene and fashionable **St-Rémy-de-Provence** ㊳.

IF YOU HAVE 5 DAYS

Expand the above itinerary to include a night in ⚏ **Les Baux-de-Provence** ㊲ or ⚏ **St-Rémy-de-Provence** ㊳, and consider a night in the vibrant university city of **Montpellier** ⑫–⑲ to the west; it's a good alternative base for forays into the Camargue. Out of ⚏ **Arles** ㉒–㉝, you can make a day trip to the medieval fortress rivals **Tarascon** ㉞ and **Beaucaire** ㉟.

IF YOU HAVE 7 DAYS

Base yourself for three nights in ⚏ **Arles** ㉒–㉝ and invest a day enjoying its museums, ruins, and Latin ambience. Then spend a half-day visiting the antiquities in ⚏ **Nîmes** ②–⑪ and head north to the Pont du Gard. Devote day three to exploring the **Camargue,** where you can stop in both **Aigues-Mortes** ⑳ and the resort town of **Stes-Maries-de-la-Mer** ㉑, which draws Gypsies to the shrine in its Romanesque church

and tourists to its beaches. Then break camp for three nights in ⊡ **St-Rémy-de-Provence** ㊳, from where you can explore **Les Baux-de-Provence** ㊲ and make excursions to **Tarascon** ㉞, **Beaucaire** ㉟, and **Fontvieille** ㊱, whose windmill inspired writer Alphonse Daudet (*Letters from My Mill*). Allow a half day for the magnificent **Abbaye de Montmajour,** just north of Arles.

When to Tour

July and August are very much the high season, especially along the coast, and are best avoided if possible, both because of the crushing crowds and the grilling heat. In winter (from November through February, even into March) you'll find a lot of tourist services closed, including hotels and restaurants, and much of the terrace life driven indoors by rain and wind. Around Easter, the plane trees begin to leaf out and the café tables to sprout. This easy midseason period maintains its lazy, pleasant pace from Easter through June and September to late October.

THE LANGUEDOC FRONTIER

Nîmes holds forth in the département of Gard and Montpellier in Hérault; both are considered more a part of the Languedoc culture than that of Provence. Yet because of their proximity to the heart of Provence and their similar climate, terrain, and architecture, they are included as kindred southern spirits. After all, the *langue d'oc* (language of oc) refers to the ancient southern language Occitane, which evolved from Latin; northern parts developed their own *langue d'oïl*. Their names derive from their manner of saying yes: *oc* in the south and *oïl* in the north. By an edict from Paris, the oïls had it in the 16th century, and *oui* and its northern dialect became standard French. Languedocien and Provençal merely went underground, however, and still crop up in gesticulating disputes at farmers' markets today.

Pont du Gard

★ ❶ *24 km (15 mi) northeast of Nîmes, 25 km (16 mi) north of Arles, 25 km (16 mi) west of Avignon.*

No other sight in Provence rivals the Pont du Gard, a mighty, three-tiered aqueduct midway between Nîmes and Avignon (☞ Chapter 3). Erected some 2,000 years ago as part of a 48-km (30-mi) canal supplying water to Roman Nîmes, it is astonishingly well preserved.

If you come to the Pont du Gard very early in the morning—before dawn is ideal—you can discover Provence in its purest blend of natural beauty and antiquity. As the silhouettes of olives emerge from the darkness and the diamond-sharp air wells up slowly with birdsong, you can see the ancient tiers as they were in the days when they carried water to Nîmes. The aqueduct is shockingly noble in its symmetry, the rhythmic repetition of arches resonant with strength, testimony to an engineering concept that was relatively new in the 1st century AD, when it first was built under Emperor Claudius. And, unsullied by tourists and by the vendors of postcards and Popsicles that dominate the site later in the day, the natural setting is just as resonant, with the river flowing through its rocky gorge unperturbed by the work of master engineering that straddles it.

Later in the day, however, crowds become a problem, even off-season; no one wants to miss this wonder of the world. You can approach the aqueduct from either side of the Gardon River. If you choose the north side (Rive Gauche), you'll be charged 22 francs to park (stay as close to the booth as possible because unfortunately break-ins are a problem). The walk to the *pont* is shorter, and the views arguably better from here. It costs less (18 francs) to park on the south side (Rive Droite), and there's a tourist office with information and postcards—but this is also the side the tour buses prefer. Access to the spectacular walkway along the top is currently blocked for restoration work.

Nîmes

29 km (18 mi) northwest of Arles, 42 km (26 mi) northeast of Montpellier.

If you have come to the south to seek out Roman treasures, you need look no further than Nîmes (pronounced neem): The Arènes and Maison Carrée are among continental Europe's best-preserved antiquities. But if you have come to seek out a more modern mythology—of lazy, graceful Provence—give Nîmes wide berth. It's a feisty, run-down rat race of a town, with jalopies and Vespas roaring irreverently around the ancient temple, and rock bands blasting sound tests into the arena's wooden stands. Its medieval old town has none of the gentrified grace of those in Arles or St-Rémy. Yet its rumpled and rebellious ways trace directly back to its Roman incarnation, when its population swelled with soldiers, arrogant and newly victorious after their conquest of Egypt in 31 BC.

Already anchoring a fiefdom of pre-Roman *oppidums* (elevated fortresses) before ceding to the empire in the 1st century BC, this ancient city bloomed to formidable proportions under the Pax Romana. A 24,000-seat coliseum, a thriving forum with a magnificent temple patterned after Rome's temple to Apollo, and a public water network fed by the Pont du Gard attest to its classical prosperity. Its next golden age bloomed under the Protestants, who established an anti-Catholic stronghold here and wreaked havoc on iconic architectural treasures— not to mention the papist minority. Their massacre of some 200 Catholic citizens is remembered as the Michelade; many of them were priests sheltered in the évêché, now the Museum of Old Nîmes. Chapels throughout the surrounding countryside were damaged by Calvin's righteous rebels.

A locally produced lightweight serge brought fame to Nîmes more than once. Legend has it that Christopher Columbus admired its durability and used it for sails; its reputation spread, and it was exported worldwide from the ports of Genoa (Gênes in French). Levi Strauss found its sturdy texture strong enough for gold miners' pants and Americanized its name from *bleu de Gênes*. The now-ubiquitous fabric's name traces back to its origins: de Nîmes.

Perhaps inspired by the influx of architects who studied its antique treasures, Nîmes has opted against becoming a lazy, atmospheric Provençal market town and has invested in modern architecture. Smack-dab across from the Maison Carrée stands the city's contemporary answer, the modern art museum dubbed the Carré d'Art (Art Square), after its ruthlessly modernist four-square form—a pillared, symmetrical glass reflection of its ancient twin. Other investments in contemporary art and architecture confirm Nîmes's commitment to modern ways.

★ ❷ Start out at the **Arènes** (Arena), which is considered the world's best-preserved Roman amphitheater. A miniature of the Colosseum in Rome, it stands more than 520 ft long and 330 ft wide, with a seating capacity of 24,000. Bloody gladiator battles and theatrical wild-boar hunts drew crowds to its bleachers. As barbarian invasions closed in on Nîmes, it was transformed into a fortress by the Visigoths. Later, medieval residents found it provided comfort and protection for tight-packed thatch-and-timber houses (as well as a small château and chapel). Nowadays the amphitheater has been restored almost to its original look, including exit signs marked VOMITORIUM (from the Latin for "to go out"). An inflatable roof covers it in winter, when various exhibits and shows occupy the space, and concerts and tennis tournaments are held here in summer. Its most colorful use is the *corrida*, the bullfight that transforms the arena (and all of Nîmes) into a sangria-flushed homage to Spain (☞ Outdoor Activities and Sports, *below*). ⊠ *bd. Victor-Hugo,* ☎ *04-66-76-72-77.* ⊡ *26 frs; joint ticket to Arènes and Tour Magne 32 frs.* ⊙ *May–Sept., daily 9–6:30; Oct.–Apr., daily 9–noon and 2–5.*

❸ At the **Musée des Beaux-Arts** (Fine Arts Museum), a few blocks south of the Arènes, you can admire a vast Roman mosaic; the marriage ceremony depicted provides intriguing insights into the Roman aristocratic lifestyle. Old-master paintings (by Nicolas Poussin, Pieter Brueghel, Peter Paul Rubens) and sculpture (by Auguste Rodin) form the mainstay of

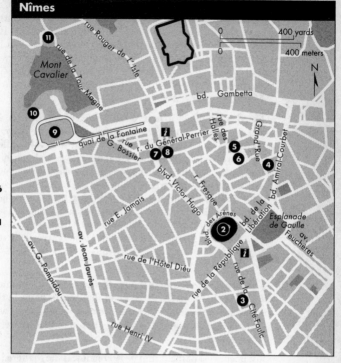

Nîmes

the collection. ⊠ *rue de la Cité-Foulc,* ☎ *04–66–67–38–21.* 🎫 *26 frs.* ⊙ *Tues.–Sun. 11–6.*

❹ The **Musée Archéologique et d'Histoire Naturelle** (Museum of Archaeology and Natural History), a few blocks northeast of the Arènes, is rich in local archaeological finds, mainly statues, busts, friezes, tools, glass, coins, and pottery. ⊠ *bd. de l'Amiral-Courbet,* ☎ *04–66–67–25–57.* 🎫 *26 frs.* ⊙ *Tues.–Sun. 11–6.*

❺ Destroyed and rebuilt in several stages, with particular damage by rampaging Protestants who slaughtered eight priests from the neighboring *évêché* (bishop's house), the **Cathédrale Notre-Dame et St-Castor** (⊠ pl. aux Herbes) still shows traces of its construction in 1096. Is that fragment of classically symmetrical pediment an 11th-century reference to the Maison Carrée? Within its fluted lines, a miraculously preserved Romanesque frieze dates, for the most part, from the year of construction. Its lively Old Testament portraiture—reminiscent in style to its contemporary, the Bayeux tapestry—portrays Adam and Eve's cowering shame, the gory slaughter of Abel, a flood-weary Noah. Inside, look for the 4th-century sarcophagus (third chapel on the right) and a magnificent 17th-century chapel (in the apse), recently restored.

❻ The **Musée du Vieux Nîmes** (Museum of Old Nîmes), opposite the cathedral in the 17th-century Bishop's Palace, has embroidered garments in exotic and vibrant displays. Look for the 14th-century jeans jacket made of blue serge "de Nîmes." ⊠ *pl. aux Herbes,* ☎ *04–66–36–00–64.* 🎫 *26 frs.* ⊙ *Tues.–Sun. 11–6.*

★ ❼ Lovely and forlorn in the middle of a busy downtown square, the exquisitely preserved **Maison Carrée** (Square House) strikes a timeless balance between symmetry and whimsy, purity of line and richness of decor. Built around 5 BC and dedicated to Caius Caesar and his grandson Lucius, it has survived subsequent use as a medieval meeting hall, an Augustine church, a storehouse for Revolutionary archives, and a horse shed. It was modeled on the Temple to Apollo in Rome, and so inspired Thomas Jefferson that he had its chaste line of columns copied for the Virginia state capitol in Richmond. Alas, its interior now serves as a slapdash display space for temporary exhibitions. ⊠ *bd. Victor-Hugo,* ☎ *04–66–36–26–76.* 🎟 *Free.* ☉ *May–Oct., daily 9–12 and 2–7; Nov.–Apr., daily 9–12 and 2–6.*

The glass-fronted Carré d'Art (it's directly opposite the Maison Carrée) was designed in 1993 by British architect Sir Norman Foster as its neighbor's stark contemporary mirror: It literally reflects the Maison Carrée's creamy symmetry and figuratively answers it with a featherlight deconstructed colonnade. References aside, it looks like an

❽ airport terminal. It serves as home to a library, archives, and the **Musée d'Art Contemporain** (Contemporary Art Museum). The permanent collection falls into three categories: French painting and sculpture; English, American and German work; and Mediterranean styles, all dating from 1960 onward. There are often temporary exhibits of new work. ⊠ *pl. de la Maison Carrée,* ☎ *04–66–76–35–70.* 🎟 *26 frs.* ☉ *Tues.–Sun. 10–6.*

❾ The **Jardin de la Fontaine** (Fountain Garden), an elaborate formal garden, was landscaped on the site of the Roman baths in the 18th century, when the Source de Nemausus, a once-sacred spring, was channeled into pools and a canal. It's a shady haven of mature trees and graceful stonework.

Just northwest of the Jardin de la Fontaine is the shattered Roman ruin
❿ known as the **Temple de Diane** (Diana's Temple), which dates from the 2nd century BC. The temple's function is unknown, though it is thought to be part of a larger Roman complex that is still unexcavated. In the Middle Ages Benedictine nuns occupied the building before it was converted into a church. Destruction came during the Wars of Religion.

⓫ At the far end of the Jardin de la Fontaine is the **Tour Magne** (Magne Tower)—the remains of a tower that the emperor Augustus had built on Gallic foundations; it was probably used as a lookout post. Despite having lost 30 ft during the course of time, it still provides fine views of Nîmes for anyone energetic enough to climb the 140 steps. ⊠ *quai de la Fontaine,* ☎ *04–66–67–29–11.* 🎟 *Tour Magne 12 frs, joint ticket with Arènes 32 frs.* ☉ *May.–Oct., daily 9–7; Nov.–Apr., daily 9–5.*

Dining and Lodging

$$–$$$ ✕ **L'Enclos de la Fontaine.** Nîmes's most fashionable post-corrida gathering spot is in the Impérator hotel (☞ *below*), with warm-weather dining in an idyllic garden court. Chef Jean-Michel Nigon provides such inventive luxuries as lobster salad with citrus vinaigrette, sole rolled with truffles, and Charolais beef sautéed with cèpes. Have an after-dinner drink in the bar Hemingway loved; they named it for him. ⊠ *15 rue Gaston-Boissier,* ☎ *04–66–21–90–30. AE, DC, MC, V.*

$$ ✕ **Le Jardin d'Hadrien.** This chic enclave, with its quarried white stone, ancient plank-and-beam ceiling, and open fireplace, would be a culinary haven even without its lovely hidden garden, a shady retreat for summer meals. Generous portions of simple but sophisticated dishes seem like so much gravy when the setting's this nice: mussel soup with saffron and cream, cod crisped in salt with peppers, or zucchini flowers filled with *brandade* (the creamy, light paste of salt cod and olive oil) all show chef Alain Vinouzé's subtle skills. ⊠ *11 rue Enclos Rey,* ☎ *04–66–21–86–65. AE, MC, V.*

$ **✕ Chez Jacotte.** Duck into an old-town back alley and into this cross-
★ vaulted grotto that embodies Nîmes's Spanish-bohemian flair. Candlelight
flickering on rich tones of oxblood, cobalt, and ochre enhance the warm
welcome of red-haired owner Jacotte Friand, who coddles her guests
and artist friends with blackboard specials. Watch for scrambled eggs
with truffles and asparagus, rich ravioli with basil, bulgur wheat with
chicken fricassee—updated with a Far East tang of coriander or red
peppercorn. The homemade cakes and pastries are irresistible. ⊠ *15
rue Fresque (Impasse),* ☎ *04–66–21–64–59. MC, V. Closed Sun.–
Mon. No lunch Sat.*

$ **✕ Nicolas.** You'll hear the noise of this homey place before you open
the door. A friendly, frazzled staff serves up delicious *bourride* (a thick
fish soup) and other local specialties at tightly packed tables, with plastic menus—and at low prices. ⊠ *1 rue Poise,* ☎ *04–66–67–50–47.
AE, DC, MC, V. No lunch Sat. and Mon.*

$ **✕ Vintage Café.** This popular old-town wine bar draws a loyal crowd
of oenophiles for serious tastings and simple, compatible foods—hot
lentil salad with smoked haddock, crisped *confit de canard* (preserved
duck), and fresh goat cheese drizzled with olive oil. The bar dominates—
all the better for bellying up to a glass of *côstières de Nîmes*—and the
six or seven tables squeezed in as an afterthought provide for intimate
conversation (by next year, the dining area may have expanded into
the adjoining building). Bright ceramics and warm-colored lamplight
enhance the artful Mediterranean decor. Summer nights on the terrace
are idyllic. ⊠ *7 rue de Bernis,* ☎ *04–66–21–04–45. MC, V. Closed
Sun. No lunch Sat. and Mon.*

$ **✕ Le Wine Bar/Chez Michel.** This classic mahogany and brass wine bar,
owned and managed by a former sommelier, features good seafood—
including *brandade de morue* (salt-cod paste)—as well as brasserie classics: foie gras salad, fried calamari, simple steaks. You may opt to dine
on the sidewalk terrace, adjacent to the square. Menus start at 80 francs.
⊠ *11 square de la Couronne,* ☎ *04–66–76–19–59. AE, MC, V. Closed
Sun., no lunch Mon.*

$$–$$$ **⊞ Impérator.** Despite its standing as the top hotel in Nîmes, this mem-
ber of the Concorde group has a bourgeois, businessy feel about it, without the luxurious excesses of more glamorous top hotels. Still, the newest
room decors have a pampered, Laura Ashley look, and those overlooking
the lovely garden court need no further frills. ⊠ *15 rue Gaston-Boissier,
30900,* ☎ *04–66–21–90–30,* 🖷 *04–66–67–70–25. 62 rooms.
Restaurant, bar, air-conditioning. AE, DC, MC, V.*

$$ **✕ La Baume.** In the heart of scruffy old Nîmes, this noble 17th-century
hôtel particulier (mansion) has been reincarnated as a chic hotel with
an architect's eye for mixing ancient detail with modern design. The
balustraded stone staircase is a protected historic monument, and sten-
ciled beam ceilings, cross vaults, and archways counterbalance hot ochre
tones, swagged raw cotton, leather, and halogen lights. The hip decor
dates from 1992 but already shows wear and tear. See if one of the
wood-ceiling rooms (the largest and prettiest) is available instead.
⊠ *21 rue Nationale, 30000. 33 rooms. Breakfast room, air-conditioning.
AE, DC, MC, V.*

$$ **✕ Clarine Plazza.** Despite a modular '80s look (lacquered wood, geometric prints), the scruffy, familial clutter that marks Nîmes has crept
in to make this chain hotel feel comfortably local: unframed bullfight
posters are taped to the walls, and hats and magazines clutter the
lobby bar. The breakfast is unusually generous, with cheese, cereal, and
yogurt. ⊠ *10 rue Roussy, 30000,* ☎ *04–66–76–16–20,* 🖷 *04–66–
67–65–99. 28 rooms. Breakfast room, air-conditioning. AE, DC,
MC, V.*

$$ 🖫 **Royal Hôtel.** Jazz, Art Deco ironwork, and caged birds set the Latin
★ tone at this bohemian, shabby-chic urban hotel, where whitewash and
scrubbed concrete set off 1930s details and trendy flea-market finds.
Bathrooms are newly tiled, and amenities reasonably up to date. Its
Spanish restaurant serves tapas on the pedestrian place d'Assas, but
the lobby bar is where you'd expect to run across Picasso slumming
over absinthe. ⊠ *3 bd. Alphonse Daudet, 30000,* ☎ *04–66–67–28–
36,* FAX *04–66–21–68–97. 27 rooms. Restaurant, bar. AE, MC, V.*

$ ✕ **Amphithéâtre.** Just behind the arena, this big, solid old private
home has fortunately fallen into the hands of a loving owner, who has
stripped 18th-century double doors and fitted rooms with restored-wood
details and antique bedroom sets. A generous breakfast buffet is served
in the dining room. Ask for one of the two rooms overlooking the place
du Marché, where you can observe café life from your balcony. ⊠ *4
rue des Arènes, 30420,* ☎ *04–66–67–28–51,* FAX *04–66–67–07–79.
17 rooms. Breakfast room. AE, MC, V.*

Outdoor Activities and Sports

The *corrida* (bullfight) is the quintessential Nîmes experience, taking
place as it does in the ancient Roman arena, and is worth working into
your schedule. There are usually three opportunities a year, always dur-
ing the carnival-like citywide *férias* (festivals): in early spring (mid-
February), at Pentecost (end of May), and during the wine harvest (end
of September). These include parades, a running of the bulls, and gen-
tle Camargue-style bullfights (where competitors pluck floral rosettes
from the bull's horns), but the focal point is a twice-daily Spanish-style
bullfight, complete with *l'estocade* (the final killing) and the traditional
cutting of the ear. For tickets and advance information, contact the
Arena's *bureau de location* (ticket office; ⊠ 1 rue A. Ducros, Nîmes
30900, ☎ 04–66–67–28–02).

Aquatropic (⊠ 39 rue de la Hostellerie, ☎ 04–66–38–31–00) is a
swimming spot with a difference: an indoor and an outdoor pool, wave
machines, slides, water cannons, and bubble baths add to the fun for
kids and adults. It's open weekdays 10–8 and weekends 10–7, for a
cost of 40 francs. Since it's south of the city, it's best to exit the au-
toroute at Nîmes Ouest.

Shopping

The Monday-morning *marché* (⊠ bd. Jean-Jaurès) stretches the length
of the boulevard Jean-Jaurès and features bright regional fabrics,
linens, pottery, and *brocante* (collectibles). The permanent covered mar-
ket called **Les Halles** is at the heart of the city and puts on a mouth-
watering show of olives, fresh fish, cheeses, and produce. The colorful
marché aux fleurs (flower market; parking in the Stades des Costières),
though far from the center, is worth seeking out by car.

The only authentic maker of brandade, Nîmes' signature salt-cod-
and-olive-oil paste, is **Raymond** (⊠ 24 rue Nationale, ☎ 04–66–67–
20–47). It's paddled fresh into a plastic carton or sold in sealed jars
so you can take it home.

In Nîmes's old town, you'll find interior-design **boutiques** and fabric
shops selling the Provençal cottons that used to be produced here en
masse (Les Indiennes de Nîmes, Les Olivades, Souleiado). **Antiques** and
collectibles are found in tiny shops throughout the city's back streets,
especially in the old town.

Montpellier

42 km (26 mi) southwest of Nîmes.

Vibrant Montpellier (pronounced monh-pell-YAY), capital of the
Languedoc-Roussillon region, has been a center of commerce and
learning since the Middle Ages, when it was crossroads for pilgrims
on their way to Santiago de Compostela in Spain and an active shipping center trading in spices from the East. With its cargo of exotic
luxuries, it also imported Renaissance learning, and its university—
founded in the 14th century—has nurtured a steady influx of ideas
through the centuries. Its faculty of medicine—still thriving—dates to
the early 13th century. Its reputation was so renowned that the great
Renaissance writer and humanist Rabelais left his native Loire Valley
to study medicine here.

Though the port silted up by the 16th century, Montpellier has never
become a backwater, and as a center of commerce and conferences, it
keeps its focus on the future. An imaginative urban planning program
has streamlined the 17th-century old town, and monumental perspectives dwarf passersby on the 17th-century Promenade du Peyrou.
An even more utopian venture in urban planning is the Antigone district: a vast, harmonious 100-acre complex designed in 1984 by Catalan architect Ricard Borfill. With all this inspired architecture, Montpellier
is anything but a living museum: A student population of some 65,000
keeps things lively, especially on the place de la Comédie, the city's social nerve center. And Montpellier's cultural sophistication manifests
itself in an intensive music scene and a superior art museum, the Musée
Fabre.

★ **12** **13** The **Promenade du Peyrou** is easy to find: Its enormous **Arc de Triomphe**
looms majestically over the peripheral highway that loops around the
city center. Both were dedicated to Louis XIV at the end of the 17th
century. The noble scale of the harmonious stone constructions and
the sweeping perspectives they frame make for an inspiring stroll.

14 Boulevard Henri IV runs north from the Promenade du Peyrou to
France's oldest botanical garden, the **Jardin des Plantes** (Botanical Garden), planted on order of Henri IV in 1593. An exceptional range of
plants, flowers, and trees grows here. ▱ *Free.* ☉ *Gardens Mon.–Sat.
9–noon and 2–5. Greenhouses weekdays 9–noon and 2–5, Sat. 9–
noon.*

15 After taking in the broad vistas of the Promenade de Peyrou, cross over
into the Vieille Ville (Old Town) and wander its maze of narrow streets,
full of pretty shops and intimate restaurants. At the northern edge of
the old town, visit the imposing **Cathédrale St-Pierre** (✉ pl. St-Pierre),
its fantastical and unique 14th-century entry porch alone worth the
detour: Two cone-topped towers—some five stories high—flank the
main portal and support a groin-vaulted shelter. The interior, despite
18th-century reconstruction, maintains the formal simplicity of its
14th-century origins.

16 Next door to the cathedral, peek into the noble **Faculté de Médecine**
(rue de l'École de Médecine), one of France's most respected medical
schools, founded in the 14th century. The infusion over the generations
of international learning—especially Arab and Jewish scholarship—raised
research here to the forefront of world medicine.

From the medical school, follow rue Foch, which slices straight east.
The number of bistros and brasseries increases as you leave the old town
to cross place des Martyrs; veering right down rue de la Loge, you spill

32

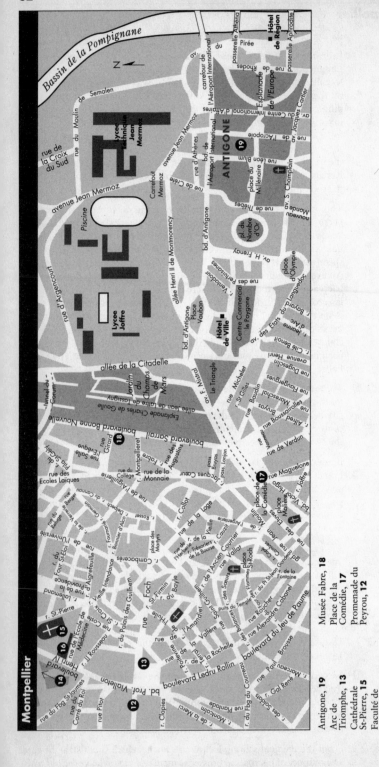

Montpellier

Bassin de la Pompignane

ANTIGONE

Hôtel de Région

⑰ out onto the festive gathering spot known as **place de la Comédie.** Anchored by the neoclassic 19th-century **Opéra-Comédie,** this broad square is a beehive of leisurely activity, a cross between Barcelona's Ramblas and a Roman *passagiata* (afternoon stroll, en masse). Brasseries, bistros, fast-food joints, and cinemas draw crowds, but the pleasure is getting there and seeing who came before, in which shoes, and with whom.

★ ⑱ From place de la Comédie, boulevard Sarrail leads north past the shady esplanade Charles de Gaulle to the **Musée Fabre.** A mixed bag of architectural styles (a 17th-century *hôtel,* a vast Victorian wing with superb natural light, and a remnant of a Baroque Jesuit college), this rich art museum has a surprisingly big collection, thanks to its namesake. François-Xavier Fabre, a native of Montpellier, was a student of the great 18th-century French artist David, who established roots in Italy and acquired a formidable collection of masterworks—which he then donated to his hometown, supervising the development of this fine museum. Among his gifts were the *Mariage mystique de sainte Catherine,* by Veronese, and Poussin's coquettish *Venus et Adonis.* Later contributions include a superb group of 17th-century Flemish works (Rubens, Steen), a collection of 19th-century French canvases (Géricault, Delacroix, Corot, Millet) that inspired Gauguin and van Gogh, and a growing group of 20th-century acquisitions that buttress a legacy of paintings by early Impressionist Frédéric Bazille. ⊠ *3 bd. Bonne Nouvelle,* ☎ *04–67–14–83–00.* 🎫 *20 frs.* ☉ *Tues.–Fri. 9–5:30, weekends 9:30–5.*

⑲ At the far-east end of the city loop, Montpellier seems to transform itself into a futuristic ideal city, all of one smooth, low-slung postmodern style. This is the **Antigone** district, the result of city planners' efforts (and local industries' commitment) to pull Montpellier up out of its economic doldrums. It worked. The ideal neighborhood designed by the Catalan architect Ricard Borfill covers 100-plus acres with plazas, esplanades, shops, restaurants, and low-income housing, all constructed out of stone-color, prestressed concrete. Be sure to visit **Place du Nombre d'Or**—symmetrically composed of curves—and the 1-km-long (½-mi-long) vista that stretches down a mall of cypress trees to the glass-fronted **Hôtel de Region** (⊠ av. du Pirée).

Dining and Lodging

$$–$$$ ✕ **Le Chandelier.** On the sixth and seventh floors of a building in the Antigone district, this restaurant has dramatic views, impeccable service, and bold blue-and-yellow Mediterranean decor. Chef Gilbert Furlan's inventive cuisine takes Provençal ingredients to sophisticated levels: Sample his squid sautéed in fresh thyme, dried mullet eggs with brandade mousse, and pigeon roasted with cinnamon and nutmeg. The licorice-honey ice cream makes a fine dessert. There's a good range of Languedoc wines available. ⊠ *267 av. Léon Blum,* ☎ *04–67–15–34–38. Reservations essential. AE, DC, MC, V. Closed Sun. No lunch Mon.*

$$ ✕ **Alexandre.** If you're making a run out to the seaside, this is a good choice for lunch. Tons of nutty, salty oysters are cultivated in the nearby *étangs* (ponds); you can sample them in the elegant surroundings of Louis XV furnishings while gazing out over the Mediterranean. Other choices include a splendid array of seafood dishes. ⊠ *Esplanade de la Capitainerie, La Grande-Motte (21 km [13 mi] southeast of Montpellier),* ☎ *04–67–56–63–63. AE, MC, V. Closed Mon. No dinner Sun.*

$ ✕ **Le Petit Jardin.** On a quiet old-town back street, this simple restaurant lives up to its name: You dine looking over (or seated in) a lovely, deep-shaded garden with views of the cathedral. A simple omelet with pepper sauce, spicy bourride, or hearty *osso buco* (veal shanks in saffron-tomato sauce) mirror the welcome, which is warm and unpretentious. ✉ *20 rue Jean-Jacques Rousseau,* ☎ *04–67–60–78–78. AE, DC, MC, V. Closed Mon.*

$ ✕ **Restaurant de la Maison des Vins.** This simple, atmospheric spot, in an 18th-century winery, is headquarters to the Syndicat des Vignerons Côteaux du Languedoc—the folks who ensure that the region's wines are up to standard. Straightforward regional dishes—foils to a well-chosen bottle—are served in the pleasant, stone-vaulted cellar or on the terrace. Watch for sardine beignets, octopus in spicy *rouille* (cayenne mayonnaise), or fresh grilled fish. Afterward, visit the Maison du Vin, where the *syndicat*'s best wines are sold at good prices. ✉ *Mas de Saporta, Lattes (from downtown Montpellier follow signs to des Prés D'Arènes; the restaurant is near the Montpellier Sud interchange of Autoroute A9),* ☎ *04–67–06–88–66. MC, V. Closed Sun. No dinner Sat.*

$$$$ ✕⊡ **Le Jardin des Sens.** This spot is Montpellier's *grande table*—its
★   great restaurant—and a new darling in the gastronomic star wars. Blink and look again: Twins Laurent and Jacques Pourcel, trained under separate masters, combine forces here to achieve a quiet, almost cerebral cuisine based on southern French traditions. At every turn are happy surprises: foie gras crisps, dried-fruit risotto, and lamb sweetbreads with *gambas* (prawn) tail. A modest lunch menu (in the **$$** category) lets you indulge on a budget. Now that there are luxurious, ultra-modern Relais & Châteaux rooms on site, complete with pool and solarium, it doesn't matter that you're far from the historic center. ✉ *11 av. St-Lazare,* ☎ *04–67–79–63–38,* ⨳ *04–67–72–13–05. 12 rooms, 2 apartments. Reservations essential. AE, DC, MC, V. Both restaurant and hotel closed Sun. No lunch Mon.*

$$ ⊡ **Le Guilhem.** On the same quiet back street as the restaurant Le Petit
★   Jardin, this jewel of a *hôtel de charme* beads together a chain of 16th-century houses. Rebuilt from ruins to include an elevator and state-of-the-art white-tile baths, it nonetheless retains original casement windows (many overlooking the extraordinary old garden), slanting floors, and views toward the cathedral. Soft yellows and powder blues add to its gentle, *temps passé* atmosphere. Tiny, garret-style rooms at the top are great if you're traveling alone; if not, ask for the largest available. ✉ *18 rue Jean-Jacques-Rousseau, 34000,* ☎ *04–67–52–90–90,* ⨳ *04–67–60–67–67. 33 rooms. Air-conditioning, parking (fee). MC, V.*

Nightlife and the Arts

La Croisière (✉ Espace Latipolia, rte. de Palavas, ☎ 04–67–64–19–52), a lively disco, is in Lattes, on the south side of Montpellier. **Gyssertin** (✉ rte. de Palavas, ☎ 04–67–22–45–82), another dance club, is also in Lattes. In the center of town, **Le Petit Negreso** (✉ 6 pl. Jean Jaurès, ☎ 04–67–66–02–10) serves up tapas and live music.

Concerts are performed in the 19th-century **Théâtre des Treize Vents** (✉ allée Jules-Milhau, ☎ 04–67–58–08–13). **The Orchestre Philharmonique de Montpellier**(☎ 04–67–61–66–16) is a young and energetic group of some reputation, performing regularly in the Opéra Berlioz in the Corum conference complex. The resident **Opéra de Montpellier** (☎ 04–67–60–19–99) performs in the Opéra-Comédie on pl. de la Comédie.

Outdoor Activities

Although Montpellier's medieval port may have been silted in, it's still a quick jaunt to the nearest **beach,** via the narrow causeway that straddles the ponds and open coastline to the city's south. You can abandon the car in the low dunes to clamber over to the water, or make a beeline for the architectural monstrosities—pyramidal residential pods—that have transformed **La Grande-Motte** and **La Grau-du-Roi** into extremely popular sandy-beach resorts.

ARLES AND THE CAMARGUE

Reigning over the bleak but evocative landscape of the marshlands of the Camargue, the small city of Arles is fiercely Provençal, nurturing its heritage and parading its culture at every colorful opportunity. Warming the wetlands with its atmosphere, animation and culture, it is a patch of hot color in a sepia landscape—and an excellent home base for sorties into the raw natural beauty and eccentric backwater culture of the Rhône delta.

Aigues-Mortes

★ **⓴** *30 km (19 mi) east of Montpellier, 39 km (24 mi) south of Nîmes, 45 km (28 mi) southwest of Arles.*

Like a tiny illumination in a medieval manuscript, Aigues-Mortes (pronounced ay-guh-MORT-uh) is a precise and perfect miniature fortress-town, contained within perfectly symmetrical castellated walls, with streets laid out in geometric grids. Now awash in a flat wasteland of sand, salt, and monotonous marsh, it once was a major port town from whence no less than St-Louis himself (Louis IX) set sail to conquer Jerusalem in the 13th century. In 1248 some 35,000 zealous men launched 1,500 ships for Cyprus, engaging the infidel on his own turf and suffering swift defeat; Louis himself was briefly taken prisoner. A second launching in 1270 led to more crushing loss, and Louis succumbed to the plague.

But Louis's state-of-the-art **fortress-port** remains intact, astonishingly well preserved in salt sea winds. Its stout walls now contain a small Provençal village milling with tourists, but the visit is more than justified by the impressive scale of the original structure.

If you're driving, park in one of the lots outside the formidable walls and enter by the main **Porte de la Gardette**; the tourist office is left of the entrance. To your right, you'll see the town's stronghold, called the **Tour de Constance**. Its 20-ft-thick walls date from 1241–1244, when it was built to protect a larger building lost to history. Enter via the 17th-century **Logis du Gouverneur** (Governor's Lodging), itself a conglomerate of several centuries' construction. The tower still contains a small votive chapel dedicated to St-Louis and an upper hall that served as prison to generations of political outcasts. (One Protestant, the heroic Marie Durand, survived 38 years in the tower without relinquishing her faith; she carved the word *résister*—resist—on her cell wall. Her endurance and courage so impressed the Languedoc governor, he had her released along with a handful of her colleagues.) You can climb all the way to the top of the steepled tower, which once served as a lighthouse lantern: From here you can appreciate the rigorous geometry of the fortifications and imagine medieval fleets surging out to sea. ⊠ *Porte de la Gardette,* ☎ *04–66–53–61–55.* ▧ *32 frs.* ☉ *Easter–late May, daily 10–6; late May–mid-Sept., daily 9:30–8; mid-Sept.–Easter, daily 10–5.*

It's not surprising that the town within the rampart walls has become tourist oriented, with the usual plethora of gift shops and postcard stands. But **place St-Louis,** where a 19th-century statue of the father of the fleur-de-lis reigns under shady pollards, has a mellow village feel, and the pretty bare-bones **Église Notre-Dame des Sablons** that corners it has a timeless air (it dates from the 13th century, but the stained glass is ultramodern).

Dining and Lodging

$$$ ✕🏠 **Les Arcades.** Long a success as an upscale seafood restaurant, this
★ beautifully preserved 16th-century house now offers big, airy rooms, some with tall windows overlooking a green courtyard. Pristine white-stone walls, color-stained woodwork, and rubbed-ochre walls frame antiques and lush fabrics, and bathrooms are all new, in white tile. There's even a little courtyard terrace with small pool. Classic cooking features lotte (monkfish) in saffron and poached turbot in hollandaise. ⊠ *23 bd. Gambetta, 30220,* ☎ *04–66–53–81–13,* FAX *04–66–53–75–46. 9 rooms. Restaurant, air-conditioning, pool. AE,DC, MC, V.*

$$ 🏠 **St-Louis.** Within the rampart walls, close to the Tour de Constance and just off place St-Louis, this homey little hotel warms its medieval construction of cool stone with Provençal charm and comfort. Rooms, which are pleasantly decorated if not stylish, look out on the garden below the ramparts or on to the sunny street. In winter dinner is served in the beamed restaurant, and in summer, in the shady garden. ⊠ *10 rue Amiral Courbet, 30220,* ☎ *04–66–53–72–68,* FAX *04–66–53–75–92. 22 rooms. Restaurant, parking. AE, DC, MC, V.*

$$ 🏠 **Les Templiers.** In a 17th-century residence within the ramparts, this delightful hotel sets the stage with stone, stucco, and terra-cotta floors. Furnishings are classically simple and softened with antiques. On the ground floor are two small, cozy sitting areas; breakfast, weather permitting, is served in the small courtyard. ⊠ *23 rue de la République, 30220,* ☎ *04–66–53–66–56,* FAX *04–66–53–69–61. 11 rooms. Air-conditioning, parking. MC, V. Closed Nov.–Mar.*

Festivals

At the end of August, Aigues-Mortes celebrates the **Fêtes du St-Louis** with a town fair, including a medieval pageant and market, strolling musicians, and fire-eaters. In early October, the **Fêtes Votive d'Aigues-Mortes** (town festival) features bull races, parades, and dancing in the main square.

The Camargue

For 777 sq km (300 sq mi), the vast alluvial delta of the Rhône known as the Camargue stretches to the horizon, an austere marshland unrelievedly flat, scoured by the mistral, swarmed by mosquitoes. Between the endless flow of sediment from the Rhône and the erosive force of the sea, its shape is constantly changing. Even the Provençal poet Frederic Mistral described it in bleak terms: *"Ni arbre, ni ombre, ni âme"* (Neither tree, nor shade, nor a soul).

Yet its harsh landscape harbors a concentration of exotic wildlife unique in Europe, and its isolation has given birth to an ascetic and ancient way of life that transcends national stereotype. It is a strange region, one worth discovering slowly, either on foot or by horseback—especially as its wildest reaches are inaccessible by car.

If people find the Camargue interesting, birds find it irresistible. Its protected marshes lure some 400 species, including more than 160 in migration. Not only will you come across pockets of little egrets, gray herons, spoonbills, bitterns, cormorants, redshanks, and grebes, but also ivory-pink flamingoes, which are as common as pigeons on a city square. Their gangly height, dodolike bill, and stilty legs give them a cartoonish air, and their flight style—the long neck slumping downward, legs trailing heavily—seems comic up close. But the sight of a few hundred—or a few thousand—of these broad-winged creatures taking flight in unison above the reeds is one you won't forget.

As you drive the scarce roads that barely crisscross the Camargue, you'll usually be within the boundaries of the **Parc Regional de Camargue.** Unlike state and national parks in the United States, this area is privately owned and utilized within rules imposed by the state. The principal owners: the famous *manadiers* (the Camargue equivalent of a small-scale rancher) and their *gardians* (a kind of open-range cowboy), who keep it for grazing their wide-horned bulls and their broad-bellied, dappled-white horses. It is thought that these beasts are the descendents of ancient, indigenous wild animals, and though they're positively bovine in their placidity today, they still bear the noble marks of their ancestors. The strong, heavy-tailed Camargue horse has been traced to the Paleolithic period (though some claim the Moors imported an Arab strain) and is prized for its stolid endurance and tough hooves. The curved-horned *taureau* (bull), if not indigenous, may have been imported by Attila the Hun. When it's not participating in a bloodless bullfight (mounted players try to hook a red ribbon from between its horns), a bull may well end up in the wine-rich regional stew, called *gardianne de taureau.*

Riding through the marshlands in leather pants and wide-rimmed black hats and wielding long prongs to prod their cattle, the gardians themselves are as fascinating as the wildlife. Their homes—tiny whitewashed, cane-thatched huts with the north end raked and curved apselike against the vicious mistral—dot the countryside. The signature wrought-iron crosses at the gable invoke holy protection, and if God isn't watching over this treeless plain, they ground lightning.

The easiest place to view bird life is in a private reserve just outside the regional park called the **Parc Ornithologique du Pont de Gau** (Ornithological Park of the Pont de Gau). On some 150 acres of marsh and salt lands, birds are welcomed and protected (but in no way confined); injured birds are treated and kept in large pens, to be released if and when able. A series of boardwalks (including a short, child-friendly inner loop past the easy-viewing invalids) snake over the wetlands, the longest leading to a blind, where a half hour of silence, binoculars in hand, can reveal unsuspected treasures. ☎ 04–90–97–82–62. 🎟 33 frs. ☉ Oct.–Mar., daily 10–sunset; Apr.–Sept., daily 9 to sunset.

If you're an even more committed nature lover, venture into the inner sanctum of the Camargue, the **Réserve Nationale de Camargue.** This intensely protected area contains the central pond called **Le Vaccarès,** mostly used for approved scientifc research. The wildlife—birds, nutria, fish—is virtually undisturbed here, but you won't come across the cabins and herds of bulls and horses that most people expect from the Camargue. Pick up maps and information at the **Centre d'Information** (☎ 04–90–97–86–32, FAX 04–90–97–70–82), open April–September, daily 9–6, October–March, Saturday–Thursday 9:30–5; it is located just up the D570 from the Parc Ornithologique at Pont de Gau. To explore this area, you'll have to strike out on foot, bicycle, or horseback (the **Association Camarguaise de Tourisme Equestre** publishes a list of stables where you can rent horses, available at the centre d'information or the Stes-Maries tourist office). Note that you are not allowed to diverge from marked trails.

Stes-Maries-de-la-Mer

㉑ *31 km (19 mi) southeast of Aigues-Mortes, 40 km (25 mi) southwest of Arles.*

The principal town within the confines of the Parc Régional de Camargue, Stes-Maries is a beach resort with a fascinating history. Provençal legend has it that around 45 AD a band of the very first Christians were rounded up and set adrift at sea in a boat without a sail and without provisions. Their stellar ranks included Mary Magdalene, Martha, and Mary Salome, mother of apostles James and John; Mary Jacoby, sister of the Virgin; and Lazarus, risen from the dead. Joining them in their fate: a dark-skinned servant girl named Sarah. Miraculously, their boat washed ashore at this ancient site, and the grateful Marys built a chapel in thanks. Martha moved on to Tarascon (☞ *below*) to tackle dragons and Lazarus founded the church in Marseille. But Mary Jacoby and Mary Salome remained in their old age, and Sarah stayed with them, begging in the streets to support them in their ministry. The three women died at the same time and were buried together at the site of their chapel.

A cult grew up around this legendary spot, and a church was built around it. When in the 15th century a stone memorial and two female bodies were found under the original chapel, the miracle was for all practical purposes confirmed, and the Romanesque church expanded to receive a new influx of pilgrims.

But the pilgrims attracted to Stes-Maries aren't all lighting candles to the two St. Marys: The servant girl Sarah has been adopted as an honorary saint by the Gypsies of the world, who blacken the crypt's domed ceiling with the soot of their votive candles lighted in her honor.

Two extraordinary festivals take place every year in Stes-Maries, one on May 24–25 and the other on the Sunday nearest to October 22. On May 24 Gypsy pilgrims gather from across Europe and carry the wooden statue of Sarah from her crypt, through the streets of the village, and down to the sea to be washed. The next day they carry a wooden statue of the two St. Marys, kneeling in their wooden boat, to the sea for their own holy bath. The same ritual is repeated by a less colorful crowd of non-Gypsy pilgrims in October, who carry the two Marys back to the sea.

★ On entering the damp, dark, and forbidding fortress-church, **Église des Stes-Maries,** what is most striking is its novel character. Almost devoid of windows, its tall, barren single nave is cluttered with florid and sentimental ex-votos (tokens of blessings, prayers, and thanks) and primitive and sentimental artworks of the famous trio. On the wall to your left, you'll see the wooden statue of the Marys in their boat; in the crypt below, Sarah glows to the light of dozens of candles.

Another oddity brings you back to the 20th century: A sign on the door forbids visitors to come *torso nu* (topless). For outside its otherworldly role, Stes-Maries is first and foremost a beach resort, dead-flat, whitewashed, and more than a little tacky. (Although Aigues-Mortes's access to the sea has silted in over the centuries, Stes-Maries, once more than 3 mi from the coast, finds itself smack on the waterfront these days; indeed, the encroaching Mediterranean has to be held off with concrete.) Unless you've made a pilgrimage to the sun and sand, don't spend much time in the town center; if you've chosen Stes-Maries as a base for viewing the Camargue, stay in one of the discreet *mas* (country inns) outside its city limits.

Lodging

$$ ⊞ **Mas de Cacharel.** On 170 acres of private marshland, many of
★ them bordering the Réserve Départemental de Camargue, this low-slung,
low-keyed haven greets you with a flutter of egrets as you roll up the
drive. Made up of a group of whitewashed buildings, set back from
D85 just north of Stes-Maries, this is a simple retreat for nature lovers.
It has a lodgelike central dining hall (really just a gathering spot for
breakfast, drinks, or cold cuts) complete with Provençal furniture and
a pleasantly smoky grand fireplace. Rooms are arranged motor-court
style, so most have windows that overlook the eternal stretch of reeds
and birds; their furnishings are spartan (electricity was only added in
the 1960s), with terra-cotta tiles, jute rugs, and cotton throws. Even
the pool is enclosed in glass walls to cut the wind but not the view toward
the resident horses. You can arrange for a guided tour on horseback
into the marshes, though you might be more content to curl up by the
pool with binoculars next to your drink. ⊠ *13460 Stes-Maries de la
Mer, 4 km (2 mi) north of town on D85,* ☎ *04–90–97–95–44,* FAX
*04–90–97–87–97. 15 rooms. Bar, breakfast room, pool, horseback
riding. MC, V.*

Arles

*29 km (18 mi) southeast of Nîmes, 40 km (25 mi) northwest of Stes-
Maries.*

If you were obliged to choose just one city to visit in Provence, lovely
little Arles would give Avignon and Aix a run for their money. It's too
chic to become museumlike yet has a wealth of classical antiquities and
Romanesque stonework, quarried-stone edifices and shuttered town
houses shading graceful old-town streets and squares, and pageantry,
festivals, and cutting-edge arts events. Its variety of atmospheric restau-
rants and picturesque small hotels makes it the ideal headquarters for
forays into the Alpilles and the Camargue.

Yet compared to Avignon and Aix, it's a small town. You can zip into
the center in five minutes without crossing a half hour's worth of
urban sprawl. And its monuments and pretty old neighborhoods are
conveniently concentrated between the main artery Boulevard des
Lices and the broad, lazy Rhône.

It wasn't always such a mellow site. A Greek colony since the 6th cen-
tury BC, little Arles took a giant step forward when Julius Caesar de-
feated Marseille in the 1st century BC. The emperor-to-be designated
Arles a Roman colony and lavished funds and engineering know-how
on it, transforming it into a formidable civilization—by some accounts,
the Rome of the north. Fed by aqueducts, canals, and solid roads, it
profited from all the Roman modern conveniences: straight paved
streets and sidewalks, sewers and latrines, thermal baths, a forum, a
stadium, a theater, and an arena. It became an international crossroads
by sea and land and a market to the world, with goods from Africa,
Arabia, and the Far East. The emperor Constantine himself moved to
Arles and brought with him Christianity.

The remains of this golden age are reason enough to visit Arles today.
Yet its character nowadays is as gracious and low-key as it once was
cutting edge. Seated in the shade of the plane trees on the place du Forum,
sunning at the foot of the obelisk on the place de la République, med-
itating in the cloister of St-Trophime, or strolling the rampart walk-
way along the sparkling Rhône, you'll see what enchanted Gauguin
and drove van Gogh mad with inspiration. It's the light: intense, vivid,
crystalline, setting off planes of color and shadow with prismatic con-

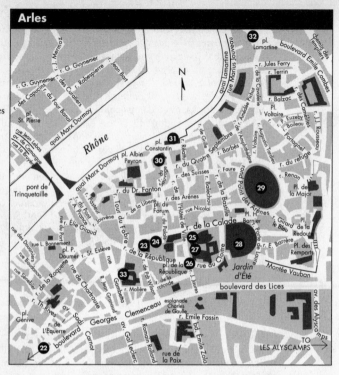

Arles

centration. As a foil to this famous light, multihued Arles—with its red and gold ochre, cool gray stone, and blue-black shade—is unsurpassed.

Note: If you plan to visit many of the monuments and museums in Arles, buy a *visite generale* ticket for 55 francs. This covers the 35-franc entry fee to the Musée de l'Arles Antique and any and all of the other museums and monuments (except the independent Museon Arlaten), which normally charge 15 francs each per visit. It's good for the length of your stay.

★ ㉒ Though it's a hike from the center, a good place to set the tone and context for your exploration of Arles is at the state-of-the-art **Musée de l'Arles Antique** (Museum of Ancient Arles). You can use the free museum shuttle from boulevard Clemenceau; there's an adjacent parking lot if you're day-tripping by car. The building itself is anything but ancient: A bold, modern triangular-shape structure, it was built in 1995 on the site of an enormous Roman *cirque* (chariot-racing stadium). It secrets its prehistoric collections in a womblike interior but bathes displays of the Roman Renaissance in wall-to-wall daylight. Natural materials and earth colors provide counterpoint to the high culture on display, and a preconceived viewing plan enhances the narrative flow of history (ask for the English-language guidebook). And there's more here than glass cases full of toga buckles: You'll learn about all the aspects of Arles in its heyday, from the development of its monuments to the details of daily life in Roman times. Perhaps the most instructive and fascinating aspect of this museum is its collection of tiny, precise models: a miniature cirque shows tiny chariots charging around its track, with an unfinished cross section that demonstrates building techniques; the amphitheater, forum, and theater as they were used; and a sophisticated 16-wheel water mill used to grind grain. The quantity of art treasures gives an idea of the extent of Arles's importance: Seven superb floor mosaics can be viewed from an elevated platform, and you exit via a hall packed tight with magnificently detailed paleo-Christian sarcophagi. The last thing you see: the belt of St-Césaire, the last bishop of Arles, who died in 542 AD as the countryside was over-whelmed by the Franks and the Roman era met its end. ⊠ *Presqu'île du Cirque Romain (follow bd. Clemenceau to N113 and cross over),* ☎ *04–90–18–88–88.* 🖃 *35 frs.* ⊙ *Apr.–mid-Sept., daily 9–7; mid-Sept.–Mar., daily 9:30–noon and 2–5:45.*

Whether you take the shuttle from the Musée de l'Arles Antique to the first stop at boulevard Georges-Clemenceau or arm yourself with lit-erature at the tourist information center just up the road (⊠ boule-vard des Lices), a good way to plunge into post-Roman Arles is through ★ ㉓ the quirky old **Museon Arlaten** (Museum of Arles). Created by the father of the Provençal revival, turn-of-the-century poet Frédéric Mistral (he paid for it with his Nobel Prize winnings), it enshrines a seemingly bot-tomless collection of regional treasures. There are spindled-oak bread boxes (mounted high on the wall like bird cages); the signature Arlésienne costumes, with their pretty shoulder scarves crossed at the waist; dolls and miniatures; an entire Camargue gardian hut, with reconstructed interior; and dioramas with mannequins—tiny tableaux of Provençal life. Following Mistral's wishes, women in full Arlésienne costume over-see the labyrinth of lovely 16th-century halls. ⊠ *29 rue de la République,* ☎ *04–90–93–58–11.* 🖃 *20 frs.* ⊙ *Apr.–May, Tues.–Sun. 9–noon and 2–6; June, Tues.–Sun. 9–noon and 2–6:30; July-Aug., daily 9–noon and 2–7; Sept., daily 9–noon and 2–6; Oct., Tues.–Sun. 9–noon and 2–5:30; Nov.–Mar., Tues.–Sun. 9–noon and 2–5.*

㉔ At the entrance to a 17th-century Jesuit college, you can access the an-cient underground galleries called the **Cryptoportiques.** Dating from 30 BC to 20 BC, this horseshoe of vaults and pillars buttressed the an-cient forum from underneath. Yet openings let in natural daylight, and artworks of considerable merit and worth were unearthed here, adding to the mystery of these passages' true function. ⊠ *rue Balze,* ☎ *04–90–49–36–74.* 🖃 *15 frs.* ⊙ *Dec.–Jan., daily 10–noon and 2–4:30; Feb., daily 10–noon and 2–5:30; Mar., daily 9–12:30 and 2–5:30; Apr.–mid-June, daily 9–12:30 and 2–7; mid-June–mid-Sept., daily 9–7; late Sept., daily 9–12:30 and 2–7; Oct., daily 10–12:30 and 2–5:30; Nov., daily 10–12:30 and 2–5.*

★ ㉕ Classed as a world treasure by UNESCO, the extraordinary Ro-manesque **Église St-Trophime** alone would justify a visit to Arles, though it's continually upstaged by the antiquities around it. Its transepts date from the 11th century and its nave from the 12th; the church's aus-tere symmetry and ancient artworks (including a stunningly Roman-style 4th-century sarcophagus) are fascinating in themselves. But it is the church's 12th-century **portal**—its entry facade—that earns it in-ternational respect. Superbly preserved and restored sculptures with high-relief modeling, complex layers of drapery, and a detail of expression that are nearly classical embellish every inch of the portal's surface. Indeed, it is that classicism that marks it as late Romanesque; Chartres Cathedral, of the same era, had long since ventured into fluid Goth-icism. The **tympanum** (the half-moon over the door) tells the story of the Last Judgment, inherently symmetrical, with its separation of the blessed who surge toward Christ and the damned who skulk, naked and in chains, toward hell. Christ is flanked by his chroniclers, the evan-gelists: the eagle (John), the bull (Luke), the angel (Matthew), and the lion (Mark). ⊠ *pl. de la République.*

㉖ Nowadays, the slender, expressive saints of St-Trophime overlook the wide steps that attract only sunners and foot-weary travelers who enjoy the modern perspective over the **place de la République,** flanked by the classical symmetry of the 17th-century **Hôtel de Ville.** This noble Italianate landmark is the work of the great 17th-century Parisian architect François Mansart (as in mansard roofs); a passageway allows you to cut through its graceful vestibule from rue Balze. The **obelisk,** of Turkish marble, used to stand in the Gallo-Roman cirque and was hauled here in the 18th century.

★ ㉗ Tucked discreetly behind St-Trophime is a peaceful haven, the **Cloître St-Trophime** (St-Trophime Cloister). A Romanesque treasure worthy of the church, it is one of the loveliest cloisters in Provence. Next to the church portals, enter via broad wooden doors that open onto the place de la République and cross a peaceful courtyard to the entrance. The slender elegance of its pillars contrasts gracefully with the florid decorations of the capitals, each carved with fine detail and a painterly hand. Even drapery and feathers pop into high relief. The clear dichotomy of Gothic and Romanesque styles—curving vaults versus delicate cross vaults—harmonizes beautifully, as does the cloister as a whole: You wouldn't be surprised to come upon Cyrano's Roxanne embroidering quietly in the light dappling through the oleander. ☎ 04–90–49–36–74. ▭ 15 frs. ☉ Dec.–Jan., daily 10–noon and 2–4:30; Feb., daily 10–noon and 2–5:30; Mar., daily 9–12:30 and 2–5:30; Apr.–mid-June, daily 9–12:30 and 2–7; mid-June–mid-Sept., daily 9–7; late Sept., daily 9–12:30 and 2–7; Oct., daily 10–12:30 and 2–5:30; Nov., daily 10–12:30 and 2–5.

㉘ Directly up rue de la Calade from the place de la République, you'll come across the picturesque ruins of the **Théâtre Antique,** built by the Romans under Augustus in the 1st century BC. Now overgrown and a pleasant, parklike retreat, it once served as an entertainment venue to some 20,000 spectators. None of its stage walls and only one row of arches remain of its once high-curved back (it was not a natural amphitheater): Its fine local stone was borrowed to build early Christian churches. Nonetheless, it serves today as a concert stage for the Festival d'Arles (in July and August) and a venue for the Recontres Internationales de la Photographie (Photography Festival). ☎ 04–90–49–36–74. ▭ 15 frs. ☉ Dec.–Jan., daily 10–noon and 2–4:30; Feb., daily 10–noon and 2–5:30; Mar., daily 9–12:30 and 2–5:30; Apr.–mid-June, daily 9–12:30 and 2–7; mid-June–mid-Sept., daily 9–7; late Sept., daily 9–12:30 and 2–7; Oct., daily 10–12:30 and 2–5:30; Nov., daily 10–12:30 and 2–5.

㉙ Rivaled only by the even better-preserved version in Nîmes, the **Arènes** (Arena) dominates old Arles. Its four medieval towers are testimony to its transformation from classical sports arena to feudal fortification in the middle ages—at the sacrifice of a full row of arches and much of the original structure. Younger than Arles's theater, it dates from the 1st century AD, and unlike the theater, seats 20,000 to this day. Its primary function: as a venue for the traditional spectacle of the corridas, or bullfights, which take place annually during the *feria pascale,* or Easter festival. Climb to the top of the tallest medieval tower, by the entry, to see the arena as a whole and take in old Arles. ☎ 04–90–49–36–74. ▭ 15 frs. ☉ Dec.–Jan., daily 10–noon and 2–4:30; Feb., daily 10–noon and 2–5:30; Mar., daily 9–12:30 and 2–5:30; Apr.–mid-June, daily 9–12:30 and 2–7; mid-June–mid-Sept., daily 9–7; late Sept., daily 9–12:30 and 2–7; Oct., daily 10–12:30 and 2–5:30; Nov., daily 10–12:30 and 2–5.

㉚ Along the riverfront stand the **Thermes Constantin,** the remains of vast and sophisticated Roman baths, luxurious social centers that once included sports facilities and a library—the Barnes & Noble of the 4th century. ☎ 04–90–49–36–74. ▭ 15 frs. ☉ Dec.–Jan., daily 10–noon *and 2–4:30; Feb., daily 10–noon and 2–5:30; Mar., daily 9–12:30 and 2–5:30; Apr.–mid-June, daily 9–12:30 and 2–7; mid-June–mid-Sept., daily 9–7; late Sept., daily 9–12:30 and 2–7; Oct., daily 10–12:30 and 2–5:30; Nov., daily 10–12:30 and 2–5.*

Though it makes every effort today to make up for its misjudgment, Arles treated Vincent van Gogh very badly during the time he passed here near the end of his life—a time when his creativity, productivity, and madness all reached a climax. It was 1888 when he settled in to work in Arles with an intensity and tempestuousness that drove away his colleague and companion Paul Gauguin and alienated his neighbors. In 1889 the people of Arles circulated a petition to have him evicted, a shock that left him more and more at a loss to cope with life and led to his eventual commitment to an insane asylum in nearby St-Rémy. The houses he lived in are no longer standing, though many of his subjects remain as he saw them (or are restored to a similar condition). Arles can't boast a single van Gogh painting—excusable, given that his works sell for $20 million today—but did they have to name their art museum after Jacques Réattu, a local painter of dazzling mediocrity? **③** The **Musée Réattu** lavishes three rooms on his turn-of-the-19th-century ephemera but redeems itself with a decent collection of 20th-century works, including paintings by Léger, Vlaminck, and Rousseau, and a gathering of bits and pieces by Picasso, all dating from 1971. The best thing about the Réattu may be the building, a Knights of Malta priory dating from the 15th century, with its fortress-facade overlooking the Rhône. ⊠ *rue Grand Prieuré,* ☎ *04–90–49–36–74.* ▧ *15 frs.* ☉ *Dec.–Jan., daily 10–noon and 2–4:30; Feb., daily 10–noon and 2–5:30; Mar., daily 9–12:30 and 2–5:30; Apr.–mid-June, daily 9–12:30 and 2–7; mid-June–mid-Sept., daily 9–7; late Sept., daily 9–12:30 and 2–7; Oct., daily 10–12:30 and 2–5:30; Nov., daily 10–12:30 and 2–5.*

Thus you'll have to go to Amsterdam or Moscow to view van Goghs. But don't despair: Though it takes some imagination, true pilgrims can glean something of van Gogh's Arles from a theme-tour of the modern town. In fact, the city has provided helpful markers and a numbered itinerary to guide you from one landmark to another—many of **②** them recognizable from beloved canvases. You can stand on **place Lamartine** (between the rail station and the ramparts) where he lived in the famous Maison Jaune (Yellow House); it was destroyed by bombs in 1944. *Starry Night* may have been painted from the quai du Rhône just off Place Lamartine, though a panel outside St-Rémy claims credit for this ambiguous landscape. The Café La Nuit on Place Forum is an exact match for the terrace platform, scattered with tables and bathed in gaslight under the stars, for the painting *Terrace de café le Soir*; Gauguin and van Gogh used to drink here. Both the Arènes (☞ *above*) and Les Alyscamps (☞ Off the Beaten Path, *below*) were featured in paintings.

But the most strikingly resonant site, impeccably restored and landscaped to match one of van Gogh's paintings, is the courtyard garden **③** of what is now the **Espace van Gogh,** featured in *Le Jardin de l'Hôtel-Dieu.* This was the hospital to which the tortured artist repared after cutting off his ear, and its cloistered grounds have become something of a shrine for visitors. The hospital has been divided up into a municipal library, book shops, and a souvenir shop—none of them directly related to van Gogh, all of them reasonably discreet. ⊠ *pl. Dr. Félix Rey.*

OFF THE BEATEN PATH — Though **Les Alyscamps,** the romantically melancholy Roman cemetery, lie away from the old town, it's worth the hike if you're in a reflective mood. Follow the boulevard des Lices past the Jardin d'Été, the post office, and the *gendarmerie* (police station), then cut right. This long necropolis amassed the remains of the dead from antiquity to the Middle Ages; bodies were shipped up the Rhône to this prestigious resting place. Greek, Roman, and Christian tombs line the long shady road that was once the entry to Arles—the Aurelian Way—and the ruins of chapels and churches are scattered among the sarcophagi. The finest of these stone coffins were offered as gifts in feudal times, and tombstones were mined for building stone. Thus no one work of surpassing beauty remains, but the ensemble has an aura of eternity. ☎ *04–90–49–36–74. ☒ 15 frs. ☉ Dec.–Jan., daily 10–noon and 2–4:30; Feb., daily 10–noon and 2–5:30; Mar., daily 9–12:30 and 2–5:30; Apr.–mid-June, daily 9–12:30 and 2–7; mid-June–mid-Sept., daily 9–7; late Sept., daily 9–12:30 and 2–7; Oct., daily 10–12:30 and 2–5:30; Nov., daily 10–12:30 and 2–5.*

Dining and Lodging

$$$ ✕ **Lou Marguès.** Whether you dine indoors, surrounded by glowing woodwork and rich Provençal fabrics, or amid the greenery of this former Carmelite cloister, atmosphere figures large in your evening at this Arles institution, in the Jules César Hotel. Chefs Pascal Renaud and Joseph Kriz mix classical grandeur with Provençal rusticity: scallop and truffle risotto, roast pigeon with turnip confit, salsify with bacon and truffled polenta, and rice pudding with honey and orange. The wine list is as ambitious as Caesar himself. ☒ *In Jules César Hotel, bd. des Lices,* ☎ *04–90–93–43–20. Reservations essential. AE, DC, MC, V. Closed mid-Nov.–Dec.*

$$ ✕ **Brasserie Nord-Pinus.** With its tile-and-ironwork interior straight
★ out of a design magazine and its place du Forum terrace packed with all the right people, this cozy-chic retro brasserie features the superb but unpretentious cooking of Jean-André Charial, trained at the hallowed L'Oustau de la Baumanière (☞ Les Baux-de-Provence, *below*). The cuisine is light, simple, and purely Provençal, and made with such ingredients as fresh asparagus, seafood, and local wines. And wasn't that Christian Lacroix (or Kate Moss or Juliette Binoche. . .) under those Ray-Bans? ☒ *pl. du Forum,* ☎ *04–90–93–44–44. Reservations essential. AE, DC, MC, V. Closed Feb. and Wed. Nov.–Mar.*

$$ ✕ **La Gueule du Loup.** Serving as hosts, waiters, and chefs, the ambitious couple who own this restaurant tackle serious cooking—monkfish and squid in saffron, lamb in pastry lined with *tapenade* (olive-and-caper spread) and crème brûlée perfumed with orange blossoms—and maintains a supercool ambience. Jazz music and vintage magic posters bring the old Arles stone-and-beam setting up to date. ☒ *39 rue des Arènes,* ☎ *04–90–96–96–69. MC, V. Closed Sun. No dinner Mon.*

$$ ✕ **Le Vaccarès.** Claim a shaded table on the place du Forum at this sought-after summer spot and enjoy the 98-franc lunch with other Arles elite; by night it's downright glamorous. The Dumas men—grandfather, father, and son—have been creating sophisticated Provençal specialties for aeons without going stale. Watch for steamed sea bass in a pool of nutty local olive oil, or garlic-rich pigeon with foie gras risotto. ☒ *pl. du Forum,* ☎ *04–90–96–06–17. MC, V. Closed mid-Jan.–mid-Feb. and Mon. No dinner Sun.*

$ ✕ **L'Affenage.** A vast smorgasbord of Provençal hors d'oeuvres draws
★ loyal locals to this former fire-horse shed. They come here for heaping plates of fried eggplant, green tapenade, chick-peas in cumin, a slab of ham carved off the bone, and roasted potatoes and lamb chops grilled in the great stone fireplace. In summer you can opt for just the first-course buffet and go back for thirds; reserve a terrace table out front.

✉ *4 rue Molière,* ☎ *04–90–96–07–67. AE, MC, V. Closed Sun. and 3 wks in Aug. No dinner Wed.*

$ ✗ **Lou Caleu.** In a charming 16th-century building behind the Arena, this popular, unpretentious place serves regional specialties (brandade, or salt-cod paste, and tough but authentic bull steak) at good prices. The lunch deals are terrific, and you can gaze at the arena's arches if you dine on the terrace. ✉ *27 rue Porte de Laure,* ☎ *04–90–49–71– 77. AE, DC, MC, V.*

$ ✗ **Vitamine.** If you're unaccustomed to French-scale eating (even the lighter southern cuisine), you'll be relieved to find this pretty, Provençal-looking eatery that puts all its energy into fresh, crisp full-meal salads—50 varieties for under 50 francs each. There are pasta options, too, and a friendly, laid-back staff. ✉ *16 rue du Docteur Fanton,* ☎ *04–90–93–77–36. MC, V. Closed Sun. No dinner Sat.*

$$$$ ✗🏠 **Le Mas de Peint.** This may be the ultimate mas experience, set as
★ it is in a 17th-century farmhouse on some 500 hectares (1,250 acres) of Camargue ranch land. Luxurious Provençal fabrics and antiques grace the old stone floors, and burnished beams warm the firelit salon and library. Rooms are lavished with brass beds, monogrammed linens, even canopied bathtubs. At dinner time, guests gather in the kitchen to chat with the cook and settle in for sophisticated specialties using home-grown products (ratatouille and lamb dishes as well as Camargue rice and bull). Diners not staying in the hotel are welcomed into the kitchen, too, just for lunch or dinner; the restaurant ($$) is closed Wednesday and advance reservations are required. In summer (mid-June–mid-Sept.) a light lunch is served by the pool. You're only 20 km (12 mi) south of Arles here, but you should plan on a relaxing immersion in the country rather than a heavy sightseeing itinerary, as other towns are well out of the way. But who would want to leave when you can ride the private grounds on Camargue horses, or take a tour in a four-wheel drive? ✉ *Le Sambuc, 13200 Arles,* ☎ *04–90–97–20–62,* ⓕ𝔸𝕏 *04–90– 97–22–20. 8 rooms, 2 apartments. Restaurant, air-conditioning, pool, horseback riding. AE, DC, MC, V. Closed mid-Jan.–mid-Mar.*

$$$$ 🏠 **Jules César.** This elegant landmark, once a Carmelite convent but styled like a Roman palace, anchors the lively boulevard des Lices. Low-slung, with rooms on the small side, it's not a grand luxury palace; rather, it's an intimate, traditional hotel, conservatively decorated with richly printed fabrics and burnished woodwork. Rooms are pure Souleiado, from the flower-sprigged wallpaper to the bathroom tiles; the antiques are classic, curvy Provençal. Some windows look over the pool and some over the pretty cloister, where breakfast is served under a vaulted stone arcade. ✉ *bd. des Lices, 13200,* ☎ *04–90–93–43–20,* ⓕ𝔸𝕏 *04–90– 93–33–47. 55 rooms. Restaurant, air-conditioning, pool. AE, DC, MC, V. Closed mid-Nov.–late Dec.*

$$$$ 🏠 **Nord-Pinus.** J. Peterman would feel right at home in this quintessen-
★ tially Mediterranean hotel on the place du Forum; Hemingway did. Travel relics, kilims, oil jars, angular wrought iron and colorful ceramics create a richly atmospheric stage-set for literati (or literary poseurs), decor magazine shoots, and people who refer to themselves as "travelers." Its scruffy insider-chic is not for everyone: Traditionalists should head for the mainstream luxuries of the Jules César. But this is where you might brush past a *Vogue* editor on the way to breakfast, and the brasserie is the *dernier cri* (last word) in shoulder-rubbing (☞ *above*). ✉ *pl. du Forum, 13200,* ☎ *04–90–47–17–16,* ⓕ𝔸𝕏 *04–90–93–34– 00. 26 rooms. Brasserie, bar. AE, DC, MC, V.*

$$$ 🏠 **Arlatan.** Once home to the counts of Arlatan, this noble 15th-cen-
★ tury stone house stands on the site of a 4th-century basilica, and a glass floor reveals the excavated vestiges under the lobby. Digging an excavation in your lobby is just another aristocratic pastime for the friendly

owners of this jewel of a hotel, with rows of rooms that horseshoe around a lovely fountain courtyard and with breakfasts served in the antiques-filled family dining hall. Rooms are decorated with a chic, light hand, with quarry tiles and Pierre Frey fabrics, and the intimate lobby bar is a cool, quiet haven. ⊠ *26 rue du Sauvage, 13200,* ☎ *04–90–93–56–66,* FAX *04–90–49–68–45. 33 rooms, 7 suites. AE, DC, MC, V.*

$–$$ 🏨 **Le Calendal.** The cheery Provençal colors of this small hotel next to the Arènes reflect the spirit of the hotel and its staff, most of whom speak English. Rooms overlook the amphitheater or the courtyard garden; some sleep four. Light meals are served in the cozy tearoom. ⊠ *22 pl. du Docteur Pomme, 13200,* ☎ *04–90–96–11–89,* FAX *04–90–96–05–84. 27 rooms. Restaurant, air-conditioning. AE, MC, V.*

$ 🏨 **Le Cloître.** Built as the private home for the head of the Cloisters, this grand old medieval building has luckily fallen into the hands of a couple devoted to making the most of its historic details—with their own bare hands. They've chipped away plaster from pristine quarried stone walls, cleaned massive beams, restored tile stairs, and mixed natural chalk and ochre to plaster the walls, which are prettily decorated with stencils. The resulting charm more than makes up for a few tired bathrooms. Bargain hunters should opt for the sweet little top-floor rooms, sans WC, with views over the ancient rooftops. ⊠ *16 rue du Cloître, 13200,* ☎ *04–90–96–29–50,* FAX *04–90–96–02–88. 30 rooms. AE, MC, V.*

$ 🏨 **Hôtel Gauguin.** Of several concrete budget hotels that sprang up in this section of the old town after World War II erased its original structures, this is the nicest. The rooms, well scrubbed and decked in pretty olive prints and sponge-paint, are small, but so is the price; those with full bathrooms are a little more. Ask for a room in front; they look onto the square. The welcoming owner, Madame Dugand, is happy to try her English. ⊠ *5 pl. Voltaire, 13200,* ☎ *04–90–96–14–35,* FAX *04–90–18–98–87. 18 rooms, 9 with bath. MC, V.*

$ 🏨 **Muette.** With 12th-century exposed stone walls, a 15th-century spi-
★ ral stair, weathered wood, and an old-town setting, a hotelier wouldn't have to try very hard to please. But the couple who own this place do: Hand-stripped doors, antiques, fresh white-and-blue-tile baths, hair dryers, good mattresses, Provençal prints, and fresh sunflowers in every room show that Alain and Brigitte Deplancke care. ⊠ *15 rue des Suisses, 13200,* ☎ *04–90–96–15–39,* FAX *04–90–49–73–16. 18 rooms, 17 with bath. AE, MC, V.*

$ 🏨 **Le Rhône.** Simple and plain, with fresh pastel paint and a few balconies overlooking the place Voltaire, this small hotel's main attraction is its value for money: The most expensive doubles are 200 francs, and those without bathrooms (sink and bidet only) cost 130 francs. The young, friendly owners offer a warm welcome. ⊠ *11 pl. Voltaire,* ☎ *04–90–93–87–03,* ☎ *04–90–96–43–70. 12 rooms, 5 with bath. AE, DC, MC, V.*

Festivals

Arles is a true festival town, offering a stimulating mix of folklorique and contemporary arts events. The **férias,** with traditional corridas, or bullfights, vie with the **Fêtes du Riz** (with corrida) in September and the **Fêtes d'Arles,** from the end of June to the beginning of July. All feature traditional games and races in the Arena, parades, folk-dance events, and—their raison d'être—the beautiful traditional costumes of Arles.

In July, the famous **Rencontres Internationales de la Photographie** bring movers and shakers in international photography into the théâtre antique for five days of highly specialized colloquiums and homages. Ordinary folks can profit, too, by attending the photography exhibits displayed in some 17 venues in Arles, open to the public throughout July and August. If you're under 25 with an I.D., you can get in free. (For information, call ☎ 04–90–96–76–06 or write to ✉ 10 rond-point des Arènes, BP 96, 13632 Arles Cedex.)

Nightlife and the Arts

To find out what's happening in and around Arles (even as far away as Nîmes and Avignon), the free weekly *Le César* lists films, plays, cabaret, jazz and rock events. It's distributed at the tourist office, in bars, clubs and cinemas. Or consult its website agenda at www.cesar.fr.

Though Arles seems to be one big sidewalk café in warm weather, the place to drink is the hip bar **Le Cintra,** in the also-hip hotel Nord-Pinus (☞ *above*); it's decorated with bullfight paraphernalia. In high season, the cafés stay lively till the wee hours; in winter, the streets empty out by 11. **Le Cargo de Nuit** (✉ 7 av. Sadi-Carnot, ☎ 04–90–49–55–99) is the main venue for live jazz, reggae and rock, with a dance floor next to the stage. There are three concerts per week (Thursday, Friday, and Saturday), and the restaurant serves food until 2 AM.

Shopping

Despite its chicness and its popularity, Arles hasn't sprouted the rows of designer shops found in Aix-en-Provence and St-Rémy. Its stores remain small and eccentric and feature an overwhelming variety of Provençal goods. Regional fabric is available at every turn (☞ Close-Up Box: Those Ubiquitous Provençal Cottons, *below*), including boutiques for the principal makers (and rivals) **Les Olivades** (✉ 2 rue Jean Jaurès) and **Souleiado** (✉ 18 bd. des Lices).

Though the charming terra-cotta folk miniatures called *santons* originate from around Marseille, the **Maison Chave** (✉ 14 Rond Point des Arènes), across from the Arena, is a good place to find them. There's always someone painting tiny fingernails or tying impossibly tiny kerchiefs, and you're welcome to watch without buying.

Arles's colorful **markets,** with produce, regional products, clothes, fabrics, wallets, frying pans, and other miscellaneous items, take place every Saturday morning along the boulevard des Lices, which flows into the boulevard Clemenceau. On the first Wednesday of the month there's a **brocante market** where you can find antiques and collectibles, many of them regional.

Abbaye de Montmajour

★ *6 km (4 mi) north of Arles, direction Fontvieille.*

An extraordinary structure looming over the marshlands north of Arles, this magnificent Romanesque abbey stands in partial ruin, with shrieking rooks ducking in and out of its empty stone-framed windows. Begun in the 12th-century by a handful of Benedictine monks, it grew according to an ambitious plan of church, crypt, and cloister; under corrupt lay monks in the 17th century, it grew more sumptuous; when those lay monks were ejected by the church, they sacked the place. When, after the Revolution, it was sold to a junkman, he tried to pay the mortgage by stripping off and selling its goods. A 19th-century medieval revival spurred its partial restoration, but its 18th-century portions remain in ruins.

Ironically, because of this mercenary history, what remains is a spare and beautiful piece of Romanesque architecture, bare of furniture and art—an abstraction of massive stone arches, vaults and flowing curves that seem to be poured and molded instead of quarried and fitted in chunks. And its **cloister** rivals that of St-Trophime in Arles for its bal-

THOSE UBIQUITOUS PROVENÇAL COTTONS

(or, If I Wake Up to One More Hotel Decor of Blue-and-Yellow Olive Sprigs I'll Cut My Ear Off)

VIVID MEDALLION PRINTS, soft floral sprigs, assertive paisley borders: They've come to define the Provençal Experience, these bright-patterned fabrics, with their sunny colors, naive prints, and country themes redolent of sunflowers and olive groves. And the southern tourist industry is eager to fulfill that expectation, swagging hotel rooms and restaurant dining rooms with gay Provençal patterns in counterpoint to the cool yellow stucco and burnished terra-cotta tiles. Nowadays in Provence and on the coast, it's all about country—back to the land with a vengeance.

These ubiquitous cottons are actually Indian prints *(indiennes)*, first shipped into the ports of Marseille from exotic trade routes in the 16th century. Ancient Chinese lost-wax techniques—indigo dyes taking hold where the wax wasn't applied—evolved into wood-block stamps, their surfaces painted with mixed colors, then pressed carefully onto bare cotton. The colors were richer, the patterns more varied than any fabrics then available—and, what's more, they were easily reproduced.

They caught on like a wildfire in a mistral, and soon mills in Provence were creating local versions en masse. Too well, it seems: By the end of the 17th century, the popular cottons were competing with royal textile manufacturers. In 1686, under Louis XIV, the manufacture and marketing of Provençal cottons was banned.

All the ban did was contain the industry to Provence, where it developed in Marseille (franchised for local production despite the ban) and in Avignon, where the Papal possessions were above royal law. Their rarity and their prohibition made them all the sexier, and fashionable Parisians—even insiders in the Versaille court—flaunted the coveted contraband.

By 1734, Louis XV cracked down on the hypocrisy, and the ban was sustained across France. The people protested: The cottons were affordable, practical, and brought a glimmer of color into the commoner's daily life. The king relented in 1758, and the peasants were free to swath their windows, tables, and hips with a limitless variety of color and print.

But because of the 72-year ban and that brief burgeoning of the southern countermarket, the tight-printed style and vivid colors remained allied in the public consciousness as "Provençal," and the region has embraced them as its own. If once they trimmed the windows of basic stone farmhouses and lined the quilted petticoats of peasants to keep off the chill, nowadays the fabrics drape the beveled-glass French doors of the finest *hôtel particuliers* (private mansions) and grandest Riviera hotels.

Two franchises dominate the market and maintain high-visibility boutiques in all the best southern towns: Souleiado and Les Olivades. Yet every tourist thoroughfare presents a hallucinatory array of goods, sewn into every salable form from lavender sachets to placemats to swirling skirts and bolero jackets. There are even toilet-paper holders.

But never mind: Now as you lie in your hotel bed and contemplate the interplay of folksy patterns, you'll know why they greet you at every Provençal turn.

ance, elegance, and air of mystical peace: Van Gogh was drawn to its womblike isolation, and came often to the abbey to paint and reflect. ☎ 04–90–54–64–17. 🖃 32 frs. ☉ Apr.–Sept., daily 9–7; Oct.–Mar., Wed.–Mon. 10–1 and 2–5.

Tarascon

34 18 km (11 mi) north of Arles, 16 km (10 mi) west of St-Rémy.

Tarascon's claim to fame is as home to the mythical Tarasque, a monster that would emerge from the Rhône to gobble up children and cattle. Luckily, Saint Martha (Ste-Marthe), who washed up at Stes-Maries-de-la-Mer, tamed the beast with a sprinkle of holy water, after which the inhabitants slashed it to pieces. This dramatic event is celebrated on the last weekend in June with a parade and immortalized by Alphonse Daudet, who lived in nearby Fontvieille, in his tales of a folk hero known to all French schoolchildren as *Tartarin de Tarascon.* Unfortunately, a saint has not yet been born who can vanquish the fumes that emanate from Tarascon's enormous paper mill, and the hotel industry is suffering for it.

★ Nonetheless, with the walls of its formidable **Château** plunging straight into the roaring Rhône, this ancient city on the river presents a daunting challenge to Beaucaire, its traditional enemy across the water. Begun in the 13th century by the noble Anjou family on the site of a Roman *castellum,* it grew through the generations into a splendid structure, crowned with both round and square towers and elegantly furnished. René the Good (1409–1480) held court here, entertaining luminaries of the age. Nowadays the castle owes its superb preservation to its use, through the ensuing centuries, as a prison: It first served as such in the 17th century, and released its last prisoner in 1926. Complete with a moat, a drawbridge, and a lovely faceted spiral staircase, it retains its beautiful decorative stonework and original window frames. ☎ 04–90–91–01–93. 🖃 32 frs. ☉ Apr.–Sept., daily 9–7; Oct.–Mar., Wed.–Mon. 9–noon and 2–5.

Beaucaire

35 19 km (12 mi) north of Arles, 2 km (1 mi) northwest of Tarascon.

Though Beaucaire's castle glowering across the Rhône at its ancient enemy Tarascon doesn't hold a candle to its neighbor, this riverside town has an ambience all its own. Virtually unvisited by tourists, its labyrinthine old town retains an ancient, empty air—with superb old buildings and its **Hôtel de Ville** (🖃 pl. Clemenceau) by 17th-century architect François Mansard. Also of note is the fabulous **Hôtel de Margailler** (🖃 23 rue de la République) dating from 1675 and featuring a porch complete with caryatids. Pick up a "Guide du Patrimoine" at the **tourist office** (🖃 quai Général de Gaulle) and wander at will.

Beaucaire's **Château** was built on the site of a Roman camp in the 11th century but was remodeled 200 years later and then dismantled in the 17th century on the orders of Cardinal Richelieu. What is left are the ramparts, two towers, the restored Romanesque chapel, and the barbican that defended the castle's entrance. You can visit the remains freely and wander in the peaceful garden, stopping in briefly to tour the Musée Auguste Jacquet, a collection of archeological finds from the castle and environs. Another way to experience the château: attending the spectacle called Les Aigles de Beaucaire—when birds of prey are handled by falconers in medieval costume. 🖃 pl. du Château, ☎ 04–66–59–47–61. ☉ Museum and château grounds open Wed.–Mon. 10–noon and 2–6. 🖃 Château: free; museum entrance: 12.50 frs.; bird show:

45 frs. ☼ Late Mar.–early Nov., Thurs.–Tues., with bird shows at 2, 3, 4, 5 (July–Aug. 3, 4, 5, 6).

Shopping

Beaucaire's picturesque **markets** hold forth Thursday and Sunday mornings in front of the Hôtel de Ville (produce) and along the Canal du Rhône à Sète (dry goods), with boats bobbing alongside the fabric stands.

THE ALPILLES

Whether approaching from the damp lowlands of Arles and the Camargue or the pebbled vineyards around Avignon, the countryside changes dramatically as you climb into the arid heights of the low mountain range called the Alpilles (pronounced ahl-PEE-yuh). A rough-hewn, rocky landscape rises into nearly barren limestone hills, the fields silvered with ranks of twisted olive trees and alleys of gnarled *amandiers* (almond trees). It's the heart of Provence and is appealing not only for the antiquities in St-Rémy and the feudal ruins in Les Baux, but also for its mellow pace when the day's touring is done. Here, as much as anywhere in the south, is the place to slip into espadrilles, nibble from a bowl of olives, and attempt nothing more taxing than a lazy game of *pétanque* (lawn bowling). Hence, the countryside around St-Rémy is peppered with gentrified *gîtes* and *mas*, and is one of the most sought-after sites for Parisiens' (and Londoners') summer homes.

Fontvieille

36 *19 km (12 mi) northeast of Arles, 20 km (12½ mi) southeast of Taras-con.*

The village of Fontvieille (pronounced fohn-VYAY-uh), among the limestone hills, is best known as the home of writer Alphonse Daudet. In the well-preserved, charming **Moulin de Daudet** (Daudet's Windmill), just up D33 on a hill in the outskirts of the village, 19th-century writer Alphonse Daudet dreamed up his short stories, *Lettres de Mon Moulin*. Inside there's a small museum devoted to Daudet, and you can walk upstairs to see the original milling system. ☎ 04–90–54–60–78. 📧 *10 frs. ☼ Apr.–Oct., daily 9–12:30 and 1:30–7; Nov.–Dec. and Feb.–Mar., daily 10–noon and 2–6.*

Dining and Lodging

$$$–$$$$ 🏨 **La Regalido.** In an old olive oil mill covered with vines, this extravagant Relais & Chateaux property has cosseted floral-print rooms that look over the Alpilles. The enchanting, stone-terraced garden full of flowering plants is reason enough to stay here. The restaurant continues to get mixed reviews for its concentration on the raw, new olive oil of the region, featured to the point of saturation; there's even a menu devoted to it. ✉ *rue F. Mistral, 13990,* ☎ *04–90–54–60–22,* 📠 *04–90–54–64–29. 13 rooms, 2 suites. Restaurant. AE, DC, MC, V. Closed Jan.*

Les Baux-de-Provence

37 *9 km (6 mi) east of Fontvieille, 19 km (12 mi) northeast of Arles.*

When you first search the craggy hilltops for signs of Les Baux-de-Provence (pronounced boh), you may not quite be able to distinguish between bedrock and building, so naturally do the ragged skyline of towers and crenellation blend into the sawtooth jags of stone. As dramatic in its perched isolation as Mont-St-Michel and St-Paul-de-Vence, this tiny château-village ranks as one of the most visited tourist sites in France. Its car-free main street (almost its *only* street) is thus jammed with shops and galleries and, by day, overwhelmed with the smell of scented souvenirs. But don't deprive yourself for fear of crowds: Stay late in the day, after the tour buses leave; spend the night in one of its modest hotels; or come off-season, and you'll experience its spectacular character—a tour-de-force blend of natural setting and medieval ambience of astonishing beauty.

From this intimidating vantage point, the lords of Baux ruled throughout the 11th and 12th centuries over one of the largest fiefdoms in the south, commanding some 80 towns and villages. Mistral called them "a race of eagles, never vassals," and their virtually unchallenged power led to the flourishing of a rich medieval culture: courtly love, troubadour songs, and knightly gallantry. By the 13th century the lords of Baux had fallen from power, their stronghold destroyed. Though Les Baux experienced a brief renaissance and reconstruction in the 16th century, the final indignity followed hard upon that: Richelieu decided to eliminate the threatening eagle's nest once and for all and had the castle and walls demolished in 1632. Its citizens themselves were required to pay the cost.

Only in the 19th century did Les Baux find new purpose: The mineral bauxite, valued as an alloy in aluminum production, was discovered in its hills and named for its source. A profitable industry sprang up that lasted into the 20th century before fading into history, like the lords of Baux themselves.

Today Les Baux offers two faces to the world: its beautifully preserved medieval village and the ghostly ruins of its fortress, once referred to as the *ville morte* (dead town). In the village, lovely 12th-century stone houses, even their window frames still intact, shelter the shops, cafés, and galleries that line the steep cobbled streets.

Vestiges of the Renaissance remain as well, including the pretty **Hôtel de Manville,** built at the end of the 16th century by a wealthy Protestant family. Step into its inner court to admire the mullioned (stone-framed) windows, Renaissance-style stained glass, and vaulted arcades. Today it serves as the *mairie* (town hall). Up and across the street, the striking remains of the 16th-century Protestant temple still bear a quote from Jean Calvin: POST TENEBRAS LUX, or "after the shadows, light."

In the Hôtel des Porcelet, which dates from the 16th century as well, the **Musée Yves-Brayer** shelters this local 20th-century artist's works. Figurative and accessible to the point of naivete, his paintings feature Italy, Spain, even Asia, but demonstrate most of all his love of Provence. Brayer's grave lies in the château cemetery. ⊠ *pl. Hervain,* ☎ *04–90–54–36–99.* 🎟 *20 frs.* ☉ *Apr.–Sept., daily 10–12:30 and 2–6:30; Oct.–Mar., daily 10–12:30 and 2–5.*

The main site to visit, however, is the 17-acre cliff-top sprawl of ruins contained under the umbrella name **Château des Baux**. Climb the rue Neuve and continue up rue Trancat to the Tour du Brau, which contains the **Musée d'Histoire des Baux**. Entry to this small collection of relics and models gives access to the wide and varied grounds, where Romanesque chapels and towers mingle with skeletal ruins. A numbered program (available in English) guides you from site to site—the 16th-century hospital, the windmill, the 13th-century donjon—many of which are recognizable only by their names. Kids are especially fascinated by reconstructions of gigantic medieval siege machines. But be sure to stop into the cemetery; a more dramatic resting place would be hard to find. And the tiny **Chapelle St-Blaise** shelters a permanent music-and-slide show, *Van Gogh, Gauguin, Cézanne au Pays de l'O-livier,* of artworks depicting olive orchards in their infinite variety. You can see painterly views over patchwork olive orchards, as well as vineyards, almond orchards, and low-slung farmhouses, from every angle of the Château cliff top—reason enough alone to pay entry. ☎ 04–90–54–55–56. ▣ 35 frs. ☉ Daily Mar.–June and Sept.–Nov. 9–7; July–Aug. 9–8:30; Nov. and Feb. 9–6; Dec.–Jan. 9–5.

About half a mile north of Les Baux, off D27, is the **Cathédrale d'Images** (Cathedral of Images), where the majestic setting of the old limestone quarries, with their towering rock faces and stone pillars, is used as a colossal screen for nature-themed films (Jacques Cousteau gets frequent billing). Bring a sweater. ⊠ *rte. de Maillane,* ☎ 04–90–54–38–65. ▣ 43 frs. ☉ Mid-Mar.–mid-Nov., daily 10–7; winter, daily 10–6. Some special exhibitions are held mid-Dec.–mid-Jan.

Dining and Lodging

$ ✕ **Café Cinarca.** The tiny dining room is nice enough, but the garden courtyard of this small, unpretentious restaurant is a shady haven from the steady flow of tourists climbing the hill. A limited blackboard menu features a simple fixed-price meal, including *tartes* and salads embellishing one or two hearty meat dishes: beef *daube* (stew), or *caillette aux herbes* (pork meat loaf) served hot or cold. It's also worth coming for afternoon tea, as the cakes and pastries are homemade and delicious. ⊠ *rue Trencat,* ☎ 04–90–54–33–94. MC, V. Closed Tues. Sept.–June.

$$$$ ✕▤ **L'Oustau de la Baumanière.** Sheltered by rocky cliffs below the village of Les Baux, this hotel, with its formal landscaped terrace and broad swimming pool, has the air of a Roman palazzo. Chef Jean-André Charial's hallowed reputation continues to attract culinary pilgrims, despite ups and downs. Ups include ravioli *de truffes aux poireaux* (stuffed with truffles and leeks), asparagus with olives and diced foie gras, and his famous *gigot de sept heures* (lamb cooked for seven hours), which must be tasted to be believed. (Be sure to make reservations and note that the restaurant is closed Thursday lunch and all day Wednesday from November to Christmas, then closed altogether January–February.) Breezy, private rooms are scattered like bungalows and are beautifully furnished with antiques. Those in the main house convey grandeur—enormous chimneys, sumptuous fabrics, and solid armoires. A few hundred yards away are 15 less formal rooms, and in a third, small, vine-covered building are three more simple but charming ones. ⊠ *Val d'Enfer, 13520,* ☎ 04–90–54–33–07, ⅢX 04–90–54–40–46. 25 rooms. Restaurant, pool, 2 tennis courts, horseback riding. AE, DC, MC, V. Closed mid-Jan.–early Mar.

$ ✕▤ **La Reine Jeanne.** Jacques Brel and Winston Churchill were loyal to this modest but majestically placed inn right at the entrance to the village, where they could stand on balconies and look over rugged views worthy of the châteaux up the street. Rooms are small, simple, and—despite the white, vinyl-padded furniture—fondly decorated with terracotta tiles and stencil prints. Reserve in advance for one of the two rooms with a balcony, though even one of the tiny interior rooms gives you the right to spend a quiet evening in lovely Les Baux after the tourists have drained away. Good home-style cooking is served in the restaurant, which has views both from inside and outside on the pretty terrace; it's the best setting for a meal in Les Baux. ⊠ *13520,* ☎ 04–90–54–32–06, ⅢX 04–90–54–32–33. 10 rooms. Restaurant. MC, V.

$$$ 🏨 **La Benvengudo.** With manicured grounds shaded by tall pines, this graceful shuttered mas feels centuries old but was built to look that way 30 years ago. Its heavy old beams, stone fireplace, and terra-cotta tiles enhance the homey, old-fashioned decor (though bathrooms date from the '70s). The resident dogs greet you just before the friendly owners do. Dine by the olive-shaded pool or have a drink on the stone-tabled terrace. ⊠ *Below Les Baux, direction Fontvieille. Vallon de l'Arcoule, 13520,* ☎ *04–90–54–32–54,* 𝖥𝖠𝖷 *04–90–54–42–58. 25 rooms. Restaurant, air-conditioning, pool, tennis. AE, MC, V. Closed Nov.–Feb.*

$$$ 🏨 **Mas de L'Oulivié.** Another mas built to look ancient, with recycled roof tiles and hand-waxed chalk walls, the Oulivié is clarity itself, with a cool, clean look and a low-keyed ambience. There's no upscale restaurant—just easy and unpretentious lunches by the pool (grilled meats, salads, and goat cheese seasoned with the house-label olive oil); you can dabble your feet with an aperitif in hand. Eight rooms on the upper floor of the main house are pretty enough, with floral print curtains and rich carpet, but ask for one with doors opening onto the lavender gardens and olive groves; there's even one with a private terrace and access to the pool. ⊠ *Below Les Baux, D27 direction Fontvieille, Les Arcoules,* ⊠ *13520,* ☎ *04–90–54–35–78,* 𝖥𝖠𝖷 *04–90–54–44–31. 23 rooms, 1 suite. Restaurant, air-conditioning, pool, tennis. AE, DC, MC, V. Closed Dec.–Feb.*

$ 🏨 **Mas de la Fontaine.** No imitations here: This lovely old mas, under gorgeous cliffs and ancient pines, dates from the 15th century. As a hotel it's modest enough; *familiale* instead of deluxe, it has all the basics, plus exposed beams, a vaulted breakfast room, and a pool. Rooms are spare but have fresh carpet and wallpaper. ⊠ *Below Les Baux, on D78 direction Fontvieille, Val d'Enfer 13520,* ☎ *04–90–54–34–13. 7 rooms, 6 with bath. Breakfast room, pool. No credit cards. Closed Nov.–Easter.*

Outdoor Activities and Sports

Les Baux has a serious 18-hole golf course at **Domaine des Manville** (☎ 04–90–54–37–02), on D27 south of Les Baux.

Shopping

An extravagant choice of souvenirs ranging from kitsch (Provençal-print toilet-paper holders) to class (silk challis shawls from Les Olivades) virtually reach out and grab you as you climb the hill lined with tempting (and not-so) shops. But come with cash: Only the post office is equipped to change money, and there's no bank.

St-Rémy-de-Provence

❸❽ *10 km (6 mi) northeast of Les Baux, 25 km (15½ mi) northeast of Arles, 24 km (15 mi) south of Avignon.*

There are other towns as pretty as St-Rémy-de-Provence, and others in more dramatic or picturesque settings. Ruins can be found throughout the south, and so can authentic village life. Yet something felicitous has happened in this market town in the heart of the Alpilles—a steady infusion of style, of art, of imagination—all brought by people with a respect for local traditions and a love of Provençal ways. Here more than anywhere you can meditate quietly on antiquity, browse redolent markets with basket in hand, peer down the very row of plane trees you remember from a van Gogh, and also enjoy urbane galleries, cosmopolitan shops, and specialty food boutiques. An abundance of chic choices in restaurants, mas, and even châteaux awaits you; the almond and olive groves conceal dozens of stone-and-terra-cotta gîtes, many with pools. In short, St-Rémy has been gentrified through and through, and is now sort of an arid, southern Martha's Vineyard or, perhaps, the Hamptons of Provence.

St-Rémy has always attracted the right sort of people. First established by an indigenous Celtic-Ligurian people who worshiped the god Glan, the village Glanum was adopted and gentrified by the Greeks of Marseille in the 2nd and 3rd centuries before Christ. They brought in sophisticated building techniques—superbly cut stone, fitted without mortar, and classical colonnades. Rome moved in to help ward off Hannibal, and by the 1st century BC Caesar had taken full control. The Via Domitia, linking Italy to Spain, passed by its doors, and the main trans-Alpine pass emptied into its entrance gate. Under the Pax Romana there developed a veritable city, complete with temples and forum, luxurious villas and baths.

The Romans eventually fell, but a town grew up next to their ruins, taking its name from their protectorate abbey St-Remi in Reims. It grew to be an important market town, and wealthy families built fine hôtels (mansions) in its center—among them the family De Sade (whose black-sheep son held forth in the Lubéron at Gordes). Another famous native son: the eccentric doctor, scholar and astrologist Michel Nostradamus (1503–1566), who is credited by some as having predicted much of the modern age. Catherine de Medici, like Princess Diana and Nancy Reagan, consulted him on every life decision.

Perhaps the best known of St-Rémy's visitors was the ill-fated Vincent van Gogh. Shipped unceremoniously out of Arles at the height of his madness (and creativity), he was committed to the asylum St-Paul-de-Mausolé and wandered through the ruins of Glanum during the last year of his life. It is his eerily peaceful retreat as well as the ruins that draw visitors by the busload to the outskirts of modern St-Rémy, but the bulk of them snap their pictures and move on to Les Baux for the day, leaving St-Rémy to its serene, sophisticated ways.

To approach Glanum, you must park in a dusty roadside lot on D5 south of town (in the direction of Les Baux). But before crossing, you'll be confronted with two of the most miraculously preserved

★ classical monuments in France, simply called **Les Antiques.** Though dating from around 30 BC, they could be taken for Romanesque, so perfectly intact are their carvings and architectural details. The **Mausolée** (Mausoleum), a wedding-cake stack of arches and columns, lacks nothing but its finial on top, yet it is dedicated to a Julian (as in Julius Caesar), probably Caesar Augustus. Allegorical scenes in bas-relief represent myths of Greek origin but most likely refer to Julius Caesar's military triumphs. Two sculptured figures, framed in its column-ringed crown, must surely be the honorees; the dedication reads SEX. L.M. IVLIEI C.F. PARENTIBUS SUEIS, or "Sextius, Lucius, Carcus son of Caius, of the family of Julii, to their parents." A few yards away stands another marvel: the **Arc Triomphal,** dating from the same era. All who crossed the Alps entered Roman Glanum through this gate, decorated with reliefs of battle scenes depicting Caesar's defeat and the capture of the Gauls.

Across the street from Les Antiques, a slick visitor center, set back from

★ D5, prepares you for entry into **Glanum** with scale models of the site in its various heydays. A good map and an English brochure guide you stone by stone through the maze of foundations, walls, towers, and columns that spread across a broad field; Greek sites are helpfully noted by numbers, Roman by letters. At the base of rugged white cliffs and shaded with black-green pines, it is an extraordinarily evocative site and inspires contemplation in even the rowdiest busload of schoolchildren. ⊠ *Off D5, direction Les Baux, info phone at Hôtel de Sade (☞ below),* ☎ *04–90–92–64–04.* 🎫 *32 frs. (36 frs. includes entry to Hôtel de Sade).* ⊙ *Apr.–Sept., daily 9–7; Oct.–Mar., daily 9–noon and 2–5.*

You can cut across the fields from Glanum to **St-Paul-de-Mausolée,** the lovely, isolated asylum where van Gogh spent the last year of his life (1889–90), but enter it quietly: It shelters psychiatric patients to this day—all of them women. You're free to walk up the beautifully manicured garden path to the church and its jewel-box Romanesque cloister where the artist found womblike peace. A small boutique features works of current patients—*art brut* reminiscent of Munch and Basquiat—for sale. You can climb a stairway to a memorial bust of van Gogh and a picture window that frames a garden view he loved and painted. ⊠ *Next to Glanum, off D5 direction Les Baux,* ☎ *04–90–92–77–00.* 🎫 *10 frs.* ⊙ *May–Sept., daily 8–7; Oct.–Apr., daily 8–5.*

St-Rémy itself is wrapped by a lively, commercial boulevard, lined with shops and cafés and anchored by its 19th-century church **Collégiale St-Martin.** Step inside to see the magnificent organ, one of the loveliest in Europe. Rebuilt to 18th-century specifications in the early '80s, it has the flexibility to interpret new and old music with pure French panache; you can listen to it Saturday afternoon at 5:30 from July through September. ⊠ *pl. de la République.*

Within St-Rémy's fast-moving traffic loop, a labyrinth of narrow streets leads you away from the action and into the slow-moving inner sanctum of the **Vieille Ville** (old town). Here high-end, trendy shops mingle pleasantly with local life, and the buildings, if gentrified, blend unobtrusively.

Make your way to the **Hôtel de Sade,** a 15th- and 16th-century private manor now housing the phenomenal abundance of sculptural treasure unearthed with the ruins of Glanum. The De Sade family built the house around remains of 4th-century baths and a 5th-century baptistery, now nestled in its courtyard. ⊠ *rue du Parage,* ☎ *04–90–92–64–04.* 🎫 *15 frs (36 frs. includes Glanum entry).* ⊙ *Feb.–Mar. and Oct., Tues.–Sun. 10–noon and 2–5; Apr.–Sept., Tues.–Sun. 10–noon and 2–6; Nov.–Dec., Wed., Sat., and Sun. 10–noon and 2–5.*

Dining and Lodging

\$\$–\$\$\$ ✕ **Maison Jaune.** This modern retreat in the old town draws crowds of summer people to its pretty roof terrace, with a decor of sober stone and lively contemporary furniture both indoors and out. The look reflects the cuisine: With vivid flavors and a cool, contained touch, chef François Perraud prepares grilled sardines with crunchy fennel and lemon confit, ham-cured duck on lentils with vinaigrette, and veal lightly flavored with olives, capers, and celery. Prices are high but one bargain lunch menu offers a minimalist smorgasbord of tastes, and wine is included. ⊠ *15 rue Carnot,* ☎ *04–90–92–56–14. Reservations essential. MC, V. Closed Mon. No dinner Sun.*

\$–\$\$
★ ✕ **L'Assiette de Marie.** Though life is lived outdoors in St-Rémy, there are rainy days and winter winds, and this is the place to retreat: Marie Ricco is a collector, and she's turned her tiny restaurant into an art-directed bower of attic treasures: unscrubbed, unrestored, as is. Fringed lampshades are artfully askew, ancient wallpaper curls from a door, the coatrack sags with woolen uniforms, and classic jazz and candlelight complete the scene. Seated at an old school desk, you choose from the day's specials, all made with Marie's Corsican-Italian touch—marinated vegetables with tapenade, a cast-iron casserole of superb pasta

(made in Marie's neighboring shop, ☞ Shopping, *below*), satiny *pane-tone* (flan). The house red is Corsican, but there's a wide choice of St-Rémy wines as well. ⊠ *1 rue Jaume Roux,* ☎ *04–90–92–32–14. Reservations essential in high season. MC, V. Closed Tues. Nov.–Easter. No lunch Mon., Tues., and sometimes Thurs. in summer (except July–Aug.).*

$ ✕ **La Gousse d'Ail.** Another intimate, indoor old-town hideaway, this family-run bistro lives up to its name (The Garlic Clove), serving robust, highly-flavored southern dishes in hearty portions: eggplant and zucchini timbale in a shower of cumin, rich homemade pasta in powerful pesto with almonds, and homemade nougat ice cream pungent with honey. A ceramic pitcher of ice water and a thick flask of house wine offer counterbalance, and the bill is delivered with much-needed mints. The cozy decor (dark timbers, niches full of puppets) matches the warm welcome. Aim for Thursday night when there are Gypsy music and jazz. ⊠ *25 rue Carnot,* ☎ *04–90–92–16–87. AE, MC, V. Closed Jan.–Feb. except occasional weekends.*

$$$$ ✕🏨 **Domaine de Valmouraine.** This genteel mas-cum-resort, beauti-
★ fully isolated on a broad park, offers guests a panoply of entertainment, from billiards to a Jacuzzi. Inside, soft, overstuffed English-country decor mixes cozily with cool Provençal stone and timber, and massive stone fireplaces warm public spaces. The restaurant features chef Pierre Walter, who vies to please with fresh game, seafood, local oils, and truffles; his desserts have won him national standing. But it's the personal welcome from English owner Judith McHugo that makes clients feel like weekend guests in a manor house. ⊠ *Petite rte. des Baux (D27), 13210,* ☎ *04–90–92–44–62,* FAX *04–90–92–37–32. 14 rooms. Restaurant, outdoor pool, hot tub, steam room, tennis court, billiards. AE, DC, MC, V.*

$$$$ ✕🏨 **Vallon de Valrugues.** This luxurious villa, replete with uniformed footmen and canopy beds, makes no bones about its pretensions to aristocracy, but you might like it for its beguiling views into the Alpilles and the olive groves. Chefs come and go, all with stellar resumés, but Philippe Boucher shows signs of taking root: Watch for his tender lamb sizzled with bacon. The restaurant atmosphere is formal, pampered, and a trifle stuffy; the bill a blow. ⊠ *chemin Canto-Cigalo, 13210,* ☎ *04–90–92–04–40,* FAX *04–90–92–44–01. 35 rooms, 15 suites. Restaurant, pool, hot tub, sauna. AE, MC, V. Closed Feb.*

$ ✕🏨 **Auberge de la Reine Jeanne.** With all the luxurious mas and châteaux to choose from, you don't have to be scared away if you're on a budget. This charming Logis-de-France property in a 17th-century stone building that surrounds a green courtyard, offers more conventional lodgings, right in the heart of town. Its strong point is its restaurant, where modestly priced, mainstream French cooking is served in the courtyard in summer and in a firelighted, dark-timber hall in winter. Room decor isn't up to St-Rémy style (it has blue carpeting and polyester quilts), but the best ones overlook the court and are clean and comfortable. ⊠ *12 bd. Mirabeau, 13210,* ☎ *04–90–92–15–33,* FAX *04–90–92–49–65. 11 rooms. Restaurant. AE, DC, MC, V.*

$$$$ 🏨 **Château des Alpilles.** At the end of an alley of grand old plane trees, this early 19th-century manor house lords over a vast park off D31. If public spaces and atmosphere are cool and spare to the point of sparseness, rooms are warm and fussy, with lush Provençal prints and polished antiques. Outer buildings offer jazzy-modern apartments with kitchenettes, and the poolside grill gives you a noble perspective over the park. ⊠ *Ancienne rte. du Grès, 13210,* ☎ *04–90–92–03–33,* FAX *04–90–92–45–17. 15 rooms, 4 suites. Pool, sauna, 2 tennis courts. AE, DC, MC, V. Closed mid-Nov.–mid-Dec. and Jan.–mid-Feb.*

$$$ ⌂ **Mas de Cornud.** An American mans the wine cellar and an Egyptian runs the professional kitchen (by request only), but the attitude is pure Provence: David and Nito Carpitras have turned their farmhouse, just outside St-Rémy, into a bed-and-breakfast. The house and the rooms are filled with French country furniture and objects from around the world, and guests and hosts unwind with a nightly pastis and a pétanque match. Without drop-in clients barging in (rooms must be reserved), guests feel like . . .well, guests. Table d'hôte dinners, cooking classes, and tours can be arranged. Breakfast is included. ⊠ *rte. de Mas-Blanc, 13210,* ☎ *04–90–92–39–32,* FAX *04–90–92–55–99. 5 rooms, 1 suite. Dining room, pool. No credit cards. Closed Jan.–Feb.*

$$ ⌂ **Château de Roussan.** In a majestic park shaded by ancient plane trees (themselves protected landmarks), its ponds and canals graced by swans and birdsong, this extraordinary 18th-century château is being valiantly preserved by managers who (without a rich owner to back them) are lovingly restoring it, squatter style. Glorious period furnishings and details are buttressed by brocante and bric-a-brac, and the bathrooms, toggled into various corners, are in dire need of updating (except for four all-new installations upstairs). Cats abound. Yet if you're the right sort for this place—backpackers, romantic couples on a budget, lovers of atmosphere over luxury—you'll blossom in this three-dimensional costume drama. ⊠ *rte. de Tarascon, 13210,* ☎ *04–90–92–11–63,* FAX *04–90–92–50–59. 22 rooms. Restaurant. MC, V.*

Festivals

St-Rémy is fond of festivals, borrowing traditions of bull-races and ferias from its lowland neighbors and creating a few of its own. On Pentecost Monday (the end of May), the **Fête de la Transhumance** celebrates the passage of the sheep from Provence into the Alps, and costumed shepherds lead some 4,000 sheep, goats and donkeys through the streets. The **Grande Feria,** in mid-August, brings the Camargue to the hills, with bull games, fireworks, and flamenco guitar. Three weekends a year (Ascension in May, late June, and mid-September) are devoted to the **Fête de la Route des Peintres de la Lumière en Provence** (Festival of the Route of Painters of Light in Provence), an enormous contemporary art fair.

Nightlife and the Arts

La Forge des Trinitaires (⊠ ave. de la Libération, ☎ 04–90–92–31–52) draws the young and restless for African and Antillaise music every Friday and Saturday night from 11 PM to 4:30 AM. **Jazz concerts** (⊠ across from St-Paul de Mausole, ☎ 04–90–92–00–81) take place once a month in summer at the Mas de la Pyramide, a natural stone grotto.

At 5:30 every Saturday in July, August, and September, you can hear the magnificent **organ of St-Martin Collégiale** (☞ *above*) in a free recital, often featuring the boy-wonder *organiste-titulaire* Jean-Pierre Lecaudey.

Shopping

Every Wednesday morning St-Rémy hosts one of the most popular and picturesque **markets** in Provence, during which the place de la République and narrow old-town streets overflow with fresh produce, herbs and spices, olive oil by the vat, and tapenade by the scoop, as well as fabrics and *brocante* (collectibles).

Interior design is a niche market in this region of summer homes, so **decor shops** abound, not only featuring Provençal pottery and fabrics but also a cosmopolitan blend of Asian fabrics, English garden furniture, and Italian high-design items. Individual artisans fill gallery-style boutiques with their photography, picture frames, and wrought-iron furniture. The common denominator is high here, so good taste has stonewalled tourist kitsch. The design shops, fabric shops and art-gallery-cum-gift-shops are scattered throughout the Vieille Ville and along the boulevards that surround it.

With all the summer people, food shops and *traiteurs* (take-out caterers) do big business in St-Rémy. Local goat cheeses are displayed like jewels and wrapped like fine pastries at **Fromagerie du Mistral** (⊠ 1 pl. Joseph-Hilaire). There are pasta makers, such as **L'Épicerie de Marie** (⊠ 1 pl. Isidore Gilles) and hand-rolled sweets at **Chocolaterie Joel Durand** (⊠ pl. Jean de Renaud). Olive oils are sold like fine old wines and the breads heaped in boulangerie windows are as knobby and rough-hewn as they should be. The best food shops are concentrated in the Vieille Ville.

THE ALPILLES, ARLES, AND THE CAMARGUE A TO Z

Arriving and Departing

By Car
The A6/A7 toll expressway (*péage*) channels all traffic from Paris towards the south. It's called the Autoroute du Soleil (Highway of the Sun) and leads directly to Provence. From Orange, A9 (La Languedocienne) heads southwest to Nîmes and Montpellier. Arles is a quick jaunt from Nîmes via A54.

By Plane
Marseille (an hour's drive from Arles) and Montpellier are served by frequent flights from Paris and London, and daily flights from Paris arrive at the smaller airport in Nîmes. In summer, Delta Airlines flies direct from New York to Nice, 200 km (134 mi) from Arles.

By Train
There's regular rail service from all points north to Avignon and then to nearby towns, and the TGV (Trains à Grande Vitesse) connects Paris to Avignon in 3 and a half hours, stopping at Orange as well. From these cities you must transfer to local trains to get to Montpellier, Nîmes, Tarascon or Arles, the only other cities served by rail lines. Overnight trains run daily to Avignon from Paris, Strasbourg, and other cloud-bound cities, allowing soggy travelers to stretch out on a couchette and wake up to indigo skies (☞ Train Travel *in* the Gold Guide).

Getting Around

By Bus
A moderately good network of private bus services links places not served, or badly served, by trains. Ask for bus schedules at train stations and tourist offices, and head for the *gare routière* (bus station).

By Car
With its swift autoroute network, it's a breeze traveling from city to city by car in this region. But some of the best of Provence is experienced on back roads and byways, including the isolated Camargue and the Alpilles. Navigating the flatlands of the Camargue can feel unearthly, with roads sailing over terrain uninterrupted by hills or forests; despite this, roads don't always run as the crow flies and can wander wide of a clean trajectory, so don't expect to make time. Rocky outcrops and switchbacks keep you a captive audience to the arid scenery in the Alpilles; to hurry—impossible as it is—would be a waste.

By Train

Although good rail service connects Avignon to Montpellier, Nîmes, Tarascon, L'Isle-sur-la-Sorgue, and Arles, trains don't penetrate the Alpilles; connections to St-Rémy and Les Baux must be made by bus.

Contacts and Resources

Bed and Breakfasts

Chambres d'hôtes (bed & breakfasts) offer simple lodging, usually in the hosts' home, with breakfast and a warm, regional welcome often included. There are lots to be found in this region, especially in the Alpilles around St-Rémy. The French national network **Gîtes de France** (☞ Lodging *in* the Gold Guide) lists bed & breakfasts that have been rated. For chambres d'hotes regulated by the national network, contact the local branches, divided by *départements* (administrative regions). Addresses are listed under Vacation Rentals, *below.*

Car Rentals

ARLES

Avis (⊠ at the train station, ☎ 04–90–96–82–42), **Europcar** (⊠ 2 bis av. Victor Hugo, ☎ 04–90–93–23–24), and **Hertz** (⊠ 4 av. Victor-Hugo, ☎ 04–90–96–75–23).

ISLE-SUR-LA-SORGUE

Avis (⊠ 58 zone industrielle Grande Marine, ☎ 04–90–38–03–60) or **Budget** (⊠ rue André Autheman, ☎ 04–90–20–64–13).

MONTPELLIER

Budget (⊠ at the train station, ☎ 04–67–92–69–00), **Europcar** (⊠ 6 rue Jules Ferry, ☎ 04–67–06–89–00), or **Hertz** (⊠ 18 rue Jules Ferry, ☎ 04–67–58–65–18).

NÎMES

Avis (⊠ 1800 av. Mar. Juin, ☎ 04–66–29–05–33), **Budget** (⊠ 225 rte. Rouquairol, ☎ 04–66–38–01–69), **Europcar** (⊠ 1 bis rue de la République, ☎ 04–66–21–31–35), or **Hertz** (⊠ 5 bd. Prague, ☎ 04–66–21–25–90).

Guided Tours

The tourist office in **Arles** (☎ 04–90–18–41–21) offers individual tours of the town, including visits to the Roman monuments, during the summer season. Dates and times vary depending on demand; check with them regarding English-speaking guides.

In addition to publishing map itineraries that you can follow yourself, **Montpellier**'s tourist office (☎ 04–67–60–60–60) provides guided walking tours of the city's neighborhoods and monuments daily in summer, and on Wednesdays and Saturdays during the school year (roughly, Sept.–June). They leave from the pl. de la Comédie. There also are **horse-drawn carriages** running tours between the place and the Esplanade Charles de Gaulle; you can go for fifteen minutes or up to an hour and a half (information ☎ 04–67–92–47–60). A small **tourist train** with broadcast commentary leaves from the Esplanade from 2 to 9, Monday through Saturday (information ☎ 04–67–60–60–60).

To learn more about **Nîmes**' monuments and old town and to arrange a guided tour in English, contact the Service des Guides at the tourist office (☎ 04–66–67–29–11). For about 150 francs, you can tour the town in a taxi for an hour; when you stop in front of a monument, the driver slips in a cassette with commentary in the language of your choice. For 250 francs, you can take a round-trip taxi ride to the Pont du Gard (he'll wait while you explore for 30 minutes). Contact **Taxis T.R.A.N.** (☎ 04–66–29–40–11).

Outdoor Activities and Sports

To penetrate the isolation of the Camargue beyond the limited access available to cars, rent a VTT (mountain bike) at Stes-Maries-de-la-Mer and follow one of the itineraries in the booklet "Camargue Naturellement." Rentals are available through **Le Vélo Santois** (⊠ 19 av. de la République, ☎ 04–90–97–74–56) or at two outlets of **Le Vélociste** (⊠ pl. des Remparts, ☎ 04–90–97–83–26; ⊠ 7 av. de la République, ☎ 04–90–97–86–44).

The most popular transport, of course, is the Camargue horse, and there are some 30 places to rent them for a *promenade equestre* (horseback tour). The **Association Camarguaise de Tourisme Equestre** publishes a list of names and numbers, available at the Stes-Maries tourist office (⊠ 5 av. van Gogh) or by writing to the association (⊠ Centre de Gènes, Pont de Gau, 13460 Stes-Maries-de-la-Mer). An hour's ride averages 70 or 80 francs, a whole day 350 francs.

Travel Agencies

ARLES

Havas Voyages (⊠ 4 bd. des Lices, 13200 Arles, ☎ 04–90–96–13–25); **Provence-Camargue Tours** (⊠ 1 rue Émile Fassin, 13200 Arles, ☎ 04–90–49–85–58).

MONTPELLIER

Havas Voyages (⊠ 2 pl. de la Comédie, 34000 Montpellier, ☎ 04–67–91–31–70).

NÎMES

Cap Horizons (⊠ 3 bd. Amiral Courbet, 3000 Nîmes, ☎ 04–66–36–19–90). **Havas Voyages** (⊠ 44 bd. Victor Hugo, 3000 Nîmes, ☎ 04–66–36–99–99).

Vacation Rentals

Gîtes de France (☞ Vacation Rentals *in* the Gold Guide) is the national network of vacation rentals, many of them in restored buildings with real regional character. The region west of Nîmes lies in the département of Hérault. Gîtes de France offices for this department are based in Montpellier (⊠ B.P. 3070, 34034 Montpellier Cedex 1, ☎ 04–67–67–71–66, FAX 04–67–67–71–69). Nîmes itself and environs are processed by the Gard office (⊠ 3 pl. des Arènes, B.P. 59, 30007 Nîmes Cedex 4, ☎ 04–66–27–94–94, FAX 04–66–27–94–95). Arles and the Alpilles gîtes are handled by the Bouches-du-Rhône departmental office (⊠ Domaine du Vergon, B.P. 26, 13370 Mallemort, ☎ 04–90–59–49–40, FAX 04–90–59–16–75).

Each of the tourist offices for towns in the region usually publishes lists of independent rentals (*locations meublés*), many of them inspected and classified by the tourist office itself.

Visitor Information

Regional tourist offices prefer written queries only. The **Comité Régional du Tourisme du Languedoc-Roussillon** (⊠ 20 rue République, Montpellier 34000, ☎ 04–67–22–81–00, FAX 04–67–22–80–27) provides information on all towns west of the Rhône. The remainder of towns covered in this chapter are handled by the **Comité Regional du Tourisme de Provence-Alpes-Côte d'Azur** (⊠ Espace Colbert, 14 rue Ste-Barbe, 13001 Marseille, ☎ 04–91–39–38–00, FAX 04–91–56–66–61).

Local tourist offices for major towns covered in this chapter can be phoned, faxed or addressed by mail. **Arles** (⊠ 35 pl. de la République, 13200 Arles, ☎ 04–90–18–41–21, FAX 04–90–93–17–17). **Les Baux** (⊠ 30 Grand-rue, 13520 Les Baux, ☎ 04–90–54–34–39, FAX 04–

90–54–51–15). **Montpellier** (✉ 30 allée Jean de Lattre de Tassigny, Esplanade Comédie, 34000 Montpellier, ☎ 04–67–60–60–60, FAX 04–67–60–60–61). **Nîmes** (✉ 6 rue Auguste, 3000 Nîmes, ☎ 04–66–67–29–11, FAX 04–66–21–81–04). **St-Rémy** (✉ pl. Jean-Jaurès, 13210 St-Rémy, ☎ 04–90–92–05–22, FAX 04–90–92–38–52). **Tarascon** (✉ 59 rue Halles, 13150 Tarascon, ☎ 04–90–91–03–52, FAX 04–90–91–22–96).

3 The Vaucluse

Avignon, the Luberon, and Mont Ventoux

Anchored by the magnificent papal stronghold of Avignon, the Vaucluse spreads luxuriantly east of the Rhône. Its famous vineyards, such as Châteauneuf-du-Pape and Beaumes-de-Venise, seduce connoisseurs, and its Roman ruins in Orange and Vaison-la-Romaine draw scholars and arts lovers. Arid lowlands dotted with orchards of olives, apricots, and almonds give way to a rich and wild mountain terrain around the formidable Mont Ventoux and flow into the primeval Luberon, made a household name by Peter Mayle.

FOR MANY, this is the only true Provence, with its sun-bleached hills and fields that are tapestries of green-and-black grapevines and silver-gray olives, and its rolling rows of lavender that harmonize with the mountains looming purple against the indigo sky. It is here, in his beloved Luberon, that British author Peter Mayle discovered and described the simple pleasures of breakfasting on melons still warm from the sun, buying fresh-dug truffles from furtive farmers in smoke-filled bars, and life without socks. The world shared his epiphany, and vacationers now flock here in search of the same sensual way of life, some retreating to lavishly renovated farmhouses with cypress-shaded pools, others making pilgrimages to the luxurious inns that cater to refugees from city smog.

Thus the golden *villages perchés* (perched villages) that lord over the patchwork valleys—Gordes, Bonnieux, Ménerbes—have become bijou boutique towns, and the markets (for food at Avignon, antiques at l'Isle-sur-la-Sorgue) have become must-do events. A ticket to the summer opera festival in the Roman theater in Orange is as réccherché as a case of 1982 Châteauneuf-du-Pâpe. But there are still quiet trails that leave the gentrification behind, winding up labyrinthine back alleys to pollard-shaded squares resonant with the splashing of ancient fountains, climbing into misty blue-black forests unaltered in spirit since the time of the Gauls.

And all this lies a stone's throw from thriving Avignon, its feudal fortifications sheltering a lively arts scene and a culture determinedly young.

Pleasures and Pastimes

Dining

The Vaucluse is the home of the famous Cavaillon melon, that globe of juicy pulchritude that hefts in the hand of marketing matrons, turned and sniffed and squeezed with the expertise of an Antwerp jeweler. The right melon, once found and sliced, yields like butter, pours a rich, perfumed nectar onto the cutting board, and melts on the tongue. Half the size of a cantaloupe and twice as flavorful, these melons are labeled, tissue-wrapped, and stacked in market pyramids of acrobatic proportion. Whether draped with a veil of musky *jambon cru* (cured ham) or cupping a pool of ruby port, eating them is a summer ritual throughout Europe, but especially on the melon's native turf.

When the undulating rows of green that spread through the Sorgue Valley's fertile fields aren't yielding melons, they're nurturing prize asparagus, fat stalks of purple-tipped white bound in bands of red, white, and blue. Pampered under mounds of cool earth from the rays of light that would cause photosynthesis and ruinous traces of green, these albino beauties retain a pure, sweet flavor and enough juice to run down your chin. Unlike the shriveled exports that wither in city supermarkets around the world, the local product is smooth and plump, and once its barky skin is stripped off (time-consuming but indispensable), it's as tender as, well, melon. In season (early March–May) restaurants go asparagus-crazy, some offering multicourse menus based entirely on this regional treasure.

Olives, of course, figure large in the Vaucluse culinary scene, from the ubiquitous *tapenade* (olive and caper spread) on toast to the requisite bowl of the pungent black pearls served with your aperitif. But the real attention getter here is the truffle, snuffled up beneath Luberon oaks by trained pigs and dogs driven wild by their smell. The Vaucluse produces 74% of all truffles sold commercially in France; even more are sold like smuggled drugs in backroom deals. Vaucluse chefs showcase the truffle in humble ways, the better to highlight its redolent charms: The classic vehicle is a simple *omelette aux truffes*.

CATEGORY	COST*
$$$$	Over 400 frs
$$$	250 frs–400 frs
$$	125 frs–250 frs
$	Under 125 frs

per person for a three-course meal, including tax (20.6%) and tip but not wine

Lodging

One of the most popular vacation regions in France outside the seaside, the Vaucluse has a plethora of sleek and fashionable converted *mas* (farmhouses), landscaped in lavender, cypress, and oil-jars full of vivid flowers. Given the crushing heat in high summer, the majority have swimming pools and, these days, air-conditioning (but it's wise to check ahead if you're counting on it). Reservations are essential most of the year, and many hotels close down altogether in winter.

Because of the pleasures of simple Provençal cooking and the joys of going to the market, as well as the privacy and independence that come with having a house of your own, booking a *gîte* (vacation rental) for your stay (by the week only) makes a lot of sense. Many in the luxury category are adding swimming pools to their comforts. All bookings for Gîtes-de-France rentals are handled through the Vaucluse branch (☞ The Vaucluse A to Z, *below*).

CATEGORY	COST*
$$$$	Over 800 frs
$$$	550 frs–800 frs
$$	300 frs–550 frs
$	Under 300 frs

All prices are for a standard double room for two, including tax (20.6%) and service charge.

Markets

Browsing through the *marché couvert* (covered food market) in Avignon is enough to make you regret all the tempting restaurants around; its seafood, free-range poultry, olives, and produce cry out to be gathered in a basket, arranged lovingly in pottery bowls, and cooked in their purest form. And the village markets, which are carefully organized to cover in turn all the days of the week, are a visual feast as well.

But at one of the most famous markets in Provence, food plays second fiddle: l'Isle-sur-la-Sorgue draws crowds of bargain hunters and collectors to its Sunday antiques and *brocante* (collectibles) fair, strung in picturesque disarray along its water mills and canals. Some of the best pickings in linen sheets, silverware, engravings, pewter, oak furniture, and quirky collectibles can be had if you arrive early, though the after-lunch stroll-and-browse is a fashionable tradition.

Perched Villages

Although there are pretty hilltop villages throughout the south of France, the Luberon has a surprising concentration of them, each with a personality of its own, some less gentrified (and more atmospheric) than others. Gordes, Menérbes, Roussillon, and Bonnieux have become boomtowns in real estate and tourism but still retain their original honey-gold stone and the majesty of their extraordinary positions overlooking the countryside. Others that are less well-known—Seguret, Le Barroux—offer less to buy and eat, but allow you to experience the quiet isolation of these ancient retreats; around Mont-Ventoux, it's worth it to turn off toward whatever cluster of hilltop houses catches your eye.

Vestiges of the Past

The best Roman ruins in this region are in Vaison-la-Romaine, where a theater, grand villas, and an entire village complete with boutiques and toilets remain in skeletal form. In Orange the magnificent theater has retained its great stone stage wall and still serves as an inspiring venue for the summer opera festival.

Avignon's old town still stands within the 14th-century wall that protected its rebellious popes from angry skeptics; their luxurious palace crowns the city center. And the magnificently preserved Romanesque Abbaye de Senanque, outside Roussillon, floats in a sea of lavender.

But the most unusual and fascinating antiquities in the Vaucluse are the tiny stone beehive-huts called *bories,* of mysterious origin but in use, it is thought, since the Iron Age. Some 3,000 are scattered over the hillsides of the Luberon and environs, and an entire village has been preserved outside Gordes.

Wine

The most serious wine center in the south of France is the southern portion of the Côtes du Rhone, home to the muscular reds of Gigondas and of its more famous neighbor Châteauneuf-du-Pape, as well as the fruity Grenache-based rosé of Tavel. Nearby Beaumes-de-Venise is famous for its sweet, light muscat. But not to be overlooked are the wines of the Côtes du Luberon, with drinkable and inexpensive reds and rosés and a notable white from Lourmarin.

Exploring the Vaucluse

Avignon as well as the Roman centers and papal vineyards to its north lie in arid lowlands, and getting from point to point can be uninspiring. It's to the east that the real Vaucluse rises up into the green-studded slopes of Mont Ventoux and the Luberon. Here, the back roads are beautiful—the temptation to abandon your rental car and go on foot is often irresistible. Give in; the smells of wild thyme, lavender, wet stone, and dry pine are as heady as a Châteauneuf-du-Pape.

Great Itineraries

Avignon is a must, and if you're a wine lover, you'll enjoy exploring the vineyards above it. If you're a fan of things Roman, you need to see Vaison-la-Romaine and Orange. The antiques market in L'Isle-sur-la-Sorgue is a Sunday must, and (outside drought season) the dramatic spring cascade in Fontaine-de-Vaucluse is a major stop nearby. But the Luberon and its villages perched high up in the hills are a world of their own and worth allowing time for—perhaps even your whole vacation. Note that the Pont de Gard, the superbly preserved Gallo-Roman aqueduct, is just 30 minutes west of Avignon, and that Arles, Nîmes, and the windswept Camargue are only a stone's throw to the south and west (☞ Chapter 2).

Numbers in the text correspond to numbers in the margin and on the Vaucluse and Avignon maps.

IF YOU HAVE 3 DAYS
Base yourself in the old town of ▣ **Avignon** ①–⑫. Make excursions to **L'Isle-sur-la-Sorgue** ㉒ and **Fontaine de Vaucluse** ㉓ on the first day, and to **Gordes** ㉔ or **Bonnieux** ㉙ in the Luberon, the next day. On the

The Vaucluse

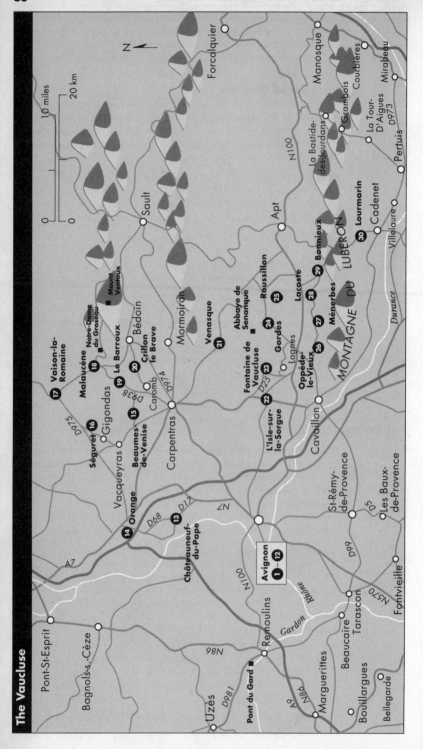

N

10 miles
20 km

Forcalquier

Manosque
Courbières
Grambois
Mirabeau
La Tour-
D'Aigues
Pertuis

Sault

N100

Apt

Cadenet
Lourmarin
Villelaure

30

Bonnieux
la Bastide-
desJourdans

29

Roussillon
25
Lacoste
28
Ménerbes
27
Gordes
24
26
Oppède-
le-Vieux

MONTAGNE DU LUBERON

Durance

Mount
Ventoux

Notre-Dame
du Groseau
Bédoin
Le Barroux
Malaucène
Crillon
le Brave
Caromb

Mormoiron

Venasque
21

Abbaye de
Sénanque

Fontaine de
Vaucluse
23
Lagnes
22

Vaison-la-
Romaine
17

Gigondas
18
19
20
16
Séguret
Beaumes-
de-Venise
15

D975

Carpentras

L'Isle-sur-
la-Sorgue

Cavaillon

Vacqueyras

Orange
14
13
D68
D17
Châteauneuf-
du-Pape

N7

St-Rémy-
de-Provence
D5
Les Baux-
de-Provence

Avignon
1 - 12

N100

Rhône

Tarascon
Fontvieille
N570

Pont-St-Esprit

Bagnols-s.-Cèze

A7

Remoulins
Gardon

98N

Uzès
D981

Pont du Gard
A9
N86

Marguerittes
Beaucaire

Bouillargues
Bellegarde

third day, head up to see the antiquities in **Orange** ⑭ and **Vaison-la-Romaine** ⑰.

IF YOU HAVE 7 DAYS

Spend three nights in 🏨 **Avignon** ①–⑫, exploring its museums and making a day trip into **Châteauneuf-du-Pape** ⑬ and Gigondas for door-to-door tastings (the designated driver must sniff, rinse, and spit, of course). On day four, head up to **Orange** ⑭ and **Vaison-la-Romaine** ⑰, then dawdle along the scenic roads at the base of Mont Ventoux, wandering up into any hill villages that look intriguing. Spend the night in 🏨 **L'Isle-sur-la-Sorgue** ㉒ or 🏨 **Fontaine de Vaucluse** ㉓. Then head into the Luberon, stopping to explore **Roussillon** ㉕ and the Abbaye de Senanque, spending night five in 🏨 **Gordes** ㉔. The next day meander through Peter Mayle country: **Oppède** ㉖, **Ménerbes** ㉗, **Lacoste** ㉘, and 🏨 **Bonnieux** ㉙, where you can spend night six overlooking the countryside. From here it's easy to cut over the crest and head on south to Aix-en-Provence and Marseille (☞ Chapter 4), or head west via Cavaillon to Les Alpilles or Nîmes (☞ Chapter 2).

IF YOU HAVE 10 DAYS

Take more time in each of the places in the seven-day itinerary, checking on concert tickets in 🏨 **Avignon** ①–⑫ or 🏨 **Orange** ⑭ and spending a night or two in the lovely medieval old town of 🏨 **Vaison-la-Romaine** ⑰.

When to Tour the Vaucluse

High heat and high season hit in July and August with an impact you won't forget: This lovely region is anything but undiscovered, thanks in part to Peter Mayle's revelations (he finally moved away from Provence to avoid the crowds he inspired). June and September are still intense but better. Low season falls between mid-November and mid-March, when many restaurants and hotels take two or three months off. That leaves spring and fall: If you arrive after Easter, the flowers are in full bloom, the air cool, and the sun warm, and you'll still be able to book a table on the terrace. The same goes for October and early November, when the hills of the Luberon turn rust and gold, and the first truffles surface.

AVIGNON

Of all the monuments in France—cathedrals, châteaux, fortresses—the ancient city of Avignon (pronounced ah-veen-YONH) is one of the most dramatic. Wrapped in a crenellated wall punctuated by Gothic slit windows, its old center stands distinct from modern extensions, crowned by the Palais des Papes (Popes' Palace), a 14th-century fortress-castle nothing short of spectacular. Standing on the place du Palais under the gaze of the gigantic Virgin that reigns from the cathedral tower, with the palace sprawling to one side, the bishops' Petit Palais to the other, and the long, low bridge of childhood song fame stretching over the river ("Sur le pont d'Avignon on y danse tous en rond . . ."), you can beam yourself briefly into the 14th century, so complete is the context, so evocative the setting.

Yet you'll soon be brought back with a jolt by the skateboarders leaping like dolphins over the smooth-paved square. Avignon is anything but a museum; it surges with modern ideas and energy and thrives within its ramparts as it did in the heyday of the popes—like those radical church lords, sensual, cultivated, cosmopolitan, with a taste for lay pleasures.

Avignon was transformed into the Vatican of the north when political infighting in the Eternal City drove Pope Clement V to accept Philippe the Good's invitation to start afresh. In 1309 his entourage arrived, preferring digs in nearby priories and châteaux; in 1316 he was replaced by Pope Jean XXII, who moved into the bishop's palace (today the Petit Palais). It was his successor Pope Benoit XII who undertook construction of the magnificent palace that was to house a series of popes through the 14th century.

During this holy reign Avignon evolved into a sophisticated, cosmopolitan capital, attracting artists and thinkers and stylish hangers-on. Founded in 1303, the university burgeoned, with thousands of students making the pilgrimage from across Europe. As the popes' wealth and power expanded, so did their formidable palace. And its sumptuous decor was legendary, inspiring horror and disdain from the poet Petrarch, who wrote of "towers both useless and absurd that our pride may mount skyward, whence it is sure to fall in ruins." The abandoned Italians dubbed Avignon a "second Babylon."

After a dispute with the king, Pope Gregory XI packed up for Rome in 1376, but Avignon held its ground. On his death in 1378, they elected their own pope, Clement VII, and the Great Schism divided the Christian world. Popes and antipopes abused, insulted, and excommunicated each other to no avail, though the real object of dispute was the vast power and wealth of the papacy. When the king himself turned on the last antipope Avignon lost to Rome, and the extravagant court dispersed.

Though it's merely the capital of the Vaucluse these days, Avignon's lively street life, active university, and colorful markets present a year-round spectacle. Every summer its arts life steps up to world-class status with the famous Avignon Theater Festival, which fills the city with devotees of its 300-some stage productions, all on the cutting edge.

An accompanied **tour of Avignon's old town** is given by the tourist office from April through October, leaving from its headquarters (⊠ 41 cours Jean-Jaurès, ☎ 04–90–82–65–11) Tuesday and Thursday at 10 AM.

The Historic Center

You can take in the best of 14th-century Avignon in a half-day's walk, but allow time to linger in the museums, restaurants, and atmospheric squares.

A Good Walk

Begin your walk at the train station (there's a good parking garage). Crossing the busy ring road, walk through the Porte de la République, an opening in **Les Remparts** ①, the magnificent ramparts surrounding the entire old town. Head straight north up rue de la République. Past the post office on your left, duck left into a backstreet and peek into the **Hospice St-Louis** ②, a 17th- and 18th-century retreat that retains its magnificent courtyard shaded by gigantic plane trees. Today it's home to the Centre National du Théâtre (National Theater Center) and the hotel-restaurant Cloître St-Louis (☞ Dining and Lodging, *below*).

At the corner of rue Joseph-Vernet, stop in at the tourist office for maps and information. A block up from the tourist office, a lovely little 17th-century Jesuit chapel shelters a fascinating jumble of classical stonework in the **Musée Lapidaire** ③. Double back and turn right (west) onto rue Joseph-Vernet; two blocks up, you can stop into the tiny, eccentric **Musée Requien** ④, with its very personal displays on natural history.

Cathédrale Notre-Dame-des-Doms, **8**
Les Halles, **12**
Hospice St-Louis, **2**
Musée Calvet, **5**
Musée Lapidaire, **3**
Musée Requien, **4**
Palais des Papes, **7**
Petit Palais, **9**
Place de l'Horloge, **6**
Pont St-Bénézet, **11**
Les Remparts, **1**
Rocher des Doms, **10**

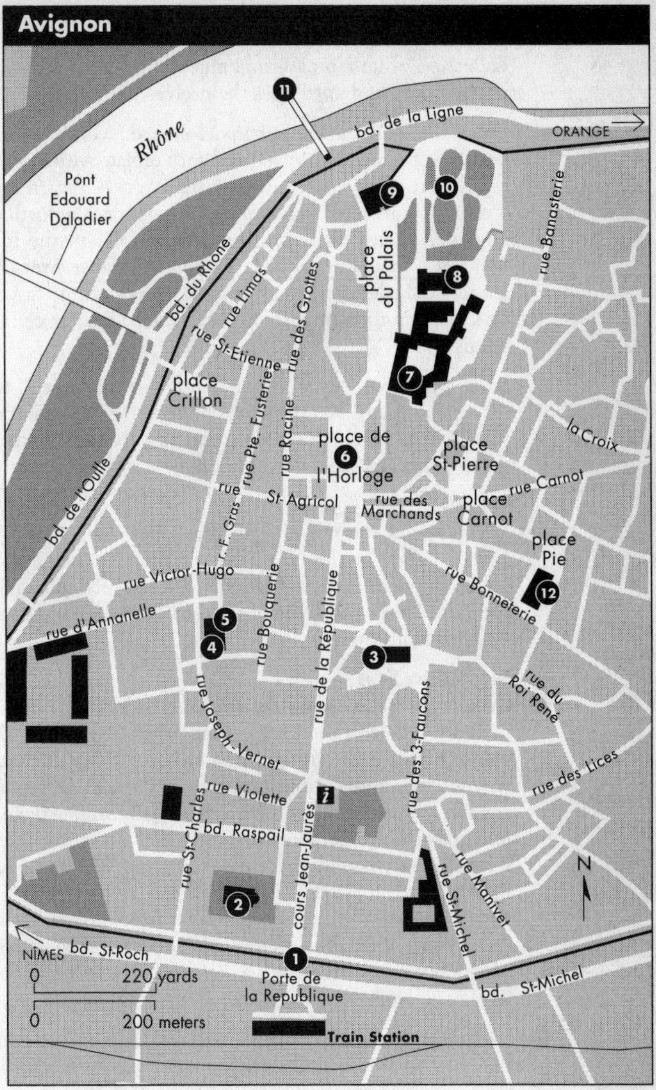

Next door, don't miss the **Musée Calvet** ⑤, a lovely neoclassic stone mansion housing a collection of 17th- and 18th-century French art, much of it created in Avignon. Double back past the Musée Requien, turn left up rue Horace Vernet, and left again up rue de la Bouquerie. Continue straight up rue Racine and turn right into the animated heart of the city, the **place de l'Horloge** ⑥, anchored by the imposing 19th-century Hôtel de Ville and its gothic Tour de l'Horloge (Clock Tower).

Tear yourself away from the sidewalk cafés, merry-go-round, jugglers, and mimes on the square and continue north to Place du Palais. Walk straight up the square and bear left until you're opposite the entry gate, so you can take in the full, wide-angle view of the magnificent **Palais des Papes** ⑦. After an hour or two touring the awesome interior, recross the square to study the magnificent facade of the Hôtel des Monnaies, a heavily sculpted Baroque masterpiece from the 17th century. Then cut across to the relatively humble but evocative **Cathédrale Notre-Dame-des-Doms** ⑧.

At the far end of Place du Palais, the **Petit Palais** ⑨—once home to Avignon's bishops and the first of its resident popes—houses a marvelous collection of Italian painting, much of it (coincidentally) from the era of the popes and antiPopes themselves.

Leave the square and climb up Montée du Moulin into the **Rocher des Doms** ⑩, a serene hilltop garden park replete with sculptures and black swans. From here you can look out over the city, the palace, and the river to the ancient enemy of papal Avignon, the fortified town of Villeneuve. Above all, you'll be able to take in the famous **Pont St-Bénézet** ⑪ in its stunted state and imagine dancers turning *tous en rond* (round and round). (From the park, you can climb down past the Tour de Chiens in the ramparts to reach the bridge; or cut behind the Petit Palais.)

Follow the scenic Escaliers Ste-Anne down and head right on rue Banasterie, but don't let the shops lining the winding backstreets around place Carnot keep you from stopping in to salivate over the delicious goods in **Les Halles** ⑫, the indoor market on place Pie (pronounced *pee*).

TIMING

If you spend the morning in the Popes' Palace and visit either the Musée Calvet or the Petit Palais in the afternoon, you can see these basics in a light day's sightseeing. If you're pressed, make a beeline for the Palace, then climb the Rocher des Doms for an overview that takes in the famous bridge.

Sights to See

❽ **Cathédrale Notre-Dame-des-Doms.** First built in a pure Provençal Romanesque style in the 12th century, then dwarfed by the extravagant palace beside it, this relatively humble church rallied in the 14th century with a cupola—that promptly collapsed. As rebuilt in 1425, it's a marvel of stacked arches with a strong Byzantine flavor and is topped nowadays with a gargantuan Virgin Mary lantern—a 19th-century afterthought—that glows for miles around. The Baroque styling in the nave dates from 1670. That's the tomb of Pope Jean XXII in the center-left chapel—but not his likeness, as his *gisant* (recumbent funeral statue) was wrecked in the Revolution and replaced with the likeness of a mere bishop, which he was before his rise to infamy. ⊠ *Pl. du Palais,* ☎ *04–90–86–81–01.* ☯ *Mon.–Sat. 7–7, Sun. 9–7.*

⑫ **Les Halles.** By 7 every morning the merchants and artisans have stacked their herbed cheeses and arranged their vine-ripened tomatoes with surgical precision in pyramids and designs that please the eye before they tease the salivary glands. This permanent covered market is as far from a farmers' market as you can get, each booth a designer boutique of *haute gamme* (top-quality) goods, from jewel-like olives to silvery mackerel to racks of hanging hares worthy of a Flemish still life. Even if you don't have a kitchen to stock, consider enjoying a cup of coffee or a glass of (breakfast) wine while you take in the sights and smells and spectacle. ⊠ *Pl. Pie,* ☎ *04–90–27–15–15.* ☯ *6AM–1PM.*

❷ **Hospice St-Louis.** Though not officially open to tourists, you can slip in for a peek at this graceful old 17th-century Jesuit cloister, converted for use as a hospital in the 19th century. Its symmetrical arches (now enclosed as a sleek hotel) are shaded by ancient plane trees. ⊠ *20 rue du Portail Boquier,* ☎ *04–90–27–55–55.*

❺ **Musée Calvet.** Worth a visit for the beauty and balance of its architecture alone, this fine old art museum contains a rich collection of art, acquired and donated by an 18th-century Avignon doctor with a hunger for antiquities and an eye for the classically inspired. Later acquisitions are neoclassic and Romantic, and almost entirely French, including works by Manet, Daumier, and David, such as *La Mort du Jeune Bara* (*The Death of Young Bara*). The main building itself is a Palladian-style jewel in pale Gard stone dating from the 1740s; and the garden is so lovely that it may distract you from the paintings. ✉ *65 rue Joseph-Vernet,* ☎ *04–90–86–33–84.* 🎟 *30 frs.* ⊙ *Wed.–Mon. 10–1 and 2–6.*

❸ Musée Lapidaire. Housed until after the year 2000 in a pretty little Jesuit chapel on the main shopping street (it will move eventually to a wing of the Musée Calvet), this collection of classical sculpture and stonework features funeral stones and works from Gallo-Roman times (1st and 2nd centuries), as well as items from the Musée Calvet's collection of Greek and Etruscan works. They are haphazardly labeled and insouciantly scattered throughout the noble chapel, itself slightly crumbling but awash with light. ✉ *27 rue de la République,* ☎ *04–90–85–75–38.* 🎟 *10 frs.* ⊙ *Wed.–Mon. 10–noon and 2–6.*

❹ Musée Requien. Don't bother to rush to this eccentric little natural history museum, but since it's next door to the Calvet Museum and free, you might want to stop in and check out the petrified palm trunks, the dinosaur skeleton, the handful of local beetles and mammals, and the careful and evocative texts (French only) accompanying them. The museum is named for a local naturalist and functions as an entrance to the massive **library** of natural history upstairs. ✉ *67 rue Joseph-Vernet,* ☎ *04–90–82–43–51.* 🎟 *Free.* ⊙ *Tues.–Sat. 9–noon and 2–6.*

★ **❼ Palais des Papes** (Popes' Palace). The Renaissance chronicler Jean Froissart called this palace "the loveliest and strongest house in the world," while Petrarch sneered, "The houses of the apostles crumble as (popes) raise up their palaces of massy gold." Within these magnificent Gothic walls, one of the heydays (or low points) in French history took place, a period of extraordinary sacred and secular power and, to skeptics, outrageous wealth. Once densely decorated in tapestries, frescoes, and sumptuous fabrics, it hosted feasts of Romanesque extravagance and witnessed intrigues of Gothic proportion. The pope ruled within as half god, half prince, eating alone at an elevated table in the crowded dining hall, sleeping in a lavishly decorated bedroom distinctly devoid of sacred reference. His chamberlain's bedroom had eight hiding holes, complete with trapdoors concealed under carpets; who knows to what use they were put?

But don't expect to see eye-boggling luxury today: Resentful Revolutionaries hacked away most traces of excess in the 1780s, and and ironically what remains has a monastic purity. Most of all you may be struck by the scale; either one of its two wings dwarfs the cathedral beside it, but between them they cover almost 50,000 ft of surface. And the grand-scale interiors are evocative as well, with a massive wooden barrel vault arching over the dining hall like a boat belly and a kitchen with fireplaces big enough to house a family. The **Grande Audience** (Grand Audience Hall) and the **Grande Chapelle,** too, are as vast as cathedrals.

From your first exterior view note the difference between the palace's two wings: The north end, toward the cathedral, is the Palais Vieux (Old Palace), a severe Cistercian bastion built by the sober Pope Benedict XII between 1334 and 1342; the south end was built over the next ten years with slightly airier fantasy by Pope Clement VI, who prized his creature comforts.

An enthusiastic patron of the arts, Clement VI brought in a team of artists from Italy to decorate his digs. It was led by no less than Simone Martini himself, imported from Siena and Assisi (where he had worked with Giotto). On his death, Mattheo Giovanetti took the lead, and the

frescoes that covered every surface must have been one of the wonders of the world. Some of the finest traces remain in Clement's study,
called the **Chambre du Cerf** (Stag's Room), where the walls still retain
the lovely frescoes he commissioned in 1343. Unlike the Raphael masterpieces that decorate the Vatican chambers in Rome, which feature
lofty classical themes and powerful Christian images, these paintings
depict simple hunting scenes: a stag hunt, bird snaring, and fishing.
They're graceful, almost naive in style, and intimate in scale, but the
attempts at perspective in the deep window frames remind you that
this was an advanced center of culture and learning in the 14th century, and perspective was then downright avant-garde, fresh from the
sketchbooks of Giotto. Among many fragments, one other example
of Giovanetti's work can be viewed in its entirety in **Chapelle St-Jean**
(St. John's Chapel), a masterpiece of composition, in which the interplay of hands and the implied lines of gazes create a silent dialogue.

Though you may be anxious to see the more famous spaces, take time
on entering to study the scale model of the palace in its medieval context. Only then can you take in its enormity, looming like Olympus
over the tiny half-timber houses that crowded the Place du Palais—a
palace worthy of a royal dynasty and a temple to holy hubris.

A note of warning: This is one of those grand, must-see monuments
that can be overwhelmed by shutter-popping bus tourists but should
be seen nonetheless; aim for opening time, lunchtime, or evenings if
you are there in the middle of summer. ⊠ *Pl. du Palais,* ☎ *04–90–*
27–50–00. ⌧ *40 frs. entry includes choice of guided tour or individual*
audio guide. ⊙ *Jan.–Mar. and Nov.–Dec., daily 9:30–5:45; Apr.–Oct.,*
daily 9–7 (to 9 during theater festival in July; to 8 in Aug.–Sept.).

★ ❾ **Petit Palais.** This former residence of bishops and cardinals houses a
large collection of old-master paintings, the majority of them Italian
works from the Renaissance schools of Siena, Florence, and Venice—
styles with which the Avignon popes would have been familiar. It's a
coincidence: The paintings were acquired in the 19th century by the
extravagant Italian marquis Campana and bought, on his bankruptcy,
by Napoléon III. Divided among provincial museums throughout
France, they remained scattered until after World War II; then the 300-
some treasures were reunited under this historic roof. But even though
the works weren't amassed by the popes, as you move through hall
after hall of exquisite 14th-century imagery, you'll get a feel for the elevated tastes of the papal era. A key piece to seek out in the 15th-century
rooms is Sandro Botticelli's *Virgin and Child,* a masterpiece of tenderness
and lyric beauty created in his youth; 16th-century masterworks include Venetian works by Carpaccio and Giovanni Bellini. ⊠ *Pl. du Palais,*
☎ *04–90–86–44–58.* ⌧ *30 frs (free Sun. Oct.–Feb.).* ⊙ *Sept.–June,*
Wed.–Mon. 9:30–noon and 2–6; July–Aug., Wed.–Mon. 10:30–6.

❻ **Place de l'Horloge** (Clock Square). This square is the social nerve center of Avignon, where the concentration of bistros, brasseries, and restaurants draws swarms of locals to the shade of its plane trees. After a
play, the doors of the **Théâtre Municipal** open onto the square and the
audience spills into the nearest sidewalk café for a postperformance
drink. The **Hôtel de Ville** (Town Hall) on the west side of the square
was built in the 19th century around its dominating gothic clock tower,
from which the square gets its name.

★ ⓫ **Pont St-Bénézet** (St. Bénézet Bridge). "Sur le pont d'Avignon on y
danse, on y danse . . ." Unlike London Bridge, this other fragment of
childhood song still stretches its arches across the river, but only part-

way: Half was washed away in the 17th century. Its first stones allegedly laid with the miraculous strength granted St-Bénézet in the 12th century, it once reached all the way to Villeneuve. It's a bit narrow for dancing "tous en rond" (round and round), though: The traditional place for dance and play was under the arches. ⊠ *Port du Rocher.*

❶ Les Remparts (The Ramparts). More than 4 km (2 mi) long, these protective crenellated walls and towers were built by the popes in the 14th century to keep out rampaging brigands and mercenary armies attracted by legends of papal wealth. It's extraordinarily well preserved, thanks only in part to the efforts of Viollet-le-Duc, who restored the southern portion in the 19th century. Modern Avignon roars around its impervious walls on a noisy ring road that was once a moat.

❿ Rocher des Doms (Rock of the Domes). This ravishing hilltop garden, with statuary and swans under grand Mediterranean pines and subtropical greenery, would be a lovely retreat anywhere. But its views make it extraordinary: From side to side you can look over the palace, the rooftops of old Avignon, the Pont St-Bénézet, and formidable Villeneuve across the Rhône. On the horizon looms Mont Ventoux, the Luberon, and Les Alpilles. ⊠ *Montée du Moulin, off Pl. du Palais.*

Dining and Lodging

$$$$ ✕ **La Vieille Fontaine.** Summer-evening meals around the old fountain and boxwood-filled oil jars in the courtyard would be wonderful with *steak-frites* alone, but combine this romantic setting with the stellar cuisine of Jean-Pierre Robert, and you have an event. Give yourself over to crabs in saffron-perfumed sauce; fat, white asparagus sautéed in vanilla; rosy lamb on a bed of red peppers and olives; the best regional wines; and an army of urbane servers—and hope for moonlight. It's in the lovely old Hôtel d'Europe. ⊠ *12 pl. Crillon,* ☎ *04–90–14–76–76. Reservations essential. AE, MC, V.*

$$$ ✕ **Brunel.** In a dull neighborhood just west of place du Palais and in a bland, overlighted setting, people come in loyal droves to enjoy the passionate Provençal cooking of Avignon-born and -bred chef Roger Brunel. It's down-home bistro cooking from a sophisticated larder: parchment-wrapped mullet with eggplant and tomatoes, chicken roasted with garlic confit (preserves), and caramelized apples in tender pastry. ⊠ *46 rue de la Balance,* ☎ *04–90–85–24–83. Reservations essential. AE, MC, V.*

$$$ ✕ **Le Jardin des Frênes.** Within the quiet confines of this bucolic Relais & Châteaux retreat, enjoy a garden meal that carries you far from Avignon and even the suburban sprawl around it. Chef Antoine Biancone continues to invent dishes that are modern yet purely Provençal: ravioli filled with *brandade* (a light salt-cod paste) and baked with eggplant, cod perfumed with truffles, and beef with a jolt of anchovy. Browse the list of Côtes-du-Rhônes and consider switching hotels: The pool does look inviting. ⊠ *645 av. des Vertes-Rives, Montfavet (5 km [3 mi] outside Avignon),* ☎ *04–90–31–17–93. AE, DC, MC, V. Closed Nov.–mid-Mar.*

$$$ ✕ **La Mirande.** Whether you dine under the 14th-century coffered ceilings, surrounded by Renaissance tapestries, or in the intimate garden under the Popes' Palace walls, the restaurant of the luxurious Hôtel de la Mirande transports you to another time. Only the soigné cuisine of chef Daniel Hébet recalls the modern age: delicate sea snail ravioli in shellfish sauce, roast pigeon in ginger, and herbed saddle of lamb. Foodies take note: Hébet teams up with guest chefs to teach casual, multilingual cooking classes around the kitchen table, followed by a feast. ⊠ *Pl. de la Mirande,* ☎ *04–90–85–93–93. Reservations essential. AE, DC, MC, V.*

$$ ✕ **La Cuisine de Reine.** Glassed into the white-stone cloister of the trendy
★   art gallery called Les Cloître des Arts, this chic bistro sports a theatrical dell'arte decor and a young, laid-back waitstaff. The blackboard lists eclectic dishes that are simple and sunny but serious in execution: duck in rosemary honey, rosy herbed lamb chops, and salmon tartare with eggplant caviar and citrus vinaigrette. Or join the cashmere-and-loafer set for the 120-franc Saturday brunch buffet. ⊠ *83 rue Joseph-Vernet,* ☎ *04–90–85–99–04. AE, DC, MC, V. Closed Sun. No dinner Mon.*

$$ ✕ **Hiély-Lucullus.** From the tiny street-level plaque marking the entry, you might expect a dentist's office. But this restaurant numbers among the best in France—despite André Chaussy taking over as chef for the legendary Pierre Hiély. The upstairs dining room has a quiet, dignified charm that matches in mood the meticulous cooking: crayfish tails in scrambled eggs tucked in a puff pastry, roast cod with juniper berries, and a very serious dessert cart. The price ceiling still holds at 210 francs for the main menu—an excellent value for money. ⊠ *5 rue de la République,* ☎ *04–90–86–17–07. Reservations essential. AE, MC, V. Closed most of Jan., last 2 wks in June, and Mon. No lunch Tues. (except July–Sept.)*

$ ✕ **Le Grand Café.** Behind the Popes' Palace, in a massive former fac-
★   tory—a setting of carefully preserved industrial decay—is a hip entertainment complex with an international cinema, a bar, and this popular bistro. Gigantic 18th-century mirrors and dance festival posters hang on crumbling plaster and brick, and votive candles half-light the raw metal framework—an inspiring environment for intense film talk and a late supper of foie gras, goat cheese, or marinated artichokes, served under terra-cotta covers. ⊠ *La Manutention, 4 rue des Escaliers Ste-Anne,* ☎ *04–90–86–86–77. MC, V. Closed Mon. (except July).*

$ ✕ **NaniType.** Crowded inside and out with trendy friends and young professionals, this pretty lunch spot serves stylish home-cooking in generous portion without the fuss of multiple courses—a comfortable Anglo-American approach. There are heaping dinner salads sizzling with fresh meat, enormous kebabs, and a creative quiche du jour. Rich homemade desserts include fruit cobblers, chocolate cakes, and puddings. Prices are remarkable, averaging 55 francs for one large course. It's just off rue de la République. ⊠ *29 rue Théodore Aubanel,* ☎ *04–90–82–60–90. No credit cards. Closed Sun. No dinner Mon.–Thurs.*

$$$$ 🏨 **Hôtel de la Mirande.** Superbly restored and richly decorated with
★   exquisite reproduction fabrics and beeswaxed antiques, this designer's dream of a hotel is just below the Popes' Palace in a car-free zone. Its enclosed garden is a breakfast and dinner oasis and its central lounge is a skylit and jazz-warmed haven. Rooms are both gorgeous and comfy, and the bathrooms with their Victorian touches are luxurious. Half the rooms face the garden, the other half the palace facade; a few even have tiny ultraprivate balconies with rooftop views. ⊠ *Pl. de la Mirande, 84000,* ☎ *04–90–85–93–93,* FAX *04–90–86–26–85. 19 rooms, 1 suite. Restaurant, bar. AE, DC, MC, V.*

$$$–$$$$ 🏨 **Hôtel d'Europe.** Napoléon slept here, and so did Robert and Elizabeth Browning and any number of artists and writers right up to the theater luminaries who stay here today: This splendid 16th-century home, built by the Marquis of Graveson, resonates with history. With discreet, classic decor—polar opposite to the cutting-edge luxe of the Mirande—and a seasoned staff, this place will be lodging festival guests for centuries to come. Rooms are vast, with two suites overlooking the Popes' Palace. The restaurant, La Vieille Fontaine (☞ *Dining, above*), is one

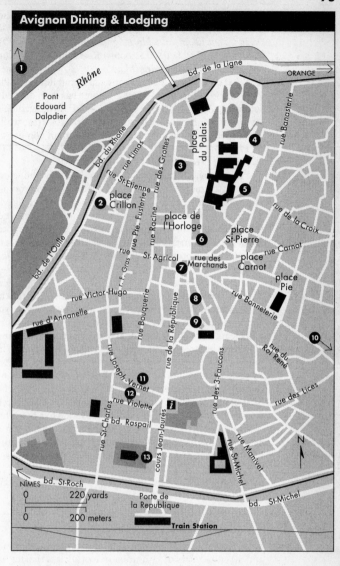

Avignon Dining & Lodging

of Avignon's finest. ⊠ *12 pl. Crillon, 84000,* ☎ *04–90–14–76–76,*
FAX *04–90–85–43–66. 47 rooms. Restaurant. AE, DC, MC, V.*

$$$ ★ 🏨 **Cloître St-Louis.** Standing serene and noble within its sturdy 17th-century walls, this sleek hotel encloses a cloistered square lined with grand old plane trees. The early Baroque building, erected by the Jesuits in 1611, was a theological school for novitiates and later a hospital before it became a hotel at the beginning of the decade. Now interiors are stripped and modernist, playing up the cool old stone; facilities and staff cater graciously to a business clientele as well as upscale tourists. There's a small roof-top pool, and it's a block's walk from the train station. ⊠ *20 rue du Portail-Boquier, 84000,* ☎ *04–90–27–55–55,* FAX *04–90–82–24–01. 80 rooms. Restaurant, bar, pool. AE, DC, MC, V.*

$$$ 🏨 **Hostellerie les Frênes.** This Relais & Châteaux hotel in a 19th-century country house two miles from the center has lovely gardens and a pool surrounded by manicured greenery. But despite recent redecoration in

Provençal style, rooms can feel spare and uninspired, and some of the public areas need freshening up. ✉ *645 av. des Vertes-Rives, Montfavet (5 km [3 mi] outside Avignon) 84140,* ☎ *04–90–31–17–93,* FAX *04–90–23–95–03. 15 rooms. Restaurant, pool, sauna. AE, DC, MC, V. Closed Nov.–early Mar.*

$$ ★ **Hôtel du Blauvac.** Just off rue de la République and Place de l'Horloge, this 17th-century nobleman's home has been divided into 16 guest rooms, many with pristine exposed stonework, aged oak details, and lovely tall windows that look, alas, onto backstreet walls. Pretty fabrics and a warm, familial welcome more than compensate, however. ✉ *11 rue de la Bancasse, 84000,* ☎ *04–90–86–34–11,* FAX *04–90–86–27–41. 16 rooms. Bar. AE, DC, MC, V.*

$ **L'Anastasy.** On the long, low island on the Rhône called Ile de la Barthelasse, this pretty farmhouse inn offers just five rooms, home cooking, and an interesting social mix if you care to mingle: Madame Manguin lets guests withdraw or join in as they like, whether during meals, poolside chats, or while having drinks in the cozy kitchen-salon. Modest-priced meals (not included in the room price) must be reserved, and are prepared for guests on request only. ✉ *Ile de la Barthelasse, 84000,* ☎ *04–90–85–55–94,* FAX *04–90–82–59–40. 5 rooms. Pool. No credit cards.*

$ **Hôtel Innova.** With the family living just off the breakfast room and the champion-scale Persian cat glowering at you as you breakfast, you'll feel like a boarder in this tiny budget lodging. But rooms are big and clean, freshly decorated, and equipped with phone and TV, and miniature bathrooms fit neatly into closets. It's just up the street from the Musée Calvet. ✉ *100 rue Joseph-Vernet, 84000,* ☎ *04–90–82–54–10,* FAX *04–90–82–52–39. 11 rooms, 5 with bath, 6 with shower only. Breakfast room. AE, DC, MC, V.*

$ **Hôtel de Mons.** Off place de l'Horloge, this little hotel was built as a 13th-century chapel, then in 1821 converted to a home for Napoléon's chaplain, Étienne Morel de Mons. Its transformation took some maneuvering, but 11 rooms with bathrooms (with adventurous modern decors) have been fitted into nooks and crannies, while retaining some period detail. Breakfast is served in a groin-vaulted stone crypt. ✉ *5 rue de Mons, 84000,* ☎ *04–90–82–57–16,* FAX *04–90–85–19–15. 11 rooms. MC, V.*

Nightlife and the Arts

Small though it is, Avignon's inspiring art museums, strong university, and 60-some years of saturation in world-class theater have made the city an antenna for the arts south of Paris.

Held annually in July, the Avignon festival, known officially as the Festival Annuel d'Art Dramatique (Annual Festival of Dramatic Art), has brought the best of world theater to this ancient city since 1947. Some 300 productions—some official, some "off" and "off-off"—take place every year; the main performances are at the Palais des Papes. Overflowing with traveling players and audiences of every kind, the city takes on the look of a medieval festival or a grand party thrown by Clement VI. (For tickets and information, contact ☎ 04–90–82–67–08.)

In the year 2000 Avignon will serve its turn as the **Ville Européenne de la Culture** (European City of Culture), which means the city's art patrons will dig deep into their pockets to fund every imaginable form of music, dance, theater, public sculpture, and art exhibition. It couldn't be a better time to plan an evening out. Tickets for many events can be purchased at the Office de Tourisme (✉ 41 rue Jean-Jaurès, ☎ 04–90–82–65–11).

A winter festival known as **Les Hivernales** celebrates French dance here every January and February. Its central venue is the Maison Jean Vilar (✉ 8 rue de Mons, ☎ 04–90–85–45–24).

Two cinema complexes show first-run, mainstream movies in *v.o.* (*version originale*, meaning in the original language with French subtitles) as well as hard-to-find international independent works: **Utopia Manutention** (✉ 4 rue des Escaliers Ste-Anne) and **République** (✉ 5 rue Figuière). For schedules call 04–90–82–65–36.

At **AJMI** (Association Pour le Jazz et la Musique Improvisée, ✉ 4 rue Escaliers Ste-Anne, ☎ 04–90–86–08–61), in La Manutention, you can hear live jazz acts of some renown.

Within its fusty old medieval walls, Avignon teems with modern nightlife well into the wee hours. **Pub Z** (☎ 04–90–85–42–84) is the hot spot for rock, sometimes live; the black-and-white decor is dominated by a zebra theme. At **Bistroquet** (✉ Ile de la Barthelasse, ☎ 04–90–82–25–83), Saturday night brings rock concerts or dance music of all kinds. The **Bistrot du Cinéma** (☎ 04–90–82–65–36) serves drinks in a dark, intimate space just outside the cinema in La Manutention.

At the cabaret **Dolphin Blues** (✉ chemin de l'île Piot, ☎ 04–90–82–46–96), a hip mix of comedy and music dominates the repertoire. **Le Rouge Gorge** (✉ 10 bis rue Peyrollerie, behind the palace, ☎ 04–90–14–02–54) presents a dinner show featuring singers, dancers, and comedians and after-dinner dancing every Friday and Saturday night. On other nights other comedy and music groups perform.

Shopping

Avignon is too big and too resident oriented to be full of boutiques for tourists, so it doesn't have an unusual concentration of Provençal gifts and products. Rather it has a cosmopolitan mix of French chains, youthful clothing shops (it's a college town), and a few plummy dress shops. **Rue des Marchands,** off place Carnot, is one shopping stretch, but **rue de la République** is the main artery.

If you're hungry for books in English, find **Shakespeare** (✉ 155 rue Carreterie, ☎ 04–90–27–38–50); in addition to new and used books in English, it has a tearoom, café, and terrace.

If you're a fan of fine French cookware, head to **Jaffier-Parsi** (✉ 42 rue des Fourbisseurs, ☎ 04–90–86–08–85), a professional cooking supply store that has been stocking heavy copper pots, stainless steel ladles, mortar-and-pestle sets, and great knives since 1902. Among the myriad vendors of Provençal pottery throughout the region, **Terre è Provence** (✉ 26 rue République, ☎ 04–90–85–56–45) maintains a high esthetic standard, with lovely pitchers, platters, and tureens.

Mouret Chapelier (✉ 20 rue Marchands, ☎ 04–90–85–39–38) has a treasure trove of old-fashioned, Old-World, and marvelously eccentric hats in a jewel-box setting.

HAUT VAUCLUSE

North and northeast of Avignon, this land of rolling orchards and vineyards spreads lazily at the foot of Mont Ventoux, redolent of truffles, lavender, and fine wine. Perhaps that's why the Romans so firmly established themselves here, raising grand theaters and luxurious villas that still remain in part. From Avignon head north into the vineyards, making a brief tour of Châteauneuf-du-Pape, even if you don't stop to drink and buy wine. Orange is just up the highway; though the town isn't the most picturesque, its Roman theater is a must-see. Cutting south-east through Carpentras, drive up toward Vaison-la-Romaine, stop-ping, if you're inclined, in the picturesque hilltop villages (Vacqueyras and Séguret) and wine centers (Beaumes-de-Venise and Gigondas) along the way. Return to Carpentras via Malaucène, which the first French pope preferred to Avignon, and via pretty, perched Le Barroux.

Châteauneuf-du-Pape

⓭ *18 km (11 mi) north of Avignon, 22 km (13 mi) west of Carpentras.*

The countryside around this very famous wine center is a patchwork of rolling vineyards, of green and black furrows striping the landscape in endless, retreating perspective. Great gates and grand houses punc-tuate the scene, as symmetrical and finely detailed as the etching on a wine label, and signs—discreet but insistent—beckon you to follow the omnipresent smell of fermenting grapes to their source. Behind barn doors, under cellar traps, and in chilly caves beneath châteaux, colos-sal oak vats nurture this noble Rhône red to maturity.

Once the table wine of the Avignon popes, who kept a fortified sum-mer house here (hence the name of the town, which means "new cas-tle of the pope"), the vineyards of Châteauneuf-du-Pape had the good fortune to be wiped out by phylloxera in the 19th century. Its revival as a muscular and resilient mix of up to thirteen varietals has moved it to the forefront of French wines, with an almost portlike intensity (it can reach 15% alcohol content). The whites, though less significant, are also to be reckoned with. To learn more, stop in at the **Musée des Outils de Vignerons Père Anselme,** a private collection of tools and equip-ment displayed in the *caveau* (wine cellar) of the Brotte family. ⊠ *rte. d'Avignon,* ☎ *04–90–83–70–07.* ☒ *Free.* ☉ *Daily 9–12 and 2–6.*

If you're disinclined to spend your holiday sniffing and sipping in a dark basement, climb the hill to the ruins of the **Château.** Though it was destroyed in the Wars of Religion and its remaining donjon (keep) blasted by the Germans in World War II, it still commands a magnif-icent position. From this rise in the rolling vineyards, you can enjoy wraparound views of Avignon, the Luberon, and Mont Ventoux.

Dining and Lodging

$–$$ ✕ **Le Pistou.** Recently discovered by sun-starved Parisians in search of the life we all dream about, this friendly little auberge (inn) serves so-phisticated cooking by a chef in love with things Provençal, such as sea bass roasted in pesto and lamb chops with thyme flowers. The wel-come is warm, the fixed-price menus start cheap, and there are even winter evenings of music and storytelling. ⊠ *15 rue Joseph-Ducos,* ☎ *04–90–83–71–75. MC, V. Closed Mon. No dinner Sun.*

$$ ✕▦ **La Garbure.** With four rooms decked in soft pastel ruffles upstairs and a new, low-priced menu *terroir* (prix-fixe menu of regional spe-cialties), this pretty auberge aims to please. Look for potted quail in Carpentras truffles, stuffed rabbit with subtle thyme sauce, and a heady sorbet of marc de Châteauneuf-du-Pape (the eau-de-vie made of local grapes). The more expensive menus feature hearty dishes from the chef's native southwest; all the more reason to opt for the local dishes—and splurge on the local wine. (The restaurant is closed Sun. Oct.–June and Sun. lunch in season.) ⊠ *3 rue Joseph-Ducos,* ☎ *04–90–83–75–08. MC, V.*

Orange

⓮ *12 km (7 mi) north of Châteauneuf-du-Pape, 31 km (19 mi) north of Avignon.*

Even less touristy than Nîmes (☞ Chapter 2) and just as eccentric, the city of Orange (pronounced oh-RAWNZH) nonetheless draws thou-
★ sands every year to its spectacular **Théâtre Antique,** a colossal Roman theater built in the time of Caesar Augustus. Its vast stone stage wall, bouncing sound off the facing hillside, climbs four stories high, and the niche at center stage contains the original statue of Augustus, just as it reigned over centuries of productions of classical plays. Today this theater inspires and shelters world-class theater, as well as concerts of dance, classical music, poetry readings, and even rock. Orange's sum-mer opera festival is one of Europe's best and one of its best known. ⊠ *pl. des Frères-Mounet,* ☎ *04–90–34–70–88.* ⊡ *30 frs; joint ticket with Musée Municipal.* ⊙ *Apr.–Oct., daily 9–6:30; Nov.–Mar., daily 9–noon and 1:30–5.*

Across the street from the theater, the small **Musée Municipal** (Town Museum) displays antiquities unearthed around Orange, including three detailed marble *cadastres* (land survey maps) dating from the 1st century. Upstairs are Provençal fabrics manufactured in local mills in the 18th century, and a collection of faïence pharmacy jars. ⊠ *pl. des Frères-Mounet,* ☎ *04–90–34–70–88.* ⊡ *30 frs; joint ticket with theater.* ⊙ *Apr.–Oct., daily 9–6:30; Nov.–Mar., daily 9–noon and 1:30–5.*

North of the city center is the notable **Arc de Triomphe** that once strad-dled the via Agrippa between Lyon and Arles. Three arches support a heavy double attic (horizontal top) floridly decorated with battle scenes and marine symbols, referring to Augustus's victories at Actium. The arch, which dates from about 20 BC, is superbly preserved, particularly the north side, but to view it on foot you'll have to cross a roundabout seething with traffic. ⊠ *North of the center on ave. de l'Arc, direction Gap.*

Vieil Orange, the old-town neighborhood you must cross to hike from one Roman monument to the other, carries on peacefully when there's not a blockbuster spectacle in the theater. Lining its broad squares, under heavy-leaved plane trees, are sidewalk cafés, which are perfect for pic-turesque repose.

Dining and Lodging

$ ✕ **La Yaka.** At this intimate, unpretentious bistro, you are greeted by the beaming owner/host/waiter, then pampered with an embarrassment of riches in menu choices. The home cooking draws local regulars: Spe-cialties are emphatically *"style grandmère"*—slow cooked and heav-ily seasoned—and include rabbit stew, *caillette* (pork-liver meat loaf), and even canned peas with bacon. It's all in a charming stone-and-beam setting, complete with a Gothic archway. ⊠ *24 pl. Sylvian,* ☎ *04–90–34–70–03. MC, V. Closed Wed. and Nov. No dinner Tues.*

$$ ⊡ **Arène.** On a quiet square in the old-town center, this comfortable old hotel features attentive owners and a labyrinth of rooms densely decorated in rich colors and heavy fabrics. The nicest ones look out over the square. As it's built between several fine old houses strung to-gether, there's no elevator, but a multitude of stairways compensates. ⊠ *pl. de Langues, 84100,* ☎ *04–90–11–40–40,* ⨳ *04–90–11–40–45. 30 rooms. Air-conditioning. AE, DC, MC, V.*

Nightlife and the Arts

To witness the torches of *Nabucco* or *Aida* flickering against a 2,000-year-old Roman wall and to hear the extraordinary sound play around the hemicycle of ancient seats is one of the great summer festival ex-periences in Europe. Every July, **Les Chorégies d'Orange** echo tradi-tion and amass operatic and classical music spectacles under the summer stars. (For information call ☎ 04–90–34–24–24 or fax F̄AX̄ 04–90–11–00–85; or write to ✉ Chorégies, B.P. 205, 84107 Orange Cedex well in advance.)

Beaumes-de-Venise

⑮ *23 km (14 mi) east of Orange, 9 km (5½ mi) north of Carpentras.*

Beaumes-de-Venise is the source of a delicately sweet Muscat wine sought after as an aperitif as well an accompaniment to desserts. Though the village itself is unremarkable, it's set at the foot of the Dentelles de Montmirail, a small range of rocky chalk cliffs eroded to lacy pinnacles—whence their name *dentelles* (lace). From tiny D21, east of town, are the prettiest views. Just up the main road you can dip a toe into Vacqueyras and Gigondas, names of fine Rhône Valley wines as well as villages.

Séguret

⑯ *14 km (9 mi) north of Beaume-de-Venise, 23 km (14 mi) north of Carpentras, 10 km (6 mi) southwest of Vaison-la-Romaine, 21 km from Orange.*

Nestled into the sharp rake of a rocky hillside and crowned with a ruined medieval castle, Séguret is a picture-book hilltop village that is only moderately commercialized. Its 14th-century clock tower, Romanesque St-Denis Church, and bubbling Renaissance fountain highlight steep little stone streets and lovely Dentelles de Montmirail views.

Dining and Lodging

$$$ ✕🏠 **La Table du Comtat.** Clinging to the top of the village—thus taking in the most breathtaking of Ségurat's valley views—this 15th-century former hospice functions nowadays as a simple hotel and serious restaurant. A purist for superior ingredients with a weakness for the tour de force, chef Frank Gomez may present you with a layered charlotte of eggplant and brandade or roast pigeon with licorice sauce. Côtes-du-Rhônes naturally dominate the wine list. (The restaurant is closed Tuesday night and Wednesday except July–September.) Upstairs, eight little rooms look over the valley or the pretty garden. ✉ *Just after pl. de l'Église, 84110,* ☎ *04–90–46–91–49,* F̄AX̄ *04–90–46–94–27. 8 rooms. Restaurant. AE, DC, MC, V. Closed Feb.*

Vaison-la-Romaine

⑰ *27 km (17 mi) northeast of Orange, 44 km (27 mi) northeast of Avignon.*

In a river valley green with orchards of almonds and apricots, this ancient town thrives as a modern market center. Yet it retains an irresistible Provençal charm, with medieval backstreets, lively squares lined with cafés and, as its name implies, remains of its Roman past. Vaison's well-established Celtic colony joined forces with Rome in the 2nd century BC and grew to powerful status in the empire's glory days. No gargantuan monuments were raised, yet the luxurious villas surpassed those of Pompeii.

There are two broad fields of **Roman ruins,** both in the center of town: Before you pay entry at either of the ticket booths, pick up a map (with English explanations) at the **Maison du Tourisme et des Vins** (☎ 04–90–36–02–11), which sits between them; it's open daily 9–12 and 2–5:45.

Like a tiny Roman forum, the **Quartier de Puymin** spreads over the field and hillside in the heart of town, visible in passing from the city streets. Its skeletal ruins of villas, landscaped gardens, and museum lie below the ancient theater, all of which are accessed by the booth across from the tourist office. Closest to the entrance, the foundations of the **Maison des Messii** (Messii House) retains the outlines of its sumptuous design, complete with a vast gentleman's library, reception rooms, an atrium with a rain-fed pool, a large kitchen (the enormous stone vats are still there), and baths with hot, cold, and warm water. It requires imagination to reconstruct the rooms in your mind (remember all those toga movies from the '50s), but a tiny detail is enough to trigger a vivid image: The thresholds still show the hinge holds and scrape marks of swinging doors.

A formal garden echoes a similar landscape of the time; wander under its cypress and flowering shrubs to the **Musée Archéologique Théo-Desplans.** In this newly renovated, streamlined venue, the accoutrements of Roman life have been amassed and displayed by theme: pottery, weapons, gods and goddesses, jewelry, and of course sculpture, including full portraits of the emperor Claudius (1st century) and a strikingly noble nude Hadrian (2nd century). The findings of recent digs have been incorporated into new displays. Cross the park behind the museum to climb into the bleachers of the 1st-century **theater**, which is smaller than Orange's but is still used today for concerts and plays.

★ Across the parking lot is the **Quartier de la Villasse,** where the remains of a lively market town evoke images of main-street shops, public gardens, and grand private homes, complete with floor mosaics. The most evocative image of all is in the *thermes* (baths): a neat row of marble-seat toilets lined up over a raked trough that rinsed waste instantly away. Sic transit gloria mundi (thus passes the glory of the world). ⊠ *Av. Gén. de Gaulle at Pl. du 11 Novembre,* ☎ *04–90–36–02–11.* 🎟 *Ruins, museum, and cloister 40 frs.* ⊙ *Ruins and cloister: June–Sept., daily 9:30–7; Mar.–May and Oct., daily 10–12:30 and 2–6; Nov.–Feb., 10–noon and 2–4:30. Museum: Mar.–May and Oct. daily 10–12:30 and 2:30–6; June–Sept. 9:30–7; Nov.–Feb. 10–11:30 and 2–4. Villasse: June–Sept., daily 9:30–12 and 2–7; Mar.–May and Oct., daily 10–12:30 and 2–6; Nov.–Feb., 10–noon and 2–4:30.*

Take the time to climb up into the **Haute Ville,** a medieval neighborhood perched high above the river valley. Its 13th- and 14th-century houses owe some of their beauty to stone pillaged from the Roman ruins below, but their charm is from the Middle Ages: a trickling stone fountain, a bell tower with wrought-iron campanile, soft-color shutters, and blooming vines that create an atmosphere of a film set of an old town.

If you're in a medieval mood, stop into the sober Romanesque **Cathédrale Notre-Dame-de-Nazareth,** based on recycled fragments and foundations of a Gallo-Roman basilica. Its cloister is the key attraction: Created in the 12th and 13th centuries, it remains virtually unscarred, and its pairs of columns retain their deeply sculpted, richly varied capitals. ⊠ *Av. Jules-Ferry.* ⊙ *June–Sept., daily 9:30–noon and 2–6:30; Mar.–May and Oct., daily 10–noon and 2–5:30; Nov.–Feb., daily 10–noon and 2–4.*

One last highlight: The remarkable single-arch **Pont Romain** (Roman Bridge), built in the 1st century, stands firm across the River Ouvèze; it was one of the few structures to survive the devastating flood that roared through Vaison in 1992, destroying 150 homes and killing 37 people. It's a living testimony to Roman engineering and provokes reflection: Had it not been "quarried" for medieval projects, how much of Roman Vaison would still be standing today?

Dining and Lodging

$$ **✕☵ Le Beffroi.** Perched on a cliff top in the old town, this gracious
★ 16th-century mansion functions as a fine little hotel. Rooms are spacious, comfortable, and filled with antique furniture; the best have views of the gardens. From April through October dine at night under the fig tree in the intimate enclosed garden court on such dishes as rabbit terrine with hazelnut and tarragon, breast of duck in Provençal honey, and nougat glacé with fruit confit. By day you can enjoy a simple salad on the garden terrace. ✉ *rue de l'Évêché, 84110,* ☎ *04–90–36–04–71,* FAX *04–90–36–24–78. 22 rooms. Restaurant. AE, DC, MC, V. Closed mid-Feb.–mid-Mar. and mid-Nov.–mid-Dec.*

$$ **☵ Évêché.** If you want to base yourself in the medieval part of town, stay in one of the four rooms in this turreted 16th-century former bishop's palace, owned by the friendly Verdiers. The warm welcome and rustic charm—delicate fabrics, exposed beams, wooden bedsteads—have garnered a loyal following among travelers who prefer B&B character to modern luxury. Summer breakfast is served in a bower of greenery overlooking the Ouvèze Valley. Make sure to stop into the groin-vaulted art gallery across the street. Advance reservations are essential. ✉ *rue de l'Évêché, 84110,* ☎ *04–90–36–13–46,* FAX *04–90–36–32–43. 4 rooms. No credit cards.*

Malaucène

⑱ *10 km (6 mi) southeast of Vaison-la-Romaine, 44 km (27 mi) northeast of Avignon.*

Yet another picturesque composition of plane trees, fountains, and *lavoirs* (public laundry fountains), crowned by a pretty church tower with campanile, this market town began as a fortified church-village. Its 14th-century church follows classic Provence Romanesque form (a broad vaulted nave, a semicircle apse) and houses an ornate carved-oak organ from the 18th century.

Just east of town, the **Chapelle Notre-Dame-du-Groseau** is the only remains of the mighty 12th-century Benedictine abbey that Pope Clement V preferred as lodging before he settled into Avignon. The setting of cliffs and woodlands is just as wild and wonderful today. ✉ *Off of D974 direction Col des Tempêtes.*

From Malaucène you can take a spectacular scenic drive along the crest of **Mount Ventoux** (D974), looking out over the broad panorama from its peak at 6,263 ft. Barring the possibility of high-summer haze, you'll take in views of the Alps, the Rhône Valley, the Luberon, and even Marseille. Loop south and west to complete your circular tour, stopping into pretty perched **Bédoin**, with its 18th-century Jesuit church, then heading south on D938 to see Le Barroux on your way to Crillon or points south.

Le Barroux

⑲ *6 km (4 mi) southwest of Malaucène, 16 km (10 mi) south of Vaison-la-Romaine, 34 km (21 mi) northeast of Avignon.*

Of all the marvelous hilltop villages stretching across the south of France, this tiny ziggurat of a town may be unique: It is 100% boutique-and-gallery-free and has only one tiny old *épicerie* (small grocery) selling canned goods, yellowed postcards, and today's *Le Provençal*. You are forced, therefore, to look around you and listen to the trickle of the ancient fountains at every labyrinthine turn.

Its **Château** is its main draw, though its Disney-perfect condition reflects a complete restoration after a World War II fire. Vaulted rooms and chapels serve as venues for contemporary art exhibits. ☎ 04–90–62–35–21. ⌨ 20 frs. ☉ Apr.–May weekends 10–7; June, Mon.–Fri. 2–7, weekends 10–7; July–Sept. daily 10–7; Oct. daily 2:30–7.

Dining and Lodging

$ ✕☒ **Les Géraniums.** Though it has simple, pretty rooms, many with views sweeping down to the valley, this family-run auberge emphasizes its restaurant ($–$$), where the owner wears the toque. A broad garden terrace stretches along the cliff side, where you can sample herb-roasted rabbit, a truffle omelet, quail pâté, and local cheeses. Demi-pension is strongly encouraged, because after the dishes are washed up, the owners go to bed; don't expect to come dashing back at midnight after dinner at Baumanière. New rooms in the annex across the street take in panoramic views. ✉ Pl. de la Croix, 84330, ☎ 04–90–62–41–08, FAX 04–90–62–56–48. 22 rooms. Restaurant, bar. AE, DC, MC, V. Closed Jan.–Feb.

Crillon le Brave

⓴ 12 km (7 mi) south of Malaucène (via Caromb), 21 km (13 mi) southeast of Vaison-la-Romaine.

The main reason to come to this tiny village, named after France's most notable soldier hero of the 16th century, is to stay or dine at its hotel, the Hostellerie de Crillon le Brave (☞ Dining and Lodging, below). But it's also pleasant—perched on a knoll in a valley shielded by Mont Ventoux, with the craggy hills of the Dentelles in one direction and the hills of the Luberon in another. Today the village still doesn't have even a boulangerie (bakery), let alone a souvenir boutique; the wrecker's ball has been held at bay. The village makes a good base camp for exploring the region if you can afford to stay at the hotel; with no other commercial establishments in the village, and little more to visit than a tiny music-box museum and an ochre quarry, you're a captive audience.

Dining and Lodging

$$$$ ✕☒ **Hostellerie de Crillon le Brave.** The views from this Relais & Châteaux's nine interconnected hilltop houses are as elevated as its prices, but for this you get a rarefied atmosphere of medieval luxury. A cozy-chic southern decor informs book-filled salons and brocante-trimmed guest rooms, some with terraces looking out onto infinity. Fountains splash in the garden overlooking the pool. In the stone-vaulted dining room, refined French cuisine is served—pan-roasted foie gras on peppered toast, fresh asparagus with garlic vinaigrette, and Sisteron lamb lightly flavored with green anise. ✉ pl. de l'Église, 84410, ☎ 04–90–65–61–61, FAX 04–90–65–62–86. 21 rooms. Restaurant, pool. AE, DC, MC, V. Closed Jan.–mid-Mar.

Venasque

㉑ 36 km (23 mi) southeast of Mont Ventoux, 16 km (12 mi) north of Gordes, 12 km (7 mi) southeast of Carpentras, 35 km (22 mi) northeast of Avignon.

Once the bishopric and capital of Comtat Venaissin, the large agricultural region east of Avignon, Venasque now only has a population of about 675 inhabitants. The village, tucked inside fortified walls, stands proudly on a hill overlooking the Carpentras Plain. With its sweeping views, stonework and masses of flowers, it's pretty enough to visit for atmosphere alone.

But if you're interested in early churches, head straight for the Merovingian **baptistery** behind the Église de Notre-Dame; it dates from the 6th century and is thus one of the oldest religious structures in France. Thought to be built on the site of a Roman temple to Diana or Venus, of which you can see columns recycled into chapel form, it retains its Greek-cross shape despite reconstruction in the 11th century. ⌑ *10 frs.* ☉ *Mon.–Tues., Thurs.–Sat., and Sun afternoon.*

Dining and Lodging

$$$ ✕⌑ **Auberge de la Fontaine.** This graceful old 18th-century house has been converted into a clever complex of apartments, each with a bedroom and fireplace salon, all but one in classic style, one contemporary. There are even kitchenettes, though the restaurant merits your full attention: Owner-chef Christian Soehlke brings Provençal sunshine to local lamb and pigeon, and knows the goats that provide his tiny cabri cheeses by name. There's a ground-floor bistro, too, for lighter meals. ⌑ *84210,* ☎ *04–90–66–02–96,* ℻ *04–90–66–13–14. 5 apartments. Air-conditioning, 2 restaurants, kitchenettes. MC, V.*

THE SORGUE AND MONTS DE VAUCLUSE

This gentle, rolling valley east of Avignon follows the course of the River Sorgue, which wells up from caverns below the arid hills of the Vaucluse plateau, gushes to the surface at Fontaine-de-Vaucluse, and rolls down to turn the mossy waterwheels in picturesque L'Isle-sur-la-Sorgue. The red-ochre terrain around Roussillon, the Romanesque symmetry of the Abbaye de Senanque, and the fashionable charms of Gordes punctuate a rugged countryside peppered with ancient stone bories.

L'Isle-sur-la-Sorgue

㉒ *23 km (14 mi) east of Avignon.*

Crisscrossed with lazy canals and alive with moss-covered waterwheels that once drove its silk, wool, and paper mills, this charming valley town retains its gentle appeal. Except on Sunday: Then this easygoing old town transforms itself into a Marrakech of marketeers, its streets crammed with antiques and brocante, its cafés swelling with crowds of chic bargain browsers making a day of it. Even hardcore modern types inured to treasure hunts enjoy the show as urbane couples with sweaters over shoulders squint discerningly through half lenses at monogrammed linen sheets, zinc washstands, china spice sets, Art Deco perfume bottles, tinted engravings, and the paintings of modern almost-masters. There are also street musicians, food stands groaning under rustic breads, vats of tapenade, cloth-lined baskets of spices, and miles of café tables offering ring-side seats to the spectacle.

On a non-market day, life returns to its mellow pace. There are plenty of antiques dealers holding forth year-round, but also fabric and interior design shops, bookstores, and food stores to explore. People curl up with paperbacks on park benches by shaded fountains and read international papers in cafés.

The token sight to see is L'Isle's 17th-century church, the **Collégiale Notre-Dame-des-Anges,** extravagantly decorated with gilt, faux marbre, and sentimental frescoes. Its double-colonnaded facade commands the center of the old town.

Dining and Lodging

$$–$$$ ✕ **La Prévôté.** With all the money you saved bargaining on that chipped Quimper vase, splurge on lunch at this discreet, pristine lavoir hidden off a backstreet courtyard. The cuisine is anything but bargain bin and has won top awards for chef Roland Mercier—try his creamed lentils with truffles, cannelloni filled with salmon and fresh chèvre, and tender duckling with lavender honey. The wine list is succinct and favors reasonably priced local reds. But evening and à la carte meals are an investment best suited to buyers of antiques rather than brocante. ⊠ *4 rue Jean-Jacques-Rousseau,* ☎ *04–90–38–57–29. Reservations essential. MC, V. Closed Mon. (Dec.–June), Nov., and two wks in Feb. No dinner Sun.*

$ ✕ **Lou Nego Chin.** In winter you'll sit shoulder to shoulder in the cramped but atmospheric dining room (chinoiserie linens, brightly hued tiles), but in summer tables are strewn across the quiet street, on a wooden deck along the river. Ask for a spot at the edge so you can watch the ducks play and order the inexpensive house wine and the 60-franc menu du jour, often a goat-cheese salad and a good and garlicky stew. ⊠ *12 quai Jean Jaurès,* ☎ *04–90–20–88–03. MC, V. Closed Mon. No dinner Sun.*

$–$$ ✕🏠 **Le Mas de Cure-Bourse.** This graceful old 18th-century postal-coach **★** stop is well outside the fray, snugly hedge-bound in the countryside amid fruit trees and fields. Here you can relax on 6 acres of green landscape, read by the large pool, and sleep in rooms freshly decked out in Provençal prints and painted country furniture. M. and Madame Pomarède, the new owners of this popular landmark, have kept their kitchen team and a loyal local following. Thus the meals are as memorable as ever: Whether by the grand old fireplace or on the terrace, you'll be served sophisticated home cooking with a local touch: stuffed zucchini flowers, pumpkin gnocchi, goat cheese with pistou (pesto) or tapenade (olive paste), and deliciously gooey chocolate cake with cherries. The restaurant is closed Monday; there's no lunch Tuesday. ⊠ *Route de Caumont,* ☎ *04–90–38–16–58,* 🗏𝖠𝖷 *04–90–38–52–31. 13 rooms. Restaurant, pool. MC, V. Closed 3 wks in Nov., first 2 wks in Jan.*

$ ✕🏠 **La Gueulardière.** After a Sunday glut of antiquing along the canals, you can dine and sleep in a setting full of collectible finds, from the school posters in the restaurant to the oak armoires and brass beds that furnish the simple lodgings, just up the street. Each room has French windows that open onto the enclosed garden courtyard, where you can enjoy a private breakfast in the shade. ⊠ *1 rue d'Apt, 84800,* ☎ *04–90–38–10–52,* 🗏𝖠𝖷 *04–90–20–83–70. 5 rooms. Restaurant. AE, DC, MC, V.*

Outdoor Activities and Sports

The **Provence Country Club** (in Saumane, ☎ 04–90–20–20–65) standing idyllically in the valley between L'Isle and Fontaine de Vaucluse, has a 18-hole (par 72) golf course, as well as a "compact" with nine holes and both grass and carpet practice ranges. Take D25 in the direction of Fontaine.

Shopping

Throughout the pretty back streets of L'Isle's old town (especially between place de l'Église and avenue de la Libération), there are boutiques spilling baskets full of tempting goods onto the sidewalk to lure you inside; most concentrate on home design and Provençal goods. **Sous l'Olivier** (⊠ 16 rue de la République, ☎ 04–90–20–68–90) is a food boutique crammed to the ceiling with precious bottles and jars of tapenade, fancy mustards, candies shaped like olives, and the house olive oil.

Of the dozens of antiques shops in L'Isle, one conglomerate concentrates some 40 dealers under the same roof: **L'Isle aux Brocantes** (⊠ 7 av. des Quatre Otages, ☎ 04−90−20−69−93). It's open Saturday−Monday. Higher end antiques are concentrated next door at the twinned shops of **Xavier Nicod and Gérard Nicod** (⊠ 9 av. des Quatre Otages, ☎ 04−90−38−35−50 or 04−90−38−07−20), arranged with a designer's eye for tasteful clutter. **Van Halewyck** (⊠ 15 quai de Rouget de L'Isle, ☎ 04−90−38−65−25) is a tiny shop crammed with old-masterly paintings.

Espace Béchard (⊠ 1 av. Jean-Charmasson, ☎ 04−90−20−81−40) throws 11 different dealers together, all with fabulously overscaled objects too big to carry home on the plane. **Maria** (⊠ across from the train station, 4 av. Julien Guigue, ☎ 04−90−38−58−02) features beautifully restored linens, including monogrammed linen sheets, lacy pillowcases, piqué throws, and *boutis* (Provençal quilts).

Fontaine de Vaucluse

❷❸ *7 km (4 mi) east of L'Isle sur la Sorgue, 30 km (19 mi) east of Avignon.*

★ The **Fontaine de Vaucluse,** for which the town is named, is a strange and beautiful natural phenomenon that has been turned into a charming yet slightly tacky tourist center—like a tiny Niagara Falls—and should not be missed if you're either a connoisseur of rushing water or a fan of foreign kitsch. There's no exaggerating the magnificence of the *fontaine* itself, a mysterious spring that gushes from a deep underground source that has been explored to a depth of 1,010 ft . . . so far. Framed by towering cliffs, a broad, pure pool wells up and spews dramatically over massive rocks down a gorge to the village, where its roar soothes and cools the tourists who crowd the riverfront cafés.

You must pay to park, then run a gauntlet of souvenir shops and tourist traps on your way to the top. But even if you plan to make a beeline past the kitsch, do stop in at the legitimate and informative **Moulin Vallis-Clausa.** A working paper mill, it demonstrates a reconstruction of a 15th-century waterwheel that drives timber crankshafts to mix rag pulp, while artisans roll and dry thick paper *à l'ancienne* (in the old manner). Observation is fascinating and free of charge, though it's almost impossible to resist buying note cards, posters, even lampshades fashioned from the pretty stuff. Fontaine was once a great industrial mill center, but its seven factories were closed by strikes in 1968 and never recovered. All the better for you today, since now you can enjoy this marvelous natural setting in peace. ☎ 04−90−20−34−14. ☺ *Nov.−Feb., Mon.−Sat. 9−12:30 and 2−6; Mar.−Apr. and Oct., Mon.−Sat. 9−12:30 and 2−6:30; May−June and Sept., Mon.−Sat. 9−12:30 and 2−7; July−Aug., Mon.−Sat. 9−7:30. Sun. open from 10 AM throughout the year.*

Fontaine even has its own ruined **Château,** perched romantically on a forested hilltop over the town and illuminated at night. First built around the year 1000 and embellished in the 13th century by the bishops of Cavaillon, it was destroyed in the 15th century and forms little more than a saw-tooth silhouette against the sky.

The Renaissance poet Petrarch, driven mad with unrequited love for a beautiful married woman named Laura, retreated to this valley to nurse his passion in a cabin with "one dog and only two servants."

He had met her in the heady social scene at the papal court in Avignon, where she was to die years later of the plague. Sixteen years in this wild isolation didn't ease the pain, but the serene setting inspired him to poetry, and his *Canzoniera* were dedicated to Laura's memory. The small **Musée-Bibliothèque Pétrarch,** built on the site of his stay, displays prints and engravings of the virtuous lovers, both in Avignon and Fontaine de Vaucluse. ☎ *04–90–20–37–20.* 🖃 *20 frs.* ☉ *Apr.–Sept., Wed.–Mon. 10–noon and 2–6; Oct., weekends only.*

Dining and Lodging

$$ ✕🖩 **Le Parc.** In a spectacular riverside setting in the shadow of the ruined château, this solid old hotel has basic, comfortable rooms (whitewashed stucco, all-weather carpet) with clean baths and no creaks. Five take in river views. The restaurant (closed Wednesday) spreads along the river in a pretty park with tables shaded by trellises heavy with grapes and trumpet vine. Moderately priced daily menus include river-fresh salmon, de rigueur in this setting. 🖃 *rue de Bourgades, 84800,* ☎ *04–90–20–31–57,* 🖷 *04–90–20–27–03. 12 rooms. Restaurant. AE, DC, MC, V. Closed Jan.–mid-Feb.*

$–$$ 🖩 **La Maison aux Fruits.** Before you enter, you know an artist lives here and that this small B&B run by Roseline Giorgis is no ordinary lodging. The carved front door and the painted woodwork set the tone for the faux marbre, murals, painted ceilings, and the owner's art collection inside. A lovely oval staircase takes you up to a sitting and dining room and a terrace; some rooms overlook the roaring river. There are also two little apartments that you may rent by the week. Some of the art works are for sale; aficionados may even be seduced to sign up for an art class here. 🖃 *rue de l'Isle de Sorgue, 84800,* ☎ *04–90–20–39–15,* 🖷 *04–90–20–27–08. 2 rooms, 2 apartments. No credit cards.*

$ 🖩 **Le Grand Jas.** In a renovated farmhouse just outside the nearby village of Lagnes, this little B&B has four comfortable, rustic rooms with exposed beams and Provençal prints. There's also a pleasant, high-ceilinged common area. With arrangements you can enjoy a table d'hôte dinner in the large kitchen/dining room. Lagnes makes a good base: it's a sweet hilltop village with a couple of small restaurants and a café-bar. 🖃 *rue du Bariot, Lagnes (5 km [3 mi] from Fontaine de Vaucluse via D100) 84800,* ☎ *04–90–20–25–12,* 🖷 *04–90–20–29–17. 4 rooms. Dining room. No credit cards.*

Gordes

㉔ *10 km (6 mi) east of Fontaine de Vaucluse, 39 km (24 mi) east of Avignon.*

Gordes is only a short distance from Fontaine de Vaucluse, but you need to wind your way south, east, and then north on D100A, D100, D2, and D15 to skirt the impassable hillside. It's a lovely drive through dry, rocky country covered with wild lavender and scrub oak and may tempt you to a picnic or a walk. How surprising, then, to leave such wildness behind and enter resort country. Gordes was once a famous, unspoiled hilltop village; it has now become a famous, unspoiled hilltop village surrounded by luxury vacation homes, modern hotels, restaurants, and B&Bs. No matter: The ancient stone village still rises above the valley in painterly hues of honey gold, and its mosaiclike cobbled streets—lined with boutiques, galleries, and real estate offices—still wind steep and narrow to its Renaissance château.

The only way to see the interior of the **Château** is to view its collection of mind-stretching photo paintings by pop artist Pol Mara, who lived until his death in Gordes. It's worth the price to look at the fabulously decorated stone fireplace, created in 1541; it covers an entire wall with neoclassic designs and stretches to frame two doors. ☎ 04–90–72–02–75. ⊒ 25 frs. ⊘ Wed.–Mon. 10–noon and 2–6.

Head downhill from the château and follow signs to the **belvédère** overlooking the miniature fields and farms below. From this height all those modern vacation homes blend in with the ancient mas—except for the aqua blue pools.

★ Just outside Gordes, on a lane heading north from D2, follow signs to the **Village des Bories.** Found throughout this region of Provence, the bizarre and fascinating little stone hovels called *bories* are concentrated some 20 strong in an ancient community. Their origins are provocatively vague: Built as shepherds' shelters with tight-fitting, mortarless stone in a hivelike form, they may date back to the Celts, the Ligurians, even the Iron Age—and were inhabited or used for sheep through the 18th century. ☎ 04–90–72–03–48. ⊒ 30 frs. ⊘ Daily 9–sunset or 8, whichever comes first.

★ In a wild valley some 4 km (2 mi) north of Gordes (via D177), the beautiful 12th-century **Abbaye de Sénanque** floats above a redolent sea of lavender (in July and August). An architecture student's dream of neat cubes, cylinders, and pyramids, its pure Romanesque form alone is worth contemplating in any context. But in this arid, rocky setting the graystone building seems to have special resonance—ancient, organic, with a bit of the borie about it. Its **church** is a model of symmetry and balance. Begun in 1150 and completed at the dawn of the 13th century, it has no decoration but still touches the soul with its chaste beauty. The adjoining **cloister**, from the 12th century, is almost as pure: Its barrel-vaulted galleries frame double rows of discreet, abstract columns and pillars; you'll find no child-devouring demons or lurid biblical tales here. Next door, the enormous vaulted **dormitory** contains an exhibition on the abbey's construction, and the **refectory** shelters a display on the history of Cistercian abbeys. In 1969 the abbey's Cistercian monks moved to St-Honorat Island, off the shore of Cannes, and the buildings here, under the stewardship of a few remaining monks, are now part of a cultural center presenting concerts and exhibitions. ☎ 04–90–72–05–72. ⊒ 20 frs. ⊘ Mar.–Oct., Mon.–Sat. 10–noon and 2–6, Sun. 2–6; Nov.–Feb., weekdays 2–5, weekends 2–6.

Dining and Lodging

$$$ ✕ **Comptoir du Victuailler.** Directly across from the château, this tiny but deluxe bistro serves an international clientele without a trace of condescension, but rather a real enthusiasm for France's—and Provence's—best. At lunch time, when tables spill out onto the square, the menu features daily aïoli, a smorgasbord of fresh cod, and lightly steamed vegetables crowned with pestled garlic mayonnaise. Evenings are reserved for intimate, formal indoor meals à la carte—roast Luberon lamb, beef with truffle sauce, or a salty-sweet raspberry-sauced pintade (guinea fowl). Leave room for the chocolate cake and St-Honoré (airy vanilla-cream pastry), and take the owner's advice on lesser known, local finds in wine. The '30s-style bistro tables and architectural lines are a relief from Gordes' ubiquitous rustic-chic. ⊠ Pl. du Château, ☎ 04–90–72–01–31. Reservations essential. MC, V. Closed mid-Nov.–Easter, and Wed. Sept.–May. No dinner Tues.

$$ ✕🛏 **Ferme de la Huppe.** This 17th-century stone farmhouse with a well in the courtyard, a swimming pool in the garden, and rooms decked with pretty prints and secondhand finds is all alone in the lavender-scented countryside outside Gordes. What more could you want? How

about roast guinea fowl in saffron and ginger and an icy bottle of local rosé? The family chef will be glad to serve you by the poolside terrace, but reserve ahead: The restaurant (closed Thursday) is as popular as the hotel. ⊠ *Les Pourquiers (3 km/2 mi east of Gordes), 84220,* ☎ *04–90–72–12–25,* FAX *04–90–72–01–83. 8 rooms. Restaurant, pool. MC, V. Closed Nov.–Mar.*

$–$$ ✕☷ **La Renaissance.** Whether you eat in the grand beamed dining hall, complete with Renaissance fireplace, or lounge under the plane trees by the fountain, you'll find an easy mix of city bistro and country Provençal. A blackboard menu lists regional specialties—aïoli, bourride—and live piano jazz livens things up at night. Six rooms upstairs have quarry tile, pristine white quilts, and double windows that open over the place du Château, but two of them share a toilet down the hall. Top-floor rooms are slick and modern, but windows are low and cheat the view. ⊠ *Pl. du Château, 84220,* ☎ *04–90–72–02–02,* FAX *04–90–72–05–11. 6 rooms, 4 with bath. Restaurant, bar. MC, V. Closed Jan.–mid-Feb.*

$$$ ☷ **Domaine de l'Enclos.** A thorough face-lift in the winter of 1998 has left this cluster of private stone cottages looking lovelier than ever, with newly laid antique tiles and fresh faux-patinas to keep it looking fashionably old. There are panoramic views and a pool, babysitting services and swingsets, and an atmosphere that is surprisingly warm and familial for an inn of this sophistication. Half-board arrangements (even for one night stays) keep costs down; in winter, when the popular restaurant calms down, the demi-pension guests are treated like house guests. Though they've owned it since 1982, Serge and Nadia Lafitte have moved on-site now, making it all the more a chambre-d'hôte experience. ⊠ *rte. de Sénanque, 84220,* ☎ *04–90–72–71–00,* FAX *04–90–72–03–03. 7 rooms, 6 apartments. Restaurant, pool. AE, MC, V.*

$$–$$$ ☷ **Les Romarins.** At this small inn in a converted 18th-century *bastide* (country house), you can gaze across the valley at Gordes while you breakfast on a sheltered terrace. Rooms are clean, well lighted, and feel spacious. Be sure to ask for a room with a valley view, especially No. 1, in the main building, from whose white-curtained windows you can see forever, or the one in the atelier that has a terrace; front rooms overlook a busy road. Warm Oriental rugs, antique furniture around the fireplace in the sitting room, and a pool add to your contentment. ⊠ *rte. de Sénanque, 84220,* ☎ *04–90–72–12–13,* FAX *04–90–72–13–13. 10 rooms. Pool. AE, MC, V. Closed mid-Jan.–mid-Feb.*

Roussillon

㉕ *14 km (9 mi) southeast of Gordes, 43 km (27 mi) southeast of Avignon.*

In shades of deep rose and russet, this hilltop cluster of houses blends into the red-ochre cliffs from which its stone was quarried. The ensemble of buildings and jagged, hand-cut slopes are equally dramatic, and views from the top look over a landscape of artfully eroded bluffs that Georgia O'Keeffe would have loved.

Unlike neighboring hill villages, there's little of historic architectural detail here; the pleasure of a visit lies in the richly varied colors that change with the light of day, and in the views of the contrasting countryside, where dense-shadowed greenery sets off the red stone with Cézanne-esque severity. There are pleasant *placettes* (tiny squares) to linger in nonetheless, and a Renaissance fortress tower crowned with a clock in the 19th century; just past it, you can take in expansive panoramas of forest and ochre cliffs.

This famous vein of natural ochre, which spreads some 25 km (15 mi) along the foot of the Vaucluse plateau, has been mined for centuries. You can visit the old **Usine Mathieu de Roussillon** (Roussillon's Mathieu Ochre Works) to learn more about ochre's extraction and its modern uses; though it has long since been closed as a mine, it functions today as the Conservatoire des Ocres et Pigments Appliqués (Conservatory of Ochres and Applied Pigments). There are explanatory exhibits, ochre powders for sale, and guided tours in English with advance request. ⊠ *On D104 southeast of town,* ☎ *04–90–05–66–69.* ☾ *Mar.–Nov. daily 10–7.*

THE LUBERON

" 'Have you ever been to the Luberon? Between Avignon and Aix. It's getting a little chichi, specially in August, but it's beautiful—old villages, mountains, no crowds, fantastic light. . . Leave the autoroute at Cavaillon, and go towards Apt.'. . . Murat poured the red wine and raised his glass. '*Bonnes vacances,* my friend. I'm serious about the Luberon; it's a little special. You should try it.' "

When Peter Mayle, no doubt barefoot by the pool, typed these words in his first novel *Hotel Pastis*, the world took a map in hand. They had already taken note when his chronicles *A Year in Provence* and *Toujours Provence* painted a delicious picture of backcountry sunshine, copious feasts and cartoonishly droll local rustics; now they had directions to get there.

They came. They climbed over Mayle's hedges for autographs. They built pink and yellow houses, booked his favorite restaurant tables, traced his footsteps with the book in hand. And not only the English: *A Year in Provence* sold 4 million copies and was translated into 20 languages, including French (where its sequel corrected his grammar to *Provence Toujours*). His name is a household word here (Peet-aire Mayeel) and doesn't always bring the oft-described grin and shrug from the locals. Perhaps that's why Mayle abandoned his idyll for greener pastures, and the fields of asparagus and grapevines he sharecropped now serve strangers at the oft-described table of immovable stone.

The dust has settled a bit, and despite the occasional Mayle Country bus tour rattling through from Cavaillon, the Luberon has returned to its former way of life. There were always Lacoste shirts here, and converted mas with pools (after all, Mayle's mas was already gentrified when they installed central heating), and sophisticated restaurants catering to seekers of the Simple Life. They're all still here, but so are the extraordinarily beautiful countryside, the golden perched villages, the blue-black forests, and the sun-bleached rocks.

The broad mountain called the Luberon is protected nowadays by the *Parc Naturel Régional du Luberon,* but that doesn't mean you should expect rangers, campsites, and his-and-hers outhouses. It has always been and remains private land, though building and forestry are allowed in moderation and hiking trails have been cleared.

Although the Luberon is made up of two distinct regions, only the more civilized Petit Luberon west of Apt is covered in this chapter. If you're a nature lover, you may want to venture into the wilder Grand Luberon, especially to the summit called Mourre Nègre.

OLD AS THE HILLS

SINCE THE CAVE PAINTINGS of Lascaux, man has extracted ochre from the earth, using its extraordinary palette of colors to make the most of nature's play between earth and light. Grounded in these earth-based pigments, the frescoes of Giotto and Michelangelo glow from within, and the houses of Tuscany and Provence seem to draw color from the land itself—and to drink light from the sky.

The rusty hues of iron hydroxide are the source of all this luminosity, intimately allied with the purest of clays. Extracted from the ground in chunks and washed to separate it from its quartz-sand base, it is ground to fine powder and mixed as a binder with chalk and sand. Applied to the stone walls of Provençal houses, this ancient blend gives the region its quintessential repetoire of warm yellows and golds, brick, sienna, and umber.

In answer to the acrylic imitations slathered on new constructions in garish shades of hot pink and canary yellow (following a Côte d'Azur trend), there is an ochre revival underway, and you can easily spot the difference in the way naturally stuccoed buildings blend organically with their setting. Even the fashionable faux-weathered facades created by London and Paris designers can't hold a candle to the refracted light and velvety matte tones of the real thing, drawn from the very earth that supports its walls, sensual, essential, and primordial.

Oppède-le-Vieux

㉖ *25 km (15½ mi) southeast of Avignon, 15 km (9 mi) southwest of Gordes.*

Heading toward Apt on D22 out of Avignon, follow signs right into the vineyards, toward Oppède. You'll occasionally be required to follow signs for Oppède-le-Village, but your goal will be marked with the symbol of *monuments historiques*: Oppède-le-Vieux. A Byronesque tumble of ruins arranged against an overgrown rocky hillside, Oppède's charm—or part of it—lies in its preservation. Taken over by writers and artists who choose to live here and restore but not develop it, the village offers a café or two but little more. Bring a lunch, wander, and contemplate.

Cross the village square, pass through the old city gate, and climb up steep trails past restored houses to the church known as **Notre-Dame-d'Alydon.** First built in the 13th century, its blunt buttresses were framed into side chapels in the 16th century; you can still see the points of stoned-in gothic windows above. The marvelous hexagonal belltower sprouts a lean, mean gargoyle from each angle. It once served as part of the village's fortifications; the views from the plateau it dominates overlook the broad valley toward Ménerbes.

Head left past the cliff-edge wall, plunge into the rock tunnel, and clamber up to the ruins of the **Château,** first built in the 13th century and transformed in the 15th century. From the left side of its great square tower, look down into the dense fir forests of the Luberon's north face.

Ménerbes

㉗ *5 km (3 mi) east of Oppède-le-Vieux, 30 km (19 mi) southeast of Avignon.*

As you drive along D188 between Oppède and Ménerbes, the rolling rows of grapevines are punctuated by stone farmhouses. But something is different: These farmhouses have electric gates, tall arborvitae hedges, and swimming pools. Peter Mayle isn't the only outsider to have vacationed here and contrived to stay.

The town of Ménerbes itself clings to a long, thin hilltop over this sought-after valley, looming over the surrounding forests like a great stone ship. At its prow juts the **Castellet,** a 15th-century fortress. At its stern rears up the 13th-century **citadelle.** These redoubtable fortifications served the Protestants well during the War of Religions—until the Catholics wore them down with a 15-month siege.

A campanile tops the Hôtel de Ville (Town Hall) on pretty **Place de l'Horloge** (Clock Square), where you can admire the delicate stonework on the arched portal and mullioned windows of a Renaissance house. Just past the tower on the right, you'll reach an overlook taking in views towards Gordes, Roussillon, and Mont Ventoux.

But what you really came to see is **Peter Mayle's house,** right? Do its current owners a favor and give it wide berth: After years of tour buses spilling the curious into the private driveway to crane their necks and snap pictures, the heirs to the stone picnic table, the pool, and Faustin's grapevines wish the books had never been written.

Dining and Lodging

$$$ ⊞ **Le Roy Soleil.** In the imposing shadow of the Luberon and the hilltop village of Ménerbes, this luxurious country inn has pulled out all stops on comfort and decor: marble and granite bathrooms, wrought-iron beds, and coordinated fabrics. But the integrity of its 17th-century building, with thick stone walls and groin vaults and beams, redeems it just short of pretentiousness and makes it a lovely place to escape. ⊠ *rte. des Beaumettes, 84560,* ☎ *04–90–72–25–61,* ⅏ *04–90–72–36–55. 19 rooms. Restaurant, bar, pool, tennis court. MC, V. Closed mid-Nov.–mid-Mar.*

Lacoste

㉘ *7 km (4 mi) east of Ménerbes, 37 km (23 mi) southeast of Avignon.*

Little but jagged ruins remain of the once magnificent **Château de Sade,** where the Marquis de Sade (1740–1814) spent some 30 years of his life, mostly hiding out. Exploits both literary and real, judged obscene by various European courts, kept him in and out of prison despite a series of escapes. His mother-in-law finally turned him in to authorities, and he was locked away in the Paris Bastille, where he passed the time writing stories and plays. Written during his time in the Bastille, *120 journées de Sodome (120 Days of Sodom)* featured a Black-Forest château suspiciously similar in form and design to his Lacoste home. The once-sumptuous château was destroyed with particular relish in the Revolution. It is privately owned now, and being restored wall by wall; you can only view it from the outside. But the village itself is worth a side trip for its pretty car-free streets and eagle's-nest views.

Bonnieux

㉙ *5 km (3 mi) southeast of Lacoste, 42 km (26 mi) south east of Avignon.*

The most impressive of the Luberon's hilltop villages, Bonnieux rises out of the arid hills in a jumble of honey-color cubes that change color subtly as the day progresses. The village is wrapped in crumbling ramparts and dug into bedrock and cliff. Most of its sharply raked streets take in wide-angle valley views, though you'll get the best view from the pine-shaded grounds of the 12th-century church, reached by stone steps that wind past tiny niche houses. Shops, galleries, cafés, and fashionable restaurants abound here, but they don't dominate: It's possible to lose yourself in a back *ruelle* (small street) most of the year.

Dining and Lodging

$$–$$$ ✕ **Le Fournil.** In a natural grotto deep in stone, lighted by candles and arty torchères, this restaurant would be memorable even without trendy decor (jade and gold cement tiles, mix-and-match jacquard linens) and stylishly-presented Provençal cuisine. But add adventurous dishes such as tomato-crisped pigs'-feet *galette* (patty), subtle seafood, an informed wine list, and the option of sitting on the terrace by the fountain, and you have an experience to note in your travel diary. ⊠ *5 pl. Carnot, 84480,* ☎ *04–90–75–83–62,* 🗺 *04–90–75–96–19. MC, V. Closed mid-Nov.–mid-Dec., mid-Jan.–mid-Feb., and Mon. No lunch Sat. July–Aug.*

$$–$$$ 🏨 **Hostellerie du Prieuré.** Not every hotel has its own private chapel,
★ but this gracious inn holds forth in an 18th-century abbey and has kept its noble details. The decor is vivid and warm, from the saffron-color bar to the leather chairs in the firelighted salon to the dining room glowing with Roussillon ochre. Summer meals and breakfasts are served in the enclosed garden oasis, which makes you feel like you're no longer in the village center. Rooms have plush carpets and antiques; one has a very small, sheltered terrace overlooking the chapel bell. Ask about the tiny, low-priced room with a toilet down the hall: Its double windows open over the garden. The Coutaz family has been in the hotel business since Napoléon III, and it shows. ⊠ *In center of village, 84480,* ☎ *04–90–75–80–78,* 🗺 *04–90–75–96–00. 10 rooms. Restaurant. MC, V. Closed Nov.–Feb.*

$$ 🏨 **Le Clos du Buis.** At this Gîtes de France B&B, whitewash and quarry
★ tiles, lovely tiled baths, and carefully juxtaposed antiques create a regional look in rooms. Public spaces, with scrubbed floorboards, a fireplace, and exposed stone, are free for your use around the clock. It even has a pool and a pretty garden, and it's all overlooking the valley from the village center. ⊠ *rue Victor Hugo, 84480,* ☎ *04–90–75–88–48,* 🗺 *04–90–75–88–57. 6 rooms. Pool. MC, V.*

$–$$ 🏨 **Caesar.** With its avocado-green carpet and creaky '60s decor, this small hotel near the top of the village is nothing special in itself. But seven of its rooms have private balconies with views across the valley to hilltop villages and the Luberon Hills. The hotel's restaurant also serves up the same marvelous view and prix-fixe menus starting at 99 francs. ⊠ *pl. de la Linerté, 84880,* ☎ *04–90–75–80–18,* 🗺 *04–90–75–99–35. 15 rooms. Restaurant. MC, V.*

En Route Between Bonnieux and Lourmarin, the *départemental* roads D36 and D943 wind dramatically through deep backcountry, offering the only passage over the spine of the Luberon. Bone-dry and bristling with scrub oak, pine, coarse broom, and wild lavender, it's a landscape reminiscent of Greece or Sicily. If you climb into the hills, you won't get views; this is landlocked, isolated terrain, but it's wildly beautiful.

Lourmarin

 12 km (7 mi) southeast of Bonnieux, 54 km (33 mi) southeast of Avignon.

The village of Lourmarin itself lies low-slung in the valley, a sprawl of manicured green. Its **Château** is its main draw, privately restored in the 1920s to appealing near-perfection. Of the old wing (15th century) and the new (begun in 1525), the latter is prettiest, with a broad-ranging art collection, rare old furniture, and ornate stone fireplaces—including one with exotic Aztec caryatids. ☎ *04–90–68–15–23.* ✆ *30 frs.* ☉ *Guided tours (45 minutes long) daily 11, 2:30, 3:30, and 4:30; July–Aug. every half hour.*

Albert Camus loved Lourmarin from the moment he discovered it in the 1930s. After he won his Nobel prize in 1957 he bought a house here, and lived in it until his death in 1960. He is buried in the village **cemetery.**

THE VAUCLUSE A TO Z

Arriving and Departing

By Bus

There's a good bus network out of Avignon to most points in the Luberon and the Alpilles; check the posted schedules at Avignon's **gare routière** (bus station; ☎ 04–90–82–07–35) next to the train station.

By Car

The A6/A7 toll (*péage*) expressway channels all traffic from Paris to the south. At Orange A7 splits to the southeast and leads directly to Avignon and N100 (in the direction of Apt), which dives straight east into the Luberon. To reach Vaison and the Mont-Ventoux region, exit before Avignon going toward Carpentras on D42. D36 jags south from N100 and leads you on a gorgeous chase over the backbone of the Luberon, via Bonnieux and Lourmarin; from there it's a straight shot to Aix and Marseille or to the Côte d'Azur. Or you can shoot back west up D73 to Cavaillon and Avignon.

By Plane

Marseille's **Marignane Airport** (an hour's drive from Avignon) is served by frequent flights from Paris and London. The smaller **Avignon Airport** itself has frequent daily flights from Paris. In summer Delta Airlines flies direct from New York to Nice, itself 200 km (124 mi) and about two hours' drive from Marseille.

By Train

Trains arrive from all points north—Paris, Strasbourg, Nantes, and Bordeaux—in Marseille; those from Paris and Strasbourg pass through Orange and Avignon. Many of these routes have overnight runs, with *couchettes* (sleeper bunks) and, sometimes, *wagons-lits* (minicabins with hotel-like service). A high-speed TGV (*Trains à Grande Vitesse*) line connects Paris and Orange (3 hrs 20 mins) and then Avignon (3 hrs 30 mins). After that, secondary connections in this area are slim to nonexistent: Only Tarascon rates a rail stop near the Alpilles, while L'Isle-sur-la-Sorgue is the farthest you'll get into the Luberon. (☞ Train Travel *in* the Gold Guide for more information.)

Getting Around

By Bus

A reasonable network of private bus services (called, confusingly enough, *cars*) links places not served or poorly served by trains. Ask for bus schedules at train stations and tourist offices, or head for Avignon's **gare routière** (bus station; ☎ 04–90–82–07–35). Avignon has a sizable one, with posted schedules; buses branch out into every corner of the Vaucluse from here. **Cars Lieutaud** (☎ 04–90–86–36–75) has a booth just outside the Avignon train station, offering daily bus excursions into different regions—for instance, the Luberon, Vaison, and the Alpilles. Some of them are one-way runs, useful as simple transport; others are round-trip guided tours.

By Car

With spokes shooting out in every direction from Avignon and A7, you'll have no problem accessing the Vaucluse. The main *routes nationales* (national routes, or secondary highways) offer fairly direct links via D942 toward Orange and Mont Ventoux and via N100 into the Luberon. Negotiating the roads to L'Isle-sur-la-Sorgue and Fontaine de la Vaucluse requires a careful mix of map and sign reading, often at high speeds around suburban *giratoires* (rotaries). But by the time you strike out into the hills and the tiny roads—one of the best parts of the Vaucluse—give yourself over to road signs and pure faith: As is the case throughout France, directions are indicated by village name only, with route numbers given as a small-print afterthought. Of course, this means you have to recognize the minor villages en route.

By Train

The Vaucluse is not a territory to explore in depth by train, though if you're passing through, you can venture out of Avignon as far as Orange, L'Isle-sur-la-Sorgue, Cavaillon, and Tarascon; buses connect from Cavaillon into the Luberon and Les Alpilles.

Contacts and Resources

Bed & Breakfasts

Chambres d'hôtes (bed-and-breakfasts) offer simple lodging, usually in the hosts' home, with breakfast and a warm, regional welcome often included. This region has a plethora of B&Bs, perhaps because of the onslaught of English and Americans looking for a simpler way of life, and all that extra space in the barn; if you prefer to speak English, there's a good chance you'll find a lodging owned by an "Anglo-Saxon." The French national network, **Gîtes de France** (☞ Lodging *in* the Gold Guide) lists B&Bs that have been rated. For chambres d'hôtes regulated by the national network, contact **Vaucluse Gîtes de France** (✉ pl. Campana, by the Papal Palace in Avignon; B.P. 164, 84008 Avignon cedex 1, ☎ 04–90–85–45–00).

Car Rental

AVIGNON

Avignon, as a major rail crossroads and springboard for the Vaucluse, has plenty of car rental agencies, and it's fairly easy to get out of town toward other destinations. **Avis** (☎ 04–90–27–96–10) has an office in the Avignon rail station. **Budget** (✉ bd. St-Roch, ☎ 04–90–86–63–36) is to your left just as you leave the train station. **Hertz** (✉ 4 bd. St-Michel, ☎ 04–90–82–37–67) is on the station's right, by the bus station.

L'ISLE-SUR-LA-SORGUE

You can even penetrate as far as L'Isle-sur-la-Sorgue by train and then rent from **Avis** (✉ 58 Zone Industrielle Grande Marine, ☎ 04–90–38–03–60) or **Budget** (✉ rue André Autheman, ☎ 04–90–20–64–13).

ORANGE

In Orange, **Avis** (✉ 19 av. Charles de Gaulle, ☎ 04–90–34–11–00) has a location by the train station; cars must be reserved in advance.

If you telephone **Budget** (⊠ 42 bd. Edouard Daladier, ☎ 04–90–34–00–34), they'll pick you up at the station and transport you to the office.

Guided Tours

A guided tour of the **Popes' Palace** (⊠ pl. du Palais, ☎ 04–90–27–50–00) in Avignon is worth the effort, as the structure was stripped during the Revolution and requires some degree of historic background to fully appreciate. Entry is 40 francs and includes the choice of a guided tour or an individual audio guide.

An accompanied tour of **Avignon's old town** is given by the tourist office from April through October, leaving from its headquarters (⊠ 41 cours Jean-Jaurès, ☎ 04–90–82–65–11) Tuesday and Thursday at 10 AM.

Daily **bus excursions** into different regions, with commentary, are offered by Cars Lieutaud (☎ 04–90–86–36–75); there's a booth just outside the Avignon train station.

Outdoor Activities and Sports

Two *grandes randonnées* (national hiking trails GR9-97 and GR92) follow the slopes and crest of the Luberon; head out from Oppède, in the northwest, or Lourmarin, in the southeast. For regional information, write to the Comité Départemental de la Randonnée Pédestre (⊠ 307 av. Foch, Orange, ☎ 04–90–51–14–86). For more information, *see* Hiking *in* the Gold Guide.

If you want to see the countryside by bike, **Vélo Loisir en Luberon** (⊠ B.P. 14, 04280 Cereste, ☎ 04–92–79–05–82) suggests itineraries (principally between Cavaillon and Forcalquier) and accommodations; they will even transport your luggage.

Travel Agencies

AVIGNON

Havas/American Express (⊠ 35 rue de la République, ☎ 04–90–80–66–80. **Nouvelles Frontières** ⊠ 14 rue Carnot, ☎ 04–90–82–31–32).

L'ISLE-SUR-LA-SORGUE

Rév'Alizés Voyages (⊠ 25 quai Jean Jaurès, ☎ 04–90–20–80–40).

ORANGE

Havas (⊠ 34 rue de la République, ☎ 04–90–11–44–44).

VAISON-LA-ROMAINE

Lieutaud Voyages (⊠ av. Choralies, ☎ 04–90–36–09–90).

Vacation Rentals

Gîtes de France is a nationwide organization that rents vacation housing, often of exceptional regional charm (☞ Lodging *in* the Gold Guide and Close-Up Box: The Gîte Way *in* Chapter 1). The Vaucluse is especially well disposed to rentals, as part of the appeal of a visit here means escaping from the usual rush of obligatory sightseeing to enjoy mouthwatering produce markets and low-key walks through the countryside. A few houses even have private pools and cost up to 7,000 francs per week, but most are reasonably priced compared to hotel stays, even for two people. For information about rentals in this region, contact the **Vaucluse Gîtes de France** (⊠ pl. Campana, by the Popes' Palace in Avignon; B.P. 164, 84008 Avignon cedex 1, ☎ 04–90–85–45–00); you can get a catalog at the office (for next time) or request one in writing or by phone.

Visitor Information

The **Comité Départemental du Tourisme de Vaucluse** (⊠ B.P. 147, 84008, Avignon Cedex 1) accepts written queries only; streamline your request and specify your needs by category (lodging, restaurants, general sights, biking).

The tourist offices of major towns covered in this chapter can be visited, phoned, faxed, or addressed by mail. **Avignon** (✉ 41 cours Jean-Jaurès, 84008, ☎ 04–90–82–65–11, FAX 04–90–82–95–03). **Bonnieux** (✉ 7 pl. Carnot, 84480, ☎ 04–90–75–91–90). **Cavaillon** (for information on smaller villages in the Luberon; ✉ pl. François Tourel, 84300, ☎ 04–90–71–32–01). **Châteauneuf-du-Pape** (✉ pl. du Portail, 84230, ☎ 04–90–83–71–08, FAX 04–90–83–50–34). **Gordes** (✉ Salle des Gardes du Château, 84220, ☎ 04–90–72–02–75, FAX 04–90–72–04–39). **L'Isle-sur-la-Sorgue** (✉ pl. de l'Église, 84800, ☎ 04–90–38–04–78, FAX 04–90–38–35–43). **Orange** (✉ 5 cours A. Briand, 84100, ☎ 04–90–34–70–88, FAX 04–90–34–99–62). **Roussillon** (✉ pl. de la Poste, 84220, ☎ 04–90–05–60–25). **Vaison-la-Romaine** (✉ pl. du Chanoine Sautel, B.P. 53, 84110, ☎ 04–90–36–02–11, FAX 04–90–28–76–04).

4 Aix, Marseille, and the Central Coast

Aubagne, Cassis, and the Iles d'Hyères

This is the land of Cézanne and Pagnol—a rough-hewn and fiercely beautiful landscape that tapers to a coastline of pine-studded cliffs and enchanting fishing ports. Sophisticated Aix-en-Provence stands aloof from Marseille, tough, gorgeous, and larger than life, yet the backcountry between them ambles along at a 19th-century pace of boules, pastis, and country markets. Cassis and Bandol mean wine to some and waterfronts to others. Off the mainland, the Iles d'Hyères are a car-free paradise.

CÉZANNE painted this countryside in daubs of russet and black-green, the rough-cut structure of bluff and twisted pine inspiring a building-block approach to painting that for others jelled into Cubism. Marcel Pagnol painted pictures with words: the smells of thyme and rosemary crunching underfoot, the sounds of thunder rumbling behind rain-starved hills, the quiet joy of opening shutters at dawn to a chorus of blackbirds in the olive grove. Both Cézanne and Pagnol were native sons of this region east of the Rhône who were inspired to eloquence by the primordial landscape and its echoes of antiquity—and the world continues to seek out the understated wonders they described.

A visit to this region involves the best of cities, seaside, and arid backcountry. Aix is a small, manageable city with a leisurely pace and a concentration of arts, due in part to its university life. Marseille offers the yang to Aix's ying: Its brash style, bold monuments, and spectacular sun-washed waterfront center are reminiscent of Naples or modern Athens; it is much maligned and unfairly neglected by visitors. Up in the dry inland hills, Pagnol's hometown of Aubagne gives a glimpse of local life, with a big farmers' market in the plane-tree-lined town center and makers of *santons* (terra-cotta figurines) at every turn. The lovely port-village of Cassis and the busy beach town of Bandol allow time to watch the tides come and go, though for the ultimate ocean retreat, take the boat that leaves for the almost tropical Iles d'Hyères.

Pleasures and Pastimes

Beaches
Wherever there's water in France, beaches of every shape and substance fill with sun lovers from June to September. The most popular beach resort is Bandol, but for a quieter retreat, head for genteel Cassis. The shipbuilding port town of La Ciotat has the most sandy-beach surface at the Clos des Plages, just beyond the pleasure-boat port.

Boat Rides
If you find yourself without a yacht on this wild and lovely coastline, it's easy to jump on a tourist cruiser, whether you putter from *calanque* (rocky finger inlet) to *calanque* between Marseille and Cassis or commute to the car-free Iles d'Hyères. Many are glass-bottomed for underwater viewing, and most allow you to climb into the top deck and face the bracing wind as you buck the waves.

Dining
Aix is one of the capitals of olive-oil production in Provence, and its market tables groan with the weight of industrial-scale jugs of the stuff. Far more than a medium here, it takes center stage at the table: a pool of chartreuse encircles goat cheese, a fillet of sea bass shimmers on a mirror of green-gold. The olives themselves—gleaming beads of briny salt fruit—figure everywhere, in every degree of ripeness and marinade imaginable, scooped from vats into tiny bowls to accompany the aperitif. Ground into a caviarlike spread called *tapenade,* made even more pungent by the mix of capers, anchovies, and garlic, the local olives appear on toast or grace a rosy leg of lamb.

But it's in leaving the highlands that you come upon the star cuisine of this region: Marseille and its environs have some of the finest seafood dishes in France, cooked robustly with garlic and flush with the fruits of the adjacent sea. It's here, more than anywhere on the southern coast, that you find authentic bouillabaisse, the quintessential fish stew of Provence. In it, chunks of Mediterranean fish otherwise too ugly to market—*rascasse, congre, grondin*—float with shellfish in a powerful broth of tomato-red fish stock, perfumed with garlic, onion, fennel, herbs, and—a must—orange peel and saffron. The simmered concoction (*bouillir,* for boiled, and *abaisser,* for reduced) is served in two courses: First the broth is poured over bread slices; it is then followed by a parade of tender fish. A dollop of *rouille* (chili peppers and garlic whipped into olive-oil paste) gives an extra jolt to the broth. Because of the price of fresh seafood, an authentic bouillabaisse will set you back from 200 to 250 francs; order a bottle of chilled Cassis and enjoy the ritual.

If bouillabaisse is too rich for your blood, the ubiquitous *soupe de poisson* (fish soup) is an affordable alternative: Less subtly seasoned and stirred to a thick velouté, it appears as a first-course option on just about every regional menu. Spread the oil-brushed croutons with rouille and float them in the soup with a sprinkle of ground cheese.

Where you eat in this region is often as wonderful as what you eat: Outdoor tables pepper the sidewalks of Marseille and Aix nearly year-round, and coastal restaurants vie to give you the best sea views.

CATEGORY	COST*
$$$$	over 400 frs
$$$	250–400 frs
$$	125–250 frs
$	under 125 frs

per person for a three-course meal, including tax (20.6%) and tip but not wine

Hiking

The walk from Cassis to the Calanques is one of the most dramatic in France, with cliff-top views over the ocean and clambering descents to intimate inlet beaches. In the hills above Marseille, so beloved by Pagnol, you can still follow his childhood trails and stand on the spot from which Ugolin screamed, *"Manon, je t'aime!"* (Manon, I love you!) in *Manon des Sources* (*Manon of the Springs*). The mountain called Ste-Victoire, often painted by Cézanne, affords beautiful hikes and views despite being burned by wildfires in 1989. Contact the Bouches-du-Rhône departmental tourist office (☞ Aix, Marseille, and the Central Coast A to Z, *below*) for information about hikes and walks in the area.

Lodging

This is no longer converted *mas* (farmhouse) country. Nonetheless, hotels in this region favor Provençal decor and aim to provide outdoor space at its loveliest, from gardens where breakfast is served under parasols of pines shading pools. As in all of France, hotels book up well in advance for July and August. If you plan to spend at least a week in the region, look into renting a *gîte* (vacation rental); those managed by Gîtes de France in the Bouches-du-Rhône and Var are often in inviting old houses and are always in rural settings (☞ Chapter 1 and the Gold Guide for more information).

CATEGORY	COST*
$$$$	Over 800 frs
$$$	550–800 frs
$$	300–550 frs
$	Under 300 frs

All prices are for a standard double room for two, including tax (20.6%) and service charge.

Wine

In the heart of the **Côtes de Provence** region, this area is summer wine country, with its fresh, unpretentious rosés chilling in buckets at every table. There are also reds, rather Italian in their hearty, fruity strength, and negligible whites, too, but the category always conjures rosés first and foremost. The smaller **Côteaux d'Aix** region, surrounding Aix-en-Provence, produces highly drinkable, unsensational rosés, as well as minor reds and whites.

Yet this region concentrates the very best of Provence, indeed its only fine wines, labeled by their place name rather than the umbrella title of Côtes de Provence. **Bandol**, famous as the best-rounded and most viable of all the rosés, makes a crisp white and a strong red, too. **Cassis** (not to be confused with the black-currant liqueur produced in Burgundy) creates marvelous whites with distinct shades of almond; it's the wine of choice with a spicy bouillabaisse, and it won't overwhelm a simple fillet. But the lone contender for the title of Great Wine comes from a tiny region around Aix, called **Palette**. Here Château Simone produces a magnificent red redolent of *garrigue*, the wild thyme, rosemary, and pine that flavor its soil, as well as a wonderful, substantial white; by all means, splurge.

Exploring Aix, Marseille, and the Central Coast

Aix lies at a major crossroads of autoroutes: one coming in from Bordeaux and Toulouse, then leading up into the Alps toward Grenoble; the other a direct line from Lyon and Paris. Aix is extremely well placed for trips to the Luberon, Avignon, and Arles, and it's only a quick half hour from Marseille. All of the coastal towns line up for easy access between Marseille and Toulon, so you can cruise along A50, which follows the coastline, and take in all the sights. Although Marseille is one of the biggest cities in France, it's a matter of minutes before you're lost in deep backcountry on winding, picturesque roads that lead to Cassis or Aubagne and beyond.

Great Itineraries

To make the most of your time in this region, plan to divide your days between big-city culture, backcountry tours, and waterfront leisure. You can "do" Marseille in an impressive day trip, but its backstreets and tiny ports reward a more leisurely approach. Aix is as much a way of life as a city charged with tourist must-sees; allow time to hang out in a cours Mirabeau café and shop the backstreets. (Note: Aim for a Tuesday in Aix if you want to see the Froment Triptych open in the cathedral, though that's the day the main art museum is closed.) Aubagne must be seen on a market day (Monday, Tuesday, Friday, or Sunday) to make the most of its charms. Cassis merits a whole day if you want to explore the calanques and enjoy a seaside lunch; Bandol is less appealing unless you're committed to beach time. The complete seaside experience, with rocky shoreline, isolated beaches, a picturesque port, and luxurious near-tropical greenery, can be found on the island of Porquerolles, one of the Iles d'Hyères; if your budget and schedule allow, spend a night or two in one of its few hotels and have much of the island to yourself.

Numbers in the text correspond to numbers in the margin and on the Aix and the Central Coast, Aix-en-Provence, and Marseille maps.

IF YOU HAVE 3 DAYS

With limited time, base yourself in ⊡ **Aix-en-Provence** ①–㉒ and explore the city first and foremost. Make a day trip to **Aubagne** ㊷, for the morning market, and **Cassis** ㊸, for an afternoon cruise to the

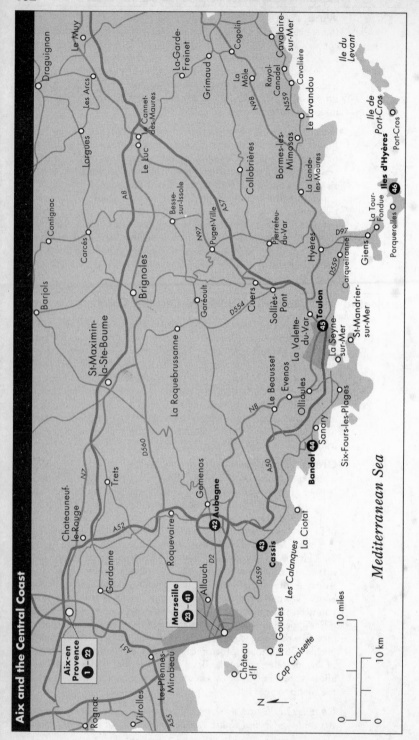

calanques. You could make a foray into **Marseille** ㉓–㊶; consider taking the train from Aix to avoid the traffic and having to find parking.

IF YOU HAVE 7 DAYS

Spend two nights in ⌖ **Aix-en-Provence** ①–㉒, seeing the old town and cathedral, and two nights in ⌖ **Cassis** ㊸, exploring the calanques and going to the market in **Aubagne** ㊷. Two nights in ⌖ **Marseille** ㉓–㊶ should give you time to wander its colorful neighborhoods and visit its museums. A seventh night could be well spent in a hotel (and an evening bike ride) on the ⌖ **Iles d'Hyères** ㊻.

IF YOU HAVE 10 DAYS

Tackle all of the sights in the seven-day itinerary and take extra time to wander Pagnol country above **Aubagne** ㊷, to taste wines around **Bandol** ㊹, and visit the hilltop village of Le Castellet. If you're brave enough to cross the traffic-clogged city of **Toulon** ㊺ you'll find that its old town is full of picturesque backstreets (just avoid them at night).

When to Tour Aix, Marseille, and the Central Coast

High season falls between Easter and October, but if you come in the winter, you may be pampered with warm sun and cool breezes. When the mistral attacks (and it can happen year-round), it channels all its forces down the Rhône Valley and blasts into Marseille like a one-way tornado. But, happily, the assault may only last one day. This is not the day, however, to opt for a boat ride from Cassis or Porquerolles; aim instead for the sheltered streets of Aix.

AIX-EN-PROVENCE

Gracious, cultivated, and made all the more cosmopolitan by the presence of some 30,000 university students, the lovely old town of Aix-en-Provence (pronounced ex) was once the capital of Provence. The vestiges of that influence and power—fine art, noble architecture, and graceful urban design—remain beautifully preserved today. That and its thriving market, vibrant café life, and world-class music festival, makes Aix tie with Arles and Avignon as one of the towns in Provence that shouldn't be missed.

The Romans were first drawn here by mild thermal baths, naming the town Aquae Sextiae (Waters of Sextius) in honor of the consul who founded a camp near the source in 123 BC. Just 20 years later some 200,000 German invaders besieged Aix, but the great Roman general Marius flanked them and pinned them against the mountain known ever since as Ste-Victoire. Marius remains a popular first name to this day.

Under the wise and generous guidance of Roi René (King René) in the 15th century, Aix became a center of Renaissance arts and letters. Under his auspices and discerning eye, a veritable army of artists flourished here and left a handful of masterpieces, including Nicolas Froment's Triptych of the Burning Bush. At the height of its political, judicial, and ecclesiastic power in the 17th and 18th centuries, Aix profited from a surge of private building, each grand *hôtel particulier* (mansion) meant to outdo its neighbor. Its signature *cours* (promenade) and *places* (squares), punctuated by grand fountains and intriguing passageways, date from this time.

It was into this exalting elegance that artist Paul Cézanne (1839–1906) was born, though he drew much of his inspiration from the raw countryside around the city and often painted Ste-Victoire. A writer and poet as well as a painter, he was barely recognized in his native Aix but drew the admiration of Impressionists on frequent trips to Paris.

If he dabbled briefly in Impressionism, he moved quickly on to paint in bold, building-block strokes, deconstructing the colors into multi-hued patches. It was this geometric dissection of form and color that laid the way for the 20th-century art revolution; Cubism, Fauvism, Constructivism, and all abstract modern art styles have been dismissed, by his most zealous admirers, as "Cézanne misunderstood."

A schoolmate of Cézanne's made equal inroads on modern society: the journalist and novelist Emile Zola (1840–1902) attended the Collège Bourbon with Cézanne and described their friendship as well as Aix itself in several of his works.

You can sense something of the ambience that nurtured these two geniuses in the streets of modern Aix, not only charged with its large university population but continually injected with new blood from exchange programs: Vanderbilt, California State, Michigan, and Wisconsin all send students to this stimulating city. There's also a British-American Institute and an American Center: in short, enough students and intellectuals to keep the crêperies and cafés crowded into the wee hours and to sustain a branch of The Gap.

It's not just the universities that keep Aix young: its famous Festival International d'Art Lyrique (International Festival of Opera) has imported and created world-class opera productions as well as related concerts and recitals since 1948. Most of the performances take place in elegant, old-Aix settings, and during this time the cafés, restaurants, and hotels spill over with *beau monde* who've come to Aix especially for the July event.

The Historic Heart

The famous cours Mirabeau, a broad, shady avenue that stretches from one grand fountain to another, bisects old Aix into two distinct neighborhoods. Below the cours, the carefully planned and imminently rational Quartier Mazarin is lined with fine 17th and 18th-century hôtels particuliers. Above, the old town twists and turns from square to fountain to square, each mysterious turn leading to another row of urbane boutiques and another cluster of café tables. If you turn a blind eye to these enticing distractions, you can see the best of Aix in a day's tour—but you'll be missing the point. The music of the fountains, the theater of the café crowds, and the painterly shade of the plane trees are what Aix is all about.

A Good Walk

Begin at the tourist office, which anchors the cours Mirabeau at Place du Général de Gaulle. The spiraling traffic, kiosks, newsstands, events posters, and crowds of students contrast sharply with **La Rotonde** ①, the monumental sculpture-fountain that towers over the swirl of modernity. Walk up the **cours Mirabeau** ② itself. With vibrant café life to your left and grand old mansions to your right, you pass a series of fountains, including the magnificently mossy **Fontaine d'Eau Chaude** ③. At No. 55 are traces of the hat shop founded by Cézanne's father, now worn away by time: The sign still reads CHAPELLERIE CÉZANNE DU COURS MIRABEAU, GROS ET DÉTAIL (Cézanne hatshop of the Cours Mirabeau, wholesale and retail). Cézanne himself hung out at the **Café les Deux Garçons** ④, the landmark café-restaurant that still serves gold-rimmed cups of espresso to artists and dreamers, nowadays armed with mobile phones.

Now cut right down the lively market street rue d'Italie and turn left at the **Église St-Jean-de-Malte** ⑤, once the chapel for a Knights of Malta priory. Just across the way, the **Musée Granet** ⑥ houses a

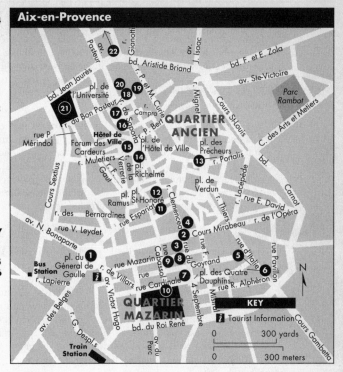

Aix-en-Provence

formidable collection of French art and archeology. Follow rue Cardinale to the **Fontaine des Quatre Dauphins** ⑦, a graceful obelisk
framed by curving dolphins; it sets off the patrician symmetry of the
lofty homes around it. Turn right up rue du 4 Septembre to the **Musée
Paul Arbaud** ⑧, with its highly personal collection of faïence and regional books. Then continue west down rue Goyrand to rue Cabassol; No. 3 is the imposing **Hôtel de Caumont** ⑨, now home to the
Conservatoire de Musique Darius-Milhaud. Head down rue Cabassol
(away from cours Mirabeau) to rue Cardinale, and you may see students of the Lycée Mignet crossing the courtyard of the former **Collège Royal-Bourbon** ⑩, just as alumni Cézanne and Zola once did.

Now head back up rue Cabassol and cross cours Mirabeau to enter
the lovely labyrinth above it. Plunge straight in and veer left; on your
right is the graceful **Place d'Albertas** ⑪, lined with fine old shuttered
mansions. The **Muséum d'Histoire Naturelle** ⑫, with its collection of
dinosaur fossils, is just behind you in the Hôtel Boyer d'Eguilles. Follow rue Espariat to place de Verdun, where the Palais de Justice looms
over an antiques market held three times a week. Walk the length of
the square and the adjoining place des Prêcheurs to the **Église de la
Madeleine** ⑬, where you'll find the Flemish Annunciation Triptych.

Next wind your way back via rue de Montigny to place Richelme and
the **Ancienne Halle aux Grains** ⑭, these days a post office. Walk around
to the front and admire its allegorical frieze of the rivers Rhône and
Durance. Up and to the left stands the **Hôtel de Ville** ⑮ with its imposing clock tower.

Continue up rue Gaston de Saporta to the **Musée du Vieil Aix** ⑯, which
houses eclectic memorabilia from Aix's past. Just beyond it on the left
is the **Hôtel de Châteaurenard** ⑰, where fabulous trompe-l'oeil murals
are concealed around a grand staircase; peek in, as it's a public build-

ing. Next door in the **Hôtel Maynier d'Oppède** ⑱ is a French-language
school; its courtyard is where concerts are held during the July opera
festival. Across the street, the luxurious Palais de l'Archevêché (Bishop's
Palace) houses the **Musée des Tapisseries** ⑲, containing a rich collection of Beauvais tapestries. Next to it, the **Cathédrale St-Sauveur** ⑳ provides a survey course in architectural history, from its 5th-century
baptistery to its Gothic-Romanesque double nave, and shelters the magnificent *Triptyque du Buisson Ardent*.

You're not far now from the very last traces of the medieval ramparts
that once surrounded this ancient city; they're just up from the cathedral and to the left. Continue past this old stone wall, and you'll reach
an even older landmark: the **Thermes** ㉑ (Thermal Baths), now a high-
tech treatment center. From here, you may want to make a pilgrimage
across the busy boulevard Jean-Jaurès to the **Atelier Cézanne** ㉒, built
by the artist when the beloved country house in which he worked was
sold.

TIMING

If you only want to take in the big picture, you can easily stroll this
broad circuit in a half day, browsing through shops and morning markets in the old town, then crossing cours Mirabeau to the Quartier
Mazarin to admire the fine old architecture. If you want to visit one
of the Mazarin's museums, spend a half day in this neighborhood, then
devote the afternoon to the old town and the cathedral north of cours
Mirabeau. A visit to Cézanne's Atelier requires extra walking time beyond the town center. And don't forget that the Froment Triptych is
only open on Tuesday afternoons between 3 and 4.

Sights to See

⓮ **Ancienne Halle aux Grains** (Old Grain Market). Built in 1761, this former grain market serves as a post office today—a rather spectacular
building for a humble service. The frieze, portraying an allegory of the
Rhône and Durance rivers, is the work of Aix sculptor Jean Chaste
(1726–1793); he also created the fountain out front. That's a real Roman
column at the fountain's top. ⊠ *pl. Mairie.*

㉒ **Atelier Cézanne** (Cézanne's Studio). After the death of his mother
forced the sale of Paul Cézanne's (1839–1906) beloved country retreat
known as Jas de Bouffan, he had this studio built just above the town
center. In the upstairs work space, the artist created some of his finest
paintings, including *Les Grandes Baigneuses* (*The Large Bathers*). But
what is most striking is the collection of simple objects that once featured prominently in the still lifes he created: the tin milk can, plates
in pure white faïence, bottles and glasses from *La Nature Morte aux
Oignons* (*Still Life with Onions*), and a tin coffee pot from *La Femme
à la Cafétière* (*The Woman with the Coffee Pot*). Also here are Cézanne's
clothes, brushes, paint tubes, and the engravings with which he surrounded himself—works by Courbet, Delacroix, and Poussin. ⊠ *9 av.
Paul-Cézanne,* ☎ *04–42–21–06–53.* ⊡ *25 frs.* ☉ *Apr.–Sept., daily
10–noon and 2:30–6; Oct.–Mar., daily 10–noon and 2–5. Guided
tours Wed. and Sat. at 10 and 3 (English on request).*

❹ **Café les Deux Garçons.** Cézanne enjoyed his coffee and papers here,
as have generations of *beau monde*, intellectuals, and neighborhood
habitués (regulars) since its founding in 1792. The gilt-and-muraled
decor inside is original, but you may not see it unless you're on your
way to the bathroom: The *très recherché* (much sought-after) sidewalk
terrace is *the* place to sit to see and be seen (☞ Dining and Lodging,
below). ⊠ *53 cours Mirabeau.*

★ ⑳ **Cathédrale St-Sauveur.** This marvelous hodgepodge juxtaposes so many eras of architectural history, all clearly delineated and preserved, it's a survey course in itself. There's a double nave, Romanesque and Gothic side by side, and a Merovingian (5th-century) **baptistery,** its colonnade mostly recovered from Roman temples to other gods. Shutters hide the ornate 16th-century carvings on the **portals,** opened by a guide on request. The guide can also lead you into the tranquil Romanesque cloisters next door so you can admire the carved pillars and slender columns.

As if these treasures weren't enough, the cathedral also contains a remarkable 15th-century triptych, painted by Nicolas Froment in the heat of inspiration from his travels in Italy and Flanders. Entitled *Triptyque du Buisson Ardent* (Burning Bush Triptych), it depicts the generous art patrons King René and Queen Jeanne kneeling on each side of the Virgin, who is poised above a burning bush. The extraordinary details are charged with biblical references—for example, the imperfect mirror in the Virgin's hand (Saint Paul to the Corinthians: "For now we see through a glass, darkly…") and Moses barefoot in the thorns and thistles (the burning bush to Moses: "Put off thy shoes from off thy feet, for the place whereon thou standest is holy ground"). There's even a complete trio of Adam, Eve, and a serpent in an angel's cameo. Froment was eager to show off his newly acquired perspective technique in the rippling planes of red drapery and the juxtaposition of the king and queen: If you imagine the side panels fitted together at a 45-degree angle, the background detail falls into one plane—and the king and queen kneel side by side before the Virgin. The painting owes its extraordinary condition to being hidden away in a Carmelite convent for centuries and opened only once a year. Now it's only opened for viewing Tuesday from 3 to 4 to prevent its delicate oil and tempera mix from being damaged (flash photography is not allowed). ✉ *rue Gaston de Saporta.*

⑩ **Collège Royal-Bourbon.** It's within these walls, which now belong to the Lycée Mignet, that Cézanne and his schoolmate Emile Zola discussed their ideas. Cézanne received his baccalauréat *cum laude* here in 1858 and went on to attend a year of law school to please his father. ✉ *rue Cardinale at rue Joseph-Cabassol.*

❷ **Cours Mirabeau.** In the deep shade of tall plane trees interlacing their heavy leaves over the street, cours Mirabeau is the social nerve center of Aix. One side of the street is lined with dignified 18th-century hôtels particuliers; you can view them from a comfortable seat in one of the dozen or so cafés and restaurants that spill onto the sidewalk on the other side. The street is named for the Count de Mirabeau, a rake in his youth who scandalized the world by leaving his carriage—*all night*—outside the home of his fiancée before their wedding. He went on, nonetheless, to be elected to the quasi-noble Third Estate in Aix in 1789.

⑬ **Église de la Madeleine.** Though the facade is modern now, this small 17th-century church still contains the center panel of the fine 15th-century *Triptych of the Annunciation,* attributed to the father of Jan Van Eyck. Some say the massive painting on the left side of the transept is a Rubens. ✉ *pl. des Prêcheurs.*

❺ **Église St-Jean-de-Malte.** This 12th-century chapel of the Knights of Malta, a medieval order of friars devoted to hospital care, was Aix's first attempt at the Gothic style, and its delicately groin-vaulted ceilings and tall windows have a touching purity of style. It was here that the counts of Provence were buried throughout the 18th century; their tombs (in the upper left) were attacked during the Revolution and only partially repaired. ⊠ *At intersection of rue Cardinale and rue d'Italie.*

❸ **Fontaine d'Eau Chaude** (Hot Water Fountain). Deliciously thick with dripping moss, this 18th-century fountain is fed by Sextius's own thermal source. It seems representative of Aix at its artfully negligent best. ⊠ *cours Mirabeau.*

❼ **Fontaine des Quatre Dauphins** (Four Dolphins Fountain). Within a tiny square at a symmetrical crossroads in the Quartier Mazarin, this lovely 17th-century fountain features four graceful dolphins at the foot of a pine-cone-topped obelisk. Under the shade of a chestnut tree and framed by broad, shuttered mansions, it makes an elegant ensemble worth contemplating from the park bench. ⊠ *pl. des Quatre Dauphins.*

❾ **Hôtel de Caumont.** The elegant facade of this mansion built in 1720 contains the **Conservatoire de Musique Darius-Milhaud** (Darius-Milhaud Music Conservatory). A native of Marseille, the composer Milhaud (1892–1974) spent several years of his childhood in Aix and returned here to die. He was a member of the group of French composers known as Les Six and created fine-boned, transparent works influenced by jazz and Hebrew chant. Aix has yet to make a museum of his memorabilia. ⊠ *3 rue Joseph-Cabassol,* ☎ *04–42–26–38–70.*

⓱ **Hôtel de Châteaurenard.** Across from a commercial gallery that calls itself the Petit Musée Cézanne (actually more of a tourist trap), this 17th-century mansion once hosted Louis XIV—and now houses government offices. This means that during business hours you can slip in and peek at the fabulous 18th-century stairwell, decorated in flamboyant trompe-l'oeil. Pseudostone *putti* (cherubs) and caryatids pop into three-dimensions—as does the false balustrade that mirrors the real one in stone. ⊠ *19 rue Gaston de Saporta.* ☉ *Weekdays, 9–4.*

⓲ **Hôtel Maynier d'Oppède.** This ornately decorated mansion houses the **Institut d'Etudes Françaises** (Institute of French Studies), where foreign students take French classes. During the July opera festival, its courtyard serves as venue to a series of classical concerts. ⊠ *23 rue Gaston de Saporta.*

⓯ **Hôtel de Ville** (City Hall). This 1655 landmark sports elaborate ironwork and frames a pretty pebble-paved courtyard. But it's the 16th-century **tour d'horloge** (clock tower) with a open ironwork belfry that draws the eye: It used to serve as the town's bell tower. The tree-lined square in front—with cafés setting up tables right into the center of the square—is a major gathering place. ⊠ *pl. Mairie.*

❻ **Musée Granet.** Once the Ecole de Dessin (Art School) that granted Cézanne a second prize in 1856, this former priory of the Église St-Jean-de-Malte is now an art museum of some substance. Cézanne's drawings and watercolors have been moved here from his studio, and there are eight of his paintings as well. You'll also find Rubens, David, Ingres, and a group of sentimental works by the museum's namesake, François Granet (1775–1849). In the archeology section are statues and busts recovered from the early Roman settlement. ⊠ *pl. St-Jean-de-Malte,* ☎ *04–42–38–14–70.* 🎟 *10 frs.* ☉ *Wed.–Mon., 10–noon and 2–6.*

❽ **Musée Paul Arbaud.** A rich and varied collection of Provençal faïence is displayed in this grand mansion in the Mazarin quarter. It also contains a library full of books on Provençal culture (only open to the public on Tuesday and Thursday from 2 to 5). ⊠ *2 rue du 4-Septembre,* ☎ *04–42–38–38–95.* 🎟 *15 frs.* ☉ *Mon.–Sat. 2–5.*

⑲ **Musée des Tapisseries** (Tapestries Museum). Housed in the 17th-century **Palais de l'Archevêché** (Archbishop's Palace), this sumptuous collection of tapestries actually decorated the walls of the bishops' quarters. Their taste was excellent: There are 17 magnificent hangings from Beauvais and a series on the life of Don Quixote from Compiègne. In the broad courtyard, the main opera productions of the Festival International d'Art Lyrique take place. ⊠ *pl. de l'Ancien-Archevêché,* ☎ *04–42–23–09–91.* ⊞ *10 frs.* ⊙ *Wed.–Mon., 10–noon and 2–5:45.*

⑯ **Musée du Vieil Aix** (Museum of Old Aix). An eclectic assortment of local treasures resides in this 17th-century mansion, from faïence to *santons* (terra-cotta figurines). There are 19th-century puppets displayed in historic tableaux, and ornately painted furniture. The building itself is lovely, too, from the dramatic stairwell to the painted beams and frescoes. The lovely boudoir is capped with a cupola decked with garlands of flowers, painted by artists who worked on the trompe l'oeil in the Châteaurenard. ⊠ *17 rue Gaston-de-Saporta,* ☎ *04–42–21–43–55.* ⊞ *15 frs.* ⊙ *Apr.–Oct., Tues.–Sun. 10–noon and 2–6:30; Nov.–Mar., Tues.–Sun. 10–noon and 2–5.*

⑫ **Muséum d'Histoire Naturelle** (Natural History Museum). The unusual collection of dinosaur eggs is this museum's claim to fame. Even if these don't interest you, the 17th-century Hôtel Boyer d'Eguilles's interiors are magnificent, with ornate woodwork and sculpture scattered among the fossilized bones. ⊠ *6 rue Espariat,* ☎ *04–42–26–23–67.* ⊞ *10 frs.* ⊙ *Daily 10–noon and 2–6.*

⑪ **Place d'Albertas.** Of all the elegant squares in Aix, this one is the most evocative and otherworldly. Set back from the city's fashionable shopping streets, it forms a horseshoe of shuttered mansions, with cobbles radiating from a simple turn-of-the-century fountain. No wonder chamber music concerts are held here in summer. ⊠ *At intersection of rue Espariat and rue Aude.*

❶ **La Rotonde.** If you've just arrived in Aix's center, this sculpture-fountain is a spectacular introduction to the town's rare mix of elegance and urban bustle. It's a towering mass of 19th-century attitude: That's Agriculture yearning toward Marseille, Art leaning toward Avignon, and Justice looking down on the cours Mirabeau. But don't study it too closely; you'll likely be sideswiped by a speeding Vespa. ⊠ *pl. de Gaulle.*

㉑ **Thermes** (Thermal Baths). First discovered under the leadership of Sextius, the Roman city's founding father, in the 2nd century BC, these warm springs are still popular with modern clients. The original site is now covered by a posh, high-tech treatment center called Les Thermes Sextius; it was recently (1998) remodeled to incorporate pressure showers, mud treatments, and underwater massage. Call for an appointment. ⊠ *55 cours Sextius,* ☎ *04–42–23–81–81.* ⊙ *Daily 9–7.*

Dining and Lodging

$$$$ ✕ **Le Clos de la Violette.** Whether you dine under the chestnut trees or
★ in the airy, pastel dining room, you'll get to experience the cuisine of one of the south's top chefs, Jean-Marc Banzo, known internationally as an ambassador for Provençal cooking. Banzo spins tradition into gold, from pressed crab on a humble chick-pea salad to *langoustine* (prawn) tails on shortbread with coral ravioli to smoked rabbit with almond puree. The wine list is devoted to the best of the region, too. The restaurant isn't far from the Atelier Cézanne, outside the old-town

110

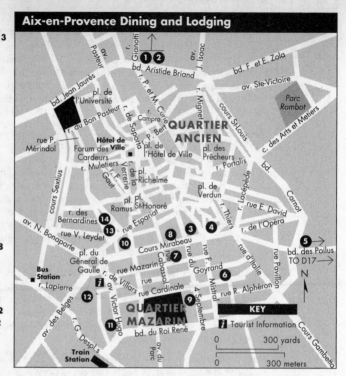

Aix-en-Provence Dining and Lodging

ring. ⊠ *10 av. de la Violette,* ☎ *04–42–23–30–71. Jacket required. AE, MC, V. Closed Sun. No lunch Mon.*

\$\$ ✕ **Les Bacchanales.** Despite a slightly self-important air and a position on a tourist-trap street off cours Mirabeau, this is a pleasant, intimate restaurant with inviting decor of daub-filled beams, yellow-ochre stucco, and Louis XIII chairs. The broad range of fixed-price menus may include a delicate octopus salad, stuffed guinea hen, *rouget* (mullet) perfumed with sage and fennel, and caramelized pears over pistachio ice cream. As the name implies, wine figures large here, and the list is extensive. ⊠ *10 rue de la Couronne,* ☎ *04–42–27–21–06. AE, MC, V.*

\$\$ ✕ **Brasserie Les Deux Garcons.** The food is rather ordinary—stick to the *coquillages* (oysters and clams) or the smoked-duck salad—but eating isn't what you come here for. It's the linen-decked sidewalk tables facing onto the cours Mirabeau, the fresh flowers, the frosted ice buckets, the white-swathed waiters snaking between the chairs, the blackboard menu, and the little gilt-edged espressos at the end of an atmospheric meal. Dining inside is less glamorous, but the murals and gilt-ivory decor date to the restaurant's founding, in 1792. Cézanne, Zola, and Cocteau were devoted regulars; call it the 2G (and remember to pronounce that *zhay*), and everyone will think you're a regular, too. ⊠ *53 cours Mirabeau,* ☎ *04–42–26–00–51. MC, V.*

\$\$ ✕ **Brasserie Léopold.** If you're more interested in the food than in regional atmosphere, this is the brasserie of choice in Aix. The cuisine is classic—steak tartare, *choucroute* (sausage and sauerkraut), and chocolate mousse—and the portions generous. Alas, the look of the place is contrived Art Deco revival—done to the hilt, as a good theme restaurant should. Provence this is not, but it's French through and through. It's across from La Rotonde, by the tourist office. ⊠ *In the*

Hôtel St-Christophe, 2 av. Victor-Hugo, ☎ 04–42–26–01–24. AE, MC, V.

$$ ✕ **Le Grillon.** Another contender for the mobile-phone set on this lively stretch of cours Mirabeau, this brasserie gives sun baskers and hair tossers a place to see and be seen. It also has waiters in black and white, crisp linens, and—incidentally—a varied menu that's especially strong at lunch. Items include the hors d'oeuvre buffet (a salad bar of crudités, anchovies, and beans), and a sliding scale of fixed-price menus featuring salmon tartare, lamb, and simple grilled fish. For a more intimate atmosphere, slip upstairs to the tiny jewel-box dining parlor, with cozy banquettes and an ornate wedding-cake decor. ✉ 49 cours Mirabeau, ☎ 04–42–27–14–35. MC, V.

$–$$ ✕ **Le Bistro Latin.** Making the most of Aix's abundant markets, this unpretentious little restaurant has only two menus, both working with fresh ingredients and equally fresh ideas. Consider a subtle terrine of chickpeas and fresh cheese with balsamic vinegar, a hearty lamb *daube* (stew) perfumed with juniper berries, or a novel flan of rabbit with crisp grilled pistachios. The two dining rooms, upstairs and down, are downright intimate, the ambience is laid-back, and the waiters are easy-going to an almost American degree. ✉ 18 rue de la Couronne, ☎ 04–42–38–22–88. AE, MC, V. Closed Sun. No lunch Mon.

$ ✕ **Le Verre Bouteille.** If you're keen on tasting rare local wines that you can't find at home, consider a simple lunch at this low-key bistro. Come here for a token platter of cold meats or cheeses to accompany the wine of the day. One or two home-cooked dishes—a fresh quiche, a pasta, or stew, as well as good cakes and fruit tarts—are served by the owners with a smile. A local clientele lunches here daily, so it's top quality. ✉ 1 bis rue Joseph-Cabassol, ☎ 04–42–27–96–66. MC, V. Closed Sun. No dinner Mon.–Thurs.

$$ ✕⊡ **Relais Ste-Victoire.** In this pretty country inn, nestled at the foot ★ of Ste-Victoire, you can dine on chef René Bergès's impeccably fresh Provençal cuisine, such as poached eggs with truffles, sardine *rillettes* (spread), and curried lamb lasagna. The restaurant ($$$) is closed Monday and has no lunch Friday or dinner Sunday. In guest rooms, tile floors shine and bright floral fabrics cover the walls; ask for a private balcony to enjoy the rugged countryside. From Aix take scenic D17 toward Le Tholonet and Cézanne country; turn right on D46 into Beaurecueil. ✉ 13100 Beaurecueil, ☎ 04–42–66–94–98, ℻ 04–42–66–85–96. 10 rooms. Restaurant, pool. AE, DC, MC, V. Closed 1st wk Jan., 2 wks Feb., and 1st 2 wks Nov.

$$$$ ⊡ **Villa Gallici.** Shaded by ancient cypress and plane trees and land- ★ scaped with jars of laurel and topiary boxwood, this luxurious hilltop garden retreat stands serenely apart from the city center—yet it's only steps away. Have breakfast on the shaded terrace, tea by the pool, then retreat to your extravagantly decorated room swagged with rich florals or plaids. The salons are design-magazine gorgeous, too. Hotel guests can enjoy light, unpretentious meals prepared by Jean-Marc Banzo, the chef of Le Clos de la Violette; for the full experience, try the restaurant, 100 yards away (closed Sunday). ✉ av. de la Violette, 13100, ☎ 04–42–23–29–23, ℻ 04–42–96–30–45. 18 rooms, 4 suites. Restaurant, pool. AE, DC, MC, V.

$$$ ⊡ **Augustins.** The best aspect of this old-town hotel, just a half block back from cours Mirabeau, is its reception area: The groin-vaulted stone, stained glass, and ironwork banister date from the 15th century, when the house was an Augustinian convent (Martin Luther was once a guest). The rooms are perfectly nice but a bit of a letdown: Instead of monastic oak and pristine linens, you get heavy carpeting and fabric-covered walls. Bathrooms are all-white tile and marble, and a few rooms have private balcony-terraces with views of the steeple of St-Esprit. The staff is efficient and eager to please. ⊠ *3 rue de la Masse, 13100,* ☎ *04–42–27–28–59,* FAX *04–42–26–74–87. 29 rooms. Breakfast room, air-conditioning. AE, DC, MC, V.* ◄

$$–$$$ 🏨 **Nègre-Coste.** Its prominent cours Mirabeau position and its lavish public areas make this 18th-century town house a popular hotel. But rooms, with all-weather carpet, cheap spindle beds, linoleum-floored bathrooms, and cheap prints of ponies, need updating badly. It might nonetheless be worth the price to open your shutters in the morning and lean out over the cours Mirabeau with a cup of café crème in hand. ⊠ *33 cours Mirabeau, 13100,* ☎ *04–42–27–74–22,* FAX *04–42–26–80–93. 37 rooms. Breakfast room, air-conditioning. AE, DC, MC, V.*

$$ 🏨 **Cardinal.** In a lovely 18th-century house in the Quartier Mazarin, this eccentric and slightly threadbare inn is the antithesis of the slick Saint Christophe. Its large rooms are furnished gracefully enough with secondhand finds, but much of it is shabby and worn, with torn carpeting and bubbling plaster. But if you're blinded by charm, you may only notice the novel furniture, the elegance of the structure, and the music of the bells of St-Jean-de-Malte. Note: Of two large kitchenette "suites" across from the Musée Granet, the ground-floor one has a private garden. ⊠ *22–24 rue Cardinale, 13100,* ☎ *04–42–38–32–30,* FAX *04–42–26–39–05. 30 rooms. Breakfast room. MC, V.*

$$ 🏨 **Mercure–Paul Cézanne.** A block from cours Mirabeau and the train station, this small, low-key hotel is run by an efficient team of friendly young women. Rooms vary enormously, from the cozy (with four-poster beds) to the wildly modern, and bathrooms are just as unpredictable. But the little lobby bar, with a mural of Provençal greenery and a TV, is a reassuringly homey spot for a nightcap. ⊠ *40 av. Victor-Hugo, 13100,* ☎ *04–42–27–20–95,* FAX *04–42–27–20–95. 55 rooms. AE, DC, MC, V.*

$$ 🏨 **Saint Christophe.** With so few midprice *hôtels de charme* in Aix and
★ a distinct lack of regional style, you might as well opt for this glossy Art Deco–style hotel, where the comfort and services are remarkable for the price. The Roaring '20s look dates from 1994, but the Cézannesque murals, burled-wood curves, and Constructivist leather chairs carry you to the Jazz Age. Rooms are slickly done in deep jewel tones, and the top-floor rooms have artisanal tiles in the bathrooms. For a pittance more, you can have a junior suite with a sleeping loft. The Brasserie Léopold (☞ *above*), though lacking cours Mirabeau chic, is the best of its kind in Aix. ⊠ *2 av. Victor-Hugo, 13100,* ☎ *04–42–26–01–24,* FAX *04–42–38–53–17. 57 rooms, 6 suites. Restaurant, air-conditioning, parking (fee). AE, MC, V.*

$–$$ 🏨 **Quatre Dauphins.** In the quiet Mazarin neighborhood below the cours
★ Mirabeau, this modest but impeccable lodging inhabits a noble *hôtel particulier.* Its pretty, comfortable little rooms have been spruced up with *boutis* (Provençal quilts), Les Olivades fabrics, quarry tiles, jute carpets, and hand-painted furniture. The top-floor rooms are even more charming but can be hot in the height of summer. The house-proud but unassuming owner-host bends over backward to please. ⊠ *55 rue Roux Alphéran, 13100,* ☎ *04–42–38–16–39,* FAX *04–42–38–60–19. 12 rooms. MC, V.*

Nightlife and the Arts

To find out what's going on in town, pick up a copy of the events calendar *Le Mois à Aix* or the bilingual city guide *Aix la Vivante* at the tourist office.

Hot Brass (⊠ rte. d'Eguilles, Celony, ☎ 04–42–21–05–57) draws an older, car-owning crowd to the suburbs for live concerts of blues, rock, and soul. **Le Mistral** (✉ 3 rue Frédéric-Mistral, ☎ 04–42–38–16–49) is a dance club where students of every nationality meet. **Le Richelme** (✉ 24 rue de la Verrerie, ☎ 04–42–23–49–29) draws a twenty-something crowd for dancing. **Le Scat Club** (✉ 11 rue de la Verrerie, ☎ 04–42–23–00–23) is the place for live soul, funk, reggae, rock, blues, and jazz.

For a night of playing roulette and the slot machines, head for the **Casino Municipal** (✉ 2 bis av. N.-Bonaparte, ☎ 04–42–26–30–33).

The **Cézanne** (✉ 21 rue Goyrand, ☎ 04–42–26–04–06) and **Renoir** (✉ 24 cours Mirabeau, ☎ 04–42–26–04–06) cinemas both show films in *v.o.* (*version originale,* i.e., not dubbed).

Every July during the **Festival International d'Art Lyrique** (International Opera Festival; ☎ 04–42–17–34–00 for information), you can see world-class opera productions in the courtyard of the Palais de l'Archevêché. It is one of the most important opera festivals in Europe, and cutting-edge productions involve the best artists available—recent guests have included director Peter Brook, choreographers Trisha Brown and Pina Bausch, and conductor Claudio Abbado. The repertoire is varied and often offbeat, featuring works like Britten's Curlew River and Bartok's Bluebeard's Castle as well as the usual Mozart, Puccini, and Verdi. The singers, however, are not celebrities, but rather an elite group of students who spend the summer with the Academie Européenne de Musique, training and performing under the tutelage of stars like Robert Tear and Yo-Yo Ma. Tickets can be purchased as early as November for the following summer, but it's usually possible to find seats a month in advance. After that, seats are scarce.

Outdoor Activities and Sports

The **Club Hippique Ste-Victoire** (✉ Chemin des Sauvaires, Meyreuil, ☎ 04–42–51–47–66) is an equestrian center from where you can take horseback sorties into the rugged countryside around Mont Ste-Victoire. Just south of Aix, off D9 (in the direction of Aeroport Marignane), the **Golf Club Aix-Marseille** (✉ Domaine de Riquetti, Les Milles, ☎ 04–42–24–20–41) has an 18-hole course. For swimming, head to the **Piscine Municipale Plein Ciel** (✉ av. Marcel-Pagnol, Jas de Bouffan, ☎ 04–42–20–00–78), a public indoor-outdoor pool open year round near Cézanne's country house west of town.

Shopping

Aix is a market town, and unlike the straightforward, country-fair atmosphere of nearby Aubagne, a trip to the market here is a gourmet event, with rarefied, high-end delicacies shoulder to shoulder with garlic braids. You'll find fine olive oils from the Pays d'Aix (Aix region), barrels glistening with olives of every hue and blend, and vats of *tapenade* (crushed olive, caper, and anchovy paste). Melons, asparagus, and mesclun salad are piled high, and dried sausages bristling with Provençal herbs hang from stands. A **food and produce market** takes place every morning on place Richelme; just up the street on place Verdun is a good, high-end *brocante* (collectibles) market Tuesday, Thursday, and Saturday mornings.

Another famous Aixois delicacy is *calissons*. A blend of almond paste and glazed melon, they are cut into geometric almond shapes and stacked high in *confiserie* windows. The most picturesque of the pretty shops specializing in calissons are **Leonard Parli** (✉ 35 av. Victor-Hugo), by the train station, and **Bechard** (✉ 12 cours Mirabeau).

In addition to its old-style markets and jewel-box candy shops, Aix is a modern shopping town—perhaps the best in Provence. The winding streets of the Vieille Ville above cours Mirabeau—focused around **rue Clemenceau, rue Marius Reinaud, rue Espariat, rue Aude,** and **rue Maréchal Foch**—have a head-turning array of goods, from high-end designer clothes, such as Sonia Rykiel and Max Mara, to Laura Ashley and The Gap. Fabric and pottery also figure large at shops such as Les Olivades, Souleiado, and Terres de Provence. Between these chain shops are dozens of fascinating one-of-a-kind boutiques, with antique and artisan jewelry, old-style hats, trendy shoes, and arts and crafts.

Particularly noteworthy is **Bleu Marine** (✉ 8 rue Maréchal Foch, ☎ 04–42–27–26–94), which sells its utterly French collection of nautical-style blazers, navy cardigans, and fisherman's stripe shirts. **Gérard Darel** (✉ 13 rue Fabrot, ☎ 04–42–26–38–45) is the shop for classic French tailoring. **Mephisto** (✉ 16 bis pl. Verdun, ☎ 04–42–38–23–23) sells its signature walking shoes and boots. **Tehen** (✉ 6 rue Clemenceau, ☎ 04–42–26–85–50) sells soft, draped knits.

MARSEILLE

Much maligned as a dirty urban sprawl plagued with impoverished immigrant neighborhoods and slightly louche politics, Marseille is often given wide berth by travelers in search of a Provençal idyll. What a waste: Its Cubist jumbles of white stone rise up over a picture-book seaport, bathed in light of blinding clarity, crowned by larger-than-life neo-Byzantine churches, and framed by massive fortifications. Its neighborhoods teem with multiethnic life, its souklike African markets reek deliciously of spices and coffees, its labyrinthine old town painted in broad strokes of saffron, cinnamon, and robin's-egg blue. Feisty and fond of broad gestures, Marseille is a dynamic city, as cosmopolitan now as when the Phocaeans first founded it, and with all the exoticism of the international shipping port it has been for 2,600 years.

The Phocaeans, an ancient people shipping out of Asia Minor some 600 years before Christ, sailed into the hill-framed inlet that is today's Vieux Port. Its white stone and dazzling sun reminded them of home, and they settled in to stay. Legend has it that their leader, Protis, paid a state visit to the Ligurians who occupied the land. It was the day of their traditional feast, where all the suitors of the princess Gyptis lined up for her to choose. When she entered, she raised her goblet to the handsome visitor, and Protis and Gyptis were married. Thus was founded Massalia, which grew to be the most important continental shipping port of antiquity. It flourished under Greek and eventually Roman rule; in the time of Christ, its university was the finest preserve of classical culture in the West and rivaled Athens for prestige.

Vital to the Crusades in the Middle Ages and crucial to Louis XIV as a military port, Marseille continued to flourish as France's market to the world. But not all its imports were good. In 1720 a Syrian ship sailed into harbor with a cargo of the plague; several of its sailors had succumbed en route. Though it was quarantined and held at bay, a greedy merchant slipped ashore to sell off the rich goods the ship carried. The infection spread through the narrow streets of Marseille, reaching as far as Arles and Toulon. More than 100,000 died in Provence—50,000 in Marseille alone—before the ship was unceremoniously sunk in the harbor now known as the Bout du Monde (End of the World).

The graceful architecture of Marseille sustained heavy damage during the Second World War, the most brutal of which was Hitler's decision to tear down a broad swath of 18th-century buildings that lined the

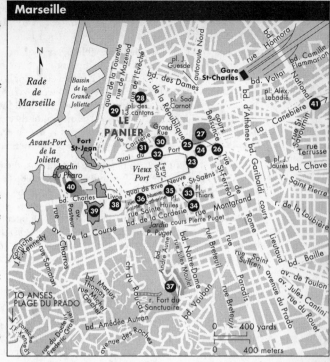

Vieux Port. It has been tastefully reconstructed in a discreet postmodern style, and the city's ensemble of urban architecture continues to be restored and renewed as Marseille makes a valiant effort to overturn its ugly reputation and show itself to the world for what it really is: A spirited international city in a spectacular setting.

The Quai du Port and Le Panier

Though Marseille is the second-largest city in France, it functions as a conglomerate of distinct neighborhoods—almost little villages. One of these microcosms—the Neapolitan-style maze of laundry-lined lanes called Le Panier—merits intimate exploration and the will to wander. There are also myriad museums tied into Marseille's nautical history, and the striking museum complex of the Vieille Charité, all worth a browse.

A Good Walk

Begin at the tourist office at the base of the Vieux Port, known as the quai des Belges. Be sure to start early because this is the stage for the first of a series of theatrical scenes that are part of Marseille's daily life: the **Marché aux Poissons** ㉓. Don't bother to come if the mistral has been roaring over the water; then the fishermen keep their boats safely tied in port. The port behind them is a show in itself, with its colorful mix of gleaming white pleasure boats, scruffy blue and green fishing boats, and even a couple of restored schooners, all bobbing together in the vast horseshoe of water.

Walk up La Canebière to the **Musée de la Marine** ㉔, where you can learn about the port's history through miniatures, paintings, and engravings. Just past the port is the unusual **Musée de la Mode** ㉕, where high-fashion clothes from the 1930s to today are on display. Head a half block over to the **Musée d'Histoire de Marseille** ㉖, which illustrates the classical history of this ancient city. Then wander into the adjoining **Jardin des Vestiges** ㉗ to see the foundations of Greek fortifications.

Next, head up broad rue de la République, past grand old apartment buildings and place Sadi Carnot. Just past the square, on the left, the elegant passage de Lorette leads you into a claustrophobic courtyard with laundry fluttering like medieval banners overhead, typical of Marseille. From here climb the steep stairs that lead into the famous neighborhood known as **Le Panier.** The anchor of the revitalization of this decaying but appealing neighborhood is the **Centre de la Vieille Charité** ㉘, once a hospice, now the home of two museums.

Follow rue du Petit Puits to place des 13 Cantons, then cross avenue Robert Schuman to the neo-Byzantine **Cathédrale de la Nouvelle Major** ㉙. Then wind back down the Montée des Accoules to place Daviel, turn right and double back right down rue du Lacydon to the **Musée du Vieux Marseille** ㉚. Housed in the Maison Diamantée, it features collections of pottery, furniture, costumes, and *santons* (terra-cotta figurines). Just a block to the left, the **Musée des Docks Romains** ㉛ displays the remains of 1st-century waterfront warehouses that lined this busy port.

Go down to the quai du Port and past the Baroque Hôtel de Ville (City Hall). At the water's edge, wait for the picturesque **Ferry Boat** ㉜ (pronounced fay-ree bow-aht) and ride across the port in style.

TIMING
Allow at least a half-day to explore the backstreets of Le Panier, a whole day if you intend to visit any of the fascinating museums at the foot of its hill; you could easily spend a morning appreciating the wonders (both architectural and archeological) of the Vieille Charité museum complex. Wear good walking shoes and be prepared to climb: Much of this district is spread over steep slopes.

Sights to See

㉙ **Cathédrale de la Nouvelle Major.** This gargantuan, neo-Byzantine, 19th-century fantasy was built under Napoléon III, but not before he'd ordered the partial destruction of the lovely 11th-century original, once a perfect example of the Provençal Romanesque style. All that remain of that now are the choir and transept—and a Della Robbia bas-relief of the deposition. You can view the flashy decor—marble and rich red porphyry inlay—in the newer of the two churches; the medieval one is being restored. ✉ *pl. de la Major.*

★ ㉘ **Centre de la Vieille Charité** (Center of the Old Charity). Designed as a hospice for the homeless, this superb ensemble of 17th- and 18th-century architecture stands at the top of Le Panier, a jewel of reason and symmetry in the midst of a romantic muddle. Even if you don't visit the museums inside, walk around its inner court, studying the retreating perspective of triple arcades and admiring the Baroque chapel with its novel egg-peaked dome. The ensemble is the work of the Marseillais artist/architects Pierre and Jean Puget. A new restaurant and *salon de thé* (tea salon) serve drinks and light meals al fresco in the courtyard or under the lovely arcades.

Under this complex's extensive roofs are two excellent museums. The
★ larger is the **Musée d'Archéologie Méditerranéenne** (Museum of Mediterranean Archaeology), with one of Europe's most complete collection from classical Mediterranean civilization, including ceramics, bronzes, funeral stelae, amphorae, and sculptures from ancient Egypt, Cyprus, Greece, the Romans, and the Etruscans. The Egyptian collec-

Earn Miles With Your MCI Card.

Take the MCI Card along on this trip and start earning miles for the next one. You'll earn frequent flyer miles on all your calls and save with the low rates you've come to expect from MCI. Before you know it, you'll be on your way to some other international destination.

Sign up for MCI by calling 1-800-FLY-FREE

Earn Frequent Flyer Miles.

Is this a great time, or what? :-)

Easy To Call Home.

1. To use your MCI Card, just dial the WorldPhone access number of the country you're calling from.
2. Dial or give the operator your MCI Card number.
3. Dial or give the number you're calling.

# Austria (CC) ♦	022-903-012
# Belarus (CC)	
From Brest, Vitebsk, Grodno, Minsk	8-800-103
From Gomel and Mogilev regions	8-10-800-103
# Belgium (CC) ♦	0800-10012
# Bulgaria	00800-0001
# Croatia (CC) ★	0800-22-0112
# Czech Republic (CC) ♦	00-42-000112
# Denmark (CC) ♦	8001-0022
# Finland (CC) ♦	08001-102-80
# France (CC) ♦	0-800-99-0019
# Germany (CC)	0800-888-8000
# Greece (CC) ♦	00-800-1211
# Hungary (CC) ♦	00▼800-01411
# Iceland (CC) ♦	800-9002
# Ireland (CC)	1-800-55-1001
# Italy (CC) ♦	172-1022
# Kazakhstan (CC)	8-800-131-4321
# Liechtenstein (CC) ♦	0800-89-0222
# Luxembourg	0800-0112
# Monaco (CC) ♦	800-90-019
# Netherlands (CC) ♦	0800-022-9122
# Norway (CC) ♦	800-19912
# Poland (CC) ÷	00-800-111-21-22
# Portugal (CC) ÷	05-017-1234
Romania (CC) ÷	01-800-1800
# Russia (CC) ÷ ♦	
To call using ROSTELCOM ■	747-3322
For a Russian-speaking operator	747-3320
To call using SOVINTEL ■	960-2222
# San Marino (CC) ♦	172-1022
# Slovak Republic (CC)	00-421-00112
# Slovenia	080-8808
# Spain (CC)	900-99-0014
# Sweden (CC) ♦	020-795-922
# Switzerland (CC) ♦	0800-89-0222
# Turkey (CC) ♦	00-8001-1177
# Ukraine (CC) ÷	8▼10-013
# United Kingdom (CC)	
To call using BT ■	0800-89-0222
To call using C&W ■	0500-89-0222
# Vatican City (CC)	172-1022

CHASE

Flying to France on Friday? Get Francs from Chase on Thursday. Call Currency To Go at 935-9935 for overnight delivery.

Or pounds for London. Or Deutschmarks for Düsseldorf. Or any of 75 foreign currencies. Call **Chase Currency To Go**[SM] at **935-9935** in area codes 212, 718, 914, 516 and Rochester, N.Y.; all other area codes call 1-800-935-9935. We'll deliver directly to your door.* Overnight. And there are no exchange fees. Let Chase make your trip an easier one.

CHASE. The right relationship is everything.[SM]

tion is the second-biggest in France, after the Louvre. And if you want to know more about the mysterious Celt-like Ligurians who peopled the Provençal coast before it was colonized, there's an extensive display of their treasures and tools upstairs. Also upstairs, the **Musée d'Arts Africains, Océaniens et Amérindiens** (Museum of African, Oceanian, and American Indian Art) provides a theatrical foil for the works' intrinsic drama: The masks and sculptures are mounted along a pure black wall, lighted indirectly, with labels across the aisle. ⊠ *2 rue de la Charité,* ☎ *04–91–14–58–80.* 🎫 *12 frs per museum.* ☉ *May–Sept., Tues.–Sun. 11–6; Oct.–Apr., Tues.–Sun. 10–5.*

㉜ Ferry Boat. To hear the natives say "fer-ry bo-at" (they've adopted the English) is one of the joys of a visit to Marseille. For a pittance you can file onto this little wooden barge and chug across the Vieux Port, which serves as handy mass transit just as it did in Marcel Pagnol's play *Marius.* It travels between place des Huiles on the quai de Rive Neuve side and the Hôtel de Ville on the quai du Port. 🎫 *3 frs.*

㉗ Jardin des Vestiges (Garden of Remains). This garden is the site of the original waterfront in Marseille's classical prime—when it was Massalia—and there are still remains of the Greek fortifications, 1st-century loading docks, paved streets, and a necropolis. It was discovered in 1967 when roadwork was being done next to the Bourse (Stock Exchange). It's now part of the Musée d'Histoire de Marseille. ⊠ *Centre Bourse,* ☎ *04–91–90–42–22.* 🎫 *12 frs includes entry to Museum of History.* ☉ *Mon.–Sat. noon–7.*

㉓ Marché aux Poissons (Fish Market). Up and going by 8 AM every day, this market puts on a vivid and aromatic show of waving fists, jostling chefs, and heaps of fish from the night's catch still twitching. You'll hear the thick soup of the Marseillais accent as blue-clad fishermen and silk-clad matrons bicker over prices, and you'll wonder at the rainbow of Mediterranean creatures before you, each uglier than the last: the spiny-headed *rascasse* (scorpion fish), dog-nosed *grondin* (red gurnet), the eel-like *congre,* and the monstrous *baudroie,* or *lotte de mer* (monkfish). The only problem with coming for the early morning show is that you have to wait so long for your bouillabaisse lunch. ⊠ *quai des Belges.* ☉ *Daily 8–1.*

㉛ Musée des Docks Romains (Roman Docks Museum). In 1943 Hitler had the neighborhood along the quai du Port destroyed—some 2,000 houses, displacing some 20,000 citizens. This act of brutal urban renewal, ironically, laid open the ground for new discoveries. When Marseille began to rebuild in 1947, they dug up remains of a Roman shipping warehouse, full of terra-cotta jars and amphorae that once lay in the bellies of low-slung ships. The museum created around it demonstrates the scale and range of Massalia's shipping prowess. ⊠ *pl. de Vivaux,* ☎ *04–91–91–24–62.* 🎫 *12 frs.* ☉ *Oct.–May, Tues.–Sun. 10–5; June–Sept., Tues.–Sun. 11–6.*

★ ㉖ Musée d'Histoire de Marseille (Marseille History Museum). With the Jardin des Vestiges in its backyard, this modern, open-spaced exhibition illuminates Massalia's history by mounting its treasure of archeological finds in didactic displays: You can learn about ancient metallurgy, pottery making, and shipbuilding. There's even a recovered wreck of a Roman cargo boat, its 3rd-century wood amazingly preserved. And that model of the Greek city should be authentic: It's based on the eyewitness description of Aristotle. ⊠ *Centre Bourse, entrance on rue de Bir-Hakeim,* ☎ *04–91–90–42–22.* 🎫 *10 frs.* ☉ *Mon.–Sat. noon–7.*

㉔ Musée de la Marine (Marine Museum). One of many museums devoted to Marseille's history as a shipping port, this one concentrates on recent times, from the 17th century to today. It's all about boats, and a model lover's dream: There are steamboats and sailboats and schooners in miniature, as well as a collection of paintings and prints of the port in action. ⊠ *Palais de la Bourse, 7 La Canebière,* ☎ *04–91–39–33–33.* ⊡ *10 frs.* ⊙ *Daily 10–6.*

㉕ Musée de la Mode (Fashion Museum). This museum is not about boats or Greeks: It's about clothes, specifically clothes from the 1930s to the present. Whether there's a temporary exhibition—on a star designer or changes in male plumage—or a display from the permanent collection (they've cornered the market on Chanel), it's executed with panache. ⊠ *11 La Canebière,* ☎ *04–91–56–59–57.* ⊡ *18 frs.* ⊙ *Tues.–Sun. noon–7.*

㉚ Musée du Vieux Marseille (Museum of Old Marseille). In the 16th-century **Maison Diamantée** (one of few buildings in this quarter that would be spared by Hitler), so called because of its beveled-stone facade, this history museum concentrates on Marseille's Provençal personality and its more prosaic traditions of recent centuries. The collection includes beautifully carved wooden furniture, crèches and santons, and 19th-century clothes. Of particular interest: a display of locally made playing cards, as Marseille was one of the medieval ports of entry for this novelty from the East, and its citizens took to it in spades. Closed at press time for renovations, it should be open by early 2000. Check with the tourist office for new hours. ⊠ *rue de la Prison,* ☎ *info 04–91–13–89–00.*

★ Le Panier. This area is the old heart of Marseille, a maze of high shuttered houses looming over narrow cobbled streets, *montées* (stone stairways), and tiny squares. Le Panier is the principal focus of the city's efforts at urban renewal, with plans for the restoration of more than 1,500 houses over the next few years. It was once home to seamen and fishermen and every kind of craftsman and laborer, all drawing a living from the sea. There were women, too, who made a living from making themselves available to sailors in port, so many that a Maison de Refuge was founded—half prison, half convent. The "fallen women" entered via the rue Déshonneur (Dishonor Street), now the rue des Honneurs! Once "reformed," they left via the rue des Repenties (Repented Street). You'll enter Le Panier through rue de Lorette and place de Lorette; an old Provençal saying had it that "the girls of Lorette can't sleep alone." Wander this seedy, atmospheric neighborhood at will, making sure to stroll along rue du Panier, the montée des Accoules, rue du Petit-Puits, and rue des Muettes; take in the smells of garlic and soap and the infinite spectrum of colors in the peeling shutters and crumbling stucco.

The Quai de Rive Neuve

If in your exploration of Le Panier and the Quai du Port, you examined Marseille's history in miniature via myriad museums, this walk will give you the "big picture." From either the crow's-nest perspective of Notre-Dame-de-la-Garde or the vast green Jardin du Pharo, you'll take in spectacular cinematic views of this great city and its ports and monuments. Wear good walking shoes and bring your wide-angle lens.

A Good Walk

From the quai des Belges, head left and up the quai de Rive Neuve, then head away from the port up rue Fortia. To your right is **place Thiars** ㉝, a lively center with restaurants and cafés. Back on rue Fortia, continue a block over to cours d'Estienne d'Orves and **Les Arce-**

naulx ㉞, a high-textured, state-of-the-art shop-and-restaurant complex in the old armory and a prime example of Marseille's commitment to renewal. Now head back to the waterfront and stop in for a pastis at the **Bar de la Marine** ㉟, scene of the salty barkeepers in Pagnol's plays *Marius, Fanny,* and *César.* This district has many popular bars and is peppered with theaters. Continue up the quai to the **Théâtre National de Marseille La Criée** ㊱, where the city's prestigious state theater company performs in a former fish-auction house.

If you're willing and able to tackle the steep (and seemingly endless) climb to the city's sentimental landmark, **Notre-Dame-de-la-Garde** ㊲, you'll be rewarded with one of the best views in Provence, panning over the brilliant white stone of the city, its complex of ports, islands, and neighboring mountains. (Hint: Bus 60 makes the run regularly from the cours Jean Ballard, between the quai des Belges and the parking Estienne d'Orves.) The church itself, another testimony to Napoléon III's megalomaniac passion for overscaled kitsch, conceals quirky treasures.

A more modest climb up rue Robert and rue Neuve Ste-Catherine brings you to the **Abbaye St-Victor** ㊳, a splendid Romanesque church-fortress. Walk past the looming walls of **Fort St-Nicolas** ㊴ to get across the boulevard and up to the **Jardin du Pharo** ㊵: From this vast green hilltop, you can take in dramatic views of the fort and its opposing **Fort St-Jean.**

TIMING

This walk involves about a half-day's worth of heavy hiking, half of it uphill. If you opt for a bus ride, you can make a beeline straight up to Notre-Dame-de-la-Garde and take in the spectacular views, all in a couple of hours.

Sights to See

★ ㊳ **Abbaye St-Victor.** Founded in the 4th century by St-Cassien, who sailed into Marseille's port full of fresh ideas on monasticism acquired in Palestine and Egypt, this ancient abbey grew to formidable proportions and influence from its vantage point on a ledge overlooking the sea. With its severe exterior of crenellated stone and the spare geometry of its Romanesque church, the structure would be as at home in the Middle East as its founder. The Saracens destroyed his first structure, so the abbey was rebuilt in the 11th century and fortified against further onslaught in the 14th. Its crudely peaked windows demonstrate the dawning transition from Romanesque arches to Gothic points; in the nave the early attempts at groin vaulting were among the first in Provence.

By far the best reason to come: the **crypt,** St-Cassien's original, which lay buried under the medieval church's new structure. Here you'll see the 5th-century sarcophagus that allegedly holds his remains, as well as the 3rd-century tomb of St-Victor himself, who was ground to death between millstones. There's a passage into the **catacombs** here, where early Christians worshiped St. Lazarus and Mary Magdalene, said to have washed ashore at Stes-Maries-de-la-Mer and carried their message inland. The boat in which they landed is reproduced in canoe-shape cookies called *navettes,* sold for an annual procession for Candlemas in February as well as year round (☞ Shopping, *below*). ▨ *Crypt entry: 10 frs.* ۞ *Daily 8:30–6:30.*

㉞ **Les Arcenaulx** (The Arsenal). In this broad, elegant stone armory, first built for Louis XIV, a complex of upscale shops and restaurant has given the building—and neighborhood—new life. Its bookstore features a large collection of publications on Marseille (as well as art, photography, history, and rare books); a boutique sells high-end cooking (and serving) goods with a southern accent; and a book-lined restaurant serves sophisticated cuisine. It's worth a peek to remind yourself that Marseille is not the squalid backwater people continue to expect. ☉ *Bookstore Mon.–Sat. 10*AM*–midnight; boutique 10:30–6:30; salon de thé 3–6.*

㉟ Bar de la Marine. Even if you've never read or seen Marcel Pagnol's trilogy of plays and films *Marius, Fanny,* and *César* (think of it as a three-part French *Casablanca*), you can get a feel for its earthy, old-Marseille atmosphere by stopping into the bar it was set in. It's been, well, "retrovated"—that is, redecorated with murals and old café chairs—to evoke the place as it was in the days the bartender César, his son Marius, the buxom fishwife Honorine, and her daughter, Fanny the shellfish girl, lived out their salty drama of love, honor and the call of the sea. Pagnol grew up in Marseille, and summered in the hills above Aubagne. ✉ *15 quai Rive-Neuve,* ☎ *04–91–54–95–47.*

㉛ Fort St-Nicolas and Fort St-Jean. This complex of brawny fortresses enclose the Vieux Port's entry from both sides. In order to keep the feisty, rebellious Marseillais under his thumb, Louis XIV had the fortresses built with the guns pointing *inward.* They're best viewed from the Jardin du Pharo.

㊵ Jardin du Pharo (Pharo Garden). The Pharo, another larger-than-life edifice built to Napoléon III's epic tastes, was a gift to his wife, Eugenie. It's a conference center now, but its green park has become a mecca for city strollers who want to take in panoramic views of the ports and fortifications. ✉ *Above bd. Charles-Livon.*

㊲ Notre-Dame-de-la-Garde. This preposterously overscaled neo-Byzantine monument was erected in 1853 by the ever-tasteful Napoléon III. Its interior is a Technicolor bonanza of red-and-beige stripes and glittering mosaics. The gargantuan Madonna and Child on the steeple (almost 30 ft high) are covered in real gold leaf. It's bread and circus for the people, who pour in (more than a million a year) to thank the Virgin for sparing them (and their ancestors before them) from cholera (and equivalent modern plagues). The results gives this otherwise contrived showpiece its profound and quirky charm: The walls of the nave are covered with ex-votos, a fascinating collection of naive art offered in thanks, most of them about shipwrecks and sea storms survived. ✉ *On foot climb up cours Pierre Puget, cross the Jardin Pierre Puget, cross a bridge to rue Vauvenargues, and hike up to pl. Edon. Or catch Bus 60 from cours Jean-Ballard.* ☎ *04–91–13–40–80.* ☉ *May–Sept., daily 7 AM–8 PM; Oct.–Apr., daily 7–7.*

㉝ Place Thiars. An ensemble of Italianate 18th-century buildings frame this popular center of activity, where one sidewalk café spills into another, and every kind of bouillabaisse is yours for the asking. At night, the neighborhood is a fashionable hangout for young professionals on their way to and from the theaters and clubs on quai de Rive Neuve.

㊱ Théâtre National de Marseille La Criée (National Theater of Marseille at "The Fish Auction"). Behind the floridly decorated facade of this grand old fish auction house, a prestigious, cutting-edge state theater company holds forth. La Criée (literally, "the screaming") is the traditional means of auctioning off the fishermen's daily catch to wholesalers; the real one now takes place near L'Estaque. ✉ *32 quai de Rive-Neuve,* ☎ *reservations 04–91–54–42–16.* ☉ *Box office Tues.–Sat. 11–6.*

OFF THE
BEATEN PATH

CHÂTEAU D'IF – François I, in the 16th century, recognized the strategic advantage of an island fortress surveying the mouth of Marseille's vast harbor, so he had one built. Its effect as deterrent was so successful, it never saw combat and was eventually converted to a prison. It was here that Alexandre Dumas locked up his most famous character, the Count of Monte Cristo. Though he was fictional, the hole Dumas had him escape through is real enough, and it's visible in the cells today. On the other hand, the real-life Man in the Iron Mask, whose cell is still being shown, was not actually imprisoned here. The boat ride (from the quai des Belges, 50 frs) and the views from the broad terrace alone are worth the trip. ☎ 04–91–59–02–30. 🎟 Château 25 frs. ☉ Apr.–Sept., daily 9–7; Oct.–Mar., Tues.–Sun. 9–5:30.

La Canebière

This famous avenue cuts a straight line north from the Vieux Port. It's easy to make forays from it through Little Tunisia along rue Longue-des-Capucins and rue d'Aubagne to the bohemian cours Julien and on to the elegant Palais Longchamp, containing a fine-arts museum.

A Good Walk

The famous **La Canebière** was the louche and lively nerve center of Marseille between the wars. From the Vieux Port, head up La Canebière and turn right on **rue Longue-des-Capucins,** narrow, lively, and crammed with tiny North African shops opening onto the street. Across from the Noaille métro station, near the intersection with La Canebière, place du Marché des Capucins makes you especially feel the North African influence in this city. Continue up the street and make a jaunt to the right down rue Vacon, where miles of Provençal cottons are sold from heavy bolts. Then double back and go right up **rue d'Aubagne,** cross the cours Lieutaud, and climb up to the **cours Julien.** At its upper end, this popular pedestrian thoroughfare opens out into a sea of restaurants, shops, and cafés, with people sunning by the modern fountain and musicians busking from table to table.

If you want to see some art or some natural history in a mega-monumental public building, hike the length of La Canebière to the **Palais de Longchamp** ㊶, where there's the Musée des Beaux Arts. It's some 3 km (2 mi) slightly uphill, but it's possible to walk it in about 45 minutes; if you wear out, catch Bus 41 from anywhere on La Canebière. It's an easy run on Bus 81 from quai des Belges.

TIMING

Allow a couple of hours to wander through the market and streets around place du Marché des Capucins. Aim for lunch or a coffee break along cours Julien. Give yourself about half a day for the Palais de Longchamp—it takes time to get there and back and to visit one of its two museums.

Sights to See

La Canebière. This wide avenue leading from the port, known affectionately as the "Can o' Beer" by American sailors, was crammed with cafés, theaters, bars, and tempting stores full of zoot suits and swell hats, and figured in popular songs and operettas. It's noisy but dull today, yet you may take pleasure in studying the grand old 19th-century mansions lining it.

Cours Julien. A center of Bohemian *flanerie* (hanging out), this is a lovely place to relax by the fountain, in the shade of plane trees, or under a café umbrella. Its low-key and painterly tableau is framed by graceful 18th-century buildings.

🕙 **Palais de Longchamp.** This extravagantly overscale 19th-century palace splays gracefully, symmetrically, and more than a little pompously around fountain-ponds to honor the confluence of the Provençal river Durance with the open sea. It houses a museum in each broad wing. The **Musée des Beaux-Arts** displays 16th- and 17th-century paintings, including several Rubens, as well as fine marble sculptures and drawings by the Baroque architect Pierre Puget, a native of Marseille. The collection of French 19th-century paintings is strong (Courbet, Millet, Ingres, and David), and there's a delightful group of sculptures by the caricaturist Honoré Daumier. In the right wing of the Palais, the **Musée d'Histoire Naturelle** (Natural History Museum) contains a collection of every kind of flora and fauna from Provence, even those in fossilized form. There's also an aquarium of fish from around the world. ⊠ *End of Boulevard Longchamp,* ☎ *04–91–14–59–50.* ⊡ *12 frs per museum.* ☉ *May–Sept., Tues.–Sun. 11–6; Oct.–Apr., Tues.–Sun. 10–5.*

Rue Longue-des-Capucins/rue d'Aubagne. Stepping into this atmospheric neighborhood, you may feel you have suddenly been transported to a Moroccan souk. Shops with open bins of olives and coffee beans and tea and spices and dried beans and chickpeas and couscous and peppers and salted sardines serve the needs of Marseille's large and vibrant North African community. Like lots of cities with large immigrant populations, there's been an unfortunate political swing to the racist right by many in Marseille: But this attitude doesn't take into account the city's 2,500-year history of input and enhancement from the outside world.

Anses East of Town

Along the coastline east of Marseille's center, a series of pretty little *anses* (ports) lead to the more famous and far-flung Calanques (☞ Cassis, *below*). These miniature inlets are really tiny villages, with pretty, balconied, boxy houses (called *cabanons*) clustered around bright-painted fishing boats. Don't even think about buying a cabanon of your own, however: They are part of the fishing community's heritage and are protected from gentrification by the outside world.

A Good Drive

Drive up the quai de Rive Neuve to the Corniche J.-F. Kennedy, which roars along the dramatic clifftop over the Mediterranean. The Art Deco **Monument aux Héros de l'Armée d'Orient et des Terres Lointaines** (Monument to the Heroes of the Army of the East and Faraway Lands) marks your turning point: Head left into the picture-perfect little fishing port called the **Vallon des Auffes.** You could paddle across it in two strokes, but this miniature inlet concentrates all the color (blue, red, and green fishing boats, azure water) of a Rossellini film set.

Continue past the wealthy **Roucas-Blanc** neighborhood and the full-scale 19th-century reproduction of Michelangelo's *David,* standing incongruously at the center of avenue du Prado: When the Marseillais do something, they do it big. The city's main beaches lie at David's feet in the **Parc Balnéaire** du Prado, including the Plage de David. From the sands, you'll have breathtaking views of the Iles de Frioul (Frioul Islands), which you can visit by boat from Marseille's port (☞ Outdoor Activities and Sports, *below*).

After David and the beaches, continue up the road to **Port de Plaisance de la Pointe Rouge** and then **La Madrague,** both postcard pretty anses wedged with bobbing boats and toy-block cabanons in saturated tints. Pursue the road to its dead end at **Les Goudes** and climb over boul-

★ ders and tidal pools to the extraordinary **Anse Croisette,** a rough inlet paradise of crashing waves and rock. It was near here, known to the Marseillais as the Bout du Monde (End of the World), where the *Grand St-Antoine*—the ship that brought the plague to Marseille in 1720—was sunk, but too late to save the 100,000 who died from its deadly cargo.

TIMING

Allow a half-day for this dramatic drive—longer if you succumb to the temptation to clamber around on barnacle-covered rocks, to sip a pastis while watching the fishing boats come in at dusk, or to settle in for a full-out bouillabaisse.

OFF THE
BEATEN PATH

L'ESTAQUE – At this famous village north of Marseille, Cézanne led an influx of artists eager to capture its cliff-top views over the harbor. Braque, Derain, and Renoir all put its red rooftops, rugged cliffs, and factory smokestacks on canvas. Pick up the English-language itinerary "L'Estaque and the Painters" from the Marseille tourist office and hunt down the sites and views they immortalized. It's a little seedy these days, but there are cafés and a few fish shops making the most of the nearby Criée (fisherman's auction): This is where the real wholesale auction moved from Marseille's quai de Rive-Neuve. A novel way to see Cézanne's famous scenery is to take a standard SNCF train trip from the Gare St-Charles to Martigue; it follows the L'Estaque waterfront and (with the exception of a few tunnels) offers magnificent views.

Dining and Lodging

$$$ ✕ **Chez Fonfon.** Tucked into a storybook film set of the tiny fishing
★   port east of the center called Vallon des Auffes, this landmark still draws the Marseillais for some of the best bouillabaisse in the world. Alexandre Pinna, the owner's son, has taken over for the late, great chef Fonfon, but the restaurant's cachet remains. A variety of plain, fresh seafood, impeccably grilled, steamed, or roasted in salt crust, are served, and two pretty pink dining rooms with picture windows overlook the fishing boats that supply your dinner. ⊠ *140 rue du Vallon des Auffes,* ☎ *04–91–52–14–38. Reservations essential. AE, DC, MC, V. Closed 2 wks in Jan. No dinner Sun.*

$$ ✕ **Les Arcenaulx.** At this book-lined, red-walled haven in the stylish book-and-boutique complex of this renovated arsenal, you can have a sophisticated regional lunch—and read while you're waiting. Seafood figures large, with classics like *soupe de poisson* (fish soup), as well as garlic-perfumed octopus stew, and lotte and baudroie from the market a block away. That diners enter via the bookstore and pass rows of burnished leather-bound antique tomes appeals to Marseille's finer side, and you'll find politicians, professors, and actors soaking in the ambience. The terrace (on the Italian-scaled cours d'Estienne d'Orves) is as pleasant as the interior. ⊠ *25 cours d'Estienne d'Orves,* ☎ *04–91–59–80–30. AE, DC, MC, V. Closed Sun.*

$$ ✕ **Baie des Singes.** On a tiny rock-ringed lagoon as isolated from the nearby city as if it were a desert island, this cinematic corner of paradise was once a customs house under Napoléon III. You can rent a mattress and lounge chair, dive into the turquoise water, and shower off for the only kind of meal worthy of such a setting: fresh fish. There's bouillabaisse, of course, but also fresh-grilled mullet and *baudroie* (monkfish), crabs and lobster, and local *cigales de mer* (shrimp-like "sea locusts"). It's all served at terrace tables overlooking the water. The expansive owner, son of a fishmonger and grandson of a fisherman, knows his craft, and includes Jacques Chirac and Catherine Deneuve among his loyal clientele. Mattress and shower access cost

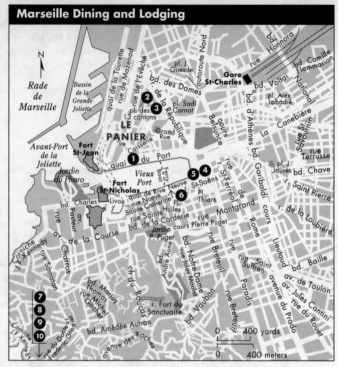

Marseille Dining and Lodging

50 francs extra. ⊠ *Anse des Croisettes, Les Goudes,* ☎ *04–91–73–68–87. AE, DC, MC, V. Closed Oct.–Mar.*

$$ ✕ **Les Galinettes/Chez Madie.** Of the dozens of seafood restaurants that actively court you as you stroll the horseshoe of the Vieux Port, this is one of the best. Seated under the shaded arcade before a white and blue panorama of boats, choose from a fish-of-the-day menu—perhaps a sardine *tartelette* (small tart) or baudroie with aïoli— selected from the stands just steps away. Bouillabaisse is a ceremony worth the required advance order. ⊠ *138 quai du Port,* ☎ *04–91–90–40–87. Closed Mon. and most of Aug. No dinner Sun.*

$–$$ ✕ **Le Panier des Arts.** Behind a saffron-color facade and lace-covered windows, this neighborhood bistro welcomes regulars and visitors alike. The cooking is straightforward but soigné—a basket of crudités with aïoli, a simple steak with shallots, and a modest local wine—and served on unpretentious olive-print oilcloths. It's all a part of the salvation and inevitable gentrification of the *quartier.* ⊠ *3 rue du Petit-Puits,* ☎ *04–91–56–02–32. MC, V. Closed Sun.*

$ ✕ **Pizzeria Etienne.** This tiny Le Panier hole-in-the-wall could be full
★ of Pagnol characters but nowadays overflows with young professionals who enjoy bathing in the abuse and rich patois of the chef. Full of Provençal prints and old photos of the neighborhood, it has more than just a good fresh-anchovy pizza from the wood-burning oven. There are also a slab of rare-grilled beef big enough for one, two, or three and the quintessential *pieds et paquets,* Marseille's earthy classic of pigs' feet and stuffed tripe. ⊠ *43 rue de la Lorette,* ☎ *no phone. No credit cards.*

$$$$ ✕▦ **Le Petit Nice.** Despite its name, this extraordinarily glamorous hide-
★ away out-Rivieras anything in Nice. On a rocky promontory overlooking the harbor and the Iles de Frioul, this fantasy villa was bought from a

countess in 1917 and converted to a hotel/restaurant, anticipating the Jazz Age rush to the Côte d'Azur. The Passédat family has been getting it right ever since. Now father and son man the exceptional kitchen (one of the coast's best), creating truffled brandade, sea anemone beignets, fresh fish cooked whole, and licorice soufflé. In summer meals are served by the saltwater pool overlooking the crashing surf. (The restaurant is closed Saturday lunch and Sunday, off-season.) Most rooms are sleek and minimalist, with some art-deco-cum-postmodern touches. All in all, it's a Hollywood set for the South of France of your dreams—but brace yourself for oblivion, as the Passédats are accustomed to catering to stars and might not notice you if you weren't featured at Cannes. ⊠ *Anse de Maldormé, corniche J.-F. Kennedy, 13007,* ☎ *04–91–59–25–92,* FAX *04–91–59–28–08. 15 rooms. Restaurant, air-conditioning, pool. AE, DC, MC, V.*

\$\$\$ ★ 🏨 **Mercure Beauvau Vieux Port.** The antiques are real, the woodwork burnished with age; add a little marble, a touch of brass, and deep carpet underfoot, and you'll have an idea of this intimate urban hotel's genuine old-world charm. George Sand kept a suite here—knowing that makes the plush retro look in all the rooms, with paisleys and moiré, seem all the more appropriate. The extensive breakfast is served in the cosseted salon overlooking the port. ⊠ *4 rue Beauvau, 13001,* ☎ *04–91–54–91–00, 1–800–MERCURE for U.S. reservations,* FAX *04–91–54–15–76. 71 rooms. Bar, breakfast room, air-conditioning. AE, DC, MC, V.*

\$\$ 🏨 **Le Rhul.** This is the Petit Nice for ordinary people: a broad, '60s-style roadside inn *left* of the corniche highway but still taking in spectacular sea views. Okay, so the stark architecture is cozied up with doilies and overstuffed chairs and the rooms are of beige built-in laminate. Nonetheless, all but three overlook the sea, and three have little balustraded balconies from which you can thumb your nose at the more famous inn below. The vaguely '50s-style restaurant banks on its magnificent panoramic views and its bouillabaisse. ⊠ *269 corniche J.-F. Kennedy, 13007,* ☎ *04–91–52–01–77,* FAX *04–91–52–49–82. 16 rooms. Restaurant, air-conditioning. AE, MC, V.*

\$–\$\$ 🏨 **Alizé.** On the Vieux Port, its front rooms taking in postcard views, this straightforward lodging has been modernized to include tight double windows, slick modular baths, and a laminate-and-all-weather-carpet look. Public spaces have exposed stone and preserved details, and a glass elevator whisks you to your floor. It's an excellent value and location for the price range. ⊠ *35 quai des Belges, 13001,* ☎ *04–91–33–66–97,* FAX *04–91–54–80–06. 37 rooms. Air-conditioning. AE, DC, MC, V.*

Nightlife and the Arts

With a population of more than 800,000, Marseille is a Big City by French standards, with all the nightlife the name entails. Arm yourself with *Marseille Poche,* a glossy monthly events minimagazine; the monthly *In Situ,* a free guide to music, theater and galleries; *Sortir,* a weekly about film, art, and concerts in southern Provence; or *TakTik,* a hip weekly on theater and new art. They're all in French.

The dance club **Metal Café** (⊠ 20 rue Fortia, ☎ 04–91–54–03–03) is the place where local celebrities and sports stars hang out. **Le Trolleybus** (⊠ 24 quai de Rive Neuve, ☎ 04–91–54–30–45) is the most happening disco in town, with live concerts, three dance "grottoes," and a young, *branché* (hip) crowd.

All the discos filled with chic, professional thirty-somethings have English names, too: **London Club** (⊠ 73 Corniche Kennedy, ☎ 04–91–52–64–64), the **Real Club** (⊠ 1 rue des Catalans, ☎ 04–91–52–76–01), and **Saint James Club** (⊠ 7 rue Venture, ☎ 04–91–33–10–63).

Rock, jazz, and reggae concerts are held at the **Espace Julien** (⊠ 39 cours Julien, ☎ 04–91–24–34–15). **L'Intermediaire** (⊠ 63 pl. Jean Jaurès, ☎ 04–91–47–01–25) and **Le May Be Blues** (⊠ 2 rue André Poggioli, ☎ 04–91–42–41–00) are also venues for live jazz, blues, and rock.

Le Pelle Mèle (⊠ 45 pl. aux Huiles, ☎ 04–91–54–85–26) has a piano bar and, on Tuesday, Wednesday, and Thursday nights, jazz combos. For a more traditional night out, have a cognac in the fine old oak-paneled **Le Cintra** piano bar (⊠ in the Hôtel Mercure Beauvau, 4 rue Beauvau, ☎ 04–91–54–91–00).

Classical music concerts are held in the **Abbaye St-Victor** (☎ 04–91–05–84–48 for information). Operas and orchestral concerts take place at the **Opéra Municipal** (⊠ 2 rue Molière, pl. Ernest Reyer, ☎ 04–91–55–00–70).

At the **Théâtre National de Marseille La Criée** (⊠ quai de Rive Neuve, ☎ 04–91–54–70–54) a strong and solid repertoire of classics and contemporary works is performed. **Théâtre Off** (⊠ quai de Rive Neuve, ☎ 04–91–33–12–92) presents alternative productions of classics. Celebrity-cast road shows and operettas are performed in the Théâtre Municipal's **Espace Odéon** (⊠ 163 La Canebière, ☎ 04–91–55–00–70).

At **Badaboum** (⊠ quai de Rive Neuve, ☎ 04–91–54–40–71), adventurous, accessible productions for children are performed. The **Théâtre des Marionettes** (⊠ Theatre Massalia, 19 rue Guibal, ☎ 04–91–11–45–65) entertains a young audience with puppets, dance, and music—ocassionally in foreign languages. It's by the Gare St-Charles.

Outdoor Activities and Sports

Marseille's waterfront position makes it easy to swim and sunbathe within the city sprawl. From the Vieux Port, Bus 83 or Bus 19 takes you to the vast green spread of reclaimed land called the **Parc Balnéaire du Prado.** Its waterfront is divided into beaches, all of them public and well-equipped with showers, toilets, and first-aid stations. The beach surface varies between sand and gravel. You can also find your own little beach on the tiny, rocky **Iles de Frioul**; boats leave from the Vieux Port and cost 50 francs.

If you want to venture into wilder coastal country, and have a car, drive it to the end of the world. Head out the coastal road to Les Goudes, then penetrate even further (up the road marked "sans issue" or dead end) until you reach Callelongue. From here you can strike out on foot, following the GR 98 to the idyllic **Calanque de Marseilleveyvre,** a rocky finger-inlet perfect for an isolated swim. From this point, the famous Calanques continue all the way to Cassis; though most of them lie on Marseille's official turf, they are most often accessed from Cassis and are thus described below (☞ Cassis, *below*).

Marseille is a major center for diving (*plongée),* with several organizations offering "baptêmes" ("baptisms," or first dives) to beginners. The coast is lined with rocky inlets, grottos, and ancient shipwrecks, not to mention thronging with aquatic life. For general information, contact the **Association Plongez Marseille** (⊠ 5 rue de Valmy, 13012,

☎ FAX 04–91–49–12–93). Two private companies specializing in initiations and day trips—and who speak English—and who can rent you the necessary equipment and provide showers and storage are: **Océan 4** (✉ 83 av. de la Pointe-Rouge, ☎ 04–51–73–91–16) and **Palm Beach Plongée** (✉ 2 promenade de la Plage, ☎ 04–91–22–10–38).

Shopping

The locally famous bakery **Four des Navettes** (✉ 136 rue Sainte, ☎ 04-91-33-32-12), up the street from Notre-Dame-de-la-Garde, makes orange-spice, shuttle-shape navettes. These cookies are modeled on the little boat in which Mary Magdalene and Lazarus washed onto continental shores (☞ Stes-Maries-de-la-Mer *in* Chapter 2) before Lazarus worked his way over to Aix and Marseille.

Savon de Marseille (Marseille Soap) is a household expression in France, often sold as a satisfyingly crude and hefty block in odorless olive-oil green. There's a world market, though, for the chichi offspring of this earth mother: dainty pastel guest soaps in almond, lemon, vanilla, and other scents. If you're not one for lingering in the odoriferous boutiques that sell these in gilt gift boxes, consider the no-nonsense outlet of **La Compagnie de Provence** (✉ 1 rue Caisserie, ☎ 04–91–56–20–97), at the foot of Le Panier: Here blocks of soap are sold in plain brown boxes, but you can have them gift wrapped on request.

For good old-fashioned big-city shopping, the rue St-Ferréol (four blocks back from the Vieux Port) is flanked with major department stores: **Galeries Lafayette** (✉ 40 rue St-Ferréol, ☎ 04-91-54-46-54) and **Marks & Spencer** (✉ 55 rue St-Ferréol, ☎ 04-91-54-46-54). **Nouvelles Galeries** (✉ Centre Bourse/Bir Hakeim, ☎ 04-91-56-82-12), a mid-priced department store, anchors the corner one block back from the port and the tourist office. Off-beat designer clothing created in Marseille can be found on cours Julien, including the home-base for the trendy, high-texture clothes and jewelry made by **Madame Zaza of Marseille** (✉ 73 cours Julien, ☎ 04–91–48–05–57).

THE CENTRAL COAST

With the floods of vacationers pouring onto the beaches from St-Tropez to Menton every summer, it's surprising that the coast between Marseille and Hyères is often dismissed. Although a few industrial pockets exist around La Ciotat and Toulon, there are just as many sections of magnificent coastline—white cliffs peppered with ragged, wind-twisted pines.

Just inland, in the dry white hills, lies the peaceful market town of Aubagne; climb to the top of its outlying hills, and you can see the ocean sparkling below. Cassis is the jewel of this region, a harbor protected by the formidable Cap Canaille, 1,300 ft high; between Cassis and Marseille stretch the extraordinary Calanques, a series of rocky fjords that probe deep into the coastline. Following the coastal highway, you come to La Ciotat, a gargantuan (but oddly picturesque) naval shipyard, and reach the popular beach resort of Bandol—incidentally the source of one of Provence's most famous wines. A popular rainy-day excursion from Bandol leads to the hilltop medieval village of Le Castellet; you may want to stop at some of the wineries along the way. Toulon is an enormous naval base and a tough big city with an inter-

esting old town for the intrepid; just east of city is where you catch the
ferry to Porquerolles, the best of the wild and beautiful Iles d'Hyères.

Aubagne

⓬ *15 km (9 mi) east of Marseille, 10 km (6 mi) north of Cassis.*

This easygoing, plane-tree-shaded market town (pronounced Oh-
BAHN-yuh) is proud of its native son, the dramatist, filmmaker, and
chronicler of all things Provençal, Marcel Pagnol, best known to An-
glophones as author of *Jean de Florette* and *Manon des Sources* (*Manon
of the Springs*). Here you can spend the morning digging through used
Pagnol books and collectibles in the old town. You can also study the
miniature dioramas of scenes from Pagnol stories at **Le Petit Monde de
Marcel Pagnol** (The Small World of Marcel Pagnol). The characters
are all santons, and there are superb portraits of a humpback Gerard
Départieu and Yves Montand, resplendent in mustache, fedora, and
velvet vest, just as they were featured in *Jean de Florette*. ⊠ *esplanade
de Gaulle.* 🔀 *Free.* ⊙ *Daily 9–noon and 2–6.*

Aubagne claims the title of the santon capital of Provence. The craft,
originally from Marseille, was focused here at the turn of the 20th century when artisans moved inland to make the most of local clay (☞
Close-Up Box: Little Santons with Feet of Clay, *below*). The more than
a dozen studios in town are set up for you to observe the production
process. Daniel Scaturro is one of the best; in 1997 he was granted status as *Meilleur Ouvrier de France* (Best French Artisan), the country's
highest honor for artisans in all fields (Paul Bocuse is another). He specializes in portraits, mostly of Pagnol's film characters—but you can
have one made of yourself for 4,000 francs. His main studio, **Daniel
Scaturro** (⊠ 20A av. de Verdun, ☎ 04–42–84–33–29) is on the edge
of town in an industrial quarter. Scaturro's son demonstrates the family craft on a smaller scale in a shop in the central old town (⊠ bd.
Jean-Jaurès/rue Martinot).

The history of the craft of santon making and other uses to which the
local clay was put—faïence and hand-painted tiles—can be studied at
the **Ateliers Thérèse Neveu,** named for Aubagne's first master *santonière*
(santon maker). Also on display are excellent temporary exhibitions
about pottery. ⊠ *chemin Entrecasteaux, at the top of the old town hill,*
☎ *04–42–03–43–10.* ⊙ *Tues.–Sun. 9–noon and 2–6.*

Even if you haven't read Pagnol's works or seen his films, you can enjoy
the **Circuit Pagnol,** a hike in the raw-hewn, arid *garrigues* (scrublands)
behind Marseille and Aubagne. Here Pagnol spent his idyllic summers,
described in his *Souvenirs d'un Enfance* (*Memories of a Childhood*),
crunching through the rosemary, thyme, and scrub oak at the foot of
his beloved Garlaban. When he grew up to be a famous playwright
and filmmaker, he shot some of his best work in these hills, casting his
wife, Jacqueline, as the first Manon of the springs. After Pagnol's
death Claude Berri came back to the Garlaban to find a location for
his remake of *Manon des Sources* but found it so altered by brush fires
and power cables, he chose to shoot in the Luberon instead. Although
the trail may no longer shelter the pine-shaded olive orchards of its
past, it still gives you the chance to walk through primeval Provençal
countryside and rewards you with spectacular views of Marseille and
the sea. *To access the marked trail by yourself, drive to La Treille northeast of Aubagne and follow the signs. For an accompanied tour with
literary commentary, contact the Office du Tourisme (☎ 04–42–03–
49–98).*

LITTLE SAINTS WITH FEET OF CLAY

THEY BECKON FROM SHOP windows in every hill town, these miniatures called *santons*, from the dialect *santouns* for "little saints." But whatever commercial role they may play today, their roots run deep in Provence.

The Christmas crèche has been a part of Provençal tradition since the middle ages, when people reenacted the tableau of the birth of Christ, wise men, shepherds, and all. When the Revolution cracked down on these pastoral plays, a crafty Marseillais decided to substitute clay actors. The tiny terra-cotta figures caught on and soon upstaged their human counterparts for good.

A Marseille tradition that eventually migrated to Aubagne in the hills above (the clay was better), the delicate doll-like figurines spread throughout Provence, and are displayed every Christmas in church crêches that resemble a rustic backcountry hill village as much as they do Bethlehem. Against a miniature background of model stone houses, dried-moss olive groves, and glass creeks, quaint, familiar characters go about their daily tasks—the lumberjack hauling matchstick kindling, the fisherman toting a basket of waxy fish, the red-cheeked town drunk leering drolly at the pretty lavender-cutter, whose basket hangs heavy with real dried sprigs. The original cast from Bethlehem gets second billing to a charming crowd of gypsies, goat herds, and provincial passersby. And wait—isn't that Gerard Depardieu? And Raimu?

And Yves Montand? Even beloved film actors have worked their way into the scene.

It's a highly competitive craft, and while artisans vie for the souvenir trade, some have raised it to an art form: Daniel Scaturro, of Aubagne, was named a Meilleur Ouvrier de France in 1997, one of the highest national honors granted to craftsmen.

Molded, dried, then scraped with sharp tools down to the finest detail—wrinkled foreheads and fingernails—the santons are baked at 1,000°C (1,832°F). Once cool, they are painted with a watchmaker's precision: eyelashes, nostrils, and gnarled knuckles. The larger ones have articulated limbs that are joined to allow for dressing; their hand-sewn costumes, Barbie-scaled, are lavished with as much fine detail as the painted features.

Many artisans maintain highly public studios so visitors can watch the process and acquire the taste for collecting. Little ones (about an inch high), without articulated limbs, run about 25 francs; big ones (8 to 10 inches), dressed and painted by the best artists, cost around 250 francs. Or you can splurge and commission a portrait of yourself for the mantel—4,000 francs at Scatturo's.

But the preferred format is the crêche tableau, and it's easy to get hooked on building a collection of Provençal rustics to be lovingly unwrapped and displayed every Christmas season.

Make sure you visit Aubagne on a **market** day, when the sleepy center is transformed into a tableau of Provençal life. For sale are fresh local asparagus, plant-ripened tomatoes, melons, and mesclun scooped by the gnarled fingers of blue-aproned ladies in from the farm. The Tuesday market is the biggest, with clothing, purses, tools, and pots and pans spilling onto the esplanade, but the Saturday and Sunday markets make more of regional products; those labeled Pays d'Aubagne must be organically raised. You won't find the social scene you'll see in Aix, but this is a more authentic farmers' market.

Another claim to fame for Aubagne: It's the headquarters for the French Foreign Legion. The legion was created in 1831 and accepts recruits from all nations, no questions asked. The discipline and camaraderie instilled among its motley team of adventurers, criminals, and mercenaries have helped the legion forge a reputation for exceptional valor—a reputation romanticized by songs and films in which sweaty deeds of heroism are performed under the desert sun. The **Musée du Képi Blanc,** named after the distinctive white caps of the *légionnaires,* does its best to polish the image by way of medals, uniforms, weapons, and photographs. ☒ *Caserne Viénot (to get there, take a left off D2 onto D44A just before Aubagne),* ☎ *04–42–03–03–20.* ◻ *Free.* ◷ *June–Sept., Tues.–Sun. 10–noon and 3–7; Oct.–May, Wed. and weekends 10–noon and 2–6.*

Dining

$ ✕ **La Farandole.** In a rustic Provençal setting of lemon-print cloths, lace curtains, and the region's typical bow-legged chairs, you can enjoy good home cooking with the local regulars who claim the same table every day. The inexpensive daily menu may feature panfried chicken livers on a green salad, rascasse with sorrel, or garlicky steak and *frites* (fries); wine is included. Homemade cakes and friendly waitresses enhance the small-town spirit. ☒ *6 rue Martino (just off cours Maréchal, on a narrow street leading into the old town),* ☎ *04–42–03–26–36. MC, V.*

Cassis

★ ㊸ *22 km (14 mi) southeast of Marseille, 10 km (6 mi) north of Aubagne.*

Surrounded by vineyards, flanked by monumental cliffs, guarded by the ruins of a medieval castle, and nestled around a picture-perfect fishing port, Cassis (pronounced cah-SEE) is the prettiest coastal town in Provence. Neighboring it are the wild Calanques that cut into the rock walls toward Marseille.

Stylish without being too recherché, it provides shelter to numerous pleasure-boaters, who restock their galleys at its market, replenish their Saint James nautical duds in its boutiques, and relax with a bottle of Cassis and a platter of urchins in one of its numerous waterfront cafés. Pastel houses at Cubist angles frame the port, and the mild rash of parking-garage architecture that scars its outer neighborhoods can't spoil the general effect, which is one of pure and unadulterated charm.

You can't visit Cassis without touring the **Calanques,** the fjord-like finger bays that probe the rocky coastline. Either take a sightseeing cruise on a double-decker, glass-bottom boat that travels across the open water and dips into each calanque in turn, or hike across the cliff tops, clambering down the steep sides to these barely accessible retreats. Or you can combine the two, going in by boat and hiking back; make arrangements at the port (☞ *Outdoor Actitives and Sports, below*).

THE S IS (HARDLY EVER) SILENT

(Or, how to brag to your friends, "we stayed in a beautiful mas outside Cassis" without mispronouncing a thing.)

THE RULE OF THUMB in Provence is to pronounce everything, even to the point of pronouncing letters that aren't there. *Pain,* in the north pronounced through the nose without a final consonant, becomes "peng" in the south. *Vin* becomes "veng," *enfin* "on feng," etc.

But there are words in constant dispute, especially among a people toilet-trained on the Academie Française, that holy arbiter of the French language. One of the words caught in the crossfire: *mas.* This old Provençal word for farmhouse is a "mahss" in the south, but Parisians hold out for a more refined Frenchification: "ma."

Cassis, on the other hand, is a booby trap. For one thing, there are two drinks named Cassis, one a black-currant liqueur made in Burgundy to be blended in white-wine *kirs,* the·other the famous wine from the coastal country east of Marseille. The liqueur is always called "cass-EESS," and northerners (who consume the most kirs) insist on pronouncing both the wine and the village "Cass-EESS" as well. But ask the locals, and they'll snort in disdain. *"C'est 'Cass-ee,' "* they'll explain, as if all the words in Provence followed the pattern.

There you have it: In Paris, it's cass-eess but mah; in Provence, it's cass-ee but mahss.

The Calanque closest to Cassis is the least attractive: **Port Miou** was a stone quarry until 1982, when the Calanques became protected sites. *Pierre de Cassis* (Cassis stone) is much sought-after in the building trade for its pink-gray whorls. Now this calanque is an active leisure and fishing port, and on the cliff top above it you can see the precarious GR98 that follows the Calanques to Marseille. **Calanque Port Pin** is prettier, with wind-twisted pines growing at angles from the white-rock cliffs. But it's the third calanque that's a corner of paradise: **Calanque En Vau** is a castaway's dream, with a tiny beach at its root and jagged cliffs looming overhead, covered with gnarled pine and scrub. Rock climbers love it. The series of massive cliffs and calanques stretch all the way to Marseille (most fall, in fact, within that city's limits) but will always be known as Les Calanques de Cassis.

The **Château de Cassis** has loomed over the harbor since the invasions of the Sarrasins in the 7th century, evolving over the centuries into a walled enclosure crowned with stout watch towers. It's private property today and best viewed from a port-side café.

If you're a wine lover, pick up a map and the brochure "Through the Vineyards" from the tourist office. There are 12 domains, all of them open for tasting and buying, but the most spectacularly sited is the **Clos Sainte Magdeleine** (⊠ av. du Revestel, ☎ 04–42–01–70–28), overlooking the sea from the slopes of the Cap Canaille.

Dining and Lodging

$$ ✕ **Monsieur Brun.** Though Cassis has many restaurants with linens and extensive menus, one of the most authentic meals you can have is a platter of raw shellfish, served a few yards from the port that supplied it. An unpretentious choice is this terrace brasserie on the west side of the port, inches from the bobbing boats and overlooking the château and Cap Canaille. A multitier tower of shellfish on a bed of kelp is served with nothing but bread, butter, and a finger towelette. Have the nutty little *bleues*, the local oyster, but *oursins* (sea urchins) are a Cassis specialty (☞ box, How to Eat a Sea Urchin, *below*). Omelets and salads are an alternative. ⊠ *2 quai Calendal,* ☎ *04–42–01–82–66. No credit cards. Closed mid-Dec.–end Jan.*

$$ ✕▥ **Jardin d'Emile.** Tucked back from the waterfront under quarried
★ cliffs and massive parasol pines, this stylish yet homey inn takes in views of the cape from the restaurant and half the rooms. View or not, rooms are intimate and welcoming, with rubbed-chalk walls, *boutis* (Provençal quilts), scrubbed pine, weathered stone, Salerne tiles, and dimmers to enhance the romantic atmosphere. The restaurant is atmospheric (closed Monday off season), on a permanently sheltered garden terrace surrounded by greenery and, by night, the illuminated cliffs. Regional specialties with a cosmopolitan twist—such as harbor-fresh tuna grilled with soy—are served on locally made pottery. ⊠ *Plage du Bestouan, 13260,* ☎ *04–42–01–80–55,* ℻ *04–42–01–80–70. 7 rooms. Restaurant. AE, DC, MC, V.*

$$$ ▥ **Les Roches Blanches.** First built as a private home in 1887, this cliff-side villa takes in smashing views of the port and the Cap Canaille, both from the best rooms and from the panoramic dining hall. The beautifully landscaped terrace is shaded by massive pines, and the horizon-line pool seems to spill into the sea. Yet the ambience is far from snooty or deluxe; rather it's friendly, low-key, and pleasantly mainstream. A bland '60s-style annex compensates for its looks with full-length balconies facing the cape. ⊠ *rte. des Calanques, 13260,* ☎ *04–42–01–09–30,* ℻ *04–42–01–94–23. Restaurant, pool. AE, MC, V.*

Outdoor Activities and Sports

To go on a **boat ride** to Les Calanques, get to the port around 10 AM or 2 PM and look for a boat that's loading passengers. Two of the best choices are the **Moby Dick III** and the **Ville de Cassis**—they have glass-bottom views and full commentary (in French only). But a slew of alternative boats won't leave you stranded. Round-trips should include at least three Calanques and average 65 francs.

To **hike** the Calanques, gauge your skills: The GR98 (marked with red-and-white bands) is the most scenic but requires ambitious scrambling to get down the sheer walls of En Vau. The alternative is to follow the green markers and approach En Vau from behind. The markers could use revision nonetheless. If you're ambitious, you can hike the length of the GR98 between Marseille and Cassis, following the coastline.

En Route From Cassis head east out of town and cut sharply right up the **Route des Crêtes.** This road takes you along a magnificent crest over the water and up to the very top of **Cap Canaille.** Venture out on the vertiginous trails to the edge, where nothing stands between you and infinity, and the whole coast stretches below. The altitude is only 1,310 ft, but that's straight up—literally—from sea level. From the **Semaphore du Bec d'Aigle,** a military lighthouse, go to the overlook that gives you the view from the cape's other side. This perspective plunges down to the

HOW TO EAT A SEA URCHIN

"**B**UT ANSWER CAME there none—/And this was scarcely odd, because/They'd eaten every one," wrote Lewis Carroll in *Through the Looking Glass*.

Urchins, those spiny little balls, are cracked open and served belly up on a platter of seaweed, usually six or a dozen at a time. To the uninitiated, they're not a pretty sight: Each black demiglobe comes with quills still. . . well, waving, but only slightly. Within this macabre natural bowl floats a dense puddle of (it must be said) muddy brown grit and bile-green slime. Supporting the rim with your left thumb and index finger (taking care not to impale yourself), scrape said slime to the sides with the point of your spoon. Here lies what the fuss is all about: There are six coral-pink strips of sea-perfumed stuff inside, more foam than flesh (you may have experienced a more substantial version in sushi). Scrape these gently up, spread them on a slice of baguette, and bite. An ocean of milky-sweet flavor is concentrated in this rosy streak. Granted, a dozen won't make a meal, but keep the little guys company with oysters, mussels, clams, sea snails, a crock of butter, a basket of bread, and an icy bottle of Cassis.

impressive shipbuilding center of **La Ciotat.** Here the Lumière brothers filmed the first moving picture, of a steam engine pulling into the train station, and screened their first film. Along the **Clos des Plages** are a series of good sand beaches. Continuing east, you'll cross out of the Bouches-du Rhône département and into the Var, which stretches nearly to Cannes.

Bandol

25 km (15½ mi) southeast of Cassis, 15 km (9 mi) west of Toulon.

Although its name means wine to most of the world, Bandol is also a popular and highly developed seaside resort town. It has seafood snack shacks, generic brasseries, a harbor packed with yachts, and a waterfront promenade. Yet the east end of town conceals lovely old villas framed in mimosas, bougainvillea, and pine. And a port-side stroll up the palm-lined allée Jean-Moulin feels downright Côte d'Azur. But be warned: The sheer concentration of high-summer crowds can't be exaggerated. If you're not a beach lover, pick up an itinerary from the tourist office and visit a few Bandol vineyards just outside of town.

Several sights around Bandol are worth pursuing. Follow D559 north of town toward **Le Castellet,** perched high above the Bandol vineyards. Its narrow streets, 17th-century stone houses, and (alas) touristy shops are designer-made for beach lovers on a rainy day.

Just east of town on D559 and past the smaller seaside resort of Sanary, turn left on D63 and follow signs to the small stone chapel of **Notre-Dame de Pépiole,** hemmed in by pines and cypresses. It's one of the oldest Christian buildings in France, dating from the 6th century and modeled on early churches in the Middle East. The simple interior has survived the years in remarkably good shape, although the colorful stained glass that fills the tiny windows is modern—composed mainly of broken bottles. ⊙ *Most afternoons 3–5.*

From Notre-Dame de Pépiole, retrace your steps toward Sanary and head south on D616 around the **Cap Sicié** for broad panoramas and a tremendous view across the Bay of Toulon. Or head north on D11 to **Ollioules**; just past the village, follow N8 (in the direction of Le Beausset) through a 5-km (3-mi) route that twists its scenic way beneath the awesome chalky rock faces of the **Gorge d'Ollioules.** Even more spectacular: Take a left at Ollioules on D20 and follow the winding road along the crest of **Le Gros Cerveau.** You'll be rewarded first with inland mountain views, then an expansive panorama of the coast.

Toulon

🅸 *67 km (41½ mi) east of Marseille, 29 km (18 mi) northwest of La Tour Fondue (departure point for the Iles d'Hyères).*

One of France's largest naval ports, Toulon is best known for the dark day in World War II when 75 French ships sunk themselves rather than fall into the hands of the attacking Germans. Though you may see nothing but monstrous apartment buildings and traffic jams in crossing through this dense and messy city of some 500,000 inhabitants, the **Vieille Ville** (Old Town) lurks behind; its nickname, "Petit Chicago," recalls the neighborhood's history (*almost* entirely in the past) as a crime-ridden, red-light district. Nowadays, it's merely run-down, with stretches of ruined medieval houses mixed with lurid neon.

Leave your car in parking lot under place de la Liberté. Head along boulevard de Strasbourg and turn right after the theater into rue Berthelot. It leads into the pedestrians-only streets that constitute the heart of the old town. Wander through **place des Trois Dauphins,** with its mossy fountain sprouting ferns and shrubs. Walk along **cours Lafayette,** with its morning market (except Sunday) shaded by rows of plane trees. And stroll past the **Hôtel de Ville,** with its Baroque figures evocatively carved by the Marseillais sculptor Pierre Puget.

Avenue de la République, an ugly array of concrete apartment blocks, runs parallel to the waterfront, where yachts and pleasure boats—some available for trips to the Iles d'Hyères or around the bay—add bright splashes of color. At the western edge of the gray is the **Musée Naval** (Naval Museum), with large models of ships, figureheads, paintings, and other items related to Toulon's maritime history. ⊠ *pl. Monsenergue,* ☎ *04–94–02–02–01.* 🎫 *22 frs.* ⊙ *Wed.–Sun. 9:30–noon and 2–6.*

Mighty hills surround Toulon, and **Mont Faron,** 1,600 ft, is the highest of all. Either drive to the top, taking the circular route du Faron in either direction, or make the six-minute ascent by cable car from boulevard de l'Amiral Jean-Vence. ☎ *04–94–92–68–25.* 🎫 *37 frs round-trip.* ⊙ *Daily July–Aug. 9:30–7:45. Closed Mon. morning. Sept.–June, Tues.–Sun. 9:30–noon and 2:15–6:30.*

Iles d'Hyères

46 *32 km (20 mi) off the coast south of Hyères. To get to the islands, follow the narrow Giens Peninsula to La Tour-Fondue, at its tip. Boats (leaving every half hour in summer, every 60 or 90 minutes the rest of the year for 75 francs round-trip) make a 20-minute beeline to Porquerolles. For Port-Cros and Levant, you'll depart from Port d'Hyères at Hyères-Plages. You can also get to all 3 islands from Port-de-Miramar or Le Lavandou—a longer boat ride to Porquerolles, but you avoid the maddening traffic bottleneck of the Giens Peninsula.*

Off the southeastern point of France's star and spanning some 32 km (20 mi), this archipelago of islands could be a set for a pirate movie; in fact, it has featured in several, thanks to a soothing microclimate and a wild and rocky coastline dotted with palms. And not only film pirates made their appearance: In the 16th century the islands were seeded with convicts to work the land. They soon ran amuck and used their adopted base to ambush ships heading into Toulon.

★ A more wholesome population claims the islands today, which consists of three main bodies: Levant, Port-Cros, and Porquerolles. **Port-Cros** is a national park, with both its surface and underwater environs protected. **Levant** has been taken over, for the most part, by nudists.
★ But **Porquerolles** (pronounced pork-uh-ROHL) is the largest and best of the lot, and a popular escape from the modern world. Off-season, it's a castaway paradise of pine forests, sandy beaches, and vertiginous cliffs over rocky coastline. Inland, its preserved pine forests and orchards of olives and figs are crisscrossed with dirt roads to be explored on foot or on bikes; except for the occasional jeep or work truck, the island is car-free. In high season (April to October) day-trippers pour off the ferries and surge to the beaches, while soap boutiques and T-shirt shops appear out of the woodwork to suit vacationers' whims. During this busy season it's worth considering staying in one of the few hotels in order to have the island to yourself when everyone else heads back to mainland.

Porquerolles is a perfect spot for a honeymoon, but it made an even better wedding gift. At the turn of the 20th century a Belgian engineer named François-Joseph Fournier made a killing on the Panama Canal, then struck gold in Mexico. To please his English bride, he bought Porquerolles at an auction and decided to create a hacienda-ranch, importing workers and founding his own school and electric company. It was only in 1970 that France nationalized the island, leaving Fournier's widow with a quarter of her original inheritance; her granddaughter runs the luxurious Mas du Langoustier (☞ Dining and Lodging, *below*).

Dining and Lodging

$$$ ✕🏠 **Mas du Langoustier.** Amid stunningly lush terrain at the westernmost
★ point of the Ile de Porquerolles, 3 km (2 mi) from the harbor, this luxurious hideout is a popular getaway for the yacht and helicopter set and a standard day trip from high-season St-Tropez. Owner Madame Richard, the granddaughter of the lucky woman who was given this island as a wedding gift, will pick you up at the port in her Dodge. Choose between big new California-modern rooms and cosseted old-style rooms in the original section. Chef Joël Guillet creates inspired southern French cuisine, to be accompanied by the rare island rosé. ✉ *Pointe du Langoustier, 83400 Ile de Porquerolles,* ☎ *04–94–58–30–09,* 🖷 *04–94–58–36–02. 51 rooms. Restaurant, tennis courts, beach, billiards. AE, DC, MC, V. Closed Nov.–Apr.*

$$–$$$ ✗▥ **La Glycine.** In soft shades of yellow ochre and sky blue, this sleekly modernized little *bastide* (country house) has an idyllic enclosed courtyard, verdant with lemon trees, ivy, and an ancient *figuier* (fig tree). Back rooms look over a jungle of mimosa and eucalyptus. Public salons have Provençal chairs and fabrics. The restaurant, where food is served on the terrace or in the garden, features port-fresh tuna and sardines. In summer (April–September) half board is obligatory; children stay (and eat) for free. The inn is just back from the port in the village center. ⊠ *pl. d'Armes, Ile de Porquerolles 83400,* ☎ *04–94–58–30–36,* ⅢX *04–94–58–35–22. 12 rooms. Restaurant, bar, air-conditioning. AE, MC, V.*

Outdoor Activities and Sports

You can rent a mountain bike (*velo tout-terrain,* or VTT) for a day to pedal the paths and cliff-top trails of Porquerolles at **Cycle Porquerol** (⊠ rue de la Ferme, ☎ 04–94–58–30–32) or **L'Indien** (⊠ pl. d'Armes, ☎ 04–94–58–30–39).

Locamarine 75 (⊠ On the port, ☎ 04–94–58–35–84) rents motor boats to amateurs with or without license. At the **Club de Plongée du Langoustier** (⊠ 7 Carré du Port, ☎ 04–94–58–34–94) you can take a diving class, hire a guide, rent diving equipment, and refill scuba tanks.

AIX, MARSEILLE, AND THE CENTRAL COAST A TO Z

Arriving and Departing

By Car

The A6/A7 toll expressway (*péage*) channels all traffic from Paris toward the south. At Orange, A7 splits to the southeast and leads directly to Aix. From there A51 leads to Marseille. Also at Aix, you can take A52 south via Aubagne to Cassis and A50, the coastal autoroute tollway; running parallel but closer to the water is the slow (but occasionally scenic) highway D559. Either of these will give you access to the coastal towns (Bandol, Toulon), inland sights (Le Castellet, Ollioules), and the Giens Peninsula for ferries to the Iles d'Hyères.

By Plane

Marseille has the second-largest airport in France, in **Marignane** (about 20 km [12 mi] northwest of the city center). Regular flights come in daily from Paris and London. In summer Delta Airlines flies direct from New York to Nice (about 190 km [118 mi] from Marseille and about 150 km [93 mi] from Toulon).

By Train

Regular rail service goes from Paris and most points north into Marseille's central station. From there it's a brief jaunt up to Aix. The main rail line continues from Marseille to Toulon, with local trains making stops at Aubagne and at Station de Cassis, about 5 km (3 mi) above the village. There are local stops in Bandol, too, and even in Hyères-Plages, where you can catch a boat to the Iles d'Hyères. The high-speed TGV (Train à Grande Vitesse) connects Paris and Marseille in 4 hours. It's also easy to take a night train from Paris and wake up in Marseille. (☞ Train Travel *in* the Gold Guide.)

Getting Around

By Bus

A good network of private bus services (confusingly called *cars*) strikes out from **Marseille's** *gare routière* (bus station; ⊠ 3 pl. Victor Hugo, ☎ 04–91–08–16–40) and carries you to points not served by train. Aix has a dense network of bus excursions; **C.A.P.** (Compagnie Autocars de Provence; ☎ 04–42–97–52–10) makes daily forays from 2 to 7 into Marseille, the Calanques by Cassis, Les Baux, the Luberon, and Arles, leaving from in front of the tourist office, at the foot of cours Mirabeau.

By Car

Although you can see this region by train, a car allows you greater freedom to visit vineyards, drive to the vertiginous edge of Cassis's Cap Canaille, and to explore the gorges, hilltop villages, and scenic countryside around Bandol and Toulon. You can also drive straight to La Tour-Fondue to take a (pedestrians-only) ferry trip to Porquerolles, one of the Iles d'Hyères; you must pay for parking, day and night.

By Train

See Arriving and Departing, *above.*

Contacts and Resources

Bed and Breakfasts

Chambres d'hôtes (bed-and-breakfasts) are simple accommodations, usually in the hosts' home, with breakfast and a warm regional welcome generally included. They are mostly concentrated around Aix, the most gentrified and touristy region in this chapter. Around Marseille and the coastal towns, they're somewhat rarer.

Gîtes de France, the French national network of vacation lodging, rate participating B&Bs for comfort and lists them in a catalogue (☞ Lodging *in* the Gold Guide). Addresses for the local listings are available through the departmental offices of Bouches-du-Rhône and the Var (☞ Vacation Rentals, *below*). Village tourist offices also publish lists of chambres d'hôtes and often rate them by objective comfort standards (shower or bath, air-conditioning, private garden, etc.). Aix's tourist office has an in-depth list of such lodgings in and around the city.

Car Rentals

AIX-EN-PROVENCE

Avis (⊠ 11 bd. Gambetta, ☎ 04–42–21–64–16); **Budget** (⊠ 16 av. des Belges, ☎ 04–42–38–37–36); and **Hertz** (⊠ 43 av. Victor Hugo, ☎ 04–42–27–91–32).

MARSEILLE

Avis (☎ 04–91–79–27–57). **Hertz** (☎ 04–91–90–14–03). Both are in the train station.

Guided Tours

Two-hour, multilingual **Aix walking tours** are organized by the tourist office (⊠ 2 pl. du Général de Gaulle, ☎ 04–42–16–11–61); tours of the old town leave at 3 on Wednesday and Saturday (50 francs). A tour of Cézanne landmarks, including a stop at the Musée Granet (and an optional finish at his Atelier), leaves from the tourist office at 9:30 Saturday morning (10 francs).

Calanques boat tours leave from Cassis; there's bullhorn commentary in French and English.

Marseille walking tours are organized by the tourist office (⊠ 4 La Canebière); these cover various neighborhoods and take place three times a week. In July and August they leave the tourist office on Monday, Wednesday, and Friday at 10AM. The rest of the year the tour leaves at 2PM on Monday and Wednesday and at 2:30 on Sunday. The tours cost 40 francs per person.

If you're feeling flush, footsore, or overwhelmed by the city, splurge on a **Marseille taxi tour** with cassette commentary in English; each taxi holds three adults or two adults and two children under 10. The drivers are selected by the tourist office and the itineraries fixed. In one and a half hours (170 francs) you'll be whisked up to the hard-to-reach Notre-Dame-de-la-Garde and Palais du Pharo; on the two-hour trip (335 francs) you'll also cruise the seaside cliff called the Corniche and duck into the picturesque fishing port Vallon des Auffes. Four hours (570 francs) shows you more ports, more monuments, and more neighborhoods. It's a good introduction to a huge city; reserve at the tourist office.

Even if you don't choose to hike the 12-km (7-mi) or 20-km (12-mi) loop through the garrigues above Aubagne, there's a **bus tour of Marcel Pagnol landmarks** that leaves from the tourist office (⊠ av. Antide Boyer, ☎ 04–42–03–49–98). It takes place in July and August on Wednesday and Saturday at 4; admission is 30 francs.

Travel Agencies

American Express (⊠ 115 rue Calude Nicolas Ledoux, Aix-en-Provence, ☎ 04–42–97–50–50). **Havas Voyages** (⊠ 20 La Canebière, Marseille, ☎ 04–96–11–26–26; ⊠ 4 av. Belges, Aix-en-Provence, ☎ 04–42–93–67–47).

Vacation Rentals

Gîtes de France is a nationwide organization that rents vacation housing, usually in homes or farmhouses with authentic regional character (☞ Lodging *in* the Gold Guide and Chapter 1 for more information). Two regional branches cover the area discussed in this chapter, so you should contact them directly. One handles the **Bouches-du-Rhône** (⊠ Domaine du Vergon, 13370 Mallemort, ☎ 04–90–59–49–39, FAX 04–90–59–16–75), as well as the Arles and Alpilles area. The other covers the **Var** (⊠ 1 bd. Maréchal Foch, ☎ 04–94–50–93–93, FAX 04–94–50–93–90). Many of the rental houses are in the wild and pretty countryside around Aix and north of Marseille.

Visitor Information

The regional tourist office, the **Comité Départemental du Tourisme du Var** (⊠ 1 bd. Maréchal Foch, 83300 Draguignan, ☎ 04–94–50–55–50, FAX 04–94–50–55–51) has extensive documentation on lodging, restaurants, rentals, hikes, and attractions in the Var. Written requests are preferred, with specific interests detailed. The same goes for the **Comité Départemental du Tourisme des Bouches-du-Rhône** (⊠ 13 rue Roux de Brignole, 13006 Marseille, ☎ 04–91–13–84–13, FAX 04–91–33–01–82).

Following are local tourist offices for towns covered in this chapter: **Aix** (⊠ 2 pl. du Général de Gaulle, B.P. 160, 13605 cedex 1, ☎ 04–42–16–11–61, FAX 04–42–16–11–62). **Aubagne** (⊠ av. Antide Boyer, ☎ 04–42–03–49–98, FAX 04–42–03–83–62). **Bandol** (⊠ pavillon du tourisme, on the waterfront, 83150, ☎ 04–94–29–41–35, FAX 04–94–32–50–39). **Cassis** (⊠ pl. Baragnon, 13260, ☎ 04–42–01–71–

17; FAX 04–42–01–28–31). **Ile de Porquerolles** (✉ carré du Port, 83400, ☎ 04–94–58–33–76, FAX 04–94–58–36–39). **Marseille** (✉ 4 La Canebière, 13001, ☎ 04–91–13–89–00, FAX 03–91–13–89–20). **Toulon** (✉ sq. William et Catherine Booth, 83000, ☎ 04–94–18–53–00, FAX 04–94–18–53–09).

5 The Western Côte d'Azur

St-Tropez to Cannes, the Haut Var, and the Gorges du Verdon

Between the watercolor port of St-Tropez and glamorous La Croisette in Cannes, this captivating stretch of the Riviera has drawn sun lovers and socialites since the days of the Grand Tour. The coastal highway hugs the spectacular waterfront, snaking past sophisticated resort towns as well as a staggering concentration of restaurants, high-rise resorts, snack shacks, gas stations, tourist traps, billboards, and beach discos. Yet just a few miles inland, picturesque Provençal villages perch above the fray; penetrate farther still, and you'll be rewarded with mountain scenery and serene little towns untouched by the tacky-chic of the commercialized scene below.

ASERIES OF PICTURE-BOOK GULFS scoop into this part of the coastline of the French Mediterranean; above them the horizon is dominated from all directions by the rugged red-rock heights of the Massif de l'Estérel and the green-black bulk of the Massif des Maures. The blue-green waters lap at the foot of thriving resort towns—St-Tropez and Cannes, of course, but also Fréjus, St-Raphaël, Mandelieu, and La Napoule. Each vies with its neighbor for vacationers craving the dependable sun and balmy temperatures. In winter these port towns are low-key, with minor pockets of glamour (Italians parading their minks up La Croisette, yachtsmen popping in for coffee in sleepy St-Tropez). But in high summer masses flood the beaches, feast on the fish, fill up the marinas, luxuriate in the spa treatments, and crowd the hotels and cafés. Bored or sun-burned or regarding each other in mutual disgust, the crowds then take to the hills—the glorious village-crowned hills that back the coast as the continent climbs gently toward the Alps.

They are a virtual subculture, these *villages perchés* (perched villages) and historic towns, which live in touristic symbiosis with the coast: Mougins, where Picasso spent his last years; Grasse, with its factories that make perfume from the region's abundant flowers; and Fayence, an 18th-century town living as much off its pottery as its spectacular views. Only 30 minutes' drive east of Cannes are also St-Paul-de-Vence (☞ Chapter 6), its maze of cobbled streets packed with shops and galleries, and Vence (☞ Chapter 6), its ancient walled center mixing medieval monuments and soap shops.

These towns make great day trips from the coast, though they're often dominated in high season by busloads of excursion-takers out of Cannes or St-Raphaël. But if you have a car and the time to explore, you can plunge even deeper into the backcountry, past the coastal plateau into the Haut Var. Here the harsh and beautiful countryside—raw rock, pine, and scrub oak—is lightly peppered with little hill villages that are almost boutique-free. You can hear the *pétanque* (lawn bowling) balls thunk, the fountains trickle, and the bells toll in their wrought-iron campaniles. If you like what you see and press on, you'll be rewarded with one of France's most spectacular natural wonders: the Gorges du Verdon, a Grand Canyon–style chasm roaring with milky-green water and edged by one of Europe's most hair-raising drives.

Pleasures and Pastimes

Art
Because the Côte d'Azur has long nurtured a relationship between artists, art lovers, and wealthy patrons, this region is blessed with a couple of superb art museums—the Musée de l'Annonciade in St-Tropez, with its collection of Impressionists and Post-Impressionists, and the Musée Fragonard, in Grasse, featuring the eponymous painter's works. You can make a pilgrimage up to Mougins, too, to see the pastoral retreat Picasso retired to.

Beaches
With their worldwide fame as the earth's most glamorous beaches, the real thing often comes as a shock to first-timers: Much of the Côte d'Azur is lined with rock and pebble, and the beaches are narrow swathes backed by city streets or roaring highways. Only St-Tropez, on this stretch of the Mediterranean, has the curving, isolated bands of sandy waterfront you've come to expect from all those '50s photographs. Other resorts, eager to please, haul in truckloads of sand to soften the lumps and bumps.

JUST WHAT IS THE CÔTE D'AZUR?

ASK FOUR FRENCHMEN to define the boundaries of the Côte d'Azur, and you'll get four (emphatic) answers. Purists will insist on limiting this stellar title to the subtropical stretch of seaside cliffs between Nice and the Italian border; this the Victorian English first called the French Riviera, and all other resorts are impostors. Another may stretch his definition to embrace palm-studded Cannes and the border of the department of Alpes-Maritimes (literally, Seaside Alps). But where does that leave sultry St-Tropez? *Alors*, expand southwest to include the democratic sandy beaches of St-Raphaël, Fréjus and Ste-Maxime and reach the elite fishing port whose name everyone loves to drop. But why stop there? After all, the sandy coast east of Toulon has unsung enclaves, and the department of Var rolls westward all the way to La Ciotat. Yet that political border cuts short of the pretty port of Cassis—and the lovely *calanques* (rocky coves) that feather the coastline all the way to Marseille.

Keep on going this way and you'll wind up in Barcelona. Suffice it to say that the resonant appellation of "Côte d'Azur" is coveted by all the coastal resorts on France's southeastern underbelly, and its application is subject to debate. Here, we have split the difference, starting with St-Tropez and following the palm trees all the way to Menton (☞ Chapters 5 and 6). The coastline west of St-Tropez— also seductively warm, and bordered with rugged pine, fig trees, and spiny succulents—we have loosely defined as the Central Coast (☞ Chapter 4). West of Marseille spans the Rhône delta, and the Languedoc coast lies beyond (☞ Chapter 2).

The beaches across from Cannes's grand hotels on La Croisette are private, renting parasols and mattresses to anyone who pays; if you're a guest of one of these hotels, you'll get a discount, but beach access is not included in the price of your stay.

Dining

Typical throughout Provence but especially at home with a cold slab of fresh coastal fish, the garlicky mayonnaise called aïoli is a staple condiment of which the poet Frédéric Mistral sang praise: "Aïoli sums up the heat, the strength, and the joy of the Provençal sun. Its other virtue: It drives off flies." Made of mortar-crushed raw garlic whipped with egg yolk and olive oil, it can bring tears to your eyes—and later, to those of your fellow travelers. Never mind: Heap it on hard-cooked eggs, on cold meat, or on raw vegetables. And watch for it as a Friday lunch special, when all of the above appear in a Provençal smorgasbord.

Even more pungent than aïoli is the powerful paste called *anchoïade*. Whether you spread it on tiny toasts or dip in raw vegetables, you'll feel the kick of concentrated salt and strong fish that characterizes the little Mediterranean anchovies that form its base.

Another staple—the Provençal version of pesto (originating from the Italian port of Genoa, nearby)—*pistou* consists of the same savory blend of basil, garlic, and pine nuts ground in olive oil. Its frequent appearance along the Mediterranean is due, in part, to the proliferation of *pin parasol* on the coast, from which the tender little nuts are produced. Although it's often served over pasta or wrapped in ravioli, its most delicious role is in a hearty vegetable *soupe au pistou,* a soup reminiscent of minestrone.

Restaurants in the coastal resorts are expensive, and often a risky investment, catering to a crowd en passage. St-Tropez prices can be higher than in Paris. Inland, you'll tap into a culture of cozy *auberges* (inns) in hilltop villages and have a better chance of finding good home-cooking for your money.

CATEGORY	COST*
$$$$	over 500 frs
$$$	250–500 frs
$$	150–250 frs
$	under 150 frs

per person for a three-course meal, including tax (20.6%) and tip but not wine

Hiking

Despite the mix of flash and glamour along the coast, the Massif des Maures and the Massif de l'Estérel are criss-crossed with excellent trails leading into rugged backcountry, often with views toward the sea. Several *sentiers du littoral* (waterfront trails) follow the water's edge along the base of the Estérel; another goes around the St-Tropez Peninsula. From the heights of the Estérel, the *grande randonée* (national hiking trail) GR51 heads into the highlands east of Draguignan, and the GR49 strikes off for Fayence, giving wide berth to the crackling cross-fire on the *camp militaire* (military camp) of Conjuers. North of the camp, the GR49 continues all the way to the Gorges du Verdon, where it intersects with France's most spectacular grande randonée, the GR4. Its star trail is the precarious Sentier Martel, which goes through the heart of the Gorges du Verdon.

Lodging

If you've come from other regions in France—even western Provence—you'll notice a sharp hike in hotel prices, costly by any standard but vertiginous in summer. In the coastal resorts you'll often find yourself far from the land of Provençal cottons and cozy country inns: The decor here is a peculiar hybrid—vaguely Jazz Age, a little Hollywood—that falls into a loose category known as Côte d'Azur style. In Cannes the grand hotels are big on prestige (waterfront position, awe-inspiring lobbies, high-price sea views) and weak on swimming pools, which are usually just big enough to dip in; their private beaches are on the other side of the busy street, and you'll have to pay for access, just as nonguests do.

Up in the hills above the coast you'll find the charm you expect from France, both in sophisticated inns with gastronomic restaurants and in friendly mom-and-pop auberges; the farther north you drive, the lower the prices.

CATEGORY	COST*
$$$$	over 1,000 frs
$$$	600–1,000 frs
$$	300–600 frs
$	under 300 frs

All prices are for a standard double room for two, including tax (20.6%) and service charge.

Shopping

On quaint old-town streets and up cobbled alleys in hilltop villages, you'll be bathed in the odor of soaps and sachets and potpourris wafting out of souvenir shops: Provence in general, but the Riviera in particular, makes the most of the flowers—especially lavender—proliferating in its sun-favored climate. In Grasse perfumes are made from the flowers on neighboring hillsides, then bottled in industrial-looking vials in its tourist-friendly factories. The most prestigious makers of Provençal fabrics have prominent spots in the main tourist centers. And Moustiers (by the Gorges du Verdon) still makes and sells its prestigious faïence, as it has since the 17th century.

Wine

Along the coast and into the hills above, vines stripe the fields in patchwork rows, destined for the unpretentious, all-encompassing wines known as Côtes de Provence. Even St-Tropez has vineyards, and the wild backcountry west of Draguignan bristles with roadside signs luring you into their *caves* (wine cellars) for *dégustations* (tastings). Most wines produced here are rosés with a few strong red table wines thrown in. Of the region's myriad versions of Côtes de Provence, one in particular gets top billing: The rosé of Domaine des Marchandises, produced outside Roquebrune-sur-Argens, is subtler than the usual coral pink blends.

Exploring the Western Côte d'Azur

You can visit any spot between St-Tropez and Cannes in an easy day trip; the hilltop villages and towns on the coastal plateau are just as accessible. Thanks to the efficient raceway, A8, you can whisk at high speeds to the exit nearest your destination up or down the coast; thus even if you like leisurely exploration, you can zoom back to your home base at day's end. Above the autoroute things slow down considerably, and you'll find the winding roads and overlooks between villages an experience in themselves. To venture farther north, either by the route Napoléon or D995, is a bigger commitment, and to be fully enjoyed, it should include at least one overnight stop.

Great Itineraries

Numbers in the text correspond to numbers in the margin and on the Western Côte d'Azur, Cannes, and the Backcountry maps.

IF YOU HAVE 3 DAYS

Spend your first day and night in **St-Tropez** ①. Pass the next day cruising (or in high summer, crawling along) the coastal highway N98, stopping to visit **Fréjus** ⑧. Still on N98, wind around the dramatic Corniche de l'Estérel, stop to dawdle by the castle and waterfront of **Mandelieu– La Napoule** ⑪. Then make a triumphant entry into **Cannes** ⑫–⑳, straight down La Croisette. Spend your third day strolling its waterfront and climbing into the old town to look over the whole of the bay.

IF YOU HAVE 7 DAYS

Follow the five-day itinerary but spend an extra night in ☷ **St-Tropez** ① so you can make an excursion into the hill towns of **Gassin** ③ and **Ramatuelle** ②. After St-Tropez, go to ☷ **Fréjus** ⑧ or ☷ **St-Raphaël** ⑨ for a night. Next, head to Cannes; with two days in ☷ **Cannes** ⑫–⑳ you can make a half day's round-trip by boat to Ile Ste-Marguerite, one of the **Iles de Lérins** ㉑. On the sixth day drive through **Mougins** ㉒ and **Grasse** ㉓ and up the Route Napoléon to the Gorges du Verdon; spend the night in ☷ **Moustiers-Ste-Marie** ㉜. On your way back down to reality, visit a few villages—such as **Aups** ㉞ and Sillans—and have lunch in old-fashioned **Cotignac** ㉟.

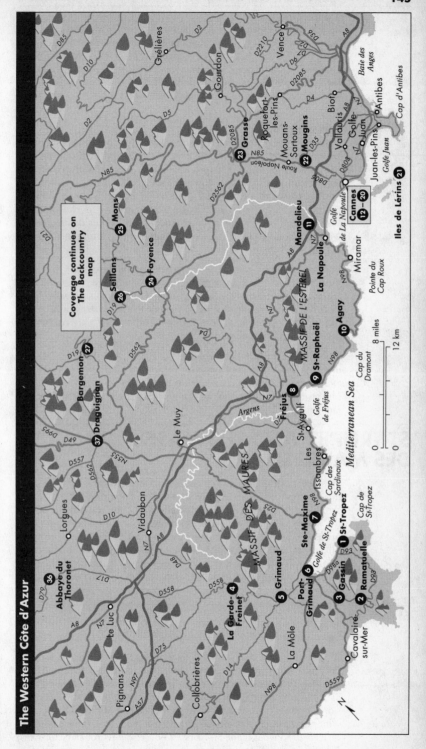

IF YOU HAVE 10 DAYS

Follow the five- and seven-day itineraries above. With your extra days take a scenic drive out of St-Tropez up to **La Garde-Freinet** ④ and spend more time in the backcountry villages—a night in ⊡ **Aups** ㉞ or ⊡ **Cotignac** ㉟, for instance—or more time on the beach. Or make a jaunt east of **Cannes** ⑫–⑳ to St-Paul-de-Vence, Vence, Antibes, or even Nice (☞ Chapter 6): A8 makes the whole coastline accessible in a day's round-trip.

When to Tour

Unless you enjoy jacked-up prices, traffic jams, and sardine-style beach crowds, avoid the coast like the plague in July and August, especially the last week of July and first three weeks of August. Many of the better restaurants simply shut down to avoid the coconut-oil crowd. Another negative about July and August: The Estérel is closed to hikers during this flash-fire season. Cannes books up early for the film festival in May, so unless you're determined to hover outside the Farfalla with an autograph book, aim for another month (April, June, September, or October).

But there are good times, even magical times, on the coast: Cannes enjoys the Côte d'Azur's gentle microclimate, protected by the Estérel from the mistral that razors through Fréjus and St-Raphaël. So with a little luck you may stroll in shirtsleeves under the palm trees on a winter day (though many places close during the off season) and even swim—if you're deeply committed.

Once you move into the highlands, you won't feel the crush of summer crowds, though the Gorges du Verdon is a mecca for rock climbers and hikers. But at altitudes averaging 3,280 ft and far from the Mediterranean that warms the coast, you may get caught in late-summer or late-spring snows.

ST-TROPEZ AND THE MASSIF DES MAURES

Shielded from the mistral by the broad, forested mass of the Massif des Maures, this small expanse of pampered coastline is crowned by the sparkling lights of St-Tropez, itself doubly protected by the hills of the Paillas. A pretty pastel port in winter, in season it becomes glamorous *"St-Trop."* For day trips you can escape to the simple life in the hill towns of Ramatuelle and Gassin or delve deep into the Maures in La Garde-Freinet. Ordinary mortals, especially vacationing families on a budget, usually aim for Ste-Maxime, across the bay, where the hyperdevelopment typical of the Riviera begins.

St-Tropez

❶ *35 km (22 mi) southwest of Fréjus, 66 km (41 mi) northeast of Toulon.*

At first glance, it really doesn't look all that lovely: There's a pretty port full of bobbing boats, but it's marred by double parking and cafés charging 23 francs for a coffee. There's a picturesque old town in sugared-almond hues, but there are many prettier in the hills nearby. There are sandy beaches, rare enough on the Riviera, and old-fashioned squares with plane trees and pétanque players, but these are a dime a dozen in Provence. So what made St-Tropez a household word? In two words: Brigitte Bardot. When this *pulpeuse* (voluptuous) teenager showed up in St-Tropez on the arm of Roger Vadim in 1956 to film *And God Cre-*

ated Woman, the heads of the world snapped around. Neither the gentle descriptions of writer Guy de Maupassant (1850–93), nor the watercolor tones of Impressionist Paul Signac (1863–1935), nor the stream of painters who followed him (including Matisse and Bonnard) could focus the world's attention on this seaside hamlet as could one voluptuous woman, in head scarf, Ray-Bans, and capris.

With the film world following in her steps, St-Tropez became the hot spot it to some extent remains, with a culture of B. B. wannabes (not all of them female) still strutting along the port side in skintight leopard-skin, toting leopard-collared terriers; they now mix with a "BCBG" ("bon-chic-bon-genre" or "well-bred yuppie") crowd in nautical togs and Gap shirts (with only golden retrievers or dalmatians, please) and a plethora of deeply tanned sixty-somethings in blazers and Gucci loafers. And then there are the others who come to see, snap photos, and say, "Oh, we spent a few days in St-Tropez, though it isn't what it was. . . . "

You will see these characters, if you come here, and pay a steep price to enjoy the carefully gentrified old town. But it's worth it if you get up early (before the 11 o'clock breakfast rush at Le Gorille Café) and wander the medieval backstreets and waterfront alone. You'll experience what the artists (who discovered St-Tropez before Bardot) first found to love and what remain the village's real charms: its soft light, warm pastels, and scent of the sea wafting in from the waterfront.

★ The legacy of the artists who loved St-Tropez has been preserved in the extraordinary **Musée de l'Annonciade** (Annunciation Museum), a 14th-century chapel converted to an art museum that alone merits a visit to St-Tropez. Works by Signac, Matisse, Signard, Braque, Dufy, Vuillard, and Rouault trace the evolution of painting from Impressionism to Expressionism, many of them painted in (and about) St-Tropez. It's at the inner corner of the port so many painters admired. ⊠ *quai de l'Épi/pl. Georges Grammont,* ☎ *04–94–97–04–01.* 🎟 *30 frs.* ☉ *June–Sept., Wed.–Mon. 10–noon and 3–7; Oct.–May, Wed.–Mon. 10–noon and 2–6.*

From the museum stroll around the **Vieux Port** (Old Port) and look over the shoulder of artists daubing their version of the view on easels that line the water's edge. Then wander past the famous port-side cafés—Le Gorille, Café de Paris, and Sénéquier's—where the cast of this living theater plays out their colorful roles from the folding director's chairs lining quai Suffren and quai Jean-Jaurès.

From the quai head up rue Laugier and rue de la Citadelle to the 16th-century **citadelle** that stands in a lovely hilltop park. Inside its *donjon* (defense tower), a **Musée Naval** (Naval Museum) displays ship models, cannons, and pictures of St-Tropez in its days as a naval port. The views from its terrace take in the whole of the gulf and the hills behind. ⊠ *Rue de la Citadelle,* ☎ *04–94–97–59–43.* 🎟 *25 frs.* ☉ *Nov.–Easter, Wed.–Mon. 10–5; Easter–Oct., 10–noon and 2–4:30.*

From the citadelle, head back down and lose yourself in the **Quartier de la Ponche,** the old-town maze of backstreets and old ramparts, daubed in shades of gold, pink, ochre, and sky blue. Trellised jasmine and wrought-iron birdcages hang from the shuttered windows, and many of the tiny streets dead-end at the sea. Wander back across rue Citadelle to the medieval rue Miséricorde, which leads under a series of stone arches to the 17th-century **Chapelle de la Miséricorde,** with its vivid glazed-tile roof, and on to rue Gambetta.

THE DOGS OF ST-TROPEZ

IN 68 AD THE ROMAN EMPEROR Nero had a centurion from Pisa decapitated for his Christian tendencies; to drive the lesson home for witnesses, he had the headless body placed in a boat with a cock and a dog, then set adrift at sea. When the boat washed ashore on St-Tropez's beach, the starving animals still kept their loyal vigil, refusing to touch the holy flesh.

Perhaps it's because of this heroic act of self-discipline that dogs are held in such high esteem in modern St-Tropez. They are clearly the companion (and accessory) of choice, as prevalent as mobile phones in the Vieux Port cafés. Whether tucked into handbags, strutted in pairs as beautifully matched as coach horses, dyed to match their mistress's hair, bounding nobly out of yachts, snarling at each other from under café tables, or lapping out of the ice bucket that chilled the champagne, they provide a spectacle almost as intriguing as their owners.

If you want to get the right port-front table at Le Gorille, consider borrowing a dog and accessorizing appropriately. Want to look like your yacht's being swabbed down for that lunch-run to Monte Carlo? A Lhasa Apso to match your ascot. Showing those canvases you daubed in the Alps last winter? Hot pants, hip-length hair, Timberlands, and an Afghan hound. Your bistro courting the Festival crowd out of Cannes? Green Lacoste sweater, red toupée, red German shepherd. Just drawn up a marriage contract to cover the London flat and Daddy's domaine in Burgundy? Matching buckskin jackets, separate phones, and a twinned team of golden retrievers.

A block up rue Gambetta you'll hear pétanque balls clicking in the sand square on **place des Lices,** the other social center of St-Tropez. A symmetrical forest of plane trees shades rows of cafés and restaurants, skateboarders, children, and grandfatherly pétanque players.

To experience up close St-Tropez's beautiful natural setting, consider walking the *sentier du littoral* (coastal path) around the peninsula. It's 12-km (7-mi) long and takes an average of four hours. Leave from the Tour du Portalet or the Tour Vieille at the edge of the old town. Follow the footpath from Plage des Graniers along the beaches and cliffs overlooking the water, often with views toward the Estérel or out to the open sea. From Cavalaire, at the southwest root of the peninsula, you can catch a bus back to St-Tropez.

Dining and Lodging

$$$ ✕ **Bistrot des Lices.** Rocked by the gentle *tonk* of pétanque balls on the Place des Lices, terrace diners at this St-Tropez landmark relish the earthy yet sophisticated cuisine of Breton-born chef Laurent Tarridec. Try his Provençal menu of, perhaps, cold roast rabbit, truffle-potato soup, lamb shoulder confit, an array of cheeses, and tender date bonbons. If you don't like the terrace scene, ask for a table in the intimate back garden. Inside, formality is softened by a warm ochre glow.

In case you want to see the world.

At American Express, we're here to make your journey a smooth one. So we have over 1,700 travel service locations in over 120 countries ready to help. What else would you expect from the world's largest travel agency?

do more®

AMERICAN EXPRESS

http://www.americanexpress.com/travel

Travel

In case you want to be welcomed there.

We're here to see that you're always welcomed at establishments everywhere. That's why millions of people carry the American Express® Card – for peace of mind, confidence, and security, around the world or just around the corner.

do more

Cards

In case you're running low.

We're here to help with more than 118,000 Express Cash locations around the world. In order to enroll, just call American Express before you start your vacation.

do more

Express Cash

And just in case.

We're here with American Express® Travelers Cheques and Cheques *for Two.*® They're the safest way to carry money on your vacation and the surest way to get a refund, practically anywhere, anytime.

Another way we help you...

do more ®

Travelers
Cheques

✉ *3 pl. des Lices,* ☎ *04–94–97–29–00. AE, DC, MC, V. Closed mid-Jan.–Mar. and mid-Nov.–Dec. 25.*

$$ ✕ **Le Girelier.** Like his father before him, chef Yves Rouet makes an effort to prepare Mediterranean-only fish for his buffed and bronzed clientele, who enjoy the casual sea-shanty decor and the highly visible Vieux Port terrace tables. Grilling is the order of the day, with most fish sold by weight, but this is also a stronghold for bouillabaisse. If you're watching your pennies, try one of the reasonable daily specials, which cost between 90 and 140 francs. ✉ *quai Jean-Jaurès,* ☎ *04–94–97–03–87. AE, DC, MC, V. Closed Oct.–Mar. (with the occasional exception).*

$$ ✕ **Lou Revelen.** Strike a pose on the throw-pillowed couch by the fireplace or people-watch from the terrace: this smart, stagy restaurant caters to the glamorous or wanna-bes. There's also, not incidentally, good Provençal cooking, with menus beginning at 160 francs. Try duck carpaccio, garlicky-sweet eggplant terrine, or basil-perfumed lamb. The fennel-grilled fish of the day is a mainstay. ✉ *bd. d'Aumale,* ☎ *04–94–97–06–34. MC, V.*

$ ✕ **Le Café.** This big, convivial brasserie with a zinc bar, an old color-tile floor, and antique posters, draws regulars for a generous plat du jour of classic bistro fare: *gigot* (leg of lamb) with *gratin dauphinois* (scalloped potatoes), salmon in juicy *poivrade* (red pepper sauce), local seafood, and homemade desserts. Tables on the square provide courtside seats to the pétanque games. ✉ *pl. des Lices,* ☎ *04–94–97–44–69. MC, V.*

$$$$ ✕🏨 **Byblos.** Arranged like a Provençal village, with ochre-stuccoed, cottagelike suites grouped around courtyards landscaped with palms, olive trees, and lavender, this landmark has undergone major renovations and changes since its days of kitschy glamour. Now it sports cool Mediterranean shades of blue and gold, and stresses fitness and beauty treatment more than ever. The new chef, Georges Pelissier, who took over the kitchen in 1998, creates artful classics with a Mediterranean touch: sea bass roasted with salsify and garlic chips, a light bouillabaisse, or rib-sticking beef tournedos with foie gras. Work on your waistline in the extensive exercise room, or sign up for a massage and skin treatment. ✉ *av. Paul-Signac, 83990,* ☎ *04–94–56–68–00,* ℻ *04–94–56–68–01. 50 rooms, 48 suites. Restaurant, air-conditioning, pool, exercise room, spa, nightclub. AE, DC, MC, V. Closed mid-Oct.–Easter.*

$$–$$$ ✕🏨 **La Résidence de la Pinède.** This balustraded white villa and its broad annex sprawl elegantly along a private waterfront, wrapped around an isolated courtyard and pool shaded by parasol pines. Pay extra for the seaside rooms, where you can lean over the balustrade and take in broad views of the coast. Fair-sized rooms and sunny colors add to the charms of this cosmopolitan resort. The restaurant is worth a visit for the skilled specialties of chef Herve Quesnel: truffle ravioli, sautéed prawns on basil-perfumed scrambled eggs, and fresh fig tarts. ✉ *Plage de la Bouillabaisse, 83991,* ☎ *04–94–55–91–00,* ℻ *04–94–97–73–64. 39 rooms, 4 suites. Restaurant, air-conditioning, pool. AE, DC, MC, V. Closed mid-Oct.–Mar.*

$$$–$$$$ 🏨 **Le Mas de Chastelas.** In a lush tropical garden full of mimosas and palms, set back from the main access road into St-Tropez, this 18th-century former silkworm farm has a handful of apartments clustered around one of two tree-lined pools. Earth-tone decor and pretty stenciling set these kitchenette suites apart from bare-bones rooms in the main house. The jury is out on the new chef in the upscale, poolside restaurant (closed Wednesday and Sunday night). ✉ *Quartier Bertaud, Gassin 83580,* ☎ *04–94–56–71–71,* ℻ *04–94–56–71–56. 12 rooms, 13 apartments. Restaurant, air-conditioning, 2 pools, tennis. AE, DC, MC, V.*

$$-$$$ ⌂ **Ermitage.** Surrounded by mimosas and lemon trees, this big, old-
★   fashioned hotel stands on a hill above town and, from backrooms and
        garden, commands striking sea views. The fireplace and cozy armchairs
        in the bar; the solid, light-bathed rooms in soft pastels; and owner Annie
        Bolloreis's friendly welcome make this a real charmer. ⊠ *av. Paul-Signac,*
        83990, ☎ *04–94–97–52–33,* FAX *04–94–97–10–43. 26 rooms. Bar.*
        MC, V.

$$ ⌂ **Le Baron.** All the simple, small, brocante-furnished rooms overlook
        the citadelle's green park, some from tiny balconies. If you're more than
        two, ask for the pretty loft suite, with its private spiral-stair entrance.
        Breakfast is served in the cozy "library" bar. ⊠ *23 rue de l'Aïoli,*
        83990, ☎ *04–94–97–06–57,* FAX *04–94–97–09–44. 11 rooms.*
        Breakfast room, bar. AE, DC, MC, V.

$–$$ ⌂ **Lou Cagnard.** Inside an enclosed garden courtyard is this pretty lit-
★   tle hotel now owned by an enthusiastic young couple who are fixing
        it up room by room. Five ground-floor rooms open onto the lovely man-
        icured garden, where breakfast is served in the shade of a fig tree. The
        newest rooms have regional-tile baths, quarry-tile floors, and Provençal
        fabrics; those not yet renovated still have chenille spreads and all-weather
        carpet. If you're willing to share a toilet down the hall, five rooms are
        real bargains. ⊠ *18 av. Paul Roussel, 83900,* ☎ *04–94–97–04–24,*
        FAX *04–94–97–09–44. 19 rooms. Parking (free). MC, V. Closed Nov.–*
        late Dec.

Nightlife and the Arts

The most elite and sought-after nightspot in St-Tropez remains the evergreen **Les Caves du Roy** in the Byblos Hotel (⊠ av. Paul-Signac, ☎
04–94–97–16–02); look your best if you want to get in. **Le Papagayo**
disco (⊠ Résidence du Port, ☎ 04–94–54–88–18) anchors the end
of the building opposite the VIP Room, and caters to a young crowd
of teens and twenty-somethings. The **VIP Room** (⊠ in the commercial
and residential building called Residence du Port, just off the main parking lot, ☎ 04–94–97–14–70) was all the rage at press time, drawing a democratic mix of young clients and baby boomers. The scene
peaks only after 2AM, and the club closes off-season (Oct.–Easter).

Every July and August, **classical music concerts** take place in the sultry gardens of the private manor house called the Château de la Moutte
(⊠ rte. des Salins). For ticket information, inquire at the tourist office
(☎ 04–94–97–45–21).

Outdoor Activities and Sports

The best *plages* (beaches) are scattered along a 5-km (3-mi) stretch
reached by the route des Plages (Beach Road); the most fashionable
are **Moorea, Tahiti,** and **Club 55.** Those beaches close to town—**Plage
des Greniers** and the **Bouillabaisse**—are accessible on foot, but many
prefer the 10-km (6-mi) sandy crescent at **Les Salins** and the long
sandy stretch of the **Plage de Pampelonne,** 4 km (3 mi) from town. Remember, they are carved up into private turf, and you must pay an average of 60 to 120 francs per day for access to these competitive
havens, which vie for your business with full restaurants, colorful
lounge chairs, hot showers, and mattress-side bar service. There are,
however, public-access beaches between the private ones, many of
them equipped with showers and toilets.

Bicycles are an ideal way to get to the beach; try **Espace 93** (⊠ 2 av.
Général-Leclerc, ☎ 04–94–55–80–00) or **Holiday Bikes** (⊠ 14 av.
Général-Leclerc, ☎ 04–94–97–09–39).

Sailboats can be rented from **Sportmer** (⊠ 8 pl. Blanqui, 04–94–97–32–33).

Shopping

Rue Sibilli, behind the quai Suffren, is lined with all kinds of trendy boutiques, many featuring those all-important sunglasses. The **Place des Lices** overflows with produce and regional foods, as well as clothing and *brocantes* (secondhand items), every Tuesday and Saturday mornings. The picturesque little **fish market** holds forth on the place aux Herbes every morning.

Ramatuelle

❷ *12 km (7 mi) southwest of St-Tropez.*

A typical hilltop whorl of red-clay roofs and dense inner streets topped with arches and lined with arcades, this ancient market town was destroyed in the War of Religions and rebuilt as a harmonious whole in 1620. Now its souvenir shops and galleries attract day-trippers out of St-Tropez, who enjoy the pretty drive through the vineyards as much as the village itself.

En Route From Ramatuelle, the lovely ride through vineyards and woods full of twisted cork oaks to the hilltop village of Gassin takes you over the highest point of the peninsula (1,070 ft).

Gassin

❸ *7 km (4 mi) north of Ramatuelle.*

Though not as picturesque as Ramatuelle, this hilltop village gives you spectacular views over the surrounding vineyards and St-Tropez's bay. In winter, before the summer haze drifts in and after the mistral has given the sky a good scrub, you may be able to make out a brilliant-white chain of Alps looming on the horizon. There's less commerce here to keep you distracted; for shops, head to Ramatuelle.

En Route The dramatic forest scenery of D558 winding west and northwest of St-Tropez merits a drive even if you're not heading up to A8: This is the **Massif des Maures,** named for the Moors who retreated here from the Battle of Poitiers in 732 and profited from its strong position over the sea. The forest is dark with thick cork oaks, their ancient trunks girdled for cork only every 10 years or so, leaving exposed a broad band of sienna brown. Looming even darker and thicker above are the chestnut trees cultivated for their thick, sweet nuts; you're not allowed to gather them from the forest floor, as signs from the growers' cooperative warn. Between wine domains' vineyards, mushroom-shape parasol pines, unique to the Mediterranean, crowd the highway.

La Garde-Freinet

❹ *20 km (12 mi) northwest of St-Tropez.*

The Moors (Arabic North Africans defeated by Charles Martel at Poitiers in 732) created a stronghold on this hilltop, building a fortress of which only ruins remain today. You can look out over the sea from there, as the Moors did, and enjoy this isolated village's quirky personality. Ramshackle but picturesque, with stacked stone visible under the ivy in some of the older buildings, it seems infinitely removed from the glamour of the coast.

Dining

$ ✕ **La Colombe Joyeuse.** Those pigeon hutches you saw lining the forest cliffs as you approach from the north aren't just for sport: They provide the dinner on your plate at this novel restaurant, where the menu revolves around fresh pigeon, potted pigeon, pigeon terrine, and pigeon roasted in honey. The fauve-tone decor inside has its charms, but the terrace in the heart of the old village feels like real Provence. ⊠ *12 pl. Vieille,* ☎ *04–94–43–65–24. MC, V. Closed Tues. Oct.– Mar.*

Grimaud

⑤ *10 km (6 mi) west of St-Tropez.*

Once a formidable Grimaldi fiefdom and home to a massive Romanesque château, the hill-village of Grimaud is merely charming today, though the romantic castle ruins that crown its steep streets still command lordly views over the forests and coast. The labyrinth of cobbled streets is punctuated by pretty fountains, carved doorways, and artisans' gallery-boutiques. Wander along the Gothic arcades of the rue des Templiers to see the beautifully proportioned Romanesque Église St-Michel, built in the 11th century.

Port-Grimaud

⑥ *5 km (3 mi) south of Grimaud, 7 km (4 mi) west of St-Tropez.*

Although much of the coast has been infected with new construction of extraordinary ugliness, this modern architect's version of a Provençal fishing village works. Begun in 1966, it has grown gracefully over the years, and offers hope for a coastal landscape scarred with pink concrete. It's worth parking and wandering up its Venicelike canals to admire the old-Mediterranean, canal-tile roofs and the pastel façades, already patinated with age. There's a boat that carries you into the heart of the complex of pretty squares and bridges. Even the church, though resolutely modern, feels Romanesque.

Ste-Maxime

⑦ *8 km (5 mi) east of Port-Grimaud, 33 km (20 mi) east of St-Tropez.*

You may be put off by its heavily built-up waterfront, bristling with parking-garage-style apartments and hotels, and its position directly on the waterfront highway, but Ste-Maxime is an affordable family resort with fine sandy beaches. It even has a sliver of car-free old town and a stand of majestic plane trees sheltering central Place Victor-Hugo. Its main beach, north of town, is the wide and sandy **La Nartelle.**

En Route   As you cling to the coastline on dramatic N98 between Ste-Maxime and Fréjus, you'll see a peculiar mix: Pretty beaches and fjordlike *calanques* (finger bays) dipping in and out of view between luxury villas (and their burglar-wired hedges), trailer-park campsites, and the fast-food stands and beach discos that define much of the Riviera. The **Calanque des Louvans** and the **Calanque du Four a Chaux** are especially scenic, with sand beaches and rocks shaded by windblown pines; watch for signs.

FRÉJUS, ST-RAPHAËL, AND THE ESTÉREL RESORTS

Though the twin resorts of Fréjus and St-Raphaël have become somewhat overwhelmed by waterfront resort culture, Fréjus still harbors a small but charming enclave that evokes both the Roman and medieval periods. Otherwise, the resorts that cluster at the foot of the magnificent red-rock Estérel are densely populated pleasure ports, with a agreeable combination of cool sea breezes and escapes into the near-desert behind.

Fréjus

8 *19 km (12 mi) northeast of Ste-Maxime, 37 km (23 mi) northeast of St-Tropez.*

Confronted with the gargantuan pink holiday high-rises that crowd the Fréjus–St-Raphaël waterfront, you may be tempted to forge onward. But after a stroll on the sandy curve along the tacky, overcommercial Fréjus-Plage (Fréjus Beach), turn your back on modern times and head uphill to Fréjus-Centre. Here you'll enter a maze of narrow streets lined with small shops—butchers, pastry makers, and slipper stores—barely touched by the cult of the lavender sachet. The farmers' market (Monday, Wednesday, and Saturday mornings) is as real and lively as any in Provence, and the cafés encircling the fountains and squares nourish an easygoing social scene.

Yet Fréjus (pronounced fray-ZHOOSS) has the honor of possessing some of the most important historic monuments on the coast. Founded in 49 BC by Julius Caesar himself and named Forum Julii, this quiet town was once a thriving Roman city of 40,000 citizens. It also was a vital shipbuilding port, where Caesar had a fleet of galleys equipped to take on Cleopatra at Actium. In its heyday Roman Fréjus had a theater, baths, and an enormous aqueduct that carried water all the way from Mons in the mountains north of town.

Today you can see the remains: a series of detached arches that follow the main avenue du Quinzième Corps (leading up to the old town). Just outside the old town is the the Roman **theater**; its remaining rows of arches are mostly intact and much of its stage works are still visible at its center. The **arènes** (often called the *amphithéâtre*) is the most impressive remains; it's still used today for concerts and bullfights. Follow avenue du Verdun west of the old town toward Puget.

★ Fréjus is also graced with one of the most impressive religious monuments in Provence: Called the **Groupe Épiscopal,** it's an enclosed ensemble of cathedral, cloisters, and baptistery. The early Gothic **cathedral** consists of two parallel naves, the narrower one from the 12th century (with barrel vaults) and the broader from the 13th century, with groin vaults supported by heavy pillars. The ensemble is spare and somber, with modern windows. Through the heavy arches of the 15th-century narthex you reach the entrance to the **baptistery,** which dates from the 5th century. This extraordinary structure retains the style of arches and columns that shows just how Roman these early Christians were. The bishop himself baptized them, washing their feet in the small pool to the side, then immersing them in the deep font at the room's center. Outside the baptistery, stairs lead up to the early Gothic **cloister,** redolent of boxwood and framing a stone well. There are two stories of pillared arcades, the lower ones pointed, the upper ones round (an odd effect, yet all were executed during one architectural pe

The capitals on the lower pillars are graceful and abstract; the grotesques and caricatures you'd expect appear instead in the unusual and striking wooden roof that covers the lower gallery: It was painted in the 15th century in sepia and earth tones with a phantasmagoric assortment of animals and biblical characters. Off the entrance and gift shop, you can peruse a small museum of findings from Roman Fréjus, including a complete mosaic and a sculpture of a two-headed Hermes. ⊠ 58 rue de Fleury. ⊠ Cathedral free; cloister, museum, and baptistery 25 frs. ☉ Cathedral: daily 8:30–noon and 4–7. Cloister, museum, and baptistery: Apr.–Sept., daily 9–7; Oct.–Mar., Tues.–Sun. 9–noon and 2–5.

OFF THE BEATEN PATH

ROCHER DE ROQUEBRUNE – Follow N7 out of Fréjus and exit south toward Roquebrune-sur-Argens, then cut right toward this massive red-rock island looming over the Argens Valley. Rough-hewn and basically unpopulated, its pine-covered slopes provide deep-country drives and walks down primeval footpaths pounded firm by thousands of passing sheep. The village of Roquebrune and its environs provide endless possibilities for purchasing local wines and olive oil; the rosé from the Domaine de Marchandise is a cut above the rest.

Dining

$ ✕ **Chez Victor.** Just off the market place and up from the cathedral, this old-town bistro serves home-cooked regional specialties under a 13th-century vaulted ceiling. If available, have the garlicky beef *daube* (stew), quail salad, or the catch of the day in Provençal tomato-and-fennel sauce. Service is friendly, and the atmosphere is low-key. ⊠ 19 rue Desaugiers, ☎ 04–94–53–89–89. MC, V. Closed Wed.

Outdoor Activities and Sports

Diving off the calanques between Fréjus and Ste-Maxime gives you interesting underwater insight into the marine life lurking in the rocks. Contact the **Centre International de Plongée** (International Diving Center; Port Fréjus, ☎ 04–94–52–34–99) for instruction, equipment rental, and guided outings.

The **beaches** around Fréjus are public and wide open, with deep sand stretches toward St-Aygulf. The urban stretch of beach draped at the foot of town, however, is backed by a commercial sprawl of brasseries, beach-gear shops, and realtors (for sunstruck visitors who dream of buying a flat on the waterfront). The calanques just south are particularly wild and pretty, with only tiny sand surfaces.

St-Raphaël

🕒 *3 km (2 mi) east of Fréjus, 30 km (19 mi) southwest of Cannes.*

Right next door to Fréjus, with almost no division between, is St-Raphaël, a sprawling resort city with a busy downtown anchored by a casino. It's also a major sailing center, has five golf courses nearby, and draws the weary and indulgent to its seawater-based thalassotherapy. Along with Fréjus, it serves as a rail crossroads, the closest stop to St-Tropez. The port has a rich history: Napoléon landed at St-Raphaël on his triumphant return from Egypt in 1799; it was also from here in 1814 that he cast off in disgrace for Elba. And it was here, too, that the Allied forces landed in their August 1944 offensive against the Germans.

Augmenting the Atlantic-City atmosphere of this modern pleasure port is the gingerbread-and-gilt dome of the neo-Byzantine **Église Notre-Dame-de-la-Victoire** (⊠ bd. Fèlix-Martin), which watches over the yachts and cruise boats sliding into the port. The neighboring **casino** (✉ bd. de la Libération), opening over the waterfront, caters to the city's many conventioneers.

But it's worth penetrating the dense city traffic and cutting inland past the train station and into the Vieille Ville (Old Town), a tiny enclave of charm crowned by the 12th-century **Église St-Pierre-des-Templiers** (✉ rue des Templiers).

On the same quiet square as St-Pierre, shaded by an old olive tree, is the intimate little **Musée Archéologique** (Archaeology Museum). Its few rooms concentrate a concise and fascinating collection of ancient amphorae gleaned from the shoals offshore, where centuries' worth of shipwrecks have accumulated; by studying this chronological progression of jars and the accompanying sketches, you can visualize the coast as it was in its heyday as a Greek and Roman shipping center. The science of exploring these shipwrecks was relatively new when French divers began probing the depths; the underwater Leicas from the 1930s and the early scuba gear from the '50s on display are as fascinating as the spoils they helped to unearth. Upstairs, a few objects—jewelry, spearheads, pottery shards, and skulls—illustrate the Neolithic and Paleolithic eras and remind you of the dense population of Celto-Ligurians who claimed this region long before the Greeks and Phocéens. A few of their dolmen and menhirs are still visible on the Estérel. ✉ *rue des Templiers,* ☎ *04–94–19–25–75.* ☉ *Mon.–Sat. 10–noon and 2–5.*

Dining and Lodging

$$ ✕ **La Bouillabaisse.** Enter through the beaded curtain covering the open doorway to a wood-paneled room decked out with starfish and the mounted head of a swordfish: This classic hole-in-the-wall has a brief, straightforward menu inspired by the fish markets in the neighborhood. You might have the half lobster with spicy *rouille* (peppers and garlic whipped with olive oil), the seafood-stuffed paella, or the generous house bouillabaisse. ✉ *50 pl. Victor-Hugo,* ☎ *04–94–95–03–57. AE, MC, V. Closed Mon.*

$$$ 🏨 **Excelsior.** This urban hotel has been under the careful management of one family for three generations. Its combination of straightforward comforts and a waterfront position in the center of town attract a regular clientele. Rooms are plush and pastel, bathrooms reasonably up to date. The café and restaurant attract nonguests for dependable fare and sea views. ✉ *promenade du Président René Coty, 83700,* ☎ *04–94–95–02–42,* FAX *04–94–95–33–82. 36 rooms. Restaurant, café, air-conditioning. AE, DC, MC, V.*

$ 🏨 **Le Thimotée.** The new owners of this bargain lodging are throwing
★ themselves wholeheartedly into improving an already attractive 19th-century villa (with double-glazing, bright-painted woodwork, and new carpet). They've also restored the garden, with its grand palms and pines shading the walk to the pretty little swimming pool. They're helpful, too: they will rent you a bike, book an excursion, pick you up at the train station, and give you seconds on coffee at breakfast. Though it's tucked away in a neighborhood far from the waterfront, top-floor rooms have poster-perfect sea views. ✉ *375 bd. Christian-Lafon, 83700,* ☎ *04–94–40–49–49. 12 rooms. Pool. AE, MC, V.*

Agay

🔟 *10 km (6 mi) east of St-Raphaël.*

Surrounded by the red rock of the Estérel, as well as the growing clutter of its own development, Agay has the best protected harbor along the Estérel coast. Traders from ancient Greece once used it as a deep-water anchorage. It was also near here that writer Antoine de St-Exupéry (*The Little Prince*) was shot down in July 1944, just after flying over his family castle in what would be his last mission.

En Route The rugged **Massif de l'Estérel,** between St-Raphaël and Cannes, is a hiker's dream. Made up of rust-red volcanic rocks (porphyry) carved by the sea into dreamlike shapes, the harshness of the landscape is softened by patches of lavender, scrub pine, and gorse. Take N7, the mountain route to the north, to lose yourself in the desert landscape far from the sea. Or stay on N98, the **Corniche de l'Estérel** (the coastal road along the dramatic corniche), past tiny calanques and sheer rock faces plunging into the sea. At Cap Roux an overlook allows you to pull off the narrow two-lane highway (where high-season sightseers can cause bumper-to-bumper traffic) and contemplate the spectacular panorama up and down the coast. Some 15 trails, leading up into the jagged rock peaks for extraordinary sea views, strike out from designated parking sites along the way; don't leave valuables in the car, as the sites are littered with glass from break-ins. For trail maps, ask at the St-Raphaël tourist office across from the train station. There is also a *sentier du littoral* (waterfront trail), leaving from the St-Raphaël port and following the rocky coast all the way to Agay; you'll see a mix of wild, rocky *criques* (little coves) and glamorous villas.

Mandelieu–La Napoule

⑪ *32 km (20 mi) northeast of St-Raphaël, 8 km (5 mi) southwest of Cannes.*

La Napoule is the small, old-fashioned port village devoured by the big-fish resort town of Mandelieu. You can visit Mandelieu for a golf-and-sailing retreat, and you can visit La Napoule for a port-side stroll, a meal, or a visit to its peculiar castle.

The **Château de La Napoule,** looming over the sea and the port, is a bizarre hybrid of Romanesque, Gothic, Moroccan, and Hollywood cooked up by the eccentric American sculptor Henry Clews. Working with his architect wife, he transformed the 14th-century bastion into something that suited his own expectations and filled the place with his fantastical sculptures. If you visit, you'll see Clews's works in their context, as he designed them. ⊠ *av. Henry Clews,* ☎ *04–93–49–95–05.* 🎫 *25 frs.* ☉ *Guided visits Mar.–Jun. and Sep.–Nov., Wed.–Mon. at 3 and 4; July–Aug., Wed.–Mon. at 3, 4, and 5.*

Dining and Lodging

$$ ✕ **Le Boucanier.** The drab, low-ceilinged dining room is upstaged by
★ wraparound plate-glass views of the marina and château at this waterfront favorite. Locals gather here for mountains of oysters and whole fish, simply grilled and impeccably filleted table-side. The seafood, market fresh, speaks for itself: No one interferes beyond a drizzle of fruity olive oil, a pinch of rock salt, or a brief flambé in pastis. ⊠ *Port La Napoule,* ☎ *04–93–49–80–51. AE, DC, MC, V.*

$$$$ ✕🎰 **Royal Hôtel Casino.** As much a resort as a hotel, this modern waterfront complex has deluxe comforts on a grand scale, with a broad beach-terrace, indoor and outdoor pools, and vast conference facilities. Streamlined rooms in soft pastels have balconies and sea views from all sides. At the informal yet glamorous restaurant-grill you can dine on such dishes as artichokes with scampi and lightly grilled *rouget* (red mullet) with kasha while you gaze out over the floodlighted swimming pool. ⊠ *605 av. Général-de-Gaulle, 06210,* ☎ *04–92–97–70–*

00, FAX *04–93–49–51–50. 211 rooms. 2 restaurants, bar, 2 pools, sauna, 2 tennis courts, exercise room, casino. AE, DC, MC, V.*

$$$ ⌂ **Le Domaine d'Olival.** Set back from the coast on its own vast land-scaped grounds along the Siagne River, this charming inn has a Provençal feel that denies its waterfront-resort situation. The sleek rooms, efficiently designed by the architect-owner, have built-in furniture and small kitchenettes. Balconies, ideal for breakfast, overlook the semitropical garden. ⌂ *778 av. de la Mer, 06210,* ☎ *04–93–49–31–99,* FAX *04–92–97–69–28. 18 apartments. Air-conditioning, kitchenettes, tennis court. AE, DC, MC, V. Closed Nov.–mid-Jan.*

$$ ⌂ **Acadia.** On a quiet gooseneck of the Siagne River, this modest hotel offers a plethora of small luxuries right on the river's edge: boat docks, a pool, a tennis court, and a shady lawn. The building itself is foursquare concrete and the decor '70s-bold, softened with lace curtains, wooden shutters, and big balconies over the river and garden. ⌂ *681 av. de la Mer, 06210,* ☎ *04–93–49–28–23,* FAX *04–92–97–55–54. 32 rooms. Pool, tennis court. AE, DC, MC, V. Closed end Nov.–end Dec.*

$$ ⌂ **Parisiana.** In the residential neighborhood of La Napoule, about 500 ft from the waterfront, is this tidy hotel with simple comforts, chenille bedspreads, and dated bathrooms. But the upkeep is impeccable. A big balcony-terrace overlooks a jungle of a garden. ⌂ *rue de l'Argentière, 06210,* ☎ *04–93–49–93–02,* FAX *04–93–49–62–32. 13 rooms. MC, V.*

Outdoor Activities and Sports

The **Golf Club de Cannes-Mandelieu** (⌂ rte. du Golf, ☎ 04–93–49–55–39) is one of the most beautiful in the south of France and is famous for its 100-year-old parasol pines that shade the greens. Posh and eccentric, it features a grand clubhouse in half-timber Normandy style and ferries golfers over the River Siagne—between holes. There are two courses—one 18 holes (par 71) and one 9 holes (par 33). The golf club is closed Tuesday except July–August.

Classified as a *station voile* (sailing resort), Mandelieu–La Napoule is a major water-sports center. To rent a boat or—what the heck—charter a yacht, contact **Cayman Yachting** (☎ 04–93–49–80–96) or **Yacht Charter Côte d'Azur** (☎ 04–93–49–86–85). Waterskiing courses and outings can be arranged through the **Ecole Privée du Ski Nautique** (☎ 04–93–49–44–19), off the plage du Sweet. For windsurfing and small sailboats contact **Maison de la Mer** (☎ 04–93–49–88–77). Lessons or supplies for scuba diving are available from **Armand Ferrand Centre de Plongée** (⌂ Port de la Rague, ☎ 04–93–49–74–33).

Two private **beaches**—Le Victoria (☎ 04–93–49–93–20) and Le Sweet (☎ 04–93–49–87–33)—have mattresses, restaurants, and bar service. They have the same fine sand as the public beaches scattered between, which provide toilets and showers.

CANNES

Backed by gentle hills and flanked to the south by the heights of the Estérel, warmed by dependable sun but kept bearable in summer by the cool breeze that blows in from the Mediterranean, Cannes is pampered with the luxurious climate that has made it one of the most popular and glamorous resorts in Europe. Its graceful curve of wave-washed sand peppered with chic restaurants and prestigious private beaches, its renowned waterfront promenade strewn with palm trees and poseurs, its status-symbol grand hotels vying for the custom of the Louis-Vuitton set, this legend is, to many, the heart and soul of the Côte d'Azur.

For 150 years the mecca of sun-worshippers, it has been further glamourized by the success of its film festival, as famous as (and, in the trade, more respected than) Hollywood's Academy Awards.

Settled first by the Ligurians and then dubbed Cannoïs by the Romans (after the cane that waved in its marshes), Cannes was an important sentinel site for the monks who established themselves on Ile St-Honorat. Its bay served as nothing more than a fishing port until in 1834 an English aristocrat, Lord Brougham, made an emergency stopover with his sick daughter and fell in love with the site. He had a home built here and returned every winter for a sun cure—a ritual quickly picked up by his peers. A railroad brought even more sun seekers, and by the turn of the century the bay glittered in the gaslight of some 50 hotels.

With the democratization of modern travel, Cannes has become a tourist and convention town, and the Croisette traffic jams slow 20 compact Twingos for every Rolls-Royce. But glamour—and the perception of glamour—is self-perpetuating, and as long as Cannes enjoys its ravishing climate and setting, it will maintain its incomparable panache.

A Good Walk

If you arrive by car, abandon it quickly in either the parking garage named La Pantiéro (on the port), or under the casino. Then pick up a map at the tourist office in the **Palais des Festivals** ⑫, the scene of the famous Festival International du Film, popularly known as the Cannes Film Festival. As you leave the information center, follow the Palais to your right to see the fountains, palm trees, and red-carpeted stairs where the stars ascend every year.

Through the palm trees and flowers and crowds of strolling poseurs (furs coats in tropical weather, mobile phones on Rollerblades, and sunglasses at night) follow the waterfront promenade known as **La Croisette** ⑬ past the broad expanse of private beaches, glamorous shops, and luxurious hotels. The most famous of these is the wide, white-masonry wedding cake called the **Carlton** ⑭.

After seeing the Carlton—have a drink in its see-and-be-seen terrace brasserie, or even, in season, lunch at one of the seductive beach restaurants—double back and right up rue Amouretti, through rond-point Duboys d'Angers, and left on rue Molière. Here you'll find an array of glittering big-name designer shops with prices that barely fit on the tag. Cut right up to rue d'Antibes, Cannes's main shopping street, and window-shop all the way back to rue du Maréchal Joffre. Turn right and immediately left on **rue Meynadier** ⑮, a lively pedestrian shopping street packed tight with trendy clothing boutiques cheek by jowl with fine food shops. Turn right briefly up rue Louis Blanc and then take a left into the covered **Marché Forville** ⑯, scene of the animated morning food market.

Leave the market via rue Dr. Gazagnaire, cut right briefly on rue Meynadier, and climb up rue St-Antoine into the picturesque old-town neighborhood known as **Le Suquet.** Wind up the steep and narrow rue du Suquet and climb the steps of avenue de la Tour to **place de la Castre** ⑰. Dominating the square is the Romanesque château known as La Castre (from the Latin castrum); within its chapel you'll find the **Musée de la Castre** ⑱, containing ethnological treasures.

On leaving the museum, angle down rue Périssol, rue de la Boucherie, and Rue St-Antoine, and head down to the port, and the broad

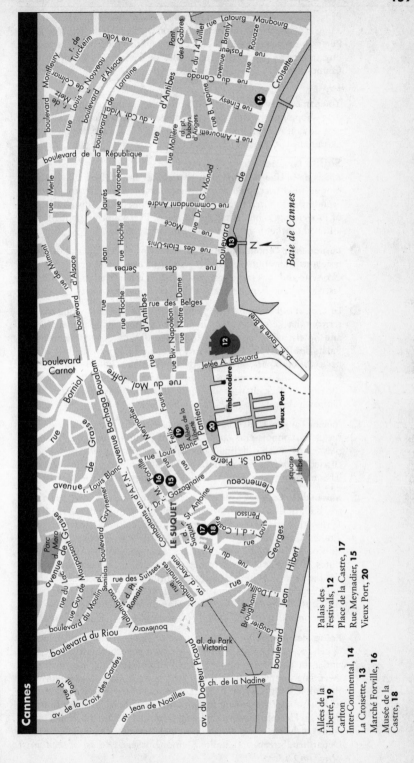

Cannes

Baie de Cannes

Allées de la
Liberté, **19**
Carlton
Inter-Continental, **14**
La Croisette, **13**
Marché Forville, **16**
Musée de la
Castre, **18**

Palais des
Festivals, **12**
Place de la Castre, **17**
Rue Meynadier, **15**
Vieux Port, **20**

Provençal-style square called the **allées de la Liberté** ⑲, where there's a flower market every morning (but Monday). Across the road the **Vieux Port** ⑳ bobs with pleasure boats and magnificent yachts; here you can buy tickets for boat trips to the Iles de Lérins (☞ Side Trip from Cannes, *below*).

TIMING

You can easily walk this tour in a morning, or make a day of it, window-shopping, watching a pétanque game in the allées de la Liberté, or studying African masks in the Musée de la Castre. If you have an extra half-day, consider the boat-trip to one of the Iles de Lérins.

Sights to See

⑲ **Allées de la Liberté.** Shaded by plane trees and sheltering a sandy pétanque field (occupied round the clock by distinctly unglamorous grandfathers inured to the scene on La Croisette), this is a little piece of Provence in a big, glitzy resort town. Every morning but Monday a flower market paints the square in vivid colors.

⑭ **Carlton Inter-Continental.** Built in 1912, this was the first of the grand hotels to stake out the superb stretch of beach and greenery on La Croisette and thus is the best positioned. It is here that most of the film festival's grand banquets take place (☞ Lodging, *below*).

⑬ **La Croisette.** For many this palm-studded promenade along the waterfront, backed by an imposing row of sumptuous apartment houses and hotels, is the epitome of the Côte d'Azur. Stretching from the Palais des Festivals to the eastern point that juts into the bay, it's the perfect spot to park on a bench overlooking the Golfe de Napoule, the beach restaurants serving wind-screened meals at the water's edge, and the rows of deck chairs under umbrellas advertising the luxury hotels that own them.

⑯ **Marché Forville.** Under the permanent shelter that every morning draws the chefs, connoisseurs, and voyeurs of Cannes, you'll see showy displays of fresh fish still flipping and glossy vegetables piled high, cheeses carried down from the mountains, sausages, olives, and flower stands. The food-shopping scene spills into the neighboring rue Meynadier.

⑱ **Musée de la Castre** (Castle Museum). In the château known as La Castre, built in the 11th century by the monks who inhabited the Iles de Lérins, this small museum is Cannes' token cultural attraction. In the vaulted Gothic chapel and a series of small castle rooms, the collection of 19th-century ethnological treasures—African drums, Asian flutes, and native clothing from America and Peru—seems out of place. But the handful of Impressionistic paintings by Provençal artists shows landscapes you may recognize. ✉ *pl. de la Castre,* ☎ *04–93–38–55–26.* 🎫 *10 frs.* ◷ *Apr.–June, Wed.–Mon. 10–noon and 2–6; July–Sept., 10–noon and 3–7; Oct.–Mar., 10–noon and 2–5. Closed most of Jan.*

⑫ **Palais des Festivals** (Festival Palace). This is where it all happens: When the Cannes Film Festival is in town, paparazzi jostle and crowd under the palm trees, popping flashbulbs at the glittering movie stars swanning up the broad, red-carpeted stairs to find out who has won the Palme d'Or (Golden Palm). Something of a shrine, these stairs are a popular spot for posing for souvenir snapshots. At the foot of the Palais and set into the surrounding pavement, the **allée des Etoiles** (Stars' Alley) enshrines some 300 autographed imprints of film stars' hands—Dépardieu, Streep, and Stallone, among others. ✉ *East of the tourist office on La Croisette.*

⑰ Place de la Castre (Castle Square). From behind the square's Romanesque 16th-century Église Notre-Dame-d'Esperance, take in magnificent views over Cannes and the Ile Ste-Marguerite. The landmark La Castre, the Romanesque château that looms over the bay, contains a museum showing ethnic treasures and local art.

⑮ Rue Meynadier. You may not notice the pretty 18th-century houses that once formed the main street of Cannes, so distracting are the boutiques they now contain. Here cheap and trendy clothes alternate with rarified food and wine shops, and some of the best butchers in town.

Le Suquet. On the site of the original Roman *castrum,* this ancient neighborhood seems to cling to the hill overlooking Cannes. Shops proffer crafts and Provençal goods and the atmospheric theme-restaurants give you a chance to catch your breath; the pretty pastel shutters, Gothic stonework, and narrow passageways are lovely distractions. Take time to lose yourself awhile on the tiny backstreets, ducking under arches and peeking into courtyards. At the top is **Place de la Castre** (☞ *above*), which is surrounded by ancient city ramparts with postcard views. The hill is crowned by the 11th-century château, housing the **Musée de la Castre** (☞ *above*), and the imposing four-sided **Tour du Suquet** (Suquet Tower), built in 1385 as a lookout against Saracen invasions.

⑳ Vieux Port (Old Port). Sparkling at the foot of Le Suquet, this narrow, well-protected port harbors a fascinating line-up of grand luxury yachts and slick little pleasure boats that creak and bob beside weathered-blue fishing barques. From the east corner, off La Pantiéro, you can catch a cruise to the Iles de Lérins.

Dining and Lodging

$$–$$$ ✕ **La Brouette de Grand'mere.** This tiny hole-in-the-wall, complete with lace curtains, painted-wood front, fireplace, and old posters, could be a set for one of the Festival's films. Yet it's true-blue bistro, with a five-course menu that includes aperitif, wine, and coffee. There's chicken steamed with taragon, pot-au-feu with beef, pork and chicken, andouillettes crisped in sweet muscadet, and sharp-aged goat cheese. It's only open evenings and feels especially right in winter. ⊠ *9 rue d'Oran,* ☎ *04–93–39–12–10. AE, DC, MC, V.*

$$ ✕ **Auberge Provençal.** Of the plethora of slightly touristy restaurants lining the long hike up into Le Suquet, this is one of the most atmospheric. This is largely due to its age, as it claims to be the oldest restaurant in town, and the heavy old beams back up the claim. For maximum effect, reserve a table in the room with the stone fireplace that crackles pleasantly on cool days. Regional specialties dominate, including bouillabaisse, aïoli, farcis niçoise, and a rich beef *estouffade* (stew). ⊠ *10 rue St-Antoine,* ☎ *04–92–99–27–17. AE, DC, MC, V.*

$$ ✕ **Chez Astoux.** For seafood, this popular spot stands out among the other restaurants overlooking the leisurely tableau of *boules* (lawn bowling), pigeons, and bandstand on allées de la Liberté. Linen-covered tables on the terrace sport showy, tiered platters of sparkling-fresh seafood, and bouillabaisse anchors the menu. You can also order seafood platters to go, with the shellfish pre-opened or not, from the same address (not to be confused with Brun, around the corner, which uses the Astoux name). ⊠ *43 rue Félix-Faure,* ☎ *04–93–39–06–22. AE, DC, MC, V.*

$$ ✕ **La Mère Besson.** Though no longer all the rage with the festival crowd, this long-standing favorite continues to please a largely foreign clientele with regional specialties such as sweet-and-sour sardines *à l'escabeche* (marinated), monkfish Provençal (with tomatoes, fennel, and onion), and roast lamb with garlic purée. The formal setting, with damask linens and still lifes, is lightened up with clatter from the open kitchen. ⊠ *13 rue des Frères-Pradignac,* ☎ *04–93–39–59–24. AE, DC, MC, V. Closed Sun. No lunch Sat. or Mon., though during festivals open daily for all meals.*

$ ✕ **Au Bec Fin.** Despite its '60s luncheonette decor, devoted regulars attest to the quality of this antichic, family-run bistro near the train station, distinguished by its steamy clatter, crowds of ordinary locals (old folks and kids, too), and homey food. The prix-fixe menus are a fantastic value for real food—grilled sardines and mesclun salad served with a liter bottle of olive oil, the day's catch grilled with fennel, and *choucroute* (sauerkraut and sausage) and lentils—even big, old-fashioned sundaes, a far cry from the chichi sorbets served along the waterfront. ⊠ *12 rue du 24-Août,* ☎ *04–93–38–35–86. AE, MC, V. Closed Sun. and mid-Dec.–mid-Jan. No dinner Sat.*

$ ✕ **Bouchon d'Objectif.** Popular and unpretentious, this tiny bistro
★ serves inexpensive Provençal menus prepared with a sophisticated twist. Watch for terrine of hare with sultanas and Armagnac, stuffed sardines, or a trio of fresh fish with aïoli. An ever-changing gallery display of photography adds a hip touch to the simple ochre-and-aqua setting. ⊠ *10 rue Constantine,* ☎ *04–93–99–21–76. AE, MC, V. Closed Mon.*

$ ✕ **Montagard.** This extraordinary newcomer serves elegant, imagina-
★ tive vegetarian cuisine—rare in France—in a chic, low-key setting. Prices, too, are startlingly low, including a copious three-course quick-lunch menu for 95 francs. A complex orchestration of crudités may include avocado, spinach, lentils, walnuts, sultanas, and fresh currants; a turnover stuffed with pumpkin and chestnuts may be trimmed with deep-fried pumpkin rings and ruby beet chips. Strains of Keith Jarrett waft through the artful mise-en-scene, with its high-design chairs and warm shades of ochre. ⊠ *6 rue Maréchal Joffre,* ☎ *04–93–39–98–38. MC, V. Closed Sun. No lunch Mon.*

$$$$ ✕⊡ **Carlton Inter-Continental.** As one of the turn-of-the-century pio-
★ neers of this resort town, this neoclassical landmark quickly staked out the best position: La Croisette seems to radiate symmetrically from its figurehead waterfront site. No discreet setback here: The Carlton sits right on the sidewalk—the better for you to be seen on the popular brasserie's terrace. The main film festival banquets take place in its gilt-and-marble Grand Salon, as do, alas, year-round conferences. Seafront rooms have a retro Laura Ashley look; those on the back compensate with cheery Provençal prints. The restaurant, La Belle Otero, next to the exclusive seventh-floor casino, is one of Cannes's finest. ⊠ *58 bd. de la Croisette, 06414,* ☎ *04–93–06–40–06,* ℻ *04–93–06–40–25. 310 rooms, 28 suites. 4 restaurants, bar, air-conditioning, health club, beach, casino. AE, DC, MC, V.*

$$$$ ✕⊡ **Majestic.** Classical statuary and tapestries set the aristocratic tone at this other La Croisette "palace"; it's grand but gracious, with a quieter feel than most of its neighbors. The (smallish) pool is behind a landscaped hillock so that breakfasting guests can't be seen. In the restaurant Villa des Lys, another of Cannes's gastronomic greats, chef Bruno Oger plays with Provençal traditions at refined levels. Its romantic poolside terrace and Egyptian/Art Deco bar give a nod to cinematic glamour. Though some rooms are fussy, most are now done in subdued tones of gold and burgundy. Ask for one of the newly redone ones, carefully renovated in retro style. ⊠ *14 bd. de la Croisette, 06400,* ☎ *04–92–98–77–00,* ℻ *04–93–38–97–90. 298 rooms, 24 apartments. Restau-*

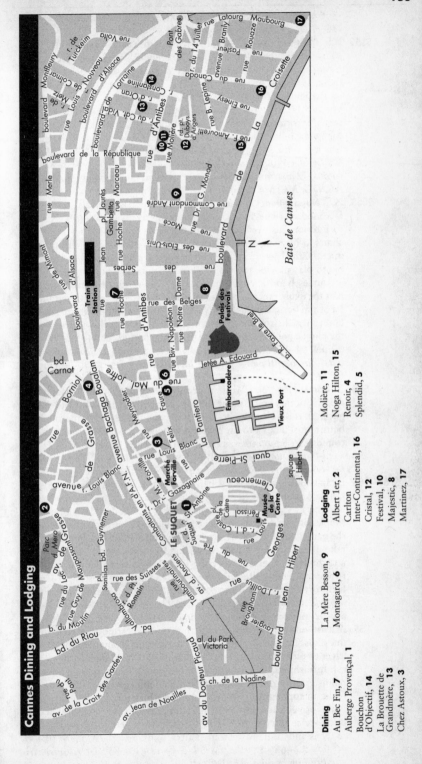

Cannes Dining and Lodging

Baie de Cannes

Dining

Au Bec Fin, **7**
Auberge Provençal, **1**
Bouchon d'Objectif, **14**
La Brouette de Grandmère, **13**
Chez Astoux, **3**
La Mère Besson, **9**
Montagard, **6**

Lodging

Albert 1er, **2**
Carlton Inter-Continental, **16**
Cristal, **12**
Festival, **10**
Majestic, **8**
Martinez, **17**
Molière, **11**
Noga Hilton, **15**
Renoir, **4**
Splendid, **5**

rant, bar, air-conditioning, pool, hairdresser, sauna, parking (fee). AE, DC, MC, V. Closed mid-Nov.–Dec.

$$$$ ✕☷ **Martinez.** A Hollywood-style face-lift has restored the Art Deco Martinez to a theatrical version of its original '30s glamour. Renovated rooms now have a splashy neo-Deco look—be sure to ask for one of these, as well as one on the seaside with gorgeous views. Avoid those on the interior overlooking the grim parking lot and the shabby still unrenovated ones on the second floor. The Palme d'Or restaurant has plush, extravagant burled-wood and ebony decor worthy of Napoléon (or Joan Collins), but despite all that, chef Christian Willer draws lavish praise for his modern Mediterranean cuisine. ⊠ *73 bd. de la Croisette, 06400,* ☎ *04–92–98–73–00,* FAX *04–93–39–67–82. 397 rooms, 12 apartments. 3 restaurants, bar, air-conditioning, pool, beach. AE, DC, MC, V. Closed mid-Nov.–mid-Jan.*

$$$$ ✕☷ **Noga Hilton.** On the site of the old Palais des Festivals, the in-your-face modern white-and-glass facade of this relative newcomer gives way to interiors just as bold and glossy, with lipstick-red leather lobby chairs, a dizzying atrium design, and high-gloss wood, chrome, and mirrors, the better to reflect the geometric-print carpets. But in refusing to play movie-set retro, the hotel maintains a posh integrity, with a seamlessly professional staff and a sense of hushed luxury that denies the exuberance of the decor. The good Mediterranean restaurant, La Scala, has tables high above La Croisette and the waterfront. Also don't miss the rooftop sunbathing terrace, with grill and bar around the plunge pool. ⊠ *50 bd. de la Croisette, 06400,* ☎ *04–92–99–70–00,* FAX *04–92–99–70–11. 184 rooms, 45 suites. 3 restaurants, 3 bars, air-conditioning, pool, 2 Jacuzzis, exercise room, beach. AE, DC, MC, V.*

$$$ ☷ **Cristal.** This Best Western property has all the comfort and predictability this brand name implies, but with a touch of Côte-d'Azur glitz: All rooms have a neo-Deco look, and the best have marble-lined bathrooms. It has a rooftop whirlpool fed by a stone fountain and surrounded by lemon trees, a bar, and a Provençal restaurant. ⊠ *13–15 rond-point Duboys-d'Angers,* ☎ *04–93–39–45–45,* FAX *04–93–38–64–66. 51 rooms. Restaurant, bar, air-conditioning. AE, DC, MC, V.*

$$–$$$ ☷ **Splendid.** If you covet a waterfront position but can't afford the grand hotels on La Croisette, consider this traditional 1873 palace overlooking La Pantiéro and the old port. It's staffed and maintained in simple comfort. Rooms are a bit creaky but sleekly decorated, and though the bathrooms have '60s tiling, they're well maintained. Small doubles take in spectacular seaside views for 50 francs extra. It's family run and thus full of personal touches: There are flowers and fruit in rooms, robes and kitchenettes in those with sea views, and pretty Provençal furniture in the breakfast room. ⊠ *allées de la Liberté, entrance on 4–6 rue Félix-Faure, 06407,* ☎ *04–93–99–53–11,* FAX *04–93–99–55–02. 64 rooms. Air-conditioning, kitchenettes. AE, DC, MC, V.*

$$ ☷ **Festival.** Completely redone in a pastel postmodern style in the mid-'90s, this small, central property benefits from an owner who is eager to please. Rooms have full marble baths and built-in Deco-style ash furnishings; five overlook the neighbor's lovely orange trees and palms. Ask for one of the two roomier doubles on the garden side, and make an appointment for the sauna and whirlpool, scheduled for maximum privacy. In addition to discount packages for long stays and reduced-price entry to the Le Calao Beach, the hotel arranges excursions to the islands and nearby tourist attractions. ⊠ *3 rue Molière, 06400,* ☎ *04–93–68–33–00,* FAX *04–93–68–33–85. 14 rooms. Air-conditioning, sauna. AE, DC, MC, V.*

$$ 🏨 **Molière.** Plush, intimate, and low-key, this hotel has pretty tiled baths
★ and small rooms in cool shades of peach, indigo, and white-waxed oak.
Nearly all overlook the vast, enclosed front garden, where palms and
cypress shade terrace tables, and breakfast is served alfresco most of
the year. ⊠ *5 rue Molière, 06400,* ☎ *04–93–68–16–16,* ℻ *04–93–
68–29–57. 42 rooms. AE, MC, V. Closed mid-Nov.–end Dec.*

$$ 🏨 **Renoir.** This graceful former mansion is on a quiet backstreet in a
residential neighborhood only a few blocks back from the center and
beach (some suites even have sea views), but it feels like another world.
A highly charged sunflower-print decor (none of the ubiquitous pink
Art Deco), the scent of lavender, and kitchenettes in every suite create
a sense of a vacation in Provence instead of on the Côte d'Azur. Sea-
view rooms overlook a busier street; for maximum quiet, ask for the
backstreet side. ⊠ *7 rue Edith Cavell, 06400,* ☎ *04–92–99–62–62,*
℻ *04–92–99–62–82. 15 rooms, 12 suites. Bar, air-conditioning,
kitchenettes. AE, DC, MC, V.*

$ 🏨 **Albert Ier.** In a quiet residential area above the Forville market—a
★ 10-minute walk downhill to La Croisette and beach—this neo-Deco
mansion has pretty rooms in pastels as well as tidy tile baths and an
enclosed garden setting. You can have breakfast on the flowered, shady
terrace or in the family-style salon. The hotel has had one owner for
18 years, and it shows in the details. ⊠ *68 av. de Grasse, 06400,* ☎
04–93–39–24–04, ℻ *04–93–38–83–75. 11 rooms. MC, V.*

Nightlife and the Arts

The Riviera's cultural calendar is splashy and star-studded, and never
more so than during the **International Film Festival** in May. The film
screenings are not open to the public, so unless you have a pass, your
star-studded glimpses will be on the streets or in restaurants—though
if you hang around in a tux, a stray ticket might come your way.

As befits a glamorous seaside resort, Cannes has two casinos. The famous **Casino Croisette** (⊠ in the Palais des Festivals, ☎ 04–93–38–
12–11), which traces its pedigree to 1907, draws more crowds to its
slot machines than any other casino in France. The **Carlton Casino Club**
(⊠ 58 bd. de la Croisette, ☎ 04–93–68–00–33), a relative newcomer
to the Cannes nightlife scene, encourages an exclusive atmosphere in
its posh seventh-floor hideaway.

To make the right entrance at the currently popular **Le Cat Corner** (⊠
22 rue Macé, ☎ 04–93–39–31–31) have yourself whisked by limo
from the steakhouse Le Farfalla. **Jimmy'z** (⊠ Palais des Festivals, ☎
04–93–68–00–07) admits celebrities, stars, and starlets, but not necessarily everyone else; the cabaret shows are legendary. After many meta-
morphoses, **Studio-Circus** is back and once again one of the main disco
draws (⊠ 48 bd. de la République, ☎ 04–93–68–13–13).

Outdoor Activities and Sports

Most of the **beaches** along La Croisette are owned by hotels and/or
restaurants, though this doesn't necessarily mean the hotels or restaurants front the beach. It does mean they own a patch of beachfront
bearing their name, from which they rent chaise longues, mats, and
umbrellas to the public and hotel guests (who also have to pay). One
of the most fashionable is the Carlton Hotel's beach (☞ *above*). Other
beaches where you must pay a fee include the stretch belonging to the
Martinez, which is the largest in Cannes, Long Beach, and Rado Plage.
You can easily recognize public beaches by the crowds; they're interspliced between the color-coordinated private beach umbrellas, and offer
simple open showers and basic toilets. To be slightly removed from the

city traffic and crowds, head west of town; the open stretches of sand run uninterrupted toward Mandelieu.

Sailboats can be rented from **Camper & Nicholson's** (⊠ Port Canto) and the **Yacht Club de Cannes** (⊠ Palm Beach Port). Windsurfing equipment is available from **Le Club Nautique La Croisette** (⊠ plage Pointe Palm-Beach) and the **Centre Nautique Municipal** (⊠ 9 rue Esprit-Violet). The **Majestic Ski Club** (Ponton du Majestic; ⊠ at the Majestic private beach, ☎ 04–92–98–77–47) can take you waterskiing, or pull you on a ski-board, an inflatable chair, or up over the water on a parachute.

Bicycles can be rented from the train station (⊠ pl. de la Gare).

Close to town are several golf courses. The venerable **Golf de Biot** (⊠ La Bastide du Roy, ☎ 04–93–65–08–48), at the foot of the village of Biot, has 18 holes and par 67. **Golf de Royal Mougins** (⊠ 424 av. du Roi, ☎ 04–93–92–49–69), beautifully landscaped and opened in 1993, has 18 holes and par 71. **Golf Cannes-Mandelieu** (☞ Mandelieu–La Napoule, *above*; ⊠ rte. du Golf, ☎ 04–93–49–55–39)—that's the pretty one with the parasol pines—has 18 holes at par 71 and 9 holes at par 33.

Shopping

Whether you're window-shopping or splurging on that little Galliano number in the Dior window, you'll find some of the best shopping outside Paris on the streets off La Croisette. For stores carrying designer names, try **rond-point Duboys-d'Angers** off **rue Amouretti, rue des Serbes,** and **rue des Belges,** all perpendicular to the waterfront. **Rue d'Antibes** is the town's main shopping drag, with every kind of clothing and shoe shop, as well as mouthwatering candy, fabric, and home design stores. **Rue Meynadier** mixes trendy young clothes with high-end food specialties.

You can find almost any item, from moth-eaten uniforms to second-hand gravy boats, at the **brocante market** (⊠ allées de la Liberté) that springs up every Saturday. The permanent **Marché Forville,** at the foot of Le Suquet, has every kind of fresh and regional food in its picturesque booths every morning but Monday, from 7 am to 1pm. On Mondays, it fills up with flea-market wares and brocante from 8 to 6. On the first and third Saturday of each month, an array of old books, posters, and postcards are sold at the **Marché du Livre Ancien et des Vieux Papiers** (Antique Books and Paper Market; ⊠ pl. de la Justice).

Side Trip from Cannes: Iles de Lérins

㉑   *15–20 minutes by ferry off the coast of Cannes.*

When you're glutted on glamour and have had enough of dodging limos, skaters, and the leavings of dyed-to-match poodles, catch a boat from Cannes's Vieux Port to one of the two Iles de Lérins (Lérins Islands). On one of these two lovely getaways, you can find car-free peace and lose yourself in a tropical landscape of palms, pines, and tidal pools. Ste-Marguerite Island has more in the way of attractions: a ruined prison-fortress, a museum, and a handful of restaurants. Smaller and wilder, St-Honorat Island is dominated by its active monastery and the ruins of its 10th-century original.

Buy your tickets from one of the ferry companies at the booths on Cannes's Vieux Port; look for the **Horizon/Caribes Company** (⊠ Jetée Edouard, ☎ 04–92–98–71–36), set back from the street, which has more comfortable boats than the more visible **Estérel Chanteclair** (⊠

promenade La Pantiéro, ☎ 04–93–39–11–82). You must decide which island (if not both) you wish to visit before you buy your tickets. Allow at least a half day to enjoy either of these islands; you can see both if you get an early start but might regret the obligation to move on once you've arrived on the first one. Although Ste-Marguerite has some restaurants and snack shops, you would be wise to bring along a picnic and drinks; you'll have to do this if you spend the day on the noncommercial St-Honorat.

It's a 15-minute, 45-franc round trip to **Ile Ste-Marguerite,** the largest of the Iles de Lérins, which is covered with dense growths of palms, pines, and eucalyptus. On arriving, head left up the tiny main street lined with restaurants and snack shops, or cut uphill and left toward **Fort Royal,** built by Richelieu and improved by Vauban. The views over the ramparts to the rocky island coast and the open sea are as evocative as the prison buildings, one of which supposedly locked up the Man in the Iron Mask. Behind the prison buildings you'll find the **Musée de la Mer** (Marine Museum), with its Roman boat dating from the first century BC and its collection of amphorae and pottery recovered from ancient shipwrecks. If you have time or prefer nature to history, head right from the port and follow the signs along the coast to the small **bird preserve,** with cormorants and gulls, and the quiet beach beyond, a paradise of tidal pools that seethe with marine life at low tide. *Museum:* ☎ *04–93–43–18–17.* 🎟 *10 frs.* ☉ *Oct.–Mar., Wed.– Mon. 10:30–12:15 and 2:15–4:30; Apr.–June, 10:30–12:15 and 2:15–5:30; July–Aug. 10:30–12:15 and 2:15–6:30. Closed three wks in Jan.*

Ile St-Honorat can be reached in 20 minutes (50 frs round trip) from the Vieux Port. Smaller and wilder than Ste-Marguerite, it is anchored by its active monastery, which traces its foundation here to the 4th century. That's when St-Honorat sought solitude on this island—and was swiftly followed by devotees also seeking solitude. The large 19th-century structure his heirs inhabit today encloses many older chapels and harbors a shop where the monks sell their herb liqueur, called Lerina. The majority of the island is covered with thick forests of pine and eucalyptus that belong to the monastery, punctuated by small chapels and criss-crossed by public paths. Wild and isolated rock-bound shores surround the island. On the island's point farthest south, just below its modern replacement, the remains of the 11th-century fortified **monastery** send thick walls plunging into the sea; the walls were built to protect the monks from marauding pirates. The monastery's complex of chapels, courtyards, and views from the crenellated rampart views are worth the climb. 🎟 *10 frs. July–Aug.; free Sept.–June.* ☉ *Sept.–June, Mon.–Sat. 9–4; Sun. afternoon only; July–Aug., daily 10–noon and 2:30–4:30.*

THE BACKCOUNTRY

The hills that back the Côte d'Azur are often called the *arrière-pays,* or backcountry, a catch-all term that applies to the hills and plateaus behind Nice as well (☞ Chapter 6). Yet this particular wedge of backcountry—specifically above and to the northwest of Cannes—has a character all its own. If the territory behind Nice has a strong Latin flavor, influenced for centuries by the Grimaldi dynasty and steeped in Italian culture, these westerly hills are deeply, unselfconsciously Provençal: undulating fields of lavender and hilltop villages so isolated and quiet you can hear a pebble drop in the mossy fountain.

The rocky swells behind Cannes and Fréjus are known loosely as the Haut Var, the highlands of the département called Var; the untamed, beautiful, and sometimes harsh landscape beyond these hills lies over the threshhold of Haute Provence.

It's possible to get a small taste of this backcountry on a day trip out of Fréjus or Cannes; a few towns—Mougins, Fayence, and Grasse—bank on the busloads that pour in from the beaches on cloudy days. On your way north you may choose to trace the steps of Napoléon himself, who followed what is now N85, today named for him, on his tentative comeback from Elba Island in 1815; it is the shortest and swiftest way between points. But if you give yourself time to wind through the back roads, stop for the views, and linger in shady perched-village squares, you may be tempted to cancel your waterfront plans and settle in for an otherworldly experience.

Mougins

㉒ *8 km (5 mi) north of Cannes, 11 km (7 mi) northwest of Antibes, 32 km (20 mi) southwest of Nice.*

Passing through Mougins, a popular summer-house community convenient to Cannes and Nice, you may perceive little more than suburban sprawl. But in 1961 Picasso found more to admire and settled into a *mas* (farmhouse) that became a mecca for artists and art lovers; he died there in 1973. Despite overbuilding today, Mougins claims extraordinary views over the coast and an old town, on a hilltop above the fray, that has retained a pretty, gentrified charm.

You can find Picasso's final home and see why of all spots in the world, he chose this one, by following D35 to the ancient ecclesiastic site of **Notre-Dame-de-Vie.** This was the hermitage, or monastic retreat, of the Abbey of Lérins(☞ Cannes, *above*), and its 13th-century bell-tower and arcaded chapel form a pretty ensemble in a magnificent setting. Approached through an alley of ancient cypress, the house Picasso shared with his wife, Jacqueline, overlooks the broad bowl of the countryside.

Dining and Lodging

$$$–$$$$ ✕🏠 **Moulin de Mougins.** In a 16th-century olive mill on a hill above
★ the coastal fray, this sophisticated inn houses one of the country's most famous restaurants: It's a de rigueur lunch trip out of Cannes, and hosts the stellar annual AIDS benefit Liz Taylor heads during the film festival. But since celebrity Chef Roger Vergé gave over most responsibility to Serge Chollet in order to teach in his nearby cooking school, the loyal clientele has begun to sigh with nostalgia for the good old days. It's still one of the best restaurants in the region, with a sun-drenched Mediterranean cuisine redolent of the market: white asparagus, sweet garlic, the freshest fish. Inside, there are intimate beamed dining rooms; in summer dine outside under the awnings. Reservations are essential for the restaurant, which is closed Monday. Rooms are elegantly rustic; the apartments are small but deluxe. ⊠ *Notre-Dame-de-Vie, 06250,* ☎ *04–93–75–78–24,* 🗚 *04–93–90–18–55. 3 rooms, 2 apartments. Restaurant. AE, DC, MC, V. Closed Feb.–Mar.*

Grasse

㉓ *10 km (6 mi) northwest of Mougins, 17 km (10½ mi) northwest of Cannes, 22 km (14 mi) northwest of Antibes, 42 km (26 mi) southwest of Nice.*

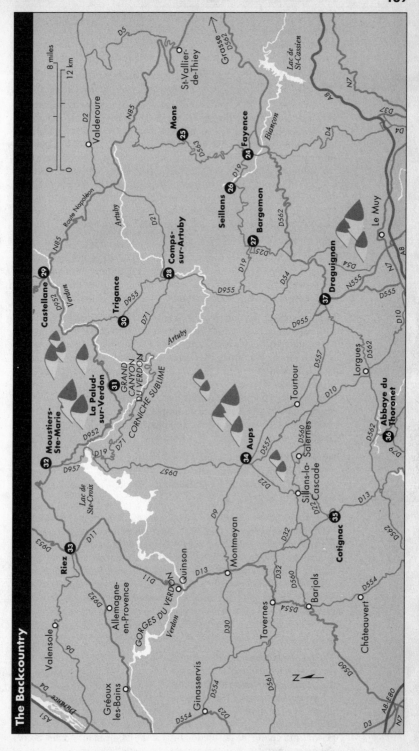

8 miles

12 km

D5

Valderoure

D2

N85

Route Napoléon

N85

Grasse D562

St-Vallier-de-Thiey

Mons **25**

D563

D19

Fayence **24**

Lac de St-Cassien

N7

D37

A8

Biançon

D4

Seillans **26**

Bargemon **27**

D562

D251

Le Muy

Artuby

D21

Comps-sur-Artuby **28**

D19

D54

Draguignan

D54

N555

N7

A8

Castellane **29**

D952

Verdon

Trigance

D955

30

D71

Artuby

D955

37

D955

D10

D555

GRAND CANYON DU VERDON

CORNICHE SUBLIME

La Palud-sur-Verdon **31**

D557

Tourtour

D10

Lorgues

D562

Abbaye du Thoronet **36**

D79

D562

Moustiers-Ste-Marie **32**

D952

D19

D77

Aups **34**

D557

D560

Salernes

Sillans-la-Cascade

D22

D13

D957

D957

Lac de Ste-Croix

D9

Montmeyan

D32

Cotignac **35**

D11

Riez **33**

D953

D11

Quinson

D13

D32

D560

Bariols

D554

Châteauvert

D952

Allemagne-en-Provence

D6

D30

Tavernes

D554

D561

D560

Valensole

GORGES DU VERDON

Verdon

N

Gréoux-les-Bains

Durance

A51

D4

D554

Ginasservis

D23

D554

D3

A8-E80

N7

High on a plateau over the coast, this busy, modern town is usually given wide berth by anyone who isn't interested in its prime tourist industry, the making of perfume. But its unusual art museum featuring works of the 18th-century artist Fragonard and the picturesque backstreets of its very Mediterranean old town round out a pleasant day trip from the coast.

It's the Côte d'Azur's hothouse climate, nurturing nearly year-round shows of tropical-hue flowers, that fosters Grasse's perfume industry. The heady, heavy scent of orange blossoms, roses, lavender, jasmine, and mimosa wrap you like silk in gardens along the coast, especially on a sultry summer night, and since time immemorial people have tried to capture that seductive scent in a bottle. In the past, perfume makers laid blossoms facedown in a lard-smeared tray, then soaked the essence away in alcohol; nowadays the scents are condensed in vast copper stills. Only the essential oils are kept, and the water thrown away—except rose water and orange water, which find their way into delicately perfumed pastries.

It takes 10,000 flowers to produce 2.2 pounds of jasmine petals and nearly one ton of petals to distill one and a half quarts of essence; this helps justify the sky-high cost of perfumes, priced by the proportion of essence their final blend contains.

In Paris and on the outskirts of Grasse, these scents are blended by a professional *nez*, or "nose," who must distinguish some 500 distinct scents and may be able to discern 3,000. Their products carry the household names of couturiers like Chanel and Dior, perfume houses like Guerlain. You can't visit the laboratories where these great blends are produced. But Grasse, to accommodate the crowds of tourists who come here wanting to know more, has met their needs with three functioning perfume factories that create simple blends and demonstrate their production techniques for free. You pass through a boutique of house perfumes on the way back to the bus and. . . well, you get the idea.

Fragonard (⌧ rte. de Cannes "Les 4-Chemins," ☎ 04–93–77–94–30) holds forth in a factory built in 1782. **Galimard** (⌧ 73 rte. de Cannes) traces its pedigree to 1747. **Molinard** (⌧ 60 bd. Victor-Hugo, ☎ 04–93–36–01–62) was established in 1849.

The **Musée International de la Parfumerie** (International Museum of Perfume), not to be confused with the small museum in the Fragonard perfume factory that calls itself the Musée de la Parfumerie but feeds directly into the gift shop, traces the 3,000-year history of perfume making. The museum has a room equipped with pot-bellied copper stills and old machines, and labels guide you through the steps of production in different eras. It also has a series of displays of exquisite perfume bottles and toiletries. There's even Marie Antoinette's *nécessaire* (travel kit). ⌧ 8 pl. du Cours, ☎ 04–93–36–80–20. ⌧ 20 frs. ☉ Apr.–Oct., daily 10–7; Dec.–Mar., Wed.–Sun. 10–noon and 2–5.

The **Musée Fragonard** isn't named for the perfume factory, rather, it's the other way around: The grand old Fragonard family of Grasse figured large in the town's 17th-century industry—that of making perfumed leather gloves. (The scents themselves eventually outstripped the gloves in popularity.) The family's most famous son, Jean-Honoré Fragonard (1732–1806), became one of the great French artists of the period, and during the Revolution lived in the family mansion that houses the museum today. The lovely villa, decorated with reproductions of the neoclassic panels he created (the originals are at the Frick Museum in New York), contains a collection of drawings, engravings, and paintings by the artist. Other rooms in the mansion display works by Fragonard's son Alexandre-Evariste and his grandson Théophile. ⊠ *23 bd. Fragonard,* ☎ *04–93–36–02–71.* 🖾 *10 frs.* 🕐 *June–Sept., daily 10–noon and 2–5; Oct.–May, Wed.–Sun. 10–noon and 2–5.*

The **Musée d'Art et d'Histoire de Provence** (Museum of the Art and History of Provence), just down from the Fragonard perfumery, has a large collection of faience from the region, including works from Moustiers, Biot, and Vallauris. Also on display in this noble 18th-century mansion are *santons* (terra-cotta figurines), furniture, local paintings, and folk costumes. ⊠ *2 rue Mirabeau,* ☎ *04–93–36–01–61.* 🖾 *10 frs.* 🕐 *Apr.–Oct., Mon.–Sat. 10–noon and 2–6; Nov.–Mar., Mon.–Sat. 10–noon and 2–5.*

Continue down rue Mirabeau and lose yourself in the dense labyrinth of the **Vieille Ville** (Old Town), its steep, narrow streets darkened on each side by shuttered houses five and six stories tall. Several little bakeries feature *fougasse à fleur d'orange,* a Grasse specialty profiting from the orange water created in its factories; the sweet, briochelike pastry is heavy with orange-blossom perfume.

On a cliff-top overlook at the old town's edge, the Romanesque **Cathédrale Ste-Marie** (⊠ pl. de la Cathédrale) contains no less than three paintings by Rubens, a triptych by the Provençal painter Louis Bréa, and *Lavement des Pieds* (*Washing of the Feet*), by the young Fragonard. Wander up rue Mougins-Roquefort and rue Droite, and cut left up stone steps to **place aux Aires,** which is lined with 17th- and 18th-century houses and their arcades. Every morning this picturesque square bursts into Technicolor hues with a flower market.

Dining

$ ✕ **Arnaud.** Just off place aux Aires, this easygoing corner bistro serves up inventive home cooking under a vaulted ceiling trimmed with grapevine stencils and pretty Provençal prints. Choose from an ambitious and sophisticated menu of à la carte specialties—a nouvelle arrangement of three kinds of fish in garlic sauce and a hearty *confit de canard* (preserved duck). At lunch there's an imaginative fixed-price regional menu, which might include tomato baked with herbed chèvre, veal with pasta, or *pieds et paquets* (pigs' feet and tripe). ⊠ *10 pl. de la Foux,* ☎ *04–93–36–44–88. MC, V.*

Route Napoléon

Extends 176 km (109 mi) from Grasse to Sisteron.

One of the most famous and panoramic roads in France is the Route Napoléon, taken by Napoléon Bonaparte in 1815 after his escape from imprisonment on the Mediterranean island of Elba. Napoléon landed at Golfe-Juan, near Cannes, on March 1 and forged northwest to Grasse, then through dramatic, hilly countryside to Castellane, Digne, and Sisteron. In Napoléon's day, most of this road (now N85) was little more than a winding dirt track. Commemorative plaques bearing the imperial eagle stud the route, inspired by Napoléon's remark, "The eagle will fly from steeple to steeple until it reaches the towers of Notre-Dame." That prediction came true. Napoléon covered the 176 km (109 mi) from the coast to Sisteron in just four days, romped north through Grenoble and Burgundy, and entered Paris in triumph on May 20.

Except for the occasional inn with the name Napoléon, there are no historical buildings or monuments, bar the plaques. There are a few lavender-honey stands and souvenir shacks, but they're few and far between. It is the panoramic views as the road winds its way up into the Alps that make this route so worth traveling.

Unless you are heading north to Grenoble, you can easily make a circular day trip along the Route Napoléon, starting from the coast at Grasse. Without stopping, you could reach **Sisteron** in 90 minutes, so take your time and stop for a picnic along the way. Sisteron, which is guarded by a medieval citadel perched 1,650 ft above the river, is the gateway between Provence and the Alpine region of Dauphine. It's also famous for its tender lamb, favored by Provençal chefs. If you forge all the way to Sisteron, pick up A51 down to Aix-en-Provence (☞ Chapter 4), and then join A6 to return to the Côte d'Azur.

You can make a bee-line up the Route Napoléon to Castellane and west to the Gorges du Verdon, the main tourist goal in the region. But if you're willing to wind and putter, the countryside west of this famous highway will reward you with a wild and rugged landscape—pine forests, ragged rock, and windswept hills—as well as tiny hill towns where life still revolves around a fountain, a café or two, and a round of boules. These are the byways of the regions known as the **Haut Var** and pre-Alpine **Haute Provence.** The villages in this area don't all lie on a neat circuit (one reason they're often tourist-free), so you'll have to make choices, or choose one—Seillans, perhaps, or tony Moustiers—as home base and make a few excursions from there. In Chapter 6 you can read about the hill towns just east of Grasse, which are much more developed and more frequented by tourists.

Fayence

㉔ *27 km (17 mi) west of Grasse, 30 km (19 mi) northwest of Cannes.*

The most touristy of all the hill towns in the Haut Var backcountry, Fayence is easiest to reach from the coast and often filled with busloads of day-trippers. Nonetheless, it has a pretty old town at the top, magnificent views from its 18th-century church down to the Massif des Maures and the Estérel, and a plethora of artisans' galleries and boutiques.

Outdoor Activities and Sports

Because of its strategic position over the broad valley slope to the sea, Fayence is a mecca for hang gliders. Anxious to leap into the void yourself? Contact the **Centre de Vol à Voile de Fayence** (Fayence Hang Gliding Center; ✉ quai Malvoisin, ☎ 04–94–76–00–68).

Mons

㉕ *15 km (9 mi) north of Fayence, 46 km (28 ½ mi) west of Grasse, 44 km (27 mi) northwest of Cannes.*

Prettier than Fayence but just that much harder to reach, this serene hilltop village stands neatly framed on the flat top of a high plateau. The breadth of its magnificent views contrasts vividly with its tidy, self-contained houses, turned inward on a warp and woof of tiny streets, dipping under arches and through arcades, ducking into courts and up cobbled steps. It's easy to see how the plague overtook this intimate enclave more than once; and it's just as easy to see why, today, Mons (pronounced mohnss) is a popular summer-home retreat, not gentrified but quietly colonized. There are almost no shops and only one restaurant, but be sure to stop into the church to see its fabulous Baroque altarpieces, entirely covered in gold leaf.

Seillans

26 *7 km (4 mi) northwest of Fayence, 36 km (22 mi) northwest of Cannes.*

With its ruined château and ramparts, fountains, flowers, and sunny maze of steeply raked cobblestone streets that suddenly break open over valley views, this is a charming old village that still smacks of the Côte d'Azur. Its church—a Renaissance remake of an 11th-century structure—is the best site for admiring the panorama. The French opera composer Gounod and the surrealist Max Ernst were regulars in Seillans; Ernst retired here.

Just east of town on the route de Fayence is the Romanesque chapel **Notre-Dame-de l'Ormeau,** containing a remarkable altarpiece dating from the 16th century. Its sculpted portraits of the wise men and shepherds adoring the Christ child, strikingly real in emotion and gesture, contrast sharply with the simple ex-votos that pepper the walls. ⊠ *rte. de Fayence.* ☉ *Sun. 10:30–6.*

Dining and Lodging

$ ✕🏠 **Deux Rocs.** Picture a tiny square with a trickling fountain, venerable plane trees, green valley views, and two massive rocks posing, sculpturelike, where they fell aeons ago: This is a magical place for a hotel. It's almost gilding the lily that the hotel should be small and personal to the point of eccentricity, and it's almost irrelevant that the bathrooms need work. From the fireplace in the salon to the bright mixed fabrics in the rooms to the homemade jam served at breakfast, the property exudes the personality of its owners. Ask for room No. 10, a corner overlooking the idyllic place. At lunch or dinner, you can dine on simple home cooking in the romantic stone-and-beam restaurant (closed on Tuesdays) or under the trees by the fountain. ⊠ *pl. Font d'Amont, 83440,* ☎ *04–94–76–87–32,* 𝖥𝖠𝖷 *04–94–76–88–68. 14 rooms. Restaurant. MC, V.*

Bargemon

27 *13 km (8 mi) west of Seillans, 25 km (15 ½ mi) northeast of Draguignan, 49 km (30 mi) northwest of Cannes.*

By the time you reach this hill village, you'll feel the Côte d'Azur dropping away and the highland winds curling over the mountains: Suddenly you'll stop craving bouillabaisse and start thinking about trout. A few mimosas and orange trees remain, but this is a mountain town, a cold stone bastion of medieval strength surrounded by traces of ramparts. Its ruined château, cobbled streets, and stone arches are softened by the fountains and plane trees of its slow, picturesque modern life.

Dining

$$ ✕ **Chez Pierrot/La Taverne.** Inside, the cottage beams, lace curtains, and oversize Armagnac on prominent display take you back to another, stuffier era, as do the courtly service and classic cuisine (beef stew with olives, local rabbit, and buttery trout). But sit in a table out front under the plane trees, listen to the splashing fountain and chiming church tower, and you'll understand why time stands still in Bargemon. ⊠ *pl. Philippe-Chauvier,* ☎ *04–94–76–62–19. MC, V. Closed Mon. No dinner Sun.*

En Route If you're feeling intrepid or you love the primeval, follow tiny D25, which winds north from Bargemon. As you leave the olive groves and lemon trees behind and approach the rocky, scrub-flecked highlands, you'll cross the **Col du Bel-Homme** (Handsome Man Pass); it's only 3,120 ft above sea level, but it's a watershed of sorts between vastly different terrains. From here you can take in the full panorama of the coastline and the blank blue horizon of the sea. Next, cross the barren, quarantined Camp Militaire de Canjuers, riddled with tank trails and crackling with distant gunfire; you are strongly advised not to leave the road. Ironically, the military camp has preserved this dramatic landscape, abandoned but for flowing masses of sheep and a few stone ghost towns. If you're inclined, you can cross D21 and continue north briefly up to the noble little hill village of **Bargèmes,** at 3,592 ft the highest in the Var. A bastion of fortified power in the 16th century, nothing remains of the village today but a few artfully restored ruins and superb views.

Comps-sur-Artuby

❷❽ *24 km (15 mi) northwest of Bargemon via Col du Bel-Homme, 26 km (16 mi) north of Draguignan.*

With D21 connecting from the Route Napoléon and D955 leading up from Draguignan and the coast, tiny Comps has long been something of a crossroads for travelers en route to the Gorges du Verdon. From here you can veer northwest on D71 and head for the famous south bank of the gorges, called the Route de la Corniche Sublime (☞ Moustiers-Ste-Marie, *below*). Lost in the isolated hills, with a few artisans' shops, it's mostly a pit stop for fuel and a memorable meal from another era.

Dining and Lodging

$–$$ ✕🏠 **Grand Hôtel Bain.** A stagecoach stopover since 1737, this plain,
★ old-fashioned restaurant and hotel has been run by the same family for eight generations, with the chef's toque passing from father to son. Its broad back dining room overlooks the hills and valleys, and travelers in hunter's lodens, biker's spandex, and trailer-tour sweat suits equally enjoy the feasts of traditional fare. From the vast regional menu overseen by young Arnaud Bain, look for hearty herbed stew, roast rabbit and mountain lamb, tripe, and homemade cannelloni, followed by local cheeses and enormous homemade desserts. Truffles are a specialty. Comfortable but simple rooms upstairs hark back to the '60s but are tidy and well-scrubbed. Many take in valley views. ✉ *Off D21 in village center, 83840,* ☎ *04–94–76–90–06,* 𝔽𝔸𝕏 *04–94–76–92–24. 18 rooms. MC, V.*

Castellane

❷❾ *26 km (16 km) north of Comps, 64 km (40 mi) northwest of Grasse, 81 km (50 mi) northwest of Cannes.*

Another juncture flanked by scenic roads, including the Route Napoléon, and a gateway to the Gorges du Verdon, this old-fashioned mountain town draws hikers, fishermen, and nature lovers. Its setting is extraordinary—curled around the roaring Verdon River and backed by a sheer rock cliff nearly 675 ft high—and its old-town streets are pleasant for strolling. Place Marcel-Sauvaire is the town's main rendezvous point, with cafés, restaurants, and hotels encircling a splashing fountain.

If you like a challenge, consider climbing the trail that zigzags up the cliff face, past ruins of the original Roman settlement, to the top. Here stands the eagle's nest **Chapelle Notre-Dame-du-Roc,** an 18th-century shrine crowned with an overscaled Virgin and lined with ex-votos left by the pilgrims who made this penitential climb before you.

Trigance

🟤 *18 km (11 mi) southwest of Castellane, 90 km (56 mi) northwest of Cannes.*

With a handful of gray-stone houses and a few artists' studios, this infinitesimal hill village between Comps and the Gorges du Verdon wouldn't merit more than a glance from the road but for its extraordinary medieval **Château de Trigance.** It was restored with a free hand and open purse by Jean-Claude Thomas, who bought it in 1971 and had it rebuilt stone by stone; it functions as a hotel-restaurant today.

Dining and Lodging

$$$ ✕⟨⟩ **Château de Trigance.** Here's a novelty for honeymooners and romantics: To stay in a fully restored medieval castle perched on a hilltop in the isolated countryside. Luggage (keep it light!) is hauled to the top by funicular, and rooms are decked in festival style, with baldachin beds and severe oak furniture. Dine under a 10th-century stone barrel vault guarded by suits of armor and fleurs-de-lis, or on the broad terrace, wrapped by crenellated walls. Naturally, the restaurant is in the novelty-banquet business and features a hefty classic cuisine (smoked duck, oysters, quail, and lamb). Half board is obligatory, which is just as well: À la carte prices are high, and the nearest alternative can't be seen, even from the guard tower. It's a Relais & Château property but is not in its luxury class—after all, it's hard to find good serfs these days. ✉ *Off D955, 83840,* ☎ *04–94–76–91–18,* ℻ *04–94– 85–68–99. 8 rooms. Restaurant, bar. AE, DC, MC, V. Closed Dec.– Feb.*

La Palud-sur-Verdon

🟤 *26 km (16 mi) southwest of Castellane, 27 km (17 mi) southeast of Moustiers.*

Though several towns bill themselves as *the* gateway to the Gorges du Verdon, this unassuming village stands in its center, on a plateau just north of the gorge's vertiginous drop. It's a hikers' and climbers' town, and—as Germans and the Dutch are more *sportif* than the French— has an international feel. You'll see more beards and Volkswagen vans here than anywhere in France, and you'll probably share a café terrace with backpackers clad in boots and fleece easing off a load of ropes, picks, and cleats. The friendly grocery store sells flashlights and *camping gaz* (cooking propane), and the central intersection flaunts six public telephones, the better to call a taxi to carry you to your hiking departure point.

★ You are here for one reason only: To explore the extraordinary **Gorges du Verdon,** also known as—with only slight exaggeration over another, more famous version—the Grand Canyon. Through the aeons the jewel green torrent of the Verdon River has chiseled away the limestone plateau and gouged a spectacular gorge lined with vertiginous white cliffs and sloping rock falls carpeted with green forest. The jagged rock bluffs, roaring water, and dense wild boxwood create a savage world of genuinely awe-inspiring beauty, whether viewed from dozens of cliff-top overlooks or explored from the wilderness below.

If you're driving from La Palud, follow the dramatic **Route des Crêtes** circuit (D23), a white-knuckle cliffhanger not for the faint of heart.

When you approach and leave La Palud, you'll do it via D952 between Castellane and Moustiers, with several breathtaking overlooks. The best of these is the **Point Sublime,** at the east end; leave your car by the hotel-restaurant and walk to the edge, holding tight to dogs and children: That's a 2,834 ft drop to the bottom.

If you want to hike, there are several trails that converge in this prime territory. The most spectacular is the branch of the GR4 that follows
★ the bed of the canyon itself, along the **Sentier Martel.** This dramatic trail, beginning at the Château de la Maline and ending at the Point Sublime, was created in the 1930s by the Touring-Club de France and named for one of the gorges' first explorers (☞ Close-Up Box, The Sentier Martel, *below*). Easier circuits leave from the Point Sublime on *sentiers de découverte* (trails with commentary) into the gorge known as Couloir Samson.

Dining

$ ✕ **Le Perroquet Vert.** In a restored house on La Palud's only street, a resourceful couple of rock climbers have opened an intimate restaurant over their sports-equipment shop. Think California 1970: Incense, jazz, and Indian cotton in fauve colors; photos of the owners suspended over a chasm; and intense discussion of the threat of a new power line to be shaved straight through the local wilderness. The cooking is as evocative and sincere, with seafood smuggled in from coastal markets and local ingredients impeccably cooked and served by the owners: Soup with tiny *favouilles* (coastal crabs), basil ravioli, and fresh goat cheese from up the road. ⊠ *rue Grande,* ☎ *04–92–77–33–39. MC, V. Closed Nov.–Mar.*

Moustiers-Ste-Marie

③② *63 km (39 ft) northwest of Draguignan, 45 km (28 mi) west of Castellane.*

At the edge of all this epic wilderness, it's a bit of a shock to find this picture-perfect village tucked into a cleft in vertical cliffs, its bluffs laced with bridges, draped with medieval stone houses, and crowned with church steeples. The Verdon gushes out of the rock at the village's heart, and between the two massive rocks that tower over the ensemble, a star swings suspended from a chain.

To most, the name *Moustiers* means faïence, the fine glazed earthenware that has been produced here since the 17th century, when a monk brought in the secret of enamel glazes from Faenza in Umbria. Its brilliant white finish caught the world's fancy, especially when the fashionable grotesques of Jean Berain, decorator to Louis XIV, were imitated and produced in exquisite detail. A colony of ceramists still creates Moustiers faience today, from large commercial producers to independent artisans. The small but excellent **Musée de la Faïence** has concise audiovisual explanations of the craft and displays a chronology of fine pieces. Currently housed in a pretty 18th-century *hôtel particulier* (private mansion) with a lovely *salle de mariage* (wedding hall) lined in painted canvas, it will soon be expanded into a new building. ⊠ *pl. du Tricentenaire,* ☎ *04–92–74–61–64.* ☎ *10 frs.* ☉ *Apr.–Oct., daily 9–noon and 2–6; Nov.–Dec. and Feb.–Mar., weekends 2–6.*

With all the faïence around, you may end up keeping your nose to the shop windows, where every form (and every quality) of the Moustiers product is for sale. But the walk through town is pretty, too, though it's little more than a double loop along the rushing stream, over a bridge

THE SENTIER MARTEL: A TOURIST'S PROVING-GROUND

I T'S NO SUNDAY-AFTER-LUNCH promenade, this trail: The famous 14 km (9 mi) stretch of the GR4 follows a steep, narrow path flanked on one side by rock wall and the other by nothingness, sometimes passing over loose rubble and sometimes over slick, mossy limestone at a 45-degree rake. And those are the easy parts. One of the trail's many engineered challenges: a series of wrought-iron ladder-stairs (240, count them if you dare) bolted deep into rock cliff and suspended over the chasm below. The grand finale: Two womb-dark tunnels through shoe-deep water, one of them 2,198 ft long. Yet, if you're an experienced hiker, you'll be able to take your eyes off your feet and appreciate the magnificence of the setting, one of the grandest canyons in Europe.

Because the Verdon is regulated by two dams, you'll often be confronted with the not-so-comforting picture of a human stick figure running for his life before a tidal wave. This is to warn you to stick to the trail and not to linger on the low, beachlike riverbed when the water is low, as it could rise suddenly at any moment. The trail itself stays above the danger line at all times, sometimes so well above it that the risk of drowning seems preferable to the risk of plunging 500 ft into the void.

The Sentier Martel takes anywhere from six to nine hours to complete. Wear good shoes with firm ankle support and textured soles. Carry plenty of water and a flashlight with good batteries; you won't be able to grope your way through the tunnels without it. Dogs and children under six won't be able to handle the metal ladders. Follow the red-and-white GR marker, and don't leave the trail. You can arrange a taxi pickup at the Point Sublime based on a rough estimate of your own abilities.

The spelunker/explorer Edouard Martel (1859–1938) couldn't arrange a taxi, but first penetrated the Gorges in 1896 with a canvas canoe, an assistant, and two local trout fishermen. Despite repeated attempts, he didn't manage to negotiate the full canyon's length before 1905. Before that first traverse, the only humans who knew the canyons at all were woodcutters who rappelled down the cliffs to chop wild boxwood—which was made into prosaic, unadventurous *boules* (lawnbowling balls).

It was in the 1930s that the Touring Club blasted fire-escape-style ladders and catwalks along the precarious rock walls, and drilled two tunnels through solid stone. They added occasional rope railings and steps, and buttressed the trail with rock supports. But much of it crosses rubble slides that shift and change with the years, and steady maintenance can't keep natural erosion from changing the limestone profile over the years. That's why it remains a challenge worthy of its intrepid namesake.

or two, and a peek into the early Gothic church, with its sliver windows in pre-Raphaelite hues.

Moustiers was founded as a monastery in the 5th century, but it was in the Middle Ages that the **Chapelle Notre-Dame-de-Beauvoir** (first known as d'Entreroches, or "between rocks") became an important pilgrimage site. You can still climb the steep cobbled switchbacks, along with pilgrims, passing modern stations-of-the-cross panels in Moustiers faience. From the porch of the 12th-century church, remodeled in the 16th century, you can look over the roofs of the village to the green valley, a patchwork of olive groves and red-tiled farmhouses. The forefather of the star that swings in the wind over the village was first hung, it is said, by a crusader grateful for his release from Saracen prison.

Despite its civilized airs, Moustiers is another gateway to the Gorges du Verdon, providing the best access to the southern bank and the famous drive along D71 called the **Route de la Corniche Sublime.** (You may also approach the corniche from the southeast at Comps.) Breathtaking views over withering drop-offs punctuate this vertiginous road that's just wide enough for two cars if you all hold your breath. The best of the vistas is called the **Balcons de la Mescla,** with viewpoints built into the cliff face overlooking the torrential whirlpool where the Verdon and the Artuby combine.

Dining and Lodging

$ ✕ **Jadis.** Whether you eat at sidewalk tables on the cobbled backstreet or climb downstairs to the tiny, cool vaulted-stone dining room, you'll get a warm welcome at this simple, family-run restaurant/pizzeria. But don't limit yourself to the excellent wood-oven pizza: Also served are fresh crudités with *anchoïade* (anchovy dip), stuffed sardines, a puff pastry of chèvre with lavender honey, fish soup, baked pastas, and hefty beef *daubes* (stews). ⊠ *rue Courtil,* ☎ *04–92–74–63–01. MC, V.*

$$$$ ✕▥ **La Bastide de Moustiers.** From the whole baguette and Opinel switchblade on your table to the folksy, wisecracking waitstaff and the recorded birdsong for callers on hold, this neo-bucolic inn is far from the regal realms chef Alain Ducasse commands in Paris and Monte Carlo. He's happily slumming here, like Marie Antoinette on her miniature farm, creating a Provençal country life for himself and for his guests. In the green valley below Moustiers, Ducasse has transformed a 17th-century *bastide* (country house) into a sleek and luxurious retreat surrounded by olive trees, chestnuts, cypress, lavender, and even a medicinal herb garden. The cuisine, under protégé Benoît Witz, has that Ducasse-in-the-country touch: A froth of pea soup with bacon bits, vegetables from the *potager* (garden) steamed and served with olive oil and sea salt, beef roasted in the fireplace, and regional cheeses. (The restaurant is closed from early January through early March, except for guests on half board.) The chestnut-shaded terrace is a small paradise. Rooms have a cool and eclectic mix of antiques and country prints without tipping into the realm of kitsch, and baths are state of the art; it's a Relais & Châteaux property. ⊠ *Chemin de Quinson, 04360,* ☎ *04–92–70–47–47,* ℻ *04–92–70–47–48. 11 rooms, 1 suite. Restaurant, air-conditioning, pool. AE, DC, MC, V.*

$ ▥ **Le Baldequin.** This tiny, somewhat eccentric little *chambre d'hôte* (bed-and-breakfast) is in a solid 17th-century bastide in Moustiers's old center. Rooms are fussy and satin-frilled, with brightly decorated all-tile baths. The light and views are serene, however, and you can hear the water trickling in the *lavoir* (stone laundry fountain) across the street. One room overlooks roofs and the hill above, another the tiny closed

courtyard with a thick lilac tree. Breakfast is served in a charming lit-
tle kitchen-bar with a whitewashed fireplace. ⊠ *pl. Clérissy, 04360,*
☎ ⅋AX *04–92–74–67–28,* ☎ *06–08–06–49–95 mobile. 6 rooms.*
Breakfast only. No credit cards.

Riez

❸❸ *15 km (9 mi) west of Moustiers on D952.*

Nowadays Riez (pronounced ree-EHZ) is modest enough, but this little market town west of Moustiers was once a Gallo-Roman colony
and a bishopric up through the Revolution. Its claim to fame is its 5th-
century baptistery, its boxy exterior concealing the classic octagon
and ring of columns that framed early Christian baptismal fonts. This
scrap of antiquity stands alone on a corner outside the town center, a
padlock on its door and its interior a jumble of broken statuary. Across
the street some casual Roman ruins with scattered chunks of column
attest to Riez's glory days. If you park next to the baptistery, you can
cross a bridge to the field where a lone quartet of Corinthian columns
stand, still supporting their architrave; they date from the 1st century AD.

It's worth puttering in the old town, too, passing through one of its
13th-century gates to enter the tangle of tiny streets. Riez's importance
as a church center shows in the stature of its hôtels particuliers: Among
the usual shuttered cubes, a handful of Renaissance showcases stand
out, with Gothic windows, jutting corbel bays, and florid decoration.

En Route From Riez, head southeast on D11 and D111 to Ste-Croiz-de-Verdon,
on the shores of the **Lac de Ste-Croix.** This vast man-made lake was
created by a dam in 1975; though its waters are brilliant blue-green,
its banks and verdure have yet to acquire the natural lines that grace
an older lake—for instance, one that can trace its pedigree to the Ice
Age. Like America's Lake Powell, it has nonetheless become a center
for water sports and swimming, and trailer campgrounds have sprung
up around its base. Follow D71 and D49 on south to D957, which
leads to Aups.

Aups

❸❹ *23 km (14 mi) south of Moustiers, 30 km (19 mi) northwest of Draguignan.*

Not perched but rather nestled artfully in a valley of olive groves
under imposing pine-covered hills, this village (pronounced ohpss)
spills in a graceful delta of towers, campaniles, and tile-roofed cubes.
Its old town, above the modern section, echoes with trickling fountains,
and the square, under heavy plane trees, remains undisturbed by
tourism. It has ruins, too, of a 12th-century château-fort with traces
of the medieval ramparts that once surrounded it. Aups's claim to fame
is the truffle, rooted up from the surrounding forests and sold in a Thursday market from November through April.

OFF THE
BEATEN PATH

TOURTOUR – At the top of a pretty winding drive of D77, the hilltop
town of Tourtour merits a side trip. Perched above the valley and
crowned by two châteaux, it has a central square with ancient olive
trees and steep-raked streets, some covered with vaulted arcades. Views
from the Romanesque church sweep down to the coastal hills.

En Route Between Aups and Cotignac, pull over for a brief turn through **Sillans-la-Cascade.** Only moderately gentrified, it has pretty backstreets and bits of old rampart walls, but its main attraction is a waterfall, the Cascade de Sillans. An easy 20-minute stroll from the village through woods and fields takes you to a viewpoint, from which you see a thick veil of water pouring over the green cliff side.

Cotignac

③⑤ *36 km (22 mi) west of Draguignan, 66 km (41 mi) northwest of St-Raphaël.*

The light changing on the stone bluff, revealing pockets of ancient stairs and dwellings tucked into shadowy hollows, give this old mountain town, nestled at the foot of a dramatic rock cliff crowned by two medieval towers, a Turner-esque quality. Life in the old town below plays out in tones of tinted sepia, in the quiet Renaissance center and along the lazy, deep-shaded cours Gambetta, where painted storefronts and cafés stand oblivious to time.

Though it's possible to make a running tour of hill villages, popping into churches, perusing the galleries, and drinking a quick one on the squares, Cotignac is a place to stop, stay, listen, and live—even briefly— the rhythm of a Provençal day. It is the place to drink a pastis slowly and practice your French with the couple at the neighboring table; they're likely to live here—and to welcome your attempts. The butcher is proud of his award-winning lamb, the bakers compete for your business, and the very few galleries maintain a low profile.

Take time to stroll through the old town, an inner sanctum within Baroque gates; here noble houses from the 16th and 17th centuries encircle a fountain and a lovely ironwork bell tower. Farther in, rue Clastre is flanked by medieval houses with shutters painted in muted hues.

If you need a concrete goal, climb up the cliff face into one of the mysterious grottoes; these ancient hollows have served as refuges and lookouts for centuries. From this vantage point you can look down over the plane trees, elms, and red roofs of the otherworldly town.

Dining and Lodging

$$ ✕🏠 **Lou Calen.** This sturdy old landmark, at the foot of cours Gam-
★ betta, conceals a secret garden where you can dine under palm trees by the pond and dipping pool. The atmosphere is comfortable and familial, and rooms have a homey, unpretentious mix of quarry tiles, knick-knacks, chenille spreads, and overstuffed chairs. Some have exposed beams, a sleeping loft, and a working fireplace, as nights get nippy up here in autumn. The traditional restaurant, featuring old-fashioned regional specialties, makes the most of the garden setting, with even its indoor tables overlooking the greenery. For drinks there's a tiny terrace out front overlooking the plane trees and the old lavoir. (The restaurant is closed Wednesday, and there's no dinner service on Tuesday.) ✉ *cours Gambetta, 83570,* ☎ *04–94–04–60–40,* FAX *04–94–04–76–64. 16 rooms. Restaurant, pool. MC, V. Closed Feb.–mid-Mar.*

OFF THE
BEATEN PATH
On pretty country roads outside Cotignac, this sight deserves a side trip. The long, lean 17th-century **Château d'Entrecasteaux** (☎ 04–94–04–43–95) is a change from the stocky medieval style in neighboring villages. You can visit the vast kitchen, salons, and garden. It's open April–October, daily 10–6, and admission is 30 francs. There's also a tiny old town with a fortified church.

Abbaye du Thoronet

36 *29 km (18 mi) southwest of Draguignan.*

This 12th-century Cistercian abbey, an extraordinary example of Romanesque architecture at its most distilled, stands in an austere, isolated valley. The purity of the structure (or severity, if you will) was a reaction in its day to the luxurious extravagance of the Cluny abbey in Burgundy. Study the dense stonework and almost total lack of wooden support and admire the near-perfect symmetry of the church's ground plan and its gentle forays into Gothic style. The cloister is stark and stolid when compared to the delicate cloisters of Fréjus and Arles. ☎ *04–94–60–43–90.* ✉ *35 frs.* ☉ *Apr.–Sept., Mon.–Sat. 9–7, Sun. 9–noon and 2–7; Oct.–Mar., 9:30–12:30 and 2–5.*

Draguignan

37 *30 km (19 mi) northwest of Fréjus, 56 km (35 mi) west of Grasse, 64 km (40 mi) nothwest of Cannes.*

Long the capital of the Var, this broad sprawl of a city suffers from intense modernization, starting with the rigid 19th-century reorganization of Baron Haussmann, who ironed out much of its charm. He spared the pretty old town, though, and it's in this charming neighborhood of shuttered houses, sculpted doors, and bubbling fountains that the animated market takes place (on place du Marché) Wednesday and Saturday mornings. At the heart of the old town, the imposing 17th-century **Tour de l'Horloge** (Clock Tower) rears up, cornered by scroll-like guard towers and topped with an elaborate campanile.

En Route   If you're heading north from Draguignan toward Comps and the Gorges du Verdun, you'll pass through the **Gorges de Châteaudouble**, a deep, winding forest canyon that prepares you for the wilderness ahead. En route you may choose to cut briefly north up to the tiny medieval hill town of **Châteaudouble**, where you can view the magnificent wooded gorge from above.

THE WESTERN CÔTE D'AZUR A TO Z

Arriving and Departing

By Car
A8 provides swift, easy access to Fréjus and Cannes. To reach resorts along the Esterel, you must follow the coastal highway N98 east; to get to St-Tropez and the resorts at the foot of the Massif des Maures, you must follow N98 southwest from Fréjus. To explore the hill towns and the Gorges du Verdon, slow and scenic roads lead north and west from Fréjus and Cannes, including the famous Route Napoléon, D85 above Grasse.

By Train
The main rail crossroads from points north and west are at Fréjus–St-Raphaël, where the rail route begins its scenic crawl along the coast to Italy, stopping in Cannes and La Napoule. There is no rail access to St-Tropez; St-Raphaël is the nearest stop. The train station nearest the Haute Var and the Gorges du Verdon is at Draguignan-Les Arcs. From there you have to rent a car or take local buses into the hills. The scenic little **Chemin de Fer de Provence** (Provence Railroad; ✉ Gare du Sud, 33 av. Malausséna, 06000 Nice, ☎ 04–93–82–10–17) leads from Nice to Digne and makes a local stop at St-André-les-Alpes, about 20 km (12 mi) north of Castellane, the eastern gateway to the Gorges du Verdon.

Getting Around

By Bus

Local buses cover a network of routes along the coast and stop at many out-of-the-way places that can't be reached by train. Timetables are available from tourist offices, train stations, and local bus stations (*gares routières*). Ask for information on commercial bus excursions, too; there are several day-trip tours out of Cannes into the most popular hill towns (Grasse, Fayence, St-Paul, and Vence).

By Car

Sailing from Fréjus and St-Raphaël to Cannes is a breeze on A8, but N98, which connects you to coastal resorts in between, can be extremely slow, though scenic. There's a tremendous amount of urban congestion between Cannes, Mougins, and Grasse; north and west of this region, you break into the country, and the roads are small, pokey, and pretty. If you want to explore any hill towns in depth and at will, a car is indispensable.

By Train

A good rail network follows the coast from St-Raphaël to Cannes, stopping at the coastal resorts. For further sightseeing you have to resort to renting a car or taking a bus excursion.

Contacts and Resources

Car Rental

If you fly into Nice, rent your car from the airport there (☞ Chapter 6). If you take the train to the coast, you'll probably stop in St-Raphaël or Cannes and can rent a car from one of the following central locations: **Avis** (⊠ 190 pl. Pierre Coullet, St-Raphaël, ☎ 04–94–83–11–41; ⊠ 69 bd. Croisette, Cannes, ☎ 04–93–94–15–86; ⊠ pl. de la Gare, Cannes, ☎ 04–93–39–26–38). **Budget** (⊠ 40 rue Waldeck, St-Raphaël, ☎ 04–94–82–24–44; ⊠ 160 rue Antibes, Cannes, ☎ 04–93–99–44–04). **Europcar** (⊠ 54 pl. Pierre Coullet, St-Raphaël, ☎ 04–94–95–56–87; ⊠ 3 rue Commandant Vidal, Cannes, ☎ 04–93–06–26–30). **Hertz** (⊠ 32 rue Waldeck, St-Raphaël, ☎ 04–94–95–48–68; ⊠ Eden Palace II, 147 rue Antibes, Cannes, ☎ 04–93–99–04–20).

Outdoor Activities and Sports

If you want to hike the hills and Grandes Randonnées of the Haut Var, contact the following agency for information and maps: **Comité Départemental de la Randonnée** (Pedestre du Var, ⊠ rue Ollivier, La Rode, 83000 Toulon, ☎ 04–94–42–15–01). For hiking around the Gorges du Verdon, contact the **Comité Départemental de la Randonnée Pedestre des Alpes-de-Haute-Provence** (⊠ L'Ubac de Chandourène, 04660 Champtercier).

If you're interested in golfing in the area, pick up the brochure and map "Les Golfs du Soleil" as well as "Destination Golf" at local tourist offices for a complete listing of golf courses and facilities along the coast.

Travel Agencies

CANNES

American Express (⊠ 8 rue des Belges, ☎ 04–93–38–15). **Nouvelles Frontières** (⊠ 19 bd. de la République, ☎ 04–92–98–80–83).

ST-RAPHAËL

Havas (⊠ 64 av. Commandant Guilbaud, ☎ 04–94–95–81–62).

ST-TROPEZ

Havas (⊠ 17 bd. Louis Blanc, ☎ 04–94–56–64–64).

Vacation Rentals

Gîtes de France is a nationwide organization that rents vacation houses by the week that are outside urban areas and usually of exceptional charm and regional character. Very few of the houses are right on the coast, as they are by definition *gîtes ruraux* (rural lodgings). For information about houses in this area, contact: **Gîtes de France Var** (⊠ Rond-Point du 3 Décembre 1974, B.P. 215, 83006 Draguignan Cedex, ☎ 04–94–50–93–93, FAX 04–94–50–93–90) and **Gîtes de France des Alpes-Maritimes** (⊠ 55 promenade des Anglais, B.P. 1602, 06011 Nice Cedex 01, ☎ 04–92–15–21–30, FAX 04–93–86–01–06, www.crt-riviera.fr/gites06). For the Verdon, contact **Gîtes de France des Alpes de Haute Provence** (⊠ 04000 Dignes les Bains, ☎ 04–92–31–52–39, FAX 04–92–32–32–63). Write or call for a catalogue, then make a selection and reservation. (For more information about renting gîtes, *see* Close-Up Box: The Gîte Way *in* Chapter 1 and Lodging *in* the Gold Guide.) The tourist offices of individual towns often publish lists of *locations meublés* (furnished rentals).

Visitor Information

For information on travel within the department of Var (St-Tropez to La Napoule) write to the **Comité Départmental du Tourisme du Var** (⊠ 1 bd. Maréchal Foch, 83300 Draguignan, ☎ 03–94–50–55–50, FAX 04–94–50–55–51). For Cannes and environs, write to the **Comité Regional du Tourisme Riviera Côte d'Azur** (⊠ 55 promenade des Anglais, B.P. 1602, 06011 Nice cedex, ☎ 04–92–15–21–30). For the Verdon, contact **Verdon Accueil** (⊠ rue Nationale, 04120 Castellane, ☎ 04–92–83–67–36, FAX 04–92–83–73–11).

Local tourist offices in major towns discussed in this chapter are as follows: **Cannes** (⊠ Palais des Festivals, Esplanade G. Pompidou, B.P. 272, ☎ 04–93–39–01–01, FAX 04–93–99–37–34). **Fréjus** (⊠ 325 rue Jean-Jaurès, B.P. 8, 83601, ☎ 04–94–17–19–19, FAX 04–94–51–00–26). **Grasse** (⊠ Palais des Congrés, 22 Cours Honoré Cresp, ☎ 04–93–36–66–66, FAX 04–93–36–86–36). **Mandelieu–La Napoule** (⊠ 340 av. Jean-Monnet, 06210, ☎ 04–93–49–14–39, FAX 04–92–97–67–79). **Mougins** (⊠ 15 av. Jean-Charles Mallet, 06251, ☎ 04–93–75–87–67, FAX 04–92–92–04–03). **St-Raphaël** (⊠ rue Waldeck-Rousseau, 83700, ☎ 04–94–19–52–52, FAX 04–94–83–85–40). **St-Tropez** (⊠ quai Jean-Jaurès, B.P. 183, F-83992, ☎ 04–94–97–45–21, FAX 04–94–97–82–66).

6 Nice and the Eastern Côte d'Azur

*Antibes, Monaco, and
the Arrière-Pays*

*This region is the heart and soul of the
Côte d'Azur. Its waterfront resorts—
Antibes, Villefranche, and Menton—
draw energy from the thriving city
of Nice, while jutting tropical peninsulas—Cap Ferrat, Cap Martin—frame
the tiny principality of Monaco. Just
behind, medieval villages mushroom
out of the nearby hills—St-Paul, Vence,
and Eze—offering refugees from the
coastal crowds a token taste of old
Provence. Deeper into the backcountry
lie scattered wild, Latin-accented
mountain towns, long cut off from the
chic scene below. And backing it all,
looming icy white on a clear day, rise
the Alps, telephoto-close behind the
palm trees.*

WITH THE ALPS AND PRE-ALPS playing body-guard against inland winds, and the sultry Mediterranean warming the sea breezes, the eastern slice of the Côte d'Azur is pampered by a nearly-tropical climate that sets it apart from the rest of France's southern coast. This is where the real glamour begins: the dreamland of azure waters and indigo sky; white villas with balustrades edging the blue horizon; evening air perfumed with jasmine and mimosa; palm trees and parasol pines silhouetted against sunsets of apricot and gold. Ideal as a Jazz-Age travel poster, this area lives up to the image of the Côte d'Azur, which seems to define happiness itself in the mind of the world.

Thus the dream confronts modern reality: On the hills that undulate along the azure water, every cliff, cranny, gully, and plain bristles with hot-pink cement-cube "villas" with balconies skewed toward the sea and the sun. Like a rosy rash they crawl and spread, outnumbering the trees and blocking each other's views. Their owners and the renters who stream southward at every vacation—Easter, Christmas, Carnaval, and All Saints'—choke the tiered highways, and on a hot day in high summer the traffic to the beach—slow going any day—coagulates and blisters in the sun.

There has always been a rush to this prime slice of the Côte d'Azur, starting with the ancient Greeks who sailed eastward from Marseille to market their goods to the indigenes. From the 18th-century English aristocrats who claimed it as one vast treatment spa, to the 19th-century Russian nobles who transformed Nice into a tropical St-Petersburg, to the 20th-century American tycoons who cast themselves as shieks, the coast beckoned like a dreamscape, a blank slate for their whims. Like the modern vacationers who have followed in their footsteps, they all have left their mark on the coast: Moroccan palaces in Menton, a neo-Greek villa in Beaulieu, the Promenade des Anglaises in Nice planted with tropical greenery introduced to suit English fancies—temples all to fantasy, inspired by the sensual pleasures of sun and sultry sea breeze.

The beauty of the coast, however, is only skin deep—a veneer of coddled glamour backed by a sharp ascent into relatively ascetic heights. True, the fantasy world spills slightly inland, as daytrippers seeking contrast have transformed the hills behind the Baie des Anges into something of a Provençal theme park. Lovely hilltowns handy to the coast have transformed themselves to fulfill visitors' dreams of backcountry villages, and galleries, souvenir shops, and snack stands crowd the cobblestones of old St-Paul, Vence, and Eze.

But the hills and deep gorges behind this hyperpopulated region are known as the *arrière-pays Niçoise* (Nice backcountry), and they have a character all their own—a world apart, not only from the coastal scene but from the hill towns of the Haut Var and Haute Provence (☞ Chapter 5). Long under the rule of the Dukes of Savoy and reminiscent of Alpine Italy, sprinkled with naively frescoed Baroque chapels and eagles'-nest villages in mellow ochre hues, they remain utterly isolated and retain their unique regional essence.

You could drive from Antibes to the Italian border in two hours and see the entire region, so small is this renowned stretch of Mediterranean coast. But like the artists and nobles who paved the way before you, you will likely be seduced to linger.

Pleasures and Pastimes

Architecture

Despite the view-hogging eyesores sprouting all over the coastal hills, the eastern Côte d'Azur retains many of the eccentric Belle Époque villas where wealthy sojourners gave their fantasies free rein. There are Moorish-style onion domes and cupolas, Gothic pastiche, glazed-tile roofs in whimsical jewel tones, friezes in Art Nouveau mosaic and trompe l'oeil frescoes.

These pleasure domes stand cheek by jowl with the extravagant symmetry of grand waterfront hotels and the classical rigor of broad Italian-style squares. There's Italy in the air, too, in the urban old towns, with dark canyonlike alleys flanked by ochre walls, pastel shutters, and laundry flying like medieval banners.

Baroque churches anchor every town, some of extraordinary sumptuousness and extravagance of scale; there's one on nearly every corner in the old quarter of Nice. Gothic chapels in the medieval hill towns—Vence and Breil-sur-Roya—have a purity of form offset by rich, often simple frescoes; their precedent inspired modern masters to decorate chapels of their own.

Art

Apart from the sun, 20th-century art is one of the main reasons to come to this region. Renoir, Picasso, Matisse, Chagall, Cocteau, Fernand Léger, and Raoul Dufy all left their mark here; there are museums devoted to their work scattered along this section of the coast. Some of them threw themselves enthusiastically into the traditions of the region, decorating chapels in intensely personal styles, just as their Gothic predecessors had: Matisse painted one in Vence, Picasso in Vallauris, and Cocteau in Villefranche. Formidable collections of modern masters and contemporary works can be seen in the museums of Nice and at the Fondation Maeght, on a hilltop garden above St-Paul.

Beaches

Despite its reputation as a beach paradise, the eastern Côte d'Azur waterfront is surfaced by stretches of smooth, round rocks the size of your fist; from Cagnes-sur-Mer to Menton, you'll spread a towel over cold lumps instead of nestling into sand. A thin foam mattress or an inflatable one can make all the difference in a day's stay. From Cannes (☞ Chapter 5) to Antibes and Cagnes, there are patches of sand between the ports and rocky shoreline. A few resorts and private beaches farther up the coast have made an effort to haul in sand to cater to the expectations of swimmers.

If you're lodging inland and plan to make a day trip to the beach, leave early: Traffic on N98, from which you'll access the waterfront throughout the length of the coast, grinds to a halt as others of like mind flow in from points north, east, and west.

Dining

This sunny, sea-warmed area mixes the best of Provençal specialties and fresh Mediterranean fish, including succulent filets of *rouget* (mullet) and *loup* (sea bass), often served with pungent garlic sauce or grilled with a crunch of anise-perfumed fennel. Along the coast and into the hills, your plate will often be garnished with ratatouille, the garlicky vegetable stew of sun-plumped eggplant, zucchini, and tomato. Zucchini flowers appear on the table, too, stuffed and fried in batter.

But the last expanse of the Riviera between the Cap d'Antibes and the Italian border draws strong culinary influence from its central city, Nice. As a gateway port intimately allied with Genoa and Liguria and influenced by input from Corsica and North Africa, Nice developed a unique cuisine that is still a part of the region's daily life. In the old town off Place Garibaldi, in street stands and *traiteurs* (food shops), you can sample Niçois specialties such as *salade Niçoise*, a confetti-bright mix of tomatoes, green beans, potatoes, eggs, anchovies or tuna, and the signature tiny, shiny black olives of Nice (the real thing is a far cry from the mainstreamed international version). Equally ubiquitous is the *pissaladière*, the father of modern pizza: Its oil-based pizza crust is topped with a golden heap of caramelized onions and garnished with a smear of *pissa* (herbed anchovy spread) and a handful of olives. It's a good picnic takeout, as is a hefty *pan bagnat*, a pita-like bun stuffed to bursting with tuna, hard-cooked eggs, tomatoes, and olives.

But venture farther to find backstreet exotica: *socca*, a paste of ground chick-peas smeared on a griddle and scraped up like a gritty pancake; it's eaten by hand with a generous shower of ground pepper; *petits farcis*, a selection of red peppers, zucchini, and eggplant stuffed with spicy sausage paste and roasted; and sardine *beignets*, fresh, whole sardines fried in a thick puff of spicy batter, crunched down bones and all. If you're a brave culinary adventurer, seek out *l'estocaficada* (pronounce it with an Italian accent, and you'll hear its roots in the word *stockfish*, or salt cod): The ammoniac dried fish is soaked and simmered with olives and strong, fresh herbs. Accompany it all with delicate Bellet, a rare Côtes-de-Provence wine produced on the slopes around Nice, which rates as one of the better rosés.

CATEGORY	COST*
$$$$	over 500 frs
$$$	250–500 frs
$$	150–250 frs
$	under 150 frs

*per person for a three-course meal, including tax (20.6%) and tip but not wine

Lodging

It's hard to find charming hotels in this overbuilt section of the coast, as the demand for rooms with sea views has exacerbated the rash of concrete-block, parking-garage-style lodgings. And the majority of visitors seem to value proximity to the sea over cachet. That said, a few treasures are worth seeking out—and reserving well in advance. Inland, hilltop villages feature small and quiet inns, some in the center of the old towns; rooms are priced accordingly.

CATEGORY	COST*
$$$$	over 1,000 frs
$$$	600–1,000 frs
$$	300–600 frs
$	under 300 frs

*All prices are for a standard double room for two, including tax (20.6%) and service charge.

Shopping

As the commercialized hilltop villages behind the eastern coast—St-Paul, Vence, and Eze—try to create Provençal atmosphere for daytrippers, the heavy-sweet smell from the ubiquitous scented-soap shops wafts through the streets (with the exception of Peillon, whose citizens wisely voted to ban boutiques). Other souvenirs include Provençal cottons (which originated around the ancient ports of Arles and Nîmes, farther west), lavender potpourris (harvested from the hills of Haute Provence), and just about anything made of olive wood. All too familiar as these charming souvenirs may be, none of them can claim roots in the coastal region.

Arts and crafts are more this region's forte. Sculpture, glass, and contemporary art in vivid colors are sold in the commercial galleries lining the streets of St-Paul-de-Vence and, to a lesser extent, Vence, but the place to go for artisanal products—sculptures, weavings, paintings—is Tourrettes-sur-Loup, where the artists have made a way of life for themselves on the tiny, raked backstreets of the old village.

Art glass and ceramics dominate the shops in two hill villages outside Antibes: Biot and Vallauris. Biot is home to the extremely popular and sought-after colored glassware that bears its name—La Verrerie de Biot. Its pitchers, goblets, and hurricane lamps are bubbled and pleasantly heavy in form as well as heft. In Vallauris, the streets are lined with ceramists' studios, and pottery is sold in every form, from useful everyday pieces to works of art.

Exploring Nice and the Eastern Côte d'Azur

It's easy to explore this part of the coast, and you can do it in depth without retracing your steps too often: There are parallel roads, especially along the Corniche between Nice and Menton, that access different towns and reveal different points of view. A8, which parallels the coast, makes zipping back to home base a breeze.

Great Itineraries

Whether you settle into one coastal home base and make day trips from there or move from resort to city to hill village, this part of the coast has an enormous variety of places to see. It's worth it to visit different resort towns, as each has a distinct personality and its own sights. Even on a short trip, you'll want to make a foray into the hills to see one of the famous perched villages; you can visit one or two in an easy day trip, but a night or two in the backcountry offers a pleasant contrast to the seaside. On a longer sojourn, consider making a day trip—or a lengthier exploration—into the hills toward the Alps.

Numbers in the text correspond to numbers in the margin and on the Eastern Côte d'Azur, Nice, and Monaco maps.

IF YOU HAVE 3 DAYS

Choose one waterfront resort town—⚄ **Antibes** ②, ⚄ **Villefranche-sur-Mer** ㊸, or ⚄ **Menton** ㊲—as your home base for three nights. Settle into the Mediterranean pace on your first day. For a big-city day, choose between the novelty of glamorous Monte Carlo in **Monaco** ㊽–㊺, with its landscaped casino and clifftop palace, or a tour of the old-town quarter of **Nice** ⑩–㉞, roving the backstreets and the market on the Cours Saleya and ambling along the waterfront on the Promenade des Anglaises. Spend your third day in the hill town of **St-Paul** ⑦, window-shopping along the cobbled streets and taking in the extraordinary sculpture garden and modern art collection at the Fondation Maeght.

IF YOU HAVE 7 DAYS

Spend two nights in ⚄ **Antibes** ②, exploring its old town, market, and waterfront the first day and either walking or driving on the alluring green **Cap d'Antibes** ③ the next morning. Make an afternoon outing to either **Vallauris** ①, to see its ceramics studios and a chapel decorated by Picasso, or **Biot** ④, to see its glass studios and a museum devoted to Fernand Léger. Move up into the hills for a night, visiting ⚄ **St-Paul** ⑦ and nearby ⚄ **Vence** ⑧, with its evocative walled old town; spend the night in either. Then move on to ⚄ **Nice** ⑩–㉞ for two nights, devot-

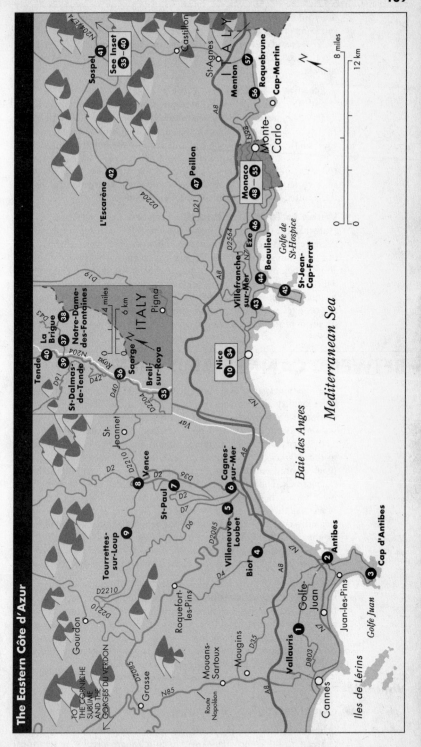

The Eastern Côte d'Azur

189

TO THE CORNICHE SUBLIME AND THE GORGES DU VERDON

Gourdon

Grasse

Route Napoléon

N85

Mouans-Sartoux

Mougins

Roquefort-les-Pins

St-Jeannet

Tourrettes-sur-Loup ⑨

Vence ⑧

St-Paul ⑦

Cagnes-sur-Mer ⑥

Villeneuve-Loubet ⑤

Biot ④

Vallauris

Golfe-Juan ①

Juan-les-Pins

Antibes ②

Cap d'Antibes ③

Golfe Juan

Cannes

Îles de Lérins

Baie des Anges

Mediterranean Sea

ITALY

Castillon

St-Agnès

Menton

Roquebrune ⑤⑦

Cap-Martin

⑤⑥

Monte-Carlo

Monaco ④⑧ — ⑤⑤

Èze ④⑥

Beaulieu ④⑤

Villefranche-sur-Mer ④④

St-Jean-Cap-Ferrat

Golfe de St-Hospice

④③

Nice ⑩ — ③④

Sospel ④①

See Inset ③⑤ — ④⑩

L'Escarène ④②

Peillon ④⑦

Inset

St-Dalmas-de-Tende

Tende ④⑩

La Brigue ③⑦

Notre-Dame-des-Fontaines ③⑧

③⑨

Saorge ③⑥

Breil-sur-Roya ③⑤

Pigna

ITALY

8 miles

12 km

4 miles

6 km

ing your second day to art museums. On your sixth and seventh days settle into the picture-pretty port towns of ☒ **Villefranche-sur-Mer** ㊸ or ☒ **St-Jean-Cap-Ferrat** ㊺, making a foray into **Monaco** ㊽–㊿ and cruising the Corniche highways, or spending a morning at the **Menton** ㊼ market.

IF YOU HAVE 10 DAYS

Spend the extra nights in ☒ **Menton** ㊼, and earlier on, when you're near Vence, head on up to **Tourrettes-sur-Loup** ⑨ for a taste of Haute Provence. Add visits to the extraordinary (and touristy) **Eze** ㊻, perched right on the coast above the sea, and drive up the quiet, boutique-free-zone in the ziggurat hilltop village of **Peillon** ㊼. Devote at least a day to an excursion into the wild gorges of the Alpine foothills northeast of Nice, stopping in the otherworldly village of **Saorge** ㊱ and visiting the painted chapel in **Notre-Dame-des-Fontaines** ㊳.

When to Tour Nice and the Eastern Côte d'Azur

Naturally the coast is in its tropical prime in July and August, but that's no secret, and the seaside resorts and hill towns are overloaded to bursting with sun seekers. If you're anxious to enjoy the beaches, aim for June or September, or you could even look for sheltered spots from March onward. Many hotels and restaurants close from November to Easter, though Nice and Monaco thrive year-round. If you're counting on exploring the mountain gorges in the arrière-pays, there may be snow in this Alpine region as late as June and as early as September.

BETWEEN CANNES AND NICE

The coastline spanning the brief distance between Cannes and Nice has a personality all its own, combining some of the most accessible and democratic waterfront resorts (Juan-les-Pins, Villeneuve, and Cagnes) with one of the most elite (Cap d'Antibes). This is vacationland, with a culture of commercial entertainment that smacks of the worst of Florida in the '60s. N98, which goes from Antibes to Cagnes, crawls past a jungle of amusement parks, beach discos, and even a gargantuan horse-racing track. The hill towns of Vallauris and Biot cater to souvenir hunting and lunch sorties. Juan-les-Pins is a party town, its cafés and brasseries thriving into the wee hours. And the glass high-rise monstrosities curving over the waterfront below Cagnes glow unnaturally bright until dawn. Yet minutes away on a peninsula jutting into the sea, the Cap d'Antibes floats aloof, its mansions and manicured gardens turning their backs on the cheaper real estate on the "mainland."

Everyone visiting this little piece of the Côte d'Azur, whether staying in a villa or a concrete cube, is after the same experience: To sit on a balcony, listening to the waves washing over the sand, and to watch the sun setting over the oil-painted backdrop of the Alps. And you are always just a 20-minute zip to Cannes (☞ Chapter 5) or Nice, and you can easily wend your way into the hills to visit the ancient villages of St-Paul and Vence and beyond.

Vallauris

❶ *6 km (4 mi) northeast of Cannes, 6 km (4 mi) west of Antibes.*

In the low hills over the coast, dominated by a blocky Renaissance château, this ancient village owes its four-square street plan to a form of medieval urban renewal. Ravaged and eventually wiped out by waves of the plague in the 14th century, the village was rebuilt by 70 Genovese families imported by the Abbaye de Lèrins in the 16th century to repopulate the abandoned site. They brought with them a taste for Roman planning—hence the grid format in the old town—but more important, a knack for pottery making. Their skills and the fine clay of Vallauris were a marriage made in heaven, and the village thrived as a pottery center for hundreds of years. In the 1940s Picasso found inspiration in the malleable soil and settled here, giving the flagging industry new life.

During his years here, sequestered in a simple stone house, Picasso created pottery art with a single-minded passion, sometimes dozens of works a day. But he was a painter first and foremost, and he returned to that medium in 1952 to create one of his masterworks in the château's Romanesque chapel, the vast multipaneled oil-on-wood composition ★ called *La Guerre et la Paix* (*War and Peace*). The chapel is part of the **Musée National "La Guerre et la Paix"** today, where several of Picasso's ceramic pieces are displayed along with a collection of pre-Columbian works. ✉ *Pl. de la Libération,* ☎ *04–93–64–16–05.* 🎫 *17 frs.* ☉ *July–Aug., Wed.–Mon. 10–7; Sept.–June, Wed.–Mon. 10–noon and 2–6.*

Shopping

Along **rue Hoche** and throughout the village center are shop and gallery windows crammed with bright pottery and ceramic art. Look for the **Galerie Madoura** (✉ av. Anciens Combattants, ☎ 04–93–64–66–39), owned by the ceramic house that Picasso worked with and that is still managed by descendants of his friends Georges and Suzanne Ramié. You can buy good reproductions of his Madoura pieces here.

Antibes

➋ *11 km (7 mi) northeast of Cannes, 15 km (9 mi) southeast of Nice.*

With its broad stone ramparts scalloping in and out over the waves and backed by blunt medieval towers and a skew of tile roofs, Antibes (Awn-*teeb*) is one of the most romantic old towns on the Mediterranean coast. Stroll promenade Amiral-de-Grasse along the crest of Vauban's sea walls, watch the cormorants diving off jagged black rock and sleek yachts purring out to sea, and you'll understand why Picasso was inspired here to paint on a panoramic scale. Yet a few steps inland you'll enter a souklike maze of old streets, its market filled with fresh fish and goat cheese, wild herbs, and exotic spices.

Named Antipolis, meaning across from (*anti*) the city (*polis*), by the Greeks who founded it in the 4th century BC, Antibes has always been the antithesis of Nice, gazing quietly across the harbor at its powerful and vital neighbor. Antibes flourished under the Romans' aristocratic rule and has an amphitheater, aqueducts, and baths. The early Christians established their bishopric here, the site of the region's cathedral until the 13th century.

It was in the Middle Ages that the kings of France began fortifying this key port town, an effort at fortification that culminated in the recognizable star-shaped ramparts designed by Vauban. The young general Napoléon once headed this stronghold, living with his family in a humble house in the old town; his mother washed their clothes in a stream. There's still a *lavoir* (public laundry fountain) today in the old town where locals, not unlike Signora Buonaparte, rinse their clothes and hang them like garlands over the narrow streets.

Antibes has its glamorous side, too: Whether you approach the waterfront from the train station or park along the avenue de Verdun, you'll first confront the awesome expanse of luxury yachts that anchor in the **Port Vauban.** Some of them stretch as much as 500 ft and swan back and forth at will between Greece, Saudi Arabia, and other ports of call. They won't find a more dramatic spot to anchor, with the tableau of snowy Alps looming behind and the formidable medieval block towers of the **Fort Carré** (Square Fort) guarding entry to the port. This superbly symmetrical island fortress was completed in 1565 and restored in 1967, but can only be admired from afar. Across the quai Rambaud, which juts into the harbor, a tiny crescent of soft sand beach called **La Gravette** offers swimmers one of the last soft spots on the coast before the famous Riviera pebble beaches begin.

To visit old Antibes, pass through the **Porte Marine,** an arched gateway in the rampart wall. Follow rue Aubernon to **cours Masséna,** where the exotic little sheltered market vaunts lemons, olives, and hand-stuffed sausages, and the vendors take breaks in the shoebox cafés flanking one side.

From cours Masséna, head left up to the **Église de l'Immaculée-Conception,** which served as the region's cathedral until the bishopric was transferred to Grasse in 1244. Its stout medieval watchtower was built in the 11th century with stones "mined" from Roman structures—one reason the town has no amphitheater or ruins today. The church's 18th-century facade, a marvelously Latin mix of classical symmetry and fantasy, has been restored in shades of ochre and cream. Inside you'll find a Baroque altarpiece of the Virgin and Child draping a protective cloak and rosary over the people, humbly underscaled, below; this central composition and the 18 fascinating miniatures that surround it were painted by the Niçois artist Louis Bréa in 1515. A moving *gisant* (full-body death portrait) of Christ, carved in wood in 1447, stands to the altar's right. ⊠ *pl. de la Cathédrale.*

Next door to the cathedral, the medieval Château Grimaldi rises on a Roman foundation, in turn constructed on a Greek base. Its square watchtower, alongside the bell tower of the neighboring church, define Antibes' silhouette. The bishops lived here in the church's heyday, and the Grimaldi family until the Revolution. But this fine old castle, high over the water, was little more than a monument until in 1946 its curator offered use of its vast chambers to Picasso, where he was to work with a singular passion against the inspiring backdrop of mountains, village, and sea. Here Picasso experimented with techniques, scale, and mediums, creating vast paintings on wood, canvas, paper, and walls. This extraordinary collection of works, alive with nymphs, fauns, and centaurs, as well as earthy fishermen, forms the core of the **Musée Picasso.** It houses more than 300 works by the artist, as well as pieces by Miró, Calder, and Léger. On the second floor (third story) is a room dedicated to the works of Nicolas de Staël (1914–1955), who spent the last winter of his life in Antibes creating more than 300 paintings before throwing himself from a window. These cool, lonely late works offer a marked contrast to Picasso's sunny joie de vivre. ⊠ *pl. du Château,* ☎ *04–92–90–54–20.* ▨ *30 frs.* ☼ *June–Sept., Tues–Sun. 10–6; Oct.–May, Tues.–Sun. 10–noon and 2–6.*

From the château you can double briefly back toward the cours Masséna and the old **Portail de l'Orme,** built of quarried Roman stone and enlarged in the Middle Ages. Inside the adjoining tower, the tiny **Musée de la Tour des Arts et Traditions Populaire** (Tower Museum of Popular Arts and Traditions) displays old photos and costumes from 18th- and 19th-century Antibes. There's even a pair of water skis, dating from 1931; the sport was invented in neighboring Juan-les-Pins. ⊠ *Tour de l'Orme,* ☎ *04–93–34–50–91.* ☼ *Apr.–Sept., Wed., Thurs., and Sat. 4–7; Oct.–Mar., Wed., Thurs., and Sat. 3–5.*

Head back to the ramparts and stroll along the promenade Amiral de Grasse, a marvelous setting for pondering the mountains and tides. The promenade leads directly to the Bastion St-André, a squat Vauban fortress now home to the **Musée Archéologique** (Archaeology Museum). In its glory days this 17th-century stronghold sheltered a garrison; the bread oven is still visible in the vaulted central hall. The museum collection focuses on Antibes's classical history, displaying amphorae and sculptures found in local digs as well as in shipwrecks from the harbor. ⊠ *av. Général-Maizières*, ☎ *04–92–90–54–35.* 🖼 *10 frs.* ☉ *Dec.– Oct., Tues.–Sun. 10–noon and 2–6.*

Double back up the promenade and turn left onto Place du Safranier, the entry to a magical little neighborhood with a character all its own: ★ the **Commune Libre du Safranier** (Free Commune of Safranier). Here the tiny houses hang heavy with flowers and vines, and neighbors carry on conversations from window to window across the stone-stepped rue du Bas-Castelet. It is said that place du Safranier was once a tiny fishing port; now it's the scene of this sub-village's festivals.

From the Commune quarter it's easy to drift farther into the old-town streets, exploring the mix of shops, galleries, restaurants, and bakeries. Aim to wind up on **place Nationale,** the site of the Roman forum. It's a pleasant place for a drink under the broad plane trees.

From old Antibes you can jump on a bus or hike over the hill to **Juan-les-Pins,** the jazzy younger-sister resort town that, with Antibes, bracelets the wrist of the Cap d'Antibes. The scene along its waterfront is something to behold, with thousands of international sun seekers flowing up and down the promenade and lying flank to flank on its endless stretch of sand. Cafés and restaurants feed the mobs, many of them right on the beach.

Dining and Lodging

$$–$$$ ✕ **La Bonne Auberge.** In a graceful inn set back from the overbuilt sprawl along N7, Chef Philippe Rostang cooks up classic, conservative specialties such as lamb slow-simmered in herbs for seven hours, lobster salad with tiny ravioli, and airy fish soufflés. The dining room is a pastel haven of exposed beams, fresh flowers, and soft light; huge glass windows allow you to view the inspired work in the kitchen. ⊠ *Quartier de la Brague (4 km [2 mi] east of Antibes),* ☎ *04–93–33– 36–65. AE, MC, V. Closed Mon., except July–Aug. Closed mid-Nov.– mid-Dec. No dinner Sun., except July–Aug.; no lunch Tues.*

$$$ ✕ **La Jarre.** You can dine under the beams or the ancient fig tree at this lovely little garden hideaway, just off the ramparts and behind the cathedral. Open only for dinner, it has an ambitious menu of Provençal specialties filtered through an international lens: tabbouleh topped with mullet and sharp black *tapenade,* sweet-and-sour duck breast, shrimp grilled in ginger, and apricot nougat. As there's no fixed-price menu, the à la carte tally runs high. ⊠ *14 rue St-Esprit, Antibes,* ☎ *04–93–34–50–12. MC, V. Closed mid-Oct.–Easter. No lunch.*

$ ✕ **Le Brûlot.** One street back from the thriving market, this bistro re-
★ mains one of the busiest in Antibes, though aperitifs are on the house if you have to wait. Burly Chef Christian Blancheri hoists anything from pigs to apple pies in and out of his roaring wood oven, and it's all delicious. Watch for the sardines *à l'escabèche* (in a tangy sweet-sour marinade), sizzling lamb chops, or grilled fresh fish. The decor is rustic and chaotic and the seating so close it's almost unavoidable to become part of one large, unruly crowd. ⊠ *3 rue Frédéric Isnard, Antibes,* ☎ *04– 93–34–17–76. MC, V. Closed Sun., last 2 wks of Aug., and last wk of Dec.–1st wk Jan. No lunch Mon.*

$$$$ ✕⊞ **Juana.** This luxuriously renovated landmark, run by the Bar-
★   rache family since it opened in 1931, retains a Gatsby feel. There are
striped awnings, white balustrades, and ornate Deco ironwork trimming the lobby. Pine trees tower over the grounds and the white-
marble pool, and rooms have a cool plain-pastel decor. Though it's two
long blocks from the waterfront, the Juana has its own private sand
beach there, with changing cabins, bar, and restaurant. But you'll want
to save room for a serious dinner at La Terrasse, where Chef Christian maintains top honors for some of the best cuisine on the Côte d'Azur.
Try scampi ravioli, or canneloni stuffed with clams and squid; sea bass
steamed with Menton lemon; lamb roasted in Vallauris clay; and
caramelized peaches, served warm in a drizzle of raspberry coulis. ⊠
av. Georges-Gallice, 06160 Juan-les-Pins, ☎ *04–93–61–08–70,* FAX
*04–93–61–76–60. 45 rooms, 5 suites. Restaurant, bar, air-conditioning,
pool. AE, MC, V. Closed Nov.–Mar.*

$$ ✕⊞ **Auberge Provençale.** The six rooms in this onetime abbey come
complete with exposed beams, canopied beds, and lovely antique fur-
niture. The dining room and the arbored garden are decorated with
the same impeccable taste; the menu features fresh seafood inventions
such as *rascasse* (rock fish) sausage with mint, as well as bouillabaisse
and duck grilled over wood coals. The restaurant is closed Monday
and for lunch Tuesday. ⊠ *61 pl. Nationale, 06600 Antibes,* ☎ *04–
93–34–13–24,* FAX *04–93–34–89–88. 6 rooms. Restaurant. AE,
DC, MC, V. Closed Jan.*

$$ ⊞ **Le Mas Djoliba.** Tucked into a residential neighborhood on the crest
between Antibes and Juan, this converted Provençal farmhouse is sur-
rounded by greenery and well protected from traffic noise. Rooms,
decked in bright colors and floral prints, have either views of the garden or the sea; from the family room on the top that sleeps four, there's
a balcony overlooking the Cap d'Antibes. ⊠ *29 av. de Provence,
06600 Antibes,* ☎ *04–93–34–02–48,* FAX *04–93–34–05–81. 13
rooms. Restaurant (summer service is half board only), pool. AE, DC,
MC, V. Closed Nov.–Jan.*

$$ ⊞ **Le Mimosa.** The fabulous setting, in an enclosed hilltop garden
studded with tall palms, mimosa, and tropical greenery, makes up for
the trafficky hike down to the beach. Rooms are small and modestly
decorated in Victorian florals, but ask for a functioning balcony: Many
look over the garden and pool—which is bigger than most in Cannes.
The lobby and lounge are warmed with Oriental rugs and terra-cotta
tiles, but you'll probably be drawn to the palm-shaded lawns to relax.
⊠ *rue Pauline,* ☎ *04–93–61–04–16,* FAX *04–92–93–06–46. 34
rooms. Pool. MC, V. Closed Oct.–Easter.*

Nightlife and the Arts

The glassed-in complex of the **Eden Casino** (⊠ bd. Baudoin, Juan-les-
Pins, ☎ 04–92–93–71–71) houses restaurants, bars, dance clubs, and
a casino, many with sea views. If you're ready to party all night, **La
Siesta** (⊠ rte. du Bord de Mer, Antibes, ☎ 04–93–33–31–31) is the
place; it's an enormous setup with seven dance floors (some on the beach),
bars, and roulette; like most of Juan, it's only open in summer.

Every July the **Festival de Jazz d'Antibes-Juan-les-Pins** (☎ 04–92–90–
50–00 for information) challenges Montreux for its stellar lineup and
romantic venue under ancient pines; it's one of the oldest festivals in
Europe and claims to have had the European debut performances of
Miles Davis (pronounce that Meels Dah-*vees*) and Ray Charles.

Outdoor Activities and Sports

Antibes and Juan together claim 25 km (15½ mi) of coastline and 48
beaches (including Cap d'Antibes). In Antibes you can choose be-

tween small sandy inlets, such as **La Gravette,** below the port; the central **Place de Ponteil;** and **Plage de la Salis** toward the Cap; rocky escarpments around the old town; or the vast stretch of sand above the Fort Carré. The Plage de la Salis may be one of the prettiest beach sites on the coast, with the dark pines of the cape to one side and the old stones of Antibes on the other, all against a backdrop of Alpine white. Juan is one big city beach, lined by a boulevard and promenade peppered with cafés and restaurants.

For information about deep-sea diving in the area, contact the **Centre Nautique d'Antibes** (☎ 04–93–67–26–22). **Guigo Marine** (✉ 9 av. du 11 novembre, ☎ 04–93–34–17–17) arranges deep-sea fishing expeditions and rents boats. **Visiobulle** (☎ 04–93–34–09–96) organizes one-hour cruises in tiny yellow glass-bottom boats leaving from the Ponton Courbet in Juan-les-Pins; study underwater life while circling the cape.

Shopping
At the **market** on Antibes's cours Masséna, you can buy fruits, vegetables, and a tempting array of other regional products daily until 1 PM. An **antiques and flea market** takes place Thursday and Saturday from 7 to 6 on place Nationale. You can also find plenty of eclectic little boutiques and gallery shops in the old town, especially along **rue Sade** and **rue de la République.**

Cap d'Antibes

❸ *2 km (1 mi) south of Antibes.*

This idyllic peninsula, protected from the concrete plague infecting the mainland coast, has been carved up into luxurious estates perched high above the water and shaded by thick, tall pines. Since the 19th century its wild greenery and isolation have drawn a glittering assortment of aristocrats, artists, literati, and the merely fabulously wealthy. Among those claiming the prestigious Cap d'Antibes address over the years: Guy de Maupassant, Anatole France, Claude Monet, the Duke and Duchess of Windsor, the Greek arms tycoon Stavros Niarchos, and the cream of the Lost Generation, including Ernest Hemingway, John Dos Passos, Dorothy Parker, Alice B. Toklas, Gertrude Stein, and Scott and Zelda Fitzgerald. Now the focal point is the famous Hotel Eden Roc, rendezvous and weekend getaway of film stars from Madonna and Robert De Niro to Arnold Schwarzenegger and Alain Delon.

You can sample a little of what draws them to the site by walking up the chemin de Calvaire from the Plage de la Salis in Antibes (about 1.2 km [¾ mi]), and taking in the extraordinary views from the hill that supports the old lighthouse, the **Phare de la Garoupe** (Garoupe Lighthouse). Next to the lighthouse, the 16th-century double chapel of **Notre-Dame-de-la-Garoupe** contain ex-votos and statues of the Virgin, all in the memory, and for the protection, of sailors. ☺ *Easter–Sept., daily 9:30–noon and 2:30–7; Oct.–Easter, daily 10–noon and 2:30–5.*

Another lovely walk (about 1½ km [1 mi]), along the **Sentier Tirepoil,** begins at the cape's pretty Plage de la Garoupe and winds along dramatic rocky shores, magnificent at sunset. The final destination of the Sentier Tirepoil is the **Villa Eilenroc,** designed by Charles Garnier, who created the Paris Opera—which should give you some idea of its style. It commands the tip of the peninsula, from a grand and glamorous garden. ✉ *At the peninsula's tip,* ☎ *04–93–67–74–33.* ☺ *Sept.–June, Wed. 9–5.*

★ Even more glorious is the **Jardin Thuret** (Thuret Garden), established by botanist Gustave Thuret in 1856 as a testing ground for subtropical plants and trees; he is solely responsible for the introduction of the palm tree, which forever changed the profile of the Côte d'Azur. On his death, the property was left to the Ministry of Agriculture, which continues to dabble in the introduction of exotic species. ⊠ *bd. du Cap,* ☎ *04–93–67–88–00.* ⌸ *Free.* ⊘ *Weekdays 8:30–5:30.*

At the southwest tip of the peninsula, an ancient battery is home to the **Musée Naval et Napoléonien** (Naval and Napoleonic Museum), where you can peruse a collection of watercolors of Antibes, lead soldiers, and scale models of military ships. ⊠ *Batterie du Grillon, av. Kennedy,* ☎ *04–93–61–45–32.* ⌸ *20 frs.* ⊘ *Weekdays 9:30–noon and 2:15–6, Sat. 9:30–noon.*

Dining and Lodging

$$$–$$$$ ✕ **Restaurant de Bacon.** Since 1948, under the careful control of the
★ Sordello brothers, who peruse the fish markets at dawn in Cannes and Antibes, this has been the spot for seafood on the Côte d'Azur. The catch of the day is presented on a tray, silver raw and still twitching; it's your decision whether to have it minced in lemon ceviche, floating in a top-of-the-line bouillabaisse, or simply grilled with fennel, crisped with hillside herbs, or baked in parchment. Such purity doesn't come cheap, but fixed-price menus help keep the bill down: The warm welcome, discreet service, sunny dining room, and dreamy terrace over the Baie des Anges justify extravagance. ⊠ *bd. de Bacon,* ☎ *04–93–61–50–02. Reservations essential. AE, DC, MC, V. Closed Mon. (except July–Aug.) and Nov.–Jan.*

$$$$ ⌸ **La Baie Dorée.** Clinging to the waterfront and skewed toward the
★ open sea, this elegant little inn provides you with private sea-view terraces off every room. The room decor is plush and subdued, the ambience discreet to the point of self-effacing, and the reception area is as small as a coat check—yet even the small standard doubles feel deluxe when you look out the window. The public grounds and terraces fall in tiers down to the water, from the shaded restaurant and bar to the boat dock to the private beach on the Baie de la Garoupe. ⊠ *579 bd. de la Garoupe, 06160,* ☎ *04–93–67–30–67,* FAX *04–92–93–76–39. 17 rooms. Restaurant, beach. MC, V. Closed Nov.–mid-Dec.*

Biot

④ *6 km (4 mi) northeast of Antibes, 15 km (9 mi) northeast of Cannes, 18 km (11 mi) southwest of Nice.*

Rising above an ugly commercial-industrial quarter up the coast from Antibes, Biot (pronounced Bee-*otte*) sits neatly on a hilltop, welcoming day-trippers into its self-consciously quaint center. For centuries home to a pottery industry, known for its fine yellow clay that stretched into massive, solid oil jars, it has in recent generations made a name for itself as a glass-art town. Nowadays its cobbled streets are lined with boutiques and galleries, their display windows flashing a staggering variety of goods in vividly colored glass.

Yet despite the commercialism, traces of the feel of old Provence remain, especially in the evening after the busloads of shoppers leave and the deep-shaded *placettes* (small squares) under the plane trees fall quiet. Then you can meander around the edges of the old town to find the stone arch-gates known as the **Porte des Tines** and the **Porte des Migraniers**; they're the last of the 16th-century fortifications that once enclosed Biot. Step into the 15th-century **église**: The church contains an early 16th-century altarpiece attributed to Louis Bréa depicting the Virgin Mary shielding humanity under her cloak; the surrounding portraits are as warmly detailed as the faces and hands in the central panel. **Place des Arcades** has an otherworldly grace, with its Gothic arcades and tall palm trees.

Long a regular on the Côte d'Azur, Fernand Léger fell under Biot's spell and bought a *mas* (farmhouse) here in 1955 to house an unwieldy collection of his sculptures. On his death his wife converted the house to a museum of his works, and in 1967 she donated it to France. The modernized structure of the **Musée National Fernand-Léger** is striking, its facade itself a vast mosaic in his signature style of heavily outlined color fields. Within you can trace the evolution of Léger's technique, from his fascination with the industrial to freewheeling abstractions. ⊠ *chemin du Val de Pomme,* ☎ *04–92–91–50–30.* 🎟 *38 frs.* ☉ *Apr.– Sept., Wed.–Mon. 10–12:30 and 2–6; Oct.–Mar., Wed.–Mon. 10– 12:30 and 2–5:30.*

On the edge of town, follow the pink signs to **La Verrerie de Biot** (Biot Glassworks), which has developed into something of a cult industry since its founding in the 1950s. Here you can observe the glassblowers at work, visit the extensive galleries of museum-quality art glass (which is of much better quality than the kitsch you find in the village shop windows), and start a collection of bubbled-glass goblets, cruets, or pitchers, just as Jackie Kennedy did when the rage first caught hold (she liked cobalt blue). The bubbles come from baking soda applied to the melted glass. Despite the extreme commercialism—there are a souvenir shop, a boutique of home decor, Walkman tours of the glassworks, a bar, and restaurant—it's a one-of-a-kind artisanal industry, and the product is made before your eyes. ⊠ *5 chemin des Combes,* ☎ *04–93–65–03–00.* ☉ *May–Sept., Mon.–Sat. 9–8, Sun. 10–1 and 3–7:30; Oct.–Apr., daily 10–1 and 3–7:30.*

☙ Marketed under the umbrella title of **Parc de la Mer** (Sea Park), this extremely commercial amusement complex provides parents with bargaining leverage for a day of Picasso and pottery shopping. There's a small **Marineland,** with a lively scripted dolphin show, dancing killer whales, and a Plexiglass walk-through aquarium that allows sharks to swim over your head; it also has a surprisingly deep and fascinating collection of old sea paraphernalia in its museum. Next door the **Jungle des Papillons** (Butterfly Jungle) presents a fluttering Butterfly Ballet that must be seen to be believed; wear colored clothing to stimulate them into a wing-flapping frenzy. There's **Aquasplash,** with a wave pool and 12 slides, and beside that, La Petite Ferme, a petting zoo. It's only a short distance from Antibes and Biot; take N7 north, then head left at La Brague onto D4, toward Biot. ⊠ *309 rue Mozart,* ☎ *04–93– 33–49–49.* 🎟 *Marineland 116 frs, Papillons 39 frs; joint ticket 129 frs. Aquasplash 89 frs. La Petite Ferme 52 frs. Two-day passport for all parks 260 frs.* ☉ *Daily 10–dark.*

Dining and Lodging

$ ✕🖪 **Galerie des Arcades.** Tucked away behind the quiet palm-lined
★ Place des Arcades in the old town, this combination hotel-restaurant-art gallery draws a chic and loyal clientele. They come to browse in the gallery, enjoy a weekend in one of the extraordinary guest rooms or dine on the serious, unpretentious, authentic Provençal food: rabbit sautéed in fresh herbs, stuffed sardines, or a Friday *aïoli* (fish and crudités served with garlic mayonnaise). Eat at the checked-cloth-covered tables either under the arcades or under the cozy beams indoors. Then ask for one of the three "*grandes chambres*" (large rooms) and revel in antiquity: four-poster beds, stone sinks and fireplaces, beams, and a tapestry-rich color scheme. (The smaller rooms are nothing to write home about.) ⊠ *14 pl. des Arcades, 06410,* ☎ *04–93–65–01– 04,* 🅵🅰🅷 *04–93–65–01–05. 12 rooms. Restaurant. AE, DC, MC, V.*

Villeneuve-Loubet

⑤ *10 km (6 mi) north of Antibes.*

This tiny village, its medieval château heavily restored in the 19th century, is best known for its sprawl of overbuilt beachfront, heavily charged with concrete high-rises with all the architectural charm of a parking ramp.

Yet, if you're a foodie, you may want to make a pilgrimage to the eccentric **Musée de l'Art Culinaire** (Museum of Culinary Arts), a shrine to the career of the great chef Auguste Escoffier (1846–1935). The epitome of 19th-century culinary extravagance and revered by the French as much as Joan of Arc and de Gaulle, Escoffier was the founding father of the school of haute cuisine Calvin Trillin calls "stuff-stuff-with-heavy," where ingredients are stripped, simmered, stuffed, sauced, and generally intervened with, sometimes beyond recognition. His was the school of food as sculpture—the famous *pièces montées*, wedding-cake spires of spun sugar, and the world of menus of staggering length and complexity. He wowed 'em at the Ritz in Paris and the Savoy and Carlton in London and is a point of reference for every modern chef—if only as a foil for rebellion. In his birthplace you'll view illustrations of his creations and a collection of fantastical menus, including one featuring the meat of zoo animals killed in the war of 1870. ⊠ *3 rue Escoffier,* ☎ *04–93–20–80–51.* ☞ *10 frs.* ⊙ *Dec.–Oct., Tues.–Sun. 2–6; July–Aug., Tues.–Sun. 2–7.*

Cagnes-sur-Mer

⑥ *14 km (9 mi) southwest of Nice, 10 km (6 mi) north of Antibes.*

Although from N7 you may be tempted to give wide berth to Cagnes-sur-Mer—with its congested sprawl of freeway overpasses, tacky tourist-oriented stores, and beachfront pizzerias—follow the signs inland and up into **Haut-de-Cagnes.** Its steep-cobbled old town is crowned by the fat, crenellated **Château de Cagnes.** Built in 1310 by the Grimaldis and reinforced over the centuries, this imposing fortress lords over the coastline, banners flying from its square watch tower. Its balustraded stairway and the triangular Renaissance courtyard, with its triple row of classical arcades, are infinitely more graceful than the exterior. Within are vaulted medieval chambers, a vast Renaissance fireplace, and a splendid 17th-century trompe l'oeil fresco of the fall of Phaeton from his sun chariot. The château also contains three highly specialized museums: the **Musée de l'Olivier** (Olive Tree Museum), an introduction to the history and cultivation of this Provençal mainstay; the obscure and eccentric **Collection Suzy-Solidor,** a group of portraits of the cabaret chanteuse painted by her artist friends, including Cocteau and Dufy; and the **Musée d'Art Moderne Méditerranéen** (Mediterranean Museum of Modern Art), which contains paintings by some of the 20th-century devotees of the Côte d'Azur, including Chagall, Cocteau, and Dufy. If you've climbed this far, continue to the **tower** and look over the coastline views in the same way that the guards once watched for Saracens. ⊠ *pl. Grimaldi,* ☎ *04–93–20–87–29.* ☞ *20 frs.* ⊙ *Oct.– Easter, Wed.–Sun. 10–noon and 2–5; Easter–Sept., Wed.–Sun. 10– noon and 2–6. Closed Nov.*

It's a pleasure to wander through Haut-de-Cagne's old streets, some with cobbled steps, others passing under vaulted arches. The houses are unusually pretty and well preserved, many dating from the 14th and 15th centuries. The **Chapelle Notre-Dame-de-la-Protection** (⊠ rue Hippolyte Guis) with its Italianate bell tower, was first built in the 13th century after the fortress had been destroyed; as a hedge against further invasion, they placed this plea for Mary's protection at the village edge. In 1936 the *curé* (priest) discovered traces of fresco under the bubbling plaster; a full stripping revealed every inch of the apse to have been decorated in scenes of the life of the Virgin and Jesus, roughly executed late in the 16th century. From the chapel's porch are sweeping sea views.

August Renoir (1841–1919) was particularly fond of the Chapelle Notre-Dame-de-la-Protection and of Cagnes as well. After staying up and down the coast, Renoir settled in a house in Les Collettes, just east of the old town, now the **Musée Renoir.** Here he passed the last 12 years of his life, painting the landscape around him, working in bronze, and rolling his wheelchair through the luxuriant garden of olive, lemon, and orange trees. You can view his home as it was preserved by his children, including his bed, his wheelchair, and of course his paintbrushes and easel. You can also view 10 of his last paintings and a bronze Venus in the garden bearing testimony to his successful ventures into sculpture. ⊠ *av. des Collettes,* ☎ *04–93–20–61–07.* ⊠ *22 frs.* ☉ *June–Oct., daily 10–noon and 2–6; Nov.–May, Wed.–Mon. 10–noon and 2–5.*

ST-PAUL, VENCE, AND TOURRETTES-SUR-LOUP

Inspired—indeed, propelled—by the clutter and crowds of the coast, forays into the famous villages on the plateau behind are an important part of the ritual of visiting the Côte d'Azur. Set high in the hills on the plateau that parallels the sea, they loom aloof to the beach crowds, redolent of wild herbs and medieval history. . . and soap shops. As they have been adopted as the most conveniently accessed of the famous hill villages, St-Paul and Vence have become commercialized to an almost overwhelming degree, especially in high season. If you're allergic, even in principle, to souvenir shops, artsy-craftsy boutiques, and middle-brow art galleries, aim to visit off-season or after hours, when the stone-paved alleys, backstreets, placettes, and rampart overlooks empty of tourists and when the scent of strawberry potpourri is washed away by the natural perfume of bougainvillea and jasmine wafting from terra-cotta jars.

St-Paul

7 *18 km (11 mi) north of Nice.*

The most commercially developed of Provence's perched villages and second only to Mont-St-Michel for its influx of tourists, St-Paul is nonetheless a magical place when the crowds thin. Artists—Chagall, Bonnard, and Miró—were drawn to its light, its pure air, its wraparound views, and its honey-color stone walls, soothingly cool on a hot Provençal afternoon. Film stars loved its lazy yet genteel ways, lingering on the garden-bower terrace of the Auberge de la Colombe d'Or and challenging the locals to a game of pétanque under the shade of the plane trees.

In the Middle Ages St-Paul was basically a city-state, and it controlled its own political destiny for centuries. Its 16th-century ramparts curved boldly over the valley, challenging Vence, Cagnes, and even almighty Nice. But by the early 20th century St-Paul had faded to oblivion—until a few penniless artists began paying their drink bills at the local auberge with paintings. Nowadays art of a sort still dominates in the myriad tourist traps that take your eyes off the beauty of its old stone houses.

It won't take you long to "do" St-Paul; a pedestrian circuit leads you inevitably through its rue-Grande to the *donjon* (fortress tower) and austere Gothic church. But break away and slip into a few mosaic-cobbled backstreets, little more than alleys; door after door, window after niche spill over with potted flowers and orange trees. The shuttered stone houses rear up over the streets, so close you could shake hands from window to window. And no matter which way you turn, you'll suddenly break into the open at the rampart walls; follow along the walkway to see the Tuscan-pretty landscape that quilts over the hills below, backed by an ivory sprawl of Alps.

On your way from the overpriced parking garages, you'll pass a Provençal scene played out with cinematic flair yet still authentic: the perpetual game of pétanque outside the **Café de la Place.** A sun-weathered pack of men in caps, cardigans, and workers' blues—occasionally joined by a passing professional with tie and rolled-up sleeves—gather under the massive plane trees and stand serene, silent, and intent to roll metal balls across the dusty square. Until his death Yves Montand made regular appearances here, participating in this ultimate southern scenario.

★ Many people come to St-Paul just to visit the **Fondation Maeght,** founded in 1964 by art dealer Aimé Maeght, and set on a wooded cliff top high above the medieval town. It's not just a small modern art museum but an extraordinary marriage of the arc-and-plane architecture of José Sert; the looming sculptures of Miró, Moore, and Giacometti; and a humbling hilltop setting of pines, vines, and flowing planes of water. On display is an intriguing and ever-varying array of the work of modern masters, including the wise and funny late-life masterwork *La Vie* (*Life*) by Chagall. ☏ 04-93-32-81-63. ▨ 45 frs. ☉ July–Sept., daily 10–7; Oct.–June, daily 10–12:30 and 2:30–6.

Dining and Lodging

$$$–$$$$ ✕ **La Colombe d'Or.** The art display here may cause a double take—are they really the Mirós, Bonnards, Légers, and Braques given in payment by the artists in hungrier days, or are they copies of the real thing, long since salted away? What matter: This idyllic old *auberge* (inn) was the heart and soul of St-Paul's artistic revival, and the cream of 20th-century France lounged together under its fig trees—Picasso and Chagall, Maeterlinck and Kipling, Marcel Pagnol (*Manon des Sources*) and Jacques Prévert (*Les Enfants du Paradis*). Yves Montand and Simone Signoret met and married here, and current film stars make appearances from time to time. They do so more in homage to the inn's resonant history and *pastorale* atmosphere than for its food, which is unambitious bordering on the ordinary, such as rack of lamb, rabbit stew, and *petits farcis* (stuffed vegetables). ✉ *pl. Général-de-Gaulle, 06570,* ☏ 04-93-32-80-02. *AE, DC, MC, V. Closed mid-Nov.–late Dec.*

$–$$ ✕ **Le Tilleul Menthe.** Before you plunge into the dense tangle of *ruelles* (little streets) in old St-Paul, stop on the ramparts under the thick-trunked, broad-leaved plane trees for a light meal or a snack at this atmospheric outdoor café. Served here are a few hot, plain dishes—roast chicken or a hot goat cheese salad, for instance—as well as drinks and sorbets, and you can idle at a table looking over the stone walls, valley, and Alps. ✉ *pl. Tilleul,* ☏ 04-93-32-80-36.

$$$$ ✕▧ **Le Saint-Paul.** Right in the center of the labyrinth of stone alleys, with views over the ancient ramparts, this luxurious inn (a Relais & Châteaux property) fills a noble 15th-century house with comfort and charm. Provençal furniture, golden quarried stone, and lush reproduction fabrics warm the salons and restaurant; rooms are decked in sleek pas-

tels and sprig prints, and a few have balconies over the valley. The restaurant, serving sophisticated regional specialties like eggplant terrine with pistou, sole with bacon and pumpkin puree, is a cut above as well. And a candlelighted meal on the terrace, where flowers spill from every niche, is a romantic's dream. (Off-season, the restaurant is closed Wednesday and lunch is not served on Thursday.) To park, you may briefly defy the ACCÈS INTERDIT (entry forbidden) signs, follow the rampart road, and drop off your baggage before parking on the other side of the village. ⊠ *86 rue Grande, 06570,* ☎ *04–93–32–65–25,* 𝖥𝖠𝖷 *04–93–32–52–94. 18 rooms. Restaurant, bar, terrace, air-conditioning. AE, DC, MC, V. Closed early Jan.–mid-Feb.*

$$ ✕⊡ **Le Hameau.** Less than a mile outside tourist-packed St-Paul, with views of the valley and the village, this lovely little inn is a jumble of terraces, trellises, archways, and honeysuckle vines. The main hotel, built in 1920, has good-size rooms and old Provençal furniture; or you can opt for the 18th-century farmhouse, with smaller, more modern rooms but wonderful views. ⊠ *528 rte. de La Colle, 06570,* ☎ *04–93–32–80–24,* 𝖥𝖠𝖷 *04–93–32–55–75. 15 rooms. Pool. MC, V. Closed mid-Nov.–mid-Feb. (except Christmas–New Year's).*

Vence

8 *4 km (2 mi) north of St-Paul, 22 km (14 mi) north of Nice.*

Encased behind stone walls inside a thriving modern market town, this jewel of an old town dates from the 15th century. Though crowded with boutiques and souvenir shops, it's slightly more conscious of its history than St-Paul—plaques guide you through its historic squares and *portes* (gates). Wander past the pretty place du Peyra with its fountains, place Clemenceau, with its ochre-color Hôtel-de-Ville (Town Hall), to Place du Frêne, with its ancient ash tree planted in the 16th century.

In the old-town center, the **Cathédrale de la Nativité de la Vierge** (Cathedral of the Birth of the Virgin; Pl. Godeau) was built on the Roman's Champ de Mars (military drilling field) and traces bits and pieces to Carolingian and even Roman times. It's a hybrid of Romanesque and Baroque styles, expanded and altered over the centuries. The carved-wood stalls are worth studying; they were sculpted between 1463 and 1467 by the Grasse cabinetmaker Jacques Bellot, and their detail and characterizations border on the risqué. In the baptistery is a ceramic mosaic of Moses in the bulrushes by Chagall.

On the outskirts of Vence, toward St-Jeannet, it's easy to bypass a humble white chapel below the road, indistinguishable from a home except for its imposing cast-iron cross. But the **Chapelle du Rosaire** (Chapel of the Rosary), decorated with beguiling simplicity and clarity by Matisse between 1947 and 1951, reflects the reductivist style of the era: The walls, floor, and ceiling are gleaming white, and the small stained-glass windows are cool greens and blues. Stylized biblical characters are roughly sketched in thick black outline; in the annex behind the chapel you can see that earlier versions were more detailed. "Despite its imperfections I think it is my masterpiece. . . the result of a lifetime devoted to the search for truth," wrote Matisse, who designed and dedicated the chapel when he was in his eighties and nearly blind. ⊠ *av. Henri-Matisse,* ☎ *04–93–58–03–26.* ▱ *Free.* ☉ *Tues. and Thurs. 10–11:30 and 2–5:30.*

Dining and Lodging

$$$ ✕ **Jacques Maximin.** This temperamental superchef has found peace of mind in a gray-stone farmhouse covered with wisteria and flanked by spikes of cypress—his home and his own country restaurant. Hav-

ing cut his teeth at La Bonne Auberge in Antibes and become a star at the Chantecler at the Negresco in Nice, he left it all for the arrière-pays. Here he devotes himself to creative country cooking, superbly prepared and unpretentiously priced—shellfish soup with crayfish ravioli, white beans in rich squid ink, Mediterranean fish grilled in rock salt and olive oil, and candied-eggplant sorbet. The yellow dining room is airy and uncluttered, with light pouring through saffron curtains; the garden, sheltered with creamy parasols, is a palm-shaded paradise. ⊠ *689 chemin de la Gaude,* ☎ *04–93–58–90–75. AE, MC, V. Closed Mon. and Nov. No dinner Sun.*

$–$$ ✕ **La Farigoule.** In a long beamed dining room that opens onto a shady terrace, this is a fine place to enjoy classic Provençal cooking in an easygoing atmosphere. You can have country classics like omelets with fresh garden herbs, ratatouille, and rabbit with thyme; contemporary spins include mullet in a lavender-fennel sauce. Reasonably priced local wines make the meal even better. ⊠ *15 rue Henri-Isnard,* ☎ *04–93–58–01–27. MC, V. Closed mid-Nov.–mid-Dec. No lunch Fri. (Oct.–Mar.) and Sat.*

$$ 🏠 **Villa Roseraie.** Although it doesn't have a rose garden, this 100-year-
★   old house has a giant magnolia that spreads its venerable branches over the terrace. The inn is a pet project of the enthusiastic young owners, Monsieur and Madame Ganier, who have scoured antiques shops for regional details and invested in fine local tiles and fabrics. Look forward to homemade bath salts and jams, and even commissioned pieces from artists and artisans in Vence and Tourrettes-sur-Loup; some of the sculptures are for sale in the garden. You can enjoy a generous breakfast on the terrace and lounge by the pool much of the year, and it's a quick walk down to old Vence. ⊠ *51 av. Henri-Giraud, 06140,* ☎ *04–93–58–02–20,* FAX *04–93–58–99–31. 12 rooms. Pool. AE, MC, V.*

En Route   On this scenic all-day drive along the **Route des Crêtes,** meander through pine forests and countryside thick with cultivated flowers, through hills woven with needlepoint-neat orchards of silvery olives and waxy-green orange trees, punctuated along the way by a string of picture-perfect perched villages. From Vence continue past the Chapelle du Rosaire and follow D2210; it leads toward the gray-stone medieval village of **St-Jeannet,** draped at the foot of the magnificent limestone cliff that rears 1,312 ft above, known as the *baou* (mesa or butte). From the top you can look out over the Esterel and the Alps. Continue on to the tiny, quiet hilltop village of **Gattières,** taking a break to climb a few twisting step streets and ponder its ancient squares. Cut north on the narrow, wild D2209 to precariously perched **Carros-Villages,** spiraled at the base of a four-square medieval château. From the top you can look out over the string of villages and panorama of mountains. Wind slowly ahead up the miniature D1 to **Le Broc,** high over the hills and valley—so high it once served as a sentinel point. Now you'll really get into backcountry as you twist over the pine-darkened hills to Bouyon and ochre-gold **Bézaudun-les-Alpes,** isolated and virtually untouched. Forge on to pretty **Coursegoules,** draped on a hill under a looming mountain, and peek into the church: It contains a graceful 16th-century altarpiece attributed to Bréa. D2 will lead you south over the climactic **Col de Vence** (Vence Pass). From this vantage point of 3,159 ft, you can pan the vast Mediterranean coast. From here it's a brief ride back to Vence and civilization.

Tourrettes-sur-Loup

➒   *5 km (3 mi) west of Vence, 24 km (15 mi) west of Nice.*

More accessible—and thus more touristy—than the little villages on the Route des Crêtes (☞ En Route, *above*), this steep-sloped old hill town stands over an invisible line that distinguishes it from the day-trip towns of Vence and St-Paul. The wind blows colder, the forest around is dense and arid, and the coast seems hours—and ages—away (though it's less than an hour's drive from Nice). From the town square that doubles as a parking lot with an on-going pétanque game on one side, to the quiet cafés lining it, to the sharp-raked, torturously twisted streets snaking down the slopes of the old town, this is old Provence without the stage makeup. Yes, there are dozens of galleries and arts-and-crafts shops, but they're owned and run by real artists and arti-sans, who have made a life for themselves in this intimate community.

Built in the Middle Ages inside a rampart of stone houses and encir-cling a 15th-century church, Tourrettes's old town crowns a rocky plateau. At its feet the olive orchards are purple with violets in spring, cultivated for the perfume industry, candied in Toulouse, or tied into nosegays and sold in flower markets across France.

NICE

As the fifth-largest city in France, sprawling from its waterfront air-port to the Cap Ferrat, this distended tangle of suburbs, modern apart-ment buildings, industry, and traffic is often avoided by travelers who expect a more leisurely experience from the south of France. Crawl-ing into town from the airport or stepping off the train at the congested commercial quarter around Gare Nice-Ville, you may be tempted to bolt for the nearest city limit, where signs encircle and slash through the name Nice—as if to say "not Nice."

They couldn't be more wrong. The vast sprawl of urbanity south of the autoroute pours inevitably toward the sea, and the waterfront, par-alleled by the famous Promenade des Anglais and lined by grand ho-tels and mansions, is one of the noblest in France. It's capped by a dramatic hilltop château whose slopes plunge almost into the sea and at whose base unfolds a bewitching warren of ancient streets reminis-cent of Italy, of Greece, of old Sardinia.

It was in this old quarter, now the Vieille Ville, that the Greeks estab-lished a market-port and named it Nikaia. After establishing Marseille as early as the 4th century BC, they branched out along the coast and founded Nice shortly thereafter. The Romans established themselves a little later on the hills of Cimiez (Cemenelum) and quickly over-shadowed the waterfront port. After falling to the Saracen invasions, Nice regained power and developed into an important port in the early Middle Ages.

So cocksure did it become that in 1388 Nice, along with the hill towns behind, effectively seceded from the county of Provence, under Louis d'Anjou, and allied itself with Savoie. Thus began its intimate liaison with the House of Savoy, and through it with Piedmont and Sardinia, as the Comté de Nice (Nice County). It was a relationship that lasted some 500 years and stained the culture, architecture, and dialect in rich Italian hues.

By the 19th century Nice was locked in rivalry with the neighboring shipping port of Genoa and flourished commercially. Another source of income: the dawning of tourism, as first the English, then Russian nobility discovered its extraordinary climate and superb waterfront po-sition. A parade of fine stone mansions and hotels closed into a nearly solid wall of masonry, separated from the smooth-round rocks of the beach by the appropriately named Promenade des Anglais (Promenade of the English).

204

Close-Up

FLOWERS, FLOATS, AND FATHEADS: CARNAVAL IN NICE

I F THE WORD CARNIVAL MEANS masked balls in Venice to most, or conjures images of feather-clad dancers writhing rhythmically through the streets of Rio, few people associate Nice with this pre-Lenten festival of excess and droll debauchery. Yet this most Latin of French cities is the capital of Carnaval in France, and transforms itself every February from a relatively sedate seaside metropolis into one vast party. The streets behind the waterfront and around Place Masséna explode in bright lights and color, and parades, masks, and impromptu street celebrations are everyday sights. Confetti brightens the gutters and no one seems to mind having colored streamers caught in their hair.

It's a tradition that dates back to pagan times, when the Romans fêted the end of winter and the dawning of spring. The festival translated easily into Christian terms, when the church established the period of partial fasting before Easter. We call it Lent; the French call it Carême; but in church Latin it was *carne levare* (crudely translated, "take out the meat"), and easily evolved into the word *carnaval*. Thus *mardi gras* (fat Tuesday) was the last chance to indulge before Ash Wednesday and the deprivations of Lent.

It wasn't long, however, before the pleasures of Carnaval outstripped those of Mardi Gras and shook free of their sacred meaning: The festival these days lasts a good two weeks and often takes place smack in the middle of Lent.

Nice's Carnaval is extremely user friendly, with a published calendar of events and easy advance ticket sales for any seated events. There's the burning of King Carnaval (in effigy, of course) on Place Masséna, transformed into an electric fantasy-land of music and blinking lights. There are parades of magnificently crafted *grosses têtes* (literally, fat heads), enormous puppetlike personages that make Macy's balloons look like so much rubber. And there are the famous *batailles des fleurs* (flower battles), really full-scale parades complete with marching bands, clowns, and samba troupes. Elaborate floats heaped with Côte d'Azur flowers cruise down the Promenade des Anglais hauling a cargo of spectacularly costumed beauty queens who toss fresh flowers into the crowd. The crowds in the bleachers lining the Promenade des Anglais toss back confetti, wave branches of lemon-yellow mimosa, and cheer for their favorite floats.

The whole of Carnaval strikes an equally wholesome tone, with revelry maintaining a polite and familial level that rarely breaks into rowdiness. This, the city claims, is due to a vigilant and discreet security source who see to it that despite the let-your-hair-down mood, things never get out of hand. For dates, schedules, and information, contact ☎ 04-92-14-48-14.

Nowadays, Nice strikes an engaging balance between old-world grace, port-town exotica, urban energy, whimsy, and, in its extraordinary museums and thriving arts life, high culture. Thanks to its two universities, there's a healthy dose of the young and hip, too. You could easily spend your vacation here and emerge days or weeks later subtly Latinized, sensually and aesthetically engaged, attuned to Nice's quirks, its rhythms, and its Mediterranean tides.

Vieux Nice

Framed by the château and cours Saleya, the old town of Nice is its strongest drawing point and, should you only be passing through, the best place to capture the city's historic atmosphere. Its grid of narrow streets, darkened by houses five and six stories high with bright splashes of laundry fluttering overhead and jewel-box Baroque churches on every other corner, creates a magic that seems utterly removed from the Côte d'Azur fast lane.

A Good Walk

Begin your exploration on **cours Saleya** ⑩, preferably in the morning so you can experience the market in full swing. Its cafés, restaurants, and market stalls throng with the sounds, smells, and sights of old Nice. At its center you'll find the florid Baroque **Chapelle de la Miséricorde** ⑪, worthy of a stop. Then make your way to the far end of the cours. The tall yellow-stone building at its end, its top floor wrapped around with a balcony, was home to Henri Matisse from 1921 to 1938; from the apartments on its top floors he took in magnificent views over the sea. Turn left up rue de la Poissonnerie to find the extravagant **Chapelle de l'Annonciation** ⑫. Continue up Poissonerie to rue de la Place Vieille, then head right to rue Droite. The **Chapelle St-Jacques-Jesu** ⑬ looms large and spare in comparison with neighboring jewel-box chapels. Turn left on rue Rossetti and cross the square to the **Cathédrale Ste-Réparate** ⑭, its restored ochre facade an inspired balance of Italianate arcs and lines.

Now take a break from the sacred, doubling back up rue Rossetti and continuing left up narrow rue Droite to the magnificent **Palais Lascaris** ⑮, whose broad classical facade squeezed onto this narrow street belies the Baroque extravagance within. Continue up rue Droite to **place St-François** ⑯, where a port-fresh fish market holds forth every morning.

Then head up rue Pairolière, but take time to duck left and right up the tiny alleys and step streets that plunge you into a concentration of popular cafés and restaurants, including the landmark street-food hang-out called Chez René (☞ Dining and Lodging, *below*). You'll emerge on boulevard Jean-Jaurès and empty onto the grand arcaded **place Garibaldi** ⑰, which would be at home in Milan or Turin. One of its five street spokes points straight to the **Musée d'Art Moderne** ⑱, a bold sculpture of a building anchoring a sleek plaza.

From place Garibaldi and boulevard Jean-Jaurès, follow rue Neuve to the **Église St-Martin** ⑲, the oldest church. From here wind your way up rue de la Providence and rue Jouane Nicolas to the **Cimetière** ⑳ and ultimately the ruins of the castle, now a park called the **Colline de Château** ㉑, with a wraparound panorama of Nice and the coast. From here you can either follow the switchback steps down or take the *ascenseur* (elevator) to the foot of the fat Tour Bellanda (Bellanda Tower), where the French composer Hector Berlioz once lived.

Next, you can either cross quai des Etats-Unis to the pebbled beach and rest your weary feet. Or you can swing left away from the old town and hike around the tidy rectangle of the **Port de Nice** ㉒, with its neat

Nice

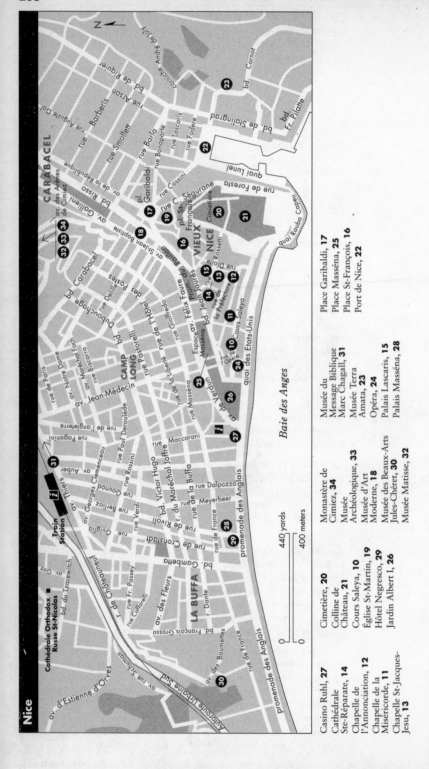

Cathédrale Orthodox Russe St-Nicolas ■

Train Station

CARABACEL

VIEUX NICE

CAMP LONG

LA BUFFA

Baie des Anges

440 yards
400 meters

Casino Ruhl, **27**
Cathédrale
Ste-Réparate, **14**
Chapelle de
l'Annonciation, **12**
Chapelle de la
Miséricorde, **11**
Chapelle St-Jacques-
Jesu, **13**

Cimetière, **20**
Colline de
Château, **21**
Cours Saleya, **10**
Église St-Martin, **19**
Hôtel Negresco, **29**
Jardin Albert I, **26**

Monastère de
Cimiez, **34**
Musée
Archéologique, **33**
Musée d'Art
Moderne, **18**
Musée des Beaux-Arts
Jules-Chéret, **30**
Musée Matisse, **32**

Musée du
Message Biblique
Marc Chagall, **31**
Musée Terra
Amata, **23**
Opéra, **24**
Palais Lascaris, **15**
Palais Masséna, **28**

Place Garibaldi, **17**
Place Masséna, **25**
Place St-François, **16**
Port de Nice, **22**

rows of pleasure boats, and from its end follow boulevard Carnot to the **Musée Terra Amata** ㉓, marking the settlement where man first flourished some 400,000 years ago.

TIMING

Aim for morning on this walk, so you'll see the markets on cours Saleya and place St-François at their liveliest. If you include a visit to the Palais Lascaris and a visit to the Musée Terra Amata, this would make a wonderful full-day's outing.

Sights to See

⑭ **Cathédrale Ste-Réparate.** Named for the 15-year-old Palestinian martyr whose body washed ashore at Nice to become the city's patron saint, this superb ensemble of columns, cupolas, and symmetrical ornaments dominates the old town, flanked by its own 18th-century bell tower and capped by its glossy ceramic tile dome. The cathedral's interior, restored to a bright color palette of ochre golds and rusts, has elaborate plasterwork and decorative frescoes on every surface. Look for the **Chapelle du St-Sacrement** in the north transept, dating from 1707; its twisted marble columns and exuberant sculpture are worthy of Bernini and St. Peter's in Rome. ⊠ *rue Ste-Réparate.*

⑫ **Chapelle de l'Annonciation.** Also known through typical Nice-lore obfuscation as St-Jaume, St-Giaume, or Ste-Rita, this 17th-century Carmelite chapel is a classic example of pure Niçoise Baroque, from its sculpted door to its extravagant marble work and the florid symmetry of its arches and cupolas. The interior concentrates every form of colored faux-stonework, rich marble inlay, gilt, and frescoes—a lot of bombast squeezed into a finite space. Though it's officially dedicated to St. James the Apostle, the people of Nice lavish flowers and candles on the statue of Ste-Rita in the first chapel on the left; having suffered from a leprous sore and a lifetime of isolation in the 14th century, she has come to represent help for the terminally ill. ⊠ *rue de la Poissonerie.*

★ ⑪ **Chapelle de la Miséricorde.** If you step inside only one Baroque chapel here, this superb 1740 structure on cours Saleya should be it. A superbly balanced pièce-montée of half domes and cupolas, decorated within an inch of its life with frescoes, faux marble, gilt, and crystal chandeliers, it's the ultimate example of Nice Baroque at its most excessive and successful. A magnificent Bréa altarpiece crowns the ensemble. ⊠ *cours Saleya.*

⑬ **Chapelle St-Jacques-Jesu.** If Nice's other chapels are jewel boxes, this is a barn: Broad, open, and ringing hollow after the intense concentration of sheer matter in the Miséricorde and Ste-Rita, this church seems austere by comparison. That's only because the decoration is spread over a more expansive surface: If it's possible, this 17th-century Baroque chapel is even more theatrical and over the top than its peers. Angels throng in plaster and fresco, pillars spill over with extravagantly sculpted capitals, and from the pulpit (to the right, at the front), the crucifix is supported by a disembodied arm. ⊠ *Corner of rue Droite and rue Gesu.*

⑳ **Cimetière** (Cemetery). This solemn cluster of white tombs looms prominently over the city below, providing a serene or macabre detail of daily life, depending on your mood. Under Nice's blue skies, the gleaming white marble and Italian mix of melodrama and exuberance in the decorations, dedications, photo portraits, and sculptures are somehow oddly life-affirming. There are three sections, to this day segregating the Catholics, the Protestants, and the Jews. ⊠ *allée François-Aragon.*

㉑ **Colline de Château** (Château Hill). Though nothing remains of this once-massive medieval stronghold but a few ruins left after its 1706 dismantling, the name château still applies to this high plateaulike park, from which you can take in extraordinary views of the Baie des Anges, the length of the promenade des Anglais, and the red-ochre roofs of the old town. ☉ *Daily 7–7.*

★ ⑩ **Cours Saleya.** This long pedestrian thoroughfare, half street, half square, is the nerve center of old Nice, the heart of the Vieille Ville (Old Town), and the stage-set for the daily dramas of the marketplace and café life. Framed with 18th-century houses and shaded by plane trees, every morning the long, narrow square bursts into the fireworks-show of color that is the flower market, as vendors roll armloads of mimosas, irises, roses, and orange blossoms into *cornets* (paper cones) and thrust them into the arms of shoppers. Cafés and restaurants, all more or less touristy, fill outdoor tables with onlookers who bask in the sun. At the far-east end, antiques and *brocante* (collectibles) draw avid junk-hounds every Monday morning. Just beyond, Place Félix seems to draw the most fashionable crowd to see and be seen, perhaps because there are no market stands to get in the way of the most visible café tables. ⊠ *2 blocks back from the quai des Etats-Unis, in the center of the old town.*

⑲ **Église St-Martin.** Also known as St-Augustin, this serene Baroque structure at the foot of the château anchors the oldest church-parish in Nice. It was built in 1405, and it was here that Martin Luther preached in 1510 and that in 1807 Garibaldi was baptized. ⊠ *rue Sincaire.*

⑱ **Musée d'Art Moderne** (Modern Art Museum). Moored by four marble-fronted towers, joined by the transparent arcs of pedestrian bridges and dramatically framing a concourse decked with outdoor sculptures, this building is a bold and emphatic statement of Nice's presence in the modern world. The art collection inside focuses intently and thoroughly on contemporary art from the late 1950s onward, featuring works of the École de Nice (Nice School), the self-dubbed *Nouveau Réalistes* (New Realists) such as artists César, Bernar Venet, Ben, Yves Klein, Daniel Spoerri, Jean Tinguely, and Niki de Saint-Phalle. The collection includes international acquisitions, too, from Jim Dine and Frank Stella to Miró and Giacometti. Be sure to climb along the rooftop sculpture terrace, a catwalk overlooking the whole of the city. ⊠ *promenade des Arts,* ☎ *04–93–62–61–62.* ▣ *25 frs.* ☉ *Mon., Wed.–Thurs., and weekends 11–6; Fri. 11–10.*

㉓ **Musée Terra Amata.** When digging the foundation for a new building in 1966, the shovels revealed the remains of a temporary settlement once used by elephant hunters around 380,000 BC. They were perhaps the oldest known inhabitants of Europe. Now the site is a museum reconstructing the ancient beach-camp known as Terra Amata ("beloved land") as it was, lodgings and all—incorporating a real human footprint, calcified in the sand. There are recorded commentaries in English, and films explaining the lifestyle of these earliest Europeans. At press time it was temporarily closed until spring 1999. ⊠ *25 bd. Carnot,* ☎ *04–93–55–59–93.* ▣ *25 frs.* ☉ *Oct.–mid-Sept., Tues.–Sun. 9–noon and 2–6.*

⑮ **Palais Lascaris** (Lascaris Palace). This aristocratic palace was built in 1648 for Jean-Baptiste Lascaris-Vintimille, marechal to the duke of Savoy, in a manner grand enough to put the neighboring chapels to shame. The magnificent vaulted staircase with its massive stone balustrade and niches filled with classical gods is only surpassed in grandeur by the Flemish tapestries (after Rubens) and the extraordinary trompe l'oeil fresco of the fall of Phaeton. On the ground floor an 18th-century pharmacy has been imported and reconstructed from Besançon, complete with built-in wooden cabinets and a lovely collection of faience jars. ✉ *15 rue Droite,* ☎ *04–93–62–05–54.* 🎫 *25 frs.* ☉ *Tues.–Sun. 10–noon and 2–6.*

⑰ Place Garibaldi. Encircled by grand vaulted arcades stuccoed in rich yellow, this broad pentagon of a square could have been airlifted out of Turin. In the center the shrinelike fountain-sculpture of Garibaldi surveys the passersby, who stroll under the arcades and lounge in its cafés. Garibaldi is held in high esteem here: The Italian general enlisted his own sons into his legion and sent them to fight beside the French in 1914.

⑯ Place St-François. Around its bubbling fountain, a lively daily fish market draws chefs and matrons to select from the day's catch.

㉒ Port de Nice. In 1750 the Duke of Savoy ordered a port to be dug into the waterfront to shelter the approach of the freight ships, fishing boats, and yachts that still sail into its safety today. Surrounded in rhythmic symmetry by the ochre facades of 19th-century houses, it makes for a pleasant walk far from the beach crowds.

Along the Promenade des Anglais

Nice takes on a completely different character west of cours Saleya. Here are broad city blocks, vast neoclassic hotels and apartment houses, and a series of inviting parks dense with palm trees, greenery, and splashing fountains. From the Jardin Albert I, once the delta of the Paillon River, the famous Promenade des Anglais stretches the length of the city's waterfront.

The original promenade was the brainchild of Lewis Way, an English minister in the growing community of British refugees drawn to Nice's climate. They needed a proper walkway to take the sea air and pooled resources to build a 2-meter-wide (6½-foot-wide) road meandering through an alley of shade trees. Nowadays it's a wide multilane boulevard thick with traffic—in fact, it's the last gasp of the coastal highway N98. Beside it runs its charming parallel, the paved pedestrian walkway with intermittent steps leading down to the smooth-rock beach; its foundation is a seawall that keeps all but the wildest storm from sloshing waves over the promenade. Only in the wee hours is it possible to enjoy the waterfront stroll as the cream of Nice's international society did, when there were nothing more than hoof beats to compete with the roar of the waves.

A Good Walk

From the west end of cours Saleya, walk down rue St-François-de-Paule past the Belle-Époque **Opéra** ㉔, constructed in classic Italian tiered loggias. Continue up the street, then head right up rue de l'Opéra to **place Masséna** ㉕, framed in broad arcades and opening onto the vast, green **Jardin Albert I** ㉖. Three long blocks past the glamorous **Casino Ruhl** ㉗, you'll reach the gates and park of the imposing **Palais Masséna** ㉘; to peruse its eclectic collection of nuggets of Nice history, walk through the grounds to enter from the rue de France side. Next door, the landmark **Hôtel Negresco** ㉙ expands its colossal facade along the waterfront, crowned at the corner by its signature dome.

Walk along the waterfront for a few blocks, past the busy boulevard Gambetta, then head inland up tiny rue Sauvan. Cross boulevard Grosso and head diagonally up the hill on avenue des Baumettes. In this quiet, once luxurious neighborhood is the **Musée des Beaux-Arts**

Jules-Chéret ⑳, built by the Ukrainian princess Kotschoubey in extravagant Italianate style.

TIMING

This walk covers a long stretch of waterfront, so it may take up to an hour to stroll the length of it. Allow a half day if you explore the Palais Massena or the Musée des Beaux Arts.

Sights to See

㉗ **Casino Ruhl.** Behind its gleaming all-glass 1970s facade, this casino thrives on the custom of summer vacationers and winter convention crowds. Some sign into the hushed gambling room for roulette and black jack, others stand at one of the 300-some slot machines. ⊠ *1 promenade des Anglais,* ☎ *04–93–87–95–87.*

㉙ **Hôtel Negresco.** This vast neoclassic palace hotel dominates a full block of the Promenade and remains, for many, the enduring symbol of Côte d'Azur luxury. Its famous Salon Royal, a broad rotunda at the hotel's center, is classed as a historic monument, with its Gustav Eiffel lead-glass dome, its Aubusson carpet, and its Baccarat chandelier commissioned by Czar Nicholas II. Like many grand hotels trying to make ends meet these days, it now caters to conferences and tour groups (☞ Lodging, *below*).

㉖ **Jardin Albert I** (Albert I Garden). This luxurious garden of tropical greenery stands over the delta of the River Paillon, underground since 1882. Every kind of flower and palm tree grows here, thrown into exotic relief by night illumination.

㉚ **Musée des Beaux-Arts Jules-Chéret** (Jules-Chéret Fine Arts Museum). Housed in a 19th-century Italianate mansion, this museum has a fine collection of paintings by Nice artists of the era, including works by the museum's namesake. A small collection of Impressionist works includes paintings by Alfred Sisley, Pierre Bonnard, and Edouard Vuillard. Two pieces by Rodin, including the original plaster of *Le Baiser* (*The Kiss*), and some ceramic pieces by Picasso round out an otherwise modest ensemble of works by lesser artists. ⊠ *33 av. des Baumettes,* ☎ *04–92–15–28–28.* ▨ *25 frs.* ☉ *Oct.–Apr., Tues.–Sun. 10–noon and 2–5; May–Sept., Tues.–Sun. 10–noon and 2–6.*

㉔ **Opéra.** Demolished by a devastating 1881 fire whose victims lie in the cemetery on the hillside of the château, this magnificent Italian-style opera house rose up from the ashes in 1885. Charles Garnier, architect of the Paris Opéra, consulted on its design. It's home today to the Opéra de Nice, with a permanent chorus, orchestra, and ballet corps. (☞ Nightlife and the Arts, *below*.) ⊠ *4 rue St-François-de-Paul,* ☎ *04–92–17–40–40.*

㉘ **Palais Masséna** (Masséna Palace). This handsome Belle Époque villa was built by a grandson of Napoléon's Marechal Masséna; his great-grandson donated it to Nice on the grounds that it house a museum of the city's history. The resulting **Musée d'Art et d'Histoire** (Museum of Art and History) is a fascinating hodgepodge of private collections reflecting every aspect of Nice's past, from Garibaldi's death sheet to Asian jewelry collected in imperial days to Empress Josephine's tiara carved entirely in cameo. It also contains extraordinary notebook sketches of Napoléon by David, as vivid and natural as a snapshot, as well as relief models of Nice in the 1930s and 1954, a desert-island wasteland compared to today's congested overbuilding. There's even a Bréa polyptich of St-Marguerite. It's a must if you love the offbeat, the obscure, and the treasure hunt. ⊠ *Entrance at 65 rue de France,* ☎ *04–93–88–11–3.* ▨ *25 frs.* ☉ *Wed.–Mon.10–noon and 2–6.*

㉕ **Place Masséna.** As cours Saleya is the heart of the old town, so this broad and noble square is the heart of the city as a whole. It's framed by an ensemble of Italian-style arcaded buildings first built in 1815, their facades stuccoed in rich red ochre. At its center is a heroic fountain in which thick-muscled bronze figures surge from the water. Here on the square the central activities of the Carnaval unfold every February, and the square is transformed with flashing lights and monstrous, Macy's-balloon-scaled puppets.

OFF THE BEATEN PATH

CATHÉDRALE ORTHODOXE RUSSE ST-NICOLAS – From the promenade, hop bus number 7 up boulevard Gambetta and get off at the Thiers-Gambetta or Parc Imperial stops, or walk west from the train station to visit this magnificent Russian Orthodox cathedral. Built in 1896 to accommodate the sizeable population of Russian aristocrats who had adopted Nice as their winter home, this Byzantine fantasy is the largest of its kind outside the motherland. The church has no less than six gold-leaf onion domes, rich ceramic mosaics on its facade, and extraordinary icons framed in silver and jewels. The benefactor was Nicholas II himself, whose family attended the inauguration in 1912. ⊠ av. Nicolas II, ☎ 04-93-96-88-02. ⊙ Apr.–Oct., Mon.–Sat. 9–noon and 2:30–6, Sun. 2:30–6; Nov.–Mar., Mon.–Sat. 9:30–noon and 2:30–5, Sun. 2:30–6.

Cimiez

Once the site of the powerful Roman settlement Cemenelum, the hilltop neighborhood of Cimiez—4 km (2 mi) north of cours Saleya—is Nice's most luxurious quarter. Villas seem in competition to outdo each other in opulence, and the combination of important art museums, Roman ruins, and a historic monastery make it worth a day's exploration.

To visit Cimiez and nearby museums, you need to combine strong legs, comfortable shoes, and either a bus pass or taxi fare. If you brave the route by car, arm yourself with a map and a navigator. Bus 15 from Place Massena or avenue Jean-Médecin takes you to both the Chagall and Matisse museums; from the latter you can visit the ruins and monastery.

A Good Walk

Begin your day at the **Musée du Message Biblique Marc Chagall** ㉛, which houses one of the finest collections of Chagall's works based on biblical themes. Then make the pilgrimage to the center of Cimiez and the **Musée Matisse** ㉜, where an important collection of Matisse's life work is amassed in an Italianate villa. Just behind, the **Musée Archéologique** ㉝ displays a wealth of Roman treasures unearthed on the site of the original colony. Slightly east of the museum is the thriving **Monastère de Cimiez** ㉞, a Franciscan monastery.

TIMING

Between bus connections and long walks from sight to sight, this walk is a half-day commitment at minimum. If you plan to really spend time in the Matisse Museum and explore the ruins and stop into the Chagall Museum, this could easily be a day's outing.

Sights to See

㉞ **Monastère de Cimiez** (Cimiez Monastery). High over Nice and its château-bearing hill, this fully-functioning monastery, originally established in the 16th century, is worth the pilgrimage. There's a lovely garden, replanted following the original 16th-century lines. There's also the **Musée Franciscain**, a didactic museum tracing the history of the Franciscan order, and a 15th-century **church.** This pretty, single-nave chapel contains three works of remarkable power and elegance by Bréa: the early *Pietà* (1475) flanked by portraits of high-Renaissance grace; the *Crucifixion* (1512); and the *Deposition* (1520), of intense suppressed emotion. ⊠ *pl. du Monastère,* ☎ *04–93–81–00–04.* ⊡ *Free.* ☉ *Mon.–Sat. 10–noon and 3–6.*

㉝ Musée Archéologique (Archaeology Museum). This contemporary building houses a dense and intriguing collection of objects extracted from the digs around the Roman city of Cemenelum, which flourished from the 1st to the 5th centuries and dwarfed its waterfront neighbor with a population of 20,000 in its prime. The examples of Greek and Italian treasures—ceramics, jewelry, and coins—attest to the cosmopolitan nature of coastal commerce. For a slight fee you can wander through the **ruins** and digs behind, including the *thermes* (baths) and an early Christian baptistery. Just beyond, the Roman *arènes* (arena) seats 4,000 for the annual jazz festival. ⊠ *160 av. des Arènes-de-Cimiez,* ☎ *04–93–81–59–57.* ⊡ *25 frs.* ☉ *Apr.–Sept., Tues.–Sun. 10–noon and 2–6; Oct.–Mar., Tues.–Sun. 10–1 and 2–5.*

★ **㉜ Musée Matisse.** In the 60s, the city of Nice bought this lovely, light-bathed 17th-century villa, surrounded by the ruins of Roman civilization, and restored it to house a large collection of Henri Matisse's works. Matisse settled in Nice in 1917, seeking a sun cure after a bout with pneumonia, and remained here until his death in 1954. During his years on the Côte d'Azur, Matisse maintained intense friendships and artistic liaisons with Renoir, who lived in Cagnes, and with Picasso, who lived in Mougins and Antibes. Settling first along the waterfront, he eventually moved up to the rarified isolation of Cimiez and took an apartment in the Hotel Regina (now an apartment building), where he lived out the rest of his life. Matisse walked often in the parklands around the Roman remains, and was buried in an olive grove outside the Cimiez Cemetery. The collection of artworks includes several pieces donated to the city by the artist himself before his death; the rest was donated by his family. In every medium and context—paintings, gouache cut-outs, engravings and book illustrations—it represents the evolution of his styles throughout the years. Even the furniture and decor speak of Matisse, from the Chinese vases to the bold-printed fabrics with which he surrounded himself. ⊠ *164 av. des Arènes-de-Cimiez,* ☎ *04–93–81–08–08.* ⊡ *25 frs.* ☉ *Apr.–Sept., Wed.–Mon. 10–6; Oct.–Mar., Wed.–Mon. 10–5.*

★ **㉛ Musée du Message Biblique Marc-Chagall** (Marc Chagall Museum of Biblical Themes). Superbly displayed in a modern structure bathed in light and surrounded by coastal greenery, this is one of the finest permanent collections of the artist's late works. Included here are 17 vast canvases on biblical themes, each in emphatic and joyous color schemes; they celebrate the stories of Adam and Eve, Noah, Abraham, Moses, and the sensual, mystical Song of Solomon, dedicated to his wife. Preparatory sketches, sculptures, and ceramic pieces enhance the exhibit, as well as a tapestry and, outside, a mosaic. ⊠ *av. du Dr-Ménard (head up av. Thiers, then take a left onto av. Malausséna, cross the railway tracks, and take the first right up av. de l'Olivetto),* ☎ *04–93–53–87–20.* ⊡ *30 frs (in summer 38 frs).* ☉ *July–Sept., Wed.–Mon. 10–6; Oct.–June, Wed.–Mon. 10–5.*

Dining and Lodging

$$–$$$ ✕ **L'Ane Rouge.** For years the best seafood restaurant in Nice, followed by a spell of resting on its laurels, this culinary landmark has found new life with a sunny, fresh decor, an expanded terrace along the port, and the experiments of chef Michel Devillers. From sardines roasted in orange butter to whole fresh fish, whether braised in olives or simmered with garlic juice and dried tomatoes, the cooking has a vitality and Mediterranean freshness it had lacked for some time. ✉ *7 quai des Deux-Emmanuel,* ☎ *04–93–89–49–63. AE, DC, MC, V. Closed Wed. and 2 wks in Jan.*

$$ ✗ **Fleur de Sel.** In a fine old residential neighborhood between the waterfront and the train station, this peculiar little white cube of a restaurant may not look appealing from the outside. But its shape creates a pretty rooftop terrace and a closed terrace, quiet oasis where you can enjoy a light, fresh meal with an emphasis on a healthy diet. The *menu dietetique* (diet menu) clocks in at 600 calories, with haddock ravioli with delicate fennel and dill sauce, fish mousse with coriander, and a light honey-filled puff pastry with a gentle counterpoint of thyme. ✉ *10 bd. Debouchage,* ☎ *04–93–13–45–45. MC, V. Closed weekends.*

$$ ✗ **Grand Café de Turin.** Whether you crowd onto a banquette in the
★ dark, low-ceilinged bar or win a coveted table under the arcaded porticoes on place Garibaldi, this is *the* place to go for shellfish in Nice. Order a bottle of something cold, spread butter on the sliced brown bread, and dive into the platters set before you: sea snails, clams, plump *fines de claires* and salty *bleues* oysters, and urchins by the dozen, their spines still waving. They've all just been pried open at the refrigerator-counters on the sidewalk, with dripping crates of fresh supplies standing by. It's packed noon and night, and there's a thriving young-pro scene after work. ✉ *5 Pl. Garibaldi,* ☎ *04–93–62–29–52. AE, DC, MC, V. Closed June.*

$$ ✗ **La Mérenda.** The back-to-bistro boom climaxed here when Dominique
★ Le Stanc retired his crown at the Negresco to take over this tiny, unpretentious landmark of Provençal cuisine. Now he and his wife work in the miniature open kitchen creating the ultimate versions of stuffed sardines, pistou, slow-simmered *daubes* (beef stews), and the quintessential stockfish (the local lutefisk). It's one man's private mission; stop by in person to reserve entry to the inner sanctum. ✉ *4 rue de la Terrasse,* ☎ *no phone. No credit cards. Closed weekends, last wk in July, 1st 2 wks in Aug., and school holidays.*

$–$$ ✗ **La Cambuse.** A marketplace greasy spoon, this friendly joint on cours Saleya packs the sunny outside tables as well as the somber, spare barroom. The cooking is straightforward and portions generous, from sardine beignets to classic petits farcis (eggplant, peppers, mushrooms, and zucchini stuffed with spicy meat and crumbs and drizzled with garlicky olive oil); watch for the fish du jour. ✉ *5 cours Saleya,* ☎ *04–93–80–12–31. MC, V. Closed Sun.*

$–$$ ✗ **Lou Pistou.** If you want to explore Nice cuisine but in a more inti-
★ mate setting than a back-alley takeout stand, this mom-and-pop shoebox of a restaurant serves real, authentically prepared home cooking. Sit elbow to elbow at checked-cloth tables and browse through framed newspaper clips praising the owners' campaign to preserve the old ways. There are *soupe au pistou* (minestrone with pesto), double-fried omelets with a touch of Parmesan, and little pissaladières, just for starters. Then choose between a rich stew or a heaping bowl of homemade pasta, and a fresh mesclun salad tossed in olive oil, followed by fresh baked fruit tarts. It's all served with sweet concern by the wife while the husband clatters and sizzles away beyond the kitchen door. ✉ *4 rue de la Terrasse (just off Espace Masséna),* ☎ *04–93–62–21–82. MC, V. Closed weekends.*

$–$$ ✗ **L'Olivier.** In this hole-in-the-wall bistro on Place Garibaldi, replete with lace curtains, checked cloths, and bentwood chairs, two brothers have gone back to their roots, and le tout Nice has followed. Frank Musso, trained at the Tour d'Argent in Paris, concentrates his sophis-

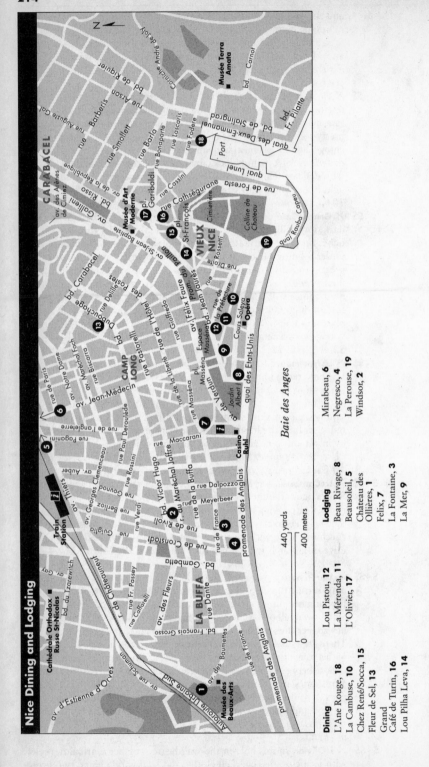

Nice Dining and Lodging

440 yards

400 meters

Baie des Anges

Dining

L'Ane Rouge, **18**
La Cambuse, **10**
Chez René/Socca, **15**
Fleur de Sel, **13**
Grand
Café de Turin, **16**
Lou Pilha Leva, **14**

Lou Pistou, **12**
La Mérenda, **11**
L'Olivier, **17**

Lodging

Beau Rivage, **8**
Beausoleil, **5**
Château des
Ollières, **1**
Felix, **7**
La Fontaine, **3**
La Mer, **9**

Mirabeau, **6**
Negresco, **4**
La Perouse, **19**
Windsor, **2**

ticated gifts on simple dishes, flawlessly prepared: tripe simmered in tomatoes, daubes and pork confits, and crêpes with homemade bitter-orange marmalade. His brother Christian provides the cheery welcome. ⊠ *2 pl. Garibaldi,* ☎ *04–93–26–89–09. Reservations essential. AE, MC, V. Closed Sun. and Aug. No lunch Wed.*

$ ✕ **Chez René/Socca.** This back-alley landmark is the most popular dive in town for the snack food unique to Nice. Rustic olive-wood tables line the street, and curt waiters splash down your drink order. For the food you get in line and carry it steaming to the table yourself. There's socca, of course, the grainy golden pancake of chick-pea flour scraped with a palette knife straight off the griddle; spicy assortments of petits farcis; pissaladières heaped with caramelized onions and shiny black olives; and sweet, quiche-like *tourta de blea,* full of chopped Swiss chard and sprinkled with pine nuts. It's off place Garibaldi on the edge of the old town, across from the *gare routière* (bus station). ⊠ *2 rue Miralhetti,* ☎ *04–93–92–05–73. No credit cards.*

$ ✕ **Lou Pilha Leva.** Its name in dialect means "tu prend et tu t'en va" ★ (take and go), but you'll be tempted to stay a while and taste everything here. Not as popular or as well known as Chez René but much more serious about the food it serves, this street stand just south of Place St-François offers good, fresh-cooked versions of petits farcis, tourta de blea, and pissaladières as well as full meals of homemade pasta, pizza, *moules-frites* (mussels with fries), soupe au pistou, and fruit tarts, all made on the premises. Order food at the window, and drinks are delivered to you at the table. ⊠ *10 rue du Collet on pl. Centrale,* ☎ *04–93–13–99–08. MC, V.*

$$$$ ✕▥ **Château des Ollières.** The genteel owner of this fantastic neo-★ Moroccan palace, once the dream house of Prince Lobnov-Rostowsky, has restored it as a luxurious manor-house inn. Its eight rooms are furnished as in a private home, with period details—herringbone parquet, crown moldings, and chandeliers—in mint condition. Deluxe rooms have vast marble baths and fine old furniture; standard rooms are filled with toile de Jouy. The candlelighted restaurant functions as a table d'hôte—one prix-fixe menu each day—and in summer expands into the extraordinary tropical garden-estate. Only the noise of the highway reminds you of the current epoch. ⊠ *39 av. des Baumettes, 06000,* ☎ *04–92–15–77–99,* ℻ *04–93–15–77–99. 8 rooms. Restaurant, air-conditioning. AE, DC, MC, V.*

$$$$ ✕▥ **Negresco.** Its pink cupola the symbol of Riviera glamour, this faded Belle Époque landmark retains much of its architectural excess, rescued by the eccentric vision of its owner of 40 years. Each floor is devoted to eras of French history, but the dominant one is the 1960s, from the plastic-glitter bathtubs to the Vasarely op-art carpet to the photos of Liz-and-Dick in the bar. Its grand restaurant, however, is still Nice's finest: Le Chantecler features the artistry of chef Alain Llorca, trained by Le Stanc (☞ La Mérenda, *above*) and Alain Ducasse. Indulge in a drink in the glorious walnut-and-velour bar, and you'll recapture some of the glamour of the old Riviera. ⊠ *37 promenade des Anglais, 06000,* ☎ *04–93–88–39–51,* ℻ *04–93–88–35–68. 122 rooms. 2 restaurants, bar, air-conditioning, beach. AE, DC, MC, V.*

$$$$ ✕▥ **La Perouse.** Just past the old town, at the foot of the château, this ★ antipalace is a secret treasure cut into the cliff (an elevator takes you up to reception). Most rooms have breathtaking views of the Baie des Anges. Some of the best not only overlook the azure sea but also look down into an intimate garden with lemon trees and a cliff-side pool. A sundeck and sauna by the pool, as well as valet parking, add to the sense of private luxury. Rooms are fairly large; some sport somber plaids, others have painted Provençal furniture. The restaurant serves meals in the candlelighted garden May–September. ⊠ *11 quai Rauba-Capeau,*

06300, ☎ 04–93–62–34–63, FAX 04–93–62–59–41. *64 rooms. Restaurant, air-conditioning, pool, sauna. AE, DC, MC, V.*

$$$–$$$$ ✕⊞ **Beau Rivage.** Occupying an imposing late-19th-century town house near cours Saleya, this hotel is just a few steps from the best parts of old Nice and the beach, though buildings have long since blocked its sea views. The room decor is standard and a bit stuffy, in pinks and teals; corner rooms have big windows and are by far the best. Le Bistrot, the house restaurant, moves to the beach every summer. Matisse lived here before moving to cours Saleya and then the hills of Cimiez. ⊠ *24 rue St-François-de-Paule, 06000,* ☎ *04–93–80–80–70,* FAX *04–93–80–55–77. 118 rooms. Restaurant, air-conditioning, beach. AE, DC, MC, V.*

$$ ⊞ **La Fontaine.** Downtown and a block from the waterfront, this immaculate, simply designed hotel offers a friendly welcome from its house-proud owners. Rooms are small and comfortable, in cheery blues and yellows and with bathrooms freshly tiled. It even has a pretty little courtyard where breakfast is served. ⊠ *49 rue de France, 06000,* ☎ *04–93–88–30–38,* FAX *04–93–88–98–11. 29 rooms. Breakfast room, air-conditioning. AE, DC, MC, V.*

$$ ⊞ **Mirabeau.** Two hundred yards from the train station on busy avenue Malausséna and a good 15-minute walk from the beach, this stylishly renovated hotel serves as a good home base for pilgrimages to the Chagall Museum and Cimiez. Plants, flowers, and leather armchairs brighten up the lobby breakfast area; rooms, with floral-pattern quilts and functional modern furniture, vary in size. The owners are friendly and always ready to assist. ⊠ *15 av. Malausséna, 06000,* ☎ *04–93–88–33–67,* FAX *04–93–16–14–08. 42 rooms. Bar, air-conditioning. AE, MC, V.*

$$ ⊞ **Windsor.** This is a memorably eccentric hotel with a vision: Most
★ of its white-on-white rooms either have frescoes of mythic themes or are works of artists' whimsy. There's also a "relaxation room" on the top floor, where you can exercise, meditate, or have a steam bath and massage. But the real draw of this otherworldly place is its astonishing city-center garden—a tropical paradise of lemon, magnolia, and palm trees. Exotic finches flutter through the leaves, and a toucan caws beside the breakfast buffet; a small pool is screened by flowering shrubs. You can breakfast or dine here by candlelight (guests only). If all this sounds like your cup of tea, then book well ahead to immerse yourself in an exoticism that is particularly Niçois. Only rooms on street side are air-conditioned; the others profit from the garden breeze. ⊠ *11 rue Dalpozzo, 06000,* ☎ *04–93–88–59–35,* FAX *04–93–88–94–57. 57 rooms. Restaurant, bar, pool. AE, DC, MC, V.*

$ ⊞ **Beausoleil.** This big, old downtown hotel on a commercial backstreet near the train station has a certain urban charm. It has French windows, ironwork balconies, and an oak cage elevator that whisks you up to pink-and-gray rooms that are impeccably maintained. A small bar and a cozy living room with TV make you feel at home. The hotel does a brisk business with bus groups, so book ahead. ⊠ *22 rue Assalit, 06000,* ☎ *04–93–85–18–54,* FAX *04–93–62–49–14. 53 rooms. Bar, air-conditioning. MC, V.*

$ ⊞ **Felix.** On popular, pedestrian rue Masséna and a block from the beach,
★ this tiny hotel is owned by a hard-working couple (both fluent in English) who make you feel welcome. It's also Nice's best bargain. Rooms are compact but neat and bright, so they don't feel as small, and four have tiny balconies with ringside seats over the pedestrian thoroughfare. There's even TV with CNN. ⊠ *41 rue Masséna, 06000,* ☎ *04–93–88–67–73,* FAX *04–93–16–15–78. 14 rooms. Air-conditioning. AE, DC, MC, V.*

$ 🏨 **La Mer.** Though rooms are downright spartan (and carpets sometimes frayed), the location can't be beat: It's right on place Masséna, near the waterfront and the old town. Prices are budget friendly, and the staff and owners are pleasant. Ask for a room away from the square to be sure of a quiet night's sleep. ⊠ *4 pl. Masséna, 06000,* ☎ *04–93–92–09–10,* FAX *04–93–85–00–64. 12 rooms. AE, MC, V.*

Nightlife and the Arts

The glamorous **Casino Ruhl** (⊠ 1 promenade des Anglais, 04–93–87–95–87) gleaming neon-bright and modern, is a sophisticated Riviera landmark. If you're all dressed up and just won big, invest in a drink in the intimate walnut-and-velvet **Bar Anglais** in the Hôtel Negresco (☞ Dining and Lodging, *above*).

L'Ascenseur (⊠ 18 bis rue Emmanuel Philibert, ☎ 04–93–26–35–30), two blocks east of Place Garibaldi, is the most popular gay and lesbian club in town. Young fans of Brit pop—especially Americans and English—drink and dance at **Chez Wayne** (⊠ 15 rue de la Préfecture, ☎ 04–93–13–46–99). At **La Douche Cyber Café** (⊠ 34 cours Saleya, ☎ 04–93–62–81–31) drink on the terrace or in the ochre-stucco bar, dance to rock, funk or rap, or hook up to the Internet. **Iguane Café** (⊠ 5 quai Deux-Emmanuels, ☎ 04–93–56–83–83), along the port, pounds with Latin rhythms and techno until 4 AM.

In July, the **Nice Jazz Festival** (☎ 04–92–17–77–77 for information) draws international performers from around the world for outdoor concerts in the Parc de Cimiez north of the center, some in the Matisse museum, and some in the Roman arena. During past festivals, big-name jazz artists have gathered in the Madisson Lounge of the **Hotel Radisson SAS** (⊠ 223 Promenade des Anglais, ☎ 04–93–37–17–17) for impromtu jam sessions into the wee hours. The **Théâtre de Verdure** (⊠ Jardin Albert I) is another spot for jazz and pop; concerts relocate to the **Arènes de Cimiez** in summer. Classical music and ballet performances take place at Nice's convention center, the **Acropolis** (⊠ Palais des Congrès, Esplanade John F. Kennedy, ☎ 04–93–92–80–00).

The season at the **Opéra de Nice** (⊠ 4 rue St-François-de-Paul, ☎ 04–92–17–40–40) runs from September to June. The **Théâtre Municipal Francis-Gag** (⊠ 4 rue St-Joseph, ☎ 04–93–62–00–03) is the place for drama, as is the **Théâtre de Nice** (⊠ Promenade des Arts, ☎ 04–93–80–52–60).

Outdoor Activities and Sports

Nice's **beaches** extend all along the Baie des Anges, backed full-length by the Promenade des Anglais and a thriving and sophisticated downtown. This leads to the peculiar phenomenon of seeing power-suited executives and secretaries stripping down to a band of Lycra, tanning over the lunch hour, then suiting back up for the afternoon's work, a block or two away. The absence of sand (there's nothing but those famous Riviera pebbles, remember?) helps maintain that dress-for-success look. The downside of the location: The otherwise stylish streets downtown tend to fill up with under-dressed, sunburned tourists caked with salt during beach season.

Posh private beaches feature full restaurants and bar service, color-coordinated mattresses and parasols, and ranks of tanners with phones glued to their ears. Several lure clients with waterskiing, parasailing, windsurfing, and jet skiing; if you're looking for a particular sport, signs are posted at the entrance with the restaurant menus. Some of the handiest private beaches are the **Beau Rivage** (☎ 04–93–80–75–06) across from the cours Saleya, which has jet skiing and a popular restaurant. Also popular is **Ruhl** (☎ 04–93–87–09–70), across from the Casino, with waterskiing and parasailing boats running steadily all day. Fees for private beaches average 40–65 francs for a dressing room and mattress, 15 to 25 francs for a parasol, and 25 to 35 fancs for a cabana to call your own. Private beaches alternate with open stretches of public frontage served by free toilets and open showers (a cold elevated faucet for rinsing off salt). Enterprising vendors cruise the waterfront, hawking ice cream, slabs of melon, coffee, ice-cold sodas, and beer.

Bicycles can be rented at the train station (✉ 17 av. Thiers). Except in July and August, the entire Promenade des Anglais is closed to traffic on the first Sunday of the month, and makes for a terrific 10-km (6-mi) ride along the waterfront.

In winter, good Alpine **skiing** is surprisingly accessible: Nice is only about 97 km (60 mi) from Valberg (4,600 to 6,300 ft), Auron (4,800 to 7,350 ft), and Isola (6,000 to 8,700 ft) in the Alps. You can practically ski into the sea.

Shopping

Nice's main shopping street, **avenue Jean-Médecin,** runs inland from Place Masséna; all needs and most tastes are catered to in its big department stores (Galeries Lafayette, Prisunic, and the split-level Étoile mall).

Olive oil by the gallon, in cans sporting colorful old-fashioned labels, is sold at tiny **Alziari** (✉ 14 rue St-François-de-Paule). Tapenade, *pistou* (pesto), and olive-wood doodads are also sold here. From November to April you can visit Alziari's oil mill (✉ 318 bd. de la Madeleine).

The venerable old **Henri Auer** (✉ 7 rue St-François-de-Paule) has sold its beautiful selection of crystallized fruit, a Nice specialty, since 1820. Another good source for crystallized fruit is the **Confiserie du Vieux Nice** (✉ 14 quai Papacino), on the west side of the port.

Seafood of all kinds is sold at the **fish market** (✉ Pl. St-François) every morning except Monday. At the daily **flower market** (✉ cours Saleya) you can find all kinds of plants and mounds of fruits and vegetables.

The **antiques and brocante market** (✉ pl. Robilante) by the Old Port is held from Tuesday through Saturday. For brocante on Monday check out cours Saleya.

THE ARRIÈRE-PAYS NIÇOISE

When you're saturated with Côte d'Azur glamour—or crowds—and you've had enough of Nice's big-city downside, consider a day or two's car trip deep into the hill country behind the coast. Within 10 minutes of cutting inland you enter a new universe—a wild, pre-Alpine terrain of rock gorges, black-green pine forests, and churning whitewater rivers sending up soft veils of mist. Along N204 you parallel a remarkable railroad, an engineering miracle of vertiginous tinker-toy bridges and model-train tunnels that drill neatly through the shaggy green cliffs; and you visit isolated mountain villages with tiny Baroque chapels decorated with the fervor of an Alpine Bernini. You may want to hike or you may want to picnic. And you may want to toss out your vacation itinerary and settle in this lost, wild world for the duration.

This circuit is only a sample of the forays to be made into the arrière-pays; the region is riddled with a series of river valleys that thread down from the Alps and the heavily protected Parc National du Mercantour. You may approach it from either end, either cutting immediately up into L'Escarène, the mountain town north of Nice, or starting, as suggested here, from the Italian border. It makes for a full day's drive, counting sorties into churches and villages, and could be difficult in heavy rain. To explore further, consider spending a night or two in St-Dalmas-de-Tende, just below Tende, the hiking center at the northernmost point covered here.

From Nice, hop on A8 and speed along the dramatic hills and in and out of tunnels. Just past the Italian customs booths (don't forget your passport) bear right toward Ventimiglia. Signs will point to Breil-sur-Roya and the Col de Tende. You'll be following E74 along the River Roya, driving only 15 km (9 mi) in Italy before crossing back into France. The territory is already radically different from the coast, resembling the mill valleys of West Virginia or the gorges of the Ozarks; the architecture, in stone and ochre stucco, seems to grow out of the rock that shores it up. At the first crossroads you'll arrive at Breil-sur-Roya, on the river's banks. Stop here and fuel up, as farther north gas stations are few and far between, then spend a little time exploring the town.

Breil-sur-Roya

③⑤ *24 km (15 mi) northwest of Ventimiglia (just over the Italian border), 58 km (36 mi) northeast of Nice via D2204.*

Draped at the foot of the forested mountains that separate it from Italy and crowding gracefully along the wide River Roya, this peaceful mountain town (pronounced bray) has survived from the Middle Ages. Its dense inner streets, basically car-free, are lined with pretty old houses, still framed by bits and pieces of old fortifications.

The main square, place Brancion, is flanked by two churches, which, with the one across the river, makes about 2% of the village's buildings sacred. On the square the town market proffers the crops from local farmers' vegetable patches and the local cheese, from cow's milk.

The facade of one of the churches, **Chapelle Ste-Catherine,** is pure Italian Renaissance. But step into the larger **Église Sancta-Maria-in-Albis,** a massive 17th-century Baroque structure turning a broad and windowless apse toward the river: The elaborate decor seems startling in these backwoods parts, especially the richly carved wood and gilt of the 17th-century organ.

Across the river is a slender Romanesque bell tower, the last vestige of a Benedictine abbey destroyed in the 18th century. Just up the hill, the town's third church, **Notre-Dame-de-l'Assomption,** retains traces of its spare Romanesque origins, though its decoration is Baroque.

En Route From Roya climb onward north to **Fontan,** from where you'll see the painterly perched village of Saorge. At Fontan cut right and double back to climb up to the village.

Saorge

★ **③⑥** *7 km (4 mi) north of Breil-sur-Roya.*

An extraordinary composition of stacked pastel cubes clinging precariously to the dark forest cliffs over the Roya gorge, Saorge is one of the most spectacular and beautiful of southern France's myriad hilltop villages. Here you'll see the first flat, stone roof tiles that signal the retreat of Mediterranean tile and the beginning of the Piedmontese Alps.

Saorge was a key Roman defense point for defending the river valley and the Alpine passes, and it remained important under the Grimaldis and the dukes of Savoy for centuries; it even figured in Alpine strategies of World War II. Yet its ancient stucco houses remain untouched by time, and its paved streets, which you must negotiate practically single file, lead to vertiginous views over the gorge. There are passageways arching over the cobblestones, and locals hauling goods home by skinny tractor-tricycles. It used to be mules: They carried every stone up the precarious paths to build the Église St-Sauveur, an eagle's aerie of a church as sumptuously decorated and furnished as any on the coast. Despite this achievement, there's nary a boutique in sight, and one pizzeria and one simple "panoramic" restaurant to meet your needs.

En Route   Farther north, turn right at St-Dalmas-de-Tende and head into La Brigue, a mountain town with interesting churches.

La Brigue

③⑦ *13 km (8 mi) northeast of Saorge.*

Dominated by the Genovese Lascaris-Grimaldis (vestiges of whose wealth and influence feature prominently in Nice and Monaco) and once a powerful medieval stronghold, La Brigue nestles under the ruins of its château. It's in a pretty valley on the River Levense that gushes toward the Roya.

Like Breil, this tiny village seems disproportionately blessed with wonderful old churches. In the village center, the **Collégial St-Martin** dates from the 15th century. It's a welcome relief from Baroque excess, yet the decor of its early Gothic structure is lavishly decorated with fine 16th-century art. Most of the works are influenced by, if not attributed to, Bréa, including a richly detailed triptych on the story of Ste-Marthe and a rare nativity scene. On the same square, two 17th-century chapels face off. The **Chapelle de l'Annonciation,** flaunts a supremely Baroque facade and a startling elipsoid shape. The **Chapelle de l'Assomption,** in contrast to the flamboyant Annonciation chapel it confronts, holds out for Renaissance purity.

En Route   From La Brigue follow D143 to its end and visit the extraordinary painted chapel of Notre-Dame-des-Fontaines.

Notre-Dame-des-Fontaines

★ **③⑧** *4 km (2 mi) east of La Brigue.*

If you make the pilgrimage to only one of the arrière-pays's famous painted chapels, this one would be a good choice. Above a roaring stream supposed to have curative powers, this spare Alpine-Gothic structure stands alone in the woods, a dead-end that's well removed from a few houses and cafés. Built in the 15th century, it was painted in an awe-inspiring series of frescoed panels, some Giotto-esque in their classical reserve, some seething with gore and the horrors of hell. The passion of Christ is depicted in 25 squares, one a vast crucifixion, another a ghastly image of Judas hanged with a demon ripping his damned soul from his bowels. The *Last Judgment* on the entrance wall combines the epic vision of Michelangelo with the morbid wit of Bosch. The works are attributed to a passionate Piedmontese named Jean Canavesio and to Jean Baleison, whose graceful Gothic style denies his provincial experience. Both worked in the mid-15th century. ⊠ *At end of D143, east of La Brigue.* ⊙ *Daily 9:30–7, officially, but hrs vary; ask for key at first restaurant below church.*

En Route   From Notre-Dame-des-Fontaines, double back on D143 to the crossroads hamlet of St-Dalmas-de-Tende, one of the gateways into the **Vallée des Merveilles,** a valley with rocks carved with figures dating from 1800 BC.

St-Dalmas-de-Tende

39 *7 km (4 mi) west of Notre-Dame-des-Fontaines.*

This tiny mountain hamlet clusters around the crossroads between the main north-south highway and the road that winds up into the departure points—on foot or four-wheel-drive—for the **Vallée des Merveilles** (☞ Tende, *below*). There's one lonely train station, a baker and a grocer, and the sound of a mountain torrent competing with the roar of passing Italian speedsters on their way up to Turin.

Dining and Lodging

$$$ ✕🖾 **Le Prieuré.** In a whitewashed Romanesque priory nestled on riverside gardens in the shadow of the mountains is this pretty inn. Thanks to an unusual arrangement, it's impeccably maintained and serviced at four-star level: The staff is handicapped, and lives and works on site. Thus the Centre d'Aide par le Travail (Center for Helping through Work) provides workers with an idyllic mountain home and on-the-job training—and guests are pampered with pristine rooms, scrubbed tile bathrooms, laundry service, immaculate grounds, and a friendly ambience. The restaurant serves good regional food to passing diners, but focuses on half-board guests who've come to hike and compare exploits with their neighbors. The results: A staff and clientele of happy campers. 🖾 *rue Jean Médicin, 06430,* ☎ *04–93–04–75–70,* 🖾 *04–93–04–71–58. 24 rooms. Restaurant. AE, DC, MC, V.*

Tende

40 *4 km (2 mi) north of St-Dalmas.*

The last stop before the climb over the pass to Italy, Tende is a market town and a center for hikers and nature lovers who come to venture into the **Parc National du Mercantour.**

Tende's striking **vieille ville** skews gracefully down from the rocky, scrub-covered mountainside, under the macabre spire of the last stone vestige of the Lascaris château; the houses, many from the 15th and 16th centuries, are built of schist with slate-slab roofs.

The modern **Musée des Merveilles** (Museum of Marvels), its facade decked out with intriguing runes, can introduce you to the wonders of the nearby **Vallée des Merveilles** (Valley of Marvels). In this high and isolated valley, enclosed on all sides by mountains, rocks are etched with thousands of Bronze Age petroglyphs depicting bulls' horns, spearheads, and lively dancers. If you want to explore these firsthand, you can hire a guide for an outing on horseback, on donkey back, on foot, or by jeep (for information, write 🖾 Val des Merveilles, 06430 Tende, or call 04–93–04–77–73). 🖾 *av. du 16-septembre-1947,* ☎ *04–93–04–32–50.* 🖾 *30 frs.* ☉ *May–mid-Oct., Wed.–Mon. 10:30–6:30; mid–Oct.–Apr., Wed.–Mon. 10:30–5.*

En Route   From Tende, you've no choice: Either double back south on the main highway or climb over the Col de Tende (Tende Pass; 6,136 ft) into Turin, Italy. If you opt to return south, just before you return to Breil-sur-Roya, cut sharply right on D2204, following directions to Sospel. Along narrow switchbacks (the signs count them for you) you climb over sparse heathered hills to the **Col de Brouis** (2,883 ft). Walk up to the overlook, and you'll be rewarded with a panorama of snowcapped mountains. Over the crest is new terrain and a new climate; the hills are grassy, sheltered from the wind, with olive trees growing on ancient step-terraced slopes. There's scarcely a house or farm in sight; by the time you descend to the banks of the River Bevera, the small mountain town of Sospel seems downright cosmopolitan.

Sospel

㊶ *21 km (13 mi) southwest of Breil-sur-Roya, 40 km (25 mi) northeast of Nice.*

With its cereal-box, six-story houses in rich-hued stucco flanking the banks of the River Bevera, its fine old fountains, and its florid Baroque church, Sospel is a picturesque old mountain town. It's difficult to imagine it as the second-largest city in the Comté de Nice and a center of medieval church power, which it was in the 13th century.

The most remarkable reminder of Sospel's fast-track past is the 11th-century **Vieux Pont** (Old Bridge), a sophisticated Romanesque bridge composed of two graceful arches spanning the waters, buttressed by a toll tower. This sturdy structure bore the steady stream of mules carrying salt from Nice to Turin along the 18th-century *route de sel* (salt route).

The **Église St-Michel,** once the cathedral in the days of the papal schism in the 14th century, bears only the bell tower from Romanesque days; the rest was built in the early 18th century and dazzles with gilt and trompe-l'oeil frescoes. From the church you can climb up to the crumbling ruins of the **fortifications** and a 15th-century watchtower.

En Route From Sospel climb back into the heights to cross the **Col de Braus** (3,287 ft), where the Alps rear back into view. The road descends sharply by *lacets,* switchbacks as tightly angled as the laces in a shoe. The perspective broadens and greenery thickens as you descend to L'Escarène, another pretty river town.

L'Escarène

㊷ *22 km (14 mi) southwest of Sospel, 18 km (11 mi) north of Nice.*

As you land safely from the switchbacks down from the Col de Braus, you roll into this serene and unassuming river town. Like Sospel, it was once a crossroads on the salt route. The **Église St-Pierre,** with two Penitent chapels standing guard at its sides, seems remarkably florid for the humble setting, yet it was designed by the same architect as Nice's cathedral.

En Route From L'Escarène, follow D2204 back down to Nice.

MONACO AND THE CORNICHES RESORTS

To many this is the true Côte d'Azur, a sun-blessed crescent from the Cap Ferrat to the Italian border backed by tropical-forested mountains and crystalline Alps, where Mediterranean breezes relieve the summer heat and the radiant light soothes midwinter days. Banana trees and date palms, cactus and figs luxuriate in the climate, and the hills, bristling with wind-twisted parasol pines, are paved with hothouses where roses and carnations profit from the year-round sun.

The lay of the land is nearly vertical, as the coastline is one great cliff, a *corniche* terraced by three parallel highways—the Basse Corniche, the Moyenne Corniche, and the Grande Corniche—that snake along its graduated crests. Woven between these panoramic routes lie the resorts, their names as evocative of luxury and glamour as a haute-couture logo: Cap Ferrat, Beaulieu, and Monte Carlo.

Yet it must be said: These pockets of elegance have long since overflowed, and it's a rare stretch of cliff side that hasn't sprouted a cluster of concrete cubes in cloying hues of pineapple, apricot, and Pepto-Bismol pink. The traffic along the Corniches routes—especially the Basse Corniche that follows the coast—is appalling, exacerbated by the manic Italian driving style and self-absorbed luxury roadsters that turn the pavement into a bumper-car battle.

But there are moments: Wrench your car out of the flow, pull over at a rare overlook on the Haute Corniche, and walk to the extremity. Like the ancient Ligurians who first built their settlements here, you can hang over the infinite expanse of teal blue sea and glittering waves and survey the resorts draped gracefully along the curves of the coast. It was from these cliffs that for 2,500 years castles and towers held watch over the waters, braced against the influx of new people—first the Greeks, then the Romans, the Saracens, trade ships from Genoa, battleships under Napoléon, Edwardian cruise ships on the Grand Tour, and the Allies in the Second World War. The influx continues today, of course, in the great waves of vacationers who storm the coast, summer and winter.

Villefranche-sur-Mer

★ **43** *10 km (6 mi) east of Nice.*

Nestled discreetly along the deep scoop of harbor between Nice and the Cap Ferrat, this pretty watercolor of a fishing port seems surreal, flanked as it is by the big city of Nice and the assertive wealth of Monaco. Genuine fishermen actually skim up to the docks here in weathered-blue barques, and the streets of the old town flow directly to the waterfront much as they did in the 13th century.

A favorite as a film location for its old-world atmosphere, this tiny port has been featured in James Bond films and *The Jewel of the Nile*. Its deep harbor was preferred by Onassis and Niarchos and royals on their yachts. But the character of the place was subtly shaped by the artists and authors who gathered at the **Hôtel Welcome** (☞ Dining and Lodging, *below*)—Diaghilev and Stravinsky, taking a break from the Ballet Russe in Monaco; Somerset Maugham and Evelyn Waugh; and above all Jean Cocteau, who came here to recover from the excesses of Paris life.

So enamored was Cocteau of this painterly fishing port that he decorated the 14th-century **Chapelle St-Pierre** with images from the life of St. Peter and dedicated it to the village's fishermen. Working in crayon and chalk fixed with paraffin, he covered the walls with earthy, simplistic drawings, heavily outlined and surprisingly—even disappointingly—realist for this master of the surreal. ✉ *Pl. Pollanais,* ☎ *04–93–76–90–70.* ✉ *12 frs.* ✆ *Mid-June–mid-Sept., Tues.–Sun. 10–noon and 4–8:30; mid-Sept.–mid-Nov., 9:30–noon and 2–6; end Dec.–Mar., 9:30–noon and 2–5:30; Apr.–mid-June, Tues.–Sun. 9:30–noon and 3–7.*

From the chapel continue down to the waterfront, where cafés and restaurants line the port. Then return through the old-town streets that parallel the water, with steep steps leading up into alleys and passageways arching over the cobbles. The extraordinary 13th-century **rue Obscure** (literally, dark street) is entirely covered by vaulted arcades; it sheltered the people of Villefranche when the Germans fired their parting shots—an artillery bombardment—near World War II's end.

The modest Baroque **Église St-Michel** (✉ Pl. Poullan), just above rue Obscure, contains a movingly realistic sculpture of Christ carved in fig wood by an anonymous 17th-century convict.

The stalwart 16th-century **Citadelle St-Elme,** restored to perfect condition, anchors the harbor with its broad, sloping stone walls. Beyond its drawbridge lie the city's offices and a group of minor gallery-museums. Whether or not you stop into these private collections of local art (all free of charge), you are welcome to stroll around the inner grounds and to circle the imposing exterior.

Dining and Lodging

$$–$$$ **Hôtel Welcome.** When Villefranche harbored a community of artists
★   and writers, this waterfront landmark was their adopted headquarters. Somerset Maugham holed up in one of the tiny crow's-nest rooms at the top, and Jean Cocteau moved into one of the corners, with windows opening onto two balconies. Evelyn Waugh and Richard Burton used to tie one on in the bar, and film directors shooting action scenes in the bay sent the guests flowers when special-effects explosions disturbed their repose. It's comfortable and modern, with the best rooms brightened with vivid colors and stenciled quotes from Cocteau, yet there's nothing glamorous about it—except that its rooms open over the port, the harbor, and the sounds of ropes ticking against masts of gently rocking yachts. The casual brasserie Carpe Diem serves light meals on the quai; the formal restaurant St-Pierre specializes, naturally enough, in fish. ⊠ *quai Courbet, 06230,* ☎ *04–93–76–27–62,* FAX *04–93–76–27–66. 32 rooms. 2 restaurants, bar, air-conditioning. AE, DC, MC, V. Closed mid-Nov.–mid-Dec.*

Beaulieu

🏿 *4 km (2 mi) east of Villefranche, 14 km (9 mi) east of Nice.*

With its back pressed hard against the cliffs of the corniche and sheltered between the peninsulas of Cap Ferrat and Cap Roux, this once-grand resort basks in a tropical microclimate that earned its central neighborhood the name "Petite Afrique." The town was the pet of 19th-century society, and its grand hotels welcomed Empress Eugénie, the Prince of Wales, and Russian nobles.

One manifestation of its Belle Époque excess is the extravagant **Villa Kerylos,** a mansion built in 1902 in the style of classical Greece. It was the dream house of the amateur archeologist Théodore Reinach, who commissioned an Italian architect so he could surround himself with Grecian delights: cool Carrara marble, alabaster, rare fruitwoods, a mosaic-lined bath/pool worthy of a 1950s toga movie, and a dining room where guests draped themselves on the floor to eat, *à la Greque.* ⊠ *rue Gustave-Eiffel,* ☎ *04–93–01–01–44.* ▦ *40 frs.* ◉ *July–Aug., daily 10:30–7; Sept.–June, Tues.–Fri. 2–6, weekends 10:30–6.*

Today Beaulieu is usually spoken of in the past tense and has taken on a rather stuffy ambience. But on the **Promenade Maurice-Rouvier,** you can stroll the waterfront, past grand villas and their tropical gardens, all the way to St-Jean-Cap-Ferrat.

St-Jean-Cap-Ferrat

★ 🏿 *2 km (1 mi) south of Beaulieu on D25.*

This luxuriously sited pleasure port moors the peninsula of Cap Ferrat; from its port-side walkways and crescent of beach you can look over the sparkling blue harbor to the graceful green bulk of the corniches. Yachts purr in and out of port, and their passengers scuttle into cafés for take-out drinks to enjoy on their private decks.

★   Between the port and the mainland, the phenomenally beautiful **Villa Ephrussi de Rothschild** stands as witness to the wealth and worldly taste of the baroness who had it built (though she only stayed here a week or two per year). Constructed in 1905 and donated to the Academy of Beaux Arts in 1934, the house was created around the artworks, decorations, and furniture brought to Beatrice de Rothschild's door by eager dealers (she rarely traveled herself). The mansion is lavished with rare tapestries and fabrics and landscaped with no less than seven theme gardens (she liked to collect). The extraordinary ensemble reigns over a hilltop at the crest of the peninsula, taking in spectacular, symmetrical views of the coastline. On the ground floor you can freely visit hall after hall exquisitely decorated with Gobelins and Beauvais tapestries, Renaissance painted-wood furniture, and wall panels painted in classical grotesques. In de Rothschild's bedroom is a ravishing collection of gowns and her travel kit for a cruise on the *Ile-de-France;* in the dining room the table is set with Sèvres tea things ready for sipping. On a guided tour of the upstairs, you can see things, things, and more things, including some fine little etchings by Fragonard, but allow yourself time to wander in the gardens: They are one of the few places on the coast where you'll be allowed to experience the lavish pleasures of the Belle Époque Côte d'Azur. ⊠ *av. Ephrussi,* ☎ *04–93–01–33–09.* ◫ *Access to ground floor and gardens 28 frs; guided tour upstairs 15 frs extra.* ☉ *Mar.–June and Sept.–Nov., daily 10–6; July–Aug., daily 10–7; Nov.–Feb., weekdays 2–6, weekends 10–6.*

Cap Ferrat itself is fiercely protected and its grand old villas are, for the most part, hidden in the depths of tropical gardens. You can nonetheless walk its entire **coastline promenade** if you strike out from the port; from the restaurant Capitaine Cook, cut right up avenue des Fossés, turn right on avenue Vignon, and follow the chemin de la Carrière. The 11-km (7-mi) walk passes through rich tropical flora and, on the west side, over white cliffs buffeted by waves. When you've traced the full outline of the peninsula, veer up the chemin du Roy past the fabulous gardens of the **Villa des Cèdres,** once owned by Leopold II, king of Belgium at the turn of the century; you'll reach the **Plage de Passable** and cut back across the peninsula's wrist.

A shorter loop takes you from town out to the **Pointe de St-Hospice,** much of the walk shaded by wind-twisted pines. From the port, climb avenue Jean Mermoz to Place Paloma and follow the path closest to the waterfront. At the point there's an 18th-century prison tower, a 19th-century chapel, and unobstructed views of Cap Martin.

Dining and Lodging

$$ ✕ **Le Sloop.** Among the touristy cafés and snack shops along the port, this sleek blue-and-white restaurant caters to the yachting crowd and sailors who cruise into dock for lunch. The focus is fish, of course: *Soupe de poisson* (fish soup), *St-Pierre* (John Dory) steamed with asparagus, or whole sea bass roasted with olives and *pistou* (pesto). Its outdoor tables surround a tiny "garden" of potted palms, and the view of the cliffs and bobbing boats is mesmerizing. ⊠ *Port de Plaisance,* ☎ *04–93–01–48–63. AE, MC, V. Closed Wed. mid-Sept.–mid-Apr. No lunch Wed. or Thurs. mid-Apr.–mid-Sept.*

$$$ ✵ **Brise Marine.** This golden-ochre 1878 villa, brightened with sky blue ★ shutters and a frieze of frescoed lemons, opens onto a broad balustraded garden and unbroken views of the sea. Though it overlooks one of the cape's many exclusive mansions, complete with vast garden and much-vaunted *chien très méchant* (very nasty dog), *this* little mansion remains unpretentious and accessible, with pretty little pastel guest rooms that feel like bedrooms in a private home. The terraces are shared, the aperitif a social occasion, and the comforts first class, including hair dryers, safes, and CNN (if you must). Honeymooners should ask for the "villa," a small room slightly set apart, with a sizable private terrace

looking straight out to sea. ⊠ *58 av. Jean Mermoz, 06230,* ☎ *04–93–76–04–36,* 𝖥𝖠𝖷 *04–93–76–11–49. 16 rooms. Bar, air-conditioning. AE, MC, V. Closed Nov.–Jan.*

Eze

🔵 *2 km (1 mi) east of Beaulieu, 12 km (7 mi) east of Nice, 7 km (4 mi) west of Monte Carlo.*

Towering like an eagle's nest above the coast and crowned with ramparts and the ruins of a medieval château, Eze (pronounced ehz) is unfortunately the most accessible of all the perched villages. Consequently, it's by far the most commercialized, surpassing St-Paul-de-Vence for the tackiness of its souvenir shops and the indifference of its waiters. Even off-season its streets pour with a lava flow of tourists, some not-so-fresh from the beach, and it earns unique status as the only town to post pictorial warnings that say, in effect, "No Shoes, No Shirt, No Service." It is, nonetheless, spectacularly sited; if you can manage to shake the crowds and duck off to a quiet overlook, the village commands splendid views up and down the coast.

From the crest-top **Jardin Exotique** (Tropical Garden), full of exotic succulents, you can pan your video cam all the way around the hills and waterfront. But if you want to have a prayer of a chance to enjoy the magnificence of this lovely stone village, come at dawn or after sunset. Or (if you have the means) spend the night—and the day elsewhere.

Dining and Lodging

$$$$ ✕🏠 **Château de la Chèvre d'Or.** Though it's directly on the main
  ★   tourist thoroughfare through Eze's raked streets—and you may be obliged to crisscross the traffic to move from room to restaurant— this extraordinary conglomerate of weathered-stone houses allows you to turn your back on the world and drink in unsurpassed sea views. More than half the creamy white rooms look over the water, and the others compensate with exposed stone, beams, and burnished antiques. The three restaurants—from the casual, affordable grill to the very medieval grand dining room—all take in the views, too, as does the Louis XIII–style bar. The swimming pool alone, clinging like a swallow's nest to the hillside, justifies the investment. So do the liveried footmen who greet you at the village entrance to wave you, VIP style, past the cattle drive of tourists. It's a member of the Relais & Châteaux group. ⊠ *rue du Barri, 06360,* ☎ *04–92–10–66–66,* 𝖥𝖠𝖷 *04–93–41–06–72. 22 rooms, 8 apartments. 3 restaurants, bar, pool. AE, DC, MC, V. Closed Dec.–Feb.*

Peillon

★ 🔵 *15 km (9 mi) northeast of Nice via D2204 and D53.*

Perhaps because it's difficult to reach and not on the way to or from anything else, this idyllic village has maintained the magical ambience of its medieval origins. You can hear the bell toll here, walk in silence up its weathered cobblestones, and smell the thyme crunching underfoot if you step past its minuscule boundaries onto the unspoiled hillsides. And its streets are utterly and completely commerce free; the citizens have voted to vaccinate themselves against the plague of boutiques, galleries, and cafés that have infected its peers along the coast.

Dining and Lodging

$–$$$ ✕🏠 **Auberge de la Madone.** With its shaded garden terrace and its
  ★   impeccable bright-colored rooms, this inn is a charming oasis on the perimeter of the village. Some windows open out over greenery, others

over spectacular views. The restaurant revels in the best local ingredients and traditions, from sea bass in fennel to pigeon stuffed with figs to local goat cheese drizzled with green olive oil; a lunch on the flowery veranda is everything the south of France should be. Yet owner Christian Millo and his partner/sister, Marie-José, continue to improve things: Now the inn has a pool and tennis court on the slope above it, and in the village annex, six little rooms offering shelter at bargain rates. ⊠ *06440 Peillon Village,* ☎ *03–93–79–91–17,* FAX *03–93–79–99–36. 23 rooms, 17 with bath. Restaurant. MC, V. Closed late Oct.–late Dec. and early Jan.–late Jan.*

Monaco

7 km (4 mi) east of Eze, 21 km (13 mi) east of Nice.

It's positively feudal, the idea that an ancient dynasty of aristocrats could still hold fast to its patch of coastline, the last scrap of a once-vast domain. But that's just what the Grimaldi family did, clinging to a few acres of glory and maintaining their own license plates, their own telephone area code (377), and their own highly forgiving tax system. Yet the Principality of Monaco covers just 473 acres and would fit comfortably inside New York's Central Park or a family farm in Iowa. And its 5,000 pampered citizens would fill only a small fraction of the seats in Yankee Stadium.

The present ruler, Prince Rainier III, traces his ancestry to Otto Canella, who was born in 1070. The Grimaldi dynasty began with Otto's great-great-great-grandson, Francesco Grimaldi, also known as Frank the Rogue. Expelled from Genoa, Frank and his cronies disguised themselves as monks and in 1297 seized the fortified medieval town known today as Le Rocher (The Rock). Except for a short break under Napoléon, the Grimaldis have been here ever since, which makes them the oldest reigning family in Europe. On the Grimaldi coat of arms are two monks holding swords (look up, and you'll see them above the main door as you enter the palace).

In the 1850s a Grimaldi named Charles III made a decision that turned the Rock into a giant blue chip. Needing revenues but not wanting to impose additional taxes on his subjects, he contracted with a company to open a gambling facility. The first spin of the roulette wheel was on December 14, 1856. There was no easy way to reach Monaco then— no carriage roads or railroads—so no one came. Between March 15 and March 20, 1857, one person entered the casino—and won two francs. In 1868, however, the railroad reached Monaco, filled with Englishmen who came to escape the London fog. The effects were immediate. Profits were so great that Charles eventually abolished all direct taxes.

Almost overnight, a threadbare principality became an elegant watering hole for European society. Dukes (and their mistresses) and duchesses (and their gigolos) danced and dined their way through a world of spinning roulette wheels and bubbling champagne—preening themselves for nights at the opera, where such artists as Vaslav Nijinsky, Sarah Bernhardt, and Enrico Caruso came to perform.

But it's the tax system, not the gambling, that's made Monaco one of the most sought-after addresses in the world—that and its sensational position on a broad, steep peninsula that bulges into the Mediterranean, its harbor sparkling with luxury cruisers, its posh mansions angling awnings toward the nearly perpetual sun. The population explosion here has allowed Monaco to break another French code, that of con-

228

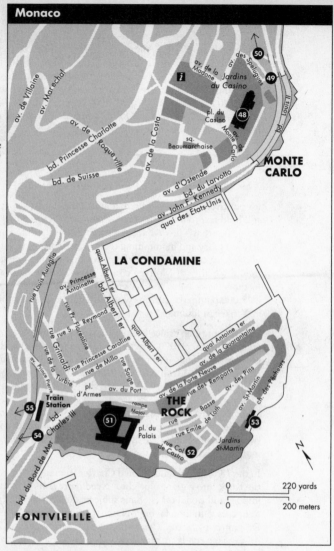

struction restraints. Thus it bristles with gleaming glass-and-concrete corncob-towers 20 and 30 stories high and with vast apartment complexes, their terraces landscaped like miniature gardens.

Its casino remains the most famous in the world, the playground of royalty, wealthy playboys, and glamorous film stars. One of the loveliest of the latter, in fact, became its princess when Hollywood's darling Grace Kelly married Prince Rainier in 1956; their wedding, marriage, and her tragic death in a car accident parallel strangely with that of another, more recent princess.

Yet all this glamour and desirability as a jet-set getaway make Monaco difficult to access as a humble tourist. Parking is as coveted as a room with a view; hotel and restaurant prices are inflated in all categories. And its two far-flung tourist centers—the lovely casino grounds of Monte Carlo, surrounded by flossy shops, and Old Monaco, the medieval town on the Rock, topped by the palace, the cathedral, and the oceanography museum—are separated by a vast port, and shuttling between them is a daunting proposition for ordinary mortals without wings.

So arm yourself with a map and a bus schedule or an excellent pair of walking shoes and start at the **tourist office** (⊠ av. de la Costa), just north of the casino gardens.

★ ❹❽ Place du Casino is the center of Monte Carlo and the **casino** is a must-see, even if you don't bet a sou. Into the gold-leaf splendor of the casino, where fortunes have been won, shirts lost, and any number of James Bond scenes filmed, the hopeful traipse from tour buses to tempt fate beneath the gilt-edged rococo ceiling. The main gambling hall is the **Salle Européene** (European Room), where for a 50-franc entry fee you can play roulette, trente et quarante, or black jack. The slot machines stand apart in the **Salle Blanche** (White Room) and the **Salon Rose** (Pink Salon), where unclad nymphs float about on the ceiling smoking cigarillos. The **Salles Privées** (Private Rooms) are for high rollers; pay another 50 frs. to play for a minimum stake of 500 francs. Jacket and tie are required in the back rooms, which open at 3 PM. Bring your passport (under-21s not admitted). ⊠ *pl. du Casino*, ☎ *377/92–16–21–21* ⊙ *Noon–the last die is thrown.*

In the true spirit of the town, it seems that the **Opéra** (⊠ pl. du Casino), with its 18-ton gilt-bronze chandelier and extravagant frescoes, is part of the casino complex. The designer, Charles Garnier, also built the Paris Opéra.

❹❾ The serious gamblers, some say, play at **Loews Casino,** by the vast convention center that juts over the water (☞ Lodging, *below*). ⊠ *12 av. des Spélugues*, ☎ *93–50–65–00.* ⊙ *Tables open weekdays at 5 PM and weekends at 4 PM; slot machines open daily at 11 AM.*

From place des Moulins there is an escalator down to the Larvotto Beach
❺⓿ complex, artfully created with imported sand, and the **Musée National,** housed in a Garnier villa within a rose garden. There's a beguiling collection of 18th- and 19th-century dolls and mechanical automatons—more than 400 altogether. ⊠ *17 av. Princesse Grace*, ☎ *93–30–91–26.* ▣ *30 frs.* ⊙ *Easter–Aug., daily 10–6:30; Sept.–Easter, daily 10–12:15 and 2:30–6:30.*

It's a hike or a ride on bus No. 6 from Monte Carlo to the **port** along boulevard Albert 1er, where pleasure boats of every shape flash white and blue. From the inner right corner of the port you climb a steep path up to the Rock. The broad place du Palais knots up with crowds at 11:55, when the poker-faded guards—in black in winter, in summer, white—change shifts, or, as the French say, relieve themselves. They
❺❶ are protecting hallowed ground: the **Palais Princier,** where the royal family resides, including on occasion Princess Stephanie. You can tell they're home if the family banner flies on the mast above the main tower. A 40-minute guided tour (summer only) of this sumptuous chunk of history, first built in the 13th century and expanded and enhanced over the centuries, reveals an extravagance of 16th- and 17th-century frescoes, as well as tapestries, gilt furniture, and paintings on a grand scale. ⊠ *pl. du Palais*, ☎ *93–25–18–31.* ▣ *30 frs; joint ticket with Musée Napoléon 40 frs.* ⊙ *June–Sept., daily 9:30–6:30; Oct.–May, daily 10–5.*

One wing of the palace, open throughout the year, is taken up by the **Musée Napoléon,** filled with Napoleonic souvenirs—including The Hat and a tricolor scarf—and genealogical charts. The Grimaldis and the Bonapartes were related, you see. ⊠ *In the Palais Princier*, ☎ *93–*

25–18–31. ☞ *20 frs; joint ticket with palace apartments 40 frs. (☞ above).* ⊙ *June–Oct., daily 9:30–6:30; Dec.–May, Tues.–Sun. 10–12:30 and 2–6.*

52 Follow the flow of crowds down the last remaining streets of medieval Monaco to the **Cathédrale de l'Immaculée-Conception** (⊠ av. St-Martin), an uninspired 19th-century version of Romanesque. It harbors nonetheless some wonderful artworks, including an altarpiece painted in 1500 by Bréa. It is, perhaps, his masterwork, depicting with tender detail the steady gaze of St-Nicolas; he is flanked by small panels portraying other saints, graceful, chastened, and demure. Despite the humility innate to the work, it's framed with unusual flamboyance in ornate gilt wood.

★ ☾ **53** At the prow of the Rock, the grand **Musée Océanographique** (Oceanography Museum) perches dramatically on a cliff. It's a splendid Edwardian structure, built under Prince Albert I to house specimens collected on amateur explorations, and it evokes the grandeur of the days of imperialist discovery and the masculine self-regard of the old National Geographic Society. It was led by Jacques Cousteau (1910–1997) from 1957 to 1988. Sumptuously decorated with mosaics of sea life, beveled-oak display cases, and gleaming brass, it nonetheless contains a collection somewhat pared down from its heyday. The main floor displays skeletons and taxidermy of enormous sea creatures, including a 6½-ft-wide Japanese crab, but many of the oak cases are empty. Also here are interesting examples of early submarines, diving gear dating to the Middle Ages, and a few interactive science displays. Upstairs are boat models, including a scale miniature of the *Titanic* sinking. But the reason the throngs pour into this landmark is its famous **aquarium**, a vast complex of backlighted tanks at eye level containing every imaginable variety of fish, crab, and eel. The wide-open piranha pond is a crowd pleaser. For a fine view and a restorative drink, take the elevator to the roof terrace. ⊠ *av. St-Martin,* ☎ *93–15–36–00.* ☞ *60 frs.* ⊙ *July–Aug., daily 9–8; Sept. and Apr.–June, daily 9–7; Oct.–Mar., daily 9:30–7; Nov.–Feb., daily 10–6.*

54 Six hundred varieties of cacti and succulents cling to a sheer rock face at the **Jardin Exotique** (Tropical Garden), a brisk half-hour walk west from the palace.

55 From the Tropical Garden, you can enter the **Musée d'Anthropologie Préhistorique** (Museum of Prehistoric Anthropology), which contains bones, tools, and other artifacts. Shapes of the stalactites and stalagmites in the cavernous grotto (entered from the gardens) resemble the cacti outside. ⊠ *bd. du Jardin Exotique,* ☎ *93–15–80–06.* ☞ *39 frs.* ⊙ *Daily 9–7 (till dusk in winter).*

Dining and Lodging

$$$$ ✕ **Le Louis XV.** This extravagantly showy restaurant, in the Hôtel de
★ Paris (☞ *below*), stuns with royal decor, yet it manages to be upstaged by its product: the superb cuisine of Alain Ducasse, one of Europe's most celebrated chefs. Ducasse often refers to his deceptively simple style as "country cooking," much as Marie Antoinette played farmer at Versailles. Glamorous iced lobster consommé with caviar and risotto perfumed with Alba white truffles slum happily with stockfish (stewed salt cod) and tripe. There are sole sautéed with tender baby fennel, milk-fed lamb with hints of cardamom, and dark-chocolate sorbet crunchy with ground coffee beans—in short, a panoply of theatrical delights using the sensual flavors of the Mediterranean. ⊠ *Hôtel de Paris, pl. du Casino,* ☎ *92–16–30–01. AE, DC, MC, V. Closed Tues. and*

Wed. (except Wed. dinner mid-June–Aug.), 2 wks in Feb.–early Mar., and late Nov.–late Dec.

$$ ✕ **Castelroc.** With its tempting pine-shaded terrace just across from the entrance to the Prince's Palace, you may take this for a tourist chaser, but it's one of the more popular lunch spots in town with locals. The cuisine is a mix of classic and regional flavors, from *anchoïade* (anchovy paste) with olive oil to tender grilled scampi, stuffed artichokes, and garlicky *stocafi* (stockfish) simmered with tomatoes and Provençal herbs. ⊠ *Pl. du Palais*, ☎ *93–30–36–68. MC, V. Closed Sat. and end-Nov.–Dec.*

$$ ✕ **Polpetta.** This popular little trattoria is close enough to the Italian
★ border to pass for the real thing, and the exuberant Guasco brothers who greet you add to the authenticity. Enjoy a parade of antipasti, ravioli sprinkled with fresh sage in a pool of green oil, seafood risotto, osso buco perfumed with saffron, and a terrific list of Italian wines. ⊠ *2 rue Paradis*, ☎ *93–50–67–84. MC, V. Closed Tues. and Feb. No lunch Sat.*

$ ✕ **La Cigale.** With a ceiling draped in fishing nets, a mounted TV, mom-and-pop serving, and timers that shut off the lights in the bathroom if you linger too long, this is the other side of Monaco, where they struggle to make ends meet and to keep the prices low. Their efforts reward you with fresh *fritto misto*, a crunchy platter of batter-fried baby fish and squid rings; hearty minestrone thick with pesto; sardine beignets; and homemade pastas sauced with a generous hand. ⊠ *18 rue Millo*, ☎ *93–30–16–14. MC, V. Closed weekends.*

$$$$ ✕🏨 **Hermitage.** Even if you're not staying, come to see the glass-dome Art Nouveau vestibule, designed by Gustav Eiffel, and the lavish dining room, where pink-marble columns hold up a gilded, frescoed ceiling. The adjacent terrace has a tinkling pianist in summer and a view of the harbor. Rooms are comfortable but far less stylish; not all face the sea—and these are priced accordingly. The hotel is one block west of the casino. ⊠ *sq. Beaumarchais, BP 277, 98005*, ☎ *92–16–40–00*, 🕿 *92–16–38–52. 197 rooms, 34 apartments. Restaurant, bar, air-conditioning, pool. AE, DC, MC, V.*

$$$$ ✕🏨 **Hôtel de Paris.** This vestige of the Belle Époque has one of the most prestigious addresses in Europe and exudes the ambience of an era in which kings and grand dukes were regulars. Yet the hallways and public areas are not as extravagant as you might expect, and the warmest welcome is reserved for a chosen few. The spacious, high-ceilinged rooms have a Louis XV look; from some you can see the sea or the casino. Dinner is served in the superb Louis XV restaurant (☞ *above*); breakfast (the Continental version runs 150 francs) is served on the terrace in Le Côte Jardin; and Mediterranean-style cuisine is served in Le Grill. ⊠ *pl. du Casino, 98000*, ☎ *92–16–30–00*, 🕿 *92–16–38–50. 143 rooms, 41 suites, and 19 junior suites. 4 restaurants, air-conditioning, pool, indoor pool, spa. AE, DC, MC, V.*

$$$$ ✕🏨 **Loews.** Big and brash, Loews has a plush extravagance on a scale Donald Trump would envy. On staff is a full-time big band, and celebrities mix with sheikhs in the bars, casino, and restaurants. The vast rooftop pool has nothing but deck chairs between it and the open sea. Contemporary rooms are decorated in ice-cream shades and angled for maximum views. The ultra-swank restaurant La Truffe (dinner only; closed Mon. and Tues.) pulls out all stops on a fixed-price truffle menu, with sole with truffle sauce, truffles spliced between slabs of foie gras and lobster, and a subtle truffle sorbet. ⊠ *12 av. des Spélugues, 98000*, ☎ *93–50–65–00*, 🕿 *93–30–01–57. 619 rooms, 69 apartments. 3 restaurants, 2 bars, air-conditioning, pool, hot tub, health club, cabaret, casino. AE, DC, MC, V.*

$$$ ⊞ **Alexandra.** The friendly proprietress, Madame Larouquie, makes you feel right at home at this central, comfortable spot, just north of the casino. Though the color schemes clash and the decor is spare, bathrooms are big and up-to-date, and insulated windows shut out traffic noise. ⊠ *35 bd. Princesse-Charlotte, 98000,* ☎ *93–50–63–13,* 🅵🅰🆇 *92–16–06–48. 55 rooms. Air-conditioning. AE, DC, MC, V.*

$$$ ⊞ **Balmoral.** This 100-year-old urban hotel makes no effort to please, keeping its walls stripped of art, its woodwork overpainted, and its bathrooms with '60s-style tiles and shower. The only reason to stay here is the view from its port-side rooms, some with wrought-iron balconies: The boats, blue water, and looming Rock make you forget the unmatched color scheme. ⊠ *12 av. de la Costa,* ☎ *93–50–62–37,* 🅵🅰🆇 *93–15–08–69. 75 rooms. Restaurant, air-conditioning in 50 rooms. AE, DC, MC, V.*

Nightlife and the Arts

There's no need to go to bed before dawn in Monte Carlo when you can go to the **casino** on place du Casino (☞ *above*) or **Loews Casino** (☞ *above*).

The **Living Room** (⊠ 7 av. des Spélugues) is a popular, crowded bar open year-round. **Parady's** (⊠ av. Princesse-Grace) is the place for dancing, with a chic, 30-something crowd. For a more low-key night, try **Sparco Café** (⊠ 19 av. Charles-III), a piano bar that often attracts good jazz singers. **Tiffany's** (⊠ 3 av. des Spélugues) is another year-round hot spot.

Monte Carlo's spring arts festival, **Printemps des Arts,** takes place from early April to mid-May and includes the world's top ballet, operatic, symphonic, and chamber performers. Year-round, ballet and classical music can be enjoyed at the **Salle Garnier** (⊠ Pl. du Casino, ☎ 92–16–22–99), the main venue of the Opéra de Monte-Carlo and the Orchestre Philharmonique de Monte-Carlo, both worthy of the magnificent hall. The **Théâtre Princesse Grace** (⊠ 12 av. d'Ostende, ☎ 93–25–32–27) stages a number of plays during the spring festival; off-season there's usually a new show each week.

Outdoor Activities and Sports

Diving equipment can be rented from the **Club d'Exploration Sous-Marine de Monaco** (Underwater Exploration Club; ⊠ quai des Sanbarbani, ☎ 92–05–91–78). Or head to the 18-hole **Golf de Monte Carlo** (⊠ rte. du Mont-Agel, La Turbie, ☎ 04–93–41–09–11), open to the public.

The **Monte Carlo Tennis Tournament** is held during the Spring Arts festival. When the tennis stops, the auto racing begins: The **Grand Prix de Monaco** (☎ 93–15–26–00 for information) takes place in mid-May.

Roquebrune–Cap-Martin

56 *5 km (3 mi) east of Monaco.*

In the midst of the frenzy of overbuilding that defines this last gasp of the coast before Italy, two twinned havens have survived, each in its own way: The perched old town of Roquebrune, which gives its name to the greater area, and Cap-Martin—luxurious, isolated, and exclusive.

With its tumble of skewed tile roofs and twisting streets, fountains, archways, and quiet squares, Roquebrune retains many of the charms of a hilltop village, but it's heavily gentrified and commercialized. Its main attraction is its **Château Féodal** (Feudal Castle): Around the remains of a 10th-century tower, the Grimaldis erected an impregnable fortress that was state of the art in the 16th century, with crenellation, watch towers, and a broad moat. Nowadays this stronghold is besieged by tourists, who invade its restored halls and snap pictures from its wraparound walkway. 🖃 *20 frs.* ☉ *Apr.–mid-Sept., daily 10–noon and 2–7; mid-Sept.–Mar., Sat.–Thurs. 10–noon and 2–5:30.*

In the **cemetery,** Swiss-French architect Le Corbusier lies buried with his wife in a tomb of his own design. He kept a humble *cabanot* (beach bungalow) on the rocky shores of the Cap-Martin, where he drowned while swimming in 1965.

★ You can visit Le Corbusier's bungalow and see the glorious fauna of the cape by walking the **Promenade Le Corbusier.** It leads over chalk cliffs and through dense Mediterranean fauna to his tiny retreat, as much indoors as out and designed along the rigorous lines he preferred. Park at the tip of the cape on avenue Winston-Churchill and follow the signs.

Menton

57 *1 km (¾ mi) east of Roquebrune, 9 km (5½ mi) east of Monaco.*

Menton, the most Mediterranean of the French resort towns, rubs shoulders with the Italian border and owes some of its balmy climate to the protective curve of the Ligurian shore. Its Cubist skew of terra-cotta roofs and yellow-ochre houses, Baroque arabesques capping the church facades, and ceramic tiles glistening on their steeples, all evoke the villages of the Italian coast. Yet there's a whiff of influence from Spain, too, in its fantastical villas, exotic gardens, and whimsical patches of ceramic color, and a soupçon of Morocco, Corsica, and Greece. It is, in fact, the best of all Mediterranean worlds—and humble to boot: Menton is the least pretentious of the Côte d'Azur resorts, and all the more alluring for its modesty.

Its near-tropical climate nurtures orange and lemon trees that hang heavy with fruit in winter. There's another Florida parallel: The warmth attracts flocks of senior citizens who warm their bones far from northern fog and ice. Thus a large population of elderly visitors bask on its waterfront benches and browse its downtown shops. But Menton has a livelier, younger side, too, and the farther you penetrate toward the east, the more intriguing and colorful it becomes.

To get a feel for the territory, start your exploration at the far-east end of the Vieille Ville and walk out to the end of the **Jetée Impératrice Eugénie** (Empress Eugenie Jetty), jutting far out into the water. Above the masts of pleasure boats, all of Menton spreads over the hills, and the mountains of Italy loom behind.

From the jetty follow quai Bonaparte right and climb up the grand tiered stairs to the **Parvis St-Michel,** a broad plaza paved in round white and gray stones patterned in the coat of arms of the family Grimaldi. It was created in the 17th century by Prince Honoré II (the letter H is mingled into the design) as a kind of signature at the base of his great gift to the city.

The **Église St-Michel,** a majestic Baroque church on Parvis St-Michel, dominates the skyline of Menton with its bell tower. A humbler Renaissance church was destroyed on the orders of the prince to create something on a grander scale, and its towering belfry secured its conspicuousness in 1701. Beyond the beautifully proportioned facade— a 19th-century addition—the richly frescoed nave and chapels contain several works by Genovese artists and a splendid 17th-century organ.

Just above the main church, the smaller **Chapelle de l'Immaculée-Conception** answers St-Michel's grand gesture with its own pure Baroque beauty, dating from 1687. Between 3 and 5 you can slip in to see the graceful trompe-l'oeil over the altar and the ornate gilt lanterns the penitents carried in processions.

From Parvis St-Michel, climb up to the **Cimetière du Vieux-Château** (Old Château Cemetery), on the terraced plateau where once stood a medieval castle. The Victorian graves here are arranged by nationality, with an entire section of Russian royalty. The birth and death dates often attest to the ugly truth: Even Menton's balmy climate couldn't reverse the ravages of tuberculosis.

Two blocks below the square, **rue St-Michel** serves as the main commercial artery of the Vieille Ville, lined with shops, cafés, and orange trees. Between the lively pedestrian rue St-Michel and the waterfront, the marvelous **Marché Couvert** (Covered Market) sums up Menton style with its Belle Époque facade decorated in jewel-tone ceramics. Inside, it's just as appealing, with merchants vaunting chewy bread, mountain cheeses, oils, fruit, and Italian delicacies in Caravaggio-esque disarray. Outside its walls, other merchants bargain away their garden vegetables and hand-wound bundles of herbs. Right by the market, the pretty little **place aux Herbes** is a picturesque spot for a drink or meal in the deep shade of the plane trees.

On the waterfront opposite the market, a squat medieval bastion crowned with four tiny watchtowers houses the **Musée Jean-Cocteau.** Built in 1636 to defend the port, it was spotted by the artist-poet-filmmaker Jean Cocteau (1889–1963) as the perfect site for a group of his works; he planned and supervised its reconstruction but never saw it finished. Outside its walls, a mosaic in round stone (an homage to the Parvis St-Michel) depicts a lizard; the inside floor answers with a salamander mosaic. There are bright, cartoonish pastels of fishermen and wenches in love, and a fantastical assortment of ceramic animals in the wrought-iron windows he designed himself. ⊠ *Vieux Port,* ☎ *04–93–57–72–30.* ▥ *20 frs.* ☉ *Wed.–Sun. 10–noon and 2–6.*

From the Cocteau Museum, stroll the length of Menton's famous beachfront **promenade du Soleil,** broad, white, and studded with palm trees. The **Casino du Soleil** (⊠ av. Félix-Faure, ☎ 04–93–10–16–16) stakes out the middle of the promenade that shares its name; it's a modest, approachable anti–Monte Carlo.

Directly behind the casino, perpendicular to the beach, the broad tropical **Jardins Biovès** (Biovès Garden) stretch the breadth of the center, sandwiched between two avenues. Its symmetrical flower beds and spires of palms are the spiritual heart of town.

The 19th-century Italianate **Hôtel de Ville** conceals another Cocteau treasure: He decorated the **Salle des Mariages** (Marriage Room), the room in which civil marriages take place, with vibrant allegorical scenes. ⊠ *17 av. de la République.* ▥ *5 frs.* ☉ *Weekdays 8:30–12:30 and 1:30–5.*

At the far west end of town, toward Roquebrune, stands the 18th-century **Palais Carnole** (Carnole Palace) in vast gardens luxuriant with orange, lemon, and grapefruit trees. It was once the summer retreat of the princes of Monaco; nowadays it contains a sizable collection of European paintings from the Renaissance to the present day. The halls of the palace themselves are as interesting as the artworks; the **Grand Salon d'Honneur** (Grand Salon of Honor) retains a rich ensemble of neoclassic grotesques and bas reliefs. ⊠ *3 av. de la Madone,* ☎ *04–93–35–49–71.* ☐ *Free.* ⊙ *Wed.–Sun. 10–noon and 2–6.*

Dining and Lodging

\$\$–\$\$\$
★
✕⌂ **Aiglon.** Sweep down the curving stone stair to the terrazzo mosaic lobby of this lovely 1880 garden villa and wander out for a drink or a meal by the pool. Or settle onto your little balcony overlooking the grounds and a tiny wedge of sea. There's a room for every whim, all soft-edged, comfortable, and romantic. The poolside restaurant, Le Riaumont, serves classic seafood by candlelight; breakfast is served in a shady garden shelter. It's a three-minute walk to the beach. ⊠ *7 av. de la Madone, 06502,* ☎ *04–93–57–55–55,* 𝔽𝔸𝕏 *04–93–35–92–39. 28 rooms, 2 apartments. Restaurant, bar. AE, MC, V.*

\$\$–\$\$\$ ✕⌂ **Royal Westminster.** This Victorian waterfront palace hotel, beautifully restored inside and out in shades of lemon, mint, and robin's egg blue, usually rents out its light-bathed, sea-view rooms to tour groups of seniors by the week. But you might get lucky on a standby basis, calling to reserve no sooner than 10 days in advance, or even dropping in. Beach mattresses and sun parasols are provided in the rooms. ⊠ *1510 promenade du Soleil, 06500,* ☎ *04–93–28–69–69,* 𝔽𝔸𝕏 *04–92–10–12–30. 92 rooms. Restaurant, bar, air-conditioning, billiards. AE, DC, MC, V.*

\$–\$\$ ✕⌂ **Londres.** This modest family-run hotel is on a small patch of greenery just a block from the beach and three blocks from the casino. It has an inexpensive traditional restaurant with outdoor tables and a tiny garden bar. Though the building dates from the turn of the century, rooms have a '70s look, with all-weather carpet, linoleum bathrooms, and acoustic tiles. But most have big French windows that open over the garden and just a sliver of sea view between the buildings. Small back rooms with shower only are a bargain. ⊠ *15 av. Carnot, BP 73, 06502,* ☎ *04–93–35–74–62,* 𝔽𝔸𝕏 *04–93–41–77–78. 27 rooms. Restaurant, bar. AE, MC, V.*

Nightlife and the Arts

The **casino** (⊠ Promenade de Soleil, ☎ 04–93–10–16–16) has the usual slot machines and roulette tables, as well as a disco and a cabaret in its Club 06.

In August the **Festival de Musique de Chambre** (Chamber Music Festival) takes place on the stone-paved plaza outside the St-Michel Church. The **Fête du Citron** (Lemon Festival), at the end of February, celebrates the lemon with Rose Bowl Parade–like floats and sculptures, all made of real fruit.

NICE AND THE EASTERN CÔTE D'AZUR A TO Z

Arriving and Departing

By Plane

The **Nice–Côte d'Azur Airport** (⊠ 7 km/4 mi from Nice, ☎ 04–93–21–30–30) sits on a peninsula between Antibes and Nice. There are frequent flights between Paris and Nice on Air Liberté, AOM, and Air France as well as direct flights on Delta Airlines from New York. The flight time between Paris and Nice is about 1 hour.

By Car

A8 flows briskly from Antibes to Nice to the resorts on the Grand Corniche; N98 follows the coast more closely. From Paris, the main southbound artery is A6/A7, known as the Autoroute du Soleil; it passes through Provence and joins the eastbound A8 at Aix-en-Provence.

By Train

Nice is the major rail crossroads for trains arriving from Paris and other northern cities and from Italy, too. This coastal line, working eastward from Marseille and west from Ventimiglia, stops at Antibes, Monaco, and Menton. To get from Paris to Nice, you can take the TGV, though it only maintains high speeds to Valence before returning to conventional rails and rates.

Getting Around

By Bus

If you want to penetrate deeper into villages and backcountry spots not on the rail line, you can take a bus out of Nice, Antibes, or Menton to the most frequented spots. Pick up a schedule for local and commercial excursion buses at the train station, at tourist offices, and at the local *gare routière* (bus station). Many hotels and excursion companies organize day trips into St-Paul-de-Vence and Vence.

By Car

The best way to explore the secondary sights in this region, especially the deep backcountry, is by car. A car also allows you the freedom to zip along A8 between the coastal resorts and to enjoy the tremendous views from the three Corniches that trace the coast from Nice to the Italian border.

By Train

You can easily move along the coast between Nice and Ventimiglia by train on the slick double-decker Côte d'Azur line, a dramatic and highly tourist-pleasing branch of the SNCF lines that offers panoramic views as it rolls from one famous resort to the next. But train travelers will have difficulty getting up to St-Paul, Vence, Peillon, and other backcountry villages; that you must accomplish by bus or car. It's still possible to climb up into the pre-Alpine arrière-pays via the tiny trestled Italian-French rail line that winds toylike from Ventimiglia in Italy to Breil-sur-Roya in the hills above Menton and on to Turin in Italy. You can catch it out of Nice.

Contacts and Resources

Car Rentals

Most likely you'll want to rent your car at one of the main rail stops, either Nice, Monaco, or Menton, or at the airport in Nice, where all major companies are represented.

Avis (⊠ 2 av. des Phocéens, Nice, ☎ 04–93–80–63–52; ⊠ Nice Airport, ☎ 04–93–21–42–80; ⊠ 9 av. d'Ostende, Monaco, ☎ 377–93–30–17–53). **Budget** (⊠ 23 rue de Belgique, Nice, ☎ 04–93–16–24–16; ⊠ Nice Airport, ☎ 04–93–21–36–50). **Europcar Interrent** (⊠ 6 av. de Suède, Nice, ☎ 04–92–14–44–50; ⊠ Nice Airport, ☎ 04–93–21–43–54; ⊠ 9 av. Thiers, Menton, ☎ 04–93–28–21–80; ⊠ 47 av. de Grande-Bretagne, Monaco, ☎ 377–93–50–74–95). **Hertz** (⊠ 12 av. de Suède, Nice, ☎ 04–93–87–11–87; ⊠ Nice Airport, ☎ 04–93–21–36–72; ⊠ 27 bd. Albert I, Monaco, ☎ 377–93–50–79–60).

Guided Tours

Santa Azur (⊠ 11 av. Jean-Médecin, Nice, ☎ 04–93–85–46–81) organizes all-day or half-day bus excursions to sights near Nice, including Monaco and Cannes, either leaving from their offices or from several stops along the Promenade des Anglais, mainly in front of the big hotels. In Antibes, **100 Tours** (⌧ 8 pl. de Gaulle, Antibes, ☎ 04–93–34–15–98) organizes similar bus explorations of the region.

The city of **Nice** arranges individual guided tours on an à la carte basis, according to your needs. For information contact the Bureau d'Acceuil (☎ 04–93–14–48–00) and specify your dates and language preferences. A small **tourist train** (☎ 04–93–92–45–59) goes along the waterfront from in front of the Casino Ruhl, along cours Saleya, and up to the Château.

Menton is particularly keen to introduce visitors to its rich architectural heritage by offering regular *visites du patrimoine* (heritage tours) to its gardens, its cemetery, its museums and villas. Details on each visit and points and times of departure are published in the city's free *programme des manifestations* (events program), published bi-monthly by the tourist office. They cost 30 francs per person, and there's a passport for four visits for 60 francs. For information contact the Service du Patrimoine (⌧ 5 rue Ciapetta, ☎ 04–92–10–33–66).

In **Antibes** there are guided walking tours of the old town only on the first Tuesday of each month, leaving at 3 PM from the Bibliotheque de l'Antiboulenc (⌧ 34 rue de la Tourraque, ☎ 04–93–34–27–60).

Outdoor Activities and Sports

This is golf country, and you can pick up the brochure and map *Les Golfs du Soleil* (*Golf Courses of the Sun*) and *Destination Golf* at local tourist offices to get a complete listing of golf courses and facilities from St-Tropez to Monaco.

For information on hiking in the mountains above the coast, contact the **Comité Départemental de la Randonée Pedestre des Alpes-Maritimes** (⌧ 2 rue Gustave-Deloye, 06000 Nice), which can furnish itineraries and maps upon written request.

Travel Agencies

MENTON

Havas Voyages (⌧ 11 av. Félix Faure, ☎ 04–92–10–54–04.

MONTE CARLO

American Express Voyages (⌧ 35 bd. Princess Charlotte, ☎ 377/93–25–74–45).

NICE

Havas Voyages (⌧ 12 av. Félix Faure, ☎ 04–93–62–90–27); **Thomas Cook** (⌧ 12 av. Thiers, ☎ 04–93–82–13–00); **American Express Voyages** (⌧ 11 Promenade des Anglais, ☎ 04–93–16–53–47).

Vacation Rentals

Gîtes de France is a nationwide organization that rents vacation housing by the week, outside urban areas, and usually of outstanding regional character. There are very few directly on the coast, as they are by definition *gîte ruraux* (rural lodgings), but there are exceptions. The prettiest represent the Italian-style stucco mountain houses and farms that cover the hills behind the coast; they provide easy access to the countryside, villages, churches, and markets that are part of the region's rhythm.

The headquarters for the region covered in this chapter is **Gîtes de France des Alpes-Maritimes** (⌧ 55 Promenadè des Anglais, B.P. 1602, 06011 Nice Cedex 01, ☎ 04–92–15–21–30, FAX 04–93–86–01–06, www.crt-riviera.fr/gites06). Write or call for a catalog, then make a selection and reservation. For general information on gîtes, *see* Close-Up Box: The Gîte Way *in* Chapter 1 and Lodging *in* the Gold Guide.

The tourist offices of individual towns often publish lists of *locations meublés* (furnished rentals), sometimes vouched for by the tourist office and rated for comfort. Select the town you'd like to be near and write or fax their tourist office (☞ Visitor Information, *below*) to a request a list.

Visitor Information

The **Comité Régional du Tourisme Riviera Côte d'Azur** (⊠ 55 Promenade des Anglais, B.P. 1602, 06011 Nice Cedex 1, ☎ 04–93–37–78–78; www.crt-riviera.fr) provides information on tourism throughout the department of Alpes-Maritimes, from Cannes to the Italian border.

Local tourist offices in major towns discussed in this chapter are as follows: **Antibes/Juan-les-Pins** (⊠ 11 pl. de Gaulle, 06600 Antibes, ☎ 04–92–90–53–00, FAX 04–92–90–53–01). **Cagnes-sur-Mer** (⊠ 6 bd. Maréchal Juin, B.P. 48, 06800, ☎ 04–93–20–61–64, FAX 04–92–20–52–63). **Menton** (⊠ Palais de l'Europe, av. Boyer, 06500, ☎ 04–92–41–76–76, FAX 04–92–41–76–78). **Monaco** (⊠ 2a bd. des Moulins, 98000, Monte Carlo, ☎ 377–92–16–61–66, FAX 377–92–16–61–66). **Nice** (⊠ 5 Promenade des Anglais, 06000, ☎ 04–92–14–48–00, FAX 04–92–14–48–03; or in person at the train station or airport). **Roquebrune-Cap Martin** (⊠ 20 av. Paul Doumer, 06190, ☎ 04–93–35–62–87, FAX 04–93–28–57–00). **St-Jean-Cap-Ferrat** (⊠ 59 av. Denis Semeria, 06230, ☎ 04–93–76–08–90, FAX 04–93–76–16–67). **St-Paul-de-Vence** (⊠ 2 rue Grande, 06570, ☎ 04–93–32–86–95, FAX 04–93–32–60–27). **Tende-Roya** (⊠ av. du 16-Septembre 1947, 06430, ☎ 04–93–04–73–71, FAX 04–93–04–35–09). **Vence** (⊠ pl. du Grand Jardin, 06140, ☎ 04–93–58–06–38, FAX 04–93–58–91–81). **Villefranche-sur-Mer** (⊠ Jardin François-Binon, 06230, ☎ 04–93–01–73–68, FAX 04–93–76–63–65).

7 Portraits of Provence and the Côte d'Azur

*Provence and the Côte d'Azur
at a Glance: A Chronology*

Postcards from Summer

Books and Videos

PROVENCE AND THE CÔTE D'AZUR AT A GLANCE: A CHRONOLOGY

ca. 600 BC   Greek colonists found Marseille.

after 500 BC   Celts appear in France.

58–51 BC   Julius Caesar conquers Gaul; writes up the war in *De Bello Gallico*.

52 BC   Lutetia, later to become Paris, is built by the Gallo-Romans.

46 BC   Roman amphitheater built at Arles.

14 BC   The Pont du Gard aqueduct at Nîmes is erected.

AD 406   Invasion by the Vandals (Germanic tribes).

The Merovingian Dynasty

486–511   Clovis, king of the Franks (481–511), defeats the Roman governor of Gaul and founds the Merovingian dynasty. Great monasteries, such as those at Tours, Limoges, and Chartres, become centers of culture.

497   Franks converted to Christianity.

567   The Frankish kingdom is divided into three parts—the eastern countries (Austrasia), later to become Belgium and Germany; the western countries (Neustria), later to become France; and Burgundy.

The Carolingian Dynasty

768–778   Charlemagne (768–814) becomes king of the Franks (768), conquers northern Italy (774), and is defeated by the Moors at Roncesvalles, Spain, after which he consolidates the Pyrénées border (778).

800   The pope crowns Charlemagne Holy Roman Emperor in Rome. Charlemagne expands the French kingdom far beyond its present borders and establishes a center for learning at his capital, Aix-la-Chapelle (Aachen, in present-day Germany).

814–987   Death of Charlemagne. The Carolingian line continues through a dozen or so monarchs, with a batch called Charles (the Bald, the Fat, the Simple) and a sprinkling of Louises. Under the Treaty of Verdun (843), the empire is divided in two—the eastern half becoming Germany, the western half, France. Provence is given to Lothair I. The Kingdom of Provence is founded in 879, joins Arles in 933.

The Capetian Dynasty

987   Hugh Capet (987–996) is made king of France and establishes the principle of hereditary rule for his descendants.

1066   Norman conquest of England by William the Conqueror (1028–87).

ca. 1100   Development of European vernacular verse: *Chanson de Roland*. The Gothic style of architecture begins to appear.

1112–1245   Provence ruled by the counts of Barcelona.

ca. 1150   Struggle between the Anglo-Norman kings (Angevin Empire) and the French; when Eleanor of Aquitaine switches husbands (from

Louis VII of France to Henry II of England), her extensive lands pass to English rule.

1245–1481 Provence ruled by the dukes of Anjou.

1270 Louis IX (1226–70), the only French king to achieve sainthood, dies in Tunis on the seventh and last Crusade.

1302–07 Philippe IV the Fair (1285–1314) calls together the first States-General, predecessor to the French Parliament. He disbands the Knights Templars to gain their wealth (1307).

1309 Pope, under pressure, leaves a corrupt and disorderly Rome for Avignon in southern France, seat of the papacy for nearly 70 years.

The Valois Dynasty

1337–1453 Hundred Years' War between France and England: fighting for control of those areas of France gained by the English crown following the marriage of Eleanor of Aquitaine and Henry II.

1348–50 The Black Death rages in France.

1428–31 Joan of Arc (1412–31), the Maid of Orléans, sparks the revival of French fortunes in the Hundred Years' War but is captured by the English and burned at the stake at Rouen.

1453 France finally defeats England, terminating the Hundred Years' War and English claims to the French throne.

1494 Italian wars: beginning of Franco-Hapsburg struggle for hegemony in Europe.

1515–47 Reign of François I, who imports Italian artists, including Leonardo da Vinci (1452–1519), and brings the Renaissance to France. The Château of Fontainebleau is begun (1528).

1562–98 Wars of Religion: Catholics versus Huguenots (French Protestants).

The Bourbon Dynasty

1589 The first Bourbon king, Henri IV (1589–1610) is a Protestant who converts to Catholicism and achieves peace in France. He signs the Edict of Nantes, giving limited freedom of worship to Protestants.

ca. 1610 Scientific revolution in Europe begins, marked by the discoveries of mathematician and philosopher René Descartes (1596–1650).

1643–1715 Reign of Louis XIV, the Sun King, a monarch who builds the Baroque power base of Versailles and presents Europe with a glorious view of France. With his first minister, Colbert, Louis makes France, by force of arms, the most powerful nation-state in Europe. He persecutes the Huguenots, who emigrate in great numbers, nearly ruining the French economy.

1660 Classical period of French culture: Dramatists Pierre Corneille (1606–84), Jean-Baptiste Molière (1622–73), and Jean Racine (1639–99), and painter Nicolas Poussin (1594–1665).

1700– onward Writer and pedagogue François-Marien Voltaire (1694–1778) is a central figure in the French Enlightenment, along with Jean-Jacques Rousseau (1712–78) and Denis Diderot (1713–84), who in 1751 compiles the first modern encyclopedia. The ideals of the Enlightenment—for reason and scientific method and against social and political injustices—pave the way for the French Revolution. In the arts, painter Jacques-Louis David (1748–1825) reinforces revolutionary creeds in his neoclassical works.

ca. 1715 Rococo art and decoration develop, typified by the painter Antoine Watteau (1684–1721) and, later, François Boucher (1703–70) and Jean-Honoré Fragonard (1732–1806).

1756–63 The Seven Years' War results in France's losing most of its overseas possessions and in England becoming a world power.

1776 The French assist in the American War of Independence. Ideals of liberty cross the Atlantic with the returning troops to reinforce new social concepts.

The French Revolution

1789–1804 The Bastille is stormed on July 14, 1789. Following early Republican ideals is the Reign of Terror and the administration of the Directory under Robespierre. There are widespread political executions—Louis XVI and Marie Antoinette are guillotined in 1793. Reaction sets in, and the instigators of the Terror are themselves executed (1794). Napoléon Bonaparte enters the Directory (1795–99) and is installed as First Consul during the Consulate (1799–1804).

1790 The départements of Bouches-du-Rhône, Var, and Basses-Alpes and the *parats* of Drôme, Alpes-Maritimes, and Vaucluse are formed from Provence.

The First Empire

1804 Napoléon crowns himself emperor of France at Notre-Dame in the presence of the pope.

1805–12 Napoléon conquers most of Europe. The Napoleonic Age is marked by a neoclassical artistic style called Empire as well as by the rise of Romanticism—characterized by such writers as François-Auguste-René de Chateaubriand (1768–1848) and Marie-Henri Stendhal (1783–1842), and the painters Eugène Delacroix (1798–1863) and Théodore Géricault (1791–1824)—which is to dominate the arts of the 19th century.

1812–14 Winter cold and Russian determination defeat Napoléon outside Moscow. The emperor abdicates and is transported to Elba.

Restoration of the Bourbons

1814–15 Louis XVIII, brother of the executed Louis XVI, regains the throne after the Congress of Vienna settles peace terms.

1815 The Hundred Days: Napoléon returns from Elba and musters an army on his march to the capital, but lacks national support. He is defeated at Waterloo (June 18) and exiled to the island of St. Helena in the south Atlantic.

1821 Napoléon dies in exile.

1830 Bourbon king Charles X, locked into a prerevolutionary state of mind, abdicates. A brief upheaval (Three Glorious Days) brings Louis-Philippe, the Citizen King, to the throne.

1840 Napoléon's remains are brought back to Paris.

1846–48 Severe industrial and farming depression contributes to Louis-Philippe's abdication (1848).

Second Republic and Second Empire

1848–52 Louis-Napoléon (nephew and step-grandson of Napoléon I) is elected president of the short-lived Second Republic. He makes a successful attempt to assume supreme power and is declared emperor of France, taking the title Napoléon III.

ca. 1850 The ensuing period is characterized in the arts by the emergence of realist painters—Jean-François Millet (1814–75), Honoré Daumier (1808–79), Gustave Courbet (1819–77)—and late-Romantic writers—Victor Hugo (1802–85), Honoré de Balzac (1799–1850), and Charles Baudelaire (1821–87).

1863 Napoléon III inaugurates the Salon des Refusés in response to critical opinion. It includes work by Édouard Manet (1832–83), Claude Monet (1840–1926), and Paul Cézanne (1839–1906) and is commonly regarded as the birthplace of Impressionism and of modern art in general.

The Third Republic

1870–71 The Franco-Prussian War sees Paris besieged by and fall to the Germans. Napoléon III takes refuge in England.

1871–1914 Before World War I, France expands its industries and builds vast colonial empires in North Africa and Southeast Asia. Sculptor Auguste Rodin (1840–1917), composers Maurice Ravel (1875–1937) and Claude Debussy (1862–1918), and poets such as Stéphane Mallarmé (1842–98) and Paul Verlaine (1844–96) set the stage for Modernism.

1874 Emergence of the Impressionist school of painting: Monet, Pierre Auguste Renoir (1841–1919), and Edgar Degas (1834–1917).

1894–1906 Franco-Russian Alliance (1894). Dreyfus affair: The spy trial and its anti-Semitic backlash shock France.

1904 The Entente Cordiale: England and France become firm allies.

1914–18 During World War I, France fights with the Allies, opposing Germany, Austria-Hungary, and Turkey. Germany invades France.

1918–39 Between wars, France attracts artists and writers, including Americans Ernest Hemingway (1899–1961) and Gertrude Stein (1874–1946). The country nourishes major artistic and philosophical movements: Constructivism, Dadaism, Surrealism, and Existentialism.

1939–45 At the beginning of World War II, France fights with the Allies until invaded and defeated by Germany in 1940. The French government, under Marshal Philippe Pétain (1856–1951), moves to Vichy and cooperates with the Nazis. French overseas colonies split between allegiance to the legal government of Vichy and declaration for the Free French Resistance, led (from London) by General Charles de Gaulle (1890–1970).

1944 D-Day, June 6: The Allies land on the beaches of Normandy and successfully invade France. Additional Allied forces land in Provence. Paris is liberated in August 1944, and France declares full allegiance to the Allies.

1944–46 A provisional government takes power under General de Gaulle; American aid assists French recovery.

The Fourth Republic

1946 France adopts a new constitution; French women gain the right to vote.

1946–54 In the Indochinese War, France is unable to regain control of its colonies in Southeast Asia. The 1954 Geneva Agreement establishes two governments in Vietnam: one in the north, under the Communist leader Ho Chi Minh, and one in the south, under the emperor Bao Dai. U.S. involvement eventually leads to French withdrawal.

1954–62 The Algerian Revolution achieves Algeria's independence from France. Other French African colonies gain independence.

1957 The Treaty of Rome establishes the European Economic Community (now known as the European Union—EU) with France as one of its members.

The Fifth Republic

1958–68 De Gaulle is the first president under a new constitution; he resigns in 1968 after widespread disturbances begun by student riots in Paris.

1976 The first supersonic transatlantic passenger service begins with the Anglo-French Concorde.

1981 François Mitterrand (1916–1996) is elected the first Socialist president of France since World War II.

1988 Mitterrand is elected for a second term.

1990 TGV (*Trains à Grande Vitesse*) train clocks a world record—515 kph (322 mph)—on a practice run. Channel Tunnel linkup between France and England begun.

1995 Jacques Chirac, mayor of Paris, is elected president.

1996 Mitterrand dies.

1997 President Chirac calls early elections, a Socialist coalition wins a majority, and Lionel Jospin is appointed prime minister.

1998 France hosts (and wins) the World Cup soccer tournament, with matches in Marseille and other parts of the country.

POSTCARDS FROM SUMMER

IT HAS TAKEN US three years to accept the fact that we live in the same house, but in two different places.

What we think of as normal life starts in September. Apart from market days in the towns, there are no crowds. Traffic on the back roads is sparse during the day— a tractor, a few vans—and virtually nonexistent at night. There is always a table in every restaurant, except perhaps for Sunday lunch. Social life is intermittent and uncomplicated. The baker has bread, the plumber has time for a chat, the postman has time for a drink. After the first deafening weekend of the hunting season, the forest is quiet. Each field has a stooped, reflective figure working among the vines, very slowly up one line, very slowly down the next. The hours between noon and two are dead.

And then we come to July and August.

We used to treat them as just another two months of the year; hot months, certainly, but nothing that required much adjustment on our part except to make sure that the afternoon included a siesta.

We were wrong. Where we live in July and August is still the Luberon, but it's not the same Luberon. It is the Luberon *en vacances,* and our past efforts to live normally during abnormal times have been miserably unsuccessful. So unsuccessful that we once considered cancelling summer altogether and going somewhere grey and cool and peaceful, like the Hebrides.

But if we did, we would probably miss it, all of it, even the days and incidents that have reduced us to sweating, irritated, overtired zombies. So we have decided to come to terms with the Luberon in the summer, to do our best to join the rest of the world on holiday and, like them, to send postcards telling distant friends about the wonderful time we are having. Here are a few.

Saint-Tropez

Cherchez les nudistes! It is open season for nature lovers, and there is likely to be a sharp increase in the number of applicants wishing to join the Saint-Tropez police force.

The mayor, Monsieur Spada, has flown in the face of years of tradition (Saint-Tropez made public nudity famous, after all) and has decreed that in the name of safety and hygiene there will be no more naked sunbathing on the public beaches. *"Le nudisme intégral est interdit,"* says Monsieur Spada, and he has empowered the police to seize and arrest any offenders. Well, perhaps not to seize them, but to track them down and fine them 75 francs, or as much as 1,500 francs if they have been guilty of creating a public outrage. Exactly where a nudist might keep 1,500 francs is a question that is puzzling local residents.

Meanwhile, a defiant group of nudists has set up headquarters in some rocks behind *la plage de la Moutte*. A spokeswoman for the group has said that under no circumstances would bathing suits be worn. Wish you were here.

The Melon Field

Faustin's brother Jacky, a wiry little man of 60 or so, grows melons in the field opposite the house. It's a large field, but he does all the work himself, and by hand. In the spring I have often seen him out there for six or seven hours, back bent like a hinge, his hoe chopping at the weeds that threaten to strangle his crop. He doesn't spray— who would eat a melon tasting of chemicals?—and I think he must enjoy looking after his land in the traditional way.

Now that the melons are ripening, he comes to the field at 6 every morning to pick the ones that are ready. He takes them up to Ménerbes to be packed in shallow wooden crates. From Ménerbes they go to Cavaillon, and from Cavaillon to Avignon, to Paris, everywhere. It amuses Jacky to think of people in smart restaurants paying *une petite fortune* for a simple thing like a melon.

If I get up early enough I can catch him before he goes to Ménerbes. He always has a couple of melons that are too ripe to travel, and he sells them to me for a few francs.

As I walk back to the house, the sun clears the top of the mountain and it is suddenly hot on my face. The melons, heavy and satisfying in my hands, are still cool from the night air. We have them for breakfast, fresh and sweet, less than 10 minutes after they have been picked.

Behind the Bar

There is a point at which a swimming pool ceases to be luxury and becomes very close to a necessity, and that point is when the temperature hits 100 degrees. Whenever people ask us about renting a house for the summer, we always tell them this, and some of them listen.

Others don't, and within two days of arriving they are on the phone telling us what we told them months before. It's so *hot,* they say. Too hot for tennis, too hot for cycling, too hot for sightseeing, too hot, too hot. Oh, for a pool. You're so lucky.

There is a hopeful pause. Is it my imagination, or can I actually hear the drops of perspiration falling like summer rain on the pages of the telephone directory?

I suppose the answer is to be callous but helpful. There is a public swimming pool near Apt, if you don't mind sharing the water with a few hundred small brown dervishes on their school holidays. There is the Mediterranean, only an hour's drive away; no, with traffic it could take two hours. Make sure you have some bottles of Evian in the car. It wouldn't do to get dehydrated.

Or you could close the shutters against the sun, spend the day in the house, and spring forth refreshed into the evening air. It would be difficult to acquire the souvenir suntan, but at least there would be no chance of heatstroke.

These brutal and unworthy suggestions barely have time to cross my mind before the voice of despair turns into the voice of relief. Of course! We could come over in the morning for a quick dip without disturbing you. Just a splash. You won't even know we've been.

They come at noon, with friends. They swim. They take the sun. Thirst creeps up on them, much to their surprise, and that's why I'm behind the bar. My wife is in the kitchen, making lunch for six. *Vivent les vacances.*

The Night Walk

The dogs cope with the heat by sleeping through it, stretched out in the courtyard or curled in the shade of the rosemary hedge. They come to life as the pink in the sky is turning to darkness, sniffing the breeze, jostling each other around our feet in their anticipation of a walk. We take the flashlight and follow them into the forest.

It smells of warm pine needles and baked earth, dry and spicy when we step on a patch of thyme. Small, invisible creatures slither away from us and rustle through the leaves of the wild box that grows like a weed.

Sounds carry: *cigales* and frogs, the muffled thump of music through the open window of a faraway house, the clinks and murmurs of dinner drifting up from Faustin's terrace. The hills on the other side of the valley, uninhabited for 10 months a year, are pricked with lights that will be switched off at the end of August.

We get back to the house and take off our shoes, and the warmth of the flagstones is an invitation to swim. A dive into dark water, and then a last glass of wine. The sky is clear except for a jumble of stars; it will be hot again tomorrow. Hot and slow, just like today.

Knee-deep in Lavender

I had been cutting lavender with a pair of pruning shears and I was making a slow, amateurish job of it, nearly an hour to do fewer than a dozen clumps. When Henriette arrived at the house with a basket of aubergines, I was pleased to have the chance to stop. Henriette looked at the lavender, looked at the pruning shears, and shook her head at the ignorance of her neighbor. Didn't I know how to cut lavender? What was I doing with those pruning shears? Where was my *faucille?*

She went to her van and came back with a blackened sickle, its needle-sharp tip embedded in an old wine cork for safety. It was surprisingly light, and felt sharp enough to shave with. I made a few passes with it in the air, and Henriette shook her head again. Obviously, I needed a lesson.

She hitched up her skirt and attacked the nearest row of lavender, gathering the long stems into a tight bunch with one arm and slicing them off at the bottom with a single smooth pull of the sickle. In five minutes she had cut more than I had in an hour.

It looked easy; bend, gather, pull. Nothing to it.

"Voilà!" said Henriette. "When I was a little girl in the Basses-Alpes, we had hectares of lavender, and no machines. Everyone used the *faucille.*"

She passed it back to me, told me to mind my legs, and went off to join Faustin in the vines.

It wasn't as easy as it looked, and my first effort produced a ragged, uneven clump, more chewed than sliced. I realized that the sickle was made for right-handed lavender cutters, and had to compensate for being left-handed by slicing away from me. My wife came out to tell me to mind my legs. She doesn't trust me with sharp implements, and so she was reassured to see me cutting away from the body. Even with my genius for self-inflicted wounds there seemed to be little risk of amputation.

I had just come to the final clump when Henriette came back. I looked up, hoping for praise, and sliced my index finger nearly through to the bone. There was a great deal of blood, and Henriette asked me if I was giving myself a manicure. I sometimes wonder about her sense of humor. Two days later she gave me a sickle of my very own, and told me that I was forbidden to use it unless I was wearing gloves.

The Alcoholic Tendencies of Wasps

The Provençal wasp, although small, has an evil sting. He also has an ungallant, hit-and-run method of attack in the swimming pool. He paddles up behind his unsuspecting victim, waits until an arm is raised, and—*tok!*—strikes deep into the armpit. It hurts for several hours, and often causes people who have been stung to dress in protective clothing before they go swimming. This is the local version of the Miss Wet T-shirt contest.

I don't know whether all wasps like water, but here they love it—floating in the shallow end, dozing in the puddles on the flagstones, keeping an eye out for the unguarded armpit and the tender extremity—and after one disastrous day during which not only armpits but inner thighs received direct hits (obviously, some wasps can hold their breath and operate under water), I was sent off to look for wasp traps.

When I found them, in a *droguerie* in the back alleys of Cavaillon, I was lucky enough to find a wasp expert behind the counter. He demonstrated for me the latest model in traps, a plastic descendant of the old glass hanging traps that can sometimes be found in flea markets. It had been specially designed, he said, for use around swimming pools, and could be made irresistible to wasps.

It was in two parts. The base was a round bowl, raised off the ground by three flat supports, with a funnel leading up from the bottom. The top fitted over the lower bowl and prevented wasps who had made their way up the funnel from escaping.

But that, said the wasp expert, was the simple part. More difficult, more subtle, more artistic, was the bait. How does one persuade the wasp to abandon the pleasures of the flesh and climb up the funnel into the trap? What could tempt him away from the pool?

After spending some time in Provence, you learn to expect a brief lecture with every purchase, from an organically grown cabbage (two minutes) to a bed (half an hour or more, depending on the state of your back). For wasp traps, you should allow between 10 and 15 minutes. I sat on the stool in front of the counter and listened.

Wasps, it turned out, like alcohol. Some wasps like it *sucré,* others like it fruity, and there are even those who will crawl anywhere for a drop of *anis.* It is, said the expert, a matter of experimentation, a balancing of flavors and consistencies until one finds the blend that suits the palate of the local wasp population.

He suggested a few basic recipes: sweet vermouth with honey and water, diluted *crème de cassis,* dark beer spiked with *marc,* neat *pastis.* As an added inducement, the funnel can be lightly coated with honey, and a small puddle of water should always be left immediately beneath the funnel.

The expert set up a trap on the counter, and with two fingers imitated a wasp out for a stroll.

He stops, attracted by the puddle of water. The fingers stopped. He approaches the water, and then he becomes aware of something delicious above him. He climbs up the funnel to investigate, he jumps into his cocktail, *et voilà!*—he is unable to get out, being too drunk to crawl back down the funnel. He dies, but he dies happy.

I bought two traps, and tried out the recipes. All of them worked, which leads me to believe that the wasp has a serious drinking problem. And now, if ever a guest is overcome by strong waters, he is described as being as pissed as a wasp.

Maladie du Luberon

Most of the seasonal ailments of summer, while they may be uncomfortable or painful or merely embarrassing, are at least regarded with some sympathy. A man convalescing after an explosive encounter with one *merguez* sausage too many is not expected to venture back into polite society until his constitution has recovered. The same is true of third-degree sunburn, *rosé* poisoning, scorpion bites, a surfeit of garlic, or the giddiness and nausea caused by prolonged exposure to French bureaucracy. One suffers, but one is allowed to suffer alone and in peace.

There is another affliction, worse than scorpions or rogue sausages, which we have experienced ourselves and seen many times in other permanent residents of this quiet corner of France. Symptoms usually appear some time around mid-July and persist until early September: glazed and bloodshot eyes, yawning, loss of appetite, shortness of temper, lethargy, and a mild form of paranoia that manifests itself in sudden urges to join a monastery.

This is the *maladie du Luberon,* or creeping social fatigue, and it provokes about the same degree of sympathy as a millionaire's servant problems.

If we examine the patients—the permanent residents—we can see why it happens. Permanent residents have their work, their local friends, their unhurried routines. They made a deliberate choice to live in the Luberon instead of one of the cocktail capitals of the world because they wanted, if not to get away from it all, to get away from most of it. This eccentricity is understood and tolerated for 10 months a year.

Try to explain that in July and August. Here come the visitors, fresh from the plane or hot off the *autoroute,* panting for social action. Let's meet some of the locals! To hell with the book in the hammock and the walk in the woods. To hell with solitude; they want people—people for lunch, people for drinks, people for dinner—and so invitations and counterinvitations fly back and forth until every day for weeks has its own social highlight.

As the holiday comes to an end with one final multibottle dinner, it is possible to see even on the visitors' faces some traces of weariness. They had no idea it was so lively down here. They are only half-joking when they say they're going to need a rest to get over the whirl of the past few days. Is it always like this? How do you keep it up?

It isn't, and we don't. Like many of our friends, we collapse in between visitations, guarding empty days and free evenings, eating little and drinking less, going to bed early. And every year, when the dust has settled, we talk to other members of the distressed residents' association about ways of making summer less of an endurance test.

We all agree that firmness is the answer. Say no more often than yes. Harden the heart against the surprise visitor who cannot find a hotel room, the deprived child who has no swimming pool, the desperate traveler who has lost his wallet. Be firm; be helpful, be kind, be rude, but above all *be firm.*

And yet I know—I think we all know—that next summer will be the same. I suppose we must enjoy it. Or we would, if we weren't exhausted.

Place du Village

Cars have been banned from the village square, and stalls or trestle tables have been set up on three sides. On the fourth, a framework of scaffolding, blinking with colored lights, supports a raised platform made from wooden planks. Outside the café, the usual single row of tables and chairs has been multiplied by 10, and an extra waiter has been taken on to serve the sprawl of customers stretching from the butcher's down to the post office. Children and dogs chase each other through the crowd, stealing lumps of sugar from the tables and dodging the old men's sticks that are waved in mock anger. Nobody will go to bed early tonight, not even the children, because this is the village's annual party, the *fête votive.*

It begins in the late afternoon with a *pot d'amitié* in the square and the official opening of the stalls. Local artisans, the men's faces shining from an afternoon shave, stand behind their tables, glass in hand, or make final adjustments to their displays. There is pottery and jewelry, honey and lavender essence, hand-woven fabrics, iron and stone artifacts, paintings and wood carvings, books, postcards, tooled leatherwork, corkscrews with twisted olive-wood handles, patterned sachets of dried herbs. The woman selling pizza does brisk business as the first glass of wine begins to make the crowd hungry.

People drift off, eat, drift back. The night comes down, warm and still, the mountains in the distance just visible as deep black humps against the sky. The three-man accordion band tunes up on the platform and launches into the first of many *paso dobles* while the rock group from Avignon that will follow later rehearses on beer and *pastis* in the café.

The first dancers appear—an old man and his granddaughter, her nose pressed into his belt buckle, her feet balanced precariously on his feet. They are joined by a mother, father, and daughter dancing *à trois*, and then by several elderly couples, holding each other with stiff formality, their faces set with concentration as they try to retrace the steps they learned 50 years ago.

The *paso doble* session comes to an end with a flourish and a ruffle of accordions and drums, and the rock group warms up with five minutes of electronic tweaks that bounce off the old stone walls of the church opposite the platform.

The group's singer, a well-built young lady in tight black Lycra and a screaming orange wig, has attracted an audience before singing a note. An old man, the peak of his cap almost meeting the jut of his chin, has dragged a chair across from the café to sit directly in front of the microphone. As the singer starts her first number, some village boys made bold by his example come out of the shadows to stand by the old man's chair. All of them stare as though hypnotized at the shiny black pelvis rotating just above their heads.

The village girls, short of partners, dance with each other, as close as possible to the backs of the mesmerized boys. One of the waiters puts down his tray to caper in front of a pretty girl sitting with her parents. She blushes and ducks her head, but her mother nudges her to dance. Go on. The holiday will soon be over.

After an hour of music that threatens to dislodge the windows of the houses around the square, the group performs its finale. With an intensity worthy of Piaf on a sad night, the singer gives us *"Comme d'habitude,"* or "My Way," ending with a sob, her orange head bent over the microphone. The old man nods and bangs his stick on the ground, and the dancers go back to the café to see if there's any beer left.

Normally, there would have been *feux d'artifice* shooting up from the field behind the war memorial. This year, because of the drought, fireworks are forbidden. But it was a good *fête*. And did you see how the postman danced?

By Peter Mayle

In his second popular book on life in Provence, *Toujours Provence*, British writer Peter Mayle wittily evokes the charms of locals and visitors alike.

BOOKS AND VIDEOS

TO SET THE TONE FOR YOUR *séjour* (stay) in the south of France, take time to look into literature and films set in the region. A few choice reads by Lost Generation ex-patriates include: F. Scott Fitzgerald's *Tender Is the Night,* in which Dick and Nicole Diver wallow in jaded decadence in Juan-les-Pins, and John Dos Passos' *The Best Times,* written in and about Antibes. Henry Miller wrote to Anaïs Nin in *Letters to Anaïs Nin* of his sojourns on the Riviera. And Peter Mayle put the Luberon on the map with his essays on southern bliss and culture shock in *A Year in Provence* and *Toujours Provence,* then wrote two novels expanding on the theme: *Toujours Provence* and *Chasing Cézanne.*

Provence produced several literary stars, from the epic poetry of Frédéric Mistral *(Miranda),* father of the revival of the Provençal language, to the austere novels of Jean Giono—*Regain* and *Jean Le Bleu*—dark with the chill of Haute Provence. Alphonse Daudet wrote folklore and tall tales from his beloved mill in Fontvieille in *Lettres de Mon Moulin.*

Changing hats from playwright to screenwriter to director to novelist to memoirist, Marcel Pagnol was the quintessential raconteur, a great storyteller with a gift for evoking the sensations and smells of Provence as well as the lilting language.

The original plays of his Marseille trilogy—*Marius, Fanny,* and *César*—were later developed into films thick with the tried-and-true Midi accent of the Provençal actor Raimu. And there are a dozen of other films of equal charm, including his own version of *Manon des Sources (Manon of the Springs),* with his wife Jacqueline cast as the young goat girl. He wrote four volumes of memoirs, the *Souvenirs d'un Enfance.* Other directors' efforts to evoke his atmospheric stories include Claude Berri's *Jean de Florette* and *Manon des Sources* (1986), filmed in the Luberon, as well as Yves Robert's version of *La Gloire de Mon Père (My Father's Glory,* 1990) and *Le Château de Ma Mère (My Mother's Château,* 1990).

To recapture the '60s glamour of the Riviera, rent a video of Hitchcock's suspense classic *To Catch a Thief* (1955), with Cary Grant and Grace Kelly; Roger Vadim's *And God Created Woman* (1957), which in turn created Brigitte Bardot and St-Tropez; *La Cage aux Folles* (1978), with scenes in the market, port, and old town of St-Tropez; and *Two for the Road* (1967), with Albert Finney and Audrey Hepburn, whose yearly vacation in France—for better, for worse—passes by the south. It's the other end of the social spectrum in the film *Marius et Jeannette* (1998), directed by Robert Guedidguan and set in working-class L'Estaque, outside Marseille.

FRENCH VOCABULARY

One of the trickiest French sounds to pronounce is the nasal final *n* sound (whether or not the *n* is actually the last letter of the word). You should try to pronounce it as a sort of nasal grunt—as in "huh." The vowel that precedes the *n* will govern the vowel sound of the word, and in this list we precede the final *n* with an *h* to remind you to be nasal.

Another problem sound is the ubiquitous but untransliterable *eu*, as in *bleu* (blue) or *deux* (two), and the very similar sound in *je* (I), *ce* (this), and *de* (of). The closest equivalent might be the vowel sound in "put," but rounded.

Words and Phrases

	English	French	Pronunciation
Basics			
	Yes/no	Oui/non	wee/nohn
	Please	S'il vous plaît	seel voo **play**
	Thank you	Merci	mair-**see**
	You're welcome	De rien	deh ree-**ehn**
	That's all right	Il n'y a pas de quoi	eel nee ah pah de **kwah**
	Excuse me, sorry	Pardon	pahr-**dohn**
	Sorry!	Désolé(e)	day-zoh-**lay**
	Good morning/ afternoon	Bonjour	bohn-**zhoor**
	Good evening	Bonsoir	bohn-**swahr**
	Goodbye	Au revoir	o ruh-**vwahr**
	Mr. (Sir)	Monsieur	muh-**syuh**
	Mrs. (Ma'am)	Madame	ma-**dam**
	Miss	Mademoiselle	mad-mwa-**zel**
	Pleased to meet you	Enchanté(e)	ohn-shahn-**tay**
	How are you?	Comment ça va?	kuh-mahn-sa-**va**
	Very well, thanks	Très bien, merci	tray bee-ehn, mair-**see**
	And you?	Et vous?	ay **voo**?
Numbers			
	one	un	uhn
	two	deux	deuh
	three	trois	twah
	four	quatre	**kaht**-ruh
	five	cinq	sank
	six	six	seess
	seven	sept	set
	eight	huit	wheat
	nine	neuf	nuff
	ten	dix	deess
	eleven	onze	ohnz
	twelve	douze	dooz

thirteen	treize	trehz
fourteen	quatorze	kah-**torz**
fifteen	quinze	kanz
sixteen	seize	sez
seventeen	dix-sept	deez-**set**
eighteen	dix-huit	deez-**wheat**
nineteen	dix-neuf	deez-**nuff**
twenty	vingt	vehn
twenty-one	vingt-et-un	vehnt-ay-**uhn**
thirty	trente	trahnt
forty	quarante	ka-**rahnt**
fifty	cinquante	sang-**kahnt**
sixty	soixante	swa-**sahnt**
seventy	soixante-dix	swa-sahnt-**deess**
eighty	quatre-vingts	kaht-ruh-**vehn**
ninety	quatre-vingt-dix	kaht-ruh-vehn-**deess**
one-hundred	cent	sahn
one-thousand	mille	meel

Colors

black	noir	nwahr
blue	bleu	bleuh
brown	brun/marron	bruhn/mar-**rohn**
green	vert	vair
orange	orange	o-**rahnj**
pink	rose	rose
red	rouge	rooje
violet	violette	vee-o-**let**
white	blanc	blahnk
yellow	jaune	zhone

Days of the Week

Sunday	dimanche	**dee**-mahnsh
Monday	lundi	**luhn**-dee
Tuesday	mardi	**mahr**-dee
Wednesday	mercredi	**mair**-kruh-dee
Thursday	jeudi	**zhuh**-dee
Friday	vendredi	**vawn**-druh-dee
Saturday	samedi	**sahm**-dee

Months

January	janvier	**zhahn**-vee-ay
February	février	**feh**-vree-ay
March	mars	marce
April	avril	a-**vreel**
May	mai	meh
June	juin	zhwehn
July	juillet	**zhwee**-ay
August	août	oot
September	septembre	sep-**tahm**-bruh
October	octobre	awk-**to**-bruh
November	novembre	no-**vahm**-bruh
December	décembre	day-**sahm**-bruh

Useful Phrases

English	French	Pronunciation
Do you speak . . . English?	Parlez-vous . . . anglais?	par-lay **voo** **ahn**-glay
I don't speak . . . French	Je ne parle pas . . . français	zhuh nuh parl **pah** frahn-**say**
I don't understand	Je ne comprends pas	zhuh nuh kohm-prahn **pah**
I understand	Je comprends	zhuh kohm-**prahn**
I don't know	Je ne sais pas	zhuh nuh say **pah**
I'm American/ British	Je suis américain/ anglais	zhuh sweez a-may-ree-**kehn**/ahn-**glay**
What's your name?	Comment vous appelez-vous?	ko-mahn voo za-pell-ay-**voo**
My name is . . .	Je m'appelle . . .	zhuh ma-**pell** . . .
What time is it?	Quelle heure est-il?	kel air eh-**teel**
How?	Comment?	ko-**mahn**
When?	Quand?	kahn
Yesterday	Hier	yair
Today	Aujourd'hui	o-zhoor-**dwee**
Tomorrow	Demain	duh-**mehn**
This morning/ afternoon	Ce matin/cet après-midi	suh ma-**tehn**/set ah-pray-mee-**dee**
Tonight	Ce soir	suh **swahr**
What?	Quoi?	kwah
What is it?	Qu'est-ce que c'est?	kess-kuh-**say**
Why?	Pourquoi?	**poor**-kwa
Who?	Qui?	kee
Where is . . .	Où se trouve . . .	oo suh **troov**
the train station?	la gare?	la gar
the subway?	la station de?	la sta-**syon** duh
station?	métro?	may-**tro**
the bus stop?	l'arrêt de bus?	la-**ray** duh **booss**
the airport?	l'aérogare?	lay-ro-**gar**
the post office?	la poste?	la post
the bank?	la banque?	la bahnk
the hotel?	l'hôtel?	lo-**tel**
the store?	le magasin?	luh ma-ga-**zehn**
the cashier?	la caisse?	la **kess**
the museum?	le musée?	luh mew-**zay**
the hospital?	l'hôpital?	lo-pee-**tahl**
the elevator?	l'ascenseur?	la-sahn-**seuhr**
the telephone?	le téléphone?	luh tay-lay-**phone**
Where are the rest rooms?	Où sont les toilettes?	oo sohn lay twah-**let**
Here/there	Ici/là	ee-**see**/la
Left/right	A gauche/à droite	a goash/a drwaht
Straight ahead	Tout droit	too drwah

Is it near/far?	C'est près/loin?	say pray/lwehn
I'd like . . .	Je voudrais . . .	zhuh voo-**dray**
a room	une chambre	ewn **shahm**-bruh
the key	la clé	la clay
a newspaper	un journal	uhn zhoor-**nahl**
a stamp	un timbre	uhn **tam**-bruh
I'd like to buy . . .	Je voudrais acheter . . .	zhuh voo-**dray** **ahsh**-tay
a cigar	un cigare	uhn see-**gar**
cigarettes	des cigarettes	day see-ga-**ret**
matches	des allumettes	days a-loo-**met**
dictionary	un dictionnaire	uhn deek-see-oh-**nare**
soap	du savon	dew sah-**vohn**
city map	un plan de ville	uhn plahn de **veel**
road map	une carte routière	ewn cart roo-tee-**air**
magazine	une revue	ewn reh-**vu**
envelopes	des enveloppes	dayz ahn-veh-**lope**
writing paper	du papier à lettres	dew pa-pee-**ay** a **let**-ruh
airmail writing paper	du papier avion	dew pa-pee-**ay** a-vee-**ohn**
postcard	une carte postale	ewn cart pos-**tal**
How much is it?	C'est combien?	say comb-bee-**ehn**
It's expensive/ cheap	C'est cher/pas cher	say share/pa share
A little/a lot	Un peu/beaucoup	uhn peuh/bo-**koo**
More/less	Plus/moins	plu/mwehn
Enough/too (much)	Assez/trop	a-say/tro
I am ill/sick	Je suis malade	zhuh swee ma-**lahd**
Call a . . . doctor	Appelez un . . . médecin	a-play uhn mayd-**sehn**
Help!	Au secours!	o suh-**koor**
Stop!	Arrêtez!	a-reh-**tay**
Fire!	Au feu!	o fuh
Caution!/Look out!	Attention!	a-tahn-see-**ohn**

Dining Out

A bottle of . . .	une bouteille de . . .	ewn boo-**tay** duh
A cup of . . .	une tasse de . . .	ewn **tass** duh
A glass of . . .	un verre de . . .	uhn **vair** duh
Ashtray	un cendrier	uhn sahn-dree-**ay**
Bill/check	l'addition	la-dee-see-**ohn**
Bread	du pain	dew pan
Breakfast	le petit-déjeuner	luh puh-**tee** day-zhuh-**nay**
Butter	du beurre	dew burr
Cheers!	A votre santé!	ah vo-truh sahn-**tay**
Cocktail/aperitif	un apéritif	uhn ah-pay-ree-**teef**

Dinner	le dîner	luh dee-**nay**
Special of the day	le plat du jour	luh plah dew **zhoor**
Enjoy!	Bon appétit!	bohn a-pay-**tee**
Fixed-price menu	le menu	luh may-**new**
Fork	une fourchette	ewn four-**shet**
I am diabetic	Je suis diabétique	zhuh swee dee-ah-bay-**teek**
I am on a diet	Je suis au régime	zhuh sweez oray-**jeem**
I am vegetarian	Je suis végé-tarien(ne)	zhuh swee vay-zhay-ta-ree-**en**
I cannot eat . . .	Je ne peux pas manger de . . .	zhuh nuh **puh** pah mahn-**jay** deh
I'd like to order	Je voudrais commander	zhuh voo-**dray** ko-mahn-**day**
I'm hungry/thirsty	J'ai faim/soif	zhay fahm/swahf
Is service/the tip included?	Le service est-il compris?	luh sair-**veess** ay-teel com-**pree**
It's good/bad	C'est bon/mauvais	say bohn/mo-**vay**
It's hot/cold	C'est chaud/froid	say sho/frwah
Knife	un couteau	uhn koo-**toe**
Lunch	le déjeuner	luh day-zhuh-**nay**
Menu	la carte	la cart
Napkin	une serviette	ewn sair-vee-**et**
Pepper	du poivre	dew **pwah**-vruh
Plate	une assiette	ewn a-see-**et**
Please give me . . .	Merci de me donner . . .	Mair-**see** deh meh doe-**nay**
Salt	du sel	dew sell
Spoon	une cuillère	ewn kwee-**air**
Sugar	du sucre	dew **sook**-ruh
Waiter!/Waitress!	Monsieur!/Mademoiselle!	muh-**syuh**/mad-mwa-**zel**
Wine list	la carte des vins	la **cart** day van

MENU GUIDE

French	English

General Dining

Entrée	Appetizer/Starter
Garniture au choix	Choice of vegetable side
Selon arrivage	When available
Supplément/En sus	Extra charge
Sur commande	Made to order

Breakfast

Confiture	Jam
Miel	Honey
Oeuf à la coque	Boiled egg
Oeufs au bacon	Bacon and eggs
Oeufs sur le plat	Fried eggs
Oeufs brouillés	Scrambled eggs
Tartine	Bread with butter or jam

Appetizers/Starters

Anchois	Anchovies
Andouille(tte)	Chitterling sausage
Assiette de charcuterie	Assorted pork products
Crudités	Mixed raw vegetable salad
Escargots	Snails
Jambon	Ham
Jambonneau	Cured pig's knuckle
Pâté	Liver puree blended with meat
Quenelles	Light dumplings
Saucisson	Dried sausage
Terrine	Pâté in an earthenware pot

Soups

Bisque	Shellfish soup
Bouillabaisse	Fish and seafood stew
Julienne	Vegetable soup
Potage/Soupe	Soup
Potage parmentier	Thick potato soup
Pot-au-feu	Stew of meat and vegetables
Soupe du jour	Soup of the day
Soupe à l'oignon gratinée	French onion soup
Soupe au pistou	Provençal vegetable soup
Velouté de . . .	Cream of . . .
Vichyssoise	Cold leek and potato cream soup

Fish and Seafood

Bar	Bass
Bourride	Fish stew from Marseilles
Brandade de morue	Creamed salt cod
Brochet	Pike
Cabillaud/Morue	Fresh cod
Calmar	Squid
Coquilles St-Jacques	Scallops
Crabe	Crab
Crevettes	Shrimp
Daurade	Sea bream

Écrevisses	Prawns/crayfish
Harengs	Herring
Homard	Lobster
Huîtres	Oysters
Langouste	Spiny lobster
Langoustine	Prawn/lobster
Lotte	Monkfish
Lotte de mer	Angler
Loup	Catfish
Maquereau	Mackerel
Matelote	Fish stew in wine
Moules	Mussels
Palourdes	Clams
Perche	Perch
Poulpe	Octopus
Raie	Skate
Rascasse	Scorpion-fish
Rouget	Red mullet
Saumon	Salmon
Thon	Tuna
Truite	Trout

Meat

Agneau	Lamb
Ballotine	Boned, stuffed, and rolled
Blanquette de veau	Veal stew with a white-sauce base
Boeuf	Beef
Boeuf à la Bourguignonne	Beef stew
Boudin blanc	Sausage made with white meat
Boudin noir	Sausage made with pig's blood
Boulettes de viande	Meatballs
Brochette	Kabob
Cassoulet	Casserole of white beans, meat
Cervelle	Brains
Châteaubriand	Double fillet steak
Côtelettes	Chops
Choucroute garnie	Sausages and cured pork served with sauerkraut
Côte de boeuf	T-bone steak
Côte	Rib
Cuisses de grenouilles	Frogs' legs
Entrecôte	Rib or rib-eye steak
Épaule	Shoulder
Escalope	Cutlet
Foie	Liver
Gigot	Leg
Langue	Tongue
Médaillon	Tenderloin steak
Pavé	Thick slice of boned beef
Pieds de cochon	Pig's feet
Porc	Pork
Ragoût	Stew
Ris de veau	Veal sweetbreads
Rognons	Kidneys
Saucisses	Sausages
Selle	Saddle

Tournedos	Tenderloin of T-bone steak
Veau	Veal
Viande	Meat

Methods of Preparation

À point	Medium
À l'étouffée	Stewed
Au four	Baked
Bien cuit	Well-done
Bleu	Very rare
Bouilli	Boiled
Braisé	Braised
Frit	Fried
Grillé	Grilled
Rôti	Roast
Saignant	Rare
Sauté/poêlée	Sautéed

Game and Poultry

Blanc de volaille	Chicken breast
Caille	Quail
Canard/Caneton	Duck/duckling
Cerf/Chevreuil	Venison
Coq au vin	Chicken stewed in red wine
Dinde/Dindonneau	Turkey/Young turkey
Faisan	Pheasant
Lapin	Rabbit
Lièvre	Wild hare
Oie	Goose
Pigeon/Pigeonneau	Pigeon/Squab
Pintade/Pintadeau	Guinea fowl/Young guinea fowl
Poularde	Fattened pullet
Poulet/Poussin	Chicken/Spring chicken
Sanglier/Marcassin	Wild boar/Young wild boar
Volaille	Fowl

Vegetables

Artichaut	Artichoke
Asperge	Asparagus
Aubergine	Eggplant
Carottes	Carrots
Champignons	Mushrooms
Chou-fleur	Cauliflower
Chou (rouge)	Cabbage (red)
Choux de Bruxelles	Brussels sprouts
Courgette	Zucchini
Cresson	Watercress
Épinard	Spinach
Haricots blancs/verts	White kidney/green beans
Laitue	Lettuce
Lentilles	Lentils
Maïs	Corn
Oignons	Onions
Petits pois	Peas
Poireaux	Leeks
Poivrons	Peppers

Pomme de terre	Potato
Pommes frites	French fries
Tomates	Tomatoes

Sauces and Preparations

Béarnaise	Vinegar, egg yolks, white wine, shallots, tarragon
Béchamel	White sauce
Bordelaise	Mushrooms, red wine, shallots, beef marrow
Bourguignon	Red wine, herbs
Chasseur	Wine, mushrooms, shallots
Diable	Hot pepper
Forestière	Mushrooms
Hollandaise	Egg yolks, butter, vinegar
Indienne	Curry
Madère	With Madeira wine
Marinière	White wine, mussel broth, egg yolks
Meunière	Brown butter, parsley, lemon juice
Périgueux	With goose or duck liver puree and truffles
Poivrade	Pepper sauce
Provençale	Onions, tomatoes, garlic

Fruits and Nuts

Abricot	Apricot
Amandes	Almonds
Ananas	Pineapple
Cacahouètes	Peanuts
Cassis	Black currants
Cerises	Cherries
Citron/Citron vert	Lemon/Lime
Figues	Figs
Fraises	Strawberries
Framboises	Raspberries
Fruits secs	Dried fruit
Groseilles	Red currants
Marrons	Chestnuts
Melon	Melon
Mûres	Blackberries
Noisettes	Hazelnuts
Noix de coco	Coconut
Noix	Walnuts
Pamplemousse	Grapefruit
Pêche	Peach
Poire	Pear
Pomme	Apple
Pruneaux	Prunes
Prunes	Plums
Raisins blancs/noirs	Grapes green/purple
Raisins secs	Raisins

Desserts

Coupe (glacée)	Sundae
Crêpe	Thin pancake
Crème brûlée	Custard with caramelized topping

Crème caramel	Caramel-coated custard
Crème Chantilly	Whipped cream
Gâteau au chocolat	Chocolate cake
Glace	Ice cream
Mousse au chocolat	Chocolate mousse
Sabayon	Egg-and-wine-based custard
Tarte aux pommes	Apple pie
Tarte tatin	Caramelized apple tart
Tourte	Layer cake

Alcoholic Drinks

À l'eau	With water
Avec des glaçons	On the rocks
Kir	Chilled white wine mixed with black-currant syrup
Bière	Beer
blonde/brune	*light/dark*
Calvados	Apple brandy from Normandy
Eau-de-vie	Brandy
Liqueur	Cordial
Poire William	Pear brandy
Porto	Port
Vin	Wine
sec	*dry/neat*
brut	*very dry*
léger	*light*
doux	*sweet*
rouge	*red*
rosé	*rosé*
mousseux	*sparkling*
blanc	*white*

Nonalcoholic Drinks

Café	Coffee
noir	*black*
crème	*with steamed milk/cream*
au lait	*with steamed milk*
décaféiné	*caffeine-free*
Express	Espresso
Chocolat chaud	Hot chocolate
Eau minérale	Mineral water
gazeuse/non gazeuse	*carbonated/still*
Jus de . . .	. . . juice
Lait	Milk
Limonade	Lemonade
Thé	Tea
au lait/au citron	*with milk/lemon*
glacé	*Iced tea*
Tisane	Herb tea

INDEX

X = restaurant, ⊡ = hotel

G

Galerie des Arcades ✕ 🖾, 197
Garden of Remains, 117
Gardens
Avignon, 73
Cap d'Antibes, 195–196
Eze, 226
Fodor's Choice, 13
Marseille, 117, 120
Menton, 234
Monaco, 230
Montpellier, 31
Nice, 210
Nîmes, 28
Garoupe Lighthouse, 195
Gasoline, *xvi–xvii*
Gassin, 151
Gattières, 202
Gay and lesbian travel, *xxiv*
Gîtes. ☞ Vacation rentals
Glanum, 54–55
Glassworks, 197
Gogh, Vincent van, 43, 55
Golf tours, *xxxviii*
Gordes, 87–89, 97
Gorge d'Ollioules, 134
Gorges de Châteaudouble, 181
Gorges du Verdon, 175–176
Governor's Lodging, 35
Grand Café de Turin ✕, 213
Grand Hôtel Bain ✕🖾, 174
Grasse, 168, 170–171, 183
Grimaud, 152
Groupe Épiscopal, 153
Group tours, *xxxvi–xxxvii*

H

Handsome Man Pass, 173
Hermitage ✕🖾, 231
Hiély-Lucullus ✕, 74
Hiking, *xxiv–xxv*
Cassis, 134
Central Coast region, 100
Fodor's Choice, 15
Western Côte d'Azur, 143
Holidays, *xxv*
Home and garden tours, *xxxviii*
Home exchanges, *xxvi–xxvii*
Horseback riding, 22
Horseback tours, *xxxviii*
Hospice St-Louis, 70
Hospitals, *xxiv*
Hostellerie de Crillon le Brave ✕🖾, 83
Hostellerie du Prieuré 🖾, 93
Hostellerie les Frênes 🖾, 75–76
Hostels, *xxvii*
Hôtel de Caumont, 108
Hôtel de Châteaurenard, 108
Hôtel de la Mirande 🖾, 74
Hôtel de Manville, 51
Hôtel de Margailler, 49
Hôtel de Mons 🖾, 76
Hôtel de Paris ✕🖾, 231

Hôtel de Sade, 55
Hôtel d'Europe 🖾, 74–75
Hôtel du Blauvac 🖾, 76
Hôtel Gauguin 🖾, 46
Hôtel Innova 🖾, 76
Hôtel Maynier d'Oppède, 108
Hotels, *xxvii–xxviii*
Hôtel Welcome ✕🖾, 224
Hot Water Fountain, 108

I

Ile Ste-Marguerite, 167
Ile St-Honorat, 167
Iles de Lérins, 166–167
Iles d'Hyères, 135–136
Impérator 🖾, 29
Institut d'Etudes Françaises, 108
Insurance
for car rentals, xvi
medical plans, xxiv
travel insurance, xxv–xxvi
International Museum of Perfume, 171
Internet services, *xv*
Itineraries, 15–17

J

Jacques Maximin ✕, 201–202
Jadis ✕, 178
Jardin Albert I, 210
Jardin Biovès, 234
Jardin de la Fontaine, 28
Jardin d'Emile ✕🖾, 132
Jardin des Plantes, 31
Jardin des Vestiges, 117
Jardin du Pharo, 120
Jardin Exotique (Eze), 226
Jardin Exotique (Monaco), 230
Jardin Thuret, 195–196
Jazz festivals, 18
Jetée Impératrice Eugénie, 233
Juana ✕🖾, 194
Juan les-Pins, 193
Jules César 🖾, 45
Jules-Chéret Fine Arts Museum, 210

L

La Baie Dorée 🖾, 196
La Bastide de Moustiers ✕🖾, 178
La Baume 🖾, 29
La Benvengudo 🖾, 53
La Bonne Auberge ✕, 193
La Bouillabaisse ✕, 155
La Bravade, 18
La Brigue, 220
La Brouette de Grand'mere ✕, 161
La Cambuse ✕, 213
Lac de Ste-Croix, 179
La Cigale ✕, 231
La Colombe d'Or ✕, 200

La Colombe Joyeuse ✕, 152
Lacoste, 92
La Cuisine de Reine ✕, 74
La Farandole ✕, 130
La Farigoule ✕, 202
L'Affenage ✕, 44–45
La Fontaine 🖾, 216
La Garbure ✕🖾, 78
La Garde-Freinet, 151–152
La Glycine ✕🖾, 136
La Gousse d'Ail ✕, 56
La Gueulardière ✕🖾, 85
La Gueule du Loup ✕, 44
La Jarre ✕, 193
La Maison aux Fruits 🖾, 87
La Mer 🖾, 217
La Mère Besson ✕, 161
La Mérenda ✕, 213
La Mirande ✕, 73–74
La Napoule, 157–158, 183
L'Anastasy 🖾, 76
L'Ane Rouge ✕, 212–213
Language, *xxvi,* 131
Languedoc Frontier, 25–35
La Palud-sur-Verdon, 175–176
La Perouse ✕🖾, 215–216
La Prévôté ✕, 85
La Regalido 🖾, 50
La Reine Jeanne ✕🖾, 52
La Renaissance ✕🖾, 89
La Résidence de la Pinède ✕🖾, 149
La Rotonde, 109
Lascaris Palace, 208–209
L'Assiette de Marie ✕, 55–56
La Table du Comtat ✕🖾, 80
La Verrerie de Biot, 197
La Vieille Fontaine ✕, 73
La Yaka ✕, 79
Learning tours, *xxxviii*
Le Baldequin ✕, 178
Le Baron 🖾, 150
Le Barroux, 82–83
Le Beffroi ✕🖾, 82
Le Bistro Latin ✕, 111
Le Boucanier ✕, 156
Le Broc, 202
Le Brûlot ✕, 193
Le Café ✕, 149
Le Calendal 🖾, 46
Le Castellet, 133
Le Chandelier ✕, 33
Le Cloître 🖾, 46
Le Clos de la Violette ✕, 109–110
Le Clos du Buis 🖾, 93
Le Corbusier, 233
Le Domaine d'Olival 🖾, 157
Le Fournil ✕, 93
Léger, Fernand, 197
Le Girelier ✕, 149
Le Grand Café ✕, 74
Le Grand Jas 🖾, 87
Le Grillon ✕, 111
Le Gros Cerveau, 134
Le Guilhem 🖾, 34
Le Hammeau ✕🖾, 201
Le Jardin des Frênes ✕, 73

NOTES

NOTES

NOTES

NOTES

With guidebooks for every kind of travel—from weekend getaways to island hopping to adventures abroad—it's easy to understand why smart travelers go with **Fodor's**.

At bookstores everywhere.
www.fodors.com

Fodor's Travel Publications

Available at bookstores everywhere. For descriptions of all our titles and a key to Fodor's guidebook series, visit http://www.fodors.com/books/

Gold Guides

U.S.

Alaska

Arizona

Boston

California

Cape Cod, Martha's Vineyard, Nantucket

The Carolinas & Georgia

Chicago

Colorado

Florida

Hawai'i

Las Vegas, Reno, Tahoe

Los Angeles

Maine, Vermont, New Hampshire

Maui & Lāna'i

Miami & the Keys

New England

New Orleans

New York City

Oregon

Pacific North Coast

Philadelphia & the Pennsylvania Dutch Country

The Rockies

San Diego

San Francisco

Santa Fe, Taos, Albuquerque

Seattle & Vancouver

The South

U.S. & British Virgin Islands

USA

Virginia & Maryland

Washington, D.C.

Foreign

Australia

Austria

The Bahamas

Belize & Guatemala

Bermuda

Canada

Cancún, Cozumel, Yucatán Peninsula

Caribbean

China

Costa Rica

Cuba

The Czech Republic & Slovakia

Denmark

Eastern & Central Europe

Europe

Florence, Tuscany & Umbria

France

Germany

Great Britain

Greece

Hong Kong

India

Ireland

Israel

Italy

Japan

London

Madrid & Barcelona

Mexico

Montréal & Québec City

Moscow, St. Petersburg, Kiev

The Netherlands, Belgium & Luxembourg

New Zealand

Norway

Nova Scotia, New Brunswick, Prince Edward Island

Paris

Portugal

Provence & the Riviera

Scandinavia

Scotland

Singapore

South Africa

South America

Southeast Asia

Spain

Sweden

Switzerland

Thailand

Toronto

Turkey

Vienna & the Danube Valley

Vietnam

Special-Interest Guides

Adventures to Imagine

Alaska Ports of Call

Ballpark Vacations

The Best Cruises

Caribbean Ports of Call

The Complete Guide to America's National Parks

Europe Ports of Call

Family Adventures

Fodor's Gay Guide to the USA

Fodor's How to Pack

Great American Learning Vacations

Great American Sports & Adventure Vacations

Great American Vacations

Great American Vacations for Travelers with Disabilities

Halliday's New Orleans Food Explorer

Healthy Escapes

Kodak Guide to Shooting Great Travel Pictures

National Parks and Seashores of the East

National Parks of the West

Nights to Imagine

Orlando Like a Pro

Rock & Roll Traveler Great Britain and Ireland

Rock & Roll Traveler USA

Sunday in San Francisco

Walt Disney World for Adults

Weekends in New York

Wendy Perrin's Secrets Every Smart Traveler Should Know

Worlds to Imagine

Fodor's Special Series

Fodor's Best Bed & Breakfasts
America
California
The Mid-Atlantic
New England
The Pacific Northwest
The South
The Southwest
The Upper Great Lakes

Compass American Guides
Alaska
Arizona
Boston
Chicago
Coastal California
Colorado
Florida
Hawai'i
Hollywood
Idaho
Las Vegas
Maine
Manhattan
Minnesota
Montana
New Mexico
New Orleans
Oregon
Pacific Northwest
San Francisco
Santa Fe
South Carolina
South Dakota
Southwest
Texas
Underwater Wonders of the National Parks
Utah
Virginia
Washington
Wine Country
Wisconsin
Wyoming

Citypacks
Amsterdam
Atlanta
Berlin
Boston
Chicago
Florence
Hong Kong
London
Los Angeles
Miami
Montréal
New York City
Paris

Prague
Rome
San Francisco
Sydney
Tokyo
Toronto
Venice
Washington, D.C.

Exploring Guides
Australia
Boston & New England
Britain
California
Canada
Caribbean
China
Costa Rica
Cuba
Egypt
Florence & Tuscany
Florida
France
Germany
Greek Islands
Hawai'i
India
Ireland
Israel
Italy
Japan
London
Mexico
Moscow & St. Petersburg
New York City
Paris
Portugal
Prague
Provence
Rome
San Francisco
Scotland
Singapore & Malaysia
South Africa
Spain
Thailand
Turkey
Venice
Vietnam

Flashmaps
Boston
New York
San Francisco
Washington, D.C.

Fodor's Cityguides
Boston
New York
San Francisco

Fodor's Gay Guides
Amsterdam
Los Angeles & Southern California
New York City
Pacific Northwest
San Francisco and the Bay Area
South Florida
USA

Karen Brown Guides
Austria
California
England B&Bs
England, Wales & Scotland
France B&Bs
France Inns
Germany
Ireland
Italy B&Bs
Italy Inns
Portugal
Spain
Switzerland

Pocket Guides
Acapulco
Aruba
Atlanta
Barbados
Beijing
Berlin
Budapest
Dublin
Honolulu
Jamaica
London
Mexico City
New York City
Paris
Prague
Puerto Rico
Rome
San Francisco
Savannah & Charleston
Shanghai
Sydney
Washington, D.C.

Languages for Travelers (Cassette & Phrasebook)
French
German
Italian
Spanish

Mobil Travel Guides
America's Best Hotels & Restaurants
Arizona

California and the West
Florida
Great Lakes
Major Cities
Mid-Atlantic
Northeast
Northwest and Great Plains
Southeast
Southern California
Southwest and South Central

Rivages Guides
Bed and Breakfasts of Character and Charm in France
Hotels and Country Inns of Character and Charm in France
Hotels and Country Inns of Character and Charm in Italy
Hotels of Character and Charm in Paris
Hotels of Character and Charm in Portugal
Hotels of Character and Charm in Spain
Wines & Vineyards of Character and Charm in France

Short Escapes
Britain
France
Near New York City
New England

Fodor's Sports
Golf Digest's Places to Play (USA)
Golf Digest's Places to Play in the Southeast
Golf Digest's Places to Play in the Southwest
Skiing USA
USA Today The Complete Four Sport Stadium Guide

Fodor's upCLOSE Guides
California
Europe
France
Great Britain
Ireland
Italy
London
Los Angeles
Mexico
New York City
Paris
San Francisco

WHEREVER YOU TRAVEL, *H*ELP IS NEVER FAR AWAY.

From planning your trip to

providing travel assistance along

the way, American Express®

Travel Service Offices are

always there to help

you do more.

do more AMERICAN EXPRESS

Travel

www.americanexpress.com/travel

American Express Travel Service Offices are
located throughout Provence and the Côte d'Azur.